# Sports Economics, Management and Policy

## Volume 12

**Series Editor**
Dennis Coates
University of Maryland, Baltimore County Dept. Economics,
Baltimore, Maryland, USA

More information about this series at http://www.springer.com/series/8343

The aim of this series is to provide academics, students, sports business executives, and policy makers with information and analysis on the cutting edge of sports economics, sport management, and public policy on sporting issues.

Volumes in this series can focus on individual sports, issues that cut across sports, issues unique to professional sports, or topics in amateur sports. Each volume will provide rigorous analysis with the purpose of advancing understanding of the sport and the sport business, improving decision making within the sport business and regarding policy toward sports, or both. Volumes may include any or all of the following: theoretical modelling and analysis, empirical investigations, or description and interpretation of institutions, policies, regulations, and law.

Christoph Breuer • Remco Hoekman
Siegfried Nagel • Harold van der Werff
Editors

# Sport Clubs in Europe

## A Cross-National Comparative Perspective

Springer

*Editors*
Christoph Breuer
German Sport University
Cologne, Germany

Remco Hoekman
Mulier Institute
Utrecht, The Netherlands

Siegfried Nagel
University of Bern Office
Bern, Switzerland

Harold van der Werff
Mulier Institute
Utrecht, The Netherlands

ISSN 2191-298X ISSN 2191-2998 (electronic)
Sports Economics, Management and Policy
ISBN 978-3-319-17634-5 ISBN 978-3-319-17635-2 (eBook)
DOI 10.1007/978-3-319-17635-2

Library of Congress Control Number: 2015943314

Springer Cham Heidelberg New York Dordrecht London


Printed on acid-free paper

Springer International Publishing AG Switzerland is part of Springer Science+Business Media (www.springer.com)

# Preface

The *European Association for Sociology of Sport* (eass) sees it as its task to bring together social researchers and to provide a platform to have scientific discussions on policy issues in the field of sport and society, such as the role of sport clubs. It is for this reason that the eass incorporates initiatives such as the *Meeting for European Sport Participation and Sport Culture Research* (MEASURE) and the *Sport Organisation Research Network* (SORN). It was during the meeting of the Sport Organisation Research Network (SORN) at the 2013 eass conference in Cordoba, Spain, that the well-received initiative was launched to develop a comparative book on sport clubs in Europe, in order to obtain a better picture of the position and societal value of sport clubs throughout Europe.

Sport clubs are to be found everywhere in Europe and can be considered as one of the main features of the European sport model. Sport clubs exist in different forms, ranging from small to large clubs and from single to multisport clubs. The overall presence of sport clubs in Europe implies that differences appear with regard to the extent to which sport clubs are present, the way they are organised and their function within our society as a whole. Moreover, the societal value of sport clubs is taken for granted, and even more and more emphasised from a European, a national as well as a local perspective.

However, when it comes to the current position of sport clubs in different societies and their contribution at large, we have to admit that we lacked a more in-depth picture from a scientific approach. It is for this reason that the idea of the present book was warmly embraced within the eass community and evoked stimulating discussions that led to an interesting theoretical and conceptual framework for the book. It is admirable how the editors succeeded in obtaining relatively comparable data of 20 European countries. In this way they managed to present a comparative book on sport clubs in Europe from a social scientific perspective.

I thank the editors and the contributing authors for their excellent work and providing insight into national data on sport clubs. I truly hope that this book will stimulate discussions on the societal relevance of sport clubs in Europe and will initiate further research and data collection both on a European and national level.

Furthermore, I hope that this book will also inspire many people from different angles and positions in the world of sport and beyond and will allow policy makers, professionals, students as well as practitioners in sport clubs and sport federations to fully use the power of sport for society, and the potential of sport clubs in particular.

Leuven, Belgium

Jeroen Scheerder
President eass

# Acknowledgement

This publication was made possible due to the support of the German Sport University Cologne, the Mulier Institute and the University of Bern. Our thanks are also due to Dennis Coates, the editor of this book series on *Sport Economics, Management and Policy*, for reflecting on our first ideas for the book. Furthermore we are grateful to Lorraine Klimowich and her team of Springer USA for transforming our manuscript into what we hope will be a valuable handbook for anybody interested in the position of sport clubs within the national sport structure, their role in policy and society, their basic characteristics and the threats and opportunities that influence the development of sport clubs. We also thank our team of authors for their invaluable contributions to this book. If it was not for them, this book would have never had a chance. Last but not least we would like to thank Pamela Wicker, Soeren Dallmeyer and Jana Vogelsang for their efforts in finalising the manuscript.

Christoph Breuer
Remco Hoekman
Siegfried Nagel
Harold van der Werff

# Acknowledgement

# Contents

# Chapter 1
# Introduction

**Remco Hoekman, Harold van der Werff, Siegfried Nagel, and Christoph Breuer**

## 1.1 Sport Clubs in a Changing Europe

Sport clubs have a long tradition in nearly all European countries. They play an important role in the sporting activities of the population, not only for elite and competitive sport but also for sport for all (e.g. Allison 2001; Lamprecht et al. 2012; Taylor et al. 2009). During the period of over a century in which sport clubs have been existent in Europe, the world around them has been changing continuously. Changes in society, in politics, in population, in economy, in leisure culture and in lifestyles have undoubtedly had an impact on sport and sport clubs all over Europe. However, sport has also influenced modern life. From a rather marginal place sport has shifted to the core of modern culture and this changed its role in society accordingly.

From a European perspective these developments have accelerated in the last two decades, not only due to the fall of the iron curtain, but also because of what could be called *the European project*: the construction of the European Community (Maastricht Treaty accepted in 1993) and European Union (Lisbon

R. Hoekman (✉) • H. van der Werff
Mulier Institute, Utrecht, The Netherlands
e-mail: r.hoekman@mulierinstituut.nl; h.vanderwerff@mulierinstituut.nl

S. Nagel
Institute of Sport Science, University of Bern, Bern, Switzerland
e-mail: siegfried.nagel@ispw.unibe.ch

C. Breuer
Department of Sport Economics and Sport Management, German Sport University Cologne, Cologne, Germany
e-mail: breuer@dshs-koeln.de



C. Breuer et al. (eds.), *Sport Clubs in Europe*, Sports Economics, Management and Policy 12, DOI 10.1007/978-3-319-17635-2_1

Treaty accepted in 2009). Since July 2013 the European Union consists of 28 Member States with approximately 507 million inhabitants living in a territory of 4.4 million $km^2$. This European project has intensified collaboration and cooperation between countries in Europe in many domains. The cooperative activities and disappearance of borders have revealed similarities between countries and cultures, for instance in the way sport is organised, but also highlighted the differences (Tokarski et al. 2004). It is interesting to see whether the development of sport clubs in different European countries is taking a convergent route in the context of overall social and cultural changes and the growing European cooperation.

A recent study on sport participation and physical activity in Europe illustrated that 12 % of the EU citizens are a member of a sport club and that this percentage has not changed in the period between 2009 and 2013 (European Commission 2014). However, the individual results of the member states do show fluctuations between the years. Furthermore, there are evident differences in sport club memberships between the member states, varying between 1 % in Romania and 27 % in the Netherlands. The differences between the countries are presumably partly the result of the differences in the position of sport clubs within the national sport structure and within sport policy, and the convergent route of sport clubs in the context of overall cultural changes.

This brings us to several interesting questions for cross-national comparisons within Europe. Can the same trends and developments be observed in sport clubs in several countries? Do sport clubs react in a comparable way to the changing social context in which they operate? How do they address the challenges and problems associated with these changes?

It is to be expected that these trends and challenges do not concern all European countries and all sport clubs in the same way. The statements of experts as well as the existing literature on sport club research show that there are similarities as well as differences between sport clubs in different European countries. However, despite a general interest in comparable data on sport clubs throughout Europe the knowledge is often fragmented and hardly comparable between countries. Many scholars in Europe have made sport clubs their central object of study and have provided insights into numerous aspects of sport clubs. Various universities and other research institutes have data on sport clubs. However, this data is hardly used for cross-national comparisons despite the fact that both policymakers and researchers have expressed an interest in more comparable data on sport clubs in Europe in the recent evaluation of the sport monitoring system in Europe (Breedveld et al. 2013).

The last book on sport clubs in Europe dates back to the previous century. In 1999, Heinemann edited the book *Sport clubs in various European countries* with research from 11 European countries on various topics related to sport clubs. However, the different chapters are characterised by a limited comparability and there is no separate chapter with a comparison of the situation of sport clubs in the different countries. With this, it lacks an up-to-date comparable portrait of sport clubs in various European countries while at the same time there is an evident interest in comparative analyses on sport clubs in Europe to obtain a better understanding of the differences.

## 1.2 Aim of the Book

Unmistakably, there will be differences between countries with regard to the position and functioning of sport clubs. With this book we aim to present an up-to-date portrait of the characteristics of sport clubs and their embedding in society and the national sport system in various European countries, using both a historical and future perspective. As a result, this book makes the research on sport clubs that is conducted in many countries available for a wider audience and with this extends the knowledge about sport clubs and their environment from one national context to another. Furthermore, we aim to present a cross-national comparative perspective of sport clubs in Europe providing insights into differences and similarities throughout Europe. A number of important benefits can be gained from undertaking cross-national comparisons. For starters, it can lead to new insights into and a deeper understanding of issues which are of central concern in different countries and that can guide future developments. Based on the country reports and the cross-national comparison we intend to identify bottlenecks and challenges for sport clubs in Europe and provide a future perspective on sport clubs in a changing Europe. Furthermore, to establish this book researchers were brought together to provide their expertise and discuss issues. By bringing together this knowledge it was also possible to identify gaps in knowledge which prevent effective cross-national comparisons. By identifying these gaps we expect to provide useful avenues for future research on sport clubs in Europe.

The book contains chapters from 20 European countries and presents both empirical data and information on the political and historical backgrounds of sport clubs. With this, the book offers interesting material on sport clubs in Europe that can serve governing bodies and policymakers and can be used for educational purposes.

## 1.3 Framework for an International Comparison

The *national* chapters are written based on a standardised structure to enable cross-national comparisons. Each chapter pays attention to the development and current situation with regard to the following questions:

1. What is the current position of sport clubs within the national sport structure and what are their historical origins?
2. Which role do they fulfil in policy and society?

3. What are their basic characteristics (e.g. size, activities, finance and professionalisation) and which threats and opportunities influence the development of sport clubs?

The combination of these three perspectives will give a multilevel description of the specific situation in every participating country (this multilevel approach will be elaborated in Chap. 2).

Besides the consideration of these three compulsive perspectives for comparison the authors had the possibility to include one additional paragraph dedicated to a specific topic. This led among others to interesting additions on the role of gender in sport clubs (Germany), the role of sport clubs in national policy programs (the Netherlands), sport clubs as health promoters (Belgium), sport clubs and social capital (Denmark), licensing system for sport clubs (England), sport policy and governance of sport clubs (Norway and Sweden) and differences between language regions (Switzerland).

## 1.4 Structure of the Book

The book consists of three parts. In the first part we present theoretical perspectives on sport clubs in connection to the changing role of sport in society and elaborate on the analytical framework that is used for the national chapters. Therefore, we will first give an overview of concepts and research approaches that have been used successfully to analyse the development of sport clubs. These concepts and approaches will be linked to the evolution of sport in society in recent decades and the pressure resulting from this to modernise the traditional sport clubs as voluntary organisations. Furthermore, we will describe the general multilevel model that is used as a framework for the analysis in the country chapters. The analytical framework will give possibilities for comparisons and promote the understanding for the readers. The second part consists of the national chapters of 20 European countries which provide a systematic overview of the knowledge on sport clubs in the given country (see Fig. 1.1). The chapters are written by experts within the field of sport club research in the specific country. The included countries represent all parts of Europe and include different political situations and different sport systems. For instance, the three sources that fed the European sport are all included in this book: (1) sport from the UK, (2) Turnen from Germany and (3) gymnastics from Sweden (Heinemann 1999).

The third and concluding part of the book offers (1) a systematic comparison of similarities and differences between the participating countries with a clear linkage to the functioning of policy systems and observed problems and possible solutions, and (2) a future perspective on sport clubs in Europe including a research agenda on sport clubs. In the cross-national comparison all the 20 contributions to this book are drawn together focusing on differences and similarities between the countries. Finally we consider trends and developments and provide a future perspective on sport clubs in Europe and identify knowledge gaps and avenues for future research.

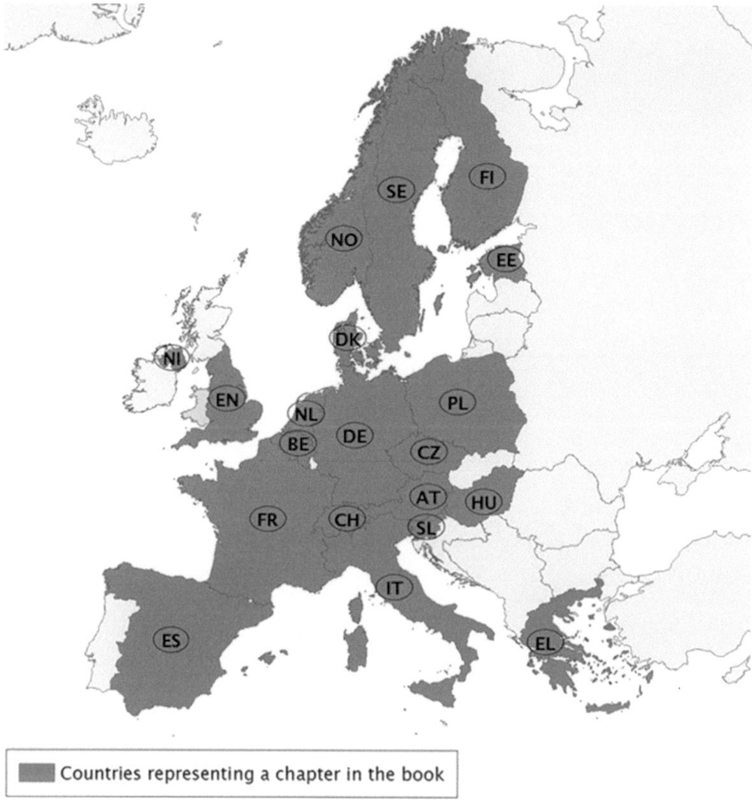


**Fig. 1.1** Countries representing a chapter in the book

# References


Allison M (2001) Sports clubs in Scotland. SportScotland, Edinburgh

Breedveld K, Gratton C, Hoekman R, Scheerder J, Stege J, Stubbe J, Vos S (2013) Study on a future sport monitoring function in the EU: final report. Mulier Institute, Utrecht

European Commission (2014) Sport and physical activity. Special Eurobarometer 412 Wave EB80.2. European Commission, Brussels

Heinemann K (ed) (1999) Sport clubs in various European countries. Hofmann, Schorndorf

Lamprecht M, Fischer A, Stamm H-P (2012) Die Schweizer Sportvereine—Strukturen, Leistungen, Herausforderungen [Sport clubs in Switzerland: structures, achievements and challenges]. Seismo, Zürich

SAZKA (2010) Výroční zpráva 2009. http://www.vyrocnizprava.cz/fotky/1_575_Sazka_VZ_09_CZ.pdf

Taylor P, Barrett D, Nichols G (2009) Survey of sports clubs 2009. CCPR, London

Tokarski W, Steinbach D, Petry K, Jesse B (eds) (2004) Two players—one goal? Sport in the European Union. Meyer & Meyer, Aachen

# Chapter 2
# Theoretical Framework

**Siegfried Nagel, Torsten Schlesinger, Pamela Wicker, Jo Lucassen, Remco Hoekman, Harold van der Werff, and Christoph Breuer**

## 2.1 Introduction

To understand the current situation of sport clubs in Europe, one has to consider the history and development of sport clubs within European society. In this chapter we briefly outline the historical roots and basic characteristics of sport clubs, as well as their development through time. We then give an overview of current research topics, presenting different theoretical approaches to form the basis for a multilevel framework of comparison for sport clubs across different European countries.

## 2.2 Historical Roots: Characteristics of Sport Clubs as Voluntary Organisations

The rise of sport clubs in Europe in the second half of the nineteenth and early twentieth century is closely connected to the emergence of a civic culture and the introduction of legal rights for civilians, especially the right to organise associations or

S. Nagel (✉) • T. Schlesinger
Institute of Sport Science, University of Bern, Bern, Switzerland
e-mail: siegfried.nagel@ispw.unibe.ch; torsten.schlesinger@ispw.unibe.ch

P. Wicker • C. Breuer
Department of Sport Economics and Sport Management, German Sport University Cologne, Cologne, Germany
e-mail: p.wicker@dshs-koeln.de; breuer@dshs-koeln.de

J. Lucassen • R. Hoekman • H. van der Werff
Mulier Institute, Utrecht, The Netherlands
e-mail: j.m.h.lucassen@mulierinstituut.nl; r.hoekman@mulierinstituut.nl; h.vanderwerff@mulierinstituut.nl



C. Breuer et al. (eds.), *Sport Clubs in Europe*, Sports Economics, Management and Policy 12, DOI 10.1007/978-3-319-17635-2_2

clubs. Voluntary organisations, like sport clubs, have deep roots and are embedded in the social structures of their society. In this context, one can assume that there are different characteristics of the voluntary sector from country to country (Salamon and Anheier 1996).

There are three different social movements that form the basis of sport clubs in European countries: (1) sports from the UK, with the concept of competition and comparison of achievement; (2) Turnen from Germany, with the idea of promoting body, health and mind and (3) gymnastics—training the human body with specific exercises—from Sweden (in detail in Heinemann 1999). The underlying ideas of these social movements influenced the creation and development of sport clubs across Europe, and these concepts still play a role in modern sports. National models of sports and sport clubs are often a mixture of these three basic notions. The specific historical context as well as the roots and development of sport clubs are described in more detail in the chapters on each country.

In contrast to other forms of organisations (especially business companies), sport clubs are voluntary organisations that are characterised by their historical base as well as the following constitutive features (Heinemann 2004; Horch 1992; Ibsen 1992):

1. *Voluntary membership:* The members can decide individually on their entry and exit. Membership is not a birth right or subject to political, legal or social constraints.
2. *Orientation towards the interests of members:* Due to the voluntary nature of the membership, the clubs only retain their members through direct incentives and joint club goals and not through monetary means. Therefore, voluntary sport clubs are characterised by the effort to realise the common interests of the members (e.g. in the form of collectively organised sport activities).
3. *Democratic decision-making structure:* To realise the members' interests, democratic decision-making structures are needed that allow the members to influence the club's goals. The individual right to vote in the general assembly creates a formal power base for members, which is then regulated by the statutes of the club.
4. *Voluntary work:* The services provided by sport clubs are mainly produced by the voluntary work of club members. Although over the last years paid jobs have increasingly been instigated in sport clubs, they still play a minor role. Without payment means that there is no contractually regulated flow of money (or the wages are below a certain threshold), and voluntarily means that the voluntary engagement is not mandatory.
5. *Autonomy:* Voluntary associations pursue their goals independently of others. Accordingly, they finance themselves primarily through internal sources of funds, mainly through membership fees. Their autonomy still allows for subsidiary promotions through public funding and the acquisition of other external resources.
6. *Not-for-profit orientation:* In contrast to companies, sport clubs do not pursue profit targets. This would work against their charitable status. Any financial surplus from a club's activities is not distributed among the members and must be reinvested to realise the purposes of the club.

7. *Solidarity:* For sport clubs, the principle of solidarity counts. This means no direct consideration in the form of rates and charges should be paid for efforts received. A flat-rate membership fee is collected. The membership fee allows for the use of all the services of the club. Membership fees also partially finance various areas of the club's work through cross-subsidisation (e.g. youth work in the club), where the paying member only indirectly benefits.

Research on sport clubs in the twentieth century has partly been focussed on the analysis of this specific type of voluntary association, sometimes in comparison with other associations for labour, religion or culture (Collins 1999; Jolles 1972; Lenk 1972; Manders and Kropman 1979; Schlagenhauf 1977; Timm 1979; Van Meerbeek 1977). In many countries over the last decades, the focus of this research has shifted along with the position of sports. Current studies often focus on the development of sport clubs in modern society and investigate to what extend these basic characteristics are still typical for sport clubs. The next section gives an overview and provides comments on these studies.

## 2.3 Sports and Sport Clubs in Transition

Sport clubs face many new challenges due to changes in society and modern sports. In this section we discuss the increasing expectations of sport policy to work towards social integration, and then present current research topics that reveal the diverse directions of sport club development.

### *2.3.1 A Changing Social Role for Sports: Increasing Expectations of Sport Clubs*

From the 1960s onward sports has become a leisure activity for an increasing number of people in many European countries, and is often promoted by governments and umbrella organisations through Sport for All campaigns. Sport clubs are encouraged to take a role in improving the accessibility of sports for additional groups of the population: youth, women, immigrants, handicapped and elderly (Baur and Braun 2003; Collins 1999). Several developments and trends can be observed in sport clubs in response to these challenges: Sport activities offered by the clubs are increasingly differentiated and opened to new groups of members. With this the number of members in sport clubs has increased considerably during the last decades. As a result, the sport clubs require staff with specific qualifications as well as extra and alternative sport facilities to meet the needs of their members.

While the emphasis in the 1970s, 1980s and 1990s in sport policy was on the enhancement of sport participation and elite sports, after the turn of the century the social role of sports has been broadened (Braun 2003; Coalter 2007a; Digel 1986;

Steenbergen et al. 2001). Sports is now expected to make a contribution to the solution of several societal problems. Major national organisations for sports, like NOCs, appear eager to embrace these opportunities for sports. UK Sport and Sport England were intensely involved in the *Game Plan* developed with the UK Government to enhance the impact of the Olympics in London 2012 (Houlihan and Green 2009). In a comparable way the Dutch Nederlands Olympisch Comité * Nederlandse Sport Federatie (NOC*NSF 2009) state in the Olympic Plan 2028:

> Our mission: with sport we want to bring the Netherlands in all respects to an Olympic level. We will all benefit from this, now and in the future, in many ways: social, economic, spatial planning and well-being. With having the Olympic and Paralympic Games in the Netherlands in 2028 as a possible result. (NOC*NSF 2009, p. 8)

As sport clubs are an important resource for sport provision, they are considered as one of the main actors in implementing this broader role of sports (Houlihan and White 2002; Skille 2008). National governing bodies for sports are stimulated by government or umbrella organisations to participate in national programs related to functions of sports for health, education, social cohesion, neighbourhood climate, labour, etc. (Houlihan and Green 2009), and they expect their member clubs to become involved. As a consequence of the economic crisis in Europe, local authorities are also changing their policy towards sport clubs and are not only demanding a contribution to public duties, but also assigning other tasks to clubs such as management of local sport facilities (Hoekman et al. 2011). For sport clubs these new tasks are quite different from their traditional undertakings and as volunteer organisations many clubs may not be equipped to fulfil such expectations.

The following developments are associated with challenges and problems for many sport clubs (e.g. Nagel and Schlesinger 2012): new tasks and increasing expectations require specific expertise and management. The clubs' services can no longer only be provided by volunteer club members, and to a certain degree, paid staff is required. Increasingly sport clubs need to cooperate with various partners (e.g. municipalities, schools; Wicker, Vos et al. 2013). Sport clubs are also in competition with other sports providers to a greater extent, and members expect the quality of the sport services to be commensurate with modern standards (Lucassen and Van Kalmthout 2011; Sport England 2009), and yet at the same time the willingness of members to volunteer has declined. Finally the number of members in sport clubs is not always increasing and sport clubs have challenges in activating the required financial resources (Breuer and Wicker 2011).

### *2.3.2 Sport Clubs Between Tradition and Ambition: Research Topics*

The connection between the growing ambition for sports and the potential of sport clubs as voluntary associations has been at the centre of many research projects conducted in several European countries over the last decades. Many scholars in

Europe from different scientific disciplines (e.g. sport sociology, sport economics, sport management) have made sport clubs their object of research and have provided valuable insights into numerous facets of sport clubs' development. Current research topics reveal that sport clubs are at a crossroad between tradition and modernisation.

- *Development of sport clubs*: In various countries, an analysis of structure is carried out at regular intervals (often through a system of monitoring the clubs). Panel data can provide a differentiated picture of the current situation of sport clubs, and enables changes and developments over the course of time to be observed (e.g. Breuer and Feiler 2013; Breuer and Wicker 2011). This provides a greater understanding of sport clubs' problems and challenges and is essential for initiating strategic decisions or specific measures by sport political actors (e.g. sport governing bodies, sport federations).
- *Change in sport clubs*: Organisational change—an inevitable feature of all organisations—has become another major area of sport club research. The need for sport clubs to change is caused externally by the dynamics and uncertainties of the environment in which sport clubs are embedded, or from inside the organisation itself (e.g. changing interests of members). In the context of such pressures for change, structural barriers that explain the resistances to modify sport clubs are also investigated (e.g. Slack and Parent 2005; Thiel and Meier 2004). Consequently, a number of different approaches for studying change processes in sport clubs have been used and developed. It is argued that societal changes (e.g. Bette 1993; Digel 1986, 1992; Flatau 2007) and the differentiation of society (e.g. Schimank 2005) have influenced the values of the club members, and as a consequence also the structure and culture of sport clubs. Furthermore, several organisational theories have been adapted to sport clubs: for example, contingency theory (e.g. Fahlén 2006; Horch and Schütte 2009), resource dependence theory (e.g. Vos et al. 2011; Wicker and Breuer 2011; Wicker, Vos et al. 2013), new institutionalism (e.g. Fahlén et al. 2008; Skille 2009) or population ecology approach (e.g. Flatau et al. 2012). Nagel (2007) has proposed the integration of the different perspectives of exogenously and endogenously determined changes into a multi-level model for the analysis of sport club development (see Sect. 2.4.1).
- *Decision-making processes*: Management practices within sport clubs are associated with decision-making processes. Various studies focus on decision-making processes in sport clubs in relation to different topics (e.g. recruitment processes, gender inequalities). Their purpose is to develop a better understanding of the (complex) decision-making processes in sport clubs by examining underlying structural conditions, mechanisms and factors of these decisions in more detail (e.g. Nagel 2006; Schlesinger et al. 2015; Thiel et al. 2006). Knowledge about club-specific decision-making processes is crucial for developing both sustainable advisory concepts and appropriate management tools for sport clubs, particularly by sport policymakers and sport associations.
- *Resources and capacities of sport clubs*: The performance of an organisation largely depends on whether it succeeds in securing a continuous flow of resources.

Based on the concept of organisational capacity (Hall et al. 2003; Misener and Doherty 2009), studies have analysed clubs' resource structures and their ability to deploy resources. Results indicate that sport clubs seem to have different types of resources at their disposal that can be ascribed to four capacity dimensions: human resources, financial resources, networks and infrastructure resources (Wicker and Breuer 2011). Furthermore, research emphasises that sport clubs are often characterised by problems in securing resources (Wicker and Breuer 2013). Much of the current research focuses on voluntary engagement as the most critical resource of sport clubs (e.g. Cuskelly 2004; Emrich et al. 2014; Østerlund 2012; Schlesinger and Nagel 2013).

- *Efforts and outcomes of sport clubs*: Along with discussions about the social significance of sport clubs, contributions of sport clubs to public welfare are analysed and evaluated (to secure and stabilise public funding). Differing social effects and benefits of sport clubs have been well documented in various studies: Sport clubs are purported to generate individual and social benefits, such as social integration of various target groups and specific groups, such as migrants and people with a disability (e.g. Reid 2012; Ulseth 2004; Wicker and Breuer 2014). Sport clubs promote the development and stabilisation of identity, values and norms, especially for children and adolescents. Through the engagement of individuals as sport club members, social capital can be accumulated (e.g. Auld 2008; Coalter 2007b; Østerlund 2013; Seippel 2006). Sport clubs are a mediator for political socialisation as they provide the conditions for participation in decision-making as well as the circumstances for civic engagement (e.g. Braun 2003). Furthermore, sport clubs facilitate physical activity and well-being for individual sport participants and, through this, also contribute to public health (e.g. Breuer and Wicker 2011).
- *Performance and effectiveness in sport clubs*: As a consequence of the broader role of sports and sport clubs in society, the provision of services by sport clubs is more heavily scrutinised. The club is now required to adhere to general quality standards in health, youth care, equality and moral conduct (Lucassen and Van Kalmthout 2009). In order to optimise the quality of service provision and to strengthen the club's position in a more competitive sport market, some studies focus on performance and service quality in sport clubs by improved (efficiency-based) managerial practices and instruments (e.g. Lucassen 2007; Van Hoecke and De Knop 2006; Van Hoecke et al. 2009). Furthermore, the professionalisation of sport clubs' structures and processes for improved rationalisation and efficiency are taken into account (Chantelat 2001). Against this background, there is critical reflection on the consequences of more formalised practices within sport clubs (e.g. social climate, interest divergences and voluntary engagement).
- *Policy interventions in sport clubs*: Sport clubs are increasingly on the political agenda and have become systematically involved in achieving desired outcomes in sport supply, health and welfare within the community, region or society. With the need for achievement of policy objectives, the relationship between the state and third-sector organisations such as sport clubs is considered one of the

major challenges facing the development of sport governance (e.g. Groeneveld 2009). A number of studies examined the relationship between political authorities (including sports) and sport clubs as policy implementers, particularly the conditions and problems of (top-down) implementation or interventions in sport clubs (e.g. Donaldson et al. 2011; May et al. 2014; Nichols et al. 2005; Skille 2008, 2009).

## 2.4 Sport Clubs and Society: Research Approaches

Within social research there are different ways of conceptualising clubs as a form of organisation with specific characteristics. Several general approaches have been advanced by various groups of researchers: some start from a disciplinary framework (sociological, economical), and some aim at integrative analysis. In the following section, different conceptual frameworks to describe sport clubs are presented in order to provide a theoretical basis for the comparison of sport clubs in different countries. In line with the framework of the previous section, we will focus on the position of sport clubs within the social and economic environment and the changes of the sport clubs within these contexts, providing sociological (Sect. 2.4.1) and economical approaches (Sect. 2.4.2) to better understand the position and logic of sport clubs.

### *2.4.1 Sociological Approaches*

#### 2.4.1.1 Sport Clubs as Social Systems

According to Luhmann's (2000) organisational sociological considerations, organisations (in this case, sport clubs) are treated as social systems consisting of (communicated) decisions. This means that organisations are continually reproduced if decisions are communicated. All other factors such as strategies and hierarchy can be seen as a result of the operation of preceding organisational decisions (Luhmann 2000). Hence, the structures of any organisation are built on a variety of principles about decisions, in other words, decisions about decision-making (Luhmann 2000; applied to sport clubs see Thiel and Meier 2004; Thiel and Mayer 2009). These principles can be initially found at the level of the programmes for decisions that define the objectives of the organisation and the methods used to achieve these objectives. They can then be found at the level of communication channels and the distribution of tasks in the club. And, finally, they can be seen in the principles that deal with human resources, for example, decisions of how positions are filled (Luhmann 2000).

If sport clubs are to be understood as self-referential, operationally closed and autonomous social systems, then the usual assumptions about change, adjustment or influence need to be revised and redefined based on an understanding of the dynamics of non-trivial systems. The consequence of this is that as social systems, sport clubs cannot be directly determined by their environment. Through the development of their individual institutional complexity and logic, sport clubs as social systems react to themselves and only deal with their environment in a selective way. Thus, environmental expectations can only lead to discussions within an organisation that might stimulate intra-organisational changes. Due to their structural specifics, voluntary sport clubs in particular are able to successfully reject expectations from their environment and intended (top-down) interventions by other institutions (Slack and Parent 2005; Thiel and Meier 2004).

Breuer (2005) describes sport clubs as organisations with a public purpose from a stakeholder perspective. These organisations can only survive when they are able to adapt to their system environment (contingency theory, Lawrence and Lorsch 1967). In this way, sport organisations can ensure that they have the resources they need. We should keep in mind that almost without exception sport clubs combine resources from internal sources with those from external sources. Internal resources provided by members and workers consist of voluntary labour, social contacts and networks and moral support and financial support, e.g. membership fees. The resources provided by external resource givers (e.g. state, community and sponsors) are mainly financial or indirectly financial such as tax reductions, reduced fares for sport facilities and subsidies. Vital sport clubs are able to keep the development of resources in balance with their ambitions, and to weigh up their dependence on internal and external resources. These relations are presented in Fig. 2.1.

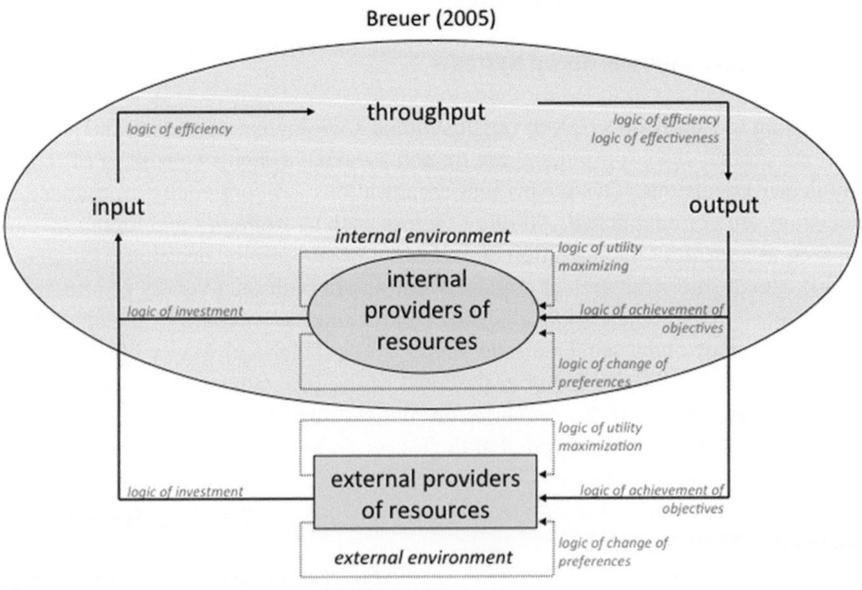


**Fig. 2.1** Model of viable sport clubs (Breuer 2005)

#### 2.4.1.2 Sport Clubs as Corporative Actors and a Multilevel Framework

To clarify a framework that can combine the different levels of sport club research (society, organisation, member), it is appropriate to analyse sport clubs using the social theory of action (Coleman 1974, 1986; Giddens 1984). The basis for actor-theoretical thinking is—according to Giddens and his structuration theory—the presumption that social acting and social structures are in a constant reciprocal connection throughout time (Giddens 1984). Each social structure is the result of the interaction of actors, and at the same time, social acting always depends on social structures.

As we specify these basic assumptions for sport organisations, we need to conceptualise sport clubs as corporative actors (Nagel 2008; Schimank 2005). The organisational logic of sport clubs is based on self-organisation and pooling resources (Coleman 1974). This means that social acting within a sport club is marked by members combining their resources in order to realise their shared interests. Their aim is to produce certain club goods (e.g. sports and social services) at a reasonable price and to provide these goods exclusively for the utility and interests of their members (Heinemann 2004). By doing so, shared interests and preferences of the members form the goals of the organisation (Coleman 1986; Schimank 2000). In order to collectively produce the club goods, club members are prepared to deliver not only financial resources (membership fees), but also temporal resources (work donations) to their club (e.g. Sandler and Tschirhart 1980). Hence, the production of club goods depends on actions based on reciprocity, and relations based on solidarity among club members (the club members are consumers and producers at the same time; Horch 1992). This assumes that club members are prepared to deliver not only financial (membership fees) but also and above all temporal resources (work donations) in order to collectively produce the club goods. Such norms and values could be defined as an unwritten contract involving individual beliefs in reciprocal or solidarity-based obligations between sport clubs and their members (e.g. Heinemann 2004).

However, sport clubs are more than just pooling of resources of their members. The sport club as a corporate actor in a supra-individual sense is characterised by the specific purpose of the association, the articles of association, the membership conditions and the internal decision-making structures. Everything that is informally anchored, such as cultural self-understanding, tradition or club history, provides the club with social stability (internally) and distinctive identity (externally). This in turn ensures the continued existence of a club, independent of its members. The specific structural conditions of a sport club are still subject to change by the corresponding impulses of the members. Nonetheless, these specific structural conditions, not the people, predominantly characterise the sport club as a corporate actor.

Based on the actor-theoretical concept of sport clubs as corporative actors and the ideas of Coleman (1986) and Esser (1999) a multilevel framework has been developed. This framework integrates the macro and meso perspective (Nagel 2006,

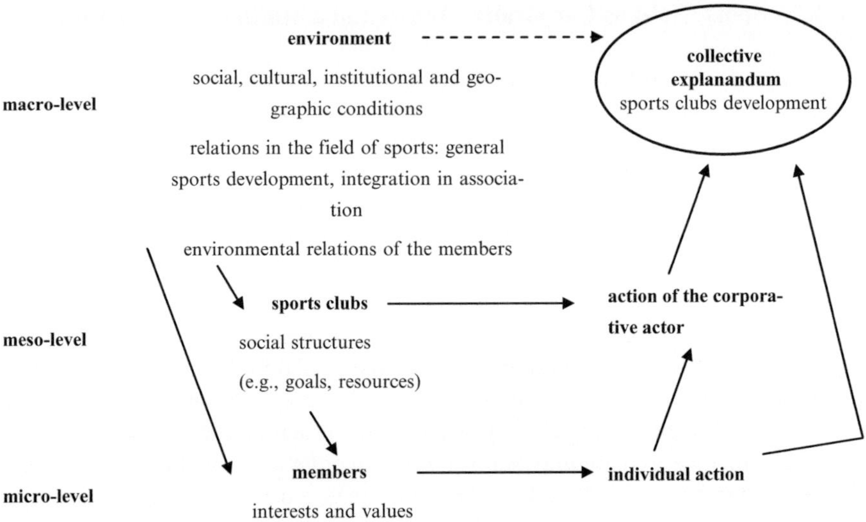


**Fig. 2.2** Multilevel model for the analysis of the development of sport clubs (Nagel 2006, 2007; Esser 1993)

2007). Three levels have been distinguished (see Fig. 2.2; conceptually the micro-level is included, but is not a focus of this book):

*Macro-level*: Sport club development has to be understood in the context of the broader development in society and modern sports. Sport clubs are embedded in several fields of society (e.g. politics, economics, the media, health system) and in specific structures of the national sport system (especially umbrella organisations), and this needs to be taken into account. For example, individualisation, commercialisation, globalisation or political changes generate so-called field-level pressures (O'Brien and Slack 2004, p. 36) and may have a strong influence on the development of sport clubs. Therefore, it is necessary to regard the societal, cultural, geographical and political embedding of sport clubs as well as their historical origins. In addition, it is interesting to note the role sport clubs play in the national and regional sport context as well as in national sport policy (e.g. Sport for All).

Other scholars have drawn attention to the way in which sport clubs as institutions cohere to the expectations of national organisations or the state (Skille 2008). Many authors have stressed the institutional volatilisation of modern societies, which would also have an effect for sport clubs (Bauman 2000; Giddens 1991; Zijderveld 2000). In particular this could threaten the traditional solidarity in associations (Schlesinger et al. 2013; Van der Roest et al. 2015).

*Meso-level*: However, not all sport clubs in certain countries reveal the same structures and changes. According to Esser (1999), to understand the cause of specific developments (such as professionalisation), it is necessary to have a closer look at the meso-level and to consider sport clubs as corporative actors. Here we can assume that the specific organisational context influences the actions and decisions of the club. For example, the number of members, the financial resources, the clubs' goals or the importance of traditions and cultures in different kinds of sports may play a crucial role for the specific activities.

(a) Furthermore, it also seems appropriate to look at the reciprocal correlations between sport clubs and their members. The specific interests of the members and their values in the context of the club could be particularly relevant to regulating action and engagement within their club (Penner 2002; Schlesinger and Nagel 2013). And with their collective actions the members constitute and change the social structure of their sport clubs (e.g. club goals, sport activities).

This multilevel framework facilitates in a broader sense the analysis of the origins and determinants of the sport clubs' development, as well as the effects and consequences of structural changes. It allows the integration of the different approaches existing in the literature in order to understand organisational change in sport clubs. In this handbook we focus mainly on a descriptive view of the macro- and meso-level and in Sect. 2.5 identify the most relevant aspects for the comparison of sport clubs in the European context.

#### 2.4.1.3 Sport Clubs as Organisations of the Third Sector

As a multidisciplinary project, third sector research attempts to analyse the structure, logic of action and social function of those organisations that in modern societies locate themselves between the different sectors of state, market and informal sphere (see also the model of four performance systems conceptualised by Jütting et al. 2003). Associations or clubs are often considered as a hybrid of the three social action logics of the market, state and private sphere. These three action logics can be seen in a simplified way as follows: the market coordinates supply and demand through price-related exchange and is dominated by the action logic of profit maximisation for individual use. The state organises the production of public services by hierarchical coordination, guided by the action logic of the right to equal treatment in the public interest; the private sphere controls the satisfaction of individual needs based on affective relations and mutual aid and follows the action logic of selfless love.

Recently, various authors have stated that voluntary associations have their own typical logic. Strob (as cited in Braun 2003, p. 50) describes this logic as "a joint action aimed at mutual, targeted benefits". Voluntary associations can be seen as communities in which individuals voluntarily unite to achieve realisation of a particular shared interest through shared commitment. Thus, sport clubs like voluntary clubs are *intermediate organisations* (Streeck 1987). In manifold ways they produce connections between individuals and complex interrelations and societal structures (Siewert 1984). Moreover, Putnam (2000) has shown that the interrelations of members within a club produce social capital, networks and trust between them. It should be noted that not only the members benefit from this interrelation. Non-members benefit from a higher level of trust in society, which means sport clubs can also produce positive externalities. With these inputs from the third sector, the public sector (policy) supports voluntary organisations, such as sport clubs, to provide sport facilities and finances.

When we consider that sport clubs belong to a specific type of institution—voluntary associations in the third sector—the development of this type of institutions can be a focal point for interest. Kikulis et al. (1992) introduce a useful categorisation of archetypes to describe specific features and developments in sport organisations. They claim that changes in sport organisations should not simply be explained as system-wide trends towards increased marketisation, professionalisation and bureaucratisation. Rather the variety in organisational design can be understood by identifying common design archetypes that exist within this institutionally specific set of organisations.

## *2.4.2 Economic Approaches*

### 2.4.2.1 Sport Clubs from an Economic Perspective

From an economic perspective, sport clubs as third-sector organisations exist because of the failure of state and market (Weisbrod 1986). Therefore, sport clubs provide services and programmes that are not covered by the state or the market (Anheier 2010; Weisbrod 1988). Typically, the state or politicians only address the interests of the mainstream to capture as many votes as possible, and the market only addresses those target groups that are sufficiently large and profitable (Anheier 2010; Weisbrod 1988).

The organisational arrangement of sport clubs fits the concept of club goods (Wicker et al. 2014). Club goods capture ownership-membership arrangements and are, thus, different from pure public or private goods (Buchanan 1965; Sandler and Tschirhart 1997). The basic idea of club goods is that members pool their resources and benefit from sharing production costs, members' characteristics and excludable benefits (Cornes and Sandler 1986; Sandler and Tschirhart 1997). However, a problem of club size occurs because the relationship between club size and reduced production costs is not linear. In fact the benefits of club production only exist up to a certain point when, for example, the club becomes too congested (Buchanan 1965).

The achievement of cost savings through increasing memberships in sport clubs can be explained by economies of scale (Wicker et al. 2014). Generally speaking, economies of scale imply that the marginal cost of one produced unit decreases with increasing number of products because the fixed costs are shared across more output units (Anheier 2010). Typically, larger organisations are more likely to benefit from economies of scale (Besanko et al. 2010). Similar to scale economies is the concept of economies of scope (Panzar and Willig 1981), which do not refer to organisational size in terms of members, but in terms of products. Economies of scope are present when production costs are lower if a set of products is produced by only one organisation, instead of each organisation producing one product separately. Such a combined production benefits from synergies (Anheier 2010; Chandler and Takashi 1990). Previous research has found evidence of scope economies in sport clubs, but not scale economies (Wicker et al. 2014).

In the context of pooling members' resources, some resources may be considered as scarce. In sport clubs, typically human resources (e.g. volunteers) and financial resources are perceived as scarce resources (Wicker and Breuer 2011). In order to mitigate resource scarcities, sport clubs tend to substitute these resources with other resources that are more accessible. Thus, substitution effects occur in order to account for such resources. For example, decreasing numbers of core volunteers are compensated by an increased workload of the remaining volunteers in the short term and the employment of paid staff in the long term (Breuer et al. 2012).

#### 2.4.2.2 Sport Clubs from a Financial Perspective

Although sport clubs are non-profit organisations that do not pursue the goal of profit maximisation and are restricted by the non-distribution constraint where profit cannot be distributed to the members (Hansmann 1980), financial health is nevertheless important to their sustenance and longevity (Young 2007). Associated with healthy finances is the concept of revenue diversification and the basic ideas stemming from financial portfolio theory, which has also been applied to non-profit organisations outside the sporting context (Kingma 1993) and within sports (Wicker and Breuer 2013). Generally speaking, sport clubs have to choose a risk/revenue package similar to standard for-profit businesses that choose a risk/return package (Kingma 1993). In doing so, relying on revenues of different risk levels is considered advantageous. For example, revenues from membership fees are considered low-risk revenues because they are projectable and split into smaller units (each member pays a fee), while revenues from government subsidies are more risky because they are typically all-or-nothing in nature and likely to be cut from one year to the next (Wicker et al. 2015). An organisation's level of revenue diversification (or concentration) is typically measured with the *Herfindahl Index* which considers both the number of different income sources and the percentage contribution of each income source to the total revenues (Chang and Tuckman 1994). Research shows that a sport club's mission affects its level of revenue diversification: Clubs that are more commercially oriented have more concentrated revenues than clubs with traditional orientations (Wicker, Feiler et al. 2013). It is assumed that organisations can improve their financial situation by diversifying their income portfolio. Existing research supports this assumption and reports that sport clubs with more diversified revenues were in a better overall financial condition (Wicker and Breuer

2013), had less volatile revenues (Wicker et al. 2015) and were less financially vulnerable (Cordery et al. 2013).

Not only is the total amount of sport clubs' revenue crucial, but also the volatility of revenues, the origin or revenue sources and the composition of the income portfolio play important roles. As opposed to simple changes in the average level of revenues, the concept of revenue volatility takes into consideration year-to-year fluctuations in revenues (Wicker et al. 2015). Large fluctuations can represent a financial threat to sport clubs, even when the average level of revenues has not materially changed over time. A club's total volatility can be split into two portions. The first portion is referred to as systematic volatility, which is subject to broader changes in the national economy, while the second portion is called club-specific (or unsystematic) volatility. While revenue diversification is a way to minimise unsystematic risk, systematic volatility cannot be simply solved through diversification (Wicker et al. 2015).

Several typologies have been advanced in regard to the origin of revenues. The most basic distinction is the one between internal and external revenue sources (Coates et al. 2014). In this context, internal revenues are revenues that stem from club members (e.g. membership fees, admission fees, service fees for members), while external revenues are generated from stakeholders outside of the club (e.g. government subsidies, sponsorship income and credits). Research shows that clubs relying on sponsorship income as one external source experience financial problems (Coates et al. 2014).

Another typology suggests a distinction between autonomous and heteronymous revenue categories (Emrich et al. 2001; Wicker, Breuer et al. 2012). In this context, autonomous revenue sources are referred to as those sources where the club has some influence on the prices and yet cannot control the overall amount of money generated from this specific source. For example, the club can set the prices for food and beverages at the club's restaurant, but it cannot ultimately control how much will be sold. Heteronymous revenue categories are characterised by the fact that the club has no control over the prices. For example, the amount of money a sponsor or a donor will give to the club cannot be determined (Wicker, Breuer et al. 2012).

Research also suggests that the composition of the income portfolio is critical because of the interactions between different income sources. Such interactions are referred to as crowd-out and crowd-in effects (Anheier 2010). Crowd-out effects occur when increases in one revenue source lead to decreases in another income source, which is *crowded out*. A typical concern in non-profit research is that public money crowds out private giving (e.g. Andreoni and Payne 2011; Kingma 1989; Payne 1998); however, this concern could not be confirmed for sport clubs (Enjolras 2002; Wicker, Breuer et al. 2012).

As sport clubs are competing for financial resources with other organisations in their environment, research on financing sport clubs has also looked at advantages or disadvantages of sport clubs over competitors such as for-profit companies. Based on property rights theory (e.g. Picot et al. 2008) it can be argued that the diffusion of property rights in sport clubs leads to financial disadvantages, in the sense that sport clubs do not have an incentive to spend their money wisely.

However, from the perspective of potential resource providers, sport clubs also have advantages over for-profit companies. For example, the attention towards a potential sponsor is higher in sport clubs and the sponsor is more protected against the hold-up risk (Wicker, Weingärtner et al. 2012). Moreover, following platform theory, sport clubs provide better platforms for sponsors than for-profit companies because for potential sponsors the networks are seen to be more open (Dietl and Weingärtner 2011). Thus, sponsors were found to be more likely to give their money to non-profit sport clubs than to for-profit companies in the same sport (Wicker, Weingärtner et al. 2012).

## 2.5 Towards a Multilevel Framework for the Comparison of Sport Clubs in Different Countries

In this theoretical section, sport clubs have been looked at from various perspectives. Historical roots as well as current developments in the context of modern sports were considered and sport clubs were conceptualised using sociological and economical approaches. Each of these theoretical concepts appears to be useful when making a comprehensive analysis of sport clubs and transnational comparisons. By integrating particular theoretical perspectives, the multilevel model for the analysis of the development of sport clubs (Fig. 2.2) can serve as a heuristic framework to assist the comparison of situations of sport clubs across different countries in Europe. For specific research questions that analyse each country covered in the chapters, two perspectives need to be differentiated: the (1) macro- and the (2) meso-level.

1. *Macro perspective:* The historical analysis of sport clubs as well as their current development reveal that they are strongly embedded in the social and political context and the national sport system. Therefore, the questions arise:

   - *What are the historical origins of sport clubs?*
   - *What is the position of sport clubs within the national sport structure?*

   Sport clubs remain the most important organisations for the participation in sports of the whole population, and play an increasingly crucial role in sport policy. Third sector research in particular emphasises the social functions of sport clubs and their contributions in social welfare: e.g. social integration, education and health promotion. In this context the following questions are important:

   - *To what extent are sport clubs able to integrate all specific groups of the population as members?*
   - *What role do sport clubs play in the context of the (local and national) sport policy?*

2. *Meso perspective:* As sport clubs are autonomous corporate actors, they are enclosed but not determined by their social and political environment. Thus, it is necessary to have a closer look at the structural characteristics of sport clubs.

When considering the different research perspectives presented in this chapter, the following aspects and questions seem relevant to any comparison between different countries.

- According to the concept of club goods, size is a relevant factor to understanding sport clubs. *Therefore, it is useful to analyse the number of members. Furthermore, it is interesting to consider whether sport clubs are organised as a single or multiple club with different sports.*
- Bearing in mind the principle that sport clubs are established to realise the shared interests of the club members, the question arises as to *what sport and non-sport activities are usually provided.*
- Volunteering of the members is a basic characteristic of sport clubs. However, in the context of professionalisation of modern sports the question can be asked *if all club activities are still organised and arranged by volunteers and what role do paid employees undertake.*
- Another important resource for a viable sport club is the finances. *What internal and external sources are relevant for sport clubs to gain revenues and what are the most significant expenses?*
- *What are the main challenges of sport clubs in the context of the current developments in modern sports and society?*

## References

Andreoni J, Payne AA (2011) Is crowding out due entirely to fundraising? Evidence from a panel of charities. J Public Econ 95:334–343

Anheier HK (2010) Nonprofit organizations. Theory, management, policy. Routledge, London

Auld C (2008) Voluntary sport clubs: the potential for the development of social capital. In: Nicholson M, Hoye R (eds) Sport and social capital. Elsevier, Amsterdam, pp 143–165

Bauman Z (2000) Liquid modernity. Polity, Cambridge

Baur J, Braun S (eds) (2003) Integrationsleistungen von Sportvereinen als freiwilligen Organisationen [Integration efforts of sport clubs as voluntary organisations]. Meyer & Meyer, Aachen

Besanko D, Dranove D, Shanley M, Schaefer S (2010) Economics of strategy, 5th edn. Wiley, Hoboken, NJ

Bette K-H (1993) Sport und Individualisierung [Sport and individualism]. Spectrum Sportwissenschaften 5:34–55

Braun S (2003) Freiwillige Vereinigungen zwischen Staat, Markt und Privatsphäre [Voluntary associations between state, market and privacy]. In: Baur J, Braun S (eds) Integrationsleistungen von Sportvereinen als Freiwilligen Organisationen. Meyer & Meyer, Aachen, pp 43–87

Breuer C (2005) Steuerbarkeit von Sportregionen [Controllability of sport regions]. Hofmann, Schorndorf

Breuer C, Feiler S (2013) Sports development report 2011/2012. Analysis of the situation of sports clubs in Germany. Abbreviated version. Sportverlag Strauß, Cologne

Breuer C, Wicker P (2011) Sports development report 2009/2010. Analysis of the situation of sports clubs in Germany. Abbreviated version. Sportverlag Strauß, Cologne

Breuer C, Wicker P, von Hanau T (2012) Consequences of the decrease in volunteers among German sports clubs: is there a substitute for voluntary work? Int J Sport Policy Polit 4:173–186

Buchanan JM (1965) An economic theory of clubs. Economica 32(125):1–14
Chandler AD, Takashi H (1990) Scale and scope: the dynamics of industrial capitalism. Belknap Press, Cambridge, MA
Chang CF, Tuckman HP (1994) Revenue diversification among non-profits. Voluntas 5:273–290
Chantelat P (2001) Professionnalisation des organisations sportives: Nouveaux enjeux, nouveaux débats [The professionalisation of sport organisations: New challenges, new debates]. L'Harmattan, Paris
Coalter F (2007a) A wider social role for sport: who's keeping the score? Routledge, London/New York
Coalter F (2007b) Sports clubs, social capital and social regeneration: 'Ill-defined interventions with hard to follow outcomes'? Sport Soc Cult Comme Media Polit 10:537–559
Coates D, Wicker P, Feiler S, Breuer C (2014) A bivariate probit examination of financial and volunteer problems of non-profit sport clubs. Int J Sport Finan 9(3):130–148
Coleman JS (1974) Power and the structure of society. Norton, New York, NY
Coleman JS (1986) Social theory, social research, and a theory of action. Am J Sociol 91:1309–1335
Collins M (1999) Sport and social inclusion: a report to the department of culture, media and sport. Loughborough University, Institute of Sport and Leisure Policy, Loughborough
Cordery CJ, Sim D, Baskerville RF (2013) Three models, one goal: assessing financial vulnerability in New Zealand amateur sports clubs. Sport Manag Rev 16:186–199
Cornes R, Sandler T (1986) The theory of externalities, public goods and club goods. Cambridge University Press, Cambridge, MA
Cuskelly G (2004) Volunteer retention in community sport organisations. Eur Sport Manag Quart 4:59–76
Dietl H, Weingärtner C (2011) The effect of professional football clubs' legal structure on sponsoring revenue. J Sponsorship 4(4):377–390
Digel H (1986) Über den Wandel der Werte in Gesellschaft, Freizeit und Sport [About the change of values in society, leisure and sport]. In: Heinemann K, Becker H (eds) Die Zukunft des Sports. Hofmann, Schorndorf, pp 14–43
Digel H (1992) Turn- und Sportvereine. Strukturen, Probleme, Trends [Gymnastic and sporting clubs. Structures, problems, trends]. Meyer & Meyer, Aachen
Donaldson A, Leggett S, Finch CF (2011) Sports policy development and implementation in context: researching and understanding the perceptions of community end-users. Int Rev Sociol Sport 46:1–18
Emrich E, Pitsch W, Flatau J, Pierdzioch C (2014) Voluntary engagement in sports clubs: a behavioral model and some empirical evidence. Int Rev Sociol Sport 49:227–240
Emrich E, Pitsch W, Papathanassiou V (2001) Die Sportvereine—Ein Versuch auf empirischer Grundlage [Sports clubs—an attempt on an empirical basis]. Hofmann, Schorndorf
Enjolras B (2002) The commercialization of voluntary sport organizations in Norway. Nonprofit Volunt Sect Quart 31:352–376
Esser H (1993) Soziologie. Allgemeine Grundlagen [Sociology. General principles]. Campus, Frankfurt
Esser H (1999) Soziologie—Spezielle Grundlagen. Band 1: Situationslogik und Handeln [Sociology–Special principles. Volume 1: situational logic and action]. Campus, Frankfurt
Fahlén J (2006) Organizational structures of Swedish elite ice hockey clubs. Sport Gesellschaft 3:57–81
Fahlén J, Stenling C, Vestin L (2008) Money talks—a qualitative analysis of the organizational change connected with the corporation formation of a voluntary sport club. Sport Gesellschaft 5:153–177
Flatau J (2007) Die Entwicklung der Leichtathletikvereine. Eine kritische empirische Analyse zur "Krise der Leichtathletik" [The development of athletics clubs. A critical empirical analysis of the "crisis of athletics"]. Sport und Strauss, Cologne
Flatau J, Pitsch W, Emrich E (2012) Zum Wandel von Sportvereinen und seinen Ursachen—Befunde einer Mehrebenen-Untersuchung [Causes of change in sports clubs. Findings from a multi-level study]. Sport Gesellschaft 9:63–92

Giddens A (1984) The constitution of society. Polity Press, Cambridge, MA
Giddens A (1991) Modernity and self-identity: self and society in the late modern age. Polity Press, Cambridge, MA
Groeneveld M (2009) European sport governance, citizens, and the state. Finding a (co-) productive balance for the twenty-first century. Public Manag Rev 11:421–440
Hall MH, Andrukow A, Barr C, Brock K, de Wit M, Embuldeniya D (2003) The capacity to serve: a qualitative study of the challenges facing Canada's nonprofit and voluntary organizations. Canadian Centre for Philanthropy, Toronto
Hansmann H (1980) The role of nonprofit enterprise. Yale Law J 33:835–901
Heinemann K (1999) Sports clubs in Europe. In: Heinemann K (ed) Sport clubs in various European countries. Hofmann, Schorndorf, pp 13–32
Heinemann K (2004) Sportorganisationen: Verstehen und Gestalten [Understanding and designing sport organizations]. Hofmann, Schorndorf
Hoekman R, Romijn D, Rutten T (2011) Een veld voor de helft: Over sociale tarieven en subsidies [A field for half price: About social rates and subsidies]. Mulier Instituut, 's-Hertogenbosch
Horch H-D (1992) Geld, Macht und Engagement in freiwilligen Vereinigungen [Money, power and engagement in voluntary associations]. Duncker & Humblot, Berlin
Horch H-D, Schütte N (2009) Pressure and obstacles to the employment of paid managers in voluntary sports clubs and federations in Germany. Eur J Sport Soc 6:101–120
Houlihan B, Green M (2009) Modernization and sport: the reform of Sport England and UK Sport. PSA, Loughborough
Houlihan B, White A (2002) The politics of sports development. Routledge, London
Ibsen B (1992) Frivilligt arbejde i idrætsforeninger [Voluntary work in sports clubs]. DHL, København
Jolles HM (1972) Sociologie van de participatie. Een onderzoek in enkele Amsterdamse verenigingen [Sociology of participation. A research in a number of sport clubs in Amsterdam]. Alphen aan den Rijn, Samson
Jütting DH, von Bentem N, Oshege V (2003) Vereine als sozialer Reichtum [Clubs as social wealth]. Waxmann, Münster
Kikulis LM, Slack T, Hinings B (1992) Institutionally specific designs archetypes: a framework for understanding change in national sport organizations. Int Rev Sociol Sport 27:343–368
Kingma BR (1989) An accurate measurement of the crowd-out effect, income effect, and price effect for charitable contributions. J Polit Econ 97:1197–1207
Kingma BR (1993) Portfolio theory and nonprofit financial stability. Nonprofit Volunt Sect Quart 22:105–119
Lawrence PR, Lorsch JW (1967) Organisation and environment. Harvard Graduate School of Business Administration, Cambridge, MA
Lenk H (1972) Probleme der Sportsoziologie [Problems of the sociology of sport]. Bundesinstitut für Sportwissenschaft, Ahrensburg
Lucassen J (2007) Service quality in a diversifying market for active participation in sport: provision of fitness centers and voluntary sport clubs compared. In: Horch H-D, Breuer C, Hovemann G, Kaiser S, Roemisch V (eds) Qualitätsmanagement im Sport. Institut für Sportökonomie und Sportmanagement, Cologne, pp 183–198
Lucassen J, Van Kalmthout J (2009) Morality management in sport clubs. Paper presented at the ISSA conference 2009, Bucharest, Romania
Lucassen J, Van Kalmthout J (2011) Sportverenigingen als maatschappelijke dienstverleners [Sport clubs as social services]. In: Boessenkool J, Lucassen J, Waardenburg M, Kemper F (eds) Sportverenigingen: Tussen tradities en transities [Sport clubs: between traditions and transitions]. Arko Sports Media, Nieuwegein, pp 55–78
Luhmann N (2000) Organisation und Entscheidung [Organization and decision]. VS, Wiesbaden
Manders T, Kropman J (1979) Kaderbehoefte bij sportverenigingen [The need for staff at sport clubs]. ITS, Nijmegen
May T, Harris S, Collins M (2014) Implementing community sport policy: understanding the variety of voluntary club types and their attitudes to policy. Int J Sport Policy Polit 5:397–419

Misener K, Doherty AJ (2009) A case study of organizational capacity in nonprofit community sport. J Sport Manag 23:457–482
Nagel S (2006) Sportvereine im Wandel. Akteurtheoretische Analysen zur Entwicklung von Sportvereinen [Sport clubs in change. Actor theoretic analyses of the development of sports]. Schorndorf, Hofmann
Nagel S (2007) Akteurtheoretische Analyse der Sportvereinsentwicklung—Ein theoretisch-methodischer Bezugsrahmen [Actor theoretic analysis of the development of sports—a theoretical-methodical reference framework]. Sportwissenschaft 37:186–201
Nagel S (2008) Goals of sports clubs. Eur J Sport Soc 5:119–139
Nagel S, Schlesinger T (2012) Sportvereinsentwicklung. Ein Leitfaden zur Planung von Veränderungsprozessen [Sport club developement. A guide for planning of change processes]. Haupt, Berne
Nederlands Olympisch Comité * Nederlandse Sport Federatie (2009) Olympisch Plan 2028. Heel Nederland naar Olympisch niveau. Plan van aanpak op hoofdlijnen [Olympic Plan 2028. All of the Netherlands to an Olympic level. Plan of action in mainlines]. NOC*NSF, Arnhem
Nichols G, Taylor P, James M, Holmes K, King L, Garrett R (2005) Pressures on the UK voluntary sport sector. Voluntas 16:33–50
O'Brien D, Slack T (2004) The emerge of a professional logic in English rugby union: the role of isomorphic and diffusion processes. J Sport Manag 18:13–39
Østerlund K (2012) Managing voluntary sport organizations to facilitate volunteer recruitment. Eur Sport Manag Quart 13:143–165
Østerlund K (2013) Foreningsidrættens sociale kvaliteter. En social kapital-inspireret undersøgelse af danske idrætsforeninger og deres medlemmer [The social benefits generated by voluntary organized sport. A study of Danish voluntary sport organizations and their members inspired by the theory of social capital]. Doctoral dissertation. University of Southern Denmark, Odense
Panzar JC, Willig RD (1981) Economies of scope. Am Econ Rev 71:268–272
Payne AA (1998) Does the government crowd-out private donations? New evidence from a sample of non-profit firms. J Public Econ 69:323–345
Penner LA (2002) Dispositional and organizational influences on sustained volunteerism: an interactionist perspective. J Soc Issues 58:447–467
Picot A, Dietl H, Franck E (2008) Organisation, 5th edn. Schäffer-Poeschel, Stuttgart
Putnam R (2000) Bowling alone: the collapse and revival of American community. Simon & Schuster, New York, NY
Reid F (2012) Increasing sports participation in Scotland: are voluntary sports clubs the answer? Int J Sport Policy Polit 4:221–241
Salamon LM, Anheier HK (1996) The international classification of nonprofit organizations: ICNPO-Revision 1, 1996 (Working papers of the Johns Hopkins Comparative Nonprofit Sector Project, no. 19). The Johns Hopkins Institute for Policy Studies, Baltimore, MD
Sandler T, Tschirhart JT (1980) The economic theory of clubs: an evaluative survey. J Econ Lit 18:1481–1521
Sandler T, Tschirhart J (1997) Club theory: thirty years later. Public Choice 93:335–355
Schimank U (2000) Handeln und Strukturen. Einführung in die akteurtheoretische Soziologie [Actions and structures. Introduction to actor-theoretical sociology]. Juventa, Weinheim
Schimank U (2005) Der Vereinssport in der Organisationsgesellschaft: Organisationssoziologische Perspektiven auf ein Spannungsverhältnis [Club sport in the organization society: organisational-sociological perspectives on a tense relationship]. In: Alkemeyer T, Rigauer B, Sobiech G (eds) Organisationsentwicklungen und DeInstitutionalisierungsprozesse im Sport. Hofmann, Schorndorf, pp 21–44
Schlagenhauf, K. (1977). Sportvereine in der Bundesrepublik Deutschland. Teil 1: Strukturelemente und Verhaltensdeterminanten im organisierten Freizeitbereich [Sport clubs in the Federal Republic of Germany. Part 1: structural elements and behavioral determinants in the organized leisure]. Hofmann, Schorndorf
Schlesinger T, Egli B, Nagel S (2013) "Continue or terminate?" Determinants of long-term volunteering in sports clubs. Eur Sport Manag Quart 13:32–53

Schlesinger T, Klenk C, Nagel S (2015) How do sport clubs recruit volunteers? Analyzing and developing a typology of decision-making processes on recruiting volunteers in Sport Clubs. Sport Manag Rev 18:193–206. doi:10.1016/j.smr.2014.04.003

Schlesinger T, Nagel S (2013) "Who will volunteer?" Analysing individual and structural factors of volunteering in Swiss sports clubs. Eur J Sport Sci 13:707–715

Seippel Ø (2006) Sport and social capital. Acta Sociol 49:169–183

Siewert H-J (1984) Zur Thematisierung des Vereinswesens in der deutschen Soziologie [For addressing clubs in German sociology]. In: Dann O (ed) Vereinswesen und bürgerliche Gesellschaft in Deutschland. Oldenbourg, Munich, pp 151–180

Skille EÅ (2008) Understanding sport clubs as sport policy implementers. Int Rev Sociol Sport 43:181–200

Skille EÅ (2009) State sport policy and voluntary sport clubs: the case of the Norwegian Sports City Program as social policy. Eur Sport Manag Quart 9:63–79

Slack T, Parent M (2005) Understanding sport organizations: the application of organization theory. Human Kinetics, Champaign, IL

Sport England (2009) Clubmark resources. Retrieved 17 October 2014 from http://www.clubmark.org.uk/clubmark/getting-clubmark/resources-and-templates/clubmark-resources

Steenbergen J, De Knop P, Elling A (2001) Values and norms in sport: critical reflections on the position and meanings of sport in society. Meyer & Meyer, Aachen

Streeck W (1987) Vielfalt und Interdependenz. Überlegungen zur Rolle von intermediären Organisationen in sich ändernden Umwelten Diversity and interdependence. Considerations of the role of intermediary organizations in changing environments. Kölner Zeitschrift für Soziologie und Sozialpsychologie 39:471–495

Thiel A, Mayer J (2009) Characteristics of voluntary sports clubs management: a sociological perspective. Eur Sport Manag Quart 9:81–98

Thiel A, Meier H (2004) Überleben durch Abwehr. Zur Lernfähigkeit des Sportvereins [Survival through resistance. About the learning capacity of sports organizations]. Sport Gesellschaft 1:103–124

Thiel A, Meier H, Cachay K (2006) Hauptberuflichkeit im Sportverein. Voraussetzungen und Hindernisse [Full-time employment in sports clubs: preconditions and obstacles]. Hofmann, Schorndorf

Timm W (1979) Sportvereine in der Bundesrepublik Deutschland. Teil II: Organisations-, Angebots- und Finanzstruktur [Sport clubs in the Federal Republic of Germany. Part II: Organizational, supply and financial structure]. Hofmann, Schorndorf

Ulseth A-L (2004) Social integration in modern sport: commercial fitness centres and voluntary sports clubs. Eur J Sport Manag 4:95–115

Van der Roest J-W, Vermeulen J, van Bottenburg M (2015) Creating sport consumers in Dutch sport policy. Int J Sport Policy Polit 7(1):105–121

Van Hoecke J, De Knop P (2006) Development of a relevant quality system for gymnastics clubs: an application of the principals of total quality and service management in traditionally organized sport. Int J Sport Manag Market 3:359–377

Van Hoecke J, De Knop P, Schoukens H (2009) A decade of quality and performance management in Flemish organized sport. Int J Sport Manag Market 6:308–329

Van Meerbeek R (1977) Structurele analyse van de sportclubs in Vlaanderen [Structural analyses of spot clubs in Vlandern]. K.U. Leuven, Instituut voor Lichamelijke Opleiding, Leuven

Vos S, Breesch D, Késenne S, Van Hoecke J, Vanreusel B, Scheerder J (2011) Governmental subsidies and coercive pressures. Evidence from sport clubs and their resource dependencies. Eur J Sport Soc 8:257–280

Weisbrod BA (1986) Toward a theory of the voluntary nonprofit sector in a three-sector economy. In: Rose-Ackerman S (ed) The economics of nonprofit institutions. Studies in structure and policy. Oxford University Press, New York, NY, pp 21–44

Weisbrod BA (1988) The nonprofit economy. Harvard University Press, Cambridge, MA

Wicker P, Breuer C (2011) Scarcity of resources in German non-profit sport clubs. Sport Manag Rev 14:188–201

Wicker P, Breuer C (2013) Understanding the importance of organizational resources to explain organizational problems: evidence from non-profit sport clubs in Germany. Voluntas 24:461–484

Wicker P, Breuer C (2014) Exploring the organizational capacity and organizational problems of disability sport clubs in Germany using matched pairs analysis. Sport Manag Rev 17:23–34

Wicker P, Breuer C, Hennigs B (2012) Understanding the interactions among revenue categories using elasticity measures—evidence from a longitudinal sample of non-profit sport clubs in Germany. Sport Manag Rev 15:318–329

Wicker P, Breuer C, Lamprecht M, Fischer A (2014) Does club size matter? An examination of economies of scale, economies of scope, and organizational problems. J Sport Manag 28:266–280

Wicker P, Feiler S, Breuer C (2013) Organizational mission and revenue diversification among non-profit sports clubs. Int J Finan Stud 1:119–136

Wicker P, Longley N, Breuer C (2015). Revenue volatility in German nonprofit sports clubs. Nonprofit Volunt Sect Quart 44:5–24. doi:10.1177/0899764013499072

Wicker P, Vos S, Scheerder J, Breuer C (2013) The link between resource problems and interorganisational relationships: a quantitative study of Western European sport clubs. Manag Leisure 18:31–45

Wicker P, Weingärtner C, Breuer C, Dietl H (2012) The effect of a sport institution's legal structure on sponsorship income: the case of amateur equestrian sports in Germany. Int J Sport Finan 7:340–357

Young DR (2007) Why study nonprofit finance? In: Young DR (ed) Financing nonprofits: putting theory into practice. AltaMira, Plymouth, pp 3–20

Zijderveld AC (2000) The institutional imperative. The interface of institutions and networks. Amsterdam University Press, Amsterdam

# Chapter 3
# Sport Clubs in Austria

**Otmar Weiss and Gilbert Norden**

## 3.1 Introduction

Austria is a democratic and federal republic. It consists of nine federal provinces, namely Burgenland, Carinthia, Lower Austria, Salzburg, Styria, Tyrol, Upper Austria, Vienna and Vorarlberg, and is presently governed by a coalition of the Social Democrats and the People's Party, which have both also been playing an important role with regard to the sport club system in Austria. Austria is well known for its cultural heritage throughout history, reaching from architectural monuments, literature and music to theatre and film. After the Second World War, skiing began to constitute a major part of the modern Homo Austriacus' sport identity.

The data used in this chapter were taken from statistics of sport associations, Austrian surveys, sociological studies and diploma theses.

## 3.2 History and Context

When considering the organisation and functions of the Austrian sport club, it is important to note that the Austrian tradition reflects a less positive attitude towards including sport as a part of the education system than the tradition in Great Britain and the USA. Since it was accepted less readily by schools and universities, sport

O. Weiss (✉)
Institute of Sport Science, Vienna University, Wien, Austria
e-mail: otmar.weiss@univie.ac.at

G. Norden
Institute of Sociology, Vienna University, Wien, Austria
e-mail: gilbert.norden@univie.ac.at



C. Breuer et al. (eds.), *Sport Clubs in Europe*, Sports Economics, Management and Policy 12, DOI 10.1007/978-3-319-17635-2_3

had to look for other fields of activity and a different organisational structure in order to operate on a broad basis. The sport clubs set-up was the result.

It started in the middle of the nineteenth century. Not until after the liberalisation of the club policies in 1861, when Emperor Franz Joseph I proclaimed the Austrian empire's constitution, did the permanent foundation of sport clubs take place.

In rapid succession, gymnastics clubs emerged, which fostered physical training in the spirit of Friedrich Ludwig Jahn (1778–1852). At the same time, sport clubs were founded, the first ones for rowing and mountain climbing in 1862, fencing in 1864, ice skating in 1867, cycling in 1869, etc. The foundation of sport clubs was succeeded by the foundation of sport federations, which—with few exceptions—only started in the early 1880s.

During these founding activities, a differentiation of the developing club and federation culture, not only regarding different sports and differing social classes of the members, but also in terms of ideological, political and religious views, soon set in. Besides liberal and German national gymnastics and sport clubs, Christian gymnastics and sport clubs emerged, and along with sport clubs which propagated the ideal of a culture of movement free from politics, working class gymnastics and sport clubs (with the aim of overcoming the capitalistic order) were founded. The ongoing differentiation of the sport club and federation culture resulted in the formation and advancement of three umbrella sport associations, which still exist to this day, the *Austrian Association for Sport and Physical Culture*, the *Austrian Sport Union* and the *Austrian General Sport Association*.

### *3.2.1 Umbrella Sport Associations*

The *Austrian Association for Sport and Physical Culture* (*Arbeitsgemeinschaft für Sport und Körperkultur Österreich*, ASKÖ) can be traced back to the *Austrian Workers Gymnastics Association* (*Österreichischer Arbeiter-Turnerbund*) founded in 1910, where the workers' gymnastics clubs, which came into being from the early 1890s and which were close to the Social Democratic Party, were pooled. Soon workers' sport clubs like-minded to the social democratic workers' gymnastics clubs also grew, initially for cycling and hiking, then for swimming, athletic sport, etc. After the end of the First World War in 1918, the workers' sport and gymnastics clubs partnered with the soldiers' sport organisations to become the *Association of Workers and Soldiers Sport Clubs* (*Verband der Arbeiter- und Soldatensportvereinigungen*), from which the *Workers' Association for Sport and Physical Culture in Austria* (*Arbeiterbund für Sport und Körperkultur in Österreich*, ASKÖ) developed. The ASKÖ saw sport as part of an unfolding workers' cultural movement and aimed at the build-up of a proletarian alternative to the bourgeois physical culture. Sport for the masses instead of bourgeois sport with the sole aim of records, healthy bodies instead of endangerment in competitive sport, collective achievements instead of individual ones and solidarity instead of individualism were its ideals. Officially, worker sportsmen were not allowed to take part in competitions of bourgeois sport. From 1934 on until the end of the Second World War, the ASKÖ was banned. After the end of the war in 1945, the ASKÖ was newly founded and it built upon its traditions of before 1934. But since then it participated in national and international competitions and sport projects without any differentiation from bourgeois sport. In 1971 the ASKÖ changed its name into its present one. The changing of the name expressed that the time of the workers' sport movement being part of the proletariat's class movement was over. The focus on the promotion of mass and leisure sport with a special emphasis on health and physical fitness was the only thing that remained from the ideology of the workers' sport. The organisation of slow-run meetings and the development of back training, spine gymnastics and health-promoting programs for children and youth have been the main activities of the ASKÖ since then. In addition, the ASKÖ offers a wide variety of sports. It is Austria's largest sport association, counting 1,089,405 members in 4,716 sport clubs. The membership number includes the members of the Social Democratic *Austrian Car and Bicycle Union* (*Auto- und Radfahrerbund Österreichs*, ARBÖ) and the politically equally aligned hiking federation *Austrian Friends of Nature* (*Naturfreunde Österreichs*).

The ideological equivalent to the ASKÖ is the *Austrian Sport Union* (*SPORTUNION Österreich*), whose history goes back as far as the history of the ASKÖ. 1914 was the founding year of a forerunner organisation of the SPORTUNION, namely the *Imperial Federation of Christian-German Gymnastics Clubs in Austria* (*Reichsverband der christlich-deutschen Turnerschaft Österreichs*). It was affiliated with the Christian-Social Party and had a Christian German purpose at its core, akin to the Austrian *fatherland* term. Since 1895 this ideology had resulted in the foundation of a number of gymnastics and sport clubs in Vienna and the crown lands of the monarchy, from the Sudetes to the Dolomites. After the breakup of the monarchy, these clubs had to reorganise themselves. The name of the association newly founded in 1921 was *Christian-German Gymnastics Union in Austria* (*Christlich-deutsche Turnerschaft Österreichs*, CDTÖ), and it experienced an enormous uplift during the time of the authoritatively administered *Christian-German corporative state* in Austria (1934–1938). The uplift was followed by an abrupt end: in the course of the annexation of Austria to the National Socialist German Reich in March 1938, the CDTÖ was dissolved.

After the Second World War was over in 1945, former officials of the CDTÖ founded an umbrella association which was ideologically allied to Christianity and to the Austrian nationality and which aimed at the fostering of all physical exercise, both at the general and the top level, expressing the organisational unity of gymnastics and sport in its naming, the *Austrian Gymnastics and Sport Union* (*Österreichische Turn- und Sport-Union*). Today the Christian ideology seems to be of subordinate importance. On the one hand, the commitment to the Catholic Church in Austria has plummeted in general, and on the other, the SPORTUNION has risen to become a major association. With 3,936 member clubs and 904,763 memberships, it constitutes the third strongest umbrella sport association in Austria after decades of ranking second (Fig. 3.1). The sport groups of the Catholic Youth and the Austrian Boy Scouts belong to the SPORTUNION and there is a close cooperation with schools today. In addition the SPORTUNION focuses on fitness sport and the association subsequently changed its name in 2002 into *Austrian Sport Union*.

In 1949, the *Austrian General Sport Association* (*Allgemeiner Sportverband Österreichs*, ASVÖ) emerged as the third umbrella sport association. The *Austrian Federation for Physical Exercise* (*Österreichischer Hauptverband für Körpersport*), which had been founded 3 years before, failed due to the hegemony of ASKÖ and SPORTUNION. Therefore the idea emerged of founding a third umbrella association on the same level as ASKÖ and SPORTUNION. This third umbrella association, the ASVÖ, declared itself as above party lines. Only politically independent sport clubs could join the association. A further requirement for admission was and still is the affiliation of the respective sport club with an internationally acknowledged sport federation.

With these requirements for admission, the ASVÖ has attracted a variety of sport clubs, including those which had been German Nationalist oriented in former times as well as Catholic sport groups which did not see a good representation of their interests in the SPORTUNION. So, the ASVÖ became a melting pot for all sport clubs which did not feel associated with SPORTUNION or ASKÖ, and spread all over Austria. Similar to the other two umbrella sport associations the ASVÖ registered a high level of growth in memberships (Fig. 3.1) especially in the 1970s until the early 1990s. Today, it unifies 5,378 sport clubs with a total of 908,763 memberships.

The rise in memberships in all of the three umbrella sport associations between the 1970s and the beginning of the 1990s was a result of favourable developments of social and economic parameters. These developments included increase of wealth

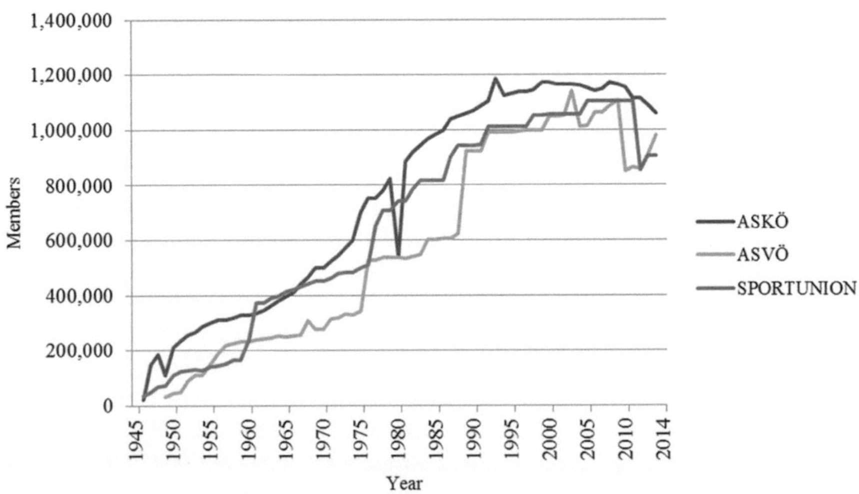


**Fig. 3.1** Development of the numbers of memberships of the three umbrella sport associations in Austria (Österreichisches Sportjahrbuch 1945–2014)

and leisure time, improved quality of life, educational expansion, decline of manual labour, improvement in mobility and better access to infrastructure. In addition, the sport for all advertisement campaigns might have positively influenced sport participation and membership growth. However, after years of growth, stagnation or even recession in membership numbers of the umbrella sport associations is noticeable (Fig. 3.1). Whether this will result in a permanent decrease, and factors such as the explosion of the canon of other attractive leisure activities, the ageing of society as a whole (sport participation is very seldom in the eighth and ninth decades of life) or the competition of commercial sport providers are finally affecting the development or not, has to be the subject of further research.

### 3.2.2 Sport Clubs Within the National Sport Structure in Austria

The sport clubs are subsumed—whether they are members in one of the three umbrella sport associations or not—in sport federations (*Sportfachverbände*), according to the sport they offer. The sport federations were reactivated immediately after the collapse of the National Socialist Regime, when the Club Reorganisation Law was passed on 31 July 1945. Today there are 81 sport federations, among them also a few multi-sports federations such as the *Austrian Military sport federation* (*Österreichischer Heeressportverband*) or the *Austrian Company sport federation* (*Österreichischer Betriebssportverband*). The aim of these sport federations is to nurture and support competitive sport, which have to be kept free from the influence of politics and ideologies. Accordingly, the federations supervise championships in their chosen sport on a provincial, national or international level and provide mandatory guidelines for their sport clubs. They also form national teams to be sent to international competitions, for example European and World championships, or Olympic Games, which require the international recognition of the sport federations as the highest national sport authority.

By far the largest of the sport federations is the *Austrian Football Federation* (*Österreichischer Fußballbund*, ÖFB) with 502,174 members in 2,296 affiliated sport clubs. The Football Federation is followed by the *Austrian Tennis Federation* (*Österreichischer Tennisverband*, ÖTV) with 173,133 members in 1,616 sport clubs, the *Austrian Ski Federation* (*Österreichischer Ski-Verband*; ÖSV) with 142,007 members in 1,182 sport clubs, the *Austrian Ice Stock Sport Association* (*Bund Österreichischer Eis- und Stocksportler*, BÖE) with 114,982 members in 1,708 sport clubs and the *Austrian Golf Federation* (*Österreichischer Golfverband*, ÖGV) with 104,736 members in 153 sport clubs.

The sport federations and the three umbrella sport associations manage sport in Austria, with the *Austrian Federal Sport Organisation* (*Österreichische Bundessportorganisation*, BSO) acting as an overall authority (Fig. 3.2). The BSO as non-governmental umbrella organisation of Austrian sport was set up in 1969. It consists of the *Austrian Federal Sport Specialist Committee* (*Österreichischer*

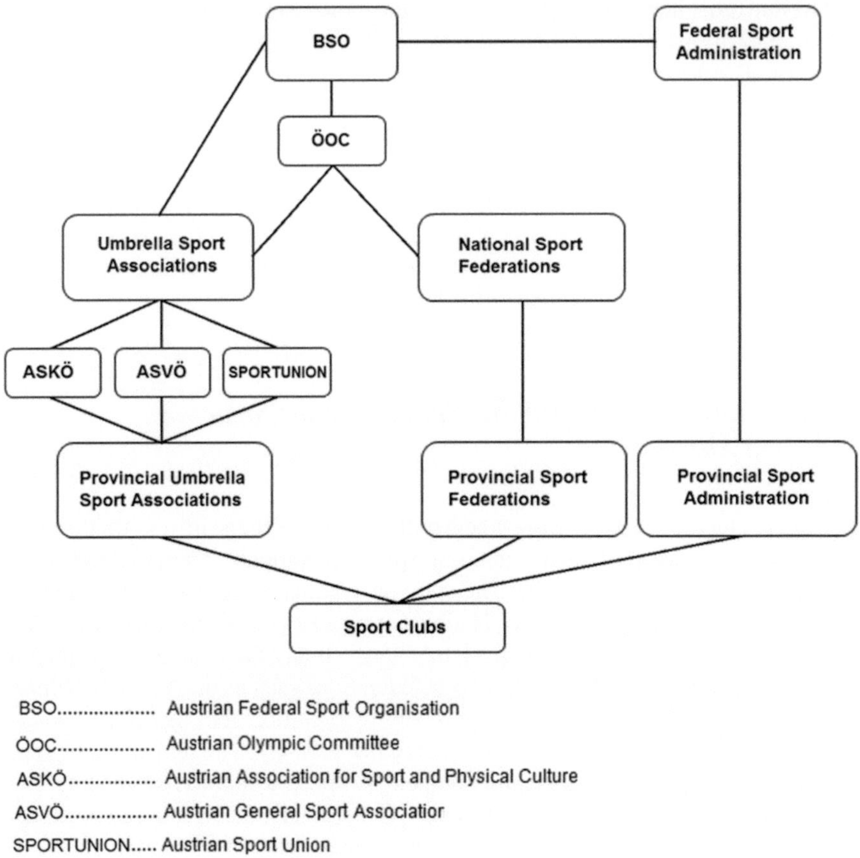


**Fig. 3.2** Overview of the national sport structure in Austria

*Bundessport-Fachrat*), which is made up of representatives from the 81 sport federations, and the *Austrian Federal Sport Committee* (*Österreichischer Bundes-Sportrat*), whose members are representatives of the federal and provincial management boards of the three umbrella sport associations and the relevant federal ministries.

The BSO is responsible for the coordination of sport activities on a nationwide basis. The BSO initiated for example anti-doping campaigns, and organised *Keep Fit Marches*, *Hiking Days* and *Cycling Days* in order to encourage people all over the country to take part in various sports. It also initiated activities for the integration of migrants in club-organised sport. In accordance with Austria's federal system, sporting affairs are the individual responsibility of the nine provinces, each of which has set up its own provincial sport associations and federations and thus sports are encouraged not only through general campaigns organised at the federal level but also at a provincial level.

## 3.3 Role of Sport Clubs in Policy and Society

### *3.3.1 Number of Sport Clubs and Club Members*

It is impossible to determine the exact number of sport clubs in Austria at the present time. Using the Association Statistics as a basis, there are 14,030 sport clubs which are members of one of the three umbrella associations. In addition there is a whole string of sport clubs outside these associations. In almost every municipality there is at least one sport club. More than half of the sport clubs are situated in rural municipalities, about a quarter in small- and medium-sized towns, and only a fifth of the sport clubs is situated in the provincial capitals. On average, there are 14 sport clubs for every 10,000 citizens, but there are significant differences when comparing the federal provinces: Burgenland has the greatest number of sport clubs in relation to the number of citizens, and Vienna the least (Weiss et al. 1999). The three umbrella sport associations have more than three million memberships in total as of today. Austria's total population is around 8.5 million. However, it cannot be concluded that about every third Austrian is a member of a sport club. Membership is not equal to member; there are a large number of multi-memberships. It can be (cautiously) estimated that there are 1.7 million persons (including children) who are members in sport clubs in Austria. Estimates of this sort are projections from poll results regarding membership in sport clubs. Recent poll results identify 13 % (2013) or 17 % (2009) of the Austrian population over the age of 14 as members of sport clubs (European Commission 2014).

### *3.3.2 Socio-Demographic Features of Members of Sport Clubs*

A fifth of the people participating in sport in Austria do so in a sport club. Within the group of club athletes, men, inhabitants of smaller towns (5,000–20,000 inhabitants) and members of the upper and middle classes are particularly common. With regard to age, no clear correlation can be observed (Table 3.1). However, 85 % of the Austrian sport clubs believe that they appeal to young people (up to the age of 30), 68 % declare they appeal also or mainly to medium age groups and 30 % appeal also or mainly to older people (over 55 years of age) (Weiss et al. 1999).

### *3.3.3 Social Significance of Sport Clubs*

Sport clubs have a prominent position in the Austrian sport scene. Because of their tradition (40 % of the sport clubs have existed for more than 50 years), their large number and their network they play a unique role which cannot be fulfilled by other sport organisations. Competitive athletic events, e.g. on an international level, are

**Table 3.1** Sport in sport clubs according to gender, age, size of place of residence and affiliation to social class in Austria, 1998

| | Sport participants in sport clubs (Percent) |
|---|---|
| *Gender* | |
| Male | 23 |
| Female | 16 |
| *Age* | |
| 16–29 | 17 |
| 30–39 | 23 |
| 40–49 | 17 |
| 50–59 | 27 |
| 60+ | 20 |
| *Size of place of residence* | |
| Up to 5,000 inhabitants | 20 |
| 5,001–20,000 inhabitants | 32 |
| Over 20,000 inhabitants | 17 |
| *Social class* | |
| Layer A | 25 |
| Layer B | 24 |
| Layer C | 21 |
| Layer D | 14 |
| Layer E | 3 |

Question: *In which form (of organisation) do you participate in sport?* I participate in sport (1) as a member of a sport club, (2) at a private sport provider; (3) I organise my sport activities by myself ($n = 1{,}000$, representative for the Austrian population over 15 years; table base 688 sport participants) (GFK 1998, unpaginated, question 6)

possible for Austria only because of the existence of sport clubs and sport associations. The sport clubs are also important for their frequently held mass sport spectacles, smaller scale national events and fitness activities, encouraged by the fitness boom and the surge of new equipment and conditioning methods. Thus, the sport clubs serve many purposes—fitness activities and competitive sports, as well as physical education, socialising, family outings, etc. Sport clubs enrich the social and cultural patrimony of every municipality or region. Especially in rural municipalities they contribute towards the safekeeping of local or regional identity.

### *3.3.4 Finance*

The important functions which sport clubs and federations serve in general are a major justification for state support. Primarily, state support in Austria means support by the federal provinces, since, in accordance with Austria's federal system, sporting affairs are the individual responsibility of the nine provinces. As Austria-wide sport issues increasingly require state support, however, the federal government has agreed to promote, within the scope of its private-sector administration, any events, projects and the like that involve more than one province and are of national interest. For tax purposes, Austria's sport associations are officially regarded as non-profit amateur organisations. However, as in every other country where sport plays an important role, adequate funds are a prerequisite for the achievement of whatever goals have been set. In the world of high-level competitive sport, true amateur status is a thing of the past.

Financial backing for sport in Austria presents problems of ever-increasing dimensions for those concerned with fundraising. The Sporttoto football pools system, introduced in 1948, provided a basic fund for the country's sport in general. In 1986 the Lotto-Toto lottery company took over the football pool system. It guaranteed annual funding for sport in Austria amounting to—in today's currency—at least 22.6 million euros. Thanks to a dramatic increase in Lotto-Toto gambling stakes 80 million euros were made available in 2013 to sport federations throughout the country (Österreichische Lotterien 2014). The sum allocated to each sport federation is dependent on the size of its membership. The fund is administered by the Federal Sport Organisation, BSO. For the distribution of fundings, the Federal Sports Promotion Fund (Bundes-Sportförderungsfond) was founded in 2014.

Further subsidies are provided by individual provinces and municipalities for the sport federations and sport clubs within their own territory, and exceptional grants are made by the federal and provincial governments for hosting of international sporting events. A high degree of involvement is noticeable between public administration and the sport federations. The *Austrian Court of Auditors* (*Rechnungshof*), for example, in its 2009 report criticised that "Officials on federal and provincial levels responsible for the granting of monetary support were at the same time employed in high positions (for example, CEO, members of the management, directorate, accountants) or on boards of receivers of grant money. Especially regarding the *Particular Federal Sport Support* (*Besondere Bundes-Sportförderung*), representatives of grant receivers played a big part in grant decisions and the control over financial aid. Thus, no continuous separation between givers and receivers of grants was given" (Lilge and Millmann 2013, p. 125).

State subsidies, however, are not enough since standards and needs are rising continuously, while income from ticket sales and broadcasting fees is still appreciably lower in Austria than in other European sporting nations. As a result, other ways of acquiring financial backing for sport have constantly to be sought. Thus, managers of sport federations and sport clubs continuously renew and extend their contracts with the advertising industry. Even top-class, long-established sport clubs would no longer be viable without these extra benefits. In some cases, sport clubs have had to go as far as changing the names of their clubs or sport fields—to include the sponsor's name—in return for financial assistance.

Another source of income is provided by sport federations' pools. One outstanding example of the success of the pools system is the Austrian Ski Pool which, for over 20 years, has been the financial mainstay of competitive skiing in Austria.

The federal government, the *Austrian Ski Federation* (ÖSV) and the *Austrian Federal Economic Chamber* joined forces to furnish a profitable source of funds. Manufacturers of skiing equipment have to buy their way into the pool. Firms that belong to the Austrian Ski Pool undertake not to interfere in the work of the ÖSV or try to exert an influence of any kind.

Many Austrian sport federations (the tennis, cycling, sailing, gymnastics, rowing, football and ice hockey federations, for example) have marketing specialists on their staff. Because of increasing expenses, particularly in the case of football and ice hockey, these experts are constantly on the lookout for new sources of income. It is worth mentioning that the *Sport Club Rapid Vienna* (*Sportklub Rapid Wien*), a Viennese football club with a long tradition and the holder of a record number of championship titles, was the first one to issue shares on the stock exchange. In an attempt to reduce the club's debts it has formed a professionally managed public limited company.

## 3.4 Characteristics of Sport Clubs

### *3.4.1 Size*

In Austria there are only a few professional sport clubs, for football, ice hockey, basketball and handball. In many other sport clubs and kinds of sport there are professional athletes as well, but they cooperate mainly with their sport federations, such as the skiing, tennis or track and field federations. Most of the sport clubs in Austria are amateur clubs. The size of membership and other characteristics of sport clubs in Austria can, according to Weiss et al. (1999) and Weiss et al. (2010), be summarised as follows. The average member count per sport club is 290. However, this number has to be seen with the fact in mind that there are several very large sport clubs with more than 1,000 members each. More than half of the sport clubs have less than 200 members. Less than a fifth of the sport clubs concentrate mainly on competitive sport. About two-fifths of the sport clubs provide opportunities for competitive sport as well as for leisure and mass sport, while the remaining two-fifths focus almost exclusively on leisure and mass sport. Although tendencies go towards mass, leisure and health sport, not even a fifth of the sport clubs provide medical assistance.

Two-fifths of the sport clubs focus on a single sport, two further fifths have up to five sports in their programme and the final fifth of sport clubs provide more than five different sports. Most sport offers of the sport clubs are placed in evenings during the week. More than two-thirds of the sport clubs also offer sport on weekends, and half of the sport clubs provide the means for sport participation during daytime during the week.

### 3.4.2 *Activities*

The sport offers of the clubs are, of course, not used by all of the members. Only in a quarter of the sport clubs do over 90 % of the members participate actively in sport. Especially in prestigious sport clubs, the number of members actually participating in sport is low. An example for this can be found in the statement of a lady working for a golf club in an Austrian village:

> The club has 227 members. Out of these, I have seen at most 60 during the last year. There are many who pay their membership fee, just to be able to proudly state that they are members of the golf club. They are members because it's prestigious, because it is chic to belong to a golf club. The membership certainly increases the reputation within the village where the golf club is seated. From this village an architect, a master-builder, medical doctors, savings bank directors, among others, are members. Some are from Vienna. Even a Count T. is on the list. The members here act like they are nobler than the rest (Girtler 2002, p. 358).

Also typical for Austrian sport clubs is socialising after sport (*Anschlussgeselligkeit*), which is, as Kleine and Fritsch (1990) point out, one of the most important forms of confraternity in sport. According to Weiss et al. (1997) there is a correlation between the motivation structure of sport participants and *Anschlussgeselligkeit*. Individuals are likely to indulge in *Anschlussgeselligkeit* if they participate in sport for competition and social motives. If their sport participation is based on nature and recreation motives *Anschlussgeselligkeit* is unlikely. In Austria there is hardly any sport club without a canteen, and members are often to be seen sitting there after sport and having a glass of beer or wine. This contributes positively towards confraternity, which is a very important goal of Austrian sport clubs (Kaiblinger 1996; Manseder 2008).

### 3.4.3 *Finance*

In terms of funding, the emphasis for sport clubs in Austria lies in celebrations and sport events. These revenues are followed, with a lower priority, by earnings from membership fees, advertising fees, sponsorships and public aid (Weiss et al. 2010). In professional sport clubs, sponsorships are the main source of income (Dachs et al. 2001). The biggest expenses of the sport clubs are generated by regular sport operation (infrastructure, travelling costs, competitions, etc.), followed by general costs (administration, rent for gyms and club houses, club premises, advertising, taxes, sociable events, etc.). Expenditure for staff is only ranked third in sport clubs of all sizes except professional sport clubs, which underlines the great value of voluntary work by functionaries and members (Weiss et al. 2010). Without this factor, sport clubs would have to have an expenditure structure akin to service companies, usually led by the item staff expenditures.

### 3.4.4 Professionalisation

Concerning personnel, 86 % of the employees of the sport clubs are volunteers and 14 % paid employees (Weiss et al. 2010). For the preponderant majority of these 14 % the job is only on the side; that is, it is not the main source of income for their support. Only 1 % of all employees have to live on the salary for their work in the club, this being their main source of income (Gerhartl 2001). The field of activity for those employees for whom it is their main job consists up to 43 % of multifunctional tasks; of these 24 % are in the area of sport (practice supervisor, trainer), 14 % in servicing and maintenance, 10 % in administrative work, 7 % in club direction and management and 2 % in technology and facilities (Gehartl 2001). From the paid employees for whom their work in the clubs is on the side, 76 % are employed in the area of sport (practice supervisor, trainer), 12 % in servicing and maintenance, 4 % in club direction and management and 1 % in other areas (Gerhartl). On average the Austrian sport club has three paid employees. Only 0.7 % of all sport clubs have paid employees exclusively (Weiss et al. 1999). Indeed, paid employees are only to be found in two-fifths of all sport clubs, a luxury the remaining sport clubs cannot afford. Accordingly, voluntary employees are the most valuable and important resource for sport clubs in Austria. On average there are 18 volunteers in each sport club, doing unpaid work for two and a half hours per week for their club. The most common activities of these volunteers are to organise or help to run a sporting event, support day-to-day club activities and to provide transport. Other common activities include being a member of a board or committee, being a coach or a trainer, doing administrative tasks and maintaining sport facilities and sport equipment (European Commission 2014). According to the Eurobarometer 2013, 12 % (European Commission 2014), or 7 %, according to a micro-census in 2006 (BMASK 2009), of the adult Austrian population fulfil such tasks. It is more common for these volunteers to be men rather than women (Fig. 3.3).

Especially the positions higher up in the hierarchy of functionaries are male dominated. An apparent problem is to find enough motivated members, regardless of gender, willing to take up voluntary work in sport clubs in the future. Especially young people are, according to older club functionaries, less willing to do honorary work.

### 3.4.5 Bottlenecks and Challenges

Sport is still a domain of youth. During the last decades the drop in birth rate has led to a drop in the number of children and young persons in almost all sport clubs. This can also be seen in the decline or stagnation of numbers of memberships of the three umbrella sport associations (Fig. 3.1). In addition, young persons do not want to do honorary work. Thus the honorary capacity of sport clubs is limited. The support of sport clubs through its members is lessening.

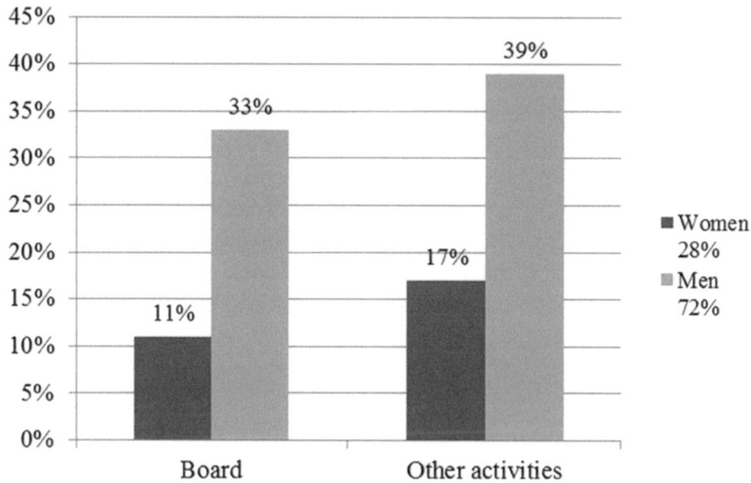


**Fig. 3.3** Voluntary workers by function and gender (Weiss et al. 2010, p. 75)

In spite of the stagnation or decline of the number of sport club members, especially in Vienna, where a fifth of the total Austrian population lives, there are not enough sport facilities. This seems to be the most serious bottleneck concerning the situation of Austrian sport clubs in general. In particular many football clubs do not have their own football pitch, and it is hard to afford the rent for such basic facilities. In discussions in online forums on this topic (OGM 2014) the word *crisis* is frequently used.

## 3.5 Consensual Sport Organisation in Austria

The specificity of sport organisation in Austria has been the political alignment of two of the three umbrella sport associations. The tripartite situation is regarded as a part of the development of the organisation of sport in Austria, and it is approved, under the aspects of diversity of opinions and positive competition. Nevertheless, since the founding of the ASVÖ, it has always been questioned why the political development of sport in Austria has not led to a single neutral and all-encompassing sport association, as has been the case in Germany. The current situation reveals deficiencies regarding concepts for future developments in sport organisations in Austria, and can only be understood from a historical point of view.

In this context, it is also worth mentioning that the ASKÖ formally cut its ties with the Austrian Social Democrats in 2013, when a new transparency law regarding funding from political parties was passed. However, the shared world view between the ASKÖ and the Social Democrats is still a given fact. Numerous functionaries of the ASKÖ also hold positions in the Social Democratic Party.

This is analogous for the SPORTUNION, which considers itself—according to its statutes—above party lines, but still leans towards the Christian-Conservative People's Party on the personnel level.

The antagonism between the Social Democratic and Conservative political movements in Austria has deeply stamped society as a whole. The intensity of contradiction in Austria permeated any number of levels of contemporary Austrian society, and it touched upon and highly influenced such disparate elements as culture, economy, labour, lifestyle, religion and ethical values. For better or worse, it gave form and substance to much in Austrian life, including sport organisation. It even took a civil war in 1934, followed by the catastrophic Second World War, for the two political camps to find a consensus and build the Second Republic—more or less together. After the First World War, the discrepancies led to martial disputes between the two political counterparts which resulted in coexistence by mutual agreement during the aftermath of the Second World War. This also manifested itself in the relations between the two Austrian umbrella sport associations ASKÖ and SPORTUNION.

After the Second World War, the reestablishment of the ASKÖ and the foundation of the SPORTUNION were given quantities. The fact of both sport associations being tied to political parties led to the demand for the founding of a third association, the ASVÖ, independent from political influence and unifying all those sport clubs which did not feel associated with the SPORTUNION or the ASKÖ. The three umbrella sport associations still influence and shape the Austrian sport sector to this day and age. Every sport club may—but does not have to—join an umbrella sport association, which mainly benefits the member sport clubs with annual funding.

At the core, the main task of the umbrella sport associations is to receive money from higher up the hierarchy and distribute it downwards while covering their own requirements and expenses in doing so. The umbrella sport associations each also has its own provincial sport associations in each of the nine federal provinces, which results in 27 provincial sport associations in total, all operating more or less expensive offices. There are also offices on a district level.

Basically, the work of the umbrella sport associations' offices is the same, and most of it is even done simultaneously. This includes, for example, fitness and health projects, advancements in mass and leisure sports and provincial, national and international sport championships. Besides these activities, the ASKÖ and the SPORTUNION also keep close connection with their respective international associations, the *Confédération Sportive International Travailliste et Amateur* (CSIT) and the *Fédération Internationale Catholique d'Education Physique et Sportive* (F.I.C.E.P.), respectively. The chief work in sport, however, is done by the sport clubs at the base of the hierarchy, and the sport federations of the respective sport disciplines. The sport federations also have their own provincial federations. This redundancy in sport organisation, as well as the large number of sport functionaries in Austria, has repeatedly become the target of criticism.

The large number of sport functionaries has not been able to meet the increased demand for sport participation opportunities. The entry into the market by commercial providers has, however, placed pressures on sport clubs on both sides of the Atlantic and more and more of these traditionally informally operated and volunteer-controlled organisations have had to become more efficient and effective. This has meant the adoption of bureaucratic methods of operating as clubs have attempted to appear more *business like* (Slack 1999). In Austria this is happening with a considerable time lag. The modernisation of sport clubs by means of specialisation and professionalisation is being prevented for the most part by functionary culture.

However, the demands upon functionaries in sport clubs have changed. While a certain enthusiasm and time commitment are still of the essence, additional qualifications (in finance matters, fundraising, coaching) are needed this day to fulfil a valuable role in the sport clubs. As Stamm and Lamprecht point out "managing a club or coaching a team is no longer just a matter of experience but in most cases involves special capabilities such as a knowledge of accounting, management skills, special training and a diploma course" (Stamm and Lamprecht 1999, p. 140).

These changing demands were also taken into account by the so-called *activation study* (Weiss et al. 2010). During the course of this study for the promotion of sport commitment in Austria, certain measures were developed, e.g. paid trainers, modern marketing strategies, valorising volunteer work, organisation of trial days, foundation of the so-called *Fitness Zone light* (improvement of the ambience and hygiene, flexible time tables, service character, etc.), offers in the form of flexible modules to improve physical fitness, relaxation ability, handling of stress (e.g. yoga, massage) and for special target groups (women, elderly, etc.). These measures aim towards an extended self-conception of sport clubs and sport associations in order to contribute better towards prevention and public health in addition to their responsibility in competitive sport.

The aforementioned activation study led to the project *Fit for Austria*, during the years 2005–2013. This was a joint initiative by the Austrian Ministry of Sport, the BSO, and the three umbrella sport associations mentioned previously. The development of the study and the initiative went hand in hand. From 2014 on, this initiative will be continued by the umbrella sport associations in the form of measures based on the activation study, which will most likely affect the members of the Austrian sport clubs (mental, physical and social well being), and also the relations between the umbrella sport associations.

## 3.6 Conclusion

Sport club culture in Austria started in the middle of the nineteenth century. Before and after the First World War, and especially in the 1970s until the early 1990s, the sport club system expanded. Nowadays estimated 1.7 million people are members of sport clubs. About 14,000 sport clubs, which in turn form 81 sport federations, and three umbrella sport associations, two of them organised according to ideological viewpoints and sporting criteria, constitute the basis of contemporary Austrian sports.

Sport clubs play a crucial role within the Austrian sport scene. They are part of the social establishment and serve important functions for society at large. These functions are described by Heinemann and Horch (1981) as integrative function (people of different ages, genders, ethnic backgrounds, etc. join together and interact in sport clubs), socialising function (members in sport clubs become familiar with values like fair play, health and democracy) and political function (sport clubs create local, regional or national identity). It is assumed that the sport clubs might fulfil these functions less expensively and bureaucratically than the state, due to their different structure of wages and honorary engagement. That is why sport clubs are supported by the state.

Tradition can be a hindrance to development, but it can also be a chance for change and new possibilities. In order to overcome the informality with its attendant structural arrangements of low specialisation within sport clubs in Austria, a move towards professionalisation and a more business-like structure would be a desirable way to more quality. In addition, sport clubs will have to integrate new target groups such as senior citizens, foreigners and other minorities. On the other hand, the typical features of the sport clubs will live on, not least because they are necessary in order to justify governmental and public support.

## References


BMASK (2009) Freiwilliges Engagement in Österreich. 1. Freiwilligenbericht. Bundesministerium für Arbeit, Soziales und Kultur, Wien

Dachs B, Macek S, Preissl M, Steindl G, Zwickl G (2001) Die wirtschaftliche Bedeutung des Sports in Österreich. IWI-Arbeitsheft 48. Industriewissenschaftliches Institut, Wien

European Commission (2014) Special Eurobarometer 412. Sport and physical activity report. Retrieved 14 July 2014 from http://ec.europa.eu/public_opinion/archives/ebs/ebs_412_en.pdf

Gerhartl M (2001) Sport und Beschäftigung im Dritten Sektor. Spectrum Sportwissenschaften 13:132–138

GfK (1998) Sportfrequenz. Im Auftrag des Instituts für Sportwissenschaft. Tabellenband. Gesellschaft für Konsumforschung, Wien

Girtler R (2002) Die feinen Leute. Von der vornehmen Art, durchs Leben zu gehen. Veritas, Wien

Heinemann K, Horch H-D (1981) Soziologie der Sportorganisationen. Sportwissenschaft 11:123–150

Kaiblinger I (1996) Die Situation der Sportvereine in Österreich. Eine empirische Untersuchung zur Bestandsaufnahme der Sportvereine. Universität Wien, Diplomarbeit, Wien

Kleine W, Fritsch W (1990) Wie gesellig ist die Geselligkeit im Sport? Zu den Folgen und Grenzen sportiver Geselligkeit aus der Sicht Sportaktiver. In: Kleine W, Fritsch W (eds) Sport und Geselligkeit. Beiträge zu einer Theorie von Geselligkeit im Sport. Meyer & Meyer Verlag, Aachen, pp 99–125

Lilge W, Millmann G (2013) Sportland Österreich. Athleten. Abzocker. Allianzen. Molden, Wien

Manseder H (2008) Sportvereine—Fit für die Zukunft? Situation, Entwicklungspotential und Perspektiven von Sportvereinen. Eine empirische Studie am Beispiel der SPORTUNION Niederösterreich. Pro-Fit Akademie. SPORTUNION Niederösterreich, St. Pölten

OGM (2014) Brand Monitor Sportvereine. Forschungsbericht. OGM, Wien

Österreichische Lotterien (2014) lotterien.at Unternehmen > Sportförderung > 80 Mio. für den Sport. Retrieved 13 May 2014 from http://www.lotterien.at/olg/CS_Grundlagen.htm?sessionID=f549b7f7-7f00-1

Österreichisches Sportjahrbuch (1945–2014) Published annually. Österreichische Bundes-Sportorganisation, Wien

Slack T (1999) An outsider looking in or an Insider looking out? In: Heinemann K (ed) Sport clubs in various European countries. Hoffmann Verlag, Stuttgart, pp 317–333

Stamm H, Lamprecht M (1999) Sports organisations in Switzerland. In: Heinemann K (ed) Sport clubs in various European countries. Hoffmann Verlag, Stuttgart, pp 119–142

Weiss O, Russo M, Norden G (1997) Gesundheitsbewusstsein, Sportengagement und Geselligkeit nach der Sportausübung. In: Weiss O (ed) Sport, Gesundheit, Gesundheitskultur. Böhlau Verlag, Wien, pp 48–58

Weiss O, Russo M, Norden G, Hilscher P (1999) Sport 2000. Entwicklungen und Trends im österreichischen Sport. Forschungsbericht. Österreichische Bundes-Sportorganisation, Wien

Weiss O, Russo M, Norden G, Hilscher P (2010a) Sport 2000. Entwicklungen und Trends im österreichischen Sport. In: Hilscher P, Norden G, Russo M, Weiss O (eds) Entwicklungstendenzen im Sport. LIT Verlag, Wien, pp 61–77

Weiss O, Braunschmid S, Grubner B, Hilscher P, Kohoutek R, Russo M (2010b) Mehr Österreicher zum Sport Eine Aktivierungsstudie zur Förderung des Sportengagements in Österreich. In: Hilscher P, Norden G, Russo M, Weiss O (eds) Entwicklungstendenzen im Sport. LIT Verlag, Wien, pp 119–133

# Chapter 4
# Sport Clubs in Belgium

**Jeroen Scheerder, Hanne Vandermeerschen, Jeroen Meganck, Jan Seghers, and Steven Vos**

## 4.1 Introduction

Belgium is a highly regulated welfare state in Western Europe with a population of about 11 million inhabitants. It has a stable, cautiously progressive, liberal democracy, strongly corresponding to the Rhineland model which is based on political consensus, a long-term policy vision, an active involvement from the government and social entrepreneurship. Because of its unique central geopolitical position at the crossroads of major European countries, Belgium has a rich but also complicated cultural and political history. Straddled along its internal boundary between Germanic and Latin cultures and lying on the external border between catholic and protestant Europe, Belgium is home to three linguistic groups, namely the Dutch-speaking, mostly Flemish population, the French-speaking, mostly Walloon population and the German-speaking population. The two largest regions are Flanders in the north and Wallonia in the south, constituting about 59 % and 31 % of the total

J. Scheerder (✉) • H. Vandermeerschen
Policy in Sports & Physical Activity Research Group, Department of Kinesiology,
KU Leuven – University of Leuven, Leuven, Belgium
e-mail: jeroen.scheerder@faber.kuleuven.be; hanne.vandermeerschen@faber.kuleuven.be

J. Meganck • J. Seghers
Physical Activity, Sports & Health Research Group, Department of Kinesiology,
KU Leuven – University of Leuven, Leuven, Belgium
e-mail: jeroen.meganck@faber.kuleuven.be; jan.seghers@faber.kuleuven.be

S. Vos
School of Sports Studies, Fontys University of Applied Sciences,
Eindhoven, The Netherlands

Policy in Sports & Physical Activity Research Group, Department of Kinesiology,
KU Leuven – University of Leuven, Leuven, Belgium
e-mail: steven.vos@faber.kuleuven.be



C. Breuer et al. (eds.), *Sport Clubs in Europe*, Sports Economics, Management and Policy 12, DOI 10.1007/978-3-319-17635-2_4

population, respectively. The Brussels-Capital Region, officially bilingual, is a mostly French-speaking enclave which comprises 10 % of the Belgian population. The German-speaking community is a small group of over 73,000 inhabitants, located in eastern Wallonia.

Due to a continuous political process of federalisation since the 1970s, Belgium emerged from a unitary state towards a balanced federal state. In 1962, according to the principle of territoriality, a Flemish-French language border was officially demarcated and, as a result, language areas and language facilities were outlined. The line separating the two main regions crosses Belgium from west to east and draws a sharp division line, not only culturally and politically, but also from an administrative, economic and social perspective. As a consequence, Belgium's complexity and diversity are also reflected in the organisation of its sport and movement culture (Scheerder and Vos 2011). Due to the divided sport policy system in Belgium, no national sport research tradition exists, in particular with regard to the active participation in (club-organised) sport. Thus, sport-related research covering Belgium as a whole is lacking. Moreover, the use of different definitions and research methods makes it difficult to compare the results from the existing regional sport studies. Because of the amplitude of available data for Flanders, the main focus of the present contribution will be on club-organised sport in this part of the country.

In this chapter a status quaestionis of club-organised sport in Flanders/Belgium is presented. More precisely, the most recent and relevant data is discussed. First, we describe the historical and societal context of sport clubs in Flanders/Belgium. Second, attention is given to the role and the position of sport clubs. Time-trend and cross-sectional data are used to give more insight into this. Third, the main features of sport clubs are presented. Here, we successively focus on the sport clubs' structural characteristics, their sport provision, their members, their volunteers, their financial situation and the role that sport clubs see for themselves. The fourth section deals with a specific topic, in this way that we provide some data with regard to the question whether sport clubs can be considered as health promoters.

## 4.2 History and Context

Thanks to its central and rather specific geopolitical position at the crossroads of different cultures and nations in Europe, Belgium has an exceptionally rich and variegated sporting culture. Different forms of movement culture with origins in neighbouring or even more distant European countries have been incorporated (Renson 1999). Several of the still existing crossbow, longbow or other guilds date back to the fourteenth century. For instance, both the archery association *Royal Saint Sebastian* founded in 1302 in Ypres and the fencing association *Royal and Chivalrous Ancient Guild of Saint Michael* founded in 1613 in Ghent can be qualified as the oldest sport clubs in the world (Renson 1976). The first international sport federation also had Belgian roots: the *Fédération Européenne de Gymnastique*—nowadays *Fédération Internationale de Gymnastique*—was established in 1881 by the liberal politician Nicolaas Jan Cupérus from the city of Antwerp. Later on, many Belgians would become chairman of international sport federations. So far, Belgium is the only country in the world that provided two presidents for the International Olympic Committee, e.g. Henri de Baillet-Latour (1925–1942) and Jacques Rogge (2001–2013). The Olympic Games of Antwerp in 1920, which were organised by de Baillet-Latour, were also the first in which the Olympic flag was raised and in which the Olympic oath was pronounced (Renson 1996).

As was already indicated by Vanreusel et al. (1999) organised sport has played a remarkable role in Belgium's divided history. Or formulated otherwise: the structuration of the Belgian state has significantly influenced the organisation of sport in Belgium (Scheerder and Vos 2013). On the one hand, sport reflects the separated structures imposed by the sociocultural and political process of division that took place during the past five decades. This is especially the case with regard to the public sport policy, as the field of sport was one of the first governmental competences to which the communities in Belgium had full authority. Thus, since the 1970s each language community has its proper sport administration, acting in a completely independent way and developing a fully separate policy for the promotion and the organisation of sport. Until the late 1970s most sport federations in Belgium were traditionally strong unitary organisations. Afterwards, these unitary organisations had to split up into two wings, namely an independent Flemish and Walloon federation. Nowadays, almost all sport federations have carried out this division according to the politically divided structure of Belgium, including a separated administration and competition system in Flanders and Wallonia.

On the other hand, sport can also highlight the alleged unity of Belgium. Since its foundation in 1906, the national Olympic committee of Belgium maintains to be a national stronghold. As a consequence, Olympic triumphs are strongly embedded in a national and even Belgicist context. Also other forms of elite sport can be considered as solid symbols of Belgian unity. The national football and hockey teams, for instance, use every occasion to create feelings of national identity and solidarity. It was not by accident that the recently inaugurated Belgian sovereign, i.e. King Philippe, attended the opening games of the Red Lions (male hockey) and the Red Panthers (female hockey), as well as a crucial game of the Red Devils (male football), at the 2013 EuroHockey Nations Championship and at the 2014 FIFA World Cup, respectively. Taking the communal tensions in Belgium into account, it is somewhat surprising however that at the occasion of such international sporting events hardly any pledges are held for regional teams in order to represent Flanders or Wallonia, as is the case for regions like Catalonia and Scotland.

## 4.3 Role and Position of Sport Clubs in Policy and Society

Parallel to its organisational virtuosity on the international sporting scene, Belgium also has a long tradition of developing and organising sport at the grass-roots level. As a result, a relatively dense network of sport clubs already existed at the end of the nineteenth century (Taks et al. 1999). It is remarkable, however, that at the time

**Table 4.1** Number of sport clubs and fitness/health clubs in Belgium (Scheerder and Vos 2013, p. 11)

| | Belgium | Brussels-Capital Region | Flanders | Wallonia |
|---|---|---|---|---|
| Sport clubs | 28,009 | 1,562 | 20,147 | 6,300 |
| Fitness clubs | 778 | 76 | 453 | 249 |

many of these sport clubs, among which gymnastics clubs, cycling clubs, rowing clubs, track and field clubs, football clubs, tennis clubs, etc., had organised themselves into national sport federations. In some sports, especially with regard to gymnastics, a structural segmentation between clubs and federations based on ideological differences (catholic, liberal and socialist) was used and would mainly persist until the beginning of the twenty-first century. As we already mentioned, since the 1970s sport clubs and sport federations are organised separately within each language community. According to the most recent, available data, Belgium counts around 28,000 sport clubs (Scheerder and Vos 2013). More than seven out of ten sport clubs are located in Flanders (Table 4.1), whereas Wallonia and the Brussels-Capital Region hold a share of 22 % and 6 %, respectively.

In Belgium, like in most Western European countries, leisure-time sport has traditionally been dominated by sport clubs, mainly driven by voluntary work. Moreover, grass-roots sport is strongly supported by public funding and policies based on the ideology of Sport for All (Scheerder et al. 2011; Vanreusel et al. 2002). Sport for All includes the principle of subsidiarity, which states that matters need to be handled by the least centralised competent authority. During the last two decades, however, the monopoly of voluntary sport associations has been broken. No longer is sport provided by sport clubs only. As a consequence, the actual provision of mass sport is characterised by a complex mixture of three main types of providers: (1) non-profit sport clubs as a prototype of the voluntary or civic sector, (2) local sport authorities as a prototype of the public or state sector and (3) for-profit fitness clubs as a prototype of the commercial or market sector (Scheerder et al. 2011). Thus, although civil society with its sport clubs still plays an important role in Belgium as regards the organisation of sport practices, it is also clear that its function is increasingly challenged by the growing impact of both public authorities and commercial organisations, among which fitness clubs, bowling centres, dancing studios and indoor kart racing clubs. At present, there are about 778 fitness clubs in Belgium (Table 4.1). Most of them are located in Flanders, in the neighbourhood of cities (Scheerder and Vos 2013). As regards the active participation in sport, findings from the 2013 Eurobarometer survey on sport and physical activity (EC 2014) show that in Belgium 53 % of the population aged 15 years and older actively partakes in leisure-time sport. The percentage of sport participants being an active member of a sport club or a fitness club equals 16 % and 11 %, respectively.

For Flanders sport participation data are available from 1969 onwards (Scheerder and Vos 2011). From Fig. 4.1 it can be seen that sport participation among 12–75-year-old people in Flanders in general has increased over the last four decades. Once considered as an exceptional form of physical behaviour, active

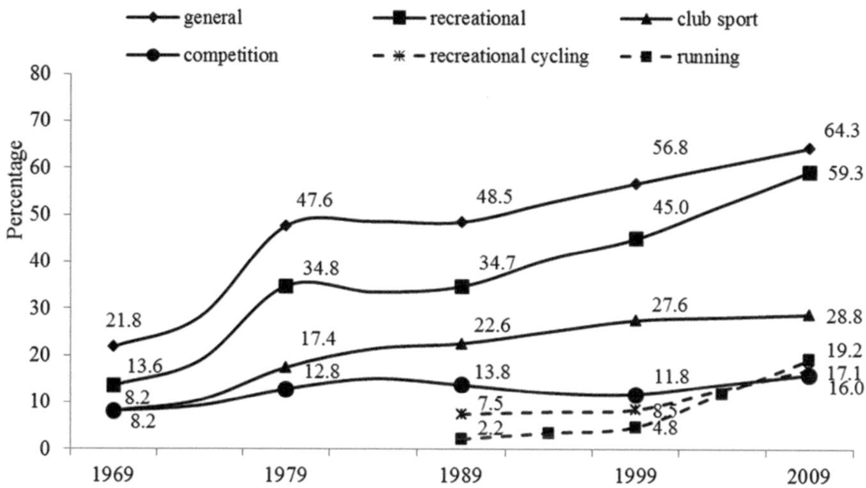


**Fig. 4.1** Time-trend analysis of active sport participation among 12–75-year-old people in Flanders, 1969–2009 (Scheerder et al. 2013, p. 77)

participation in sport nowadays has evolved to an accepted and even normative lifestyle activity. The most spectacular increase of the number of sport participants took place during the 1970s. In that period, Flanders, together with the Nordic countries, was a pioneering region in Europe that launched ambitious Sport for All campaigns in order to stimulate as many people as possible to actively participate in leisure-time sport (Scheerder et al. 2011; Vanreusel et al. 2002). Similar to the growth of sport participation between the 1960s and 1970s, also the past decade is characterised by a relatively strong increase of sport participants (see Fig. 4.1). However, there is a clear rise of non-organised sport participation. In contrast, sport club participation has only slightly risen over the past decades. This implies that the increase of sport participation in Flanders can be put mainly on the account of non-organised sport participants. Along with this development, the participation in so-called *light sport communities* has grown in popularity. *Sport light* refers to sport participation that is performed together with other people in an informal context and with rather loose forms of commitments and loyalty. Small running groups, for instance, seem to be very popular light communities (Scheerder et al. 2015).

According to the most recent data for Flanders, sport participation has become a leisure-time physical activity in which over six out of ten adults are actively involved. Almost nine out of ten children (6–12 years of age; 89.4 %) and youngsters (13–18 years of age; 86.3 %) are actively involved in leisure-time sport. In 2009, 25 % of the adults in Flanders participated in a sport club. About half of the children (50.8 %) and half of the youngsters (52.2 %) are members of one or more sport clubs (Scheerder et al. 2013).

As referred to before, apart from the traditional sport clubs, other arrangements like light sport communities and commercial sport settings arise. Recreational cyclists, runners and walkers, among others, join each other in self-organised groups and/or take part in events such as cycle rides, city runs, walking tours and the like. An overview of the ten most practiced sports confirms this evolution (see Table 4.2). Nowadays, running, recreational cycling and swimming make up the top three of most popular sport activities among adults. Fitness and recreational walking complete the top five. All of these sports can be easily practiced without the need for a rigid club structure or a (long-term) club membership. Therefore, they can be defined as typically individual and free-booting sport activities. Also among children and adolescents, recreational swimming and recreational cycling attract huge numbers of participants. Moreover, more adolescents participate in running and fitness than is the case for more formal sport activities like tennis and volleyball. Only soccer, still one of the most popular club sport activities, seems to resist somewhat to the societal trends of de-traditionalisation and de-institutionalisation.

Among children, youngsters as well as adults, the most popular sport that is practiced in a club is football (Table 4.2). Also tennis, dancing (young people and adults), gymnastics (young people only) and volleyball (youngsters and adults) seem to be popular club-organised sports. However, the participation shares of team sports, such as football, basketball and volleyball, have dwindled significantly during the last decades (Scheerder et al. 2013).

In spite of the significant increase of the general sport participation level in Flanders, the active involvement in (club-organised) sport is not yet equally common among all citizens (Scheerder et al. 2013). Differences according to sex show up, implying that sport active men (26.5 %) are more involved in a sport club compared to women (23.5 %). With regard to age, it is clear that, among adults, adults aged 50 years and older (32.6 %) are less likely to partake in club-organised sport compared to adults below the age of 50 (37.8 %). Apparently, sport participation in a club is also still clearly associated with socio-economic background characteristics. People with a higher socio-educational status (19.9 % for university graduates) are more likely to be involved in a sport club than is the case for lower educated persons (9.1 % for people with (no) primary school certificate). Thus, despite over 40 years of Sport for All policies in Flanders, a pattern of social stratification of club-organised sport activities still persists. Consequently, particular groups have less opportunities to benefit from the advantages related to sport, including, among others, health and pleasure.

## 4.4 Characteristics of Sport Clubs

In what follows, we present some main features of sport clubs in Flanders, in terms of their structural characteristics, their sport provision, their members, their volunteers, their financial situation and the role they see for themselves. The results stem from a representative survey called *Flemish Sport Club Panel*, collected in 2012 at the Department of Kinesiology of the University of Leuven (Scheerder et al. 2015). A first edition of this panel survey was held 3 years earlier, in 2009 (Scheerder et al. 2010).

**Table 4.2** Sport preferences among children youngsters and adults in Flanders in 2009 (percentages in function of sportive population) (Scheerder et al. 2013, p. 167; 170; 173)

| | Children (6–12 years of age) | | | | Youngsters (13–18 years of age) | | | | Adults | | | |
|---|---|---|---|---|---|---|---|---|---|---|---|---|
| | All sports | | Sports practiced in club | | All sports | | Sports prasticed in club | | All sports | | Sports practiced in club | |
| 1 | Recreational swimming | 46.6 | Football | 14.6 | Recreational swimming | 30.5 | Football | 16.8 | Running | 29.9 | Football | 5.3 |
| 2 | Football | 29.1 | Swimming | 8.4 | Football | 27.5 | Tennis | 8.0 | Recreational cycling | 25.8 | Tennis | 4.7 |
| 3 | Recreational cycling | 25.3 | Tennis | 7.0 | Recreational cycling | 22.8 | Dancing | 7.6 | Swimming | 15.5 | Running | 2.8 |
| 4 | Dancing | 22.7 | Dancing | 6.7 | Running | 21.0 | Volleyball | 5.1 | Fitness | 14.5 | Dancing | 2.6 |
| 5 | Gymnastics | 16.9 | Gymnastics | 5.1 | Dancing | 19.2 | Gymnastics | 3.9 | Recreational walking | 12.3 | Volleyball | 2.2 |
| 6 | Tennis | 15.2 | Martial arts | 4.8 | Fitness | 14.3 | Martial arts | 3.6 | Tennis | 7.5 | Cycle touring | 2.1 |
| 7 | Skiing | 10.2 | Basketball | 4.4 | Tennis | 13.7 | Horse riding | 3.3 | Football | 7.2 | Aerobics | 1.5 |
| 8 | Swimming | 9.9 | Track and field | 3.3 | Skiing | 11.8 | Swimming | 3.3 | Skiing | 6.4 | Badminton | 1.4 |
| 9 | Horse riding | 9.2 | Volleyball | 2.5 | Badminton | 10.4 | Badminton | 2.9 | Cycle touring | 4.6 | Zumba | 1.3 |
| 10 | Basketball | 9.0 | Horse riding | 2.0 | Volleyball | 9.6 | Track and field | 2.7 | Mountain biking | 3.6 | Spinning | 1.3 |

In other words, the 2012 survey is the second wave of a panel study among sport clubs. For this chapter, only the 2012 data are used. The selection of the clubs is done through a random stratified sample of municipalities, based on their socio-economic profile. The selected municipalities were requested to either contact the clubs in their municipality by sending an information letter provided by the researchers or to provide the researchers with the addresses of the clubs. In the first wave, 60 municipalities were selected; in 2012, the sample was extended with 30 *new* municipalities, again randomly stratified based on socio-economic profile. The clubs received a letter containing the link to the questionnaire, which was held online. In total, the resulting 2012 sample consisted of 580 clubs, of which 285 had responded to the 2009 survey as well; 295 clubs were *new* clubs for 2012. The data allow us to accurately describe and analyse the current situation of sport clubs in Flanders, the results of which are presented below.

### 4.4.1 Structural Characteristics

Flanders has a dense network of rather small-sized clubs. The data from the Flemish Sport Club Panel show that less than one in five clubs (19.0 %) can be qualified as *large clubs*, i.e. counting over 200 members. Forty-five percent of the clubs in Flanders are small in size, with 60 members or less. The remaining 37 % of the clubs is medium sized, counting between 61 and 200 members. The relatively small scale of many Flemish clubs appears to have an impact on how they operate. For example, 43 % of the sport clubs have a policy plan. This implies that this is not the case in 57 % of the clubs. Still, the small scale does not seem to impede a long-term stability of clubs, since over 50 % of the Flemish clubs originated before the 1980s. In the 1970s, a peak occurred, as over a quarter of the current sport clubs were created during that decade. Clearly, new sport clubs are still being formed. However, recent clubs are a minority in the total landscape of sport clubs: less than one in five current clubs (15.6 %) were created after the turn of the twenty-first century.

The organisation and the rather small size of Flemish clubs are also reflected in the possession of accommodation. One in four clubs (25.1 %) owns facilities, or independently manages sport infrastructure on a daily basis. For three-quarters of the sport clubs in Flanders (74.9 %), this is not the case. In other words, the share of clubs having their *own* accommodation is rather small.

### 4.4.2 Sport Provision

A large majority of the clubs in Flanders (85.4 %) can be characterised as a single-sport club, promoting one specific sport. Around 15 % of the clubs (14.6 %) declare to be multisport clubs, offering several sports at a time. However, among those clubs, there is a large share of clubs presenting various sports that are closely related

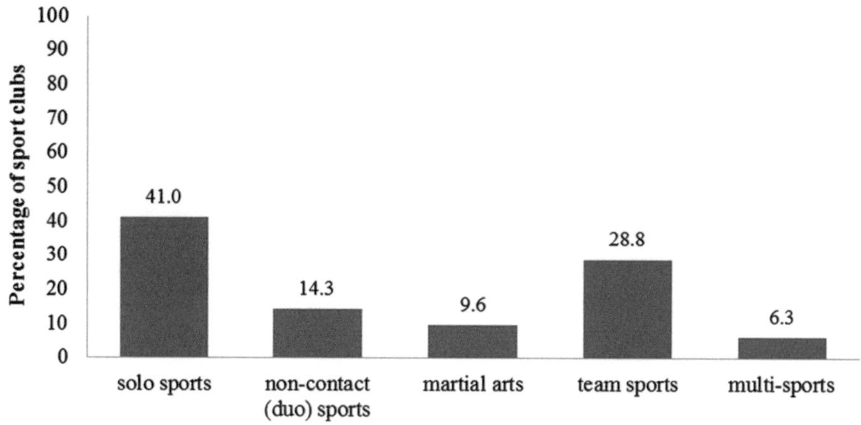


**Fig. 4.2** Type of sports practiced in Flemish sport clubs ($N=573$) (Scheerder et al. 2015)

and that belong to the same *family* of sports. Examples are jazz dance and ballet, kayak and canoe, etc. If we take only clubs offering very distinct or even unrelated sports into account, the share of multisport clubs is approximately 6 % of the clubs. In other words, Flanders has a relatively strong tradition of *single-sport* clubs.

Figure 4.2 presents the type of sports offered by clubs in Flanders. As can be observed, over four in ten sport clubs offer a *solo sport*, this is, a sport that can be practised alone, such as running, swimming and cycling. This type of sports has the largest share among the sport clubs. Approximately three in ten clubs organise a team sport (28.8 %). Fourteen percent of the clubs offer non-contact sports, which are sports that do not involve physical contact, but where an opponent is required. They are usually practiced in duo. Typical examples here are racket sports, such as badminton or tennis, but also darts or petanque are part of this category of sports. Finally, the last type of sports, martial arts, is provided by approximately one-tenth of the sport clubs (9.6 %).

Recreational sport takes a large share in the sport participation practice in Flanders. Only a small minority of the clubs (8.3 %) focuses exclusively on competitive sport activities. In a much larger share (47.1 %), both recreational and competitive sports are organised. In about 45 % of the clubs (44.5 %), only recreational sport is offered. The level of sports practice (recreational versus competitive) is closely linked to the size of the club (Fig. 4.3). Among the large clubs of more than 200 members, seven in ten sport clubs organise both recreational and competitive sports. In small clubs of 60 members or less, this holds for less than four in ten clubs. Small clubs are more likely to focus exclusively on recreational sports, as compared to large clubs. Medium-sized clubs of 61–200 members occupy an intermediate position in this regard.

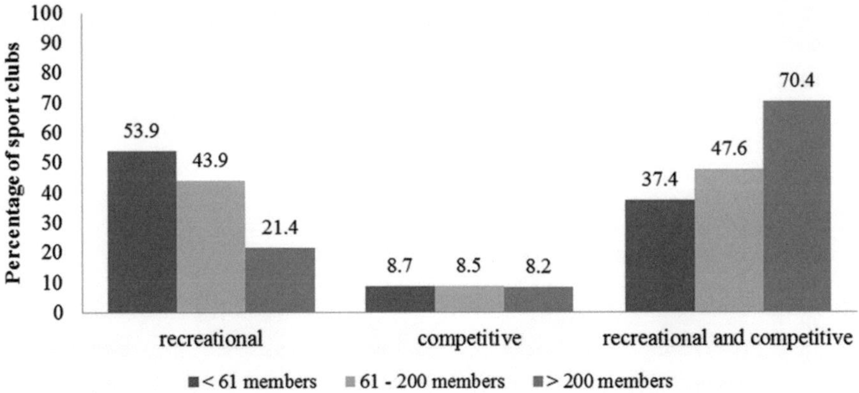


**Fig. 4.3** Share of recreational and competitive clubs in Flanders, by size of the club ($N=517$) (Scheerder et al. 2015)

Sport clubs tend to be criticised as being too demanding in terms of engagement by their members. More particularly, they are said not to allow for enough flexibility towards their members and the varying needs and aspirations of present-day sport participants (Scheerder and Van Bottenburg 2010). In this context, and in view of gathering empirical evidence in this matter, an item was included in the survey on the degree to which clubs try to respond to different expectations from members. More specifically, clubs were asked to what extent they agreed or disagreed with the statement that their club *offers alternative modes of membership for people who are only using certain services of the club (f.i. only using sport accommodation, advice for training without participating to training within the club)*. Twenty-three percent of the clubs replied positively and agreed with the statement (agree/totally agree). With 21 % of the clubs being indecisive, this leaves 55 % of the clubs disagreeing. This informs us that most clubs stick to a *standard* supply of their services, rather than tailor-made provision or innovative forms of sport practices.

Apart from the sport training sessions, a considerable number of clubs also organises non-sport activities, such as a spaghetti dinner (for fundraising purposes), a New Year's reception and information sessions on specific topics. These types of activities are organised on average four times a year. Here again, the organisation of such activities is closely related to the size of the club: the larger the club, the more frequently non-sport activities will be organised. For example, large clubs organise these activities on average 5.7 times a year, whereas small clubs will do so 2.7 times a year on average. These activities do not belong to the core of the sport practice of the clubs. However, the clubs indicated that they consider these activities as important. Whereas financial reasons are clearly a motivation for some clubs to organise these activities, the most important underlying rationale is the enhancement of social contacts and social cohesion among their members.

### 4.4.3 Members

As shown in sport participation research (cf. supra), women are underrepresented in Flemish sport clubs. This also appears from the findings of the *Flemish Sport Club Panel*. Almost half of the sport clubs (47.4 %) in Flanders have less than 25 % of women among their members. In over three-quarters (77.3 %) of the clubs, men outnumber women; 14 % of the clubs does not have any female members at all. Evidently, the share of women in a club depends on the type of sports being practiced. Some very popular sports are still largely dominated by male participants. For example, football and martial arts are traditionally much more popular among men, and together these two sports represent 25 % of the clubs in our sample, thereby reflecting reality. Nevertheless, the opposite can also occur: in nearly 10 % of the sport clubs in Flanders (9.8 %), at least two-thirds of the members are women, and in 2 % of the clubs, there are no male members. In sum, whereas women are generally underrepresented in sport clubs, the male/female balance varies largely between clubs.

With regard to age, we see a similar picture arising. As discussed earlier, there are differences in sport club participation according to age. Yet, here too, it should be added that the age distribution also varies between clubs. As indicated in Fig. 4.4, not all age groups are present in every club. For example, in almost six in ten clubs (57.0 %), there are no children younger than 12 years old, and in about one-third of the clubs (32.8 %), there are no members of 55 or older.

Most sport clubs have witnessed a stable or growing number of members over the last years. As reported by the club representatives, in half of the clubs (51.3 %) membership has remained more or less stable. In one-third of the clubs (33.1 %), on the other hand, membership has increased. This also implies, however, that about 16 % of the sport clubs have been confronted with a decrease in membership.

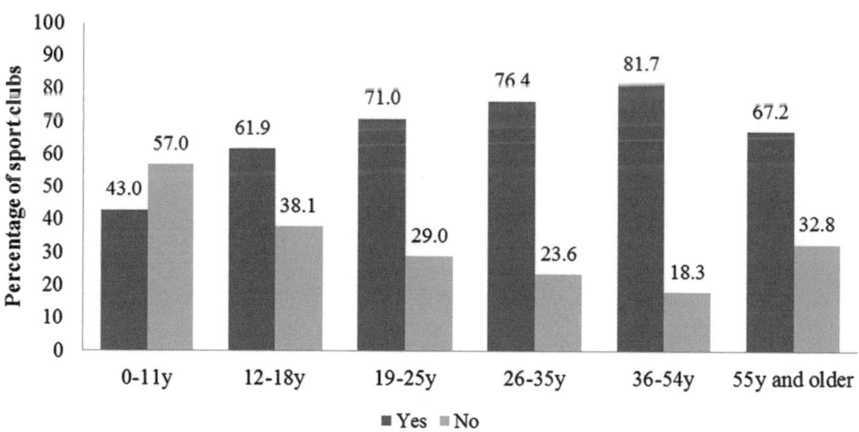


**Fig. 4.4** Presence of age groups in sport clubs in Flanders ($N$=525) (Scheerder et al. 2015)

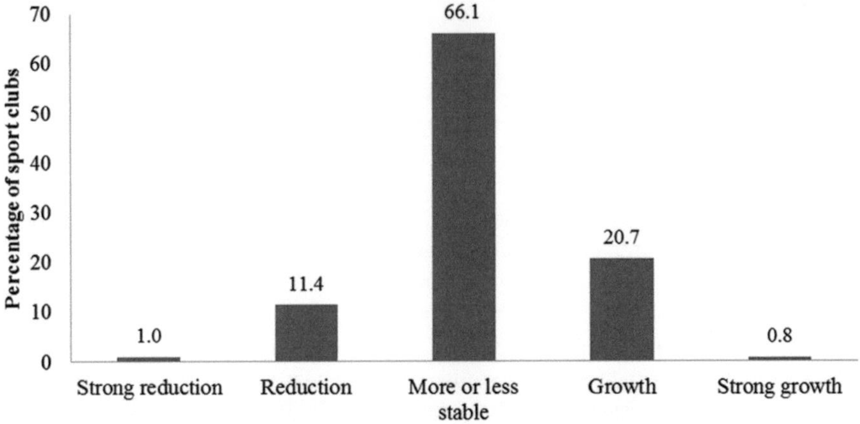


**Fig. 4.5** Expected evolution of membership in sport clubs in Flanders ($N=516$) (Scheerder et al. 2015)

When asked how they evaluate the current number of members, almost three in four clubs (73.6 %) state that they currently have sufficient members. About one in four clubs (25.6 %), on the other hand, indicate having too few members. Less than 1 %of the sport clubs answered that they have too many members. In sum, the majority of the clubs is in a comfortable position in terms of membership, with enough members, and observing a stable or positive trend in membership. Nevertheless, there is also a share of clubs for which the situation is less reassuring, being confronted with a lack of members, and/or a negative trend in membership. This is also reflected in the prognosis that clubs make for the coming years (Fig. 4.5). Two-thirds of all clubs (66.1 %) predict a stable membership in the years to come, and one in five clubs (21.5 %) expects a growth in membership. Nevertheless, 12 % of the clubs expect a decrease.

### 4.4.4 *Staff and Volunteers*

Sport clubs in Flanders rely almost exclusively on volunteers for their daily activities. In less than 2 % of the clubs, there are paid employees. In other words, in 98 % of the clubs, all members are volunteers. This implies that many volunteers are needed. We investigated to what extent this poses a problem to sport clubs. The results of the survey show that 17 % of the clubs experience a lack of volunteers. However, in the majority of the clubs, this is not the case. Approximately half of the total amount of clubs (47.3 %) state that they have enough volunteers and are not looking for new forces. The remaining 35 % of the clubs state that they do not experience a lack of volunteers, but continue looking for more people nevertheless. This implies that in total, four in five clubs (82.6 %) indicate that they currently have sufficient volunteers.

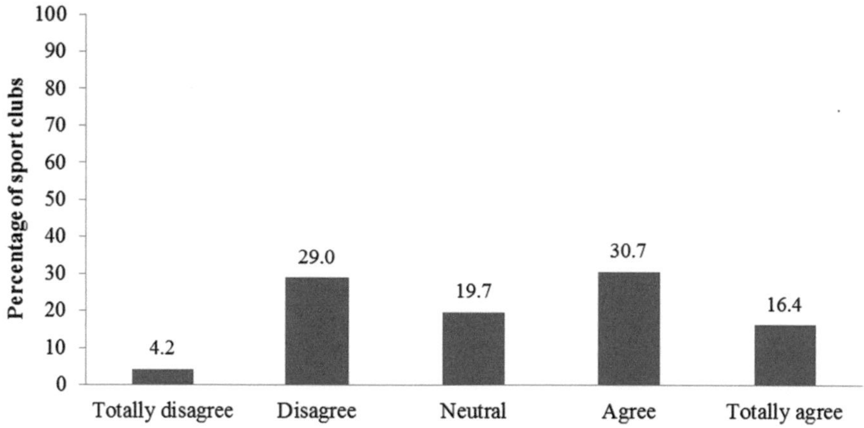


**Fig. 4.6** Agreement/disagreement among sport clubs in Flanders with the statement "our sport club never has problems in recruiting volunteers" ($N$=548) (Scheerder et al. 2015)

**Table 4.3** Non-sport-related tasks of volunteers in sport clubs in Flanders (Scheerder et al. 2015)

| | *N* of clubs | % of clubs |
|---|---|---|
| The organisation of additional activities | 296 | 51.1 |
| Referee/jury | 200 | 34.5 |
| Care | 93 | 16.1 |
| Maintenance | 203 | 35.1 |
| Canteen | 150 | 25.9 |
| Other | 62 | 10.7 |

But how difficult is it to recruit new volunteers in time? When confronted with the statement *our sport club never has problems in recruiting volunteers*, almost half of the clubs (47.1 %) agrees or fully agrees. Around 20 % of the clubs (19.7 %) gives a neutral answer. Still, one-third of the clubs (33.2 %) disagrees with this statement (Fig. 4.6), indicating that they do face problems in finding new volunteers.

To sum up, whereas the majority of the clubs do not experience problems with recruiting sufficient volunteers, one in three clubs does. Additional analyses have shown that larger clubs are more likely to be confronted with a lack of volunteers and/or to experience problems with the recruitment of volunteers, as compared to small clubs.

Volunteers in sport clubs can take very different functions, varying from board member, over trainer, to functions *on the side* such as maintenance and taking care of the canteen. Approximately seven in ten clubs (72.2 %) have voluntary workers for these types of additional functions. Table 4.3 gives an overview of non-sport-related

**Table 4.4** Attitude of sport clubs in Flanders regarding the support of volunteers through training and education, expressed on a 5-point scale, in percentages (Scheerder et al. 2015)

| | Totally disagree | Disagree | Neither agree nor disagree | Agree | Totally agree |
|---|---|---|---|---|---|
| The club invests in training and education for its volunteers ($n=540$) | 23.5 | 15.9 | 22.6 | 25.9 | 12.0 |
| Volunteers who follow courses or training that are relevant for the club, get the costs reimbursed ($n=537$) | 29.1 | 8.6 | 15.5 | 21.6 | 25.3 |
| The club reserves a yearly budget for the training of members of staff ($n=535$) | 41.5 | 21.3 | 19.1 | 12.7 | 5.4 |

functions and the share of clubs relying on volunteers for these tasks, which are mostly only indirectly sport related. The most popular tasks are the organisation of additional activities (51.1 % of the clubs count on volunteers for this task), maintenance of material or accommodation (35.1 %) and refereeing (34.5 %). Fulfilling these tasks is usually not financially rewarded. In 86 % of the clubs, nobody receives remuneration for it. Board members as well are usually not remunerated. In nine out of ten clubs (89.6 %), none of the board members receive remuneration for their voluntary work. This is different for functions such as a trainer and coach. In 27 % of the clubs (virtually) all trainers/coaches are remunerated, and in another 12 % of the clubs, some trainers/coaches receive remuneration. This remuneration can take different forms, such as a fixed amount for volunteering, a cover for expenses made, a payment in kind or a payment per hour. Still, in six out of ten clubs (60.8 %), none of the trainers/coaches is remunerated.

A drawback of relying almost exclusively on volunteers in sport clubs is that volunteers are not always well trained for the tasks they perform, which could hamper the quality of the sport provision. As can be observed in Table 4.4, in Flanders, the attitude of sport clubs with regard to providing, facilitating or encouraging training and education for their volunteers varies largely between clubs. Some clubs invest in training for volunteers, whereas other clubs do not. Still, clubs which reserve a budget for the training of their (voluntary) members represent a minority, and less than four in ten clubs (37.9 %) invest in training and education for their volunteers.

Specifically with regard to trainers/coaches, the results from the survey indicate that approximately half of the trainers (51.2 %) are non-qualified. On the other hand, 35 % of the trainers have obtained a qualification by the Flemish School for Trainers and Coaches, which means that they have obtained a certificate after following a course organised by the Flemish sport administration. The remaining 13 % of the trainers is trained as a physical education teacher and/or has a university degree in physical education or physiotherapy.

### 4.4.5 *Financial Situation*

Clubs get their revenues from a wide array of sources. Most recurring sources of revenue among sport clubs are (1) membership fees (82.6 %), (2) subsidies from the local sport authorities (75.2 %), (3) sponsoring (55.1 %) and (4) fundraising activities (46.2 %). Also cafeteria (29.9 %) and competitions (25.2 %) are frequently mentioned by the clubs. Subsidies from the federation (umbrella organisation) and other sources count for 18 % and 17 %, respectively.

Figure 4.7 presents the relative weight of the different sources of revenue in the total revenue of sport clubs. The findings indicate that membership fees are the largest source of revenue: on average, clubs draw 41 % of their revenues from membership fees. Other important sources of revenue are sponsoring (12.9 % of total revenue), fundraising activities (11.1 %), subsidies from the municipality (11.0 %) and cafeteria (11.0 %). These figures indicate that clubs rely on many different sources for their revenues, which has the advantage of decreasing their dependence on a particular source of revenue. The results also indicate that direct subsidies (from the federation and/or from the local municipality) account for a rather small part of the total revenue of the clubs. Put differently, clubs rely much more on *own* sources of revenue, such as membership fees, fundraising activities or the cafeteria, which is again beneficial in terms of independence. At the same time, it should be mentioned that clubs receive more indirect forms of support from the municipality as well, for example through the use of sport infrastructure. While essential for many clubs, this is not taken into account in the figures presented here.

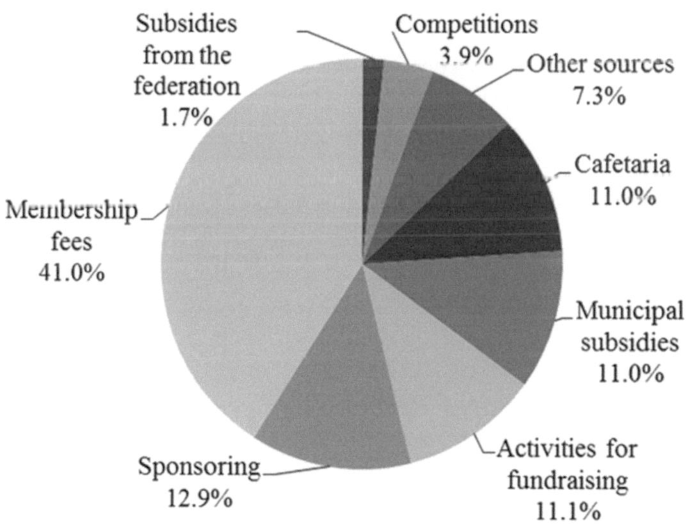


**Fig. 4.7** Average share of revenue sources in the total revenue of sport clubs in Flanders ($N=408$) (Scheerder et al. 2015)

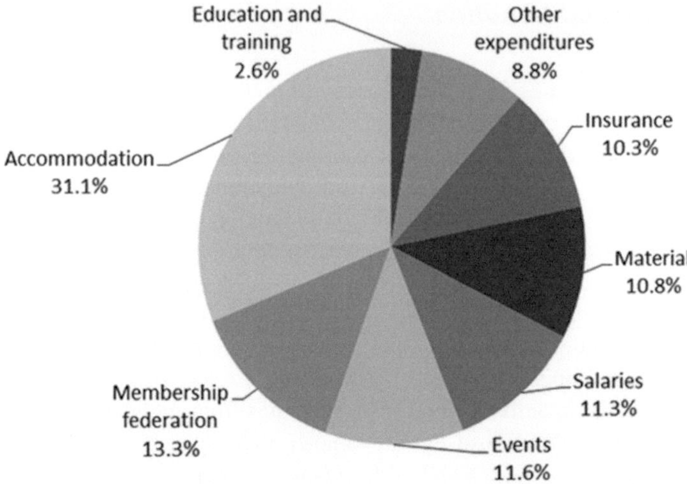


**Fig. 4.8** Average share of expenditure per source of expenditure of sport clubs in Flanders ($N$=400) (Scheerder et al. 2015)

When looking at the expenditures, sport accommodation presents the highest average cost for clubs in Flanders (Fig. 4.8). It accounts for almost one-third of the clubs' expenditures (31.1 %). Other important costs are the payment of membership fees to the federation (13.3 % of the total expenditures), the organisation of events (11.6 %), the payment of salaries (11.3 %), material (10.3 %) and insurance (10.3 %). Parallel to our observation with regard to the sources of revenue, also in terms of expenditures we may conclude that the expenditures are formed by a multitude of different, smaller costs.

By and large, most club representatives are optimistic about the financial situation of their club. Over 50 % (52.4 %) qualifies the situation of their club as *healthy* and 14 % (14.4 %) even considers it as *very healthy*. Twenty-seven percent (27.1 %) of the clubs describes the situation of their club as "in between". Six percent (6.1 %) of the Flemish clubs stated that the financial situation is unhealthy or not really healthy.

### 4.4.6 Role and Perceived Responsibilities of Sport Clubs

In addition to the collection of factual information with regard to the structure and organisation of clubs, their members, volunteers, financial situation, etc., some items in the survey were designed to investigate how clubs perceive their own role and responsibility. As shown in Table 4.5, an overwhelming majority of clubs (93.0 %) confirms that their club has social objectives, in addition to their

**Table 4.5** Opinion of sport clubs in Flanders with regard to their tasks and responsibilities as a club, expressed on a 5-point scale, in percentages (Scheerder et al. 2015)

| | Totally disagree | Disagree | Neither agree nor disagree | Agree | Totally agree |
|---|---|---|---|---|---|
| In addition to sport related objectives, our club has also social objectives (f.i. being together, making friends, solidarity) ($n=424$) | 0.0 | 1.2 | 5.9 | 51.7 | 41.3 |
| Stimulating societal integration belongs to the tasks of a sport club ($n=418$) | 5.0 | 6.9 | 32.1 | 43.8 | 12.2 |
| It is the task of a sport club to pursue maximum membership ($n=418$) | 10.1 | 35.7 | 30.6 | 17.7 | 6.0 |
| It is the task of a sport club to stimulate diversity among the members, and to try to ensure that also disadvantaged groups are part of the sport club ($n=414$) | 4.8 | 10.9 | 33.6 | 40.6 | 10.1 |

sport-related objectives. More than half of the clubs (56.0 %) also agrees that it is their task as a club to stimulate social integration. In other words, there is quite some agreement that clubs have *broader*, societal goals. There is also considerable agreement with the statement regarding the stimulation of diversity. One in two clubs (50.7 %) agrees that it is the task of a sport club to stimulate diversity, and to strive for participation of disadvantaged groups in their club. However, less than one in four clubs (23.7 %) agree that it is the task of a sport club to pursue maximum membership.

## 4.5 Sport Clubs as Future Health Promoters?

One of the core businesses of sport clubs is to provide their members with a high-quality sport experience (Casey et al. 2012). Sport clubs are also more and more called upon as an instrument for the pursuit of societal goals, such as social integration or health (Bergsgard et al. 2007). Not surprisingly, for example, they are considered important partners in the fight against obesity through their contribution to the physical activity of their members. But the potential health benefits of a sport club membership extend beyond physical into mental and social health as well (Eime et al. 2013; Geidne et al. 2013). In line with the World Health Organisation's advocacy for setting-based health promotion (WHO 1986) this resulted in the development of the health-promoting sport club concept (HPSC; Kokko et al. 2006), with experts in health and in sport collaborating to identify 22 standards for a health-promoting sport club.

**Table 4.6** Classification of sport clubs in Flanders ($n=329$) according to the level of health promotion (%) (Scheerder et al. 2015)

| | Health promotion classification | | |
|---|---|---|---|
| | Low | Moderate | High |
| Policy index | 59.0 | 25.2 | 15.8 |
| Ideology index | 5.5 | 19.5 | 75.1 |
| Practice index | 72.3 | 8.2 | 19.5 |
| Environment index | 46.2 | 15.8 | 38.0 |
| Health-promoting sports club index | 55.0 | 21.9 | 23.1 |

This instrument, the so-called HPSC index (Kokko et al. 2009, p. 29, Table 2), was used to classify Flemish sport clubs according to the extent their policy (e.g. "Health and well-being viewpoints are observed in the sport clubs' decision-making process"), their ideology (e.g. "The sport club promotes the fair play ideology"), their practices (e.g. "The sport club assures that health education is carried out") and their environment (e.g. "The sport club provides a sport environment that is free of intoxicants during junior activities") reflect the integration of health promotion as a new responsibility for sport clubs in Flanders. Previous research has tested this instrument in Flanders, indicating that Flemish sport clubs are willing to take on this new role (Meganck et al. 2014).

As shown in Table 4.6, less than a quarter of the Flemish sport clubs gain an overall high classification. The results on the ideology index are the exception with three-quarters of the clubs in the high classification category. It would, however, be too early to decide that this issue does not need any further attention, as the data collection for this study coincided with the end of a governmental campaign emphasising the fair play ideology (Flemish Government 2012). It remains to be seen whether this had a temporary or a lasting effect.

Action on the part of the sport federations and the sport government seems required if Flemish sport clubs are to become health-promoting environments in the broadest sense. These interventions could benefit from targeting the barriers as perceived by sport clubs' representatives. As one in five respondents states that health promotion is not a priority in their club (21.9 %) and about the same share indicates that their members are not interested (20.6 %), continued advocacy for this subject matter will be essential. Additional funding from local municipality or sponsorship by health-promoting organisations (e.g. Kelly et al. 2014), and/or public recognition by means of a quality label, conditional on increased health promotion activity, may also be an important incentive. Insufficient know-how (13.4 %) completes the top three of the perceived barriers. Collaborations between sport organisations and health promotion experts may be a promising strategy (Casey et al. 2009), for example to create health promotion "packages" that can easily be used by lay persons like coaches and club officials. In spite of these barriers, respondents also recognised the advantages of investing in health promotion. The top three motives to take on this new responsibility are as follows: (1) healthy athletes perform better (29.4 %), (2) we want to contribute to the health of the population (21.8 %) and (3) we want to profile our club as a healthy sport club (15.5 %). Clearly, sport clubs in Flanders need further support, but they are open to this new challenge, creating many opportunities for innovative health promotion through club-organised sport.

## 4.6 Conclusion

In this chapter both the geopolitical situation and the sociocultural position of Belgium were briefly described. From this perspective it is clear that the organisation of sport in Belgium is strongly influenced by the political system. Sport policies and sport organisations in Belgium are as divided as their embedding state structure. In spite of, or maybe thanks to, the divided nature of sport in Belgium, a viable and dense network of voluntary sport associations exists. Due to the scarcity of adequate national data, we mainly focused on club-organised sport in the northern part of the country, i.e. Flanders.

In order not to look only at the supply side, findings with regard to sport participation were presented and interpreted. Although sport participation has become a very popular leisure-time physical activity among the Flemish population, it has been indicated that only a minority of the sport participants takes part in club-organised sport activities. Apparently, active participation in commercial and rather informal sport settings is on the rise. Research findings also indicate that, despite almost five decades of Sport for All campaigns, a democratisation in terms of equal opportunities for participation in a sport club did not fully occur so far. Differences according to sex, age and socioeconomic status can still be noticed.

Based on the results from the *Flemish Sport Club Panel*, characteristics of sport clubs in Flanders were shown. Half of the clubs are small scaled, meaning that they count 60 members at maximum. About the same share of clubs (51.4 %) has been founded before the 1980s. Thus, it can be concluded that club-organised sport in Flanders is characterised by rather small and relatively long-standing clubs. The majority of the clubs (85.4 %) promote one sport, and therefore can be described as single-sport clubs, as opposed to multisport clubs. It is remarkable that 55 % of the clubs stick to their somewhat *standardised* package of services. This might hamper clubs to offer flexible sport programmes or to attract new groups of potential sport participants. Almost three in four clubs state that they have sufficient members at the moment, and only one in five clubs expects an increase in membership in the (near) future.

For their operational functioning, sport clubs highly rely on volunteers. About one-third of the clubs, however, faces difficulties in recruiting new volunteers. This is especially the case for large clubs. Sport clubs need volunteers, not only for functions such as club manager, trainer or referee, but also for non-sport-related tasks like providing care, maintaining infrastructure or managing the canteen. Professionalisation of their services, however, is a tricky problem for voluntary sport associations. For their incomes, sport clubs largely depend on membership fees and municipal subsidies. As there is a good chance that local authorities will have to save on their budgets, clubs may be urged to look more for private financial resources, for instance by means of (extra) sponsoring.

In general, sport clubs in Flanders still have a prominent position. Thanks to their large number and their significant continuity, clubs play a unique role in Flemish society. One of the potential opportunities for sport clubs is related to the health enhancing function they could fulfil in the future. As an increasing share of the population are convinced of the preventive and social benefits of physical activity, clubs can take advantage of this by offering a health-promoting environment. To make this a success, co-operations with public and private organisations will be needed. Therefore, it is argued that sport clubs should be considered as a good investment, not only for individual well-being, but for a healthy society as well.

## References

Bergsgard NA, Houlihan B, Mangset P, Nødland SI, Rommetvedt H (2007) Sport policy. A comparative analysis of stability and change. Elsevier, Oxford

Casey MM, Payne WR, Eime RM (2009) Building the health promotion capacity of sport and recreational organizations. A case study of regional sports assemblies. Manag Leisure 14(2):112–124

Casey MM, Payne WR, Eime RM (2012) Organisational readiness and capacity building strategies of sporting organizations to promote health. Sport Manag Rev 15(1):109–124

EC (2014) Sport and physical activity (Special Eurobarometer Report 412). European Commission, Brussels

Eime RM, Young JA, Harvey JT, Charity MJ, Payne WR (2013) A systematic review of the psychological and social benefits of participation in sport for adults Informing development of a conceptual model of health through sport. Int J Behav Nutr Phys Activity 10:135

Flemish Government (2012) Besluit van de Vlaamse Regering tot uitvaardiging van de thema's en de richtsnoeren betreffende ethisch verantwoord sporten voor de Olympiade 2013–2016 [Decision of the Flemish government to promulgate themes and guidelines for ethically responsible sports participation for the Olympiad 2013-2016]. Staatsblad, Retrieved 21 December 2014 from http://www.codex.Vlaanderen.be/Portals/Codex/documenten/1022640.html

Geidne S, Quennerstedt M, Eriksson C (2013) The youth sports club as a health-promoting setting. An integrative review of research. Scand J Public Health 41(3):269–283

Kelly B, King L, Bauman AE, Macniven R, Chapman K, Smith BJ (2014) Identifying important and feasible policies and actions for health at community sports clubs. A consensus-generating approach. J Sci Med Sport 17(1):61–66

Kokko S, Kannas L, Villberg J (2006) The health promoting sports club in Finland. A challenge for the settings-based approach. Health Promot Int 21(3):219–229

Kokko S, Kannas L, Villberg J (2009) Health promotion profile of youth sports clubs in Finland. Club officials' and coaches' perceptions. Health Promot Int 24(1):26–35

Meganck J, Scheerder J, Thibaut E, Seghers J (2014) Youth sports clubs' potential as health promoting setting. Profiles, motives and barriers. Health Educ J. Online publication on 23 September 2012. doi:10.1177/0017896914549486

Renson R (1976) The Flemisch (sic) archery gilds. From defense mechanisms to sports institution. In: Renson R, De Nayer P-P, Ostyn M (eds) The history, the evolution and diffusion of sports and games in different cultures (Proceedings of the 4th international HISPA seminar, Leuven, 1975). Brussels, BLOSO, pp 135–159

Renson R (1996) The games reborn. The VIIth Olympiad Antwerp 1920. Pandora, Antwerp

Renson R (1999) Physical education in Europe from a cross-national perspective. In: Bussard J-C, Roth F (eds) Quelle éducation physique pour quelle école? Welcher Sportunterricht für welche Schule? Which physical education for which school? (Proceedings of the ASEP congress; Neuchâtel, 20–23 May 1998). ASEP, Neuchâtel, pp 115–130

Scheerder J, Breedveld K, Borgers J (2015a) Running across Europe. The rise and size of one of the largest sport markets. Palgrave Macmillan, Basingstoke

Scheerder J, Seghers J, Meganck J, Vandermeerschen H, Vos S (2015b) Sportclubs in beeld. Resultaten van het Vlaamse Sportclub Panel 2.0 (VSP2.0) [Study on sport clubs in Flanders. Results from the Flemish Sports Club Panel (VSP2.0)]. University of Leuven/Department of Kinesiology, Leuven

Scheerder J, Van Bottenburg M (2010) Sport light. De opkomst van lichte organisaties in de sport [Sport light. The emergence of light organisations in sport]. In: Pattyn B, Raymaekers B (eds) In gesprek met morgen (Lessen voor de eenentwintigste eeuw 16). Universitaire Pers Leuven, Leuven, pp 89–120

Scheerder J, Vandermeerschen H, Borgers J, Thibaut E, Vos S (2013) Vlaanderen sport! Vier decennia sportbeleid en sportparticipatie [Sport in Flanders. Four decades of sport policy and sport participation]. (SBS Series 5). Academia, Ghent

Scheerder J, Vandermeerschen H, Van Tuyckom C, Hoekman R, Breedveld K, Vos S (2011a) Understanding the game: sport participation in Europe. Facts, reflections and recommendations (Sport Policy & Management 10). University of Leuven/Research Unit of Social Kinesiology & Sport Management, Leuven

Scheerder J, Vos S (2011) Social stratification in adults' sports participation from a time-trend perspective Results from a 40-year household study. Eur J Sport Soc 8(1):31–44

Scheerder J, Vos S (2013) Belgium: Flanders. In: Hallmann K, Petry K (eds) Comparative sport development. Systems, participation and public policy (Sports Economics, Management & Policy 8). Springer Science, New York, NY, pp 7–21

Scheerder J, Vos S, Breesch D, Késenne S, Van Hoecke J, Vanreusel B (2010) Sportclubs in beeld. Basisrapportering over het Vlaamse Sportclub Panel 2009 (VSP09) [Sport clubs at a glance. Report on the Flemish Sport Club Panel 2009]. Leuven: KU Leuven/Research Unit of Social Kinesiology & Sport Management

Scheerder J, Zintz T, Delheye P (2011b) The organisation of sports in Belgium. Between public, economic and social profit. In: Sobry C (ed) Sports governance in the world: a socio-historic approach. The organization of sport in Europe: a patch-work of institutions, with few shared points. Le Manuscrit, Paris, pp 84–113

Taks M, Renson R, Vanreusel B (1999) Organised sport in transition. Development, structure and trends of sports clubs in Belgium. In: Heinemann K (ed) Sport clubs in various European countries (Series Club of Cologne 1). Hofmann & Schattauer, Cologne, pp 183–223

Vanreusel B, Renson R, Tolleneer J (1999) Divided sports in a divided Belgium. In: Sugden J, Bairner A (eds) Sport in divided societies. Meyer & Meyer Sport, Aachen, pp 97–111

Vanreusel B, Taks M, Renson R (2002) Belgium—Flanders. Origins, development and trends of Sport for All. In: DaCosta LP, Miragaya A (eds) Worldwide experiences and trends in Sport for All. Meyer & Meyer Sport, Oxford, pp 379–400

WHO (1986) Ottawa charter for health promotion. World Health Organization, Geneva

# Chapter 5
# Sport Clubs in the Czech Republic

Jiri Novotny

## 5.1 Introduction

According to the Czech Statistical Office there were 10,562,214 inhabitants living in the Czech Republic in 2011.[1] In the first half of the twentieth century, the population growth was rather small. It reached its peak during the Second World War, when the number slightly exceeded 11 million people. After the Second World War, on the contrary, the population decreased by about two million inhabitants (mainly due to the expulsion of the German population). Since 2000 the Czech Republic is divided into 13 regions and exists as the unitary state. The administrative hierarchy is the Czech Government, regions and municipalities. The Czech Republic is a secular state. In 2011 it was declared that only 20.6 % of people were believers and only 13.9 % were reported to be officially recognized by the Church. Half of the believers are the Roman Catholic. The ethnic structure of the population is homogenous—nearly 95 % are Czechs.

## 5.2 History and Context

An important source of information about the current situation in sport clubs was a Master's thesis of Marek Palma: The Economics of Sports Clubs in Czech Republic, University of Economics Prague and Faculty Business Administration (2014). Palma did a survey only in the Pilsen region and had a problem with the willingness of clubs to cooperate. The questionnaire he applied was anonymous and contained out of 30

[1] Obyvatelstvo—roční časové řady, Český statistický úřad (Czech Statistical Office).

J. Novotny (✉)
University of Economics Prague, Praha, Czech Republic
e-mail: jnovotn26@gmail.com



C. Breuer et al. (eds.), *Sport Clubs in Europe*, Sports Economics, Management and Policy 12, DOI 10.1007/978-3-319-17635-2_5

questions. The aim of the questionnaire was to get information about the economic situation of sports clubs in the Pilsen region. Research sub-objectives were to explore the relationships between clubs and local municipalities, the importance of related finance resources for clubs, the use of grant programs from public budgets, membership fees and management of clubs. After removal of faulty questionnaires there were 60 valid questionnaires left to analyse. The typical sports clubs have a legal form of a citizen association based in a small village with a thousand of inhabitants, either focusing on football as the sport sector or an identical situation with clubs operating in several sports sectors/disciplines, which often include a football club.

Since 2000, the Czech sports clubs are facing two main problems, both associated with deep political and social changes, which occurred in 1990. Firstly, it was a decrease of the birth index with lower share of youth in the population and secondly, it was the bankruptcy of the lottery company SAZKA, which was one of the main sources of financing amateur's sports in the Czech Republic.

Lottery company SAZKA was established on 15 September 1956 as a state company. The main tasks were the operation of betting on sports results. A year later it was cooperating with the newly established and unified amateur organisation ČSTV. The whole profit of this business was used for funding the sport in Czechoslovakia. In 1992, SAZKA was transformed into a joint stock company, with its owners being civic associations active in the field of sports and physical education. These shareholders were the Czech Association of Physical Education (ČSTV) with 68 % share, Czech Sokol Organisation (owning 13.5 %), the Czech Association Sport for All (ČASPV, 5.55 %), Autoklub Czech Republic (4 %), Association of Sports Federations Czech Republic (3.55 %), Czech Olympic Committee (2 %), Czech Shooting Federation (1.5 %), Association of Sports Clubs Czech Republic (1 %) and Orel (0.9 %) (SAZKA 2010). The main problems of SAZKA were managerial failures during the build-up of the largest sports arena in the Czech Republic in 2004. The failures resulted in the inability to pay back the loans used for financing the construction of the arena and meet its financial commitments towards the sports associations. The bankruptcy of SAZKA in 2011 and the subsequent amendment of the Act no. 202/1990 Sb. on lotteries and other similar games in 2012 were major problems for sports clubs. The amendment of law has changed the distribution of proceeds from gambling from 2012 on and has negatively affected the Czech sports—even more than the fall of the company SAZKA itself. According to the amendment, the Ministry of Finance started sending the yields from the taxation from gambling in the Czech Republic directly to the municipalities. Sports organisations as CUS and Czech Olympic Committee were omitted from the distribution of the funds for sports clubs. Analysis has shown that municipalities in 2012 improved by 6.1 billion CZK. The comparison with the previous year indicated an increase of the budget of municipalities by about 4.3 billion CZK. Municipalities had provided grants for sport clubs in the same volume as years ago. At least Czech sports environment lost two billion CZK per year, which could previously count the sport for its activity. For sport clubs that is a hard impact.[2]

[2] In 2013 only sport clubs of ČUS had revenue of 4 billion. CZK, cca 160 million EUR.

In combination with a decrease in the number of young people that is a hard blow with a negative impact to the development of the member's base.

## 5.3 Origin of Sports Clubs

Amateur sports clubs began to emerge in the territory of the present Czech Republic (meaning Bohemia, Moravia and Silesia) in the second half of the nineteenth century. Everything was related to the revolutionary period in 1848 in Europe. With the slackening of social relations in this territory the industry began to develop rapidly and strongly and started to develop a middle class.

Sport has become a tool of emancipation for the newly emerging middle class population in the Czech lands. It was a multinational territory, where people mainly spoke Czech and German. The greatest share was represented by the Catholic religion, followed by the Evangelical and Jewish religions in a smaller scale. Before the World War II the Czech, German and Jewish sports clubs coexisted in the given territory. After the war until now there were only Czech clubs in the territory of Czechoslovakia. In 1993, the republic was split to the Czech Republic and Slovak Republic.

The first impulses for founding amateur sports clubs came from the German-speaking population living in Prague. Therefore, the first sports club was founded by Prague Germans. A few months later, on 16 February 1862 the first Czech amateur sport club Sokol Pražský was established. The statutes of the club have been processed under the German model. This sports club was the basis for the emergence of the sports association Sokol; clubs that were implemented in this organisation had been oriented in their programs on the versatility in the spirit of the ancient Greek kalokagathia. The content of the activity was mainly based on physical exercises, the spread of education and enlightenment among the population and singing and playing the theatre with building of the local Sokol libraries. The activity of the association was socially very affluent. Sokol did not agree with sports competition, which emerged at the time, especially from England. The foundation of Sokol Pražský was followed by residents in other towns and villages—first in Bohemia, and a little later in Moravia and Silesia. In 1865 there were already 25 Sokol clubs and by 1871 there were already 131 organisations. Sokol movement continued to establish new clubs across the whole territory of Habsburg monarchy, where Slavic peoples lived. The process was facilitated by the adoption of the Federal Act in 1867 No. 167 in the Reich, which is still valid in Austria. Česká obec sokolská (ČOS) as the head organisation of Sokol clubs was founded only in 1889 with headquarters in Prague.

A group of unsatisfied gymnasts went away from the Sokol federation. On 22 August 1897 the first Workers Gymnastics Club was founded as a maternal club. Another sports federation on the same basis as Sokol was established, but this one did focus on the working class. It was the second type of the sport federation in the Czech territory.

The third similar sports federation was Orel. Formally, it was founded on the initiative of the Catholic Church in 1909. Orel with about 35,000 members in 1931 represented the second largest sports organisation in the former Czechoslovakia. The Orel built its basics on the Christian principles and is mainly dedicated to Sport for All and youth work.

Until the beginning of the Second World War, the trend in clubs was to bear national ideology and emancipatory efforts of the Czech society against the German part of the Austro—Hungarian Empire and later Germany.

The second trend in the development of sports clubs, which emerged later and was inspired mainly by the English concept of sports, was a focus on sports performance. The first purely sporting club in the country—disregarded of Moravia—can be considered as Utraquist Eisklub Prager Verein, established in 1868. In 1872 it merged with Prager Ruderclub Regatta (founded 1870). This meant that Utraquist was a Czech-German sports club. The first Czech sport club of English type was founded as a rowing club Blesk, which started its sport activity in 1875 and exists until now. Major development of sport clubs occurred after 1880. For example, 1880: Smíchovský ČKV (Smíchovský Czech club Velocipede), 1890: Athletic Club Praha, 1891: Český ski klub Praha (Czech Ski Club Prague), 1892: SK Slavia Praha (football), 1893: 1. Český Lawn Tenis Klub (1. Czech Lawn Tenis Club) and 1893: Český Yacht Klub (Czech Yacht Club). Klub Českých turistů (KČT), in English the Czech Tourist Club, dates back to the year 1888, when the club was founded by a group of Czech patriots around Vojta Náprstek. Formed in 1888, the club really began going trail-marking.

Before the Second World War in Czechoslovakia there were about 120,000 sports clubs with nearly two million members. However, it is difficult to judge the accuracy of the data. The best records of its members had Sokol (and it was close to one million members). Other sports associations usually estimated the number of its members based upon the occasion of significant anniversaries of their founding. After war the number of clubs has decreased. It was the result of post-war development in Czechoslovakia, especially after 1948 and the unification of all sports associations under one single sports organisation. After the split of Czechoslovakia in 1993, only the Czech Republic has about 14,000–16,000 of sports clubs, but probably at the time the number was lower (about 11,000 sports clubs). In a difficult system of relationships of sports federations some sports sections of clubs were certainly included as separated sport clubs.

There were only amateur sports clubs until 1989 with a classic structure of club governance with registration members. Members do pay yearly membership fees and are part of the clubs' highest authority assembly. The general membership meeting elects the club bureau with a president and the Audit Commission. For the administration of the club it is important to have secretary and a treasurer or an economist. Only the largest Czech clubs have professionals workers on these positions, but in most cases such functions are being covered by volunteers. These principles are followed even nowadays.

Until 1948 there was a pluralistic system of sports associations; from 1949 to 1990 we had unitary system under one head federation. Since 1948 it began to enforce particular orientation towards sports performance. Since 1956 the name of this federation was Československý svaz tělesné výchovy (ČSTV), in English: Czechoslovak Sport Association. Now the pluralistic system is in place again. In the present system, the free organised set of sport in the Czech Republic is applied and clubs are organised in different sports federations. There are several clubs, which are independent (are not subordinated under any of the existing sports federations). Since 1990 the activities of sports associations such as Sokol or Orel were reestablished and the Czech Association Sport for All (ČASPV) was newly founded. These associations are more focused on all-round development of man.

All the sports clubs focused on sports performance in their sports associations are under the umbrella association Czech Sports Association (CSTV). In 2013 it was renamed to Česká Unie sportu (ČUS), in English: Czech Union of Sport. It is the biggest sport organisation with 74 sports or sports branches and is the biggest owner of sports facilities in the Czech Republic. Currently, the clubs have major problems with financing of sports facilities and therefore they try to convert those into municipal ownership. The clubs are mainly oriented for competitive sports.[3]

Sokol is the second biggest umbrella sports association. After 40 years the activity has been resumed in 1990. Sokol exercise was and still is addressed for everybody and most the clubs can be categorised as traditional sports clubs. It develops motoric skills—speed, strength, agility and endurance exercisers, learn to win and lose, do not give up when you fail and not to be afraid. Sokol has sport sections too; there are 57 sports overall. Sokol is the second largest owner of sports facilities in the Czech Republic after ČUS.

Česká asociace sport pro všechny (ČASPV), in English: Czech Association Sport for All, is the head sports federation and was established as a new association from 1992. The federation aim is (through physical education and sport) to keep people fit while they relax from daily worries. Therefore, the physical activity should be appropriately challenging to develop the young body and for elderly to maintain its function at an optimal level. They offer their members a varied selection of effective physical activities: general gymnastics, recreational sports, aerobics, rhythmic gymnastics, yoga, health physical education, psychomotor, exercise and outdoor activities, dance sport, step, exercise for preschool children, training parents with children, etc. ČASPV is not an owner of sport facilities. The relevant clubs are traditional sports clubs.

Klub českých turistů (KČT), in English: Czech Tourist Club, got out of union ČSTV and began to function independently since 1993. Many of these clubs are departments and operate in other umbrella federations. The association maintains and marks all hiking trails. The club really began going trail-marking after the World War II. Today more than 40,000 km of marked routes maintained by 1,350 volunteers are available. The club also coordinates the bike and skiing trails across the country. Today the hiking trails are still maintained by Czech Tourist Club members on a voluntary basis. KČT is owner of a few mountain tourist lodges.

[3] Using German typology of sport clubs.

Orel is an other sports association, a Christian sports organisation. After 40 years the activity has been resumed in 1990. The aim is to educate young people and children through sports and other activities. It is not the objective to educate the world champions; their goal is to pursue a sport that promotes positive human qualities—a sport that is fair, respecting opponents and teammates. Orel owns a range of sports facilities and gyms. The relevant clubs are traditional sports clubs.

Asociace tělovýchovných jednot a sportovních klubů (ATJSK), in English: Association of Sports Clubs, is the smallest umbrella organisation and was established as a new association from 1990. The clubs are mainly oriented for competitive sports.

In the Czech Republic, there are also many other single federations, but those are smaller and only have dozens of clubs. One of the biggest is Autoklub České republiky (AČR)—officially it is impossible to find any information about statistics of members and clubs of the federation. According to the information from the Ministry of Education the number was about 20,000 members.

## 5.4 Role of Sport Clubs in Policy and Society

### *5.4.1 Troubles with the Registration of Members and Clubs*

Each sports association in the Czech Republic has its own registry. It performs an educational role here, and in particular also a social role in a rural society. It is therefore a difficult comparison between the systems. Since the scope is on amateur sport clubs and volunteers are carrying out most of the administrative work, the quality and topciality has to be considered sometimes as problematic. They differ in the details of evidence, and terminology is not uniform. ČUS (formerly ČSTV) has the longest time series of the numbers and structure of members. Its records are from the mid-1960s and are relatively consistent. The most accurate information is from the period of socialism, i.e. up to 1989. Thanks to the fact that it was the only overarching sports organisation for the whole Czechoslovakia, there were no duplications or triplications in the registry of members. A member was firstly registered in the parent sports club (e.g. a football section in the club) and in case he or she was active in other sports section, such as an ice hockey, he or she only had a hosting in the second section of the club or other club. Identification of the members was by birth numbers and, therefore, the member could not be counted twice to the total number of members of the sports organisation in Czechoslovakia. Under the present system it does not work that way. For example, the Ministry of Education presented a number of 2.7 million of registered members, but it has been severely distorted by duplicity and triplicates. The number was also significantly increased by the so-called inactive members, who were registered, but do not pay membership fees (so they did only inflate the numbers). Currently, the clubs are in the financial crisis and begin to consistently collect member fees, so the numbers were decreased due to a reduction of inactive members. There is a purification of the member's base.

### 5.4.2 *National Data on Sport Club Participation (by Age Group, Sex, etc.)*

Participation amounted to 1.6 million members in 2010; due to a dramatic change in the conditions of the financing of sports associations and the bankruptcy of lottery company SAZKA owned by sports associations, there was a significant decline in the membership base. For example Football Association of Czech Republic had 520,000 members and now it decreased to 280,000.

Memberships in ČUS as of 31 December 2013 persist in the trend of the last few years, which is a slight decline. ČUS has 1,297,898 members and 8,731 clubs. This represents an annual loss of 298 sport clubs and approximately 130,000 members, from which the 37,000 is among the youth. Figure 5.1 shows the same trend in the overall statistics on sports branches after the inclusion of the rest of the members belonging to the line of national sports associations. This is caused by the unfavourable demographic development in the Czech Republic. In the 1990s the birth rate declined. The unfavorable trend was stooped after the year 2005. The trend may changes after a few years again (Fig. 5.2).

In the age structure and decomposition we can demonstrate unfavorable demographic development as in Fig. 5.3.

Figure 5.4 shows the development of memberships in ČUS when dividing them into three age categories with aspect of sex: to the category of students/pupils as a male or a female and fall members under the age of 15 years (whereby the member, who turned 15 years of age during 2013, is counted in adolescents), again divided to male and female. The member who during 2013 turned 19 years of age, for this year, is already counted in the category of adults with dividing to men and women.

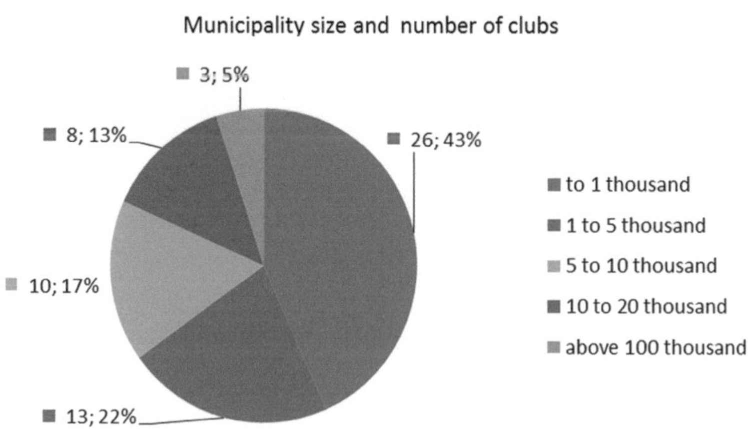


**Fig. 5.1** Municipality size and number of clubs (Palma 2014, p. 66)

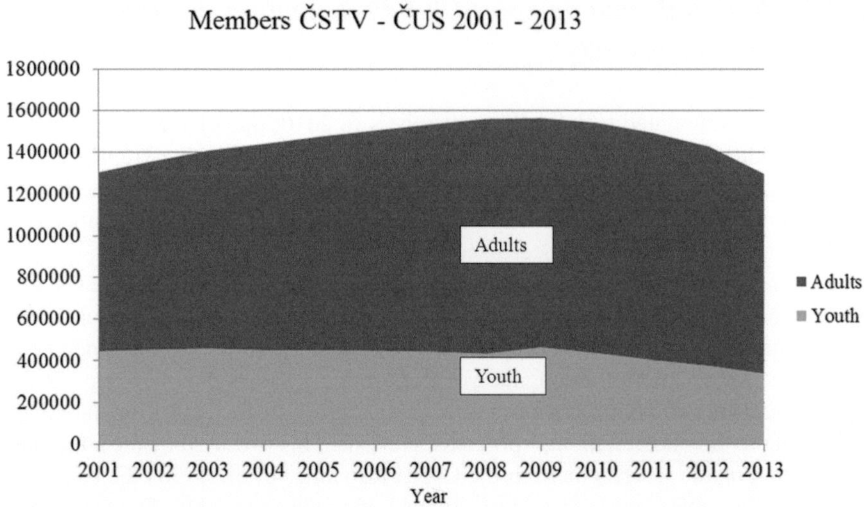


**Fig. 5.2** Membership of the ČUS in the period from 2001 to 2013 (ČUS 2014)

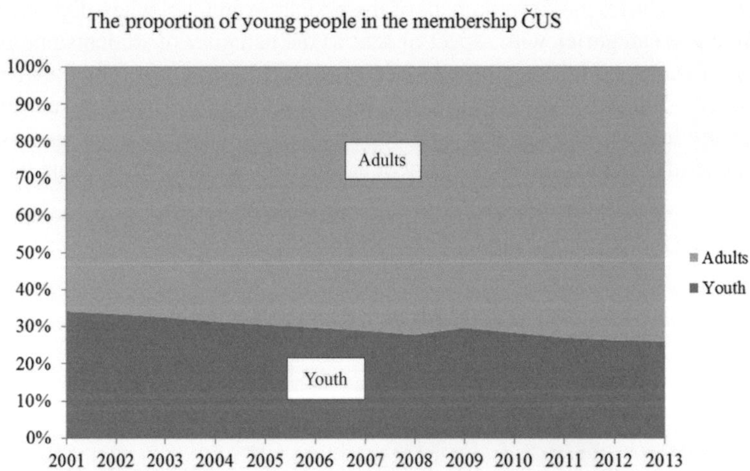


**Fig. 5.3** The share of youth in the membership base of ČUS during the years 2000–2012 (ČUS 2014)

In Fig. 5.4 we can see the decreasing share of females mainly in categories U15 and adult women. There are probably two main reasons: unfavorable demographic development and a lack of appealing sporting activities for women offered by the ČUS.

Table 5.1 captures the development of citizen's participation in the biggest sport organisation ČSTV–ČUS in the Czech Republic. In the period between years 1974

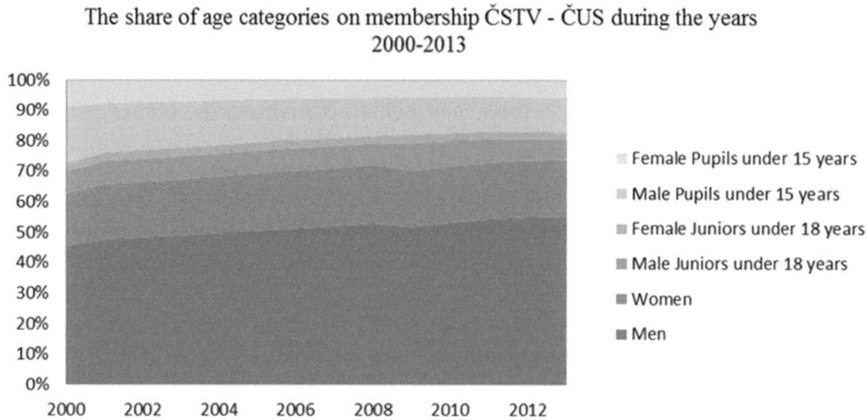


**Fig. 5.4** Development of the share of the membership base in ČSTV–ČUS during the years 2000–2012 by ages and gender (ČUS 2014)

**Table 5.1** Development of the membership in CSTV/ČUS in the period 1974–2013 (age, gender, position; Statistika ČSTV 1974, 1984, 1988)

| Year | 1974 | 1984 | 1988 | 2008 | 2013 |
|---|---|---|---|---|---|
| Memberships total | 1,134,531 | 1,341,778 | 1,423,012 | 1,535,787 | 1,297,898 |
| Number of clubs | 5,324 | 5,479 | 5,558 | 8,412 | 8,645 |
| Average size of the club | 213 | 249 | 256 | 183 | 150 |
| Men | 470,413 | 522,656 | 528,757 | 748,239 | 718,302 |
| Women | 196,593 | 260,524 | 275,732 | 269,580 | 241,092 |
| Adults male U18 | 95,990 | 102,837 | 115,208 | 176,607 | 86,450 |
| Adults female U18 | 39,187 | 40,266 | 49,467 | 59,058 | 30,080 |
| Pupils male U15 | 185,086 | 236,034 | 259,398 | 194,986 | 149,337 |
| Pupils female U15 | 146,962 | 179,461 | 194,450 | 87,317 | 72,617 |
| The share of the male (%) | 69.4 | 64.20 | 63.70 | 72.90 | 73.92 |
| The share of the female (%) | 30.6 | 35.80 | 36.30 | 27.10 | 26.49 |
| Trainers | 69,877 | 136,421 | 152,818 | 50,550 | 53,792 |
| Referees | 28,933 | 44,710 | 50,602 | 17,946 | 20,877 |

and 1988 only one umbrella sports organisation for the whole Czechoslovakia did exist. The unitary system of the sport did exist for the whole republic. Years 2008–2013 are the period of the pluralistic system of the covering sports federations in the Czech Republic. ČSTV, now ČUS, is still continuing as the biggest sports umbrella organisation until now. It is necessary to keep in mind that the last data of members are distorted by duplications and triplications.

The number of memberships was growing until 2008. In recent years it has significantly reduced. A possible cause could be the bankruptcy of the company SAZKA and troubles with funding of sport clubs. Numbers of clubs until 1988 increased slightly. In the 1990s there was a sharp increase in the number of clubs and in 2008 it was about 51 % more than it was 20 years ago. In contrast of this development, the average size of the club was reduced to 150 members and it is about 41 % lower compared with 1988. In the period of the socialisms the average size of the club has been slightly increasing (20.2 %). After political change in Czechoslovakia in 1990 a trend of increasing number of sport clubs and decreasing average size of the clubs was obvious. A possible explanation could be an increased number of single-subject clubs, emergence of new popular sports and troubles with financing. In 2008 there were 5,514 clubs while in 2013 the number increased to 5,826. 67 % of them were single-subject clubs. On the contrary the number of multidisciplinary clubs with more than six disciplinary was reduced from 574 to 555 with a share of 6 % in 2013. An unfavorable development can be observed in the structure of members by gender and age. The share of men is continually increasing. It was 73.9 % in the year 2013. In contrast of this development, the share of women is decreasing—a top share was 36.3 % in 1988 whereas in 2013 it declined to 26.5 %. The possible cause could be a lack of attractive supply for women and girls from sport clubs. In large cities it could be a competition offer of the commercial fit centres. Decreases in the number of young people could be caused by lower birth rates in the Czech population between years 1993 and 2003. The decrease in the number of trainers and referees can be explained firstly by an underestimation of the importance of the training volunteers from a side of sport federations and secondly it could be affected by the changes in the labour market. Employers do not want to free employees for the education courses organised by sport federations. Czech clubs move closer to the standards of Western Europe. It may be the result of problems with financing of sport in the Czech Republic and sports clubs trying to convert sports facilities to municipalities.

ČASPV, Sokol and Orel are in a different situation with the age and gender structure of members.

Sokol had 1,002 clubs with 160,460 members in 2013. According to the age structure 65.4 % of members are adults and 34.8 % are underaged. The gender structure is not officially listed.

ČASPV was having 770 departments or sections with 45,603 members in 2013. Only 117 of them are in the club of ČASPV; others belong under another covering sport association. For example, 629 departments are in sport sections in the clubs of ČUS. Fig. 5.5 shows the age structure of the ČASPV as the tree of life. They have a 47.8 % share of the youth from 45,603 member base. In the gender structure they have 59.55 % of female members. Since 2012 it has seen dramatic fall of members—from 240,000 to 45,000 members.

*Orel* had around 17,000 members in 250 clubs with sport facilities mainly including gymnasiums.

*Sokol* and *Orel* differ significantly from Č*ASPV* in age structures of the membership because they are associations with a very long tradition. Regarding the age

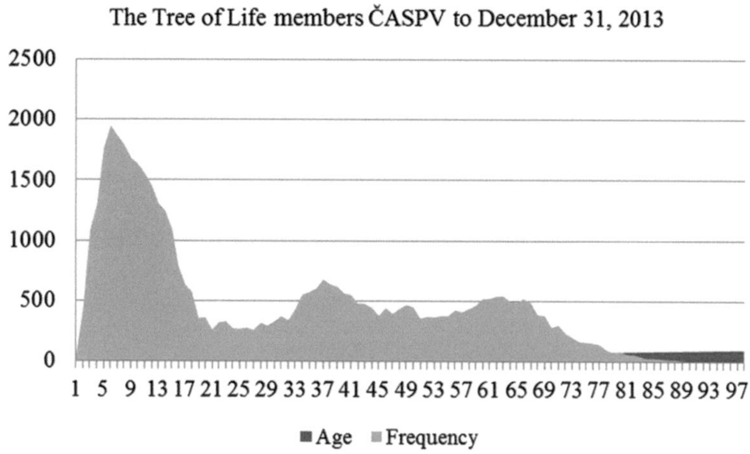


**Fig. 5.5** The Tree of Life members in ČASPV on 31 December 2013 (ČASPV 2013)

structure, clubs of these associations are in a better situation than clubs from *ČUS*. It is obvious from the fragmentary information that these organisations provide to the public.

*KČT* has around 40,000 members in 461 departments. Almost one-quarter of the members are young people.

*Asociace tělovýchovných jednot a sportovních klubů* (ATJSK) Association of Sports Clubs in 2013 encompassed 62 clubs with 14,006 members. The proportion of young and adults in the membership was 47.6 %. There were registered 33 disabled sportsmen and 1,633 seniors.

## 5.5 Societal, Political Embedding

Sports clubs are very important for the social life in municipalities. Czech amateur clubs were owners of two-thirds of all the sports facilities in the country. After bankruptcy of the lottery company SAZKA (2011), whose earnings were a very strong source of funding for non-profit sport organisations, a new situation started. Amateur sports clubs have shown an increased tendency for transfers of ownership of the large sport facilities onto municipalities. Especially in large cities the process has begun. Until now many football stadiums, ice arenas, swimming pools and multifunctional exercise halls are under the municipal ownership. This is underpinned by the value of assets of the amateur sport clubs. In 2005 ČSTV showed assets in the amount of CZK 42 billion and in 2013 it was fluctuating between 15 and 18 billion CZK. This will further allow citizens of towns and villages to access sports activities. Most municipalities do not have to take care of the maintenance and operation of sports facilities; they support clubs only by small grants. In reality there are two types of club's support. The first type is grant on sports activity, mostly related to the support of young members of clubs on the expenditures for the sport competitions (such as the rent for the use of sports facilities or sports jerseys). Second type of the support is oriented to the operating costs of sports facilities and for the maintenance. Volume of this support or the subvention should be higher than the one for sport activities. In 2013, most municipalities provided grants to clubs only for sports facilities which are owners of sports facilities and clubs must have a seat in the municipality.

### *5.5.1 Revenue Structure of the Clubs' Budgets*

KPMG studies from 2012 show that key sources for the clubs' revenues are household expenditures with 42 %. Public budgets (as the municipal, regional and governmental) are second contributing with 19 %, with the majority coming from municipal budgets. It is interesting to observe this share in a long interval through the existence of Czechoslovakia. In the long past the share was still oscillating between 17 and 20 %. The other sources as contributions from the sport federations, sponsorship and donations are relatively equal. The membership fees are hidden under the household's revenue (Fig. 5.6).

There are disproportions with the statistic of ČUS to the date 31 December 2013. According to them, the share of membership fees was at around 22 % of clubs' revenues. KPMG used different methods for estimating the different income sources. Probably more exact is the information from the statistic of ČUS.

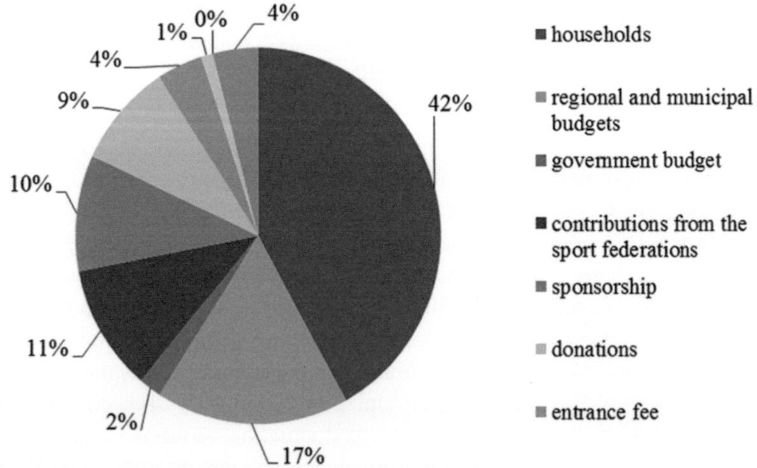


**Fig. 5.6** Revenue structure of the club budgets (KPMG 2012)

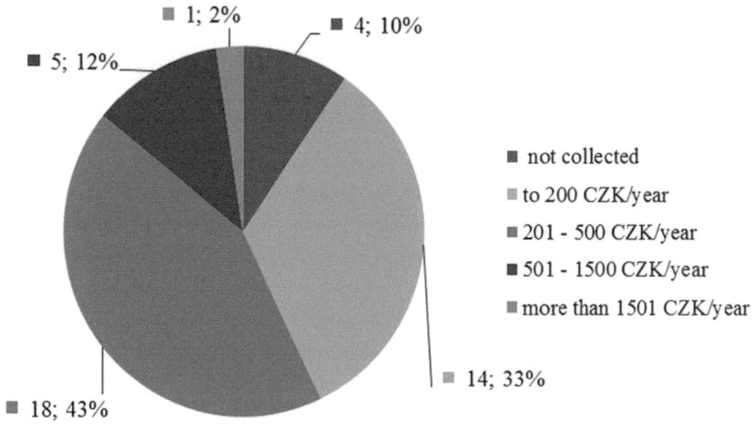


**Fig. 5.7** The amount of membership fees of clubs (Palma 2014, p. 70)

The increasing trend in member fees still exists since 1990. In the last 10 years it was accelerating.

The results of Palma (2014) indicated the fact that the primary source across the spectrum cannot be identified and the degree of importance of each resource is important for every other club. He selected the following items: membership fee—dues, grants from municipalities, grants or contributions from the sports association, sponsorship, donations and finally complementary activities of the club, for example income from hostels, rent of sports equipment and sports facilities for the general public. It depends on under which conditions the club operates and what the environment offers as income opportunities.

More than half of all surveyed clubs have chosen the membership fees ranging from 201 to 1,500 CZK per year (7–54 EUR). 6.7 % of the clubs do not collect membership fees, while over 5,000 CZK had been collected only by a golf club. It is true that rural clubs are choosing lower contributions than clubs from cities and that they play in lower leagues, which are cheaper (Fig. 5.7).

Cooperation of the club with the municipality in which it is located must be good. Support can be financial or non-financial. Here it became clear that the overwhelming majority of nearly 92 % of the relevant municipalities cooperate with the clubs, which is a good sign. It does not prove the rule *one club in the village = cooperation between the two entities* (Fig. 5.8).

### *5.5.2 Cooperation with Municipality*

Of the 83.4 % of the clubs that have requested funding 80 % were successful and only 3.4 % of clubs' applications were unsuccessful; this indicates that the relationships between clubs and municipalities are very good.

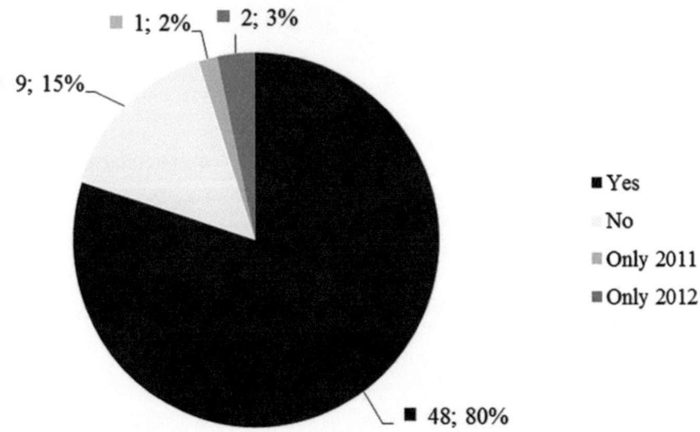


**Fig. 5.8** The request for financial assistance from the municipality in the last 2 years, 2011, 2012 (Palma 2014, p. 69)

Financial support of clubs from the sports associations is less than that from municipalities. 56 % of clubs requested the financial support and 21.6 % did not succeed. The effectiveness of this kind of support is not as high as in the case of applications from municipalities. Only 15 % of clubs had the chance to get the grant/contribution or non-financial support directly from the government (Ministry of Education) and 3 % of them got the grant in the full amount at the end.

It can be stated that 66.67 % of sport clubs consider the current system of the public finance support in the Czech Republic as unsatisfactory. Only 8.3 % clubs consider the system as adequate as well as the reasonable amount of money for them.

Most of the clubs, 67 %, were able to keep their budget balanced and keep revenues in balance with expenditures. Only 10 % of clubs found it impossible to get out from deficit, and 14.7 % of clubs operated with surplus.

In Czech sport clubs women and men, respectively girls and boys, are practising together. In 67 % of the clubs there are sporting for both together. Strictly women's representation can only be found in one of the volleyball clubs. Then 32 % has in its ranks only male representative. 26 % of them play football, 4.3 % play table tennis and the last club plays ice hockey. We do not have a precise information on specially youth-oriented sport clubs. It exists, but usually the care about the youth is carried out at a club with adults. It is one condition for obtaining grants from the sport association.

Sport clubs are still very active in the participation on the social life of community. Traditional clubs organise cultural and social events, which were always in Czech rural areas and very popular smaller towns. Such activities not only enrich the life in the village, but also contribute by income to the budget of the clubs. The responses indicate that only 10 % of the clubs do not organise any such activities

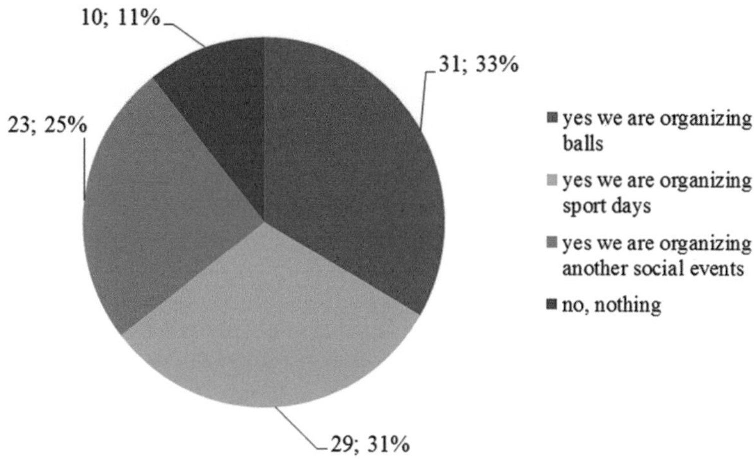


**Fig. 5.9** Participation of sport clubs in the social life of municipalities (Palma 2014, p. 78)

(could probably be very small clubs from the larger cities). Figure 5.9 shows the participation of sport clubs in the social life of municipalities.

Czech clubs perceive their work as a mission towards the development of a healthy lifestyle, transmission of moral values, socialisation of young people, youth crime prevention, etc. 88 % of clubs consider this activity as the added value.

## 5.6 Conclusion

The Czech sport movement is going through a difficult period, especially for sport clubs. The number of young people has been reduced and clubs have financial troubles. In recapitulation of available information it can be stated that the Czech Republic has 10,162 sport clubs in the five main umbrella sport associations. It does not count 461 departments of the Czech Tourist Club. It is not clear if every club exists as a sport club or as the department of bigger sport clubs in other associations. From the unreliable statistical statements of amateur sports federations we can estimate the current state of the membership base to 1.7 million registered members. Since 1990 the share of one-branch clubs has been slowly increasing, and now it is at 67 %. This reduces the size of the clubs, now at 150 members. In the ČUS, the proportion of female component falls to historic minimum of 26.5 %. Only ČASPV has a share of the female component of 59.9 % and 47.8 % share of the youth. All amateur clubs are part of social life in communities. The club is playing greater role in smaller towns and villages. The Czech sport movement has a long historical tradition and hopefully the temporal obstacles can be overcome and clubs will offer sport for all in a optimal structure.

# References

Asociace tělovýchovných jednot a sportovních klubů (2014) Anniversary reports. Retrieved 12 August 2014 from http://www.atjsk.cz/wp-content/uploads/vyrocni_zprava_.pdf

ČASPV (2014) Anniversary reports. Retrieved 09 July 2014 from http://www.caspv.cz/cz/o-nas/dokumenty/vyrocni-zpravy/

ČESKÁ UNIE SPORTU (2014) Co je ČUS?. Retrieved 14 July 2014 from http://www.cuscz.cz/o-nas/co-je-cus.html

Czech Statistical Office (2014) Population. Retrieved 12 August 2014 from http://www.czso.cz/eng/redakce.nsf/i/population

ČUS (2014). Retrieved 02 July 2014 from http://www.cuscz.cz/o-nas/statistika.html

KPMG (2012) Česká republika, s.r.o. Koncepce financování sportu v České republice: analyticko-koncepční studie. Retrieved 13 April 2012 from http://www.olympic.cz/financovani/docs/koncepce_financovani_sportu_prezentace_v9a.pdf

Orel. Retrieved 10 July 2014 from http://www.orel.cz/?ukaz=profil_orla/ [Access 2014-07-10]

Palma M (2014) The Economics of Sports Clubs in Czech Republic. Master's thesis, leader: Jiri Novotny. University of Economics Prague, and Faculty of Business Administration

SAZKA (2010) Výroční zpráva 2009. Retrieved from http://www.vyrocnizprava.cz/fotky/1_575_Sazka_VZ_09_CZ.pdf

Sokol (2014). Retrieved 10 July 2014 from http://www.sokol.cz/sokol/

Statistika ČSTV (1974) Výsledky statistického šetření k 31.12.1974. Organizační oddělení ÚV ČSTV 1975, Praha

Statistika ČSTV (1984) Výsledky statistického šetření k 31.12.1984. Organizační oddělení ÚV ČSTV 1985, Praha

Statistika ČSTV (1988) Výsledky statistického šetření k 31.12.1988. Organizační oddělení ÚV ČSTV 1989, Praha

# Chapter 6
# Sport Clubs in Denmark

**Bjarne Ibsen, Karsten Østerlund, and Trygve Laub**

## 6.1 Introduction

The kingdom of Denmark is a constitutional monarchy, consisting of Denmark and the two autonomous areas: the Faroe Islands in the North Atlantic and Greenland. This analysis does not include the latter two parts of the kingdom. Denmark has 5.6 million inhabitants spread over approx. 43,000 $km^2$.

Voluntary sport clubs form an essential element of sport and exercise in Denmark. Four out of ten adults and eight out of ten school children perform sports or take other kinds of exercise in one or more of the estimated 16,000 sport clubs in Denmark, all based on the principles of the voluntary association. An association is normally regarded as a union of people with common aims or interests, organised and managed by commonly accepted democratic rules and procedures (Ibsen and Habermann 2005).

Generally associations and voluntary work play a relatively large role in Denmark compared to other European countries. A comparative analysis of the voluntary non-profit sector in selected European countries shows that the sector's share of the total economy in Denmark is greater than in most European countries, being at the same level as in the UK, Ireland and Belgium and only clearly lower than in Holland, where the non-profit sector plays the greatest economic role (Boje 2008). An EU survey in 2008 put the Nordic countries ahead of all their European partners in terms of the proportion of their populations participating in voluntary

B. Ibsen (✉) • K. Østerlund
Department of Sports Science and Clinical Biomechanics,
University of Southern Denmark, Odense, Denmark
e-mail: bibsen@health.sdu.dk; kosterlund@health.sdu.dk

T. Laub
Danish Institute for Sports Studies, Copenhagen, Denmark
e-mail: tryge.laub@idan.dk



C. Breuer et al. (eds.), *Sport Clubs in Europe*, Sports Economics, Management and Policy 12, DOI 10.1007/978-3-319-17635-2_6

and charitable activities (McCloughan et al. 2011). Politically, there is a strong belief in Denmark in the social significance of associations and especially their impact on social inclusion and cohesion.

The aim of this chapter is therefore firstly to describe the features that characterise sport clubs in Denmark, secondly to explain the strong position of sport organised in voluntary associations and thirdly to explore the truth of the widespread assumption that participation in sport clubs contributes to social inclusion and the formation of social capital.

The analysis is based primarily on four studies. The description of specific characteristics of sport clubs is based on a comprehensive study of Danish sport clubs from 2010. The questionnaire was sent to more than 10,000 sport clubs, all members of the National Olympic Committee and Sports Confederation of Denmark, of which 50.4 % responded (Laub 2012).

The analysis of the participation in sport clubs of both children and adults is based on a number of repeated surveys of sports habits in Denmark, the most recent conducted in 2011. A comprehensive questionnaire including questions about the organisational forms of the sports activities was completed by 3,957 adults, or 44 % of those who received the questionnaire, and 2,035 children representing 50 % of those surveyed (Laub 2013).

The third study, which we refer to later in this chapter, is a major study of all types of local associations. The study included a registration of local voluntary associations in 2004 and in 2010 in a region in Denmark (the islands of Fyn, Langeland and Ærø) along with a subsequent questionnaire survey of a representative selection of the registered associations (Ibsen et al. 2013).

The last part of the chapter is based on a survey conducted at the member level in 2011 with responses from 2,023 members, volunteers and paid employees from 30 sport clubs representing five sporting activities (Østerlund 2013).

## 6.2 History and Context

The introductory chapter of this book includes a description of different theoretical explanations for the existence of voluntary associations. One of the theories explains the size and characteristics of the voluntary sector as a result of the characteristics of the welfare state. Another theory has more focus on the historical roots of the voluntary movements and organisations. The size and composition of the voluntary, non-profit sector is assumed to be historically determined and affected by the type of the welfare state within which it has developed. Inspired by these two theoretical explanations we will in this part of the chapter describe the historical development of the voluntary sector with particular focus on sports organised into clubs, and in the next part examine the societal and political embedding of the sport clubs in Denmark.

In order to understand the development of the voluntary sector in Denmark, three factors have to be taken into account: (a) the adoption of a democratic constitution,

(b) the emergence of popular movements and (c) the formation of the welfare state. When the absolute monarch gave in to pressure from the people and the new constitution was adopted in 1849, the Danish Constitutional Act prepared the ground for an expansion in civil engagement across society. Now the citizens had the freedom to join any organisation, union or association. Being a member was not in itself anything new, but the association, based as it was on free membership and democratic rules, provided a new form of participation. After the adoption of the constitution, the civil right to form associations and organisations was ensured, and *the association* became a central feature of almost all spheres of society: political party associations, interest organisations (landlords' associations, artisans' associations, smallholders' association, etc.), trade unions, economic associations (savings banks, health insurance societies and cooperatives), philanthropic associations, religious associations, sports associations and so on.

This period towards the end of the nineteenth century saw the rise of substantial popular movements: *the agricultural cooperative movement*, the labour movement, the revivals between two religious movements (the Grundtvigian movement and Evangelical movement/Home Mission), the temperance movement and the movements promoting popular sport and outdoor activities (Klausen and Selle 1996). From these derive the values and traditions that still characterise many associations. For the development of the Danish welfare state, popular movements had an enormous political significance as democratic partners and opponents.

One of the first national voluntary organisations was the Danish Rifle Shooting Association founded in 1861. The aim of the organisation was to strengthen the defence of the nation, but because of the historical events that followed in the wake of 1864, when Denmark lost a war to Germany, gymnastics (mainly a result of Swedish influence) became the rallying ground for young people, particularly in rural parts of the country, from the 1880s onwards. Throughout the nineteenth century gymnastics was central to the development of a popular sports movement in Denmark that was constantly adapting and reshaping itself organisationally as it expanded, incorporating and merging new members. The overarching sports organisation for this branch of sport and exercise in Denmark today is Danish Gymnastics and Sports Associations (DGI) founded in 1991.[1]

Parallel to the development of the popular gymnastics movement in the country, sport clubs derived from the English model emerged in and around urban centres. Initially they were home to the bourgeoisie of the industrial age, but eventually blue-collar workers also joined or united to form their own sport clubs, underlining the broad appeal of voluntary sport clubs for the Danish public. Contrary to the gymnastics movement's focus on local community and civic engagement, clubs built on the English model placed emphasis on the core values of sport itself, on performance and competition, which were also characteristic of the spirit of the industrial age (Korsgaard 1997). In 1896 these clubs joined forces to form the Sports Confederation of Denmark (DIF). Over time DIF became the central organisation

[1] The organisation was formed by an amalgamation of two organisations, both of which had roots in shooting and gymnastic movement from the 1800s.

for a wide range of sports federations and the body in charge of organising Danish championships. This led to natural ties with the Danish Olympic Committee, founded in 1905 and eventually merged into DIF in 1993.

In 1946 a third umbrella organisation entered the field in the shape of the Danish Association for Company Sports (DFIF), which organises sport clubs based around workplace communities. DFIF took the lead in developing a particularly Danish tradition of merging the personal and professional sphere by engaging in sporting activities with colleagues (Ibsen and Eichberg 2012).

According to the latest figures from 2013, DIF organises 9,287 sport clubs with 1.9 million members, DGI organises 6,331 clubs with total 1.5 million members and the Danish Association for Company Sports organises 244 sport clubs (each of which represents a number of workplaces) with 350,000 members (DGI 2013). Many clubs are, however, members of both the two largest organisations, but there are also associations that deal with sport and physical activity that are not members of a sports organisation. The total number of sport clubs in Denmark is estimated to be 16,000, which correspond to one association for every 350 inhabitants.

Although the differences between these umbrella organisations have to some extent disappeared, and although most clubs today choose sides for practical rather than ideological reasons, the two major national sports organisations, DIF and DGI, continue to exist side by side, supplemented by the more specialised DFIF. The sporting landscape in Denmark is in this way quite different from neighbouring countries, as there is not one single national organisation for voluntary sport clubs but, so to speak, two and a half. Over the years, this structural heterogeneity in the field of sports has been the topic of much debate, subject to criticism for being administratively irrational and praised for being dynamic and inclusive (Ibsen and Eichberg 2012).

Voluntary sport clubs are, however, not the only way to be physically active in an organised setting in Denmark. Many women go to various forms of training—typically non-competitive gymnastics, yoga, meditation and the like—at *evening leisure classes*, non-profit institutions that offer non-formal adult education and leisure activities with the aim of allowing the individual to develop their skills or understanding.

## 6.3 Role of Sport Clubs in Policy and Society

In this part of the chapter, we firstly look at the participation of the population in sport clubs, and secondly we focus on the societal and political embedding of the sport clubs in Denmark.

Denmark is a country with relatively high levels of general participation in sport. Among adult Danes (16 years and above), general participation in sports has been steadily on the rise for the past 50 years or so. From 1964 to 2011, participation rates rose from 15 to 64 %. Children (7–15 years) have only been monitored in 2007 and 2011, but figures indicate a stable and high level of general participation with between eight and nine out of ten children participating in sport.

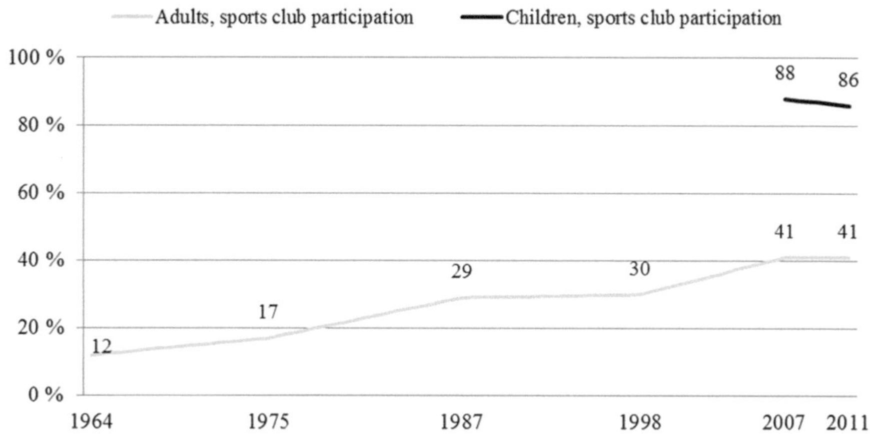


**Fig. 6.1** Historical development in participation in sport clubs among Danish children and adults

Sport club participation in Denmark is high in comparison with other European countries (European Commission 2010; Scheerder et al. 2011). In the sports participation survey of 2011, 86 % of children (aged 7–15) and 41 % of adults (16 and above) had participated in one or more sports activities in a voluntary club setting regularly during the previous year (Fig. 6.1).

As the numbers suggest, voluntary clubs are an integral part of Danish children's sports participation. Between the ages of 7 and 15, almost all children do sport in one form or another, and almost all of these in a club setting. However, sport clubs fall somewhat out of favour, and other settings grow in popularity when comparing how different age groups organise their sporting activities (Fig. 6.2).

Where children (or their parents) choose to participate in sports is linked to what they choose to do. Seven out of ten of the most popular sports among children are predominantly organised in a club, meaning that the majority of the children engaging in the specific sport do so in a sport club (Fig. 6.3).

These seven major club sports are football, swimming, gymnastics,[2] handball, badminton, dancing and horse riding. Three out of four Danish children aged 7–15 do at least one of these sports regularly in a sport club.

During adolescence, however, a significant drop in the popularity of sport clubs occurs. Club participation rates fall from 82 % among the age group 13–15 to 58 % among late teenagers aged 16–19 and fall further to 44 % among Danes in their 20s. Dropping out of sport clubs does not necessarily end sports participation in general. Large numbers of Danes between 15 and 30 years of age opt for other organisational settings, often accompanied by a change in sporting activities. The two most popular activities in the age groups 16–19 and 20–29 are running and strength training. The former is most often done alone or in self-organised groups (with friends or family).

[2] Sport clubs offering gymnastics often include a number of keep-fit activities, such as spinning, aerobics and Zumba.

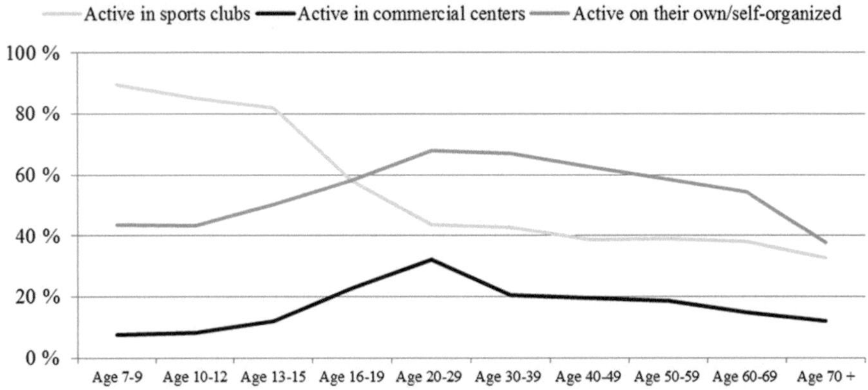


**Fig. 6.2** Proportion of population who do sports or physical activity in different organisational contexts, by age groups (percent)

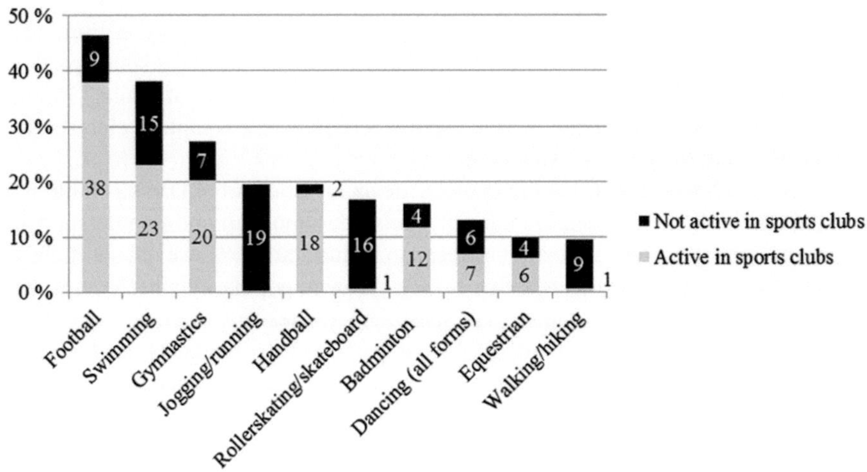


**Fig. 6.3** Proportion of children who participate in sport in a sport club, divided into the ten most popular sports (percent)

In clear contrast to Danish children's top ten, only three of the most popular activities among Danish adults take place predominantly in club settings. These are gymnastics (particularly popular among seniors), football (particularly popular among the young adults) and badminton, coming in at fifth, eighth and tenth on adults' top ten sporting activities (Fig. 6.4).

In Denmark, differences between male and female sports participation in general are insignificant. Boys and girls are often equally active in sport clubs, but they often choose different clubs to be active in. Significantly more boys than girls play football and badminton in clubs, while it is the other way around for dancing,

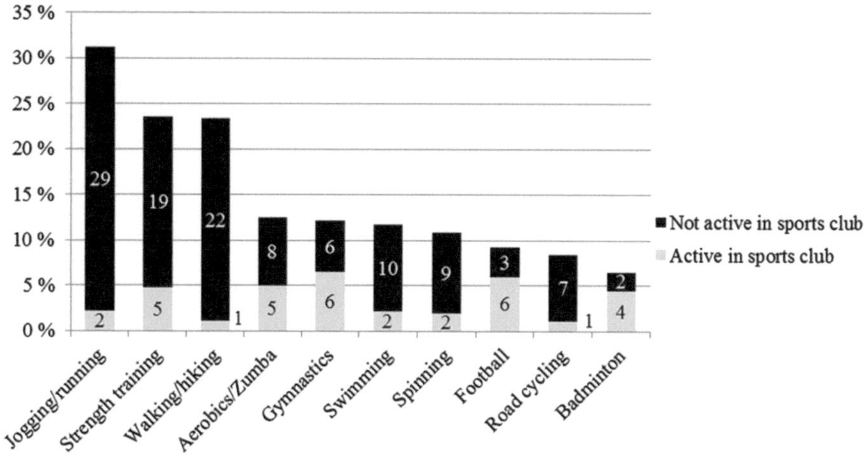


**Fig. 6.4** Proportion of adults who participate in sports in a sport club, divided into the ten most popular sports (percent)

equestrian sports and gymnastics. In only two of the seven traditional club sports for children is the boy/girl ratio roughly even: handball and swimming.

While adult men and women often participate in sport in general,[3] men are more often found in sport clubs than women. This is primarily because of men's tendency to end their club participation (most often in football clubs) later in life, than girls/women.

Young women in particular replace sport club participation with membership of commercial centres, most often doing team exercises (aerobics, spinning, yoga) or weight training. As a result, at the age of 20–29, the share of women in active commercial centres equals the share of women active in sport clubs at 35 %. But while commercial centres fall somewhat out of favour with Danes (both men and women) over 30 years of age, sport clubs participation decreases only slightly with age as shown in Fig. 6.2.

Although sports participation in general and participation in clubs specifically are relatively widespread among the Danish population, both coincide significantly with socio-economic background variables, educational level being the most significant factor.

Approximately only one in four adult Danes with primary school education as their highest level of education participates in club-organised sports. Among adults with upper secondary or equivalent vocational training, the share active in sport clubs is 42 %. When considering these numbers, it is important to bear in mind that age has an underlying influence on statistics, because low levels of education are more common in older age groups.

[3] Statistically significant differences in general participation (women > men) are found, however, when taking into account a middle response option ("I do sport, but not for the time being"), which is otherwise included as a negative answer. Significantly more women give this answer than men.

In summary, the analysis of sports participation in Denmark shows that, compared with most other European countries, a relatively large proportion of those active in sport, both children and adults, make use of a voluntary club but that the proportion decreases with age. Furthermore, the analysis shows that, although sport clubs over the past three decades have faced competition from new organisational forms, the percentage of adults who practise sport in a sport club has increased.

### 6.3.1 Societal, Political Embedding

Now we turn to question how the voluntary-organised sport is embedded in society with a particular focus on the institutional framework and conditions for the clubs.

In comparative social analyses, the Danish social model is called "the institutionalised welfare model" (Esping-Andersen 1990, p. 27), which is characterised by a large public sector and universal, egalitarian and redistributive welfare schemes. Compared with other countries, the Danish model has relatively small differences in real wages and in the position of men and women in society. Culturally, Denmark is a very homogeneous society, ethnically as well as religiously, but also a very secularised society. Sometimes Denmark and the other Nordic countries are described as *consensual democracies*. These are systems that prefer to solve problems and conflicts through talk, debate, compromise and controlled conflict, and where all types of organisations have easy access to the political decision-making process. At the same time, important social areas and sectors are characterised by considerable autonomy and self-regulation. The labour force is mainly regulated by agreements between employers and trade unions; the private commercial sector has been subject to relatively little state intervention; and in the educational field there is a strong tradition for private, non-profit, schools, for specialised boarding schools for children aged 15–16, and for so-called *folk high schools*, where people of all ages can develop particular interests. Most of them are based on Grundtvigian *learning for life* and all are funded by the state.

A large public sector combined with a relatively homogeneous society should, according to economic theory, result in a small voluntary sector (Weisbrod 1977). However, this is not the case in Denmark, and this may have something to do with the political framework and with the conditions under which associations and voluntary organisations operate. The overall assumption is that certain conditions are crucial for the actions of organisations and associations. Notably, four conditions have a decisive significance for the voluntary sector:

1. *The right to form associations:* The Danish Constitution states that *citizens have the right without preceding authorisation to form associations for any lawful purpose*, and *that citizens have the right without preceding authorisation to gather unarmed.* In other words, citizens have the right to form associations and gather for common purposes and activities that are legal. Moreover, it is easy to establish an association without having to surmount difficult, bureaucratic obstacles. In Denmark an association does not need to be approved by the government, and the government cannot ban associations unless the matter is taken to court.

2. *The responsibility of the civil society for collective tasks:* In Denmark there are several areas in which civil society is responsible for collective tasks or has the right to organise common interests. Examples of this are:

   - Citizens have (under certain conditions) the right to form free, democratic (non-profit) schools built on other values and educational principles than state schools but nevertheless funded by the state.
   - Municipalities have handed over several responsibilities in housing areas to local housing associations (e.g. maintenance of roads, observance of building regulations).
   - The Leisure Recreation Act, which governs the distribution of public funding for culture, youth and sport activities for children and youngsters, states that aid can only be given to voluntary democratic associations.

3. *Bias in favour of voluntary organisations and associations:* It is highly significant that in certain social areas the government *favours* democratic associations over commercial companies. This includes governmental aid and tax benefits. For example:

   - Cultural, youth and sports associations in Denmark do not pay to use public premises for activities for children and youngsters.
   - People who do voluntary work can receive around €650 per year to cover expenses without being taxed.
   - Cultural, youth and sports associations receive financial support from central and local government.

Since the early stages of organised sport in Denmark, the government has supported voluntary sports organisations and clubs, though support has varied substantially (Ibsen and Eichberg 2012; Ibsen and Habermann 2005). From 1849 to 1945 public sector involvement was limited, although rifle clubs and later their associated gymnastics divisions did receive financial support from the government (Nordby 2009). More importantly, local municipal involvement increased from the turn of the twentieth century, resulting in the construction of numerous sports facilities, owned entirely or in part by local authorities. From 1945 to 1970 there was a drastic increase in government support for sport, combined with relatively little political involvement in the field. The creation of a monopoly on national football pools in 1948 (including the lottery in 1989) generated substantial profit with a statutory dividend awarded to sports organisations. This system has, with minor adjustments, remained in place since its creation, and it is vital to the economic and political autonomy of sports organisations (Eichberg and Loland 2010).

In 1968 a leisure act was passed that instructed local municipalities to grant voluntary associations, the vast majority of which were sport clubs, free use of public facilities. This legislation was naturally accompanied by a massive expansion in the construction of local public sports facilities. This meant that the latter half of the twentieth century saw the creation of a Danish sports system with two parallel economic circuits. One funded national sports organisations through pools and lottery profits, and the other supported voluntary clubs, particularly through building and securing access to public sports facilities at a local level through municipal budgets.

In 2013 the pools and lottery profits funding sports organisations and bodies amounted to about €122 million (the lion's share going to DIF and DGI). This is exceeded, however, by the investments made by municipalities in the field of sports, which altogether amount to about €425 million, most of which goes to public facilities.[4]

Recent years have seen a growing municipal involvement in sport. As sport has increasingly been recognised for social and health effects, local political interest has intensified and broadened perspectives on what sport is and how it should be supported from the public sector. Having being viewed almost exclusively as an activity for young people in voluntary clubs, sport is today understood as being relevant to all sectors of the population in a wide variety of ways. These even include negative ways, as indicated by the current focus on *dark sides* of sport (social exclusion, fitness doping and so on).

4. *High degree of autonomy despite public support*: Lastly, and crucially, the public sector respects the self-determination of associations, even though they receive public funding. This means that every association determines:

   - Its ideology, goal and activities
   - How it is organised (given that it is democratic)
   - Its method of working and educational principles as determined by its members
   - How the activities are financed and funds are used (given that profit is not distributed to its members)

In summary, the analysis of the relationships between the voluntary and the public sector shows (a) that voluntary-organised sports have significant direct and indirect financial support from the public sector, (b) that despite this only minor demands are made by the public sector on associations (c) and that these principles for public support for sport clubs have existed almost unchanged for almost 50 years.

## 6.4 Characteristics of Sport Clubs

In this section we move from the perspective of individual participation in sport clubs to the perspective of the club. The focus is on central characteristics of sport clubs and their role in society. The central topics are their size and forms of participation, the structure and membership democracy, volunteering and professionalisation, finances and sports facilities, collaborations and, finally, problems and challenges.

[4]Data obtained from Statistics Denmark's publicly available data file on government cultural appropriations (BEVIL01).

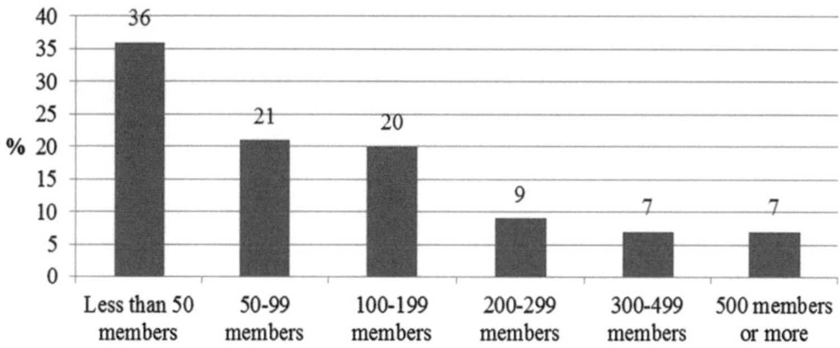


**Fig. 6.5** Size of sport clubs

On average, Danish sport clubs have 160 members, but this average figure conceals a large diversity in the membership of sport clubs. The majority are relatively small. Almost six out of ten (57 %) have fewer than 100 members, whereas less than one-tenth (7 %) have more than 500 members. In spite of this, sport clubs with more than 500 members contain more than one-third (36 %) of the total membership. Hence, large sport clubs make up a small proportion of clubs but contain a relatively large proportion of the total membership (Laub 2012) (Fig. 6.5).

Almost seven out of ten sport clubs (69 %) characterise themselves as single-sport clubs in the sense that they provide only one sports activity for their membership. Conversely, a little more than three out of ten (31 %) characterise themselves as units or sections of multi-sports clubs[5] (Laub 2012).

Regardless of sports activity, most clubs offer training for their members. Only 1 in 20 sport clubs report that none of their members participate in training, but for a little less than half of all clubs' (47 %) training involves less than half of all members (Laub 2012). This reflects the fact that even though the vast majority of sport clubs offer training, a large group of members do not take advantage of the offer, whether by choice or because training is restricted to particular groups of members depending on, for instance, age and competitive level.

Nine out of ten clubs (91 %) offer opportunities for members to participate in competitions. Sixty-one percent of sport clubs participate in competitions at the national level, 74 % participate at a regional level, while 63 % participate locally. These figures reflect the fact that many clubs compete on a number of different levels. As with training, a large group of members do not participate in competitions. In almost six out of ten clubs (59 %), less than half of the members participate in competitions (Laub 2012). Again, in some instances this reflects a deliberate

[5] In relation to the figures presented here, it is worth noting that subsidiaries of multi-sport clubs are counted as individual clubs. This is due to the manner in which they are categorised by DIF, one of the main umbrella organisations for organised sport in Denmark. This means that the proportion of multi-sport clubs is less than 31 %, but we do not have data from recent surveys telling us how much less. A study from 1997 estimated that multi-sport clubs make up around a quarter of the population of sport clubs, but since then there is evidence that the population of single-sport clubs has grown somewhat faster than the population of multi-sport clubs (Ibsen 2006).

choice from members not to participate, while in others it reflects the fact that competitions are restricted to particular groups of members.

Even though most sport clubs are single-sport clubs with a strong focus on the main sports activity, many offer a broader range of activities. An example of this is the relatively high proportion of clubs that, within the past year, have offered activities or teams targeted at specific groups, such as families (42 %), the elderly (36 %), the physically inactive (13 %), people with disabilities (13 %) and ethnic minorities (11 %). Furthermore, more than a third (35 %) have offered activities related to exercise or events that are open to groups other than members (Laub 2012).

Non-sports activities are also commonly found in sport clubs. Social activities were organised by 86 % of sport clubs for their members within the past year, and half of the clubs arranged cultural and leisure activities. Within the same time period, 44 % arranged or participated in local events with a focus other than sport (Laub 2012). Jointly, these figures indicate that most sport clubs give priority to other target areas than those closely linked to the sports activity.

Sport clubs are membership democracies. A board is elected by members at the annual general meeting, which is the highest democratic authority. Besides the annual general meeting, a little more than six out of ten sport clubs (61 %) report that they involve members in decisions that concern their team or group, and almost half (49 %) host meetings for members, where important matters are discussed (Ibsen et al. 2013).

Judging from the structure of sport clubs and from the different ways in which clubs report involving members in decision-making, therefore, it seems that members can easily influence decision-making. This is confirmed by a study showing that nine out of ten members who find it important to be able to influence decision-making report that they find ample opportunity to influence their respective sport clubs (Torpe 2003).

Another way for members to influence decision-making in their respective sport clubs and to contribute to its daily operation is to become volunteers. Seven out of ten sport clubs are run exclusively on a voluntary basis, and a little more than nine out of ten (92 %) of those who contribute to the daily operation of sport clubs are unpaid in the sense that they do not receive taxable pay for their efforts[6] (Laub 2012). It therefore seems justified to characterise volunteers as the primary resource securing the survival of sport clubs.

Volunteers can be divided into two main groups based on the nature of their contribution. First we have a group of volunteer managers, who are either enrolled in the board or on committees. Next we have coaches and instructors, who conduct the training of one or more teams or groups.[7] As an illustration of the degree of volunteer involvement in sport clubs, the volunteer-to-member ratio can be applied.

---

[6]This means that, within the group of volunteers, some receive remuneration that is not taxable. In most cases this remuneration is relatively modest, but in some cases it can be substantial, and in these instances it is debatable whether they can be categorised as volunteers. Due to the lack of data here, they will, however, be treated as volunteers.

[7]There is also a third, more indeterminable group of volunteers working with *other tasks* such as maintenance, administration and a number of ad hoc tasks. Due to large variations in the way clubs interpret this third group, it will not be included in the analyses below because the figures are subject to considerable uncertainty.

**Table 6.1** The volunteer-to-member ratio in different sports activities

| Sports activity | Volunteer-to-member ratio |
|---|---|
| Handball | 6 |
| Football | 7 |
| Badminton | 17 |
| Gymnastics | 23 |
| Tennis | 23 |
| Golf | 34 |
| Swimming | 41 |
| All sports | 10 |

The lower the ratio, the higher the level of volunteer involvement. On average, there are 19 members per volunteer manager and 13 members per volunteer coach and instructor. Including volunteer managers along with coaches and instructors, the average volunteer-to-member ratio is 10.

These average figures mask significant variations across the membership of sport clubs. The volunteer-to-member ratio increases with the size of sport clubs, meaning that they have fewer volunteers per member. There are also considerable variations as regards the nature of sports activities. Some sports demand more volunteers than others. Team ballgames, like football and handball, have a relatively high demand for volunteers, whereas recreational sports activities, such as tennis, golf and swimming, have a significantly lower demand (Laub 2012). This is illustrated in Table 6.1, where the volunteer-to-member ratios in some of the largest sports are shown.

Even though the vast majority of the workforce in sport clubs is made up of volunteers, it seems relevant to briefly describe the degree of professionalisation in sport clubs. Of their managers, coaches and instructors 7 % receive taxable pay for their efforts. Almost no managers (2 %) are paid, while it is more common for coaches and instructors (13 %) to receive taxable pay (Laub 2012). We do not have exact figures for the amounts of money paid employees in sport clubs receive, but they are in most instances relatively modest. Only a small segment of the largest and wealthiest clubs have full-time employees working as, for instance, sports managers or coaches.

Again there are significant differences between different sports activities in degrees of professionalisation. Swimming has by far the highest percentage of paid employees relative to volunteers, followed by gymnastics and tennis, while team ballgames such as football and handball are among the sports with the lowest degree of professionalisation (Table 6.2).

Another aspect of professionalisation is the degree to which volunteers receive training targeted at improving their efforts within sport clubs. In that respect, training courses have traditionally had the highest level of awareness from both sport clubs and sports organisations. A little more than half of all sport clubs (54 %) report that they give volunteers the opportunity to participate in training courses (Laub 2012). In that respect it is quite common for sport clubs to provide opportunities for volunteers to improve their knowledge and skills.

**Table 6.2** The degree of professionalisation in different sports activities

| Sports activity | Degree of professionalisation |
|---|---|
| Swimming | 38 |
| Gymnastics | 24 |
| Tennis | 19 |
| Badminton | 13 |
| Golf | 11 |
| Handball | 6 |
| Football | 6 |
| All sports | 7 |

Furthermore, data at the individual level show that among regular volunteers,[8] almost three out of four (74 %) have participated in at least one course related to the work they do in the sport club. The majority of the courses are short, lasting a day or two. Only a little more than one in ten regular volunteers (12 %) have participated in longer courses lasting for weeks or even months. At the same time, more than half of the regular volunteers (55 %) report that they have professional training relating to the work they do in their respective sport clubs. The three most prominent forms of training are in management (21 %), in PE (18 %) and in pedagogy (16 %) (Østerlund 2013).

Generally speaking, sport clubs have healthy finances. This is certainly the case if we consider financial data from 2009. That year, almost four out of ten clubs (38 %) reported surpluses, a little more than four out of ten (42 %) had broken even, while only one in five sport clubs reported losses (Laub 2012). It is important to stress here that a surplus in a sport club can only benefit the club. This is due to the structure of sport clubs as associations, which means that surpluses cannot be withdrawn from clubs.

In 2009, the average revenue of sport clubs was €55,000, and on average the clubs had a small surplus of €2,300. These figures are, however, average figures from a very diverse range of sport clubs. This range includes a large number of small clubs with correspondingly small revenues alongside a small number of large clubs with revenues in excess of one million euros.[9] More specifically, almost four out of ten sport clubs (39 %) have relatively small revenues of less than €10,000, whereas only 15 % have revenues in excess of €100,000 (Laub 2012).

The pie chart below clearly shows that the largest proportion of the income of sport clubs is self-generated. It derives primarily from membership fees, which on average make up 60 % of the total revenues, and through supporters, events and activities, which make up 10 %. Jointly, these self-generated income sources make up 70 % of total revenues (Fig. 6.6).

Apart from self-generated income sources, sport clubs also generate income through sponsorships, which make up 10 % of the total revenues. Surprisingly

[8] Regular volunteers are defined as volunteers who provide a continuous effort for the sport club at least once every second week.

[9] A large proportion of these clubs are golf clubs.

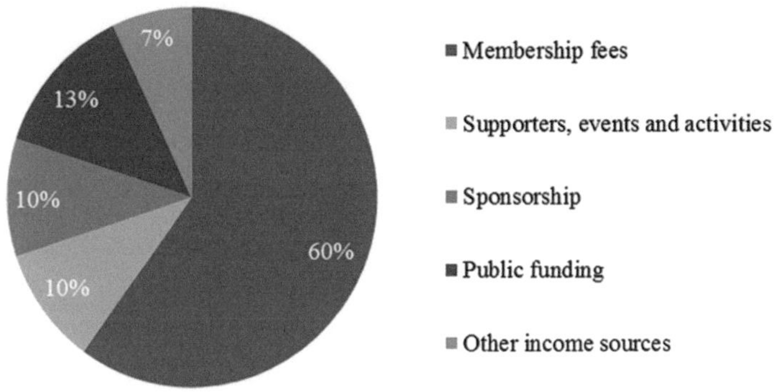


**Fig. 6.6** The distribution of revenues in sport clubs

perhaps, public funding only makes up 13 % of the total revenues (Laub 2012). The largest part of this funding comes from municipalities and is based on the number of members under the age of 25. Hence, clubs with activities for children and adolescents are those that receive the largest amounts of public funding.

The fact that public funding only makes up a small portion of total revenues is an expression of the ability of sport clubs to generate their own income, but it also reflects the funding system, whereby the greater part of public funding from municipalities to sport clubs is distributed through the provision of facilities. Municipalities are obliged by law to provide facilities free of charge for the activities of sport clubs, apart from any service fees that municipalities are permitted by law to charge within certain regulatory limits.

The facilities must be suited for the activities of the respective sport clubs, but the requirements are not specifically addressed in the law. In those cases where municipalities are not able to provide appropriate facilities, they are obliged to give subsidies to privately owned facilities run by sport clubs. Most sport clubs use facilities owned by municipalities, and it is less common for sport clubs to own their own facilities (Laub 2012). This portion of public funding, which makes up the largest portion, is not visible in the pie chart above.

As mentioned earlier, most sport clubs tend to be inward looking in the sense that their main focus is on providing activities for their members. Nevertheless, it is by no means uncommon for clubs to collaborate with stakeholders. The chart below indicates the proportion of sport clubs that have some form of binding collaboration with regard to activities, events or projects and shows a selection of the most relevant stakeholders (Fig. 6.7).

The most common collaboration is between sport clubs and sports organisations. Almost seven out of ten sport clubs (69 %) report having a binding collaboration with one or more sports organisations. Furthermore, just over half of the clubs (51 %) collaborate with other sport clubs.

Perhaps the most interesting feature is that four out of ten clubs (41 %) collaborate with the municipal administration (Laub 2012). In most cases this reflects the fact that agreements on funding and facilities are considered forms of collaboration.

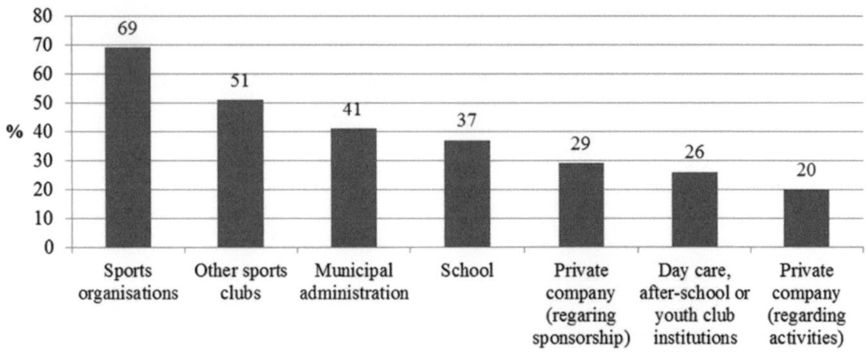


**Fig. 6.7** Proportion of sport clubs that collaborate with various stakeholders

Apart from that, however, a smaller number of clubs report having agreements with municipalities to arrange activities for specific target groups, such as the elderly, the physically inactive and ethnic minorities (Ibsen et al. 2013).

Municipalities have high hopes that such collaboration with sport clubs on the inclusion of specific target groups in voluntary-organised sport, which are often launched as projects or partnerships, will be further developed. This is a political expectation that also applies to various municipal institutions, particularly schools, where sport clubs are expected to play an even more active role in the future than they do today. There is also preliminary evidence showing that over a 6-year period from 2004 to 2010, these forms of collaboration have increased (Ibsen et al. 2013).

Generally speaking, sport clubs do not seem to experience many significant problems or challenges. This is one of the main conclusions gleaned from the questions answered by sport clubs about the relevance of a number of potential problems or challenges to their respective clubs. Some of the most relevant problems and challenges are presented in the chart below (Ibsen et al. 2013) (Fig. 6.8).

The chart illustrates how sport clubs face three main challenges: (1) ensuring members' commitment and participation, (2) recruiting volunteers and (3) raising sufficient funds. More specifically, one-third of sport clubs consider it a significant problem that few members attend the annual general meeting and other meetings. This perception is substantiated later in the paragraph on social capital, which indicates that only a minority of members take part in the membership democracy within their respective sport clubs.

The relatively low level of member commitment and participation may probably also explain why the recruitment of volunteers is one of the main challenges confronting sport clubs. Members active in the democratic decision-making and social life of sport clubs are far more likely to become volunteers than less active members (Østerlund 2013). Furthermore, we have already seen that volunteers are the main resource that underpins the survival of sport clubs. The challenges reported in recruiting volunteers may also reflect the pressing need of sport clubs to retain this important resource.

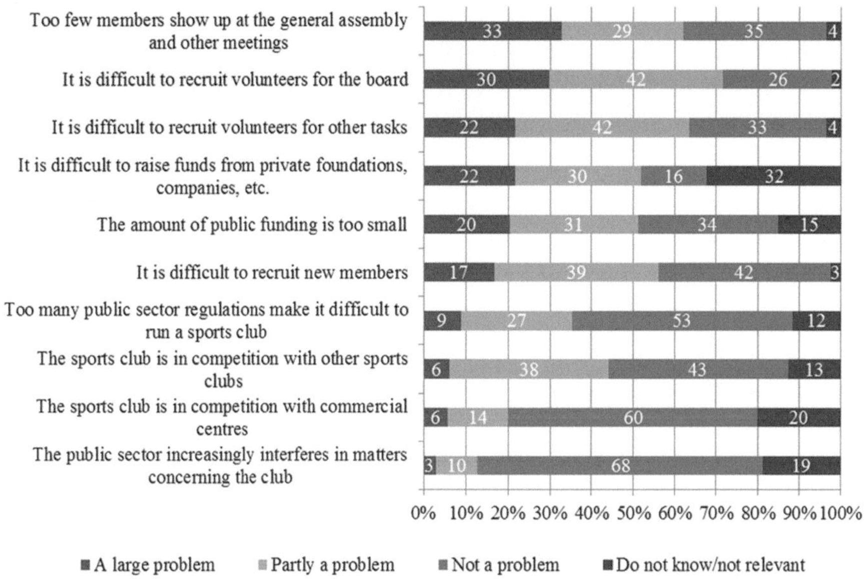


**Fig. 6.8** Problems and challenges for sport clubs (percentage of sport clubs)

It is worth noting that sport clubs find it more challenging to recruit volunteers for the board than for other tasks. A closer look at the volunteer tasks that present the greatest challenges indicates that chairperson and treasurer are by far the most difficult positions to fill. Easier to fill are coaching positions, though are also difficult, while ad hoc positions are in relative terms the easiest to fill[10] (Laub 2012).

Regarding the third main challenge, around one-fifth of sport clubs find it difficult to raise sufficient funds. For 22 %, raising funds from private foundations, companies and the like present significant difficulties, while 20 % consider it a problem that public funding is too low. This may appear somewhat paradoxical given the healthy finances of sport clubs and the high level of public funding but, as it is the case for volunteer recruitment, it probably reflects the fact that financial support is one of the principal prerequisites for the survival of sport clubs.

At the very bottom of the list we find the sport clubs' relation to the public sector. Only 3 % of sport clubs consider interference from the public sector in matters that concern sport clubs to be a major problem. This is true in spite of attempts by municipalities, described above, to use projects and partnerships to raise awareness

[10] A study on how to manage sport clubs to facilitate the recruitment of volunteers establishes some guidelines for sport clubs aiming to improve their volunteer appeal. Among other things, the study recommends sport clubs to aim at involving members in decision-making and to delegate tasks and decisions to multiple committees or to volunteers (Østerlund 2012). These recommendations are in line with the arguments presented above that active and committed members are more likely to become volunteers than less active members, and that ad hoc positions in relative terms are the easiest to fill.

among sport clubs about integrating target groups such as physically inactive people and ethnic minorities in their activities.

On the same note, only 6 % of sport clubs find competition with commercial centres a major problem, even though this might on the surface appear to present problems considering the previously presented figures for sports participation, particularly among adults. The fact that these issues are not perceived as problems or challenges may indicate that most sport clubs are narrowly focused on their own sports activity and not on developments in the general patterns of sports participation.

In summary, the analysis of the characteristics of sport clubs in Denmark shows that

- The vast majority of clubs are relatively small with less than 100 members and seven out of ten clubs are single-sport clubs.
- Nine out of ten clubs enable members to participate in competitions at various levels, but most of the clubs also run activities whose aim does not involve sports competitions and arrange social and cultural activities.
- One out of three clubs collaborate with a public school, and in general an increasing proportion of sport clubs cooperate with other clubs and their municipal institution.
- The majority of their income is self-generated, but the indirect public support in the form of sports facilities that the clubs can use for free is also very important.
- Seven out of ten clubs are run exclusively on a voluntary basis and fewer than one out of ten leaders and coaches receive taxable pay for their efforts.
- The clubs attach considerable importance to involving members in key decisions, but in most clubs it is a minority of the members who are thus engaged. Alongside the difficulty of recruiting new volunteers, this is also the clubs' main problem—according to the clubs themselves.

## 6.5 Specific Topic: Social Capital

Sport clubs are generally seen as arenas for social participation that foster bonds in communities and promote social integration. These qualities are seen as beneficial both for members of sport clubs and for society in a broader sense. This is expressed in the theory of social capital, which ascribes such qualities to voluntary associations. A thorough analysis of social capital in sport clubs is, nevertheless, long overdue and relevant, because the rhetoric surrounding sport clubs tends to take the alleged social benefits for granted. The approach to the study of social capital in sport clubs presented here originates from a PhD study on the subject (Østerlund 2013).

An important claim with regard to social capital stems from Robert D. Putnam's study on social capital in America in his famous book, *Bowling Alone*. Putnam claims that: "What really matters from the point of view of social capital and civic

**Table 6.3** Distribution of answers (%) to the question: "How often do you attempt to influence decision-making in your club in the following ways?"

| | By joining member meetings regarding the entire sport club | By joining members' meetings regarding my team/group | By sharing my views with key member of the club | By sharing my views with other members |
|---|---|---|---|---|
| Always/often | 12 | 30 | 24 | 34 |
| Sometimes | 10 | 13 | 29 | 34 |
| Rarely/never | 78 | 57 | 46 | 31 |
| Total | 100 | 100 | 99 | 99 |

engagement is not merely nominal membership, but active and involved membership" (Putnam 2000, p. 58). In this spirit, he applies different measures of social participation as indicators for the social capital in American society. Inspired by this approach, the participation of adult members (16+ years) in democratic processes, in social life and in voluntary work was examined as an indicator of social capital in sport clubs.

The overarching conclusion from the study on social capital is that a minority of members participate in democratic processes and in voluntary work, while it is more common for members to participate in the social life of their respective sport clubs.

Regarding the clubs' democratic processes, only one in five members attends the annual general meeting, and, as the table below shows, there is also a limited interest in members' meetings, especially when they concern the entire sport club. It is a bit more common informally to discuss matters regarding the sport club with key members of the club or with other members, but nevertheless the majority of members do not participate in such discussion, or at least not very frequently (Table 6.3).

When it comes to the social life of sport clubs, participation is somewhat greater. Almost four out of ten members always or often participate in social arrangements within the club, and the same percentage stays and chats with other members after training. Furthermore, data from the study show that almost eight out of ten members (79 %) have made new friends through participation in sport club activities. This shows that sport clubs, true to their reputation, are more than arenas for maintaining friendships (Table 6.4).

Finally, the participation of members in voluntary work was also examined in the study. The results showed that one in five members performs voluntary work on a regular basis (at least every second week) within the club, and that this group spend, on average, 18 h per month during the season of their sports activity. For the remaining four out of five members, the table below shows how the majority contribute by offering voluntary work either very rarely or not at all. One-third never does voluntary work, and one-third helps with ad hoc tasks only once a year at most. This is the case even though the tasks proposed were relatively modest, such as driving or helping at parties (Table 6.5).

**Table 6.4** Distribution of answers (%) to the question: "How often do you participate in your club's social life in the following ways?"

| | I participate in social arrangements | I stay and chat with other members after training |
|---|---|---|
| Always/often | 39 | 39 |
| Sometimes | 27 | 28 |
| Rarely/never | 35 | 32 |
| Total | 101 | 99 |

**Table 6.5** Distribution of answers (%) to the question: "How often do you help with ad hoc voluntary tasks in the club?"

| | |
|---|---|
| At least once a week | 3 |
| Approximately every second week | 3 |
| Approximately once a month | 7 |
| Approximately once every 3 months | 10 |
| Approximately twice a year | 11 |
| Approximately once a year | 18 |
| Less than once a year | 15 |
| Never | 33 |
| Total | 100 |

Besides examining participation patterns among adult members of sport clubs, the study also focused on the effect exerted on social capital by certain characteristics of both member and club. More specifically, the participation patterns of members within the three main areas presented above were combined into an index of social capital. The influence of various independent variables at the member and club level is displayed in the table below[11] (Table 6.6).

At the member level there is a tendency towards selective integration. Gender, age and educational level influence the propensity of members to be actively engaged in sport clubs. In addition, the analyses show how characteristics linked to the relations between members and their respective sport clubs influence their tendency to be actively engaged in the club. This applies to the duration of membership and to the impact of existing social networks within sport clubs.

At the organisational level, the nature of the sporting activity was found to have a considerable impact on the level and nature of member participation. In the analyses, team sports such as football and handball were found to be far more conducive to member participation than individual sporting activities such as tennis and gymnastics. Perhaps a bit surprisingly, however, cycling was found to be almost as productive for social capital as handball.

Taken together, the study both underpins and refines assumptions underlying the rhetoric regarding the social benefits generated by sport clubs. In support of that rhetoric, the study shows that, for their members, sport clubs are arenas for social

[11] The figures reported in the table derive from a multilevel regression analysis conducted in SPSS. The dependent variable is an index ranging from 0 to 100, with 0 referring to the lowest level of participation, and 100 referring to the highest.

**Table 6.6** The impact of member and club characteristics on social capital

| | Index for social capital ($n = 1{,}752$) | |
|---|---|---|
| *Member characteristics* | Non-standardised coefficient | |
| Intercept | 29.70 | *** |
| Gender (man) | 4.15 | *** |
| Age, 16–30 years (reference) | | |
| Age, 31–45 years | −8.86 | *** |
| Age, 46–60 years | −12.80 | *** |
| Age, 61+ years | −14.64 | *** |
| Educational level (1–5) | −1.85 | *** |
| Duration of membership (0–6) | 3.35 | *** |
| Child or children active in sport club (yes) | 13.25 | *** |
| *Club characteristics* | | |
| Gymnastics (reference) | | |
| Football | 21.38 | *** |
| Handball | 13.87 | ** |
| Cycling | 12.23 | * |
| Tennis | 0.40 | |
| Club size, 0–200 members (reference) | | |
| Club size, 201–400 members | 3.84 | |
| Club size, 401+ members | 3.30 | |
| *Model characteristics* | | |
| ICC: Intra-class correlation | 0.22 | |
| $R^2$ member level | 0.13 | |
| $R^2$ club level | 0.92 | |

***$p < 0.001$, **$p < 0.01$, *$p < 0.05$

participation and community building. At the same time it is evident that members do not automatically become volunteers, engage socially with other members or participate in the various aspects of club life that have been examined. The population of sport clubs and the membership within them are simply too diverse to make broad generalisations about social capital in sport clubs.

## 6.6 Conclusion

How do sport clubs in Denmark differ from sport clubs in most European countries? Firstly both the share of children and adults who participate in sport in a club and the number of sport clubs in relation to population are very high. The latest survey from 2012 showed that 86 % of school children and 41 % of adults participated in sport in a sport club. Secondly, more than in most countries sport clubs are oriented towards "sport for all". Most members do not participate in sports competitions, and many clubs have activities for specific groups (the elderly, the disabled and so on).

Thirdly the clubs are almost entirely based on voluntary, unpaid labour. Nine out of ten of those who work in a sport club do so unpaid.

We are convinced that the explanations for these differences between club sports in Denmark and club sports in other countries must be found in the history of the voluntary sector and the embedding of club sports in the welfare state. Since the mid-1800s, it has been deemed an ideal to organise many tasks in associations based on member democracy—including rifle shooting, gymnastics and later also sports. All over the country associations for different ideologies, goals and interests were formed. In the early stages of the development of civil society in Denmark, rifle shooting and gymnastic associations formed part of a cultural and political movement, in which self-determination and spiritual freedom were key values. From these developed a "sport for all" movement—long before it was regarded as desirable in most European countries—with ideals and targets that were different from Olympic sports ideals. Although this ideological background plays only a minor role today, it has left its mark on the public's perception of sport clubs and of activities in the clubs. Many sport clubs emphasise that both the skilled and less skilled athletes can enjoy sports at their club, and throughout the country clubs are found that primarily or exclusively are engaged in *sport for all.*

The development of a sports movement based on values other than those of Olympic sport is also one of the reasons why, in contrast to nearly all other European countries, Denmark has two almost equal and mutually independent sports organisations (DGI and DIF), which represent two different approaches to sport. In addition, there is a somewhat smaller organisation, DFIF, which organises sports for employees in workplaces. This multiplicity of organisations is due, firstly, to the historical development of a strong rifle shooting and gymnastics movement with cultural and formative goals that developed into a *sport for all* organisation. Secondly, it may also be due to the fact that the Danish state, unlike for example Norway and Sweden, has not interfered in the organisational pattern in an effort to assemble the sports movement in one organisation (Ibsen 2002). The presence of several organisations means, firstly, that there are two organisations (DGI and DFIF) whose explicit aim is to promote participation in sports and to question elite sport values and the economic resources devoted to it. Second, it means that there is competition between organisations to attract both membership of the sport clubs and the attention of the politicians.

The legislation and public aid that supports associations is undoubtedly also a contributory factor in explaining the strong position of club sport in Denmark. Firstly, the goal of public support is influenced by educational and democratic ideals, and the legislation is aimed at all kinds of leisure and cultural associations for children and adolescents; that is, public support for sport clubs is not determined by sporting goals. Secondly, access to sports facilities and municipal funding is determined by how many members an association has; that is, the club is *rewarded* if it gets more members. Thirdly, there is considerable freedom to *be an association* in the manner that is meaningful to its members and voluntary workers; that is, it is easy to form an association and there are few demands made of them, even though they are publicly funded.

If most sport clubs are entirely based on voluntary, unpaid labour the explanation is undoubtedly to be found in a strong tradition of volunteering in Denmark, which is one of the countries in Europe where the proportion of those who volunteer is greatest. This is probably enhanced by the fact that public aid is not earmarked for the salaries of managers and coaches. Finally, it can also be explained by the fact that very few sport clubs are in charge of the sports facilities that they use. Most work on sports facilities is carried out by paid staff, but the facilities are either owned by the municipality or by so-called independent non-profit institutions.

Even though voluntary-organised sport in Denmark holds a strong position, sport clubs face at least three challenges. The first challenge is the change in the pattern of sports participation. The fastest growing sports activities within the two last decades are primarily activities such as running/jogging, weight training, aerobics (and the like), spinning and road cycling, which are primarily performed as self-organised activities or in commercial centres. These are activities in which the athletes typically do not participate in sports competitions and for which no trainer or special sports facilities are required. Furthermore, the activities can be practised as and when it suits the individual.

But, although most of the athletes in the large new sports and exercise activities are active in contexts other than a sport club, many Danish clubs have adapted to this development: The modern team exercise activities (such as aerobics and Zumba) are found in most gymnastics and exercise clubs in Denmark; it is estimated that there are as many sport clubs as commercial gyms that allow for strength training, spinning and so on (club fitness centres are however typically much smaller than the commercial fitness centres); and in recent years the number of biking and jogging clubs has grown rapidly. The number of Danish adults participating in the new exercise and sports activities in a sport club is about as great as the number attending traditional sports in a club (such as football and handball) where the members take part in competitions.

The second major challenge for sport clubs is, as the clubs themselves admit, the (lack of) involvement among members in the social activities, voluntary work and democratic decision-making of the club. This is confirmed by the study of members' participation in the democratic processes in sport clubs, as reported earlier in this chapter, showing that only a minority of the members participate in meetings within the club or otherwise are engaged in the club's goals, plans and so on, and the majority of members are rarely or never involved in voluntary work in the club. Considerable differences are, however, to be found between various sports (and types of sport clubs) in the level of members' involvement in the club's social and democratic activities. The involvement is much greater in traditional team ball-games (like football and handball) than in some of the more individual sports and exercise activities that have achieved substantial growth in recent decades. This indicates that the growth in participation in new sports and exercise activities in sport club has brought with it an increase in the proportion of members with a more customer-like relationship to the club.

The third major challenge for the sport clubs is its changing relationship to the public sector. The analysis of the Danish sport clubs shows that clubs are increasingly collaborating with various local municipal institutions (state school, day care, etc.). This is probably due to the fact that over the last decade the public sector has endeavoured to involve local associations in solving a number of tasks that the state and municipalities have primary responsibility for. A change in the law for state schools thus obliges them to look for collaborations with local associations with the aim of ensuring that children get a more physically active school day. Similarly for some years municipalities have established partnerships with many sport clubs to enable physical activity for inactive children and adults, as well as sports activities for children and young people in deprived local areas. This generates on the one hand greater political focus and legitimacy for voluntary-organised sport, but it also raises the question whether this closer cooperation is at the expense of the traditional autonomy and voluntary ideal which until now has characterised sport clubs in Denmark.

## References

Boje TP (2008) Den danske frivillige nonprofit sektor i komparativt perspektiv. In: Ibsen B, Boje TP, Fridberg T (eds) Det frivillige Danmark. Universitetsforlag, Syddansk, pp 197–203

Commission E (2010) Special Eurobarometer 334. Sport and physical activity. TNS Opinion & Social, Brussels

DGI (2013) *Fælles medlemsregistrering er en realitet*. Retrieved 21 January 2014 from http://www.dif.dk/da/NYHEDER/nyheder/2013/04/20130415_faelles_medlemstal.aspx

Eichberg H, Loland S (2010) Nordic sports: from social movements via emotional to bodily movement—and back again? Sport Soc 13:676–690

Esping-Andersen G (1990) The three worlds of welfare capitalism. Polity Press, Cambridge

Ibsen B (2002) En eller flere idrætsorganisationer. Hvorfor forskelle mellem de nordiske lande? In: Eichberg H, Madsen BV (eds) Idrættens enhed eller mangfoldighed. Forlaget KLIM, Aarhus, pp 187–222

Ibsen B (2006) Foreningsidrætten i Danmark: Udvikling og udfordringer. Centre for forskning i Idræt, Sundhed og Civilsamfund, Syddansk Universitet for Idrættens Analyseinstitut, København

Ibsen B, Eichberg H (2012) Dansk idrætspolitik—mellem frivillighed og statslig styring. In: Eichberg H (ed) Idrætspolitik i komparativ belysning—national og international. Syddansk Universitetsforlag, Odense, pp 147–209

Ibsen B, Habermann U (2005) Defining the Nonprofit Sector: Denmark. Working papers of the Johns Hopkins comparative nonprofit sector project. Retrieved 21 January 2014 from http://ccss.jhu.edu/wp-content/uploads/downloads/2011/08/Denmark_CNP_WP44_2005.pdf

Ibsen B, Thøgersen M, Levinsen K (2013) Kontinuitet og forandring i foreningslivet. Movements 2013: 11. University of Southern Denmark, Institute for Sports Science and Clinical Biomechanics, Odense

Klausen KK, Selle P (1996) The third sector in Scandinavia. Voluntas 7(2):99–122

Korsgaard O (1997) Kampen om kroppen, 3rd edn. Gyldendal, Copenhagen

Laub TB (2012) Fremtidens frivillige foreningsliv i idrætten. Danish Institute for Sports Studies, Copenhagen

Laub TB (2013) Sports participation in Denmark 2011. Danish Institute for Sports Studies, Copenhagen

McCloughan P, Batt WH, Costine M, Scully D (2011) Participation in volunteering and unpaid work. Second European quality of life survey. European Foundation for the Improvement of Living and Working Conditions

Nordby I (2009) De Danske Skytteforeninger gennem 150 år: vol. 1. De Danske Skytteforeninger, Vingsted

Østerlund K (2012) Managing voluntary sport organizations to facilitate volunteer recruitment. Eur Sport Manag Quart 13(2):143–165

Østerlund K (2013) Foreningsidrættens sociale kvaliteter. En social kapital-inspireret undersøgelse af danske idrætsforeninger og deres medlemmer. Phd thesis. University of Southern Denmark, Odense

Putnam RD (2000) Bowling alone: the collapse and revival of American community. Simon & Schuster, New York

Scheerder J, Vandermeerschen H, Van Tuyckom C, Hoekman R, Breedveld K, Vos S (2011) Understanding the game: sport participation in Europe. Facts, reflections and recommendations. KU Leuven, Leuven

Torpe L (2003) Democracy and associations in Denmark: changing relationships between individuals and associations? Nonprofit Volunt Sect Quart 32(3):329–343

Weisbrod B (1977) The voluntary nonprofit sector. Lexington Books, Lexington, MA

# Chapter 7
# Sport Clubs in England

**Geoff Nichols and Peter Taylor**

## 7.1 Introduction

England is the largest of the *home countries* in the UK, with a population of 53.9 million out of 64.1 million in the UK as a whole. Despite a rich historic tradition in manufacturing industry, the economy is now dominated by services, which comprise 80 % of employment and 77 % of the nation's Gross Domestic Product. The South East of the country is recovering faster than any other European country from the economic crash of 2008, although recovery is very uneven across England as a whole. Although comparatively wealthy, England has one of the most unequal distributions of income of all the developed countries. Figures are available to compare sports participation and volunteering in the UK as a whole with European countries. Levels of formal volunteering are slightly below the European average, well below levels in the Netherlands, Germany and the Nordic countries. This is despite a strong tradition of volunteering, much of which takes place in the structure of organisations such as sports clubs, developed in the late nineteenth and early twentieth centuries. The Conservative/Liberal Democrat coalition government, which came into power in May 2010, aimed to promote volunteering within a policy labelled as *The Big Society*. There is little evidence of volunteering increasing but it will have to if volunteers are to help deliver sports and other leisure facilities which local government is less able to maintain because of funding cuts. Levels of sports participation are relatively high, still below the Nordic countries, but on a par with the Netherlands and slightly above Germany and France. This reflects a strong

G. Nichols (✉)
Management School, University of Sheffield, Sheffield, UK
e-mail: g.nichols@sheffield.ac.uk

P. Taylor
Sport Industry Research Centre, Sheffield Hallam University, Sheffield, UK
e-mail: peter.taylor@shu.ac.uk



C. Breuer et al. (eds.), *Sport Clubs in Europe*, Sports Economics, Management and Policy 12, DOI 10.1007/978-3-319-17635-2_7

sporting tradition, as described in the chapter below. However, levels of sports participation are static with a trend towards more individual participation, while obesity levels and associated illnesses climb rapidly.

The infrastructure of sport clubs in England is specific to its historical development and culture.

Traditionally opportunities to participate in sport in England have been categorised as being provided by the voluntary, public or commercial sectors, although the three overlap. For example, a cricket club run by volunteers may play on pitches hired from local government; use balls provided by a commercial sponsor; and socialise after the game in a local public house. This chapter focuses on the voluntary sector although all three components of the sporting infrastructure and their interrelationship have to be understood as reflecting the historical circumstances in which modern sport emerged in the nineteenth century. From this developed a large number of relatively small sport clubs run by volunteers, often focused on a single sport, with strong connections to a local community, and represented by national governing bodies of sport (NGBs) which had initially been established to codify *rules* of the games. The interventions of the public sector through local government direct provision of facilities were initially led by concerns for public health and promotion of dominant social values, characterised as *rational recreation*. The commercial sector in sport developed in response to demand, reflecting increasing income and leisure time from the second half of the nineteenth century but it was initially more concerned with consumption of a leisure experience (for example; gambling, professional football) than participation, although relatively recently it has grown considerably in the fitness industry.

Each of these sectors of sporting opportunities, and the relation between them, is changing in response to circumstances. In the voluntary sector an apparently stable infrastructure of clubs and facilities, supported by a tradition of volunteering, is having to adapt to trends towards more episodic and transactional volunteering, increasing competition in the leisure market for time, energy and enthusiasm, and a changed relationship with the public and commercial sectors. Since the early 1990s public sector leisure provision has become more market oriented, promoted by competition for contracts to provide services, reductions in public sector budgets and a more market-led attitude towards provision (Nichols and Taylor 1995). Since 2011 considerable reductions in local government budgets, as a consequence of national government policies to reduce public expenditure, have led to greater costs of public sector facility hire and greater competition for peak-time use, affecting the sport clubs that rely on these facilities.

Sport England's strategies (the government agency responsible for promoting community sport) have increasingly incorporated voluntary sector clubs as a means to achieving social objectives, such as increasing sports participation. NGBs need to balance Sport England's policy objectives, enshrined in performance indicators associated with public funding; with supporting and representing the needs of their clubs and the volunteers who manage them. Trends towards more individualistic sports participation have been reflected in a decline in importance of clubs led by volunteers for participation and an increase in commercial clubs—largely catering for the fitness market.

This chapter first reviews the history of sport and sport clubs in England, which is essential to understanding modern day structures and processes. It then provides evidence of participation in different types of sport clubs from a national survey, particularly for non-profit clubs largely run by volunteers, and for commercial fitness clubs. A review of the policy importance of sport clubs is followed by national evidence on their participants, demonstrating their societal embedding. Characteristics of sport clubs are summarised from another national survey, including clubs' human resources, finances, facilities used, community links and challenges faced. The chapter finishes with a specific focus on a contemporary issue for non-profit sport clubs in England—the formalisation of sport club management.

## 7.2 History and Context

Modern sport emerged in Britain from the experience of the industrial revolution. The historical context helps us to understand characteristics of the voluntary sector in sport today. This section can only identify the main historical factors in the development of sport and of volunteering; which are dealt with more comprehensively by Holt (1990) and Rochester (2013). The rapid movement of the population from a rural to an urban environment meant that previous forms of recreation, at least for the working class, had to be abandoned. An example was *folk football*, with whole villages competing against each other guided by no rules other than the need to place an object corresponding to the modern ball in a *goal* defined by local tradition. Folk football was forcibly restrained by police and troops as it was seen as a threat to public order.

However, a set of circumstances in the second half of the nineteenth century promoted the emergence of modern forms of sport. The reduction of working hours to allow a half day off on Saturday provided the time for both participation and spectating. Common rules needed to be established for sport, particularly for public, fee paying schools to play each other, and for former school boys to continue to compete at university. The prominence of sport in the curriculum in the public schools reflected a movement termed *muscular Christianity* which emphasised the role of sport in promoting desirable moral values. A concern with the moral condition of the urban poor led to the 'rational recreation movement' (Holt 1990, p. 136) which developed in the third quarter of the nineteenth century and reflected the values of evangelical Christianity. As part of this movement, organised sport was reintroduced to the urban population by men who had attended the public schools. This reflected a philanthropic tradition which has been identified as one of the roots of voluntary action (Rochester 2013). For example, football clubs were formed based on factories (e.g. Woolwich Arsenal, founded 1886) and religious missions (e.g. Aston Villa, a Methodist chapel, 1874). Holt attributes the embracing of football by the working class at this time not only to its simplicity, but also to its ability to express a local sense of community that had been lost in the move from a rural environment to the amorphous mass of the city.

A flourishing of sports teams reflected a second main impulse of voluntary activity, *mutual aid*—collective action to meet a shared need. Hoggett and Bishop (1985) describe it as *organising around enthusiasms*. A third but relatively neglected root of voluntary activity is the promotion of *conviviality* (Rochester 2013) in which socialisation is an end in itself, explaining the association of many teams with social facilities, such as pubs.

In the second half of the nineteenth century the development of professional sport was facilitated by the expanding railway network and newspapers, allowing the working class to follow the fortunes of their favourite team by travelling to games or through the press. Increased time and wages provided the demand for professional sport, especially football and rugby. This contrasted with a strong ethos of amateurism prominent in the Victorian era. A sample of NGBs was founded on the following dates:

- Football Association 1863
- Rugby Football Union 1871
- Bicyclists Union 1878
- Amateur Athletic Association 1880
- Amateur Boxing Association 1880
- Amateur Rowing Association 1882
- Amateur Swimming Association 1886
- Lawn Tennis Association 1888

This not only illustrates the dates at which the rules of modern sport were established but also the prominence of amateur in the title. Football and rugby both had to adapt to professionalism which initially came about as working class players were compensated for time away from paid work—termed *broken time*. Within rugby this led to a split in 1894 between the Northern version of the game, Rugby League, which accepted professionals; and the Southern version, Rugby Union, which was amateur. Sports maintained different traditions and as late as 1961 the score card at Lords distinguished the status of amateur and professional cricketers by their initials preceding or following their surname, respectively. There is an umbrella, representative organisation for NGBs, established in 1935 and now called the Sport and Recreation Alliance.

### *7.2.1 Origin of Sport Clubs*

This brief historical overview helps us to understand the following characteristics of sport clubs in England, illustrated in more detail later:

The large number of sport clubs, which are mainly single sport and relatively small, and with a strong identity and connection with a locality (Allison 2001). This explains, for example, why the Lawn Tennis Association has found it difficult to persuade small clubs to merge.

The role volunteers take in all the tasks required to make the clubs function; reflecting a mutual aid tradition of organising around enthusiasms. An alternative conception of grass roots volunteer led organises is as meeting an unmet need in *the market* (Nichols 2001; Gratton and Taylor 1991).

Within the mutual aid tradition there is an ethos of equality, an antipathy to distinctions of power embodied in a formal management structure, and the same volunteers will take roles of governance and delivery. This, combined with the objective of providing conviviality and a pleasant social experience, means that management practices in different types of organise will not be appropriate and will need to be adapted (Schulz et al. 2011; Rochester 2013). A tradition of amateurism may also engender an antipathy toward formal management practices.

Along with many other associational forms of group-based leisure with roots in the nineteenth century, the clubs have a strong sense of independence, history and tradition. This explains a degree of scepticism to policies of local or national government, if the club is an older and more permanent institution.

The clubs regard their NGBs as existing to represent their interests, rather than the interests of national government. This explains a tension in NGBs' positions as they balance representing the clubs affiliated to them with meeting the conditions of Sport England grants.

The expectation that local government will take a positive view towards volunteer-led sport clubs reflects the values of the rational recreation movement but there is a tension between this and a more recent market oriented approach to providing local government services and the significantly reduced ability of local government to support sport, which is a non-statutory service.

### 7.2.2 *Sport Clubs Within the National Sport Structure*

The national sport structure in England comprises three sectors: the public sector, including facilities and services provided by, or on behalf of, national and local government; the private commercial sector; and the private non-profit sector—often termed the *third sector*. Sport clubs contribute mainly to the private non-profit sector, although commercial fitness clubs are a major part of the private commercial sector in sport and many non-profit sport clubs use facilities provided by the public sector.

Evidence on sports participation for the adult population of England (16 years +) is contained in the Active People Survey (Sport England 2014a, b). This includes the participation rates in clubs and in different types of club—health and fitness clubs are largely commercial; sport clubs are largely voluntary; social clubs are largely charitable; and other clubs include multipurpose clubs. Table 7.1 shows the percentages of the adult population participating in sport at different types of club at least once in the previous 4 weeks.

There are two main features of this evidence. First, the proportion of adults participating in health and fitness clubs is larger than in sport clubs, which reflects a

**Table 7.1** Participation in sport through different types of clubs in England, 2009/10-2012/13 (Active People Survey)

| | Weighted sample | Any type of club | Health and fitness clubs | Sport clubs | Social clubs | Other clubs |
|---|---|---|---|---|---|---|
| | | *% of adult population who have been a member of a club in order to participate in sport in the previous 4 weeks* | | | | |
| 2012/13 | 46,914 | 22.1 | 10.2 | 9.2 | 2.9 | 1.6 |
| 2011/12 | 84,706 | 22.8 | 10.5 | 9.5 | 3.6 | 1.6 |
| 2010/11 | 164,026 | 23.3 | 10.7 | 8.8 | 3.4 | 2.4 |
| 2009/10 | 186,376 | 23.9 | 10.8 | 10.4 | 3.2 | 0.8 |

trend in favour of individualised, time-flexible fitness activities, and against more time inflexible, team sports, which occur mainly at voluntary sport clubs. Second, over the 4 years of data there is a declining proportion of adults participating at clubs overall, with the largest decline over the 3 years for which data is available being in voluntary sport clubs. However, it should be noted that the sport clubs' numbers in the table only includes active participants; it does not include social and other non-active members which, according to the Sport and Recreation Alliance (2013), comprise 28 % of all adult members of sport clubs. This emphasises the social as well as sporting purpose of voluntary sport clubs.

In practice it is difficult to define a club run by volunteers. A club may be regarded as one or more of: just one competitive team; a club with several teams—possibly divided by age and gender; a session in a sports centre led by a coach; a group of friends that maintain a regular booking in a facility but with no formal arrangements; or a multi-sports club with sections for each sport. The only practical way to estimate the number of clubs is to ask for figures from the NGBs of the number of affiliated clubs. One source (Erewash Sport 2014) lists 137 NGBs. Such a method will exclude clubs who do not affiliate as they do not want to compete in a league structure or see little benefit in affiliation. It will thus exclude the more informal and smaller groups which will become increasingly important if, as has been suggested, there is a trend towards more informal participation as group activities are harder to co-ordinate with individuals' increasingly fragmented lifestyles (Coalter 1999; Gratton et al. 2011). Figures from NGBs may include some clubs run by professionals for a profit although these only accounted for 2 % of clubs in a 2009 survey (Taylor et al. 2009). Relying on NGB records and identifying trends is complicated by differences in NGBs' club definitions and changes in this over time. NGBs also vary in their national boundaries (NGBs in the UK may cover any of England, Scotland, Wales and N. Ireland); their merger of NGBs for male and female participants, and there are other inconsistencies in recording. The list of 137 NGBs referred to above (Erewash Sport 2014) includes many that are British, some that are UK, and some that are English. It refers to 16 sports for which there is no recognised NGB, and at the other extreme one sport, bowls, with ten NGBs. Further, NGBs or clubs may amalgamate, so fewer clubs or NGBs does not necessarily correspond to fewer club members.

Studies conducted in 2002 (Taylor et al. 2003) and in 2009 (Taylor et al. 2009), both attempted to estimate the number of clubs by direct contact with NGB officials and NGB published reports. These methods produced figures of 106,423 clubs in England in 2002 and 85,000 in 2009. A fall in the number of clubs is consistent with a trend towards more informal participation, and has been supported by analysis of clubs in one sport (hockey) in one county, using local association handbooks (Barrett et al. 2014).

Mintel (2013) estimate the number of health and fitness clubs in England to be 3,520 in January 2013. This total comprises 2,330 gymnasia/fitness suites (largely in the local government public sector) and 1,190 private sports and leisure centres. Mintel estimates that the number of health and fitness clubs in England grew by 13 % between March 2011 and January 2013. Mintel also estimates a total membership of 5.4 million for the UK as a whole in 2013, which is 4.2 % higher than the total membership for 2007. These Mintel estimates, however, are inconsistent with the slight decline in participation in such clubs according to the Active People Survey in the table above. Nevertheless, the health and fitness club industry has proven very resilient in the post financial crash environment, partly because of the emergence and growth of budget clubs.

An important part of the voluntary sports club structure in England is in universities. According to BUCS (2013), there were 3,704 student sport clubs in 103 higher education institutions surveyed in 2012. Although there were some non-responding universities, this was a British sample and Universities UK list 107 English universities, so an estimate of around 3,800 student sport clubs in England is reasonable. In a survey of students at 52 universities TNS (2013) identify that 39 % of students were members of clubs to participate in sport, whilst 4 % had taken part in one hour a week or more of sports volunteering. A recent study for BUCS (2013) has identified the importance of participating and volunteering in university sport clubs for enhancing the employability of students.

## 7.3 The Role of Sport Clubs in Policy and Society

Sport clubs play an important role in government plans to increase sports participation for its associated health benefits and other social benefits—particularly for the young, such as reducing crime and vandalism, and increasing educational achievements. The policy importance is recognised in the current and previous strategies of Sport England (2008, 2012). Sport clubs also play a significant role in identifying and developing talent in sport, as part of a system for producing sporting excellence for national teams and international competitions.

In England, sport clubs have been incorporated into government policy to promote sports participation through NGBs agreeing their *Whole Sport Plans* with Sport England (Green 2008; Nichols 2013; Sport England 2013a). Sport England provides funding for 46 NGBs, in most cases grants in exchange for agreeing to raise participation by specific levels in their sport over a set time period. These levels of participation are measured through Sport England's annual Active People Survey. Funding of NGBs through Sport England is also conditional on the implementation of policies to promote participation by under-represented groups and to promote Sport England's (or an NGB equivalent) Clubmark accreditation (discussed in more detail below). The ability of Sport England to influence NGBs in this way has been greatly increased by its ability to distribute £2,777 m of funds from the National Lottery between 1995 and 2009; although the ability of money to buy the enthusiasm of volunteers who drive sport clubs is limited, as many clubs cherish their independence. There is thus a greater tension between NGBs' role as a policy instrument of government and their original purpose as a representative body of the clubs. The ability and willingness of sport clubs' volunteers to implement Sport England policies, or even to know what they are, has been questioned (Harris et al. 2009).

The importance of sport clubs for producing excellence in sport is that they feed their best players into their NGBs' systems for regional, national and international training and competitions. NGBs have systems of talent identification and development, which are part of their plans for Sport England and also the subject of separate funding agreements with UK Sport—the latter being entirely focussed on the development of high performance sport. At the time of writing, 36 Olympic and Paralympic sports' NGBs receive funding from UK Sport 'to protect and enhance medal prospects for Rio 2016 and Tokyo 2020' (UK Sport 2014a, b).

### *7.3.1 National Data on Sport Club Participation*

Secondary analysis of the Active People Survey data identifies the demographic structure of participation in sport clubs of different types. This helps to identify the extent to which clubs cater for different parts of society. We compare the characteristics of the two main types of clubs with non-club participants in Table 7.2, which again relates to participation at least once in the previous 4 weeks and only to active sports participants, not to non-active members of sport clubs. The population structure of England is also provided in the last column, so that the representativeness of the different modes of sports participation can be judged.

There are some key differences in the participants' characteristics of sport clubs, health and fitness clubs, and those who do not participate in clubs. Sport clubs and non-club participants have majorities of male participants, whilst health and fitness clubs have a majority of female participants. Sport clubs have higher proportions of participants who are young (16–19) or old (65+), and correspondingly who are students or retired, than either health and fitness clubs or non-club participants. Health and fitness clubs and non-club participants have a stronger representation of non-White ethnic groups. In terms of educational qualifications, income, car availability and children in the household, the two main types of clubs have similar profiles. There are obvious differences in the activities participated in at the two types of club—the highest proportions of sports club participants participated in football (18 %), golf (15 %), rugby union (6 %) and cricket (5 %), none of which are likely at health and fitness clubs.

**Table 7.2** Participation demographics for different types of clubs in England, 2011/12 (Active People Survey)

| | Sport clubs | Health and fitness clubs | Non-club participants[a] | England population |
|---|---|---|---|---|
| Gender | *% of participants* | | | % |
| Female | 28 | 56 | 47 | 51 |
| Male | 72 | 44 | 53 | 49 |
| Age | | | | |
| 16–19 | 21 | 11 | 11 | 6 |
| 20–24 | 10 | 10 | 8 | 8 |
| 25–29 | 8 | 11 | 10 | 8.5 |
| 30–34 | 8 | 11 | 11 | 8 |
| 35–44 | 13 | 19 | 19 | 17 |
| 45–64 | 26 | 31 | 32 | 31 |
| 65+ | 15 | 8 | 10 | 20 |
| Ethnicity | | | | |
| White | 93 | 88 | 89 | 85 |
| Mixed | 2 | 2 | 2 | 2 |
| Asian | 3 | 6 | 6 | 7 |
| Black | 2 | 3 | 3 | 4 |
| Other | 1 | 1 | 1 | 1 |
| Chinese | 0.1 | 0.4 | 0.3 | 0.7 |
| Work status | | | | |
| Employed | 59 | 69 | 68 | 62 |
| Unemployed | 4 | 5 | 6 | 4.5 |
| Retired | 16 | 11 | 12 | 14 |
| Other econ. Inactive | 2 | 4 | 4 | 11 |
| Student | 19 | 12 | 10 | 9 |

Some subsections sum to >or<100 % because of rounding

[a]Non-club participants = all participants excluding those who participate in any type of club

In terms of how representative different types of clubs' participants are of the English population, the table demonstrates that both the main types of club under-represent older people (65+), those of Asian and Chinese ethnicity and those who are in the category other economically inactive (e.g. full-time in the home). Sport clubs also under-represent females, 35–64 year olds, and those of Black ethnicity.

### 7.3.2 *Societal Importance of Sport Clubs*

Sport clubs led by volunteers are important because they provide the opportunity for people to take part in sport at a cheaper rate than if they had to pay for use of commercial facilities—although as reported in the paragraph above, the participants' income profiles at the two types of club are very similar. The 2013 Sport and Recreation Alliance survey of sport clubs estimated that each club had, on average,

82 playing adult members, 32 non-playing members, and 90 junior members (Sport and Recreation Alliance 2013). Combining these figures with the estimate of 85,000 clubs in England in 2009 (the latest which is available) gives 6.97 million players, 2.72 million non-playing members, and 7.65 million juniors. The figures may be an overestimate because the Sport and Recreation Alliance 2013 survey sample of 2,910 clubs over-represents those with Clubmark accreditation, 41 %, (a Sport England accreditation scheme) and with Community Amateur Sports Club (CASC) status, 23 %, which confers tax advantages. These clubs are likely to be the more formal and larger clubs (Nichols et al. 2012). It also double-counts people who are members of more than one club. However, it does not include unaffiliated clubs, although these are likely to be less important for junior participation.

It is not known how the non-playing members in clubs are split between those who support participants and those who are members primarily for the social rewards of conviviality. Volunteers supporting participants will be more significant in clubs with large junior sections (Nichols et al. 2013a). Formal volunteering has been associated with high levels of social capital in the UK and sport and exercise is the largest single area in which formal volunteering takes place (DCMS 2013). However, social capital is not an unambiguous social good. Club association may enhance 'bonding' social capital within club members, but not necessarily bridging social capital with the rest of the community (Nichols et al. 2013; Blackshaw and Long 2005). There is also an unclear relationship with the policy of the central government in the UK to promote volunteering within a *Big Society*, in which individuals take greater responsibility for their immediate environment through civic activism. An aim is to reduce the activity of the state which has been regarded as crowding out the voluntary sector by Big Government. However, the Big Society concept has been criticised as idealistic, ignoring the different propensity of social classes to volunteer and as a substitute for the considerable cuts in public sector expenditure since 2010. On the one hand government aims to increase volunteering, but on the other hand reductions in practical support to voluntary sport clubs, such as through subsidies for facility use and grants for refurbishing facilities, provide additional challenges (Nichols et al. 2013).

## 7.4 Characteristics of Sport Clubs

The Sport and Recreation Alliance has surveyed sport clubs in the UK every 2 years since 2007. The latest of these surveys, in 2013, had a sample of 2,910 clubs from over 100 sports, with over a third of the sample from cricket (15 % of the total), rugby union (12 %) and football (8 %). The survey is largely of voluntary sport clubs—90 % of the clubs surveyed are non-profit clubs—and it does not include commercial health and fitness clubs. Although it is a UK survey, nearly 95 % of the responses in 2013 are from English clubs. The survey does not sample the same clubs each time, so variations between the surveys may simply reflect different samples (Nichols 2013). The survey includes questions on staff and volunteers, members, facilities, finances and community links. This section summarises these characteristics, except for members, which are discussed in the previous section.

### 7.4.1 Club Size and Sports

Typically sport clubs in England are single sport, largely because of their historical development—see above. Whilst the average number of adult playing members is 82, according to the Sport and Recreation Alliance (2013), responses to this survey are likely to be biased towards larger clubs. Nevertheless, Table 7.3 illustrates the considerable variation in size between sports, both for adult and junior participants.

### 7.4.2 Staff and Volunteers

On average, each sports club has 24 volunteers helping the club, 9 of whom are qualified coaches; and also two paid members of staff—one of whom is typically a qualified coach. The number of volunteers in the clubs surveyed in 2013 was 20 % higher than the clubs surveyed in 2011 and 26 % higher than in 2007. A quarter of clubs surveyed in 2013 indicated that they had benefited from new volunteers after the London 2012 Olympic Games and Paralympic Games, and over three-quarters of these clubs with new volunteers were in Olympic and Paralympic sports. Volunteers take roles in administration and delivery with individual volunteers typically involved in both. Any role required to allow the club to function will be taken by volunteers, including: chair, treasurer, membership secretary, fixture secretary, welfare officer, coaches, team managers and other roles which may not have a formal definition. Roles which take the most time include those on the management committee and coaching. Typically 20 % of the volunteers contribute 80 % of the time and the volunteers who have been involved the longest create a role as their interests develop. This can lead to difficulties replacing key volunteers' whose role is defined around the person rather than a set of functions. Paid staff are more common in the larger clubs which manage their own facility and tend to be involved in facility maintenance, running a bar and in coaching roles—as above. Thus, paid staff are not usually involved in management roles.

### 7.4.3 Facilities

Clubs in different sports tend to use different facilities, as shown in Table 7.4. In the 2013 survey, 45 % of the clubs surveyed own or part-own their facilities, or have long-term leases on them.

**Table 7.3** Average adult playing members per club for different sports in England (Sport and Recreation 2013)

| Sport | Average number of adult playing members per club | Average number of junior playing members per club |
|---|---|---|
| Golf | 387 | 48 |
| Snowsports | 314 | 162 |
| Angling | 308 | 38 |
| Motor sports | 249 | 9 |
| Sailing | 176 | 91 |
| Athletics | 151 | 105 |
| Tennis | 149 | 130 |
| Bowls | 124 | 4 |
| Triathlon | 124 | 70 |
| Badminton | 110 | 38 |
| Rugby Union | 106 | 216 |
| Canoeing | 97 | 49 |
| Equestrian | 92 | 18 |
| Rugby League | 90 | 130 |
| Gliding | 83 | 10 |
| Cycling | 82 | 32 |
| Hockey | 81 | 91 |
| Rowing | 74 | 42 |
| Orienteering | 72 | 21 |
| Shooting | 71 | 9 |
| Table tennis | 62 | 35 |
| Archery | 55 | 16 |
| Volleyball | 52 | 20 |
| Cricket | 49 | 70 |
| Football | 49 | 121 |
| Netball | 38 | 40 |
| Wheelchair basketball | 34 | 65 |
| Karate | 31 | 43 |
| Basketball | 31 | 64 |
| Korfball | 29 | 4 |
| Fencing | 28 | 26 |
| Weightlifting | 24 | 16 |
| Swimming | 23 | 163 |
| Taekwondo | 21 | 61 |
| Tchoukball | 20 | 2 |
| Judo | 19 | 121 |
| Boccia | 18 | 16 |
| Gymnastics | 15 | 252 |

**Table 7.4** Sports clubs and facilities (Sports and Recreation Alliance 2013)

| Sports with more clubs owning or leasing their facilities (% of clubs) | Sports with more clubs hiring facilities (% of clubs) | Sports with more clubs using public spaces (% of clubs) |
|---|---|---|
| Golf (83 %) | Korfball (100 %) | Orienteering (100 %) |
| Squash (82 %) | Tchoukball (100 %) | Motor Sports (82 %) |
| Shooting (50 %) | Badminton (97 %) | Cycling (61 %) |
| Rugby Union (49 %) | Basketball (97 %) | Horse riding (57 %) |
| | Judo (95 %) | Canoeing (45 %) |
| | Karate (94 %) | |
| | Netball (94 %) | |
| | Fencing (91 %) | |
| | Swimming/diving (91 %) | |
| | Taekwondo (91 %) | |
| | Volleyball (90 %) | |

49 % of clubs hired a facility, with hire costs amounting to 47 % of their total expenditure on average. More than a third of all clubs, and 53 % of clubs which hire a facility, hire from their local authority. This is significant given the sharp cuts in local government spending that are occurring at the time of writing, because one implication of these cuts is increasing facility hire costs for clubs. Another implication is reduced maintenance of facilities—for 68 % of clubs hiring facilities, it is the local authorities which are responsible for maintenance. 14 % of clubs use public space for their activities.

### 7.4.4 *Finances*

On average sport clubs made an average surplus of £1,825 in 2012, which is 67 % higher than in 2010. But this average hides a lot of variation. Whilst 48 % of clubs surveyed made surpluses, 24 % made losses. The ratio of surplus to loss making clubs varied from nearly 8:1 in tennis, to 1:1 in badminton. There was considerable effort by sport clubs to improve their financial situation in the year before the 2013 survey, mostly to increase income to compensate for higher costs, as shown in Table 7.5. A key income earner for sport clubs which lease or own their facilities is the bar, which in 2012 contributed on average a third of the surveyed clubs' incomes and typically the bar made a profit. Sports with the highest average clubs' income are golf, rugby union, gliding and gymnastics; whilst sports with the lowest average clubs' income include weightlifting, baseball/softball, karate and netball. The same structure applies to clubs' expenditures—there is a strong correlation between higher or lower average income and higher or lower average expenditure, reflecting the typical financial objective of break-even.

**Table 7.5** Achieving break even—balancing increasing costs with higher income (Sport and Recreation Alliance 2013)

| Higher costs for clubs, 2011–2012 | Increasing income for clubs, 2011–2012 |
|---|---|
| Outdoor facility maintenance (33 % increase) | More fundraising (49 % of clubs) |
| Indoor facility maintenance (23 % increase) | Applying for funds from external organisations: NB national or local government, NGBs (45 % of clubs) |
| Business property tax (20 % increase) | Higher membership income: from more members (44 % of clubs) and higher membership fees (34 % of clubs) |
| Water costs (38 % increase) | More social events (40 % of clubs) |
| Electricity and gas costs (10 and 19 % increases) | Hiring out club's facilities (21 % of clubs) |

The 2009 survey of clubs was able to show the major differences in income between clubs that owned or did not own their own facilities. Owning facilities meant that a much higher income, and higher proportion of income, could be gained through bar, catering and hospitality. Owning a social facility gives the club a social focus, allowing a wider range of social rewards for its members. This is harder for sports such as swimming or athletics to achieve, because participation is as an individual and not co-ordinated at the same time, or event place. Thus, facility ownership confers additional costs and benefits, and is associated with the larger clubs (Nichols et al. 2012).

### *7.4.5 Community Links*

Over half the clubs surveyed in 2013 are working with local schools and 88 % of these clubs claim the links are successful, although the precise meaning of the terms working with and successful for the responding clubs is not explored in the survey. Links between clubs and schools have been an important aspect to a variety of government policy initiatives in recent years. The most common factors contributing to perceived success in club-school links are reported by clubs to be: students joining the clubs as members, effective communication, advertising club opportunities in schools, club coaches or officials assisting in PE lessons, and the opportunity for clubs to identify talent in schools. 54 % of clubs surveyed report that they are running programmes that engage with the wider, non-member community although again the exact nature of these programmes is not provided in survey responses. The most common are 42 % of clubs working with young people in the community, and 30 % of clubs involved in programmes to improve physical health. There is evidence, therefore, of significant minorities of clubs aligning some of their activity with government policy.

### 7.4.6 Challenges for Sport Clubs

The 2010 GHK report, *Volunteering in the European Union* used previous research in the UK (Gratton et al. 1997; Taylor et al. 2003, 2009) and three interviews to identify challenges faced by sport clubs. Challenges included: the recruitment and retention of volunteers, professionalisation of the voluntary sector (meaning requiring volunteers to adopt practices of management and service delivery comparable to those in the private or public sectors), reacting to legal and regulatory frameworks, the production of information on volunteering, achieving sustainable funding, managing a tension between state support and incorporating objectives of the state, achieving recognition for the work of volunteers, overcoming a prejudice towards voluntary engagement, and coping with a lack of a clear strategy in a fragmented political landscape (p. 254). The three most important concerns raised by sport organisations were: the complexity and administrative burden of applying for subsidies, insurance and liability, and the low level of public funding (p. 256) although this conclusion is likely to have been derived from the three interviews.

More recent information is provided by the Sport and Recreation Alliance surveys—see Table 7.6. As noted above, these surveys tend to over-represent the larger and more formal clubs. The extrapolation of trends is also limited because the surveys do not include the same sample of clubs each time.

The 2013 survey (Sport and Recreation Alliance 2013) is able to show that immediately following the London 2012 Olympic Games and Paralympic Games, clubs experienced a greater than normal increase in junior members. This is likely to have been the result of 'inspiration' due to saturation coverage of sport on television for 3 weeks (Ives 2012) rather than as a coherent government strategy for promoting sport, which has been criticised for its absence (Weed 2014). Seven in ten clubs in the Sport and Recreation Alliance survey (2013) reported the Games had no noticeable impact on adult sports participation. The Taking Part national survey shows an increase in formal volunteering rates in the UK from January 2012 to December 2012 (DCMS, 2013, p6) and the 2013 Sport and Recreation Alliance

**Table 7.6** Most common challenges faced by sport clubs in England (Sport and Recreation Alliance 2013)

| Expected challenges in the next 2 years | Percentage of sport clubs reporting (%) |
|---|---|
| Accessing funding | 52 |
| Recruiting new members | 51 |
| Improving or extending facilities | 49 |
| Generating sufficient income | 48 |
| Increasing facility costs | 47 |
| Retaining existing members | 44 |
| Retaining volunteers | 42 |
| Financial sustainability of club | 41 |
| Equipment needs improving | 40 |

survey (SARA, 2013) found that between 2011 and 2012 clubs had experienced a 20 % increase in the number of volunteers. This may have been assisted by Sport England's *Sport Makers* programme (Nichols et al. 2013) although there was no national strategy to convert the Olympic and Paralympic Games volunteers to more long-term volunteering (Nichols and Ralston 2014). Seventy three percent of clubs reported that no volunteers joined them in the 2 months immediately after the Olympic Games and Paralympic Games (Sport and Recreation Alliance 2013). The 2013 Sport and Recreation Alliance survey (p. 44) reports that clubs were experiencing above inflation utility costs, as reported above. Costs of hiring local government playing facilities increased from 2011 to 2012 for a majority of clubs (Sport and Recreation Alliance 2013) although the average proportion of total club expenditure taken by facility hiring remained the same.

## 7.5 Clubmark Accreditation and Formalisation of Management

This section describes *Clubmark*, Sport England's *licensing system* for clubs with junior participants, as an example of the formalisation of club management, which is certainly seen as an advantage by Sport England, but may be seen as a threat by some more traditional clubs with no junior members. It draws on a pilot study of the effects of Clubmark accreditation on club volunteers (Nichols and Faulkner 2013). Attaining Clubmark accreditation requires clubs to comply with defined standards across:

- 'Activity/playing programmes—this includes, for example, coaching qualifications required, insurance and 'coach to participant' ratios.
- Duty of care and welfare—appropriate risk assessments, health and safety policies, training, compliance and child protection policies.
- Knowing your club and its community—this ensures that your club is committed to fairness and equity in respect of the way in seeks to attract and retain members from your local community.
- Club management—which covers issues to do with club and committee structures and the general running of the organisation'. (Sport England 2013b).

Attaining these criteria may be a 2 years process involving considerable effort from volunteers. It may require new roles, new training—particularly to attain coaching qualifications—as well as additional volunteer roles and the formalisation of management practices such as role descriptions. Some of these requirements, such as gaining coaching and first aid qualifications, can be costly. These costs are likely to be passed on to participants. Benefits of Clubmark accreditation include providing a badge of quality for parents of junior members and assuring club members that they are implementing *good practice*. Clubmark accreditation is a condition for funding support from local and national government and from NGBs; and also, in some local authorities, preferential access to facilities. Clubmark was introduced in 2002. By August 2013, 11,711 clubs had obtained it and 3,972 were working towards it. Clubmark requires reassessment every 3 or 4 years.

As an example of formalisation and 'professionalisation of club management, one can argue that Clubmark has both benefits and costs. The new procedures will enable the club to compete more effectively for the time, enthusiasm and subscriptions of junior members (and their parents). It will enable new volunteers to more easily see their role in the club and thus may aid recruitment. Yet there is also an argument that adopting management procedures from service delivery organisations may be inappropriate for a mutual aid organisation which also has objectives of providing conviviality (Schulz et al. 2011; Rochester 2013). They may change the very nature of a club from mutual aid with conviviality towards a service delivery organisation. Is this what volunteers want to happen, or is it a change imposed upon them, overtly or covertly?

It is possible that the clubs with Clubmark status will expand and those without it contract as, where a choice is available, parents of new junior members gravitate towards the accredited clubs. As NGBs and local government focus their support on Clubmark clubs this will also help them develop at the expense of others. In this respect clubs without junior sections, but possibly with a large number of adults, are also disadvantaged.

## 7.6 Conclusion

Sport clubs in England face a number of considerable challenges now and in the foreseeable future. The apparent stability of an infrastructure which emerged from the conditions of the nineteenth century may be deceptive. First, the nature of participation in sport and physical activity is undergoing a long-term change, from traditional, time-bound sporting activities, often organised by teams, to individualised, time-flexible fitness activities. Thus, voluntary sport clubs are being overtaken in terms of participation numbers by health and fitness clubs, which are a source of significant growth for the commercial sector. If this change in relative importance is to be arrested by voluntary sport clubs, they will need to adopt a more flexible approach to the needs of potential members and volunteers. Participants will continue to want more opportunities for fitness activities, so sport clubs need to consider whether or not to accommodate this important source of demand. Clubs may not choose to do this if the collective enthusiasm binding volunteers to the club is love of a particular sport, rather than a desire to serve a particular community.

Second, while volunteers are sport clubs' lifeblood, the management of volunteers presents challenges. In seeking to recruit volunteers, normally from club members and parents of members, clubs may have to accommodate a trend towards *episodic* volunteering, which is limited in time duration (Rochester et al. 2010). Managing a larger number of episodic volunteers presents a more complex task of volunteer coordination for the traditional 'long-term' volunteers (Cuskelly 2005) who may themselves become harder to replace. Further, the management practices advocated by Sport England, as embodied in Clubmark accreditation criteria, are based on a conception of the club as a competitor to provide a service for new participants in a leisure market. The key is to find management practices which allow clubs to do this, if they want to, but at the same time retain traditional practices which maintain the function of providing *conviviality*. Volunteering is a form of leisure, and the volunteers have to experience it as such. A danger of regarding the club as a service provider is that new members may also regard it as just that: a place to satisfy a need to play sport with no moral obligation to contribute to the *collective enthusiasm*.

Third, a large number of voluntary sport clubs struggle for financial security, which is influenced by their success or otherwise in attracting members and income, and their ability to contain costs. An important moderating influence in this relationship is facilities, particularly when they are hired. For those clubs which hire facilities from local authorities, there is a real threat of increasing costs and/or reduced quality of facilities as local government is forced to cut spending. Financially, voluntary sport clubs in England appear quite fragile—they make a very modest financial surplus on average. Yet it should be remembered that they are also reasonably durable and resilient and that they are in the main non-profit organisations, so operating to a break-even requirement is the norm. There are considerable financial challenges, however, in the form of increasing costs, which underpin widespread efforts by clubs to increase their income.

Fourth, there is a tension between the traditional independence of voluntary sport clubs and the increasing pressure to adhere to government policy. This is particularly the case in those sports which are in receipt of government funding for their NGBs. These sports are accountable to participation plans which rely largely on sport clubs to achieve them. At one level, this tension is in principle restricted to the 46 sports funded by the government's agency, Sport England. Nearly a hundred other sports do not have such funding, so they are less directly tied to government objectives. However, the Sport and Recreation Alliance survey evidence suggests 45 % of clubs have applied for funding from external organisations, and over half of clubs have links with schools and/or programmes stretching into their local communities. Clubmark accreditation is regarded as a key criterion for a club applying for funding, thus obliging clubs to obtain it. There is evidence that NGB support through sports development officers is directed at clubs who have, or are trying to obtain, Clubmark (Nichols and Faulkner 2013). These suggest less independence than would previously have been the case. If more participation is taking place outside traditional sport clubs, NGBs may have to work through other organisations to achieve their Whole Sport Plan participation targets. However, this will divert their role from the traditional one of representing and supporting the clubs. So while Sport England see sport clubs as playing a major role in its strategy to increase participation, at the same time Sport England policies may be making NGBs less representative of clubs. It is interesting to speculate how the influence of Sport England might wane if it is forced to make the same expenditure cuts proportionately as local government and if the revenue it distributes from National Lottery proceeds also declines.

The net effect of these challenges is that voluntary sport clubs in England are in a period of potentially significant change. Whether this results in the continued importance of such clubs for participation and policy remains to be seen. But if current trends continue, it is the private health and fitness clubs and informal participation out of the club structure altogether which will attract increasing attention, by participants and policy makers alike.

## References

Allison M (2001) Sports clubs in Scotland, research report no. 75. Sportscotland, Edinburgh
Barrett D, Nichols G, Woods C (2014 unpublished) Hockey clubs in Yorkshire, 1990–2011: understanding falling participation in the UK national context
Blackshaw T, Long J (2005) What's the big idea? A critical exploration of the concept of social capital and its incorporation into leisure policy discourse. Leisure Stud 24(3):239–258
BUCS (2013) Graduate employability research. http://www.bucs.org.uk/page.asp?section=16992&sectionTitle=Graduate+Employability+Research. Accessed 2 Oct 2014
Coalter F (1999) Sport and recreation in the United Kingdom: flow with the flow or buck the trends? Manag Leisure 4(1):24–39
Cuskelly G (2005) Volunteer participation trends in Australian sport. In: Nichols G, Collins M (eds) Volunteers in sports clubs. Leisure Studies Association, Eastbourne, pp 86–104
Department for Culture, Media and Sport (2013) Meta-evaluation of the impacts and legacy of the London 2012 Olympic Games and Paralympic Games. Report 5 post-games evaluation, community engagement evidence base. https://www.gov.uk/government/uploads/system/uploads/attachment_data/file/224146/Report_5_Community_Engagement_Evidence_Base_FINAL.pdf. Accessed 1 Aug 2014
Erewash Sport (2014) National Governing Body list, Erewash Borough Council. http://www.erewashcsn.org.uk/index.php?option=com_content&view=article&id=74&Itemid=76. Accessed 2 Oct 2014
GHK (2010) Volunteering in the European Union. Directorate General Education and Culture. http://ec.europa.eu/sport/library/doc/f_studies/volunteering_final_report.pdf. Accessed 22 June 2010
Gratton C, Rowe N, Veal AJ (2011) International comparisons of sport participation in European countries: an update of the COMPASS project. Eur J Sport Soc 8(1–2):99–116
Gratton C, Nichols G, Shibli S, Taylor P (1997) Valuing volunteers in UK sport. Sports Council, London
Gratton C, Taylor P (1991) Government and the economics of sport. Longman, Harlow
Green M (2008) Non-governmental organisations in sports development. In: Girginov V (ed) Management of sports development. Elsevier, London, pp 89–107
Harris S, Mori K, Collins M (2009) Great expectations: voluntary sports clubs and their role in delivering national policy for English sport. Voluntas 20:405–423
Hoggett P, Bishop J (1985) The social organisation of leisure. Sports Council, London
Holt R (1990) Sport and the British. Oxford University Press, Oxford
Ives J (2012) Leisure review editorial – hanging out the bunting? Not just yet. http://www.theleisurereview.co.uk/editorial/editorial58.html. Accessed 2 Apr 2013
Mintel (2013) Health and fitness clubs UK. http://academic.mintel.com/display/669872/. Accessed 2 Oct 2014
Nichols G (2013) Voluntary sports clubs and sport development. In: Hylton K (ed) Sport development: policy, process and practice. Routledge, London, pp 213–230
Nichols G (2001) The UK voluntary sector. In: Wolsey C, Abrams J (eds) Understanding the leisure and sport industry. Pearson, Harlow, pp 33–49

Nichols G, Ralston R (2014) Volunteering for the games. In: Girginov V (ed) Handbook of the London 2012 Olympic and Paralympic Games. Volume two: celebrating the games. Routledge, London, pp 53–70

Nichols G, Taylor P, Barrett D, Jeanes R (2013a) Youth sport volunteers in England: a paradox between reducing the state and promoting a Big Society. Sport Manag Rev 17(3):337–346

Nichols G, Tacon R, Muir A (2013b) Sports clubs' volunteers: bonding in or bridging out? Sociology 47:350–367

Nichols G, Ferguson G, Grix J, Griffiths M (2013) Sport makers – developing good practice in volunteer and sports development. http://cms2.shef.ac.uk/polopoly_fs/1.274199.1368460426!/file/ec1gn_Sport_Makers_Report_4-13.pdf. Accessed 1 Aug 2013

Nichols G, Faulkner A (2013) The impact of gaining Clubmark accreditation on sports club volunteers – a pilot study. http://svrn.group.shef.ac.uk/previous-meetings/. Accessed 13 Feb 2014

Nichols G, Padmore J, Taylor P, Barrett D (2012) The relationship between types of sports club and English government policy to grow participation. Int J Sport Pol Polit 4(2):187–200

Nichols G, Taylor P (1995) The impact on local authority leisure provision of compulsory competitive tendering, financial cuts and changing attitudes. Local Govern Stud 21(4):607–622

Rochester C (2013) Rediscovering voluntary action; the beat of a different drum. Palgrave Macmillan, Basingstoke

Rochester C, Ellis Paine A, Howlett S, Zimmeck M (2010) Volunteering and society in the 21st century. Palgrave Macmillan, Basingstoke

Schulz J, Nichols G, Auld C (2011) Issues in the management of voluntary sports organisations and volunteers. In: Houlihan B, Green M (eds) Handbook of sports development. Routledge, London, pp 432–445

Sport and Recreation Alliance (2013) Survey of sports clubs 2013. Sport and Recreation Alliance, London

Sport and Recreation Alliance (2011) Survey of sports clubs 2011. Sport and Recreation Alliance, London

Sport and Recreation Alliance (2011b) Red card to red tape: how sport and recreation clubs want to break free from bureaucracy. http://www.sportandrecreation.org.uk/sites/default/files/web/documents/pdf/Sport%20and%20Recreation%20Alliance%20Red%20Card%20to%20Red%20Tape%20%28Full%20report%2C%20low%20res%29.pdf. Accessed 4 Jan 2014

Sport England (2008) Sport England strategy 2008–11. http://www.sportengland.org/about_us/what_we_do.aspx. Accessed 30 Dec 2011

Sport England/DCMS (2012) Creating a sporting habit for life: a new youth sport strategy. https://www.sportengland.org/media/130949/DCMS-Creating-a-sporting-habit-for-life-1-.pdf. Accessed 25 Sept 2013

Sport England (2013a) Whole sport plans 2013–17. http://www.sportengland.org/funding/ngb_investment/whole_sport_plans_2013-17.aspx. Accessed 1 Aug 2014

Sport England (2013b) Clubmark web site. http://www.clubmark.org.uk/what-clubmark. Accessed 1 Aug 2014

Sport England (2014) Who plays sport – the national picture. http://www.sportengland.org/research/who-plays-sport/national-picture/who-plays-sport/. Accessed 2 Oct 2014

Taylor P, Barrett D, Nichols G (2009) Survey of sports clubs 2009. CCPR, London

Taylor P, Nichols G, Holmes K, James M, Gratton C, Garrett R, Kokolakakis T, Mulder C, King L (2003) Sports volunteering in England. Sport England, London

TNS (2013) Higher education sport participation and satisfaction survey: national report year two. TNS BMRB and Sport England, London

UK Sport (2014) World class success. http://www.uksport.gov.uk/news/uk-sport-targets-investment-to-protect-and-enhance-medal-potential-for-rio-2016-and-beyond-040214. Accessed 5 Aug 2014

Weed M (2014) London 2012 legacy strategy: did it deliver? In: Girginov V (ed) Handbook of the London 2012 Olympic and Paralympic Games. Volume two: celebrating the games. Routledge, London, pp 281–294

# Chapter 8
# Sport Clubs in Estonia

**Kristjan Port and Peeter Lusmägi**

## 8.1 Introduction

To understand the importance and status of sports in Estonia, one has to understand the historical background of the country. The oldest known settlement in Estonia dates back to around 11,000 years ago at the beginning of the ninth millennium BC. The first mention of the people inhabiting present-day Estonia is by the Roman historian Tacitus, who in his book Germania (ca. AD 98) describes the Aesti tribe. Due to its strategically advantageous geographical location, Estonian territory was under the rule of Denmark, Sweden, Germany and Russia for several consecutive centuries. By retaining its language throughout this period of history, the effects of historical events have been absorbed into the contemporary Estonian culture and the mindset, including sports.

The World Bank considers present-day Estonia a high-income economy; however, the purchasing power per capita is below that of other long-time EU members. Roughly the size of the Netherlands, the population density of Estonia is comparatively low with 29 inhabitants per square kilometre. Contemporary Estonia is often described as one of the most *wired* countries in Europe which indicates a fast paced and technology driven mindset that dominates the culture of a high workload generation striving toward a more prosperous lifestyle—especially when compared to the country's complicated history after World War II. More than 70 % of the population lives in towns. Modern Estonia is a multinational country of 1,294,236 inhabitants

K. Port (✉)
Institute of Health Sciences and Sport, Tallinn University, Tallinn, Estonia
e-mail: kport@tlu.ee

P. Lusmägi
Estonian Sport for All Association, Estonian Olympic Committee, Tallinn, Estonia
e-mail: peeter@eok.ee



C. Breuer et al. (eds.), *Sport Clubs in Europe*, Sports Economics, Management and Policy 12, DOI 10.1007/978-3-319-17635-2_8

in which 157 languages are spoken, according to a 2012 census (Statistics Estonia 2012). 68.5 % of Estonian citizens speak Estonian and 29.6 % Russian as their native language.

Historically, Estonians consider themselves to be a sport-loving nation; however, the current level of physical activity is similar to the average for Europe (TNS Opinion and Social 2014). Strategically, Estonian sport organisation is built around the framework of sports clubs, but only 11 % of the physically active population use them for sport. The statistic does not mean that this format of sport participation does not work or that it should be discounted in the future, but more realistically the picture serves as an indicator of the issues illustrating the development of sports in Estonia.

## 8.2 History and Context

The contemporary sports movement in Estonia has its roots in German gymnastic traditions—*Turnvereine*. The first, *Revaler Turnverein* (Tallinn, the capital, was known as Reval at that time) was established in 1863. It was followed 1 year later by a similar operation in Tartu (Doprater Turverein) and the Dorpater Ruderclub in 1875. Coinciding with national awakening, the first locally organised but unofficial wrestling and weight lifting club was established in 1888; it later became official and was named the Tallinn Voluntary Sports Club. However, the first officially recognised Estonian sports club dates from 1896 and was established by cycling enthusiasts in a small county with a lakeside spa—the Saadjärve Cyclist Association.

In this way, the sports movement gained momentum and new sporting clubs were established throughout the country. Therefore, one may consider the organisation of sports began in Estonia at the beginning of the twentieth century, at a time when Estonia was a province of Tsarist Russia. For example, in the 1912 Olympic Games in Stockholm, the Finn, Alfred Asikainen and the Estonian Martin Klein, wrestled for a record 11 h and 40 min. Klein won, and his country of residence was given as Russia. At that time, Estonians were among the best in the entire Russian empire in athletics (16 records out of 29), as well as in wrestling and weightlifting.

However, these were turbulent times in Europe due to the First World War and the Bolshevik takeover of power in Russia. Again, largely due to its geographical location, Estonia was drawn into a military conflict that had two fronts, one against Russian and the other opposed to German rule. Success in the wars against both Soviet Russia and the German Freikorps and the Baltische Landeswehr secured an opportunity to establish an independent Estonian state in 1918. The Republic of Estonia was recognised (*de jure*) in 1920.

During the Independence War, the sports movement was seen as a valuable bearer of national identity and therefore played a supportive role in the making of the new state. Not surprisingly, the first national Sports Congress was organised as early as 1919. The Sports Congress decided to establish a central coordinating body for the sports movement—*Eesti Spordi Liit* (Estonian Sports Association), and to send its own national team to the 1920 Olympic Games held in Antwerp. The first-ever national team was successful, winning one gold and two silver medals and several placements among the first six places.

The success in the Olympics encouraged progress both in the number of participants in the sports movement and in the number of sports clubs to accommodate the increasing number of interested parties. The most popular fields in sport were track and field, football, wrestling, weight lifting and winter sports. Due to the fast expansion of the popularity of sports, the principal organisation, the Estonian Sports Association, exhausted its ability to manage all the aspects and as a result, encouraged a number of sports clubs and associations to establish their own pan-national sports federations. A major shift occurred in 1921 with the establishment of the Estonian Football Association and the Estonian Winter Sport Association, which in turn, inspired several others to follow. It then became apparent that the original Estonian Sports Association was left to govern only track and field. Tension arose but was settled amicably by establishing a comprehensive Central Union of Estonian Sport in 1923. The aim of this body was to act as an umbrella organisation for all sports federations. In the same year the Estonian Olympic Committee was registered as an official partner in the international Olympic movement.

In 1925, the government formed a dedicated cultural endowment capital fund (Kultuurikapital), which incorporated physical culture. The fund was used to support the work of sports clubs, associations and organisations enabling them to employ salaried instructors and coaches. Likewise, the fund assisted by providing a bridging loan for the construction of a new and fully equipped national stadium in the capital, Tallinn, in 1925. Success in the 1928 Olympics in Amsterdam further fostered the position of sports in the local culture. During the following years, the organisation of sports at all levels evolved through reforms, adjustments and amendments in order to incorporate the growing needs and aspirations of the country. The first pan-national sports games, with 12,000 participants in various fields of sports, were held in 1934 under the auspices of the Central Union of Estonian Sport. The second pan-Estonian Games were held in 1939. Based on a general consensus among leaders in the sports movement, the Estonian sports organisation was considered to be stable and thriving. Comprehensive plans foresaw the development and building of several new sporting facilities to accommodate the growing demand.

In 1940, the Central Union of Estonian Sport incorporated ten sports federations and 11 regional sports associations. Further down the organisational ladder there were 350 sports associations, clubs, unions and sections. There were 119 sporting grounds, 63 arenas for gymnastics and 25 swimming pools. During the period 1918–1940, Estonians won a total of 21 Olympic medals and they never fell below 16th place in point classification. In various championships, Estonia's iceboat sailors, wrestlers, weightlifters and boxers won medals.

Estonia maintained its independence for 22 years. Despite mild protests from Europe, Estonia was annexed by Soviet Russia as a result of the German–Soviet Non-Aggression Pact and its Secret Additional Protocol (the so-called Molotov–Ribbentrop Pact, also known as the Hitler–Stalin Pact) of August 1939. The Government of the German Reich and the Government of the Union of Soviet

Socialist Republics decided that in the event of a territorial and political rearrangement, the areas belonging to the Baltic States would be included in the sphere of influence of the USSR.

World War II casualties of Estonia are estimated to be around 25 % of the population and include the Soviet deportations in 1941. Notwithstanding this destitution, the love for sport among Estonians remained intact. Maybe more than ever, due to late achievements and its modus operandi, sports embodied a national identity and maintained the values of freedom and independence throughout following years of Soviet occupation. The story of Kristjan Palusalu (1908–1987), the heavyweight wrestler, who won two gold medals at the 1936 Olympic Games in Berlin, will serve as a case in point. In 1941, Palusalu was deported to Russia. He managed to escape, was condemned to death, escaped again and finally reached home. Later, he was again arrested and was obliged to lead a reclusive life. However, the people of Estonia did not forget him. Perhaps because his life reflected the fate of the whole nation, Kristjan Palusalu has remained the most popular sportsman in Estonia throughout history.

In 1941, the Soviet Union regime stipulated a new sports organisation, under the controls of the Estonian Soviet Socialist Republic's Committee of Physical Culture and Sports. All previous constituents of sports organisations from the Republic of Estonia were disbanded pursuant to the clause, *being rudiments of an oppressive state.* The list of disbanded organisations included the Estonian Central Sport Association, Estonian Olympic Committee, the Cultural Endowment Capital Fund, professional and county associations, former sports associations and clubs. As in the example of Kristjan Palusalu, the new governors put in place from Moscow declared a number of representatives of the previous sports era as enemies of the nation and they were either shot or deported.

There was a short but essential and seminal interlude between 1941 and 1944 when Germany invaded the Soviet Union in June of 1941. The Wehrmacht was able to reach Estonia within days, and the Soviets were driven from the country. Although initially the Germans were welcomed, it soon became apparent that they were but another occupying power whose aim was to use local resources for the war effort. Despite the on-going war, old sports organisations were somewhat successfully re-established and several sports federations were allowed to operate actively through clubs and associations. A number of Estonians, unwilling to side with the Nazis, joined the Finnish Army to fight against the Soviet Union. Although many Estonians were recruited into the German armed forces, the majority of them did so only in 1944 when the threat of a new invasion of Estonia by the Red Army had become imminent.

The Soviet forces re-conquered Estonia in the autumn of 1944. In the face of the country being re-occupied, tens of thousands of Estonians, including a majority of the professionals in education, culture, science, and political and social spheres, (estimated at up to 80,000) chose to either retreat with the Germans or flee to Finland or Sweden. Later, in January 1949, the Soviet Council of Ministers issued a decree *on the expulsion and deportation* from Estonia of *all kulaks and their families, the families of bandits and nationalists*, and others. Overall, more than 10 % of the entire adult Baltic population was deported or sent to Soviet labour camps, and in response to the continuing insurgency against Soviet rule more than 20,000 Estonians were forcibly deported to labour camps in Siberia known as Gulags. Mass deportations were followed by the policy of encouraging Soviet immigration when hundreds of thousands of migrants were relocated to Estonia from other parts of the Soviet Union to assist in the industrialisation and militarisation process, accounting for an increase of about half a million people within 45 years.

From 1944 to 1990, sports organisations in Estonia were founded basically on the same framework as in the rest of the Soviet Union. The political objective of the Sports Committee was to create a scientifically proven system for the physical education of the population, preparation of highly qualified athletes, with wide-scale involvement of citizens in physical culture and development of the necessary infrastructure and financial support. All sporting events were under the management and control of the Sports Committee.

Sport clubs were organised by the state. The majority were based on trade unions or institutions including the army, heavy industries, agriculture etc. Sport clubs were seen as builders of human resources for a planned economy. Not all organisational forms were named *sport club* as there were local councils, institutions, companies and organisations who managed the activities of *sport collectives*, *sports circles* and *sport societies*. By 1989, a total of 9,507 various athletics collectives with 300,000 members existed in Estonia, only 37 of which bore the name of a *sports club* (regardless of being mostly built on the concept of a sport club). On the other hand they did not have the characteristics of a democratic club: freedom of organisational judgment, self-financing, non-formal membership (only the employees of the institution were allowed to become members) etc. Participation was free of charge while costs were covered by the originating organisation and ultimately by the state, since there were no private companies. With the exception of one big trade union, all sports societies had their own network of sports schools (mainly for competitive sport among youth), making a total of 59 sports schools in Estonia.

Despite local representations, basically all the so-called sport collectives were part of a centrally governed trans-border network of clubs and associations. There were also sporting clubs belonging to the Soviet republics to promote friendly competition between nations. However, the meaning of a nation was an extremely dangerous concept, trifling with the heavily guarded domain of nationalism. Therefore, self-organising voluntary associations in sports were seen as working against the central command ideology and carried the potential danger of portraying nationalism.

In spite of this state of affairs, real life provided the occupied republics a form of balance to keep alive culturally valued, traditional sports and ways of participation in sports. While the overall organisation of sports in Soviet Estonia followed the general Soviet framework, real life carried the tell tale signs of old and long-established traditions in sports and its organisation. Between 1940 and 1988, Estonians won 11 gold medals at the Olympics. At the chess Olympics, Paul Keres received a team gold medal seven times. The Soviet Union naturally took credit for all of these achievements.

The achievement of Estonian sovereignty in 1991 reconstituted the pre-1940 state of sports organisation with its formal structure of governance. It was understood that the new organisational structure needed to embrace several new sport entities that had been established during the Soviet era. As a result, the National Sport Congress decided that sport should be developed on the premise of legal entities that are non-profit organisations and would be named as *sports clubs*. Sports clubs were built around major sport associations like the Union of Estonian Sport, the Estonian Olympic Committee and Sport Federations. Until 2005, sport clubs were legally required to be solely non-profit entities.

## 8.3 Role of Sport Clubs in Policy and Society

The last 25 years have seen the distribution of roles in sport organised between central and local authorities and sports organisations. The public sector creates conditions for sports activities, in particular through legislation, development of infrastructure, the provision of allowances and financing the education of professionals as well as exercising oversight over the use of public funds. Sports federations, associations and clubs connect people, provide services in the field of sports and organise sports activities.

The recent development of sport in Estonia has been most affected by deeds and charters such as the Estonian Sports Concept (adopted in 1989), Estonian Sports Charter (adopted in 1994), *Sport For All* Development Plans 2006–2010 and 2011–2014, and Estonian Sports Act (the most recent being adopted in 2005 by the Estonian Parliament) (Riigikogu 2005). The Act defines a *sport club* as the building block of a sport organisation. *Sport club* is a legal person governed by private law and its principal activity is the development of sport. The Act outlines regional and municipal sports associations that are comprised of local sport clubs and hold the right to organise local championships. Sport federations embody sport clubs on the national level within their corresponding field of sport, and have the right to hold national championships as well as serving as a connection to international sport. Sport unions bring together sport clubs that act in a specific area such as physical activity for recreation, health promotion, sport in schools, age group sport and sport for the disabled. The Estonian Olympic Committee serves as the umbrella organisation for all sport associations and is responsible for protecting and developing sport in Estonia. The Sport Act also specifies the status of the coach as a specialist in sports with a compulsory certified qualification according to the Professions Act.

Statistics covering sport organisation is by law, part of the national statistics maintained by the Estonian Sport Register (Eesti Spordiregister) (Estonian Sports Register 2014). Individuals and representatives of sport organisations enter data using a secure and identifiable access, comparable to online banking, utilising the national ID-card infrastructure. Data from the register is used for monitoring club activity, composition of membership, qualification of coaches, and it also enables decisions regarding club financing and the development of various policies. Sports in Estonia is further governed by several distinct stakeholders and corresponding strategic government whitepapers including the National Health Plan 2009–2020, Fundamentals of Cultural Policy until 2020, Strategy for Active Ageing 2013–2020, Estonian Regional Development Plan for 2014–2020 and at least 13 decrees from diverse government ministries and offices.

In July 2014, according to the official Estonian sports statistics, there were 1,871 sports clubs, 63 sports federations, 19 regional and municipal sports associations, and a total of 106 sport organisations based on various other forms (altogether 2,059 sport related organisations). Overall the sport organisations provide services for 81,000 children and young people aged up to 19 years, in addition to all other age groups. In the official register of coaches (licensed by law in six levels of proficiency) there were 3,400 specialists, and the sports facilities registry records a total of 2,559 sporting objects with 4,145 individual sporting pitches.

To understand the logic behind the evolution of diverse organisational forms of sport, one needs to differentiate between several different scenarios for the creation of sport clubs in contemporary Estonia.

The first is related to the state-maintained or municipality-maintained sport schools that were established during the time of the Soviet Union. Sport schools had thousands of participating children and hundreds of coaches. However, due to the status as a branch or department of a public organisation without independent legal status, sport schools were not able to join federations of specific sports. This effectively caused participation in sports on the international level to be cut off, as well as being unfeasible to receive private financial aid or sponsorships etc. As a result, sport schools established specialised *spin-off* sport clubs (i.e. a track and field sport club of a particular sport school or region). One of the outcomes was the rapid evolution of the newly established sport club organisations from a rigid structure to a dynamic, self-motivated and often financially sounder organisation. The overall dynamics of sport schools in the context of new sport clubs between 1988 and 1997 is given in Table 8.1.

The second scenario of sport club growth was built around a municipal sport school due to the shortage of funds, where a municipality backed the activities in a limited number of fields of sport. Consequently, locally active people launched new sport clubs in their favourite field of sport. Remarkably, as a result of basically starting from zero, several of these sport clubs evolved to become the most resilient and

**Table 8.1** Characteristics of sport schools between 1988 (start of reorganisation of post-Soviet sport organisation) and 1997 showing departure of children to newly established sport clubs

| | Training groups | Children (<19 years) | Coaches |
|---|---|---|---|
| 1988 | 2,994 | 45,606 | 1,401 |
| 1992 | 1,979 | 27,499 | 951 |
| 1996 | 1,670 | 21,221 | 775 |
| 1997 | 1,614 | 20,614 | 768 |

National census in 1989—1,565,662—in 2000—1,370,052 (Estonian Sports Register 2014)

successful sport clubs. It is worth mentioning that the state supported the development of sport in clubs for youth through monetary incentives on a per capita basis.

The third circumstance for establishing legally sovereign sport clubs, after 50 years of a central command, was based on organised physical activity within bigger, state owned and later private companies. In this case, members of a company established a sport club as an independent body of the company that typically bore its name.

The fourth scenario stems from the law of delegation of public services to civic organisations that motivate deprived municipalities to support the establishment of sport clubs via non-profit organisations.

Lastly, the fifth and maybe the most natural way, sport clubs were established as a civic initiative.

The first scenario mentioned above is linked to the previously stated law, which until 2005, mandated that sport clubs were legally allowed to be only non-profit entities. Even if there were few for-profit fitness clubs, they were left out from official statistics of sport organisation and they also posed problems for the framework of sports regulations. Therefore, the rule was relaxed and a few privately held and for-profit clubs, mainly emerging from the fitness gym business, entered the sport club scene. Their proportion is still small, consisting of a few dozen of such entities.

Therefore, sport clubs in Estonia have a short history, even if a number of them are technically legal descendants of old organisations from the beginning of the century. Realistically, the continuity between the two generations of sport organisations is based on few cultural artefacts and mainly written traditions as the bearers of the traditions were wiped out by the war and occupation.

Thus, the number of sport clubs began to grow. The number of sport clubs at the end of the first Republic of Estonia at the time of the Occupation in 1939 was just over 500. Roughly the same number of clubs was on the official register within a few years of regaining Independence in 1991. Table 8.2 describes the development of sport clubs between 1994 and 2012.

The Estonian census in 2012 gave a population figure of 1,294,236. Using this figure, Table 8.2 gives an estimate for the participation of the population in organised sports of 10 % of the total population. The latest *Eurobarometer 2014* indicates that Estonia has 36 % of respondents who never exercise or play sport at all. When comparing the results with the 2009 survey, there has been a 5 % decrease in the proportion of respondents that never exercise or play sports. At the same time, 39 % of the respondents indicated they participate in sport regularly or with some regularity, which is an increase of 5 %.

Participation in sports based on a personal, non-organised basis is significantly greater when compared to organised forms of sport that service roughly one in every ten people who label themselves as physically active. The same conclusion is further supported with the recent 2014 study of consumption of culture in Estonia (Unpublished Manuscript), which found that among the physically active population, 11 % participate in organised sport through training groups in sport clubs. Twenty-one percent of respondents joined a group of friends, 16 % were with family while 51 % preferred to train alone and on their own.

**Table 8.2** Statistics of sport clubs in Estonia—between 1994 and 2012 (Estonian Sports Register 2014)

| Sport clubs in Estonia | Number of registered clubs | Number of members | Number of children (<19 years) | Number of females | Total number of personnel | Number of coaches and instructors |
|---|---|---|---|---|---|---|
| 1994 | 592 | 44,257 | 17,622 | 9,013 | 1,614 | 757 |
| 1995 | 747 | 36,493 | 14,549 | 8,712 | 1,607 | 763 |
| 1996 | 930 | 60,066 | 26,100 | 12,660 | 2,427 | 1,077 |
| 1997 | 978 | 70,171 | 30,490 | 14,990 | 2,997 | 1,260 |
| 1998 | 734 | 67,763 | 29,897 | 17,024 | 2,642 | 1,130 |
| 1999 | 856 | 83,723 | 37,194 | 20,427 | 3,057 | 1,340 |
| 2000 | 866 | 79,802 | 37,483 | 22,873 | 3,270 | 1,487 |
| 2001 | 1,056 | 109,416 | 58,886 | 31,365 | 4,202 | 2,091 |
| 2002 | 1,038 | 100,876 | 49,198 | 28,169 | 4,017 | 1,973 |
| 2003 | 1,327 | 121,757 | 60,231 | 34,201 | 5,124 | 2,449 |
| 2004 | 1,513 | 142,429 | 69,142 | 41,768 | 6,279 | 2,878 |
| 2005 | 1,599 | 152,242 | 69,066 | 46,233 | 6,063 | 2,845 |
| 2006 | 1,521 | 153,875 | 74,450 | 54,812 | 6,271 | 3,100 |
| 2007 | 1,519 | 148,668 | 71,932 | 54,780 | 5,939 | 3,108 |
| 2008 | 1,528 | 130,763 | 71,335 | 48,704 | 5,916 | 3,130 |
| 2009 | 1,603 | 133,136 | 69,818 | 47,987 | 7,064 | 3,613 |
| 2010 | 1,629 | 129,839 | 68,941 | 50,930 | 6,931 | 3,488 |
| 2011 | 1,692 | 129,402 | 72,873 | 46,101 | 6,740 | 3,899 |
| 2012 | 1,744 | 130,839 | 76,066 | 47,398 | 7,049 | 4,248 |

### *8.3.1 National Data on Sport Club Participation*

Sport club membership in Estonia is male dominated as is illustrated in Fig. 8.1. Female and youth (5–19 years) share of the participation in the sport club membership has been steadily growing and coincides with the overall trend in the membership enlargement.

Inflow of the portion of the younger population to the sport clubs will likely start to stall due to the fall in the birth rate (see Fig. 8.2). For illustration in 1998 the population segment of 5–19 year olds was 305,000 people and in 2013 the same segment had fallen to 194,000 young individuals. On the other hand, in 1998 out of the total youth population only 9.8 % were enrolled in the sport clubs while in 2013 the same relative indicator was 41 % and in absolute numbers had increased by 2.5-fold reaching more than 81,000 youngsters.

Low fertility and a rapidly ageing population, as shown in Fig. 8.2 (Statistics Estonia 2014), will have an impact on the needs and ways of doing sport, as well as on the organisation that will coordinate the provisioning of the required services. It is already acknowledged that there is an increasing necessity for the development of appropriate services for sport and other modes of managed physical activity for the more mature age groups. Sadly, the older population at the time of writing consists

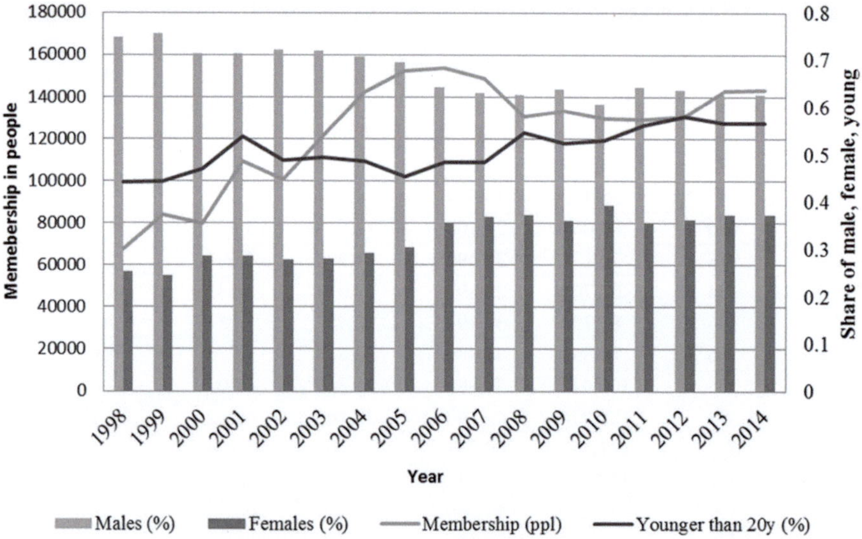


**Fig. 8.1** Yearly trends between 1998 and 2014 in sport club membership and percentage share of male, female and younger than 20 years (Estonian Sports Register 2014)

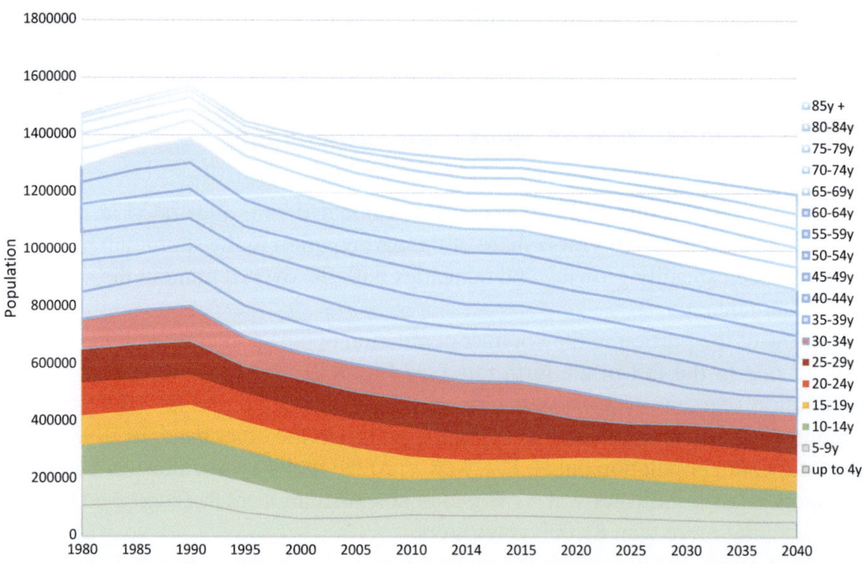


**Fig. 8.2** Demographics of Estonia (between 1980 and 2014) and projection until 2040 with division of the age groups. Coloured sections mark the younger and mainly healthy population strata up to 34 years of age and *light blue* shows layers of ages between 35 and 64 who together with younger cohort would be representative consumers of sport related services (Estonian Sports Register 2014)

mainly of the people who lived through difficult times and therefore have not accumulated wealth that could have had a stimulus effect on the development of services for healthy and active living.

On the other hand the age groups that are currently employed show growing interest toward both the disease preventive and health sustaining but also to the hedonistic sides of the sport. The actual conversion from the passive daydreamer to the active participant depends on overcoming of the perceived and the real obstacles. Preliminary studies among employees of various companies in Estonia indicate toward the perception that sport clubs are meant for the fitter, younger and/or affluent people. Knowing that, commercial sport clubs have started to reinforce more health-aware image of a member in their ad campaigns. They also provide free or low-cost options for the elderly at the times of lower usage. Particularly in the first half of the day, that seems to be also best for the retired people.

However, the fast responding, customer oriented, commercially founded sport clubs comprise only a small share of the existing sport organisation and are mainly available in the bigger townships. Beyond commercial footing the majority of sport clubs are still heavily dependent on the subsidies from the state and the municipalities, the money of which is earmarked for young members. Therefore, there is a tangible obstacle for the involvement of the wider population in the majority of today's youth oriented sport clubs.

In current vision the sport club will be the building block of the sport in Estonia. Therefore, the emergent trend compared to the *old* or traditional goals for sport clubs is the shift from the top athletic competitiveness to provision of services that support quality of life through active living. However, the majority of the physically active population still prefers to train and participate in sports alone or in some informal alliance outside of the organised sport. Both schemes provide access to competitions on various levels of proficiency and there are estimated to be 40,000–50,000 people regularly participating in competitions such as the mass starts, various cups and games. It is estimated that one third of the population competing in the sporting events comes from the sport clubs.

## 8.4 Characteristics of Sport Clubs

### *8.4.1 Finance*

Regarding the structure of the membership, the governing social policy has been towards the promotion of sport among young participants in sport clubs that have been channelled through the system of direct financial support per person until 19 years of age (see Table 8.3). This may also explain the relatively low number of physically active people from higher age groups utilising the club format in their pursuit of physical activity.

However, as seen in Table 8.3, there has been a continuously increasing trend of financing from club membership fees and from growth of business activities as well

**Table 8.3** Funding of sport clubs: total revenue (incl. economic activities), money from membership and from local government in 2000–2013 (Estonian Sports Register 2014)

| Year | Number of registered clubs | Number of members | Number of children (<19 years) | Total revenue (mil Euro) | From member-ship (mil Euro) | From local Gov. (mil Euro) |
|---|---|---|---|---|---|---|
| 2013 | 1,861 | 142,888 | 81,057 | 60,853 | 25,123 | *10,500* |
| 2012 | 1,744 | 130,839 | 76,066 | 56,114 | 19,976 | 10,210 |
| 2011 | 1,692 | 129,402 | 72,873 | 49,006 | 17,997 | 8,324 |
| 2010 | 1,629 | 129,839 | 68,941 | 43,266 | 13,606 | 7,623 |
| 2009 | 1,603 | 133,136 | 69,818 | 43,515 | 12,352 | 9,242 |
| 2008 | 1,528 | 130,763 | 71,335 | 46,920 | 11,090 | 10,254 |
| 2007 | 1,519 | 148,668 | 71,932 | 42,523 | 9,374 | 9,301 |
| 2006 | 1,521 | 153,875 | 74,450 | 34,719 | 7,164 | 7,858 |
| 2005 | 1,599 | 152,242 | 69,066 | 31,358 | 4,469 | 7,187 |
| 2004 | 1,513 | 142,429 | 69,142 | 27,032 | 3,967 | 5,998 |
| 2003 | 1,327 | 121,757 | 60,231 | 20,625 | 2,377 | 5,145 |
| 2002 | 1,038 | 100,876 | 49,198 | 16,068 | 1,765 | 3,846 |
| 2001 | 1,056 | 109,416 | 58,886 | 13,409 | 1,274 | 3,534 |
| 2000 | 866 | 79,802 | 37,483 | 6,540 | 0.678 | 1,643 |

as from sponsorships. A significant shift towards a new financing model was created in 2005 when the requirement was removed for sport clubs to be non-profit entities. Despite the ensuing downturn in the world economy, membership fees began to surpass the state support, which is also an indicator of the change in the structure of membership toward the employed (i.e. paying) adult population.

The current core value proposition for sport clubs is to serve as a vehicle for training knowledge through trainers, coaches and instructors (the qualification framework specifies only coach or trainer—*treener* in Estonian) and to organise training groups for various demographic segments of the population. The essential infrastructure and facilities are received or rented (generally subsidised) on an *as-needed* basis from local government or the state (stadiums, arenas, school and university facilities, etc.), or they belong to an organisation that owns their own facilities. Furthermore, there are a few successful examples of sport clubs building their own facilities (with help from local governments and the state who channel earmarked EU support). The last mentioned trend is possibly reflected in the structure of financing of sport by local governments, as shown in Table 8.4.

The above figures demonstrate the policy of decline in financing for the erection of new buildings and the concurrent increase of maintenance costs endured by local governments sport budgets. The trend of increased maintenance costs is to be anticipated with the concurrent deceleration of building new facilities, but it also kindles the need for rapidly developing sport clubs (mainly football) to consider constructing their own facilities (mainly football fields with financial support from the international federation i.e. UEFA).

**Table 8.4** Structure of financing of sport by local government (in mil EUR) 2004–2012 (Estonian Sports Register 2014)

| Year | 2004 | 2005 | 2006 | 2007 | 2008 | 2009 | 2010 | 2011 | 2012 |
|---|---|---|---|---|---|---|---|---|---|
| Building and renovation | 16.9 | 22.7 | 22.8 | 16.6 | 22.6 | 13.5 | 5.8 | 9.3 | 11.0 |
| Maintenance | 7.0 | 7.9 | 11.8 | 13.0 | 16.2 | 15.1 | 18.1 | 13.9 | 16.1 |
| Sport activities | 13.0 | 15.6 | 18.9 | 20.2 | 23.6 | 20.3 | 16.8 | 20.5 | 17.1 |
| Total | 36.9 | 46.2 | 53.5 | 49.8 | 62.4 | 48.9 | 40.7 | 43.7 | 44.2 |

### *8.4.2 Professionalisation*

The majority of sport clubs serve the amateur sport and recreational interests of the population. Professional sport (where sport provides the sole income for the person) is mainly developed in sport clubs specialising in team sports such as football, basketball, handball and volleyball. Approximately 50 clubs (out of about 1,800) support professional teams and/or individual athletes. Based on a rough estimate, there are about 300 full-time professional athletes among all club members. The real number of professionals in Estonia is higher, as some of them receive income from the state (members of the national team), various sponsorship deals, and there are also a number of athletes signed with overseas clubs.

The Estonian Sports Act stipulates that the coach must have a certified occupational qualification. One organisational instrument of compliance has been the prerequisite of receiving state or sport federation support (directly or indirectly). The awarding body for a coaches' qualification is the Estonian Olympic Committee, which also serves the function of a central sport organisation. Therefore, as an example, coaches who work under the auspices of sport federations and train children in sport clubs must possess certified qualifications. On the other hand, several privately held fitness clubs employ instructors who lack corresponding certified education. In 2013, there were 4,436 coaches and instructors on the official register (Estonian Sports Register 2014). Of these individuals, 482 had full tenure, 831 were working on a contract and 3,123 were registered as voluntary workers. The last figure does not correspond to reality because of the taxation related matters when several coaches receive salary in the form of a non-taxable stipend. Again, this arrangement served the purpose in the nineties to kick-start the development of sport clubs organisation in economically tight settings, but it also meant less social guarantees and could not endure per se. As a result, the current focus of revitalising sport clubs is via new taxation policies that also motivates and supports real voluntary work in sport.

### *8.4.3 Club Size*

According to data from the Estonian Sports register, 79.7 % of Estonian sports clubs have less than 100 participants (Table 8.5). In the sports concept approved at the Estonian Sports Congress, a sports club should be the main form of organising

**Table 8.5** Distribution of participants in the Estonians Sports Clubs in 2013 (Estonian Sports Register 2014)

| Membership (ppl) | 2013 |
|---|---|
| 1–9 | 13.4 % |
| 10–49 | 47.2 % |
| 50–99 | 19.1 % |
| 100–499 | 18.5 % |
| 500+ | 1.8 % |

sporting life, and should serve as a fundamental unit in the system of competitions. Nevertheless, at this point in time, only a few Estonian sports clubs have developed into socialising institutions involving the general population.

The range of activities is generally narrow and the social side of the clubs is underdeveloped. Due to the small size most sports clubs cover only one discipline and the primary goal for further development is the advancements in competitive achievements.

### *8.4.4 Bottlenecks and Challenges*

A unique characteristic bottleneck in the development of sport clubs has only recently become evident. The need of jumpstarting the club-based sport organisations in the nineties also coincided with the need for encouragement and support for sport among the youth in society. As a result, the monetary support from the state and the municipalities based on the so-called *head money*, favoured the development of small clubs with one or just a few enthusiastic coaches and therefore a limited number of children. It is good that club formation was actually set in motion, but they were surviving mainly on state sponsorship and could not develop the clubs into self-sustainable entities. It was estimated that up to 80 % of centrally supported club financing was underutilised and thus limited the club development. The characteristics of these circumstances were persistently low salaries (coaching often became a second job), lack of possibilities for young talent to move beyond the local athletic challenges and opportunities, unattractive financial investments by third parties (i.e. sponsorships), hindering the formation of adult sport and an overall stagnation in competitiveness. As a consequence of the mounting frustration, various organisational and financial efforts have been introduced to promote the consolidation of smaller sport clubs, to promote economic sustainability through further enlargement in membership and development of services etc.

Therefore, in the present day the majority of sport clubs are motivated and actively involved in training children and youth, whereas the age groups of middle-aged and older people are generally dismissed from the activities of the club. Noteworthy after-effect of the above circumstance is surfacing of the municipality supported and project based services of physical activity for mainly adult population. New strategic plan for sport (Estonian Sport 2030) that is currently in preparatory stage will try to challenge some of the inefficiencies regarding role of sport clubs in the service of the general public. Key instruments are amendments in policies, monetary incentives and improved cooperation with the stakeholders currently beyond domain of sport (health care, social care, youth work etc.).

### 8.4.5 Activities and Sports

Tables 8.6 and 8.7 depict most popular sports by the number of the clubs in the field and by the number of registered participants. General sentiment after the World War II hold basketball, volleyball, Nordic skiing and athletics as the national sports and did not regard football high on the list. Balance in popularity fell quickly towards the football in the nineties, partly due to the need for something new and unburdened from the former sport system. Other reasons were related to economic depression that hit the sport schools and various other forms of sport organisation with the resulting fall in popularity of the disciplines of sport nurtured in them. With newly established sport clubs and with the help of international federation, football gained momentum and then surpassed locally time-honoured disciplines of sport.

High participation rate in gymnastics (Table 8.7) reflects another trend that was absent from the pre-nineties sports scene—namely the aerobics. Since the aerobics have a need of a room and the instructor, this form of exercise became one of the building blocks for hundreds of sport clubs many of which became before long full service commercial gyms with conforming facilities for body building (yet another popular form of sport in club statistics) and other life style sports. Popularity of a sport based on the participation rate in sport clubs (Table 8.7) indicate the need of the specific facilities that are more efficiently provided via a sports club or a gym than through a less-organised and individually pursued alternatives. Hence, the Nordic skiing and cycling that one can practise in outdoors, for example, are also activities of high participation rate in the physically active population, but are not reflected through the statistics of sport clubs.

**Table 8.6** Most popular sport by the number of clubs (Estonian Sports Register 2014)

| Sport | Sport clubs |
|---|---|
| Football | 194 |
| Volleyball | 169 |
| Basketball | 167 |
| Skiing | 129 |
| Track and field | 124 |

**Table 8.7** Most popular sport by the participants (Estonian Sports Register 2014)

| Sport | Participants |
|---|---|
| Gymnastics | 18,760 |
| Football | 17,290 |
| Swimming | 11,421 |
| Body building | 9,495 |
| Basketball | 8,035 |

## 8.5 Conclusion

The above delineation of the awakening and development of modern sports in Estonia and its complex journey through the twentieth century should be taken into account in any pan-European comparison of cultural participation in sports and its organisational spirit. Estonia regained its independence in 1991. There was and is a lapse of two generations between the *old republic*, with its then Europeanised principles for organising sports, and the contemporary multinational state. On the one hand, the contemporary state wants to reclaim old traditions in order to build a continuum between the two stages of the Republic, but on the other hand, has in its distinctive cultural settings, the goal to invent or learn new, advanced, maybe even enlightened ways of performing sports and enjoying physical activity. However, there is something in our culture that perhaps no other society would have been willing to endure, but it has left something of value worth keeping, including our popular attitudes regarding sports. A similar line of thought befits the other Baltic countries as well.

## References

Estonian Sports Register. https://www.spordiregister.ee/. Accessed 9 Oct 2014

Riigikogu EV (2005) Spordiseadus. Teataja, Riigi

Statistics Estonia (2012) Population and Housing Census 2011. http://estonia.eu/about-estonia/country/population-census-2011.html. Accessed 9 Oct 2014

Statistics Estonia (2014) Population Census. http://www.stat.ee/population. Accessed 15 Sept 2014

TNS Opinion Social (2014) Special Eurobarometer 412. European Commission, Directorate-General for Education and Culture, Brussels

# Chapter 9
# Sport Clubs in Finland

**Pasi Koski, Hannu Itkonen, Kati Lehtonen, and Hanna Vehmas**

## 9.1 Introduction

Finland is one of the Nordic countries, situated in between the Scandinavian Peninsula and the Kola Peninsula of north Russia. A quarter of its total area lies north of the Arctic Circle. Finland is a member of the European Union since 1995 and is the northernmost member state of the Union. Finland is the sixth largest country in Europe by area, but in terms of population, Finland is one of the smallest countries in Europe with a population of 5.4 million and the population density as low as 17 persons per square kilometre.

Finland is the most heavily forested country in Europe, with 23 million hectares under forest cover. Europe's largest archipelago, which includes the self-governing province of the Aland Islands, lies off the south-west coast of Finland. Although Finland is located in the far north in comparison with most other countries, the climate is much milder than other countries, Canada for example, at the same latitudes. This is due to the warming effect of the Gulf Stream on this part of Europe.

Finland is an advanced industrial economy: the metal products, engineering and electronics industrial sectors account for 50 % of Finland's export revenues, and the forest products for 30 %. Finland is one of the leading countries in Internet use.

P. Koski (✉)
Department of Teacher Education, University of Turku, Rauma Unit, Rauma, Finland
e-mail: pasi.koski@utu.fi

H. Itkonen • H. Vehmas
Department of Sport Sciences, University of Jyvaskylä, Jyväskylä, Finland
e-mail: hannu.itkonen@jyu.fi; hanna.m.vehmas@jyu.fi

K. Lehtonen
Research Center for Sport and Health Sciences, Jyväskylä, Finland
e-mail: kati.lehtonen@likes.fi



C. Breuer et al. (eds.), *Sport Clubs in Europe*, Sports Economics, Management and Policy 12, DOI 10.1007/978-3-319-17635-2_9

The GDP per capita in Finland was 47,625 USD in 2013 (ranking 21st). Since 2002 Finland has had Euro as the currency.

The Finnish language belongs to the Finno-Ugric group of languages. Finland has two official languages, Finnish and Swedish, the latter spoken as a mother tongue by about 5 % of the people.

Sport and physical activities have a significant role in the Finnish society. They are widely recognised as health promoters of the citizens; as means of socialisation, especially for youth and children; and as providers of different forms of employment and economic opportunities. In addition, elite sport has been a major factor for contributing national identity (Vehmas and Ilmanen 2013).

The Finnish sport system consists of three major elements: firstly, voluntarism in sport clubs, secondly, public sector involvement with government-subsidising municipalities (e.g. sport facilities) and thirdly, private sector offering sport-related business opportunities and enhancing professional sport. Volunteer associations and the civic sector act as the backbone of Finnish physical culture, but the public sector, namely the state, the municipalities and the political system, still forms an essential factor with steering mechanisms and financial resources. Professional sport on the other hand is relatively marginal when compared internationally, even though competitive sport is visible in the media and Finns have succeeded markedly in a number of international sport events (Heikkala 2009; Vehmas and Ilmanen 2013).

Sport is the most popular form of citizen activity in Finland. Finland has ranked among the highest levels of sport participation and the highest percentage of sport participants in Europe over the years (Gratton et al. 2011; European Commission 2013, 2010). Also the National Sport Surveys reveal that Finnish children and youth, adults and senior citizens are active in leisure sport participation (Vehmas and Ilmanen 2013).

There are more than 10,000 sport clubs and 130 sport federations and other national sports organisations in Finland (Koski 2013b). Annually 350,000 children and young people and 500,000 adults use the services of sports clubs and federations. About four out of five Finnish young people participate in sport club's activities before their 19th birthday (Lämsä and Mäenpää 2002; Koski and Tähtinen 2005). Ninety-seven percent of the clubs are non-profit-making. However, most Finns engage in physical activities self-sufficiently, spontaneously and recreationally (Vehmas and Ilmanen 2013).

This chapter introduces the current state of the Finnish sport clubs. The chapter aims to highlight firstly how sport and physical culture in Finland are historically based on the civil society and volunteer activities; secondly what are the characteristics of sport clubs in Finland and finally what kind of challenges sport clubs are facing at the moment and in the future.

## 9.2 History and Context

In order to understand the changes and the current state of the Finnish sports club institutions, a broader look at the changes of the civic society needs to be taken.

The formation of the civic society dates back to the second half of the nineteenth century (Alapuro and Stenius 1987). In its early organisation three different phases can be seen. In the first phase (1855–1880) the mobilising forces were represented by the upper class elite where the most visible actors came from the relatively small group with the ideals of popular enlightenment (Stenius 1977).

In the second phase (1880–1896) of the civic society formation, the association activities expanded rapidly and became influential also in other strata. Temperance, labour and youth movements became the most important social movements. The starting points of these movements were to find solutions to the general societal problems (Stenius 1977). These were for example contagious diseases, infant mortality, low level of public health and overuse of alcohol. In the third phase (1896–1905) a wide net of associations was formed in Finland. A number of regional and local departments of civic society were established in the whole country (Stenius 1977).

Sport clubs have been and still are among the most central organisations in the civic society in Finland. The roots of the Finnish sport club activities stem from three different directions. Firstly, in the rural society sport was played as a form of living, frolic and games (Kärkkäinen 1992). Secondly, sport was a form of pastime for the upper class and gentry with promenades and other physical activity-related trips and excursions (Heikkinen 1992). Thirdly, sport was played in conjunction with various folk festivals organised by different associations (Itkonen and Knuuttila 1992).

By the beginning of the 1900s there were 341 clubs in Finland that were mostly single-sport clubs founded by the gentry. On the other hand clubs that were founded by other associations were often multi-sport clubs. Gymnastics for instance was very popular and it was exercised in most of the clubs (Itkonen 1996). The very first and still active sport club in Finland was a sailing club called Segelföreningen I Björneborg (SFB) that was founded in 1856. That time it had a defensive role by controlling the shipping nearby the coast. The club still actively operates in enhancing sailing and other forms of boating activities.

There were major changes in the Finnish sport club activities during the twentieth century, which is illustrated in four distinctive ages. The age of organisation culture was characteristic in the Finnish civic society from the beginning of 1900 until the 1930s. During that time sport and physical activity became tightly connected with organisations outside of sport such as workers' movement, women's movement, ideology of sober lifestyle and voluntary fire brigade. The following age from 1930s until 1960s is labelled as the age of hobby competition. Characteristics of this era were the specification of sport and the foundation of single-sport clubs. The formerly tight connections with the non-sport-specific organisations started to dissolve (Itkonen 2000).

The age of intense competition was prevailing in the Finnish physical culture from the 1960s until the 1980s. During that time, the clubs continued to became more sport specific. In addition, scientific knowledge and effective planning were utilised in training and coaching more than before. Moreover, the concept and progress of an athlete's career from childhood to the top athlete were launched. The last distinctive age from the 1980s until today is called the age of divergent activity, when the number of different sports and forms of physical activities have increased tremendously. At the same time the aims and goals of the physical culture have become more diverse. As a result of the diversification, a clearer gap is seen in between professional top-level sport and voluntary-based civic sport, as well as in between competition sport and non-competitive fitness sport (Itkonen 2000).

One of the characteristics of the Finnish physical culture has been a multiform civic society. Most of the organising sport and physical activity has happened voluntarily. The public sport sector has also been relatively strong in Finland. Sport affairs have been taken care of by the Ministry of Education and Culture at the state level, and by the municipalities at the local level (Itkonen 2011). The foundation of this division of tasks is that the public sector is responsible for providing the sport facilities, and the sport club sector is in charge of organising the activities.

## 9.3 Role of Sport Clubs in the National Policy and Society

### *9.3.1 National Data About Sport Club Participation*

The participation of the Finns in the sport clubs has been mainly observed through the researches about population's health and leisure behaviour. These studies reveal information not only about leisure participation in general in Finland, but also about participation in the sport clubs or in other organised sports. National Sport Surveys produced trend information about Finns' sport participation in 1995–2010. Eurobarometers on the other hand have revealed information about sport participation of the population over 15 years. However, large scientific studies covering sport *club* participation of the whole population have not been conducted recently.

Sport participation in the clubs has steadily increased among children and youth (under 14) in Finland since the mid-1990s (Fig. 9.1). In 2009 approximately one-third of the Finnish children under 6 years and every other child between 7 and 14 years participated in the sport clubs. Most actively children participate in the sport clubs at the age of 11–14 years. The number of children of 15–18 years was steadily growing until the beginning of the new millennium. During the last decade approximately 35 % of the Finnish youth between 15 and 18 years have participated in sport clubs. All along boys have been more active club participants than girls. On the other hand, no major changes have occurred in adults' sport participation during the last 15 years as 15–20 % of the Finnish men and 10–15 % of Finnish women participate in sport clubs. The amount of senior citizens (65+) in sport clubs is approximately 5 % (Lehtonen and Hakonen 2013).

At the same time (with sport clubs representing the core of the physical culture) Finns' sport participation does not rely on organised sport, i.e. club participation. In 2009–2010, as many as 16 % of the Finns participated in sport clubs and spent on average 10 h per month in voluntary activities. However, most Finns, especially adults, prefer to exercise independently outside of the organised sports (either in with company or alone). In 2009, on average 13–14 % of the Finns indicate that they engaged in sport and physical activity in a sport club whereas nearly 80 % of the adults exercised independently. According to the latest Eurobarometer (2014), only

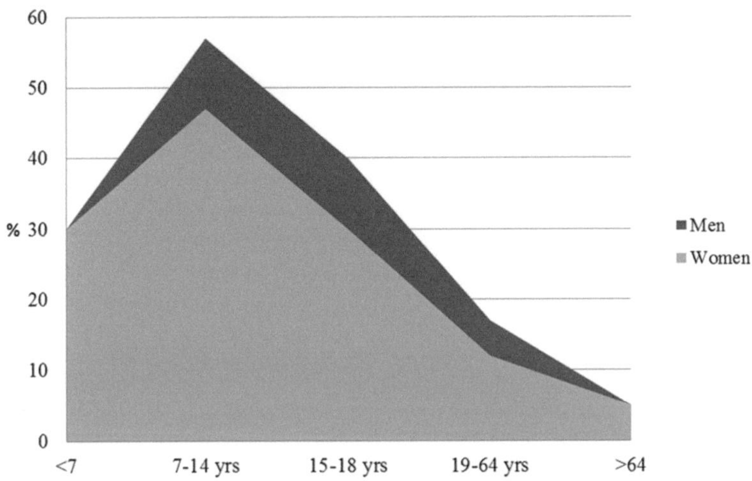


**Fig. 9.1** Sport club participation of the Finns in the end of 2010 (Lehtonen and Hakonen 2013)

7 % of the Finns actually engage in sport and physical activity in sport clubs, whereas 72 % (which is most per item on the EU28) exercise or play in parks and other outdoors (European Commission 2014, 2010; SLU 2010).

The most popular sports among adult Finns have long been walking, bicycling, cross country skiing, jogging, swimming, Nordic walking and floor ball. In order to even intensively participate in these physical activities, sport organisations are not necessarily needed to support it. Except for football, gymnastics and ice hockey many of the most popular children and youth sports are also such that they can and they are often participated without a sport club attachment. This might have twofold consequences. From the general populations' physical activity and health promotion perspective it is good that Finns find themselves in the physically active leisure environments independently and without always needing to have activities organised. The same can be said about the sport club participation of the children and youth in the economically challenging current situations where organised sport participation has become a financial challenge/burden to many families, and thus adding social inequality (Puronaho 2014).

According to the studies (for example Time use survey, World Values Survey 2000: Finnish data, Youth Barometer 2012) about voluntary work 15 % of the Finnish men and 10 % of the women took part in the voluntary work in the sport clubs during the last decade (Lehtonen and Hakonen 2013). According to the latest Eurobarometer (European Commission 2014) the number of Finns doing voluntary work has decreased. This, however, applies not only to voluntary work in sport clubs.

Inclination to do voluntary work is associated with the sport club participation of one's own children. According to the *Study of young people's leisure activities 2013* approximately 65 % of the parents whose children participated in the sport clubs were involved in the club activities almost daily. Parents with higher economic status are doing more voluntary work in sports clubs than those with lower incomes. The most active parents are the ones with children at the age of 10–14 years. Common way to do voluntary work is to take part in fundraising. This concerns 15 % of the parents. 9 % of the parents work as officials and 8 % as coaches. 4 % of the parents work voluntarily as team leaders or in the boards of the clubs. About one-third of the 10–29-year-old children and youth who exercise or play in the sport club himself/herself also work as a volunteer in the club. The most common forms of voluntary work are to take part in fundraising and coaching (Berg and Myllyniemi 2013).

### *9.3.2 Public Funds for Physical Activities in Finland*

At the beginning of the 1900s sport and physical activity began to differentiate into an independent organisational activity. National sport organisations were subsidised for the first time in the beginning of 1910. Already then the financial basis of both national and local sport organisations was founded on the extensive health benefits and taking care of the community responsibility (Vasara 2004). The financing of the elite sport on the other hand has been justified by the national identity formation and the importance of the idols.

The relationship between sport clubs and the local government is defined in the Sports Act. When writing this the Act is being renewed. According to the effective Act (2§, 1998/1054):

> Creating general preconditions for physical activity is the responsibility of the state and the municipalities. Sport organises have the main responsibility in organizing sport and physical activity. The Ministry of Education and Culture is in charge of the general directing, developing and reconciliation of the sport sector in the state administration. The municipalities must create physical activity conditions for the inhabitants of the municipality by developing the local and regional co-operation and by taking the needs of the special groups into account.

The Sports Act also defines the state subsidies for sport and physical activity. According to the Act the municipalities are state subsidised for the operating costs of the sport sector. These costs include for instance subsidies for the sport clubs and personnel expenses of the municipal sport sectors (OKM 2013).

In 2012, the state's sport allowance/appropriation was 153.7 million euro and was almost totally made up of the National Lottery Funds (Fig. 9.2). Almost one-third of the sport allowances were directed to the civic sector of sport. In practice the money was distributed to the annual funding of the operations of the sport organisations. There are nearly 130 sport organisations in Finland that receive government support. The state subsidies for the municipalities are 19.5 million euro. This is approx. 3 % of the operational costs of the local sport sectors. The municipalities allocate every year approximately 600–700 million tax revenue euro to sport and physical activity (OKM 2013).

The use of state subsidies varies in different municipalities. At the end of 2013 there were 320 autonomous municipalities in Finland (Kuntaliitto 2014) who could

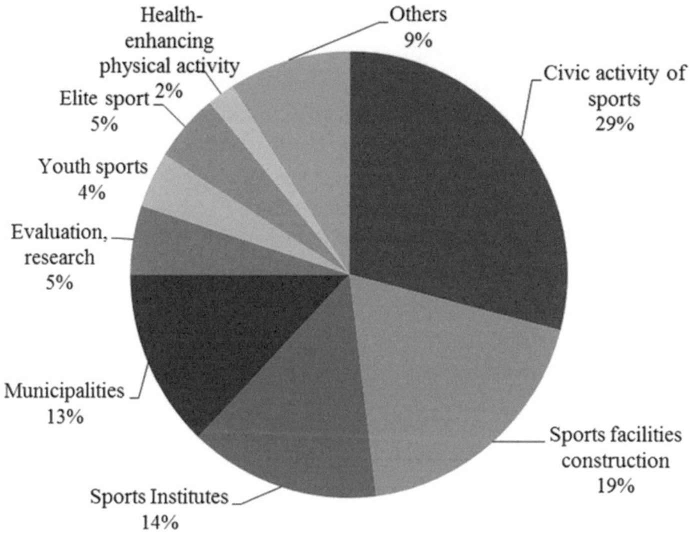


**Fig. 9.2** Distribution of the state subsidies for sport in 2012 (OKM 2013, p. 16)

all independently decide how to use the state subsidies. Thus, sport clubs were not funded in every municipality. Also the fees for using municipal sport facilities varied. According to Koski (2013b), close to 4,700 sport clubs received public support through their home towns in 2011. This is less than half of the sport clubs in the country. The financing directed to the sport clubs is heterogeneous, because the state does not give exact instructions how to use the state subsidies and thus the municipalities can independently decide how to use the municipal tax revenues.

The Ministry of Education and Culture has financially subsidised, with the National Lottery Funding, 300–400 sport clubs in Finland for the last 15 years. The total amount of annual support was 300,000–400,000 euro until 2009. After that the amount of state subsidy has increased almost every year (Lehtonen 2012). In 2013, the total amount of subsidy was 3.85 million euro. The number of funded clubs has not increased. National sport organisations were responsible for the application process and the selection of the funded clubs until 2013. Nowadays the Ministry of Education and Culture is in charge of the distribution process in total (Lehtonen et al. 2014).

## 9.4 Characteristics of Sport Clubs

### *9.4.1 Size and Amount of Sport Clubs*

It is somewhat difficult to exactly estimate how many actively functioning sport clubs there are in Finland at the moment. This is despite the fact that all officially registered associations in Finland need to be compiled in the records. In some occasions however, the officially kept records may include information about the clubs that have ceased to exist or are active only on paper. With this mind, it can be stated that there are altogether some 20,000 sport-related associations in Finland. These include a broad range of (physical) activities, such as chess or different forms of boating or motor sport activities (Koski 2013b).

In addition to the register of associations, the total amount of sport clubs can be traced through the municipalities. In Finland, every registered association needs to define itself a ‘home town’ whose sport officials then have the access to the information about the clubs. The number of these municipally operating sport clubs (when the club receives municipal subsidies and/or uses municipal facilities) is approximately 6,000–7,000, which can be considered as the bottom line of the amount of actually functioning clubs in the country. Moreover, there are clubs in Finland that do not apply/receive public subsidies nor use municipal sport facilities (Koski 2013b). It is also worth mentioning that 75 % of the sport facilities in Finland are constructed and maintained by the municipalities (OKM 2013). Based on the information of the municipal sport officials, it can be estimated that the above-mentioned two groups of sport-related associations altogether comprise some 10,000–11,000 actively operating sport clubs in Finland (Koski 2013b).

The average size of the sport clubs in Finland has decreased. In 1986 there were on average 356 members in the clubs, whereas in 1996 the amount was 328. By 2006 the size had diminished to 292 members (Koski 2009). What is characteristic nowadays is that the club membership is not as binding as it used to be in the previous times. Today people may be involved in the club activities even if they are not members and vice versa (Koski 2000). Thus the membership numbers and figures reveal only one part of the truth.

The membership numbers of the Finnish sport clubs show that the distribution is skew. The proportion of small clubs is relatively large. Especially the share of clubs with only a few dozen members has increased during the past few years. In 2006, for example, the share of the clubs with the maximum of 25 members was 10 %, and the share of the clubs with the maximum of 50 members was 20 %. Clearly over one-third of the clubs had the maximum of 100 members. On the other hand, the largest club on record has over 13,000 members. The skewness of the club distribution can be also approached by the membership volumes. In Finland, 45 % of the club members belong to the 10 % of the biggest clubs (Koski 2009).

### 9.4.2 Activities

The hegemony of the competitive sport was seen clearly in the club activities during the 1970s. However along with the economic development in Finland the citizens’ demands for physical activities increased and diversified. It meant that the sustaining and promoting of other types of physical culture gained ground in the clubs. In the other words the diversification of the physical culture in Finland is also seen in the increasing variety of the supply that the clubs offer. In the 1980s, the emphasis in the clubs was mainly in training and practicing sessions. Later on however, this

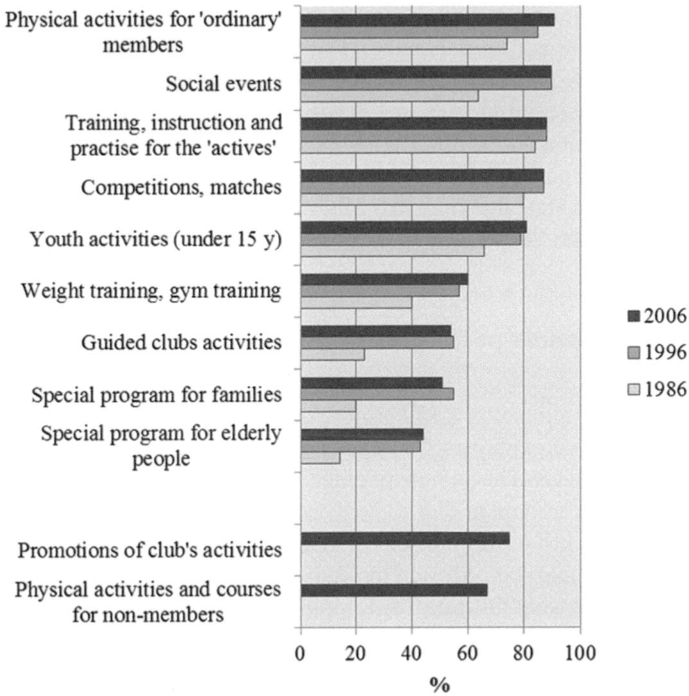


**Fig. 9.3** Supply of activities in the sport clubs in 1986, 1996 and 2006 (%) (Koski 2009)

has been complemented with other types of target groups, forms of action and new sports (Fig. 9.3) (Koski 2009, 2012).

In 2006, approximately 25 % of the clubs were aiming at the minimum of national level competition success. Another 25 % was satisfied with the lower level success and the rest, i.e. every other club, considered the promotion of physical activity and youth education as the main purpose of action (Koski 2009). All in all, goal-oriented competitive forms of activities have gotten other forms of activities alongside. In 2006, half of the clubs answered that they offer physical activity to families, and more than 40 % regarded senior citizens as their target group as well (Fig. 9.3). When asked about their future emphasis, about 60 % of the clubs regarded children and youth sport as a very important target group. Health-enhancing physical activity was regarded as very important for a third of the clubs and competition sports for 15 % of the clubs (Koski 2009).

The increasing variety of the club activities is also seen in the increasing amount of different sports. This idea got evidence when the amount of sports that was exercised or played at least in 1 % of the responding clubs was counted from the data of three decades. The amount of sports increased from 34 disciplines in 1986 to 38 sports in 1996 and further to 43 sports in 2006 (Koski 2009, 2013a).

On the other hand, the amount of sports in the individual clubs has not generally increased, on the contrary. During the first half of the last century it was typical that there were at the minimum of two different sports in the program. Multi-sport clubs with 4–8 sports were not unusual either. During the 1960s and 1970s, the share of newly found single-sport clubs was almost 50 %. After that a clear majority of the clubs ended up concentrating on a specific discipline of sport. This is an illustration of what differentiation and specialisation mean in the field of sport clubs. In 2006, the share of single-sport clubs was 43 %, but as we know that small clubs are under-represented, we can state that over half of the sport clubs in Finland concentrate on one sport only (Koski 2009).

### 9.4.3 Professionals in the Clubs

In 2012, there were altogether 1,150 professional athletes in Finland (Lämsä 2012). Most of them were team players. The share of ice hockey players was nearly half of all professional athletes. The amount of clubs with professional athletes is low compared with the total amount of clubs.

Professionalism has become more common in the Finnish sport clubs, because they started to hire paid staff. Most of the clubs, however, still work on the voluntary basis. In 1986, there were full-time paid employees in about 7 % of the Finnish sport clubs, which equals about 1,500 workers. Twenty years later in 2006 the share of the clubs with paid staff had increased to 12 % and the number of employees to nearly 3,000. The number of part-time employees has been generally higher. In 1986, there were part-time workers in 15 % of the Finnish sport clubs, which equals some 6,000 employees. In 2006, the share was 19 % and the number 15,000 (Koski 2009). In addition, different kinds of compensations of expenses and fees became more common in the clubs between 1986 and 2006.

In 2009, the Ministry of Education (nowadays Ministry of Education and Culture) provided 200 clubs with a possibility to hire a full-time worker for 22 months. At first this government subsidy covered half of the employment expenses. The aim was to see how this type of action would develop clubs' activities, and if the clubs were able to secure the continuation of the employment also after the subsidy period. According to a club survey ($n = 155$) the results were mainly encouraging as 80 % of the clubs were able to continue with the employment after the support period (Koski 2012). Nevertheless, the state has continued to support the clubs after this experimentation. In 2014, for instance, the state uses five million euro for this purpose. Almost 400 clubs were supported with a sum ranging from 2,500 to 30,000 euro. Many of the clubs use the money for the employment.

### 9.4.4 Finance

The amount of money needed for running the activities of the clubs has increased significantly during the last couple of decades. The economic recession in the beginning of 1990s was also seen in the clubs' resources. In 1986 and 1996, the gross income raised by the clubs was about 35,000–40,000 euro per club,[1] and during the first decade of the 2000s close to 60,000 euro. However, when the largest club is written off the average in 2006 remains at about 49,000 euro. Nevertheless, the economic volumes of the clubs have increased since the 1980s and especially from the mid-1990s onwards. When observed proportionally by the amount of the clubs, it can be stated that the money needed per club increased nearly 1.5-fold. In 1986, the clubs raised money about 100 euro per a member and 20 years later the amount was close to 150 euro. There was a clear increase in the numbers also with regard to the participant numbers. One interesting observation is that the differences between clubs were clearly increasing. The standard deviation of the total income proportioned by the club members had nearly doubled during the mentioned 20 years (Koski 2009). This increase has also meant that the costs of youth's sport participation have become one of the challenges in the sport club environment/setting (Puronaho 2014). The trend is an indication of the increased level of standards and expectations in relation to sport club activities.

Changes have also occurred in the distribution of the club's income during the past 20 years. The proportional shares of the fundraising and primary activities have explicitly dropped. In 2006, both of their shares were approximately one-third lower than in 1986 (fundraising 38 % → 27 %, primary activities 38 % → 26 %). During that time, Finns learned to be customers, which is seen in the club procedures. The proportion represented by direct payments as a source of income increased from 5 % in 1986 to 27 % in 2007 (Koski 2009, 2013a).

### 9.4.5 *Bottlenecks and Challenges*

International comparisons on happiness and life satisfaction have often indicated that Nordic countries are among the highest ranked countries (e.g. Inglehart et al. 2008). One of the explanations could be that in those countries the structure of society is based on the balance of three main sectors. The workable civil society consists of the appropriate public sector and active business sector and in addition there are enough room and good conditions for the third sector, i.e. civil activity with voluntary associations. The recent societal development in Finland has more weakened than strengthened the preconditions of the last mentioned.

Still the number of clubs and associations in sport and physical activities has increased during past decades. About one-fourth of all new associations operate in that domain. It is difficult to imagine that the popular movement around sport and physical activities would wither rapidly even by purpose. However its future is not without shadows, for instance the age structure of the sport clubs' members is ageing. This trend is reflected by the fact that Finland is among the fastest ageing coun-

[1] The numbers presented in this paper are based on the monetary value of 2006. This means that the 1986 and 1996 currency values (of the Finnish Mark prior to 2002) have been converted by the Statistics Finland's rate converter into 2006 euro (Tilastokeskus 2007).

tries in Europe (Giannakouris 2008). The process is clearly seen especially when looking the presidents of the clubs. From 1986 to 2006, the proportion of the presidents older than 60 years became seven times greater (Koski 2012). This change is not very flattering to the dynamic civic movement which main target group is youth.

Due to the development of individualisation and the process where the Finns started to be more customers than humble citizens have increased the demands for the services and supply of sport clubs both quantitatively and qualitatively. Linked to these processes the main problem in sport clubs is the continuous lack of volunteers. This is true in spite of the fact that recently the number of volunteers has been higher than ever. There is a crowd of people but their commitment is not always strong enough. In the clubs there is more than enough work and the volunteers commit themselves temporarily and like in projects (Koski 2009; Koski 2012). According to the new Eurobarometer (European Commission 2014) the proportional share of sport club volunteers in Finland was in 2013 5 % smaller than 4 years before. Especially the middle group where volunteers work 6–20 h for the club was smaller which trend has been seen already for some years (Koski 2009).

When the participants have customer's attitudes that means that errands are run with straight payments without personal contribution, emotional ties or commitment. The process of consumer-supplier relationship has chipped away at volunteerism as well as communality. From the future perspective, probably the most worrying issue is that Finnish youth do not have memberships in associations as often as the former generations. Some years ago Finnish youth was in the international comparison among the least interested when they were asked about joint liability and readiness to participate in civil activities (Suutarinen et al. 2001). One trend which is not increasing the youth participation in sport clubs is the rise of costs. According to Puronaho's (2014) findings the increase of participation costs is high during the past 10 years. The costs of participation in competitive sport are two or three times higher than in 2001. Especially some sports such as horse riding, dancing, ice hockey and figure stating are expensive sports in Finnish context.

## 9.5 Conclusions

Sport clubs have a somewhat controversial role in the Finnish physical culture. Historically, clubs can be regarded as the core elements of the voluntary-based civic society where Finns' sport participation has been built on during the last 150 years. Traditionally attached to many other forms of social and political movements the clubs have become a solid part of the civic society that emphasises amateur activities. This then may be seen as having had an impact in the fact that sport participation rates in Finland are among the highest when compared internationally. Sport and physical activity have been traditionally seen as natural parts of people's life and leisure.

From the sport clubs' point of view on one hand independent and unorganised activities may become a challenge as less citizens want to commit themselves in the clubs. On the other hand consumer orientation is seen in the increase of the participation numbers in private fitness and health centres (European Commission 2014). Both of these may lead to the difficulties in finding active volunteers, and to the diminishing of the membership fees. In this respect, the future of Finnish sport club has challenges. In addition the whole structure of Finnish sport organisations is at the moment under the renewing process and because of the many diverse interests, the future role and status of sport clubs are undefined.

## References


Alapuro R, Stenius H (1987) Kansanliikkeet loivat kansakunnan. [Folk movements creating the Nation]. In: Alapuro R, Liikanen I, Smeds K, Stenius H (eds) Kansa liikkeessä. Kirjayhtymä, Vaasa, pp 7–53

Berg P, Myllyniemi S (2013) Nuoria liikkeellä! Nuorten vapaa-aikatutkimus 2013. [Young people on the go! Study of young people's leisure activities 2013]. Nuorisoasiain neuvottelukunta, Helsinki

European Commission (2014) Special Eurobarometer 412. Sport and physical activity. Conducted by TNS opinion & social at the request of the Directorate-General for Education and Culture.http://ec.europa.eu/public_opinion/archives/ebs/ebs_412_en.pdf. Accessed 17 Apr 2014

European Commission (2013) Sport and physical activity. Special Eurobarometer 412. European Commission, Brussels

European Commission (2010) Special Eurobarometer 334. European Commission, Brussels

Giannakouris K (2008) Population and social conditions. Eurostat, European Commission. http://epp.eurostat.ec.europa.eu/cache/ITY_OFFPUB/KS-SF-08-072/EN/KS-SF-08-072-EN.PDF. Accessed 1 Oct 2011

Gratton C, Rowe N, Veal A (2011) International comparisons of sports participation in European countries. An update of the COMPASS project. Eur J Sport Soc 8(1–2):99–116

Heikkala J (2009) Sports governance in Finland. Finnish Sports Federation, Helsinki

Heikkinen A (1992) Promenadeja ja terveyskylpyjä. [Promenades and health spas]. In: Pyykkönen T (ed) Suomi uskoi urheiluun. Suomen urheilun ja liikunnan historia. Liikuntatieteellisen Seuran julkaisu nro. Liikuntatieteellinen Seura, Helsinki, p 131

Inglehart R, Foa R, Peterson C, Welzel C (2008) Development, freedom, and rising happiness. Perspect Psychol Sci 3(4):264–285

Itkonen H (1996) Kenttien kutsu. Tutkimus liikuntakulttuurin muutoksesta. Gaudeamus, Helsinki

Itkonen H (2000) Sport and civil society. Sociological perspectives. Karelian Institute University of Joensuu, Joensuu

Itkonen H (2011) Changing roles and practices of sport actors in local context. In: Pereira AL, Garcia L (eds) A social perspective on sport, health and environment. Portuguese J Sport Sci 11(1). Faculdade de Desporto da Universidade do Porto, Porto

Itkonen H, Knuuttila S (1992) Sankareista mediatähtiin. Urheilujulkisuuden muodonmuutos. [From heroes to media starts. Changes in media publicity]. In: Olin K, Itkonen H, Ranto E (eds) Liikunnan muutos, murros vai kaaos? Työväen Urheiluliitto, Helsinki, pp 145–161

Koski P (2000) Liikunta kansalaisaktiivisuutena. [Sport as a civil activity]. In: Itkonen H, Heikkala J, Ilmanen K, Koski P (eds) Liikunnan kansalaistoiminta – muutokset, merkitykset ja reunaehdot. Liikuntatieteellinen Seura, Helsinki, pp 40–55

Koski P (2009) Liikunta- ja urheiluseurat muutoksessa. [Sports clubs in the change]. SLU, Helsinki

Koski P (2012) Palkattu seuraan – Mitä seuraa? Seuratoiminnan kehittämistuen tulokset. [Paid professional in the club – What are the consequences?]. LIKES, Jyväskylä

Koski P (2013a) Finnish sports clubs as a mirror of society. Int J Sport Pol Polit 4(2):257–275

Koski P (2013b) Liikunta ja urheiluseuroja koskeva tietopohja ja sen kehittäminen. [Basic information about sports clubs and its development]. In: Liikunnan kansalaistoiminnan tietopohja. Valtion liikuntaneuvoston julkaisuja. Valtion liikuntaneuvosto, Helsinki, pp 18–42

Koski P, Tähtinen J (2005) Liikunnan merkitykset nuoruudessa. [The meanings of sport and physical activities in youth]. Nuorisotutkimus 23(1):3–21

Kuntaliitto (2014) Kuntaliiton verkkosivut: Kaupunkien ja kuntien lukumäärä. [The number of towns and municipalities in Finland]. www.kunnat.net/fi/tietopankit/tilastot/aluejaot/kuntien-lukumaara/Sivut/default.aspx. Accessed 27 Jan 2014

Kärkkäinen P (1992) Voimainkoetuksia ja kisailuja. [Trials of strengths and frolics]. In: Pyykkönen T (ed) Suomi uskoi urheiluun. Suomen urheilun ja liikunnan historia. Liikuntatieteellisen Seuran julkaisu nro. Liikuntatieteellinen Seura, Helsinki, p 131

Lehtonen K (2012) Nuorten harrasteliikunnan kehittäminen 1999–2011. [The developments of the recreational youth sports]. Valtion liikuntaneuvosto, Helsinki

Lehtonen K, Hakonen H (2013) Basic information on civic activity in Finnish sports: Participation and volunteer work in sports clubs. LINET research unit. http://www.likes.fi/filebank/803-Civic_activity_english_summary_112013.pdf. Accessed 27 Jan 2014

Lehtonen K, Paukku J, Hakamäki M, Laine K (2014) Seuratuki 2013. Haku-ja jakoprosessin arviointi. [Club subsidies in 2013. The evaluation of the application and distribution processes]. LIKES, Jyväskylä

Lämsä J (2012) Finnish elite sport – from class-based tensions to pluralist complexity. In: Andersen SS, Ronglan LT (eds) Nordic elite sport. Same ambitions – different tracks. Universitetsforlaget, Oslo, pp 83–106

Lämsä J, Mäenpää P (2002) Kuinka moni lopettaa? Tietoja ja näkemyksiä nuorten urheiluharrastuksen aloittamisesta ja lopettamisesta. [How many quit? Facts and outlooks about youth sport participation]. Nuori Suomi, Helsinki

OKM (2013) Liikuntatoimi tilastojen valossa. Perustilastoja vuodelta 2012. [Basic statistics of the field of sports in Finland in 2012]. Opetus-ja kulttuuriministeriö, Helsinki

Puronaho K (2014) Drop-out vai throw-out. Tutkimus lasten ja nuorten liikunnanharrastusten kustannuksista. [Drop-out or throw-out. A study about the costs of sport participation of children and youth]. Opetus- ja kulttuuriministeriö, Helsinki

SLU (2010) Kansallinen liikuntatutkimus 2009–2010: Aikuiset. [National sports survey 2009–2010. Adult population]. Finnish Sport Federation, Helsinki

Sports Act. www.finlex.fi/fi/laki/ajantasa/1998/19981054. Accessed 27 Jan 2014

Stenius H (1977) Järjestö-Suomen kehityspiirteitä. [Development features of the Organisational Finland]. In: Kuusi M, Alapuro R, Klinge M (eds) Maailmankuvan muutoksen kehityspiirteitä. Keuruu, Otava, pp 77–97

Suutarinen S, Brunell V, Poutiainen A, Puhakka E, Saari H, Törmäkangas K (2001) Suomen peruskoulun päättövaiheessa olevien nuorten yhteiskunnalliset tiedot, käsitykset, asenteet ja toiminta 28 maan kansainvälisessä vertailussa. [Social Knowledge, Skills, Attitudes and Activity of Young People Completing Finnish Basic Education in an International Comparison of 28 Countries. Summary of Results]. http://ktl.jyu.fi/arkisto/civics/civics.htm. Accessed 18 Oct 2007

Tilastokeskus (2007) Rahanarvonkerroin 1860–2007. [Coefficient of monetary value 1860–2007].http://www.stat.fi/til/khi/2007/khi_2007_2008-01-14_tau_001.html. Accessed 27 Jan 2014

Vasara E (2004) Valtion liikuntahallinnon historia. [History of State Sport Governance]. Liikuntatieteellinen Seura, Helsinki

Vehmas H, Ilmanen K (2013) Finland. In: Hallman K, Petry K (eds) Comparative sport development. Systems, participation and public policy. Springer, New York, pp 47–59

Youth Barometer (2012) Ministry of Education and Culture, Youth Research Network Advisory & Council for Youth Affairs. Publications (Finnish Youth Research Society) No. 127, Internet publications (Finnish Youth Research Society) 53. Hakapaino, Helsinki.https://tietoanuorista.fi/wp-content/uploads/2013/05/Nuorisobarometri_2012_Verkkojulkaisu.pdf. Accessed 1 May 2015

World Values Survey (2000) Finnish data. Finnish Social Science Data Archive, Tampere University

# Chapter 10
# Sport Clubs in France

**Sabine Chavinier-Réla, Emmanuel Bayle, and Eric Barget**

## 10.1 Introduction

France is a unitary constitutional republic which has a parliamentary system with a semi-presidential tendency. Historically, the country has defended democratic, non-religious and republican values. Its motto *Liberté, égalité, fraternité* means *Liberty, equality* and *fraternity*. The capital of France is Paris, French being the official language with the euro as its currency.

The major part of the French territory and population is located in Western Europe. However, owing to its colonial heritage, France also comprises several overseas regions and territories worldwide. With a population approaching 67 million people, it is the largest country in the European Union (EU) and the third in Europe.

S. Chavinier-Réla (✉)
Centre de Droit et d'Economie du Sport, Université de Limoges, Limoges, France
e-mail: chavinier@cdes.fr

E. Bayle
Institut en sciences du sport, Université de Lausanne, Lausanne, Switzerland
e-mail: emmanuel.bayle@unil.ch

E. Barget
OMIJ CDES Équipe d'Accueil 3177, Université de Limoges, Limoges, France
e-mail: eric.barget@unilim.fr



C. Breuer et al. (eds.), *Sport Clubs in Europe*, Sports Economics, Management and Policy 12, DOI 10.1007/978-3-319-17635-2_10

## 10.2 History and Context

### 10.2.1 Origin of Sport Clubs

At their early stages, the French sport clubs got directly inspired from a strong Anglo-Saxon influence. They were initially established in Paris and in the major cities of the country. Their members were exclusively well-bred students. Then, during the last third of the nineteenth century, physical and sporting activities started to set up massively in France. This is how a physical culture was born first. Originally, such a physical culture did not have unity. We could identify a value system and/or a set of objectives for each social group (Arnaud and Camy 1986). There were different types of practices: playful, sporting, gymnastic, competitive, athletic, etc., depending on the groups that could be localised and identified. Sociability with peers was a core issue but each set of sport clubs was pursuing its own goals. For instance, Catholic sport was considered as a means to master modernity and it met a need to compensate for the Church which was affected by the social and political changes (Lagrée 1986).

The beginning of the twentieth century was marked by the advent of a fundamental law for sport clubs. On 1st July 1901, Pierre Waldeck-Rousseau passed the law *related to the contract of association*. Its scope is significant as it guarantees one of the greatest republican freedoms. Every citizen has the right to freedom of association without prior authorisation. The following decree, on 16th August 1901, represents the basis of the functioning of French associations. For the sport association movement, the effects of those laws were observed as of from 1910 (Garrigou 1986).

The sport clubs were gradually established in rural areas in the course of a diffusion phenomenon including the republic, the school, the labour unions and the agricultural cooperatives (Garrier 1986). The sport associations were considered as institutional intermediaries for education with a specific role in the "republicanisation process" in France (Arnaud and Camy 1986, p. 408). The competition between young Catholic, Protestant and lay youth groups favoured the spreading of sport associations, as shown by Jean-Pierre Augustin (Augustin 1992) with the example of basketball in the Chalosse region (south-west of France). Thereafter, the First World War played a significant role in increasing the number of sport clubs, as shown by Pierre Lanfranchi in the case of football in the Languedoc region (Lanfranchi 1986) or by Sabine Chavinier-Réla with the example of basketball around the American bases.

During the twentieth century, a period of internationalism contributed to the modernisation of the sport association movement (Arnaud and Camy 1986). With the first international matches and the creation of French federations for each sport, France moved from an activist approach falling within the scope of popular education or close to industrial paternalism to a competitive approach, focused on sport as such. During the interwar period, Délétang described sport as a steamroller unifying all the sporting practices, whether they have the same affinities[1] or not (Délétang 1986). Then, during the Second World War, the Vichy government helped to increase the number of sport associations (Garrigou 1986).

During the second part of the twentieth century, an evolution of social demand quickened. Throughout the advent of the *leisure civilisation* (Dumazedier 1962), the expectations of the French population towards sport competition turned into new aspirations related to sensations (Loret 1995) but also to health concerns. The Eurobarometer 412 (2014) has thus highlighted that the motivations of the French to practise a physical or sporting activity are mainly related to their will of improving their shape, relaxing or being with friends.

A quick analysis would lead us to think that *history seems to be repeating itself.* The origin of the sport association movement has merged with the history of associations. In the nineteenth century, the associations were multifunctional, and then they became monofunctional during the twentieth century (Agulhon 1978). But, during the twenty-first century, expectations towards associations have been multifunctional again, the only difference being that a strong demand for synergies and partnerships has been observed. While the expansion of sport associations is one of the effects of the predominance of sporting ends and sport competition, their future seems now to be depending on their ability to fulfil social functions (integration, education, inclusion, cohesion), health functions (against obesity, epidemics, fighting chronic diseases) and economical functions (professionalisation, financial impacts of events, lever of territorial development). From the bourgeois, male student of the Parisian universities to the millions of sport club members and people practising a sporting activity, the evolution is significant. However, the transition to sport for all is still unachieved. Given the societal challenges, the French public authorities have been encouraging sport associations to welcome new members and adapt their offers to people still remote from sport. Different priority target groups have thus been identified and public funding is oriented towards specific actions that the sport clubs can implement for them.

### *10.2.2 A Brief Overview of Position of Sport Clubs Within the National Sport Structure*

The position of the French sport clubs is part of a vertical organisation, which is a reflection of a highly structured sport association movement. A network of 164,137 sport clubs thus forms the base of a pyramid on top of which are the national sports federations and the French National Olympic Committee (CNOSF).

---

[1] The French Ministry of Sports and Youth provides the following definition for the sports federations considered as *affinitaires* (French Ministry of Sports): they aim in priority at a multipurpose sporting practice, with several activities, based on different affinities focused on the human being as a whole (e.g.: the French federation "UFOLEP" has a double objective: to be a multisport federation and to promote the movement of ideas in today's society and in the future).

**Table 10.1** Number of clubs depending on the type of federations (French Ministry of Sports 2012)

| | Single-sport federations | Multisport federations |
|---|---|---|
| Olympic federations | 67,927 | X |
| Non-Olympic federations | 42,187 | 54,031 |

In France, the ministry responsible for sports[2] classifies sports federations in two categories: multisport or single sport. Besides, among the single-sport federations, a distinction is made for the Olympic federations. The Olympic single-sport federations gather almost 68,000 clubs in France, which represents around 41 % of the overall. The clubs affiliated to the multisport federations come after with 54,000 clubs (i.e. one-third) (Table 10.1).

The French Sports Code provides a definition for the sports federations considered as *délégataires*: in each sport discipline, and for a defined period of time, only one authorised federation receives the delegation of authority from the ministry responsible for sports. The *delegate* federations organise sports competitions at the outcome of which are awarded the international, national and regional titles. They conduct then the corresponding selections, and make suggestions for the registration of elite athletes, coaches, referees and senior judges on the elite lists, but also on the list of athletes under 22 years old (called *Espoirs*, which means prospects) and on the list of training partners. These federations enact the technical rules that are specific to their sport discipline as well as the regulations related to the organisation of any event open to their members (French Sports Code, articles L131-14 to 16).

Based on the model of the French public administrations, the sport association movement exists on the regional and the local level (department level specific to France). These bodies are both ascending/descending communications relays and points of contact for the local authorities corresponding to the administrative level. In broad outline, each of the 115 national sports federations has 22 regional leagues in mainland France (including Corsica, but excluding the French Overseas departments (Guadeloupe, Martinique, French Guiana, Reunion Island, Mayotte) and territories (French Polynesia, Saint-Pierre and Miquelon, Wallis and Futuna, Saint-Martin, Saint-Barthelemy) as well as New Caledonia and the French Southern and Antarctic Lands). They take care of the organisation of interdepartmental championships; provide federal training for sport coaches, referees and managers; collect public funding from the Regional Council (*Conseil régional*); manage the high-level training centres and much more. We currently observe at the regional level a trend to mutualise human resources for administrative and financial positions as well as development jobs at the service of the clubs. At a lower level, each national sports federation governs a hundred of departmental committees. They are mainly in charge of organising local championships; they can provide services to mutualise

[2] In France, the designation of the ministry in charge of sports has changed many times since its creation: sometimes associated to other fields such as youth, health, associative life and gender equality.

human resources or payroll outsourcing services; they collect the public funding from the General Council (*Conseil Général*), manage the sport classes (special section at school with a specific timetable for sporting activities) and much more. Nowadays, some of these departmental committees get involved in the development of a complementary offer to sport clubs, more focused on institutions (leisure centres, prisons, retirement homes, medico-educational institutes (IMEs) and so on).

Sport clubs themselves rank fourth at the national level (behind the federations, regions and departments). Their members are generally both subscribing members of the club (subscription fee) and members of a sports federation (sport licence). The clubs can be affiliated to one or several federations. Their role is to organise a sporting practice on a daily basis (trainings) and the club participation in sports competitions (championships, trials, tournaments). At this position, sport clubs are at a crossing point between two principles: a vertical approach (as part of the federal sport movement, but also with a link with the state and its decentralised bodies) and a horizontal approach (being established in a territory with local authorities (town, department, region) and audiences with specific expectations and demographic, economic and social characteristics).

The pyramid which traditionally represents the French association movement is nowadays weakened. On the one hand, a part of the sports elite is trying to distance itself from the new trend which consists in teaming up individual sports athletes or organising professional clubs shaped like sports companies with a mere statutory link with the support association which organises a mass practice. On the other hand, national sports federations have the possibility since 2007 to authorise professional sports institutions as part of their affiliated members, in addition to the traditional sport clubs. Within 5 years, the number of these institutions has increased from 5,000 to 7,000. Moreover, 80,000 non-affiliated associations can be counted outside the federations' scope, which represents almost one-third of the overall sports offer provided by associations (CNAR-Sport March 2009). Besides, even the athletes start to practise a sporting activity outside the sport movement: there is now a sports supply provided by municipalities at competitive prices, but also an increase in the private, for-profit offer as well as the development of self-organised sporting practices. In 2013, 43 % of the French population declared that they practise a physical activity on a more or less regular basis, whereas only 16 % claimed that they were practising sport in a club (Eurobarometer March 2014).

## 10.3 Role of Sport Clubs in Policy and Society

### *10.3.1 National Data on Sport Club Participation (by Age Group, Sex, Etc.)*

According to a survey on the sports practices conducted in 2010 (Ministère des sports 2011), 65 % of the population aged 15 and over living in France stated that during the past 12 months they had been practising one or several physical activities at least once a week. If we count all the people practising sport, including the ones who do it on an occasional basis and those who only practise a physical activity during the holidays, 89 % of the French population are concerned by the practice of a physical or sporting activity. In 10 years, the practice of a physical or sporting activity has slightly increased. Taking into account the same coverage (population aged from 15 to 75) having the same socio-economic structure status and being asked similar questions, the practice rate has grown by 5 points, increasing from 83 % in 2000 to 88 % in 2010. Over a decade, the women's sporting practice in particular has expanded as well by 6 points. The affiliation to an organisation (whether it is an association or a private, for-profit club) has slightly increased, but the practice of a physical and sporting activity generally takes place outside any kind of sports organisation, and resorting to a coaching structure still represents a minority of cases. The most spectacular growth in terms of practice has been reached in the activities of nature sport. If we take all the practice modes into account, whether they are institutional or not, almost 25 million people declared practicing an activity similar to nature sports (hiking and cycling being the ones stated most often). The development of nature sports events witnesses the public's enthusiasm for these kinds of sporting practice.

We should undoubtedly also mention the number of people who practice a physical of sporting activity more than three times a week, among the few activities that are representative of the new forms of commitment to sports: indeed, there are about 600,000 joggers and 500,000 weightlifters. Besides, France is not unified in sport, as illustrated by the predominance of rugby union in the south-west, or *pétanque* (bowls) in the south-east, or traditional practices related to specific territories like *Basque pelota* in the Basque Country, but also *courses camarguaises* (bloodless bullfighting) in the Camargue region as well as the so-called *joutes languedociennes* (water contests on boats in the Languedoc region).

Concerning the sporting practice in club specifically, a study conducted by the French Ministry of Sports (Cléron 2013) in 2013 shows that the number of sporting licences issued by the official sports federations—authorised by the French ministry responsible for sports—increased by 11 % between 2001 and 2011, up to 15,659,500 licences. The number of other sporting participation certificates (for example temporary sport licences or *discovery passes*) multiplied by 2.5, reaching 1,842,000 units. If we make a comparison on the same period of time, the growth of the French population was considerably lower (+7 %). The growth of the number of licences issued was higher for the single-sport federations than for the multisport ones: 12 % compared with 9 %. Over a period of 10 years, some federations like the French federations of hockey and weightlifting have more than doubled their number of licences. However, in terms of impact on the total number of delivered licences, the highest increases have been observed in Olympic federations like the French horse riding federation (+273,285 licences), the French handball federation (+140,812 licences) and the French golf federation (+116,438 licences). In the same period of time, the French federation of football, which is the biggest in France, has lost more than 150,000 members, dropping below two million members; this seems to be mainly due to the negative image of football given by the French national team in 2010. In 10 years, the women's licences have significantly increased (+3 points) reaching about 37 % of total licences in 2011. The competitors are estimated to be about nine million and the top of the pyramid is represented by 10,000–12,000 professional and top-level athletes who dedicate most of their time to sport.

On one hand, when one takes all the federations into account[3] (Ministère des sports 2013), the number of male members goes over 63 % whereas, in the French population, women are more numerous (52 %). On the other hand, we estimate that in 2011 more than half of the memberships have been given to people 20 years old or younger. In comparison, they represent only 25 % of the French population. Furthermore, 4.4 million people live in low-income urban zones (sensitive urban zones: around 7 % of the French population), and they represent only 4 % of the sport members. The level of education (diplomas) as well as income level have an effect on the practice level. Concerning this aspect, statistics are available for players only even if they do not belong to a sport club (Muller 2005) and not for the members.

Even if people aged 15–24 years are the most athletic ones, being graduated, studying or working and having a high level of living make it easier for people to practise sports. The difference in the practising rate between men and women is less important for people with privileged backgrounds. Furthermore, the number of sports increases along with the level of life, so does being a member of a club or taking part into sport competition. As far as the other variables are concerned, one must know that in France: *It is forbidden to collect or process personal data which precise, directly or indirectly, the ethnic origins, the political, philosophical or religious opinion or the trade union membership of people, or which refers to their health or sexual life.*

*Societal, political embedding (why do sport clubs exist, importance of sport clubs for society, contribution to the local municipality —incl. national special programs, special interests).*

The massification of the sports phenomenon explains the major societal role played by sport and clubs, especially in local social life.

The affiliation of a sport club to a national sports federation allows it to be eligible for the federal activities and to receive public funding. Some sports federations —but very few clubs—are considered as public-interest organisations and such recognition allows them to receive donations and legacies.

The significance of public funding, whether it is direct or indirect (free-of-charge sports facilities), and of volunteering allows clubs to offer services that are much cheaper than the market price (see Sect. 4.6 afterwards). As a consequence, their offers are accessible to people with very limited creditworthiness and even to people who are excluded or away from the sporting practices. In addition, some specific public helps like the sports voucher (worth €10) supplement the access to the sporting practice in a club. Some regions like Poitou-Charentes have made the accessibility

[3] Atlas national des fédérations sportives, 2012 (Atlas of the national sport federations).

of youth to sport a priority.[4] Other public helps like the ones from the family allowances fund (*Caisse d'Allocations Familiales*) are intended for teenagers whose parents have low incomes. More generally, the state and the public actors consider sport as an essential tool for social cohesion and encourage policies with priorities for the people kept away from the sporting practice (like women, sensitive urban and periurban neighbourhoods, rural areas and disabled people) or policies fighting violence and uncivil behaviours. The agency for education through sport (APELS) is a national association in France that was created to enhance and recognise the utility of sport as a tool for education and integration. To this end, this association conducts many calls for projects, brings technical resources through publications and organises meetings and discussions as well as enhancing events. Thanks to the programme *Fais-nous rêver-Fondation GDF Suez* (Make us dream-GDF SUEZ foundation), the APELS organisation has been detecting, enhancing and helping initiatives of education through sport for 17 years.

Furthermore, the clubs can host school groups and this process could increase significantly with the reform plan of the school pace (allowing more time for cultural and sporting activities). More generally, clubs can work as service providers for the municipalities, as part of projects for hosting sporting and leisure activities for the youth. The public funding for sport tends to target more the dimension of social cohesion/inclusion/education through sport and less the help to the general functioning of clubs. These public funds thus try to give more value to the social and educational role of sport clubs. The French National Olympic Committee (CNOSF) supports this phenomenon and struggles against the expansion of the auto-organised sports practices through its campaign called *Le sport, c'est mieux dans un club* (It is better to practice sport in a club). It is associated since 2009 with another public campaign called *Sentez-vous sport* (Feel sport (Comité National Olympique et Sportif Francais)). Its goal is to encourage the French population to practise a physical activity on a regular basis while being supervised by a sport coach. This event offering thousands of activities during 1 week aspires to be a sustainable meeting, a great sports party symbolising the annual period of restart for sports in France. The importance of using sporting and physical activities in the health programmes has raised national awareness in France which has been translated at the national level by sport, health and well-being. This plan was launched in 2012 and consists in promoting and developing the practice of physical and sporting activities as a public health factor. It lies on 15 principles forming a range of 47 actions organised towards two different typologies of people (general public/public with specific needs). The expansion of the physical and sporting activities for health opens new possibilities for the sport movement, as showed by the implementation since the end of the 2000 of new positions as sports and health coaches in the French Athletics Federation, as well as quite similar initiatives within the French Federation for Physical Education and Voluntary Gymnastics (FFEPGV) (Fédération d'Education Physique et de Gymnastique Volontaire).

[4]For example, with the *sports voucher*, a teenager aged between 15 and 18 can have a €25 discount on the membership fee in the club of his or her choice.

## 10.4 Characteristics of Sport Clubs

### *10.4.1 Characteristics of Sport Clubs: Size, the Way They Are Organised, Roots (Independent, Religion, Company, Single- or Multiple-Sport Club)*

The decrease in the number of clubs together with the increase of the number of licences resulted in a growth in the average size of clubs, from 84 licences in 2001 to 96 in 2012. This number reveals a 20 % increase in comparison to 2000 (French Ministry of Sports and Youth 2012) but we can note some territorial variations. The biggest clubs (about 123 licences each) are established in the Ile-de-France region (whose biggest town is Paris). The smallest clubs (about 65 licences per club) are established in a rural region: Limousin (whose capital is Limoges). Four regions can be highlighted thanks to a size ranking for clubs which do not respect the ranking according to the number of inhabitants. They are territories where the associative movement is particularly active around towns like Lille, Nantes, Rennes and Strasbourg (Table 10.2).

*Variations between sport disciplines*—The clubs affiliated to the French Federation of *Giraviation* (rotor crafting) have the highest number of members with 1,305 licences, whereas the smallest clubs are affiliated to the French federation of sand yachting with 6 licences on average. The French sailing federation ranks 5th (taking into consideration all types of federations all together) with an average of 284 licences per club. The French football federation which has the highest number of clubs (15,696) has reached an average of 126 licences per club (French Ministry of Sports and Youth 2012).

*Variations depending on the level of competition*—The clubs competing at the highest level are fewer (6 %) but their average number of members (257 licences) is significantly higher than the other clubs. They can be easily distinguished from the clubs that participate in national, regional and local (departmental) competitions. The clubs that do not attend competitions are the most numerous (31 %) and generally have an average of 94 members (Table 10.3).

**Table 10.2** Overview of the size of sport clubs and the size of regions in France (The French Ministry of Sports 2012)

| Region | Number of licences per club | Rank | Population | Rank |
|---|---|---|---|---|
| France | 96 | | 64,933,400 | |
| Alsace/Strasbourg | 100 | 4 | 1,852,325 | 14 |
| Rhône-Alpes/Lyon | 100 | 4 | 6,283,541 | 2 |
| Bretagne/Rennes | 100 | 4 | 3,217,767 | 7 |
| Pays de la Loire/Nantes | 103 | 3 | 3,601,113 | 5 |
| Nord-Pas de Calais/Lille | 108 | 2 | 4,042,015 | 4 |
| Île-de-France/Paris | 123 | 1 | 11,852,851 | 1 |

**Table 10.3** Number of members according to the clubs' level of practice (Beretti E, Calatayud P 2006, p. 5)

| Highest level of practice | Average number of members | Percentage of associations |
|---|---|---|
| Leisure/no competition | 94 | 31 % |
| Departmental competition | 103 | 18 % |
| Regional competition | 151 | 22 % |
| National competition | 180 | 23 % |
| International competition | 257 | 6 % |

**Table 10.4** Estimation of volunteering in sport associations (Ministère des sports 2006, p. 4)

| Roles of the volunteers | Average number per club | Estimation of the annual number of hours per volunteer | Estimation of the total number of volunteering hours per year |
|---|---|---|---|
| President | 1.1 | 254 | 279 |
| Treasurer | 1.1 | 156 | 203 |
| General Secretary | 1.3 | 167 | 217 |
| Coach | 5.9 | 379 | 2,236 |
| Other | 3.9 | 219 | 854 |
| Total | 13.5 | 224 | 3,789 |

*Variations between single-sport clubs and multisport clubs*—The clubs affiliated to Olympic single-sport federations are the biggest with 124 licences each. The multisport federations have clubs with an average of 94 licences. Finally, the non-Olympic single-sport federations barely exceed 52 licences per club (French Ministry of Sports and Youth 2012).

In accordance with the French law on the freedom of association of 1901, sport clubs are run in a democratic way. They are traditionally managed by a board composed of volunteers. The president, treasurer and general secretary share the main functions. Other volunteers get involved in the field as coaches or playing supporting roles (refer to Table 10.4). Some clubs pay the sport coaches. The best structured clubs have also employees for administrative, management or development missions.

### *10.4.2 Experienced Bottlenecks and Challenges by Sport Clubs*

The sporting practice organised within associations and the *smooth* running of clubs depend a lot on public funding whether it is direct or indirect (provision of sport facilities belonging to the municipality, often free of charge) and on volunteering. These items are often not enough clarified in the clubs' budgets (refer to Sect. 4.6 related to finance) and yet, they represent the pillars of the organisational model of finance for French associative clubs. This dependence leads to greater risks in the context of the growing economic and social crisis since 2008.

On the one hand, the increasing public debt for municipalities and public actors indeed raises queries on the ability of towns to continue to bear the free provision of sport facilities despite the growing interest in local sport as a social cohesion factor. Indeed, the French Ministry of Sports has identified more than 260,000 sport facilities and most of them (80 %) belong to the municipalities and 70 % of their management is performed directly by the municipality, whereas 15 % are granted to associations. On the other hand, the decrease of commitment for long-term volunteering (Schlesinger et al. 2013) seems to be an issue which, more globally, echoes individualism and the growing hopping of social behaviours observed in the developed countries. The potential costs related to these two elements can weigh on the clubs' finances as well as on their identity, encouraging them to act more as service providers (Chantelat et al. 2001).

Another recurring threat for the sport association movement is the difficulty to adapt to the development of demand, especially the high increase of *sports for health* and the practices of nature sports. The sport clubs often face both direct and indirect multifaceted competition: public and private for-profit offers, as well as prevalent self-organised practices in most of sports. Educational and marketing innovations are required to emerge from the traditional competitive offers for adults and children, and thus, to better meet the various expectations of the different market segments (from the very young children to the oldest people). While some federations start to diversify their sporting practice offers, the ability of the federal network and clubs to implement these offers is often partial and fragile because of the lack of professionalisation.

Professionalisation is a very sensitive matter in the sport associations. It could be defined as directing project management aiming at increasing the efficiency and effectiveness of an organisation without necessarily resulting in hiring employees (Chantelat 2001). In fact, it is more about rationalising the functioning: using tools, management and human resources practices in order to develop a real ability to provide services. It often implies the challenge of managing volunteers and employees whose expectations and forms of commitment are very different, which could create potential risks of conflicts (Amis et al. 1995; Cuskelly et al. 1999).

The challenges to respond to the identified threats are often taken on but not always fully exploited by many sport clubs and/or disciplines:

Pooling of means (human resources, material, projects, etc.) which sometimes results in clubs' gatherings and even club mergers in order to achieve a minimum critical size: The national sports federations as well as local public actors are generally the driving forces to encourage this pooling of means.

Quality approach through an increased professionalisation and sometimes through the labelisation of associative clubs (generally attributed according to the specifications) that are proposed by some federations, based on a method of self-assessment (Pigeassou 1997).

Enhancement of the positive externalities of the associative sport clubs activities: It is a major challenge, especially to legitimise public funding. This requires developing tools in order to understand the social, economic and environmental impact of clubs.

### *10.4.3 Recreational Sport and Professional Sport in Sport Clubs*

Recreational sport concerns more individual sports, whereas the evolution of competitive sport towards professional sport rather concerns team sports. This distinction is of course too brief, insofar as the dimension of recreational sport (health, well-being …) is a strong tendency of the evolution of sporting practices which should be assimilated by all the federations and their clubs because this practice is largely dominant (walking, swimming, cycling) and a 76 % increase in the number of subscriptions to the federations of nature sports for nautical activities between 2000 and 2011: according to the French Ministry of Sports and Youth (Cléron 2013). The survey on the sporting practices of the French in 2000 suggests two poles of sporting worlds: one marked by the diligence, or even a strong commitment in terms of participation in competitions, of membership to a club, or in terms of frequency of practice (rugby, martial arts, handball), and the other being more related to leisure activities and relaxation (skiing, sailing, table tennis). For a number of recreational and/or touristic sports, some federations have decided to accept commercial structures that offer sporting practices as part of federations like canoe-kayak, horse riding and sailing, for example. In some sports like golf, tennis or judo among others, it is more likely to find clubs acting as service providers that are very close to the model of service companies described by Chantelat et al. (2001). The growth of recreational sports partly explains the strong employment growth during the last 20 years and more recently the number of employees in clubs has increased from 74,000 to 81,000 between 2005 and 2010, according to the data collected by the French Ministry of Sports and Youth (Cléron 2013).

All the professional clubs emanate from the historical associative clubs. At the club level, the professional club is integrated into the supporting association, most often in the form of public limited company (except for volleyball where the associative status remains very dominant). We can count around 200 professional clubs, essentially in six team sports organising a professional championship in France (ranked by order of economic importance: football, rugby, basketball, handball, ice hockey and volleyball). Unlike in football, most professional clubs are small- or medium-sized companies valued at less than ten million euros, of which most contracts concern sport professionalisation (players and technical staff). As for the marketing and administrative positions, they are sometimes fulfilled by volunteers in the least wealthy clubs (Table 10.5).

In these professional sports, a league under the administrative supervision of a federation organises the competitions on both economical and sport sides (Bayle 2000). The originality of the French organisation model is the financial and direct relationship between professional sport and amateur sport. This financial link is reflected by the existence of a mandatory convention between the supporting association and the professional club, in the same way as between the federation and the professional league. Moreover, the legislation imposes financial retrocessions that come from television rights (from entertainment sports) to amateur sport (see Sect. 4.6

**Table 10.5** Average budget of the professional team sport clubs for men playing in the first division in France (CDES)

| | Football | Rugby | Basketball | Handball | Ice hockey | Volleyball |
|---|---|---|---|---|---|---|
| Number of clubs | 20 | 14 | 16 | 14 | 14 | 13 |
| Average budget | €64,866,000** | €18,325,000* | €4,301,000* | €3,349,000** | €1,368,000** | €1,414,000* |

Report from management control authorities. sport seasons 2011–2012* and 2012–2013**—data processing by CDES above) regarding the National Sport Development Centre (CNDS). It is important to note interesting evolutions for the women's elite football in France, since the French football federation now obliges professional clubs to have a women's section, thus developing the original concept of *mixed club* which is not very present in the other women's elite clubs in basketball, handball or volleyball (Bayle et al. 2013).

### 10.4.4 Activities for Sport Club Members: Training, Competition, Other Sport Activities, Non-sport Activities

Naturally, French sport clubs offer sport activities to their members. Traditionally, the offer of sport clubs is mainly composed of training sessions and competition. For the first one, depending on the sport disciplines, the French clubs offer collective practices with a coach during determined time slots, individual lessons or courses (or for limited-sized groups) on demand or the bare rental of sport facilities. For the second one, as part of their performance goals, the French clubs make sure that the teams and individual athletes are registered to the competitions, and they can even organise the trip, supervision and coaching during the events. Many of them schedule tournaments and internal training courses.

In addition, French sport clubs are less or more active beyond sport. Most of them try *to be a living place again*. In a society that is increasingly individualistic, several sport clubs are willing to offer other services to their members (joint purchasing, repairs, rental, sale of equipment), as well as other more friendly sporting activities (petanque tournament (bowls), road racing, hiking, rally) or non-sporting activities (sale of second-hand equipment, club house, organisation of friendly evenings, trips to attend sports events and so on). Intergenerational offers are emerging to allow families to practise a sporting activity all together, or grandparents to devote themselves to an activity while waiting for the children they look after doing their own activity.

Furthermore, clubs assert themselves as a vector of education and citizenship. Through a sporting activity, the clubs can also achieve other goals related to people's self-fulfilment or civic commitment. Some clubs also offer awareness campaigns about health food or the risks of all addictions, but also first-aid classes, as well as classes about the various volunteer functions related to sport coaching, refereeing and administration management. Some of them organise after-school tutoring or networking services: car sharing, babysitting, exchange of expertise, etc.

Finally, sport clubs get requests from the public authorities. The reform of the school pace encourages the municipalities to request sport clubs to supervise extracurricular workshops during the lunch break or after school. More broadly, sport clubs are increasingly offering their services to the surrounding establishments: retirement homes, leisure centres, medico-educational institutes and prisons. The challenge is mainly to secure permanent jobs by optimising the working hours of the employed sport coaches in addition to Wednesdays and evenings. At the state level, the demand consists in reaching the people who are remote from sport. The sport clubs are thus encouraged to increase the range of age groups they welcome. The offers are targeted to increasingly young children (under 3 years old) and increasingly old people (aged more than 50, more than 65 and so on). Specific efforts towards women are also required through various feminisation plans elaborated by the federations, at the request of the French ministry responsible for sports.

According to the figures of the last Eurobarometer dealing with physical and sporting activities, the answers of the French may seem paradoxical:

- 43 % of the French population indicated that they practise a sporting activity or do physical exercise on a regular or occasional basis.
- 16 % are members of a sport club; 4 % of them are members of another type of club, 4 % are members of a fitness centre, whereas 74 % are not members of any type of clubs.
- Yet, 88 % declared that they agree with the statement: Local sport clubs and other local providers offer many opportunities to be physically active.

### 10.4.5 *Professionalisation (Paid Employees and Volunteers, Training)*

The professionalisation of sport clubs has been a strong tendency during the last 20 years. It is reflected by the arrival of a higher number of employees as well as by a consideration given to training, but more largely, by the support provided to volunteer managers who hire employees.

This employment growth can be explained by the fact that the associative sport sector has been perceived by the political authorities, especially since the 1990s, as a recruiting ground with potential job opportunities to contribute, at its scale, to reduce unemployment. A lot of employment aid measures offered to the youth,[5] the associative sector[6] and the associative sport[7] have thus been mobilised to drastically decrease the employment costs.

The employment in the associative sport sector and clubs is characterised by the huge predominance of jobs for sport coaches (nine jobs out of ten in clubs; Camy, 2004) in comparison to administrative and managerial jobs. This predominance can be explained by the obligation, specifically in France within the European sporting landscape, to have diplomas which are recognised by the state whose training

[5] Contract of apprenticeship and professionalisation.

[6] "Contrat emploi-jeunes" (Youth employment contract), "contrat unique d'insertion" (single contract of occupation integration), then the so-called Contrat d'avenir (Contract for the future of people with minimum social benefits).

[7] The decision dated 27/07/1994 allowing tax exemptions of social security contributions or social security contributions on very limited flat-rate bases; the sport-employment programme (created in 1997) offers a government aid, sometimes completed by decreasing the regions, and regressive during 4 years, bearing the expenses in some cases for 80 % of the payroll during the first year and a maximum of 40 % during the last year.

courses have mainly benefited to the French Ministry of Sports.[8] Between 1995 and 2005, around 100,000 sport diplomas of this type were delivered. Between 65 and 70 % of the graduated as sport coaches from the French Ministry of Youth and Sports are probably full-time employees (Beaufils 2013), according to a survey about the occupational insertion of 2007 graduates. It seems that the contracts subsidised by the government are not dominant; nevertheless the median earning is very low (around €1,110/month) and the career development possibilities are generally poor. However, since 2006, the existence of a collective agreement about sport has allowed to provide a regulation framework to social dialogue and to start working on the management of human resources,[9] often a taboo subject in the associative sport clubs.

It must be said that the volunteer managers are generally not well prepared to fulfil their employer function. That is why, since a decade, some information and training policies, as well as supporting measures, have been implemented. The programme *Profession sport loisirs* (Recreational sport profession) (Fédération Nationale Profession Sport and Loisir), created in 1989, works almost like a temporary work agency in all the French departments. It allows the clubs to be freed from their social and administrative obligations regarding the staff management. It also avoids that employed sport coaches have recourse too often to short-term contracts, since they are usually recruited on a full-time basis directly by profession sport. At the same time as this initiative which is very close to the French Government and the Ministry of Sports, the federations have little by little supported more timidly the managers who hire employees, providing them with trainings (some federations created a training centre) and measures dedicated especially to them (as in the case of the French table tennis federation), as well as the creation—still timid—of employers' groups for each sport on determined territories (for instance, the French judo federation).

All the stakeholders that are present around the clubs, the federations, the Ministry of Sports and the regions in charge of the employment/training have therefore strongly urged to support the professionalisation movement of the associative sport. Their efforts were not sufficient to find sustainable and structuring solutions neither for the crumbling and weakness of the employment in the associative sport sector, nor for the issue related to its management in organisations having a lot of volunteers.

### 10.4.6 Finance (Revenues, Expenses, Balance)

A study conducted at the European level (European Commission 2011b) related to sport clubs of six disciplines (football, tennis, basketball, gymnastics, swimming, athletics) in eight countries (Germany, Denmark, Spain, France, the Netherlands,

---

[8] The French State certificate for Sport Coaches was replaced in 2011 by the professional certificate and advanced diplomas, respectively, for the levels 4 and 3 in the European classification.

[9] 8 pay grids, identification of the function for employees working as executives, easier access to professional training.

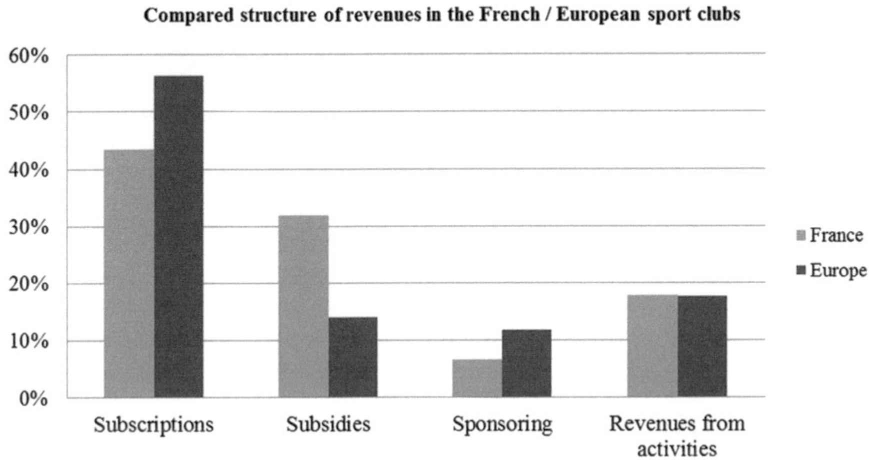


**Fig. 10.1** Compared structure of funding in the French/European sport clubs (European Commission 2011b)

Lithuania, the Czech Republic, the United Kingdom) allows to draw up the financing structure of these clubs as well as their expenses. The French sport clubs (there are more than 200,000) can be positioned in comparison to the other European Union's countries from the figures gathered during the reporting year (2009).

#### 10.4.6.1 Main Revenue Items

The average amount of funding for a club is about €64,871 in France, which has to be put into perspective because of a risk of potential bias in favour of the big clubs in the survey.[10] Besides, there are great disparities: since the median is very different from the average, it is established only at €35,098. The budgets of the richest clubs push the average up. The sport association that has the highest resources gathers €894,000 in terms of revenues. The distribution of the budget between the major revenue items shows some features specific to France (Fig. 10.1).

The breakdown of these revenues from activities divided into subcategories also shows the closeness between France and the European Union from this point of view. Yet, we can note that the subscriptions and sponsoring represent a relatively smaller part in France than in Europe, in spite of the advantageous provisions related to donations and patronage that confer entitlement to a tax reduction for 60 % of the donation. On the contrary, the subsidies have a significant relative higher weight in

[10] A study conducted by the French Ministry of Sports, Youth and Associative Life estimated in 2005 (Stat Info 2005) the average budget of the French sport associations to be around €31,000 (reference year: 2003). This confirms that we can possibly fear a bias in favour of the biggest clubs in the European study published in 2011.

France, given that the financial aid from the territorial authorities (local and regional), in particular from the municipalities, is high and widespread. This relates to the findings of the study on sport funding in general (Andreff et al. 2009). France ranks first in Europe in terms of support from the local authorities, with €163 per inhabitant. The scale of the action taken by the territorial authorities can thus be interpreted as aiming at seeking greater equity. This public contribution partially replaces private expenditure and explains that the French citizens are less consenting to pay than in other countries that have quite a similar level of GDP per inhabitant. As a result, the subscription fee is moderate, especially in comparison to Spain where subscriptions are very expensive. The revenues from activities—which show the clubs' dynamism and their ability to generate their own revenues by selling products or services—are at the same level in the French clubs as in European clubs.

The contribution from local authorities is all the more noteworthy because in addition to these financial contributions (direct) there is also an indirect support through the provision of sports facilities belonging almost entirely to the local authorities, as well as through the provision of staff, especially for maintenance tasks (Bourg and Nys 2012). The associative sector also benefits from an advantageous taxation regime in terms of VAT, and often gets an exemption for the entertainment tax (tax that applies to the sports events and which usually goes to the municipality). Employment aid programmes are also highly developed, with a gradually decreasing contribution from the public authorities over the years. There is a real challenge for the clubs: to secure the employment sustainability by developing their own resources (this challenge is often not achieved).

Volunteering is also a resource to finance sport clubs. With an average of 0.64 volunteer for 100 inhabitants France ranks second in Europe behind the Netherlands (European Commission 2011b). One may wonder about enhancing the value of volunteering, which means to think about the efficiency of voluntary work, compared to paid jobs. Andreff (2009) suggests an interval of values by enhancing the value of the volunteers' working hours according to the national average income (high assumption), on the basis of half of this salary only (low assumption). With 271,000 full-time equivalent hours, it is estimated that the French volunteers represented between 2.544 and 5.089 billion euros in 2005. France ranks first in Europe, followed by Germany (3,965 billion euros), and the Netherlands (2,327 billion euros).

#### 10.4.6.2 Main Expenditure Items

The clubs' expenditure pattern shows again some specificities of French clubs, compared to the other European clubs (Fig. 10.2). Thus, salaries have a relatively lower impact, which might show some delay in terms of professionalisation, despite the development of sport management courses in sports universities. The rental costs of sport facilities are also proportionally less significant, which can be explained by the widespread provision of sports equipment by the municipalities, unlike in other European countries where private facilities are used. On the contrary, we can observe an over-representation of the travel expenses, which deserves to be

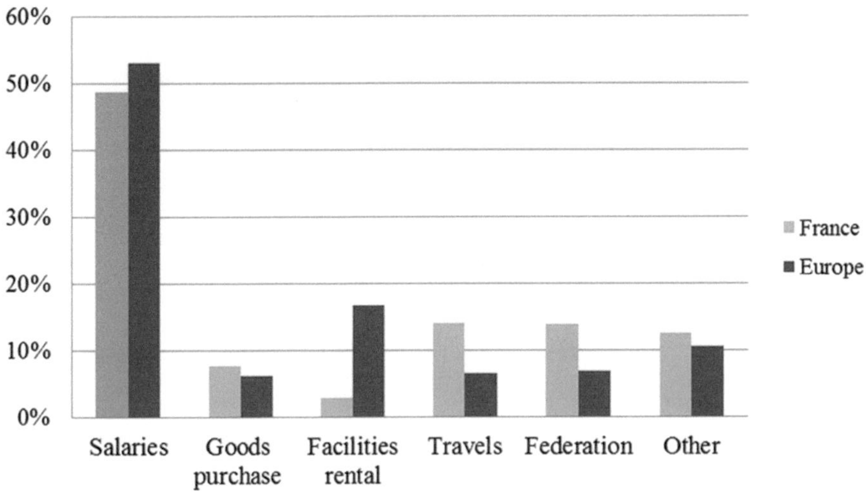


**Fig. 10.2** Compared expenditure structure of the French/European sport clubs (European Commission 2011b)

considered in a complementary study in order to identify potential undisclosed compensations paid to the managerial staff. The amounts retransferred to the French federation are also more important than in Europe, because the clubs' contribution to the French federal functioning system seems to be more substantial.

This average structure of the budget conceals something: behind it there is actually a huge heterogeneity. Both funding and expenditure of sport associations vary depending on the size of the organisation, the sport discipline, the level of competition and the presence (or not) of employees in the organisation (Barget and Chavinier-Réla 2011). Furthermore, some authors (Chantelat et al. 2001) have shown that socio-economic logics were decisive. They suggest a typology of clubs with six categories (each one referring to a socio-economic logic related to their functioning):

- The sociable club: The expenditure is planned to create social relationships.
- The traditional club: The expenditure is balanced between sociability and sporting practice.
- The club focused on sport: The main part of expenditure is for the sporting practice.
- The professionalised club: The expenditure is targeted to the delivery of sporting results.
- The community, professional club: The expenditure is balanced between sporting practice, quest for performance and sociability.
- The service-provider club: It is very close to the model of a service-provider company.
- Are French club sports funding different of French associations funding?

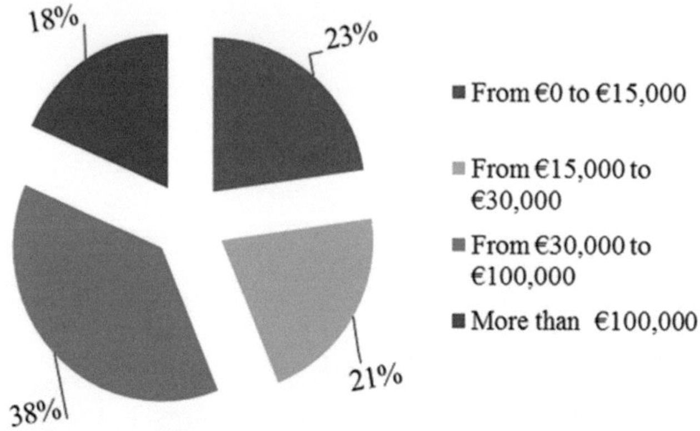


**Fig. 10.3** Distribution of French clubs according to their budget bracket (European Commission 2011b)

In the last part, we propose to focus on the French specificities vis-à-vis the sport clubs in Europe from what we learnt from the European study on the funding of grass-roots sport. Our question is as follows: Are French clubs representative of third-sector* institutions? Of course, sport clubs belong to the non-profit private sector including non-profit associations but which comparisons can we draw between the financing of associations and the financing of sport clubs? We will try to answer this question by explaining the sources of diversification of revenues and studying the sustainability of solidarity mechanisms.

The size of the budget is extremely variable, as shown in Fig. 10.3. Whereas a significant proportion of clubs (22.7 %) have a budget lower than €15,000, others (18.4 % of the sport associations) have financial resources above €100,000. The minimum amount which was announced in terms of revenues was €100 and the maximum value €894,456. The median shows that half of the clubs have a budget below €35,098.

Such disparities can be explained by many factors (Muller 2005) in the associative sector in general (Tchernonog 2007a, b) and especially in the sporting sector. According to this last publication, the fact to employ people (status of *hiring associations*), the level of practice (from leisure level to international level) and the type of sport discipline taught in the association are decisive.

First of all, the club's level of structuration and professionalisation seems to be crucial regarding its ability to develop its own resources, and especially revenues from activities. From this point of view, sporting institutions have gone through profound changes for about 30 years, and there are more than 350,000 jobs (in the sporting sector, not related to clubs) focused mainly on sport management (Leroux and Dalla-Praia 2012). The recruiting process of employees is largely conducted in sport science universities, since the number of students in sport management courses has experienced a noteworthy growth in spite of the growing competition with business schools. While 31 % of the French sport clubs have at least one employee (sometimes with a government-subsidised contract), 69 % of clubs are run only by volunteers. The fact of having employees influences the club's budget: the associations that hire employees have an average budget of €64,833, whereas the associations with no employees have an average budget of €13,255 (French Ministry of Sports 2006). The associations with employees have a budget that is four to five times higher than the others.[11] The expenditure structure is also affected because the *hiring clubs* dedicate 43 % of their financial resources to the payroll, whereas the expenditure related to the activities is preponderant in the clubs with no employee (74 % of their total expenditure). These employment aid measures exist, with a system of degression for the contributions from local authorities over several years (3–5 in general), but they raise the question of preserving these jobs when the subsidy ends.

The level of sporting practice has also a strong influence on the size of the budget, since the correlation between these two variables is positive: the higher the level achieved by the top team in collective sport or the best athletes in individual sports, the more the budget increases. The statistics from the French Ministry of Sports (2006) show that the associations whose purpose only concerns recreational sports have resources around €13,000, whereas the clubs with some athletes participating to international competitions have resources around €58,000. Again, it is difficult to establish the causal link: clubs need to have sufficient means at the beginning to compete in a high-level championship, and such participation paves the way for extra revenues, especially in terms of ticketing, sponsoring and subsidies.

In financial terms, the sports discipline is also a crucial differentiating factor (see Table 10.6). The data provided by the Statistics Unit (Beretti and Calatayud 2006) show that 30,000 of sport associations that are not affiliated to an authorised sports federation (15 % of all the French clubs) have budgets which are less than half than those of the affiliated associations. The highest budgets per members are those of team sport clubs: rugby, football, basketball and volleyball. Volleyball ranks only 13th in terms of clubs' average budget, due to the rather limited number of members per club (52). The sport associations which have the highest budget are rugby clubs (€96,550): their average budget is three times higher than the average value calculated for all the disciplines. We can observe that the financing of some individual sports is well ranked, considering the estimated budgets; it is the case for swimming and tennis. Other disciplines are emerging in terms of budget per member, especially table tennis and athletics.

These inequalities persist despite the fact that diverse mechanisms have been mobilised in order to ensure some fairness between clubs practising different disciplines with various different levels of practice. These sport policies show France's attachment to the European model of sport funding. They aim at preserving the sport pyramid starting from grass-roots sport (clubs) to high-level sport (entertainment).

[11] Based on the information available so far, it is difficult to know if the importance of the budget is a consequence of the recruitment of employees who are able to request more means to club's stakeholders or, if on the contrary, it is the triggering factor of the recruiting process. Unless it is both: when a certain resource threshold is reached, the club can recruit people, and the recruitment is a valuable asset to develop further the activities and the corresponding financial incomes.

**Table 10.6** Average budget of associations per sport discipline (Beretti and Calatayud 2006, p. 4)

| Disciplines | Average budget | Average number of members | Budget per member | Subscription per member |
|---|---|---|---|---|
| Rugby | 96,500 | 206 | 468 | 69 |
| Swimming | 69,906 | 341 | 205 | 96 |
| Football | 45,156 | 179 | 252 | 48 |
| Basketball | 36,892 | 143 | 258 | 49 |
| Tennis | 33,678 | 174 | 194 | 66 |
| Judo | 25,899 | 145 | 179 | 95 |
| Dance | 21,639 | 128 | 169 | 91 |
| Athletics | 19,341 | 88 | 220 | 38 |
| Hiking | 18,689 | 144 | 130 | 16 |
| Table tennis | 18,304 | 59 | 310 | 48 |
| Gymnastics | 16,948 | 143 | 118 | 63 |
| Karate | 16,808 | 81 | 207 | 112 |
| Volleyball | 14,917 | 52 | 286 | 37 |
| Bowl sports (bocce) | 12,819 | 78 | 164 | 17 |
| Bicycle touring | 6,915 | 52 | 133 | 14 |
| Multisport | 65,521 | 466 | 141 | 40 |

Such policies with a vocation for redistribution are sometimes implemented by the sporting institutions themselves, as illustrated by the aid fund for amateur football. Based on a protocol (contractual agreement) between the French football federation and the French professional football league, the latter pays each year a contribution to the aid fund for amateur football. The French tennis federation retransfers the profits from the Roland Garros tournament to the decentralised bodies and clubs in order to implement tennis development programmes for different target audiences (seniors, women, beginners, mini-tennis). Such retransfers are another example of the solidarity existing within the federal sport system. From a net profit of about 70 million euros (based on a budget of 160 million in 2012), 27 million euros have helped to develop grass-roots tennis. This is a unique example of this magnitude, due to the success of the tournament and to the federation's decision made during the era of Philippe Chatrier to manage the tournament itself in order to keep the profits (Bayle 2014).

Such solidarity is spread by the state's action (who redirects part of the money coming from sports betting towards grass-roots sports). If the French State ranks 6th for the amount allocated to sport by the government (€51.4 per inhabitant according to the European Commission 2011a), it is mainly due to the National Sport Development Centre (CNDS). The CNDS, which was created in 2006 (but succeeding to the FNDS which was functioning with the same funding), is a public organisation handling administrative matters that benefits from revenues assigned by the Finance Law. The revenues come from a part of tax withholding performed on the amounts at stake both for the games managed by *La Française des jeux*[12] (1.8 %)

[12] 72 % of this company is owned by the French State.

and for sport betting run by all the authorised operators (1.5 %). What is probably even more surprising is that another taxation (5 %) is applied on the transfer of broadcasting rights for sport events. This shows a certain originality, since there is both a vertical solidarity (between professional and grass-roots sport) and a horizontal solidarity (between broadcast sports, especially football, and the other sports that are not—or poorly—broadcast). These revenues are indeed broadly distributed between sport associations and decentralised federal organisations (local (i.e. departmental) and regional committees of the different sports).

As a conclusion, it should be noted that the policies aiming at reducing the funding gaps between sport clubs do not seem to be strong enough to regulate successfully the system which remains very unequal. In this context, it can be useful to bear in mind the challenges to be taken on by the French sport clubs, as they were identified in the European Commission report of 2011:

- Raise individuals' willingness to pay.
- Balance the various funding sources to have less dependence on one stream of funding, adapt the offer to the needs of households to increase membership and participation rates and increase funding from other (private) stakeholders.
- Secure the revenue from lotteries, betting and gambling and reinforce solidarity mechanisms with channel revenue from the high level to the grass-roots level: including through solidarity within the sport movement: although there are regulated mechanisms channelling the revenue from lotteries, betting and gambling and media rights to sport, these revenues represent less than 1 % of the total budget of the sport system.

## 10.5 Conclusion

Historically, the sport sector in France is characterised by a public, interventionist model in which sport clubs are the cornerstones of a truly consolidated sport movement.

Since the 1970s: an increasing number of private clubs have been opened; the individual sport practice (without supervision) has faded and the state has developed its own sport offer. Moreover, the whole organisation has become more and more professional, the regulations have been strengthened, the relationship with the local authorities has become more efficient, etc.

Today, the French sport clubs have to face several challenges. The main one is the need to adapt to the evolution of social demand both in granting a special attention to people who are not interested in sports and in adapting themselves to the increasing demands of new consumers/members.

In this context of competitiveness, making sport associations sustainable has become the main issue to come. The knowledge of the social functions fulfilled by the associative sport sector is the actual challenge.

## References


Agulhon M (1978) La France de 1914 à 1940. Nathan, Paris

Amis J, Slack T, Berett T (1995) The structural antecedents of conflict in voluntary sport organizations. Leisure Stud 4:13–26

Andreff W (2009) Public and private sport financing in Europe: the impact of financial crisis. In: 84th Western Economic Association International Conference, Vancouver

Andreff W, Montel J, Dutoya J (2009) Le modèle européen de financement du sport: quels risques? Revue juridique et économique du sport 90:75–85

Arnaud P, Camy J (1986) La naissance du mouvement sportif associatif en France: sociabilités et formes de pratiques sportives. PUL, Lyon

Augustin J-P (1992) Les espaces des sports collectifs. Mappemonde 2:29–31

Barget E, Chavinier-Réla S (2011) Analyse de la diversification des recettes des clubs. Jurisport:32–33

Bayle E (2000) La dynamique de la professionnalisation des sports collectifs: les cas du football, du basket-ball et du rugby. Revue Inter des Sc du Sport et de l'Éduc Phye, Eds AFRAPS (52):33–60

Bayle E (2014) Philippe Chatrier à l'épreuve de l'argent dans le sport. In: Bayle E (ed) Les grands dirigeants du sport. Louvain-la-Neuve, De Boeck, pp 173–190

Bayle E, Jaccard E, Vonnard P (2013) Synergies football masculin et féminin: vers un nouveau modèle stratégique pour les clubs professionnels européens? REMS 39:5–21

Beretti E, Calatayud P (2006) Le budget des associations sportives. Ministère des sports: Stat-Info n 06-05.http://www.sports.gouv.fr/IMG/archives/pdf/STAT-Info_n_06-05_avril_2006_-_Le_budget_des_associations_sportives.pdf. Accessed 05 Jan 2015

Beaufils H (2013) Le premier emploi des diplômés de la jeunesse et des sports. Ministère des sports: Stat-Info n 13-02. http://www.sports.gouv.fr/IMG/pdf/stat-info_no13-02_de_juin_2013.pdf. Accessed 05 Jan 2015

Bourg J-F, Nys J-F (2012) Clubs sportifs et stratégies des collectivités territoriales. Editions Territorial, Voiron

Camy J, A (2004) Vocasport, La formation dans le domaine du sport en Europe" Ezus/EOSE/ENSSEE, rapport pour la Commission européenne. http://eose.org/wp-content/uploads/2014/03/vocasport-Final-Report-English-Version.pdf. Accessed 05 Jan 2015

Centre de Droit et d'Economie du Sport (CDES) http://www.cdes.fr/index.php?id=uk12. Accessed 05 Jan 2015

Centre National d'Appui et de Ressources du Sport (2009) Le sport en quelques chiffres. http://cnar-sport.franceolympique.com/cnar/fichiers/File/CNAR_Sport/Fiches_de_presentation/fiche_chiffres_du_sportx.pdf. Accessed 05 Jan 2015

Chantelat P, Bouhaouala M, Champely S (2001) Les logiques socio-économiques des clubs sportifs amateurs: une analyse des budgets. STAPS:61–78

Chantelat P (2001) Professionnalisation des organisations sportives. L'Harmattan, Paris

Cléron E (2013) Dix ans de licences sportives: 2001–2011. Ministère des sports: Stat-Info n 13-03.http://www.sports.gouv.fr/IMG/pdf/stat-info_no13-03_de_aout_2013.pdf

Comité National Olympique et Sportif Français. Sentez-vous sport, annual national program. http://sentezvoussport.fr/accueil.php

Cuskelly G, Boag A, McIntyre N (1999) Differences in organisational commitment between paid and volunteer administrators in sport. Eur J Sport Manag 6:39–61

Délétang B (1986) Le mouvement sportif ouvrier ou l'enjeu idéologique du sport. In: Arnaud P, Camy J (eds) La Naissance du mouvement sportif associatif en France. PUL, Lyon, pp 309–326

Dumazedier J (1962) Vers une Civilisation des loisirs? Editions du Seuil, Paris

European Commission (2011a) Study on the funding of grassroots Sport in EU. Deutsche Sporthochschule, Köln

European Commission (2011b) EuroStrastégies, Amnyos, CDES & Deutsche Sporthochschule Köln (2011). Study on the funding of Grassroots Sport in European Union. vol. 1 and 2. This survey has been requested by the European Commission, Directorate-General for Education and Culture and co-ordinated by Directorate-General for Internal Market. http://ec.europa.eu/internal_market/top_layer/services/sport/study_en.htm. Accessed 05 Jan 2015

European Commission (2014) Special Eurobarometer 412, Sport and physical activity. Report. Fieldwork: November–December 2013. This survey has been requested by the European Commission, Directorate-General for Education and Culture and co-ordinated by Directorate-General for Communication. http://ec.europa.eu/public_opinion/archives/ebs/ebs_412_en.pdf. Accessed 05 Jan 2015

Fédération d'Education Physique et de Gymnastique Volontaire. Présentation de la fédération. http://www.sport-sante.fr/ffepgv/dossiers/english-presentation/?rub=38&dossier=english. Accessed 05 Jan 2015

Fédération Nationale Profession Sport & Loisir. Présentation de la fédération. http://www.profession-sport-loisirs.fr/presentation/federation. Accessed 05 Jan 2015

French Ministry of Sport. Chiffres clés du sport et données détaillées. http://www.sports.gouv.fr/organisation/publication-chiffres-cles/Statistiques/. Accessed 05 Jan 2015

Garrier G (1986) Introduction. In: Arnaud P, Camy J (eds) La Naissance du mouvement sportif associatif en France. PUL, Lyon, pp 9–10

Garrigou A (1986) La naissance du mouvement associatif sportif sous la troisième République. In: Arnaud P, Camy J (eds) La Naissance du mouvement sportif associatif en France. PUL, Lyon, pp 241–258

Lagrée M (1986) Sport et sociabilité catholique en France au début du XXe siècle. In: Arnaud P, Camy J (eds) La Naissance du mouvement sportif associatif en France. PUL, Lyon, pp 327–338

Lanfranchi P (1986) Apparition et affirmation du football. In: Arnaud P, Camy J (eds) La Naissance du mouvement sportif associatif en France. PUL, Lyon, pp 259–274

Leroux N, Dalla-Praia Y (2012) Quand le management du sport se professionnalise: regard croisé sur un secteur en mutation. Revue Pol et Parlementaire, juin:47–51

Loret A (1995) Génération glisse. Editions Autrement, Paris

Ministère de la Jeunesse, des Sports et de la Vie Associative (2012) Le poids économique du sport en 2012

Ministère des sports (2011) Les principales activités physiques et sportives pratiquées en France en 2010. http://www.sports.gouv.fr/IMG/archives/pdf/Stat_Info_no11-02_de_novembre_2011.pdf. Accessed 05 Jan 2015

Ministère des sports (2013) Atlas national des fédérations sportives, 2012. http://www.sports.gouv.fr/autres/atlas.pdf. Accessed 05 Jan 2015

Muller L (2005) Âge, diplôme, niveau de vie. principaux facteurs sociodémographiques de la pratique sportive et des activités choisies. Ministère des sports: Stat Info n 05-05. http://www.sports.gouv.fr/IMG/archives/pdf/STA_INFO_n_05-05.pdf. Accessed 05 Jan 2015

Pigeassou C (1997) Les organisations de services sportifs. In: Pigeassou C, Garrabos C (eds) Management des organisations de services sportifs. PUF, Paris, pp 309–331

Schlesinger T, Egli B, Nagel S (2013) "Continue or terminate?" Determinants of long-term volunteering in sports clubs. Eur Sport Manag Q 13:32–53

Tchernonog V (2007a) État du paysage associatif français. Centre d'Économie de la Sorbonne, Paris

Tchernonog V (2007b) Le paysage associatif français. Ministère des sports: Stat-Info n 07-04. http://www.associations.gouv.fr/IMG/pdf/Stat-Info_07-04.pdf. Accessed 05 Jan 2015

# Chapter 11
# Sport Clubs in Germany

**Christoph Breuer, Svenja Feiler, and Pamela Wicker**

## 11.1 Introduction

Germany is home to approximately 80.8 million people who live in 16 federal states (Destatis 2014a). Thereby, Germany is the most heavily populated country in the European Union and German is the most frequently spoken first language within the EU (EU 2014). A recent population survey reveals that 16.3 million people who live in Germany have a migration background (Destatis 2013). This shows that Germany is home to many different cultures and ethnicities. Since 1990, the former German Democratic Republic (Eastern Germany) is united with the Federal Republic of Germany (former Western Germany). Today, Germany is the biggest economy within the EU. Apart from large international companies, the German economy is characterised by consisting of many small- and medium-sized enterprises. Main sectors within the German economy include among others automobile production, mechanical and electrical engineering, and chemicals (EU 2014). Cultural-wise, Germany is known as the land of poets and thinkers and has a rich cultural scene with roughly 4,800 museums and 35 million yearly visits to theatres and orchestras (Destatis 2014b; Deutscher Bühnenverein 2014).

The non-profit sector in Germany has a long tradition and takes on greater significance for society, politics, and economy (Zimmer et al. 2013). German sport clubs are part of the third sector and amount to one-quarter of all third-sector organisations in the country (Krimmer and Priemer 2013). Although German non-profit sport clubs have to face competition from other sport providers, e.g. fitness studios, the sport clubs are still the main sport providers to a broad population in Germany. This is due to the fact that sport clubs offer affordable sport programmes, both in the

C. Breuer (✉) • S. Feiler • P. Wicker
Department of Sport Economics and Sport Management, German Sport University Cologne, Cologne, Germany
e-mail: breuer@dshs-koeln.de; s.feiler@dshs-koeln.de; p.wicker@dshs-koeln.de



C. Breuer et al. (eds.), *Sport Clubs in Europe*, Sports Economics, Management and Policy 12, DOI 10.1007/978-3-319-17635-2_11

fields of recreational and professional sport and in individual as well as team sports (Heinemann 2007). Due to the importance of sport clubs, different studies have dealt with the background, characteristics, and the situation of the clubs. In this regard, several studies focused on particular regions within Germany and the respective sport clubs (e.g. Emrich et al. 1998, 1999; Nagel et al. 2004) or on particular sports, e.g. gymnastics (Digel et al. 1992). Moreover, studies analysing the structures and finances of sport clubs were conducted (Emrich et al. 2001; Emrich 1998; Heinemann and Schubert 1994). Since 2005, the so-called *Sport Development Report—Analysis of the situation of sport clubs in Germany* gives regular information on the development of structures within German sport clubs (Breuer 2007, 2009, 2011, 2013a, b; Breuer and Wicker 2011a; Breuer and Feiler 2014). The *Sport Development Report* is a nationwide online survey among sport clubs in Germany which is conducted every 2 years and designed as a panel study. The project started in 2005 with the first wave. Until now, five survey waves have been conducted.

This country chapter gives an overview of sport clubs in Germany, starting with a short overview of the origin of sport clubs in Germany as well as the position of sport clubs in the national sport structure. The second part gives an overview of the role and relevance of sport clubs for society and policy, including sport club participation rates and political as well as societal embedding. The third part is the largest one, dealing with and displaying main characteristics of sport clubs in Germany. This includes basic characteristics such as size and organisational form as well as problems and challenges, types of sports and activities for sport club members, employment structures, as well as finances. Moreover, the fourth part concentrates on a particular topic within German sport clubs, namely gender aspects. The conclusion rounds up this chapter.

## 11.2 History and Context

The origin of sport clubs in Germany dates back to the early nineteenth century when the first so-called *Turnvereine* (meaning gymnastic clubs), initiated by Friedrich Ludwig Jahn, were established. Further sport clubs offering rowing, skating, cycling, and swimming were founded from 1836 onwards (DSB 2003; Heinemann and Horch 1981). Later on, various other clubs offering different types of sports followed. Figure 11.1 displays the years of foundation of today's sport clubs in Germany, based on data from the fifth wave of the *Sport Development Report* (Breuer and Feiler 2014). It can be seen that many of Germany's existing sport clubs have been established between 1960 and 1999.

Sport clubs in Germany are the main pillar of a broad and self-organised sport provision (Digel 1988; Hartmann-Tews 1996). Sport clubs as voluntary organisations of the third sector are characterised through certain features and can thereby be distinguished from for-profit organisations. The features can be distinguished into constitutive and economic. The five constituent features include the following: (1) membership in sport clubs is voluntary, meaning that members can freely decide

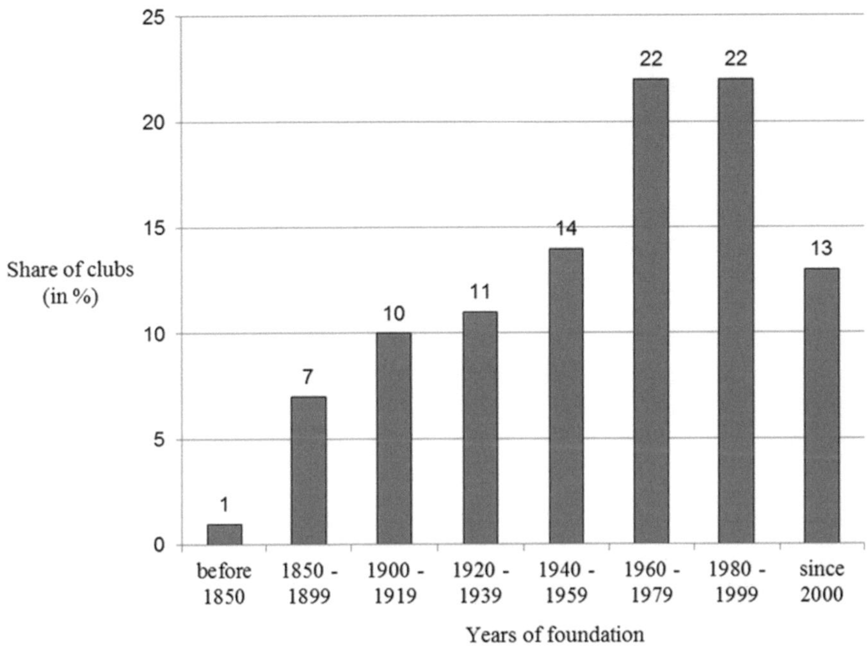


**Fig. 11.1** Establishment of sport clubs in Germany (Breuer and Feiler 2014, p. 3)

to enter into the club and to leave the club; (2) sport clubs are autonomous; (3) sport clubs focus on the interests of their members; (4) decision structures in sport clubs are democratic; and (5) sport clubs rely on voluntary work (Heinemann and Horch 1981). The economic features are a non-profit orientation, identity of member roles, autonomous revenues, and the principle of solidarity (Horch 1994). The non-profit orientation does not mean that the clubs cannot make profit. However, due to the non-distribution constraint (Hansmann 1980), they are not allowed to distribute surpluses among their members. Consequently, sport clubs are not following profit-maximising goals which for-profit organisations do.

### *11.2.1 Position of Sport Clubs Within the National Sport Structure*

The German sport system has a pyramid structure, with the non-profit sport clubs building the basis for mass sport provision in Germany (Petry and Hallmann 2013). Today, Germany is home to over 91,000 sport clubs which are spread throughout the country. The federal state with the largest number of clubs is North-Rhine Westphalia (19,496), followed by Bavaria (12,112) and Baden-Wuerttemberg (11,461) (DOSB 2012). The sport system is headed by the German Olympic Sports Confederation

(DOSB) which is the umbrella organisation of the voluntary sport sector in Germany. The middle of the pyramid consists of 98 membership organisations belonging to the DOSB, namely 34 Olympic sports federations, 28 non-Olympic sports federations, 16 regional sports confederations (analogous to the 16 federal states in Germany), and 20 federations with special tasks. The federal sport confederations represent the sport clubs' interests in politics and give assistance and support to the sport clubs in different fields, e.g. which possibilities exist to cooperate with schools. With regard to types of sports, the largest number of clubs and divisions within clubs, respectively, exists for football (25,641), followed by gymnastics (20,189), shooting (14,914), table tennis (10,685), and tennis (9,506) (DOSB 2012). Although sport is autonomous in Germany as described above (see Sect. 11.2), the non-profit sport clubs receive public subsidies from different instances, e.g. from the district or community or the federal state (also see Sect. 11.4.6).

## 11.3 Role of Sport Clubs in Policy and Society

### *11.3.1 Sport Club Participation*

In Germany, the membership numbers in sport clubs amount to 27.7 million. Taking into account that Germany has a population of roughly 80 million citizens, over one-third of the German population is a member of a sport club.[1] The integrative character of sport clubs in Germany is underlined by the fact that higher shares of the population are members of sport clubs than of other organisations of the third sector (Rittner and Breuer 2004). The latest data on sport club participation show that the share of males among members is higher than the share of females throughout all age groups and geographic regions. This is supported by the following numbers: In relation to the population, 35 % of all German males and 23 % of all females are members of a sport club. The fact that men are more likely to practice sport in German sport clubs than women is confirmed by empirical studies (e.g. Wicker et al. 2012c). Comparing the five federal states of the former German Democratic Republic (Eastern Germany) which are part of the Federal Republic of Germany since 1990 with the remaining federal states (Western Germany), some differences can be observed: relative to the respective populations in the different regions, the share of people who are members of sport clubs is lower in the Eastern part than in the Western part. This applies to all age and gender groups. The gap is particularly large in the age group of the 7–14-year-olds, both for boys and girls: in the Western federal states, 86 % of all boys in this age group are members of a sport club, whereas this applies only to 55 % in the Eastern part. Nearly the same difference can be observed for girls, with a membership rate of roughly two-thirds in this age

[1] It has to be considered that the 27.7 million refer to memberships, meaning that one person can be a member in various sport clubs and thereby accounts for more than one membership. Thus, the actual number is probably lower than one-third.

group in the Western and approximately one-third in the Eastern states (DOSB 2012). Research further showed that several characteristics such as age, the quadratic term of age (which allows measuring saturation effects), gender, migration background, working time, and time for caring for children/relatives are significant predictors of being active in a sport club. In this regard, negative effects are found for people with high working times and a high weekly workload for bringing up children or caring for relatives. Moreover, women and migrants are less likely to practice sports in a sport club. The effects of age and age squared show that age has a negative impact on sport club participation whereas age squared shows a positive effect, indicating that sport club participation first decreases with increasing age and then increases from a certain age onwards (Wicker et al. 2013c).

Going further into detail with demographic factors it can be observed that in German sport clubs, different population groups like the youth and the elderly as well as people with a migration background are represented. Regarding age it can be observed that the share of children and adolescents under 19 years relative to total club members reaches 24 % on average. Within the German population, the same group reaches a share of 15 %. Thus, German sport clubs are obviously providing attractive sport programmes for the youth since this group is overrepresented in sport clubs compared to the population (Breuer and Feiler 2013a). Although participation rates in German sport clubs among the youth are highest compared to other age groups, a longitudinal study among young people in North-Rhine Westphalia found out that there is fluctuation among young sport club members over the years (Brettschneider and Kleine 2002). Nevertheless, sport clubs have more children and adolescents among their members than any other non-profit organisations in Germany (Rittner and Breuer 2004). In contrast to high participation rates among the youth relative to the respective population group, the opposite applies to the group of seniors, i.e. people aged 60 years and older. Although the share of seniors within sport clubs amounts to nearly one-fifth of all members (19 %), this group is still stronger represented in the population, with a proportion of 27 % relative to the whole population (Breuer and Feiler 2013a). This finding is in accordance with prior studies (for an overview see Rittner and Breuer 2004). However, the share of the elderly among sport clubs members has significantly increased from 2009 to 2011 (Breuer and Feiler 2013a) and sport clubs are generally more successful in integrating seniors than other organisations of the third sector (Rittner and Breuer 2004). Regarding people with a migration background, latest survey data on sport clubs in Germany show that two-thirds of all clubs have migrants among their members. Relative to all club members, migrants reach a proportion of 6 %. The gender distribution among migrants in sport clubs reveals that nearly 70 % are male and 30 % are female. The integrative function of sport clubs is underlined by the fact that a total of nearly 20 % of German sport clubs have migrants among their volunteers, although this number has significantly decreased over the last 4 years (Breuer and Feiler 2014).

Apart from gender and age, further demographic and socio-economic factors have an impact on participation rates in sport clubs in Germany. One of the first investigating such factors was Schlagenhauf (1977). He found that particularly for women, social class plays an important role for being member of a sport club. In this context, further studies detected that income and educational level are positive predictors of sport club membership, meaning that people with a higher income and a higher educational level are more likely to be members of sport clubs (Nagel 2003).

### 11.3.2 Societal and Political Embedding

German sport clubs exist in a three-sector economy and come into play in situations of market and government failure (Heinemann 1995; Weisbrod 1986). If public sport provision (e.g. adult evening classes) and provision by commercial sport providers (e.g. fitness centres) cannot satisfy the heterogeneous demand of the population, non-profit sport providers, i.e. sport clubs, fulfil this task (Weisbrod 1998). In this role, non-profit sport clubs are the main providers for mass sport in Germany and thereby contribute significantly to public welfare (Heinemann 1995, 2007; Rittner and Breuer 2004), which makes them eligible to seek public funding (Heinemann and Horch 1981; Weisbrod 1964). Sport clubs are not only beneficial to individuals who participate in sports and thereby gather personal benefit (e.g. fitness), but they are also beneficial to the population since they are able to produce public goods such as national sporting success which fosters civic pride (Gratton and Taylor 2000). This particularly happens through the promotion of young talents within sport clubs which nurture the development of squad athletes. In Germany, 12 % of the clubs are home to squad athletes and thereby build the basis for elite sport (Breuer and Feiler 2014).

Furthermore, sport clubs, not only in Germany, are valuable to society due to the output of positive externalities such as youth promotion, social integration, crime prevention, and health (Handy and Brudney 2007; Heinemann 1995, 2007; Rittner and Breuer 2004; Ulseth 2004; Vos et al. 2012). This welfare-oriented sport supply is mirrored in the goals and objectives, i.e. the philosophy[2] of sport clubs (for a detailed overview see Breuer and Feiler 2014). The results show that German sport clubs put high value on trying to convey values such as fair play and tolerance: 92 % of the clubs show agreement with this statement which underlines the importance of this goal. Moreover, the aim of sport clubs is to offer an affordable sports supply which is also displayed in the clubs' high agreement towards this goal (86 %) as well as in fair membership and admission fees: half of the German sport clubs charge a maximum monthly membership fee of €2.50 for children, €3.10 for adolescents, and €6.20 for adults. Moreover, 61 % of the clubs offer the possibility of a family membership with a monthly fee of up to €12.00 for two adults and two children (Breuer and Feiler 2014). Through the moderate membership fees, sport clubs

[2]The club philosophy is measured on a scale from 1 (do not agree at all) to 5 (totally agree). For this analysis, the categories 4 (agree) and 5 (totally agree) were consolidated so that the share of clubs which agree and totally agree to the different philosophy items can be displayed. For reasons of simplification we name the new category 'agreement'.

**Table 11.1** Most prominent goals (philosophy) of German sport clubs (share of clubs in % that agree or totally agree)

| Our club … | Share of clubs showing agreement (in %) |
|---|---|
| Tries to convey values such as fair play and tolerance | 92 |
| Gives an inexpensive opportunity to practice sports | 86 |
| Offers sports for people with a migration background | 83 |
| Sets high value on companionship and conviviality | 82 |
| Is committed to reaching an equal participation of girls/women and boys/men | 82 |

can guarantee organised sports programmes for many different population groups and thereby stand for the idea of sport for all (Digel 1988; Enjolars 2002; Hartmann-Tews 1996). Pertaining to (social) integration, sport clubs are particularly concerned with offering sports for people with a migration background (agreement of 83 %) and with setting high value on companionship and conviviality (82 % agreement). Moreover, 82 % of the clubs are committed to reaching an equal participation of girls/women and boys/men in the clubs (see Table 11.1).

Overall, the sport clubs in Germany represent an imperative foundation for the areas of elite, mass, recreational, and health sports (Breuer and Feiler 2013c, 2014). This is supported and fostered through various projects and initiatives of the DOSB and its membership organisations (e.g. *Integration through sport*, *Fit from 50 onwards*, *Sport moves families*, *Sport pro health*, *Strong nets against violence*).

## 11.4 Characteristics of Sport Clubs in Germany

### *11.4.1 General Characteristics*

Generally speaking, size, both in regard to the number of members and the number of sports, can be regarded as a central characteristic of sport clubs (Wicker et al. 2013a). Nearly 70 % of all German sport clubs can be described as small clubs with a membership number at up to 300. One-fifth of the clubs consist of 301–800 members and can be categorised as middle-sized clubs. Moreover, roughly 8 % of German sport clubs have 801–2,000 members and only a small percentage of slightly above 2 % of all clubs are regarded as large clubs with more than 2,000 members (Breuer et al. 2013a). The majority of sport clubs in Germany is run in the form of single-sport clubs, meaning they only provide one type of sport, e.g. soccer, gymnastics, and swimming (Breuer and Feiler 2013b). However, multi-sports clubs are also common in Germany which is underlined by the fact that, on average, a sport club consists of 3.1 divisions and a division has averagely 105.4 members. Taking a look at regional differences it can be seen that the Eastern federal states have on average smaller divisions than the federal states in the West. However,

**Table 11.2** Strategic orientations of German sport clubs (Breuer et al. 2013b, p. 183)

| Strategic orientation | Share of clubs (in %) |
|---|---|
| Price leader | 79 |
| Quality leader | 74 |
| Integrative | 57 |
| Traditional | 50 |
| Convivial | 49 |
| Mass/health sport oriented | 43 |
| Elite sport oriented | 35 |
| Diversity oriented | 24 |
| Service oriented | 17 |

regarding the range of divisions, these differences cannot be observed. Pertaining to the development of the clubs' scale and scope, division size (scale) was found to have significantly increased between 2009 and 2011, whereas the range of divisions (scope) has significantly decreased over the same period (Breuer et al. 2013b).

Apart from size, sport clubs can be characterised and categorised based on their philosophy. Within the *Sport Development Report*, the club philosophy is measured by asking the sport clubs to indicate the extent to which the club's board agrees to a list of statements (from 1 = do not agree at all to 5 = totally agree). Thus, clubs with different strategic orientations can be detected by measuring the share of clubs which agree and strongly agree to certain statements. The following types of strategic orientations were observed: (1) traditional, (2) convivial, (3) service oriented, (4) integrative, (5) price leader, (6) quality leader, (7) elite sport, (8) mass and health sport, and (9) diversity. German sport clubs particularly follow the strategies of being a price leader (79 %), a quality leader (74 %), or particularly integrative (57 %; see Table 11.2). From 2009 onwards, the share of clubs which are particularly service oriented and diversity oriented has increased, whereas being focused on elite sports has become less important (Breuer et al. 2013b).

The clubs' strategies of being service oriented, integrative, a quality leader, mass/health sport oriented, and diversity oriented increase with increasing club size, meaning that larger clubs are more likely to pursue these strategies. On the other hand, smaller clubs are rather traditional, since a traditional orientation decreases with increasing club size (Breuer et al. 2013b).

In addition to size and strategic orientations, sport clubs are characterised by certain resource structures, also described as organisational capacity (Hall et al. 2003). Sport clubs particularly rely on human resources, financial resources, network resources, and infrastructure resources (Wicker and Breuer 2011). Human resource capacity in sport clubs includes volunteers and paid staff and will be described in more detail in Sect. 11.4.5. Financial resource capacity in sport clubs is mainly built by revenues, expenses, and their balance (see Sect. 11.4.6). Pertaining to network resource capacity, sport clubs are found to have relationships with other organisations in the form of cooperations. Particularly cooperating with schools in the provision of sport offers becomes more and more important for sport clubs in Germany due to policy changes in the school systems (e.g. all-day schools, 8-year

**Table 11.3** Sport clubs cooperating with other institutions in the provision of sport offers (Breuer and Feiler 2014, p. 11)

| Cooperations of sport clubs with … | Share of clubs (in %) | Index (percentage increase since 2009) |
|---|---|---|
| Schools | 35 | +42*** |
| Other non-profit sport clubs | 32 | +57*** |
| Kindergarten/nursery school | 17 | +70*** |
| Hospital | 9 | +50*** |
| Commercial enterprise | 5 | n.s. |
| Home for handicapped/disabled | 4 | n.a. |
| Commercial sport provider | 4 | n.s. |
| Youth office | 4 | +33*** |
| Employment bureau | 4 | +45* |
| Institution for senior citizens | 3 | n.s. |
| Health office | 1 | n.s. |
| Multigenerational house | 1 | n.a. |

Share of clubs in %; *** = highly significant change since 2009: probability of error is equal/less than 0.1 %; * = significant change since 2009: probability of error is equal/less than 5 %; n.s. = no significant change since 2009; n.a. = no data available in 2009

instead of 9-year high school). Therefore, the share of clubs cooperating with schools has significantly increased from 2009 to 2013. Apart from school cooperations, sport clubs are in partnerships with various other institutions. Particularly the share of clubs cooperating with other sport clubs, nursery schools, hospitals, the youth office, and the employment bureau has increased over the last 4 years (Breuer and Feiler 2014). An overview of cooperation partners of sport clubs in Germany is displayed in Table 11.3.

To offer different types of sports, sport clubs are dependent on an adequate sport infrastructure, i.e. sport facilities. Nearly half of all German sport clubs possess their own sport facilities. Pertaining to club-owned gyms, only a few clubs (3 %) own such facilities. Moreover, roughly 62 % of German sport clubs use public sport facilities, mostly gym halls and playing fields, but also indoor and outdoor swimming pools as well as track and field stadiums (Breuer and Feiler 2013c). Almost two-thirds of the sport facilities used by German sport clubs are older than 30 years. Approximately 68 % of these old facilities have been renovated or modernised during the last 10 years which shows that there is still a not-to-be-underestimated share of facilities which is in need of modernisation. This is in accordance with an increase in the perceived problem intensity regarding the condition of sport facilities (see next section).

## 11.4.2 Bottlenecks and Challenges

Although sport clubs perform remarkably in many different areas, the situation of the clubs is not without problems. Over the time period from 2005 to 2011, particularly problems relating to the recruitment and retention of volunteers, to demographic changes in the region, and to increasing competition from other non-profit sport clubs have significantly increased (Breuer et al. 2014). Based on latest data from the fifth wave of the *Sport Development Report*, problems mainly exist in the areas of the recruitment and retention of volunteers, adolescent competitive athletes, coaches/ instructors, referees/officials, and members. Moreover, challenges exist due to demographic change in the regions and the number of laws, orders, and directives facing the clubs, i.e. bureaucratic issues (see Fig. 11.2).

Compared to 2011, the perceived severity of problems relating to the recruitment and retention of volunteers has significantly increased. The same applies to problems related to the recruitment and retention of coaches/instructors and referees/ officials. On the other hand, the problem of membership recruitment and retention has slightly decreased over the same period. Apart from the problems regarding human resources, sport clubs are increasingly challenged by demographic changes, effects of all-day schools on the available time for training, the unclarity of the club's overall perspective, the condition of sport facilities, and local competition from other non-profit sport clubs (Fig. 11.2). Overall, the severity of the clubs' problems can be described as moderate, although 37 % of all sport clubs in Germany have at least one problem which threatens their existence. This number has significantly increased between 2011 and 2013. The problem which threatens the largest share of clubs (13 %) in their existence in 2013 is the recruitment and retention of volunteers (Breuer and Feiler 2014). This is particularly struggling since the majority of clubs that were facing this problem in 2011 had implemented measures to deal with before. These measures included direct persuasion of active volunteers to continue their tasks or recruit new members for voluntary positions. Moreover, clubs tried to recruit volunteers from outside the club through advertisements and announcement (Breuer and Feiler 2013c). However, these measures do not seem to have been successful for all clubs since the problem still threatens a not-to-be-underestimated share of clubs in 2013.

The problems of sport clubs in Germany are related to different structural and organisational factors (e.g. Wicker and Breuer 2013; Wicker et al. 2012b, 2013a). For example, research has shown that problems relating to sport facilities and bureaucracy increase with an increasing number of sports provided by the clubs (Wicker et al. 2013a). Regarding demographic factors it was found that clubs with an ageing membership structure (higher shares of seniors and smaller shares of youth) had bigger problems due to demographic changes in the region; in retaining and recruiting members, young athletes, and referees; and in having clarity about the general perspective of the club than clubs with a rejuvenated membership structure (Breuer and Feiler 2013a). Additionally, pertaining to problems relating to the recruitment and retention of volunteers, coaches, adolescent athletes, and members, data mining procedures have been used to detect factors impacting the severity of such problems. It was found that the types of sports offered by the clubs and the proportion of club members taking part in convivial gatherings of the club are important factors relating to the severity of problems. For example, some problems were found to be bigger in clubs offering soccer, shooting, tennis, and equestrian sport and smaller in clubs with high shares of members taking part in convivial

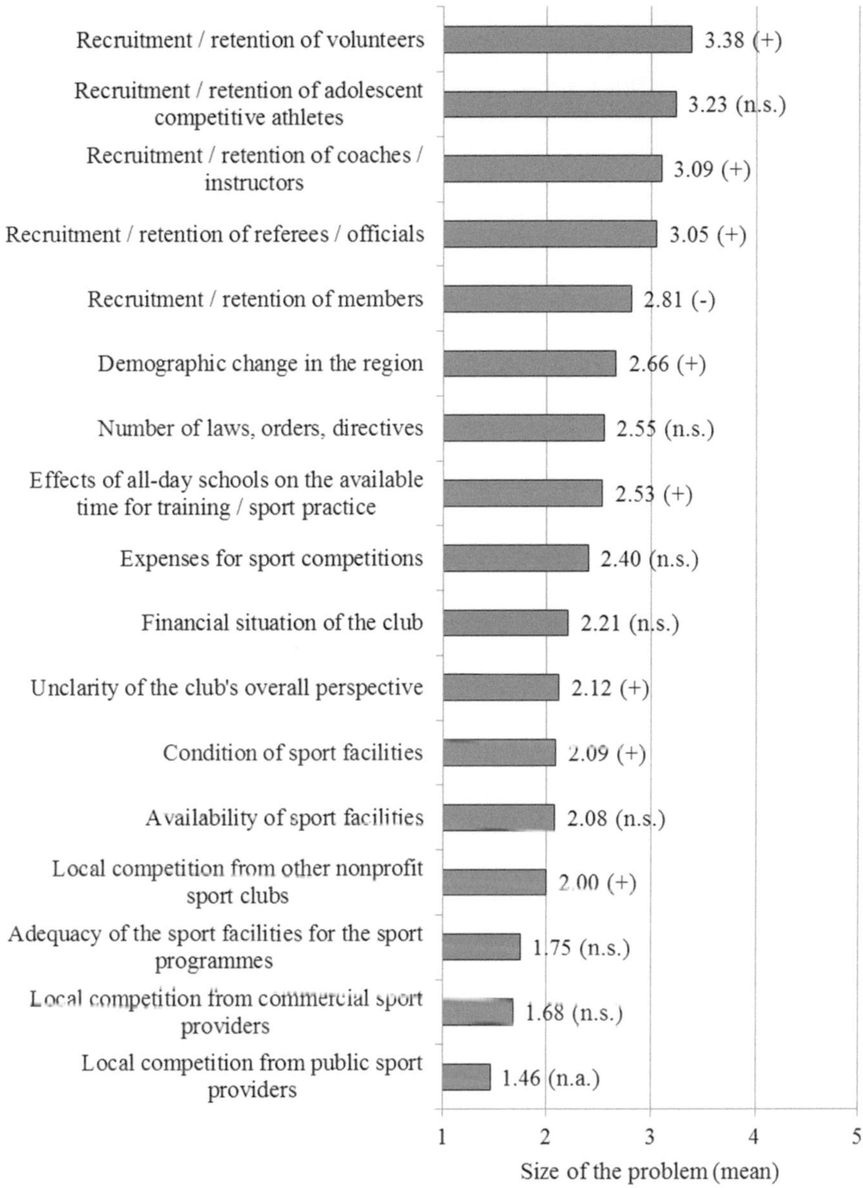


**Fig. 11.2** Problems of sport clubs in 2013, sorted by size of the problem, and their development from 2011 to 2013 (+ = significant increase; − = significant decrease; n.s. = no significant change; n.a. = no data available in 2011; Breuer and Feiler 2014, p. 25)

gatherings (Wicker and Breuer 2010). Moreover, organisational problems in general have been found to be dependent on organisational resources, i.e. the capacity of sport clubs. Organisational resources include human, financial, infrastructure, and cultural resources. The results of different regression models show that clubs with higher shares of females on the board and a high level of volunteers, clubs with policies for the strategic development and the formation of employees, and clubs caring for companionship and conviviality are likely to have smaller organiseal problems. On the other hand, clubs being situated in bigger communities were found to have larger problems in the fields of recruiting members, coaches, and pertaining to the financial situation. This might indicate that in larger communities, more substitutes for sport clubs are available, for example commercial sport providers and other leisure activities (Wicker and Breuer 2013). Apart from identifying factors impacting on sport clubs' problems, a recent study can provide evidence that certain types of problems, namely financial and volunteer problems, are interrelated (Coates et al. 2014).

### *11.4.3 Recreational and Professional Sport*

Pertaining to sport programmes and activities of German sport clubs, the clubs offer a wide range of different sports, both on the recreational and on the elite sport level. Regarding the elite/professional sport level, 12 % of the clubs have national squad athletes and thereby form the basis for elite sport in Germany. After a decrease of clubs with squad athletes between 2009 and 2011, the number of clubs with squad athletes has again significantly increased from 2011 to 2013 by roughly 2 % points (Breuer and Feiler 2013c, 2014). An interesting fact is that sport clubs with squad athletes more often cooperate with other sport clubs, schools, nursery schools, and commercial enterprises. However, compared to clubs with no focus on elite sports, problems relating to the financial situation and to sport facilities are perceived bigger in such clubs, whereas volunteer and coach problems are found to be smaller (Breuer and Wicker 2009b).

Apart from elite sport, recreational sport offers play a major role in most German sport clubs. One statement from the club philosophy (for the measurement of the club philosophy see Sect. 11.4.1) asks whether the club's board thinks of the club as a recreational or mass sport club. A high mean value of $M = 4.09$ underlines the recreational nature of most sport clubs. Nevertheless, participation in competitions and tournaments is also possible for members being active on the mass sport level, both for individual and for team sports. In 2013, 30 % of all sport club members in Germany took part in official competitions and league competitions (Breuer and Feiler 2014).

An increasingly important area for German sport clubs is the provision of health sport offers. As described above, demographic changes and particularly the ageing population are challenging many German sport clubs. Thus, health sport offers for these population groups, but also health prevention measures for the working population, take on greater significance. Sport clubs seem to react to these challenges by

**Table 11.4** Sport clubs with sport programmes in the health care section (Breuer and Feiler 2014, p. 9)

| | Share of clubs (in %) | Index (percentage increase since 2011) |
|---|---|---|
| Health promotion and primary prevention | 32 | +8*** |
| Rehabilitation/tertiary prevention | 5 | +16* |
| Disabilities/chronic diseases | 6 | +16** |
| Sum of categories related to health care | 34 | +8*** |

Share of clubs in %; ***=highly significant change since 2011: probability of error is equal/less than 0.1 %; **=very significant change since 2011: probability of error is equal/less than 1 %; *=significant change since 2011: probability of error is equal/less than 5 %

offering different types of health sports. Overall, 34 % of the clubs offer programmes related to health aspects, including health promotion and prevention, rehabilitation, and offers for disabled people as well as for people with chronic diseases. In all areas, significant increases from 2011 onwards can be observed (see Table 11.4). Related to all sport offers of the clubs, 12 % have a health care function (Breuer and Feiler 2014).

Clubs offering health sport can be distinguished from other clubs through certain characteristics: first, the share of multi-sports clubs is much higher among clubs offering health sport. This corresponds to the second characteristic, namely that clubs offering such programmes are on average larger clubs with more members. Moreover, health sport clubs more often use public sport facilities which stress the importance of an adequate public sport infrastructure (Breuer and Wicker 2009a). The importance of health sport programmes is underlined by the fact that the DOSB has developed two certificates in this area: *Sport pro health* and *Sport pro fitness*. Clubs can get certified with these two signets when they fulfil certain criteria related to health and fitness sport offers. However, in 2011 the share of clubs being certified was with 9 % still at a low level (Breuer and Feiler 2013c).

### 11.4.4 Activities for Sport Club Members

In addition to the above-described professional and recreational sport offers, sport clubs in Germany provide further sport-related and non-sport-related activities to their members. For example, in 2013, 12 % of the clubs offered their members to take part in training sessions for the so-called *German sport badge* (Breuer and Feiler 2014). The '*German sport badge*' is a certificate outside the classical competitive sport with a history of more than 100 years. It is awarded by the DOSB and can be received through completing different sport disciplines in a given time or limit, depending on gender and age. A certain focus is put on the classical motor skill endurance, strength, speed, and coordination. To receive the *German sport badge*, membership in a sport club is not necessary, although to get the badge it certainly helps to take part in offered training sessions by the clubs.

As already described in previous sections, members of German sport clubs represent different population groups, e.g. juniors, seniors, and migrants. Since demographic changes in the different regions affect sport clubs, the clubs try to particularly care about these groups by providing customised sport offers. The orientation towards these different population groups is again mirrored in the clubs' philosophy since the philosophy items show that clubs particularly care about migrants, the youth, the elderly, and families. Moreover, sport clubs put high value on companionship and conviviality (Breuer and Feiler 2014; Krimmer and Priemer 2013). Therefore, apart from sport programmes and activities, the clubs also offer non-sport activities for their members (e.g. celebrations, social gathering, carnival parties). This applies to 54 % of all German sport clubs. The importance of such activities for sport club members is documented by the fact that nearly half of all sport club members took part in social events of their clubs in 2013 (Breuer and Feiler 2014).

### *11.4.5 Professionalisation*

German sport clubs are mainly run by volunteers. Altogether, when extrapolating the mean values, the members of German sport clubs comprise 1.8 million volunteers and further 6.9 million members who are working sporadically for the club as secondary volunteers (e.g. at sport events, helping with cleaning, renovations, driving athletes to competitions). On the club level, averagely 9.7 positions are occupied by volunteers on the club's board. These positions can encompass a chairman, a deputy chairman, a voluntary director, a treasurer, a youth director, a sport director, a press spokesman, a mass sport director, and a secretary. Moreover, further 9.5 positions are averagely occupied at the executive level (coaches and instructors). The number of voluntary positions in German sport clubs has significantly increased since 2009. However, the total working hours per volunteer decreased and amounted to 13.8 h/month in 2013. Even though the voluntary engagement in German sport clubs is impressive, problems relating to the recruitment and retention of volunteers in sport clubs are evident (Breuer and Feiler 2013c, 2014; Breuer and Wicker 2011b). Therefore, longitudinal analyses in the context of German sport clubs investigated the consequences of a decreasing voluntary engagement and whether substitutes exist for the decline in voluntary work. The study indicated that in sport clubs with decreasing volunteer numbers, some substitution effects exist. Those effects differed between the short term (2 years) and the long term (4 years). Regarding the short-term period, a significant increase in secondary volunteers, i.e. people working sporadically for the club (e.g. at competitions, events), and a significant increase of clubs with low-cost employees (recruited from the employment office) could be observed. In the long term, the proportion of sport clubs employing paid staff has significantly increased (Breuer et al. 2012).

Although most of the work of German sport clubs is done by volunteers, paid staff is also employed on different club levels and in different positions (see Table 11.5).

**Table 11.5** Sport clubs with paid staff (Breuer and Feiler 2014, pp. 20–21)

| | Share of clubs (in %) | Index (percentage increase since 2007) |
|---|---|---|
| Paid staff total | 26 | n.s. |
| Paid staff full-time | 4 | n.s. |
| Paid staff part-time | 5 | −57*** |
| Marginally employed | 17 | n.a. |
| Freelancers | 10 | −32*** |
| Leading position (e.g. executive director) | 4 | +50** |
| Paid staff in direction and administration | 8 | n.s. |
| Paid staff in sports, training, supervision | 17 | n.s. |
| Paid staff in maintenance/technique | 13 | n.s. |

Share of clubs in %; ***=highly significant change since 2007: probability of error is equal/less than 0.1 %; **=very significant change since 2007: probability of error is equal/less than 1 %; n.s.=no significant change since 2007; n.a.=no data available in 2007

A small number of clubs (4 %) have people being employed in a leading position, e.g. as a manager or an executive director. However, the share of clubs employing paid staff on executive levels is higher: overall, one-quarter of the German sport clubs state to have paid staff in the areas of administration (8 %), sports (17 %), and maintenance/technique (13 %). The type of employment can be distinguished into four main categories: full-time, part time, marginally employed (also called *mini-job*: type of employment in Germany on a maximum of €450 basis/month), and freelancers. The most frequent type of paid work in German sport clubs is the form of marginal employment. This kind of paid staff can be found in 17 % of the clubs. Moreover, 10 % of German sport clubs have freelancers on their payrolls. The forms of full-time and part-time employment are only found in approximately 4 and 5 % of the clubs (Breuer and Feiler 2014).

Regarding qualifications, the volunteers and paid staff are equipped with several formal qualifications. Overall, 90 % of the German sport clubs have coaches and instructors with a formal qualification. This includes both formal certificates of the German sport system (DOSB-licence) and other formal qualifications (licence from certain confederations, university degrees, etc.). However, also half of the clubs have coaches and instructors without any formal qualification. The share of clubs with formally qualified coaches and instructors increases with increasing club size. Moreover, qualified coaches are more often found in multi-sports clubs than in single-sport clubs, although the share of single-sport clubs with qualified coaches still reaches nearly 88 % compared to nearly 94 % in multi-sport clubs. Pertaining to all coaches and instructors (with and without a formal qualification), 92 % of them work on a voluntary basis. This share is a little lower for coaches and instructors with a formal qualification (91 %). Within coaches and instructors without a formal qualification, even 96 % work on a voluntary basis. Regarding the gender distribution among coaches and instructors it can be observed that 32 % are women. The share of females is a bit higher among qualified coaches (34 %) and a bit lower

(30 %) among coaches and instructors without a formal qualification (Breuer and Feiler 2013d).

The importance of sport clubs to society is once more stressed since clubs also engage in training and education of employees. In 2013, 26 % of the clubs stated to have a person being responsible for the education and training of volunteers and paid staff within the sport club. However, this share has significantly decreased since 2009 by roughly seven percentage points (Breuer and Feiler 2014). Further analyses showed that having such a person is dependent on different factors. For example, larger clubs, clubs setting high value on the quality of their sport programmes, clubs with a strategic policy, and clubs being engaged in the health sport sector employ someone for educational tasks. In contrast, clubs which set particularly high value on companionship and conviviality and on being run solely by volunteers are rarely equipped with such a person (Breuer and Wicker 2011b). In addition to further educating existing volunteers and paid employees, almost 1 % of the German sport clubs act as a training company for apprentices (Breuer and Feiler 2014).

### *11.4.6 Finance*

Expenses and revenues in German sport clubs are manifold. Based on the fifth wave of the *Sport Development Report*, sport clubs in Germany have expenses in 19 different categories and generate revenues from 25 different income sources. Pertaining to expenses of German sport clubs, the most frequent expense categories, meaning the share of clubs which have expenses in those categories, are fees for sport organisations such as confederations and regional federations (86 %), insurances (72 %), sport equipment and clothing (69 %), administration (58 %), and coaches/instructors (58 %). Pertaining to the yearly average amount of expenses, sport clubs in Germany spend most on coaches/instructors (€7,146), followed by maintenance and service of self-owned facilities (€4,893), equipment and clothing (€2,524), organisation of own sport events (€2,034), and fees for sport organisations (€1,874) (Breuer and Feiler 2014).

With regard to revenues of the clubs, all German sport clubs generate revenue from membership fees. This is self-explaining since the payment of membership fees by members is a necessary condition for being able to join the club and for benefiting from the offers of the club. A further common income category in German sport clubs is donations: three-quarters of all clubs receive revenue from donations and donations amount to 9 % of all revenues of German sport clubs. Moreover, a nearly equal percentage of sport clubs receives public subsidies (71.4 %), with public subsidies making up 9 % of all revenues. A minor role is played by income from sponsorship in German sport clubs since the proportion of sponsorship income relative to total income only reaches 3 %. The highest revenues moneywise are generated from membership fees (€16,620), donations (€3,093), public subsidies from the district/community (€1,721), self-managed restaurants (€1,466), and sport events (€1,462) (Breuer and Feiler 2014).

The above-described sources of revenue show that sport clubs in Germany rely on a wide range of different income sources, which is typical for non-profit organisations (Young 2007). Diversified income portfolios help clubs to reach a financially healthy situation (Carrol and Stater 2009) and lead to lower revenue volatility (Wicker et al. 2015). Research on German sport clubs has shown that revenue diversification among clubs is dependent on the clubs' mission. More diversified income portfolios can be found in clubs which focus on missions like promoting elite and youth sport, conviviality, tradition, and non-sport programmes. On the other hand, clubs which focus on leisure and health sport and commercially oriented clubs have more concentrated revenues (Wicker et al. 2013b). Although the main goal of non-profit sport clubs is not to maximise profit, the clubs should nevertheless try to reach a balanced and stable financial situation. Financial health is particularly important to secure the existence of the clubs (Kearns 2007). Pertaining to the financial situation of German sport clubs it can be noted that in 2013, 76 % of the clubs have at least a balanced profit-and-loss account. However, this number has significantly decreased since 2011, implying that the overall financial situation of sport clubs has slightly deteriorated, although the perceived problems of the clubs relating to the financial situation have not significantly changed lately. Nevertheless, still 5 % of German sport clubs feel threatened in their existence because of financial problems (Breuer and Feiler 2014). Financial problems can particularly arise due to decreasing public subsidies (Breuer 2012) and a volatile nature of revenues from donations (Gronbjerg 1991) which are main income categories of German sport clubs, as described above. Thus, clubs might have to consider an increase of their membership fees to try compensating the decrease in other income sources (Wicker 2011). Membership fees can be described as an autonomous income category, meaning that clubs can decide about the price levels, but not the overall revenues (Wicker et al. 2012a). Thus, it is easier for clubs to increase membership fees than trying to gather income from other external sources. Longitudinal analyses show that the membership fees have increased in German sport clubs between 2005 and 2009. The increase between 2005 and 2007 amounted to 12 % and between 2007 and 2009 to 13 % (Breuer et al. 2014; Breuer and Wicker 2009d, 2011b). This implies that clubs have used this autonomous income source as a compensation measure. Nevertheless, this is only partly possible which underlines the importance of public support for sport clubs in Germany (Breuer 2012).

## 11.5 Specific Topic: Gender Aspects in Sport Clubs in Germany

As shown in the sport participation statistics, girls and women are generally underrepresented in sport clubs compared to their share of the population. The lowest share of female members in relation to the respective population group is found in the age category 60 plus. Here, only 14 % of the female population are members of a sport club. On the other hand, the largest share of women and girls, respectively, in relation to the corresponding population group is found in the age category of 7–14-year-olds: here, 63 % of the population in this group are members of a sport club (DOSB 2012). To investigate factors which are important for the proportion of female members, data mining analyses show that the share of female members predominantly depends on the sport offers of the clubs. Particularly sport clubs with offers in gymnastics (including aerobic), equestrian sports, and dancing have high shares of women among their members. On the other hand, this proportion is considerably lower and even beneath average in football clubs (Breuer and Wicker 2009d). In addition to certain sport offerings, regression analyses have revealed that an important factor to increase the share of women within sport clubs is to have women on the board level.[3] Women seem to particularly appreciate quality since sport clubs which care about the quality of their sport offerings are more likely to increase the share of female members (Breuer and Feiler 2012). Thus, women on the board can foster the provision of high-quality sport programmes (e.g. health sport programmes) and types of sports which are attractive to women, such as gymnastics and dancing. Thereby, the share of women within the clubs can be expanded.

Apart from lower participation rates of female members in sports clubs, women are also underrepresented in management and leadership positions on the voluntary level of sport clubs in Germany. This is particularly troubling since clubs with higher shares of women on the board level and among members in general were found to experience lower levels of organisational problems (Wicker et al. 2012b). Averagely, one-fourth of all executive board positions are held by women. The highest shares of women on the executive board of non-profit sport clubs in Germany can be found in positions such as secretaries (47 %), treasurers (33 %), and youth directors (32 %) (Breuer and Wicker 2009c). Not only on the board level of non-profit sport clubs, but also on the executive level, no equal gender distribution can be found. The latest survey of sport clubs in Germany shows that men fill more than twice as many voluntary positions in sport clubs than women: men averagely reach a total number of 13 voluntary positions in German sport clubs whereas women are only represented in averagely 6 positions (Breuer and Feiler 2014). However, a different picture can be observed with respect to paid staff in German sport clubs: two-thirds of the positions in the fields of management and administration are held by women (Breuer and Wicker 2009c). Pertaining to coaches and instructors (both voluntary and paid), roughly one-third is female. The share of female coaches was found to increase with increasing club size. The highest share of women among coaches can be found in clubs with more than 1,000 and less than 2,500 members. But still, not even half (45 %) of all coaches are women in those clubs. In addition to club size, the share of female coaches was also found to be higher in multi-sport clubs than in single-sport clubs (Breuer and Feiler 2013d).

---

[3] However, cause-effect relationships need to be taken into account at this point. This means that the relation between women on the board level and female members in sport clubs could be the other way round as well.

## 11.6 Conclusion

German sport clubs can be described as well-adaptable elements of stability in a rapidly changing society. Sport clubs in Germany are run in the form of voluntary non-profit organisations. The clubs are mainly managed by volunteers and only rely to a small degree on paid staff. The clubs' intention is to transmit values and offer an affordable sports supply for many population groups. However, not all groups are represented in sport clubs relative to their respective population groups. For example, children and adolescents are stronger represented in sport clubs than in the population, whereas seniors only reach lower shares within sport clubs relative to their share within the population. Through the combination of offering sport as well as non-sport programmes, sport clubs in Germany represent an imperative foundation for the areas of mass, recreational, elite, and health sport. Nevertheless, sport clubs also face some problems, particularly in the areas of recruiting and retaining volunteers. Analyses have shown that problems in sport clubs are related to different structural factors and resources. On the other hand, there is strong evidence that certain factors can help overcoming existing problems. Thus, to counter the threats which the clubs are facing, research has shown that a reduction of problems can be reached by increasing the percentage of women on the board, by a high level of voluntary engagement, by installing policies for the formation of the employees and the strategic development of the club, by offering quality sport programmes, and by setting high value on companionship and conviviality. On the other hand, a pure traditional orientation does not help to overcome organisational problems (Wicker and Breuer 2013).

## References


Brettschneider W-D, Kleine T (2002) Jugendarbeit in Sportvereinen. Anspruch und Wirklichkeit Hofmann, Schorndorf

Breuer C (2007) Sportentwicklungsbericht 2005/2006. Analyse zur Situation der Sportvereine in Deutschland. Sportverlag Strauß, Köln

Breuer C (2009) Sportentwicklungsbericht 2007/2008—Analyse zur Situation der Sportvereine in Deutschland. Sportverlag Strauß, Köln

Breuer C (2011) Sportentwicklungsbericht 2009/2010—Analyse zur Situation der Sportvereine in Deutschland. Sportverlag Strauß, Köln

Breuer C (2012) Wie viel Staat braucht der Breitensport? Ökonometrische Evidenzen für ein Europäisches Modell des Breitensports. In: Büch M-P, Maenning W, Schulke H-J (eds) Sport und Sportgroßveranstaltungen in Europa—zwischen Zentralstaat und Regionen. University Press, Hamburg

Breuer C (2013a) Sportentwicklungsbericht 2011/2012—Analyse zur Situation der Sportvereine in Deutschland. Sportverlag Strauß, Köln

Breuer C (2013b) Sportverbände, Sportvereine und ausgewählte Sportarten. Weiterführende Analysen der Sportentwicklungsberichte. Sportverlag Strauß, Köln

Breuer C, Feiler S (2012) Geschlechtergerechte Vereinsentwicklung—evidenzbasierte Strategien auf Basis des Sportentwicklungsberichts. In: DoSB (ed) Bewegt in die Zukunft. Sportvereine und Kommunen setzen auf Geschlechtergerechtigkeit. Deutscher Olympischer Sportbund, Frankfurt

Breuer C, Feiler S (2013a) Demographische Entwicklung. In: Breuer C (ed) Sportentwicklungsbericht 2011/2012. Analyse zur Situation der Sportvereine in Deutschland. Sportverlag Strauß, Köln

Breuer C, Feiler S (2013b) Der Sportverein und seine Abteilungen. In: Breuer C (ed) Sportentwicklungsbericht 2011/2012. Analyse zur Situation der Sportvereine in Deutschland. Sportverlag Strauß, Köln

Breuer C, Feiler S (2013c) Sport development report 2011/2012. Analysis of the situation of sports clubs in Germany. Abbreviated version. Sportverlag Strauß, Cologne

Breuer C, Feiler S (2013d) Trainer, Übungsleiter und Qualifizierung. In: Breuer C (ed) Sportentwicklungsbericht 2011/2012. Analyse zur Situation der Sportvereine in Deutschland. Sportverlag Strauß, Köln

Breuer C, Feiler S (2014) Sportvereine in Deutschland. Sportentwicklungsbericht 2013/2014. Analyse zur Situation der Sportvereine in Deutschland. Deutsche Sporthochschule Köln, Köln

Breuer C, Wicker P (2009a) Gesundheitssport im Sportverein. In: Breuer C (ed) Sportentwicklungsbericht 2007/2008—Analyse zur Situation der Sportvereine in Deutschland. Sportverlag Strauß, Köln

Breuer C, Wicker P (2009b) Leistungs- und Hochleistungssport im Sportverein. In: Breuer C (ed) Sportentwicklungsbericht 2007/2008—Analyse zur Situation der Sportvereine in Deutschland. Sportverlag Strauß, Köln

Breuer C, Wicker P (2009c) Mädchen und Frauen im Sportverein. In: Breuer C (ed) Sportentwicklungsbericht 2007/2008—Analyse zur Situation der Sportvereine in Deutschland. Sportverlag Strauß, Köln

Breuer C, Wicker P (2009d) Sport development report 2007/2008. Analysis of the sports clubs' situation in Germany. Abbreviated version. Sportverlag Strauß, Cologne

Breuer C, Wicker P (2011a) Die Situation der Sportarten in Deutschland. Eine Analyse der Sportvereine in Deutschland auf Basis der Sportentwicklungsberichte. Sportverlag Strauß, Köln

Breuer C, Wicker P (2011b) Sport development report 2009/2010. Analysis of the situation of sports clubs in Germany. Abbreviated version. Sportverlag Strauß, Cologne

Breuer C, Wicker P, von Hanau T (2012) Consequences of the decrease in volunteers among German sports clubs: is there a substitute for voluntary work? Int J Sport Pol Polit 4:173–186

Breuer C, Feiler S, Wicker P (2013a) Methode. In: Breuer C (ed) Sportentwicklungsbericht 2011/2012. Analyse zur Situation der Sportvereine in Deutschland. Sportverlag Strauß, Köln

Breuer C, Feiler S, Wicker P (2013b) Strategien und ihre Bedeutung. In: Breuer C (ed) Sportentwicklungsbericht 2011/2012. Analyse zur Situation der Sportvereine in Deutschland. Sportverlag Strauß, Köln

Breuer C, Wicker P, Feiler S (2014) Empirische Analysen zur Entwicklung der Strukturen in Sportvereinen. In: Rütten A, Nagel S, Kähler R (eds) Handbuch Sportentwicklungsplanung. Schorndorf, Hofmann

Carrol DA, Stater KJ (2009) Revenue diversification in nonprofit organizations: does it lead to financial stability? J Public Adm Res Theory 19:947–966

Coates D, Wicker P, Feiler S, Breuer C (2014) A bivariate probit examination of financial and volunteer problems of non-profit sport clubs. IJSF 9(3):130–148

Destatis (2013) Bevölkerung und Erwerbstätigkeit. Bevölkerung mit Migrationshintergrund—Ergebnisse des Mikrozensus 2012. Statistisches Bundesamt, Wiesbaden

Destatis (2014a) Wirtschaft und Statistik. März 2014. Statistisches Bundesamt, Wiesbaden

Destatis (2014b) Museen und Zahl der Besuche nach Arten und Trägerschaft. https://www.destatis.de/DE/ZahlenFakten/GesellschaftStaat/BildungForschungKultur/Kultur/Tabellen/MuseenBesucheTraegerschaft.html. Accessed 08 Aug 2014

Deutscher Bühnenverein (2014) Theater und Orchesterlandschaft. http://www.buehnenverein.de/de/theater-und-orchester/19.html. Access 08 Aug 2014

Digel H (1988) Sport im Verein und im Verband. In: Digel H (ed) Sport im Verein und im Verband. Historische, politische und soziologische Aspekte. Hofmann, Schorndorf

Digel H, Hartmann H, Singer R, Ungerer-Röhrich U, Weßling-Lünnemann G (1992) Turn- und Sportvereine. Strukturen—Probleme—Trends. Eine Analyse der Vereine im Deutschen Turner-Bund. Meyer & Meyer, Aachen

DOSB (2012) Bestandserhebung 2012. Deutscher Olympischer Sportbund, Frankfurt
DSB (2003) Sport in Deutschland. Deutscher Sportbund, Frankfurt
Emrich E (1998) Ausgewählte Ergebnisse der Finanz- und Strukturanalyse der Sportvereine 1996 (FISAS 1996). Deutscher Sportbund, Frankfurt
Emrich E, Papathanssiou V, Pitsch W (1998) Sportvereine im Sportbund Pfalz. Ergebnisse einer empirischen Untersuchung. Schors, Niedernhausen
Emrich E, Papathanassiou V, Pitsch W (1999) Sportvereine im Blickpunkt. Strukturelemente, Umweltverflechtungen und Selbstverständnis saarländischer Sportvereine. Röhrig, St. Ingbert
Emrich E, Papathanassiou V, Pitsch W (2001) Die Sportvereine—Ein Versuch auf empirischer Grundlage. Hofmann, Schorndorf
Enjolars B (2002) The commercialization of voluntary sport organizations in Norway. Nonprofit Volunt Sect Q 31:352–376
EU (2014) Wie funktioniert die EU? Deutschland. http://europa.eu/about-eu/countries/member-countries/germany/index_de.htm. Accessed 07 Aug 2014
Gratton C, Taylor P (2000) Economics of sport and recreation. E & FN Spon, London
Gronbjerg KA (1991) How nonprofit human service organizations manage their funding sources: key findings and policy implications. Nonprof Manag Leader 2:159–175
Hall MH, Andrukow A, Barr C, Brock K, De Wit M, Embuldeniya D, Jolin L, Lasby D, Levesque B, Malinsky E, Stowe S, Vaillancourt Y (2003) The capacity to serve: a qualitative study of the challenges facing Canada's nonprofit and voluntary organization. Centre for Philanthropy, Toronto, ON
Handy F, Brudney JL (2007) When to use volunteer labor resources? An organizational analysis for nonprofit management. VIO 4:91–100
Hansmann H (1980) The role of nonprofit enterprise. Yale Law J 89:835–902
Hartmann-Tews I (1996) Sport für alle!? Strukturwandel europäischer Sportsysteme im Vergleich: Bundesrepublik Deutschland, Frankreich, Großbritannien. Hofmann, Schorndorf
Heinemann K (1995) Einführung in die Ökonomie des Sports. Hofmann, Schorndorf
Heinemann K (2007) Einführung in die Soziologie des Sports. Hofmann, Schorndorf
Heinemann K, Horch H-D (1981) Soziologie der Sportorganisation. Sportwissenschaft 11:123–150
Heinemann K, Schubert M (1994) Der Sportverein. Hofmann, Schorndorf
Horch H-D (1994) On the socio-economics of voluntary associations. Voluntas 5:219–230
Kearns K (2007) Income portfolios. In: Young DR (ed) Financing nonprofits. Putting theory into practice. AltaMira Press, Lanham, MD
Krimmer H, Priemer J (2013) ZIVIZ-survey 2012. Zivilgesellschaft verstehen. Stifterverband für die Deutsche Wissenschaft, Berlin
Nagel M (2003) Die soziale Zusammensetzung der Sportvereinsmitglieder. In: Bauer J, Braun S (eds) Integrationsleistungen von Sportvereinen als Freiwilligenorganisationen. Meyer & Meyer, Aachen
Nagel S, Conzelmann A, Gabler H (2004) Sportvereine—Auslaufmodell oder Hoffnungsträger? Die WLSB-Vereinsstudie. Attempto, Tübingen
Petry K, Hallmann K (2013) Germany. In: Hallmann K, Petry K (eds) Comparative sport development. Springer, New York
Rittner V, Breuer C (2004) Gemeinwohlorientierung und soziale Bedeutung des Sports. Sport und Buch Strauß, Köln
Schlagenhauf K (1977) Sportvereine in der Bundesrepublik Deutschland. Teil I: Strukturelemente und Verhaltensdeterminanten im organisierten Freizeitbereich. Hofmann, Schorndorf
Ulseth A-LB (2004) Social integration in modern sport: commercial fitness centres and voluntary sport clubs. ESMQ 2:95–115
Vos S, Breesch D, Kesenne S, Lagae W, Hoecke JV, Vanreusel B, Scheerder J (2012) The value of human resources in non-public sports providers: the importance of volunteers in non-profit sports clubs versus professionals in for-profit fitness and health clubs. IJSMM 11:3–25
Weisbrod BA (1964) Collective-consumption services of individual-consumption goods. Q J Econ 78:471–477

Weisbrod BA (1986) Toward a theory of the voluntary nonprofit sector in a three-sector economy. In: Rose-Ackermann S (ed) The economics of nonprofit institutions. Studies in structure and policy. Oxford University Press, New York

Weisbrod BA (1998) The nonprofit mission and its financing: growing links between nonprofits and the rest of the economy. In: Weisbrod BA (ed) To profit or not to profit. The commercial transformation of the nonprofit sector. Cambridge University Press, Cambridge

Wicker P (2011) Willingness-to-pay in non-profit sports clubs. IJSF 6:155–169

Wicker P, Breuer C (2010) Analysis of problems using data mining techniques—findings from sports clubs in Germany. EJSS 7:131–140

Wicker P, Breuer C (2011) Scarcity of resources in German non-profit sport clubs. Sport Manag Rev 14:188–201

Wicker P, Breuer C (2013) Understanding the importance of organizational resources to explain organizational problems: evidence from nonprofit sport clubs in Germany. Voluntas 24: 461–484

Wicker P, Breuer C, Hennings B (2012a) Understanding the interactions among revenue categories using elasticity measures—evidence from a longitudinal sample of non-profit sport clubs in Germany. Sport Manag Rev 15:318–329

Wicker P, Breuer C, von Hanau T (2012b) Gender effects on organizational problems—evidence from non-profit sports clubs in Germany. Sex Roles 66:105–116

Wicker P, Hallmann K, Breuer C (2012c) Micro and macro level determinants of sport participation. SBM 2:51–68

Wicker P, Breuer C, Lamprecht M, Fischer A (2013a) Does club size matter? An examination of economies of scale, economies of scope, and organizational problems. J Sport Manag 28: 266–280

Wicker P, Feiler S, Breuer C (2013b) Organizational mission and revenue diversification among non-profit sports clubs. Int J Financ Stud 1:119–136

Wicker P, Hallmann K, Breuer C (2013c) Analyzing the impact of sport infrastructure on sport participation using geo-coded data: evidence from multi-level models. Sport Manag Rev 16:54–67

Wicker P, Longley N, Breuer C (2015) Revenue volatility in German nonprofit sports clubs. Nonprofit Volunt Sect Q 44(1):5–24

Young DR (2007) Why study nonprofit finance? In: Young DR (ed) Financing nonprofits. Putting theory into practice. AltaMira Press, Lanham, MD

Zimmer A, Priller E, Anheier HK (2013) Der Nonprofit-Sektor in Deutschland. In: Simsa R, Meyer M, Badelt C (eds) Handbuch der Nonprofit-Organisation. Strukturen und Management. Schäffer-Poeschel Verlag, Stuttgart

# Chapter 12
# Sport Clubs in Greece

**Kostas Alexandris and Panagiota Balaska**

## 12.1 Introduction

Greece is a country with a total population of 10,815.197 (ELSTAT 2011). It is the 15th largest economy in the 27-member European Union. Its economy is mainly based on the service sector (85 %), industry sector (12 %), and agriculture (3 %). One of the most important industries within the service sector is tourism. It is estimated that Greece will attract more than 18.5 million visitors in 2014, who will contribute more than 12 billion euro to the Greek economy. The sports industry is a very small sector within the Greek economy, contributing about 1.7 % to the country's GPD.

## 12.2 The Greek Sport Administration System and the Sport Clubs in Greece

This section presents the Greek sport administration system, and discusses the role of sport clubs within the sport system and the role of local authorities' sports departments within the sport system.

The Hellenic Ministry of Culture and Sports (2012) is responsible for developing the central government's sport policy in Greece, in cooperation with the General Secretariat of Sports, which is one of the four Secretariats of the Ministry (the other three are the Secretariats of Tourism, Culture, and Infrastructure).

K. Alexandris (✉) • P. Balaska
School of Physical Education and Sport Science, Aristotle University of Thessaloniki, Thessaloniki, Greece
e-mail: kalexand@phed.auth.gr; pmalask@phed.auth.gr



C. Breuer et al. (eds.), *Sport Clubs in Europe*, Sports Economics, Management and Policy 12, DOI 10.1007/978-3-319-17635-2_12

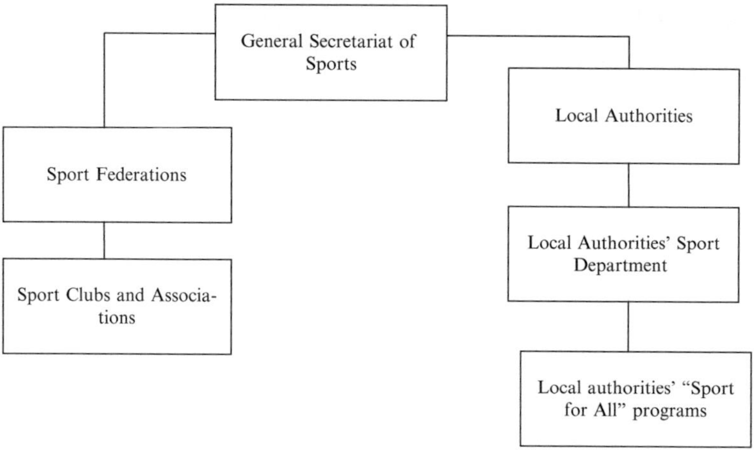


**Fig. 12.1** The Greek Sport Administration System

A graphical presentation of the Greek sport administration system in Greece is presented in Fig. 12.1.

The General Secretariat of Sports (2015) has the following objectives:

- To promote the sport culture within the society
- To promote the Olympic values in national and international levels
- To identify the *sport needs* of the country and develop the appropriate sport policy strategies
- To efficiently and effectively manage sport services and facilities
- To evaluate the national sport policy and take correcting actions
- To direct and supervise the Sport Federations and National Sport Bodies, and ensure the adherence to the laws and regulations
- To supervise the Sport Federations and National Sport Bodies in order to ensure the implementation of the national sport policy

The General Secretariat of Sports is financed by the Central Government Budget, the Greek Organisation of Football Prognostics (O.P.A.P.), the Hellenic Horse Racing Organisation, and the National Investment Program.

The Sport Federations are directed by the General Secretariat of Sports, which decides on the amount of financial help that they receive every year. Sport federations are nonprofit organizers, which are managed by an elected committee. Each federation is responsible for promoting the sport that it represents. Each federation is also responsible for supervising its sport clubs and associations, which deliver the sport services and programs.

According to the law 2725/1999 (article 78), a sport club is a union of individuals, aiming to create an environment for developing and training athletes for competition. For a sport club to be established 20 adult individuals are required to meet and sign the articles of the association; these articles define the guidelines under which the club will operate. These 20 individuals have to also select a committee, who will be in charge of following the law requirements. When a club/association is recognized by law, it can apply to become a member of a sport federation.

A different feature of the Greek sport system, in comparison to other EU countries, is that sport clubs/associations have traditionally targeted youths, providing opportunities for training of young athletes and promoting elite sports. Recreational sports have not been their main focus. Only the last couple of years there have been sport clubs and associations that have started to target *sport for all*, mainly in outdoor sports (e.g., biking, mountain running, and triathlon). The sport clubs are financed by membership fees and the General Secretariat of Sports, through funds given by their sport federations. The amount of financial help that they take depends mainly on the success of the clubs in promoting *sports for excellence* (number of elite athletes). Due to the dramatic reduction in the budget of the sport federations in the last 4 years in Greece, they have started to cut their operation costs, looking at the same time for alternative financial sources (e.g., sponsorships). The 2014 figures show that sport federations received in total 19.9 million euro, while in 2013 they had received 21.2 million euro. The Athletics Federation is one of those with the highest cuts (from 4.4 in 2013 to 3.7 in 2014) (The General Secretariat of Sports 2013-2014).

As expected, these cuts have influenced the amount of financial help that the sport clubs receive from their federations. As a result, the sport clubs have started the last couple of years to organize sport academies for children and youths and summer sport camps, which brings money to them, through fees. They have also started to work on attracting private investments with the form of sponsorships.

As previously noted, opportunities for sport participation are mainly provided by local authorities through their *sport for all* programs. Examples of these programs are *sport and women*, *sport and disabled*, *sport and children*, *sport and elderly*, *sport and individuals with chronic diseases,* etc. They also manage indoor and outdoor sport facilities for use at the community level. Furthermore, they provide a variety of different fitness-related programs and outdoor sport activities, which take place in the facilities that they manage. Sport programs within local authorities are financed by membership fees and the financial help that they receive from the General Secretariat of Sports, upon acceptance of their proposals to run them. The financial contribution of the central government to the local authorities' sport programs has been reduced during the last few years, as a result of the financial crisis in the country and the subsequent reductions in public spending. As a result, local authorities have been advised to look for alternative financial resources, in order to be financially independent. There is a general lack of published information regarding the number of participants in local authorities' sport programs at national level, as well as information regarding the evaluation of these programs (e.g., cost-benefit analysis).

Finally, opportunities for sport participation are also provided by the private sector in Greece. Private sector includes sport, health and fitness clubs, as well as outdoor recreation facilities. Although profitability is always the major objective of the commercial sector, its contribution in the provision of sport opportunities is important. It is estimated that around 3–4 % of the adult population are members of private sport, health, and fitness clubs.

## 12.3 Sport Participation in Greece

This chapter aims to present information on recreational sport participation in Greece, based on local studies, and to compare recreational sport participation figures, according to demographic data.

As previously noted, sport clubs in Greece have traditionally targeted youth and elite sports. Opportunities for organized recreational sport participation are mainly provided by local authorities' sport programs and by private sport clubs. In line with this, this chapter presents brief information on general sport participation in Greece. Greece is one of the countries that do not collect sport participation data at a national level. Subsequently, information about sport participation is limited, mainly based on local studies, conducted by individual researchers.

The latest study (Balaska et al. 2012) was based on five hundred and eighteen ($N=518$) adults, residents of the city of Thessaloniki. The majority of sport participants (66 %) reported that they participate in free/unorganized sport activities. Furthermore, 25 % reported that they were members of private health clubs, while 10 % reported that they were members of local authority sport programs (*sport for all* programs). Once again, the absence of *sport club* as a setting for sport participation should be noted.

The majority of respondents (55 %) reported that they do not participate in any recreational sport activity during their leisure time. Subsequently, 45 % of adult individuals are those that participate in some type of recreational sports during their leisure time. In terms of frequency of sport participation, 6 % stated that they participate almost every day, 14 % stated that they participated 3–5 times/week, 15 % stated that they participate 1–2 times/week, and 10 % stated that they participate less than once a week (Fig. 12.2). If we group these statistics, we can see that about 20 % of the adult population in Greece participates regularly in some type of sports, during their leisure time. This proportion is higher than the one reported by previous local studies that have used the same methodology; this shows that Greeks have started to adopt a more active lifestyle. However, it should become clear that these statistics are not representative of the whole adult population in Greece, since the sample is biased towards younger individuals (in comparison with the census data) and also the data were collected by an urban area. Considering that sport participation among older individuals and residents of rural areas is lower, it could be argued that the national sport participation rate is much lower than the 45 %, which was found in the present study. The same applies to the frequencies of sport participation.

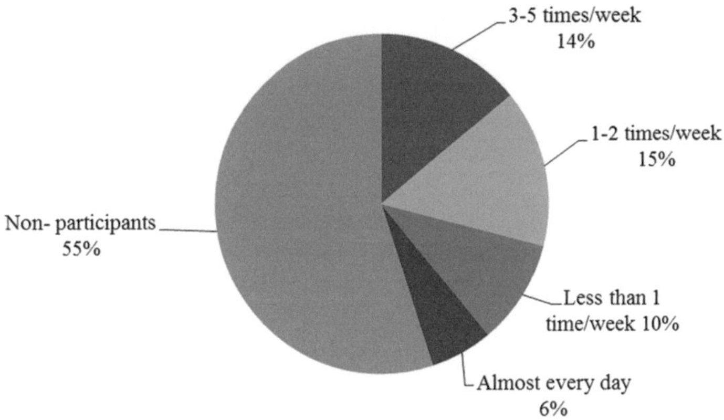


**Fig. 12.2** Sport participation rate and frequency of sport participation (Balaska and Alexandris 2014)

## 12.4 Demographic Differences in Sport Participation

The cross tabulations between demographic variables and sport participation rates revealed some trends.

First of all, males had higher sport participation rates than females. However, the difference is not statistically significant (Table 12.1). This result shows that the gap in sport participation between the two gender groups, which was reported in earlier studies, is closing. This is due to the changing role of women in the Modern Greek society, the financial independence of younger women, their increased levels of employment, as well as the provision of more opportunities for recreational sports for women. Promotion of sports for women through media and sport companies has also influenced women' increased participation rates.

Mixed results were found in terms of sport participation by age groups (Table 12.1). While the two youngest groups had the highest sport participation rates, a decrease in sport participation seems to happen after the age of 60 years old. However, the results show only trends, since the differences are not statistically significant. Considering the aging of the Greek population, it could be proposed that local authorities, sport clubs, and associations should develop strategies to promote sports within elderly in Greece, since this will be the largest group of the population soon. Educating older people about the value of sport participation is a key strategy. Cooperation with health professionals is a second strategy that could be proposed. In any case the sport programs and services provided by sport clubs should address the needs of older individuals.

Finally, the results also show a trend towards increased sport participation levels with higher education, without the differences being statistically significant (Table 12.1). This is also a finding that has been consistently reported in all the studies

**Table 12.1** Sport participation rates by demographic groups (% shows participation) (Balaska 2013)

| Gender groups | | Age groups | | Educational level groups | |
|---|---|---|---|---|---|
| Males | 50.0 % | 18–25 | 60.0 % | Primary | 33.0 % |
| Females | 41.0 % | 26–35 | 52.0 % | Secondary | 40.0 % |
| | | 36–45 | 43.0 % | Vocational | 41.0 % |
| | | 46–55 | 43.0 % | Technical | 48.0 % |
| | | 56–60 | 44.0 % | University | 50.0 % |
| | | >60 | 37.0 % | Postgraduate | 62.0 % |
| $\chi^2 = 1.71$, n.s. | | $\chi^2 = 8.5$, n.s. | | $\chi^2 = 3.6$, n.s. | |

conducted in Greece. This relates to the understanding of the benefits of sport participation among the most educated individuals. It might also reflect the economic status of the different education groups. Finally, it might also be due to the better access to information related to sport participation among the most educated individuals. Considering the higher levels of education among the younger individuals in Greece, increases in future sport participation rates should be expected.

## 12.5 Characteristics of Sport Clubs/Associations

As previously noted, nonprofit sport clubs and associations in Greece mainly promote sport for children, youth sports, and elite athletes. There are, however, some sport clubs mainly in outdoor sports (e.g., climbing, trekking, mountain biking, sailing) which have been developed in the last couple of years, aiming to promote *sport for all* (especially in outdoor sports). It could be argued that the years after the 2004 Olympic Games there has been a change in the sport culture in Greece, from elite athleticism to recreational sports. This has become clear in the changing focus of many sport clubs towards recreational programs. Sport clubs today organize children and youth sport academies/camps and some of them have started to organize active lifestyle programs targeting to adults (e.g., trekking, biking). Many of the sport clubs have been recently involved in the organization of outdoor sport events, such as city marathons, mountain marathons, mountain biking, and triathlon events. These events have shown a rapid growth during the last couple of years in terms of number of participants. Some of them achieved impressive figures and increases. In *The Athens Classic Marathon* the number of 20,000 runners in 2010 increased to 30,000 in 2013. In the *Alexander the Great Marathon*, which takes place in Thessaloniki, the number increased from 11,000 in 2013 to 15,000 in 2014. These events are organized with cooperation among local authorities, sport clubs, and the Athletics Sport Federation. As a conclusion, sport clubs in Greece have been growing in the last few years, despite the economic crisis in the country, because of their focus on recreational sports. This shows the positive perspective of the recreational sport market in the future.

The sport clubs and associations are managed by elected committees. The members of these committees do not get paid; they are volunteers. Considering the number of the sport clubs and their important contribution to the sport sector, it is clear that the sport administration system relies a lot on volunteerism. Sport coaches and instructors, who deliver the programs of each club, are Physical Education and Sport Science graduates; they are paid by the sport clubs, depending on their working status (e.g., full/part time).

Considering the changing phase of the Greek public sector (e.g., reduced budges, restructuring of the Greek public sector, and privatizations) sport clubs and associations will face specific challenges during the next few years, which are summarized below:

- Increase their financial sources
- Adopt a *recreational philosophy* to their programs
- *Catch* the trends towards a more active and healthy lifestyle
- Expand to new sports (e.g., outdoor and street sports)
- Attract financial support from the private sector (sponsorships)
- Increase their number of members (children and adults), through the provision of recreational sports
- Make their sports more attractive and competitive (e.g., fun programs)
- Market their sports
- Educate their coaches and instructors towards the philosophy of recreational culture

As previously noted, local authorities and their sport departments are the main providers of *sport for all* programs in Greece. They aim to contribute to the quality of life of residents of local communities. In order to achieve their social objectives they have low enrollment fees (in comparison with the private sport sector) and they also target the *disadvantaged*, in terms of sport participation, groups of the population (e.g., elderly, disabled, individuals with chronic diseases). They have, of course, also programs for the mainstream population (e.g., fitness classes, team sports, strength and conditioning, and outdoor sports). Traditionally these programs have been supported financially by the General Secretariat of Sports and the fees of the participants. While there have been financial reductions on the part of the General Secretariat of Sports, local authorities are still financially supported to run these programs; the central government has recognized the value of recreational sports for the quality of life of local communities. However, it has to be noted that local authorities have started to explore alternative sources of financing (e.g., sponsorships, higher membership fees, rent of facilities). The aim is to become as much as possible financially independent. It should be noted, however, that there has also been critique of the local authorities' sport programs as being old-fashioned, and delivered in poor-quality sport facilities. The quality of the sport services varies a lot among the local authorities. The lack of a performance evaluation system of these programs is one of the issues that have not been adequately addressed by the central government.

The organisational structure of the sport departments depends on the size of the local authority and how much it has invested on sport services. It is common to have a program director and a facility manager, who are responsible for organizing and managing sport services. Physical Education and Sport Science graduates are employed to deliver the sport programs. Some of them are permanent employees of the local authorities while some other are hired for some months every year to deliver the programs. They are paid either by the General Secretariat of Sports or by the local authorities themselves.

For the same reason that discussed above (changes due to economic crisis), sport departments of local authorities will also face challenges during the following years; they can be summarized as follows:

- To increase their financial sources
- To reduce operating costs
- To run their programs more efficiently
- To attract financial support from the private sector (sponsorships)
- To become less dependent on the central government
- To upgrade the quality of their sport services
- To manage their sport facilities more efficiently
- To generate income by their sport facilities (e.g., rent, events)
- To expand to new sports (e.g., outdoor and street sports)
- To modernise their sport programs
- To improve their networks within the communities
- To market their programs
- To adopt a strategic marketing approach to their sport services
- To avoid the *privatization* of their programs

## 12.6 Specific Topic: Constraints on Recreational Sport Participation

Since the main aim of sport clubs and local authorities' sport departments is to increase sport participation and reduce inactivity, studying individuals' sport decision making for participation is an important issue. A number of theoretical models have been used to study recreational sport behavior. One of the most popular theories that have been recently used in the leisure literature has been the leisure constraint theory (Crawford et al. 1991).

A number of studies have been conducted recently in Greece to investigate the factors that constrain individuals to participate in sport activities, in the context of free sport participation but also in municipal and sport club sport programs. Constraints have been defined as factors that limit or block participation in leisure, or preferences for participation in specific activities (Jackson 1991). It has been proposed (Crawford et al. 1991) and empirically supported (Alexandris et al. 2002) that constraints are categorized into the following:

- Intrapersonal constraints: They are internal to an individual, related to psychological states and attributes, such as low self-esteem, anxiety to participate in sports, body image perceptions, and fear of getting hurt during participation.
- Interpersonal constraints: They are related to an individual's social isolation, and inability to find partners to participate in sports.
- Structural constraints: They are external to an individual, and include factors related to lack of time and resources, facility and accessibility problems, and financial issues.

A hierarchical model of leisure constraints has been proposed, according to which the intrapersonal constraints are the most powerful ones, which block participation in sport activities; the structural and interpersonal constraints do not block participation but they usually modify it (participation less frequently and in alternative activities).

In the most detailed study (Alexandris et al. 2002) that investigated constraints for sport participation in Greece among the adult population (city of Thessaloniki) seven constraint factors were revealed which correspond to the three above categories of constraints, as follows:

### 12.6.1 *Intrapersonal Constraints*

- Individual/psychological (anxiety to participate, not feel comfortable in social situations, fear of getting hurt, body image perceptions)
- Lack of knowledge (limited knowledge on the opportunities to participate)
- Limited Interest/negative past experiences (sports are not a priority, experience of participation was not positive)

Although intrapersonal constraints are internal ones, they are applicable in the context of sport club participation, since they relate to how individuals perceive organized sport programs. For example, beginners and old individuals are negatively influenced by individual/psychological constraints on their decision to join organized sport programs (e.g., anxiety to participate in social situations, fear of getting hurt). Furthermore, lack of knowledge constraints might relate to ineffective promotion of sport clubs' organized programs.

### 12.6.2 *Structural Constraints*

- Sport facility/service-related issues (limited sport facilities and opportunities to participate, poor quality of facilities and services)
- Accessibility/financial (cost of participation, difficult access to sport services and facilities)
- Lack of time (limited time due to professional, family, and social commitments)

These constraints are external ones and they directly relate with the quality of the sport programs provided by the sport clubs and the sport facilities that the programs are delivered. Furthermore, financial problems relate to the cost of participation (e.g., membership fees), cost of transportation, and time cost; all these are experienced more intensely in a period of economic crisis, as previously discussed in Greece.

### *12.6.3 Interpersonal Constraints*

- Lack of partners (social isolation, inability to find partners for participation)

These constraints are not very much applicable in the context of sport clubs, since organized programs aim to create the social environment for sport participation and increase the opportunities for social interaction. Actually, promotion of sport club programs is a solution to these constraints.

Alexandris et al. (2002) found that the intrapersonal factors are the most powerful predictors of sport participation/nonparticipation, while the structural and interpersonal factors influence mainly the frequency of sport participation. Also, demographic comparisons in terms of the perception of constraints indicated that (a) females were significantly more influenced by intrapersonal constraints, in comparison to males, (b) the perception of all types of constraints significantly increased among less educated individuals; and (c) there was an inverted U-relationship between perception of constraints and age. Perception of constraints increased from young to middle-aged individuals and then decreased to old individuals, who are mainly influenced by intrapersonal constraints.

It is clear that such data should be used by local authorities and sport clubs aiming to develop appropriate strategies to remove the perceptions of these constraints. Sport clubs should take a leading role in developing such strategies. They could take the role of ambassadors for sports and contribute in areas such as diffusing information about the benefits of sport participation, providing sport education, promoting sports within the society, providing continuing training of sport instructors, promoting the social aspect of sport participation, developing informal networks for promoting sport participation and helping interactions among the members of sport clubs, and cooperating with the central government to develop recreational sport policy.

## 12.7 Conclusion

Greece is currently in a stage of changes and transformations in the public administration system, in an aim to reduce costs, and run public services more efficiently. These changes, the subsequent financial cuts, and the organisational restructuring of local authorities and sport administration system have influenced the delivery of sport services by local authorities and sport clubs. It is, however, notable that the sport sector (local authorities, sport clubs, and private sport clubs) has shown an unexpected resistance to the financial crisis, as shown by the number of sport programs continuing to run, the number of members enrolled in sport clubs and associations, and the number of employees working in sport-related associations and clubs. This shows the important role of sports within society and the strong sport values that Greeks have developed. It is in local authorities' and sport clubs' hands to adapt to the new economic, political, and social environment in Greece. This means that they have to change and modernize their organisational structure and culture with the aim to promote sports within society more effectively, and become as much as possible financially independent. Specifically, if sport clubs are to financially survive, they have to also target recreational sports, by providing opportunities for sport participation among the general population, and not focusing only to elite sports. If they achieve this, they will be able to generate income by membership fees and other commercial activities (e.g., sponsorship programs).

## References


Alexandris K, Tsorbatzoudis C, Grouios G (2002) Perceived constraints on recreational sport participation: investigating their relationship with intrinsic motivation, extrinsic motivation and amotivation. J Leisure Res 34(3):233–252

Balaska P (2013) Recreational sports in local authorities: strategies for planning and promoting sport programs. Unpublished Doctoral Dissertation, Aristotle University of Thessaloniki, Greece, Department of PE and Sport Science

Balaska P, Alexandris K (2014) Examining recreational sport participation behaviour in a period of economic crisis: the case of Greece. Paper presented at the European Association for Sport Management Conference, 9–12 September, 2014, Coventry, UK

Balaska P, Alexandris K, Kouthouris C, Polatidou P (2012) An examination of how constraints and processes of change affect stages of behavioral change for recreational sport participation. Int J Sport Manag Market 12(3/4):275–293

Crawford D, Jackson E, Godbey G (1991) A hierarchical model of leisure constraints. Leisure Sci 13(4):309–320

ELSTAT (2011) Hellenic statistical authority.http://www.statistics.gr/portal/page/portal/ESYE. Accessed 20 Jan 2015

Jackson E (1991) Leisure constraints/constrained leisure: special issue introduction. J Leisure Res 23(4):279–285

The Hellenic Ministry of Culture and Sports (2012) http://www.culture.gr/culture/eindex.jsp. Accessed 20 Jan 2015

The General Secretariat of Sports (2015) http://www.sportsnet. Accessed 20 Jan 2015

The General Secretariat of Sports (2013-2014) Sport Federations Financial Support.http://sportsnet.gr/index.php/grafeio-tupou/deltia-tupou/1377-omospondion-2014-epixorigiseis. Accessed 20 Jan 2015

# Chapter 13
# Sport Clubs in Hungary

**Szilvia Perényi and Ilona Bodnár**

## 13.1 Introduction

Based on the main political and historical changes in Hungarian society, which fundamentally restructured the economic, political and social composition of the country, such as World War II and the pluralistic changes in 1989–1990, the development of sports clubs in Hungary can be divided into the following three periods: first, the era before World War II (Bodnár and Perényi 2012), second, the state socialist era between 1945 and 1989 and third, the new democratic transition period since 1989–1990 (Földesi and Egressy 2005). Through a socio-historical analysis this chapter introduces the meanings, roles and importance given to sport, as well as how this formulated the position of sport clubs in the Hungarian sport system. It is in the characteristics of the former state-socialist countries that the pace and direction of their development differ from those of the Western European countries. Regardless of the different sporting practices in Western Europe, which were also models for implementation in Eastern and Central Europe, their historic difference was deeply ingrained in the foundation of their sporting culture and shaped their sporting practices in a special way. Before World War II, these countries were neither at such a level of development, nor did they have effective organisations in place. Following the war, political notions were strong; those influences formed the mentioned special character of sport also in Hungary. This underlines the reason for

S. Perényi (✉)
Department of Sport Economics and Management, University of Debrecen, Debrecen, Hungary
e-mail: sperenyi@hotmail.com

I. Bodnár
Eötvös Lóránt University of Sciences, Budapest, Hungary



C. Breuer et al. (eds.), *Sport Clubs in Europe*, Sports Economics, Management and Policy 12, DOI 10.1007/978-3-319-17635-2_13

a socio-historical approach when introducing the *role of sport clubs in policy and society*, and gives an answer to the question of why sport clubs exist, how important sport clubs are for society and what contributions they make to local communities.

## 13.2 History and Context

### *13.2.1 Before World War II*

The Hungarian Reform Era (1825–1848) targeted the renewal of the overall social, political and economic contexts of society, and also launched an awakening in the approaches given to the concept of body culture in our country. Playing a leading role in this movement, aristocrats felt obliged to develop the national sport as well. Influenced by examples of Western European countries, the popularisation of riding, fencing and new forms of rowing began and new sport institutions, prizes and contests were founded. Around 1820 new horse racing courts, rowing houses and fencing halls were established, financed by private funds, which institutions were surrounded by members of exclusively aristocratic descent. The founders, according to their political will and nation-loyal education, opened the opportunities for entry also for the bourgeoisie by the 1830s, and continued the operation of these establishments as joint-stock companies. Following the restructuring, the leadership still remained in the hands of the magnates, but more and more members of bourgeois origin were recruited.

The position of the National Fencing Association can be considered an average practice as it identifies future supporters "… Hungarian-born, unable to pay tuition, honest, at least 12 years old, of bourgeois descent, not working as a servant … (Zeidler 2006, p. 56)", who could create the vast majority of members of these sporting "schools". Sport that started as an aristocratic fashion gradually became an accepted leisure activity also by the upper societal segment by the 1830s. The increasing integration of members of the bourgeoisie made opportunities for the trainers in fencing and gymnastics start their own private businesses. Ignatius (Ignác) Clair (1794–1866) founded his Gymnastics School for both girls and boys in Pest in 1833, which later also became a joint-stock company (Pester Gymnastische Schule) due to the increasing interest of Pest-Buda's bourgeoisie of German descent (Zeidler 2012).

These first joint-stock companies were the first sporting entities (institutions) of Hungarian sport. Their transformation into civil organisations (clubs) were slowed by two factors. First of all, civil initiative that recognised the values of sport was weak, which can be explained by the weakness of the civilian middle class who could access these services; the second factor was the lack of political support for sport. Following the defeat of the Hungarian Revolution and War of Independence (1848–1849), the Habsburg absolutism rejected all initiatives in relation to physical education and sport. For example, the official inaugural meeting (1866) for the emergence of the previously mentioned Gymnastic School of Ignác Clair with Pesti

Torna Egylet (Budapest Gymnastic Club) took more than 3 years, due to the continued rejection by the council. The more liberal policy of the Austro-Hungarian Dual Monarchy after the Compromise of 1867, however, removed the barriers from expansion of sport in the country.

The different sports of the Hungarian Reform Era in many ways preserved their aristocratic nature, which was increasingly less able to support the development of sport institutionalisation. It was the sport of athletics that revitalised the momentum for sport development. Count Maximilian Esterhazy (1837–1883), who was an athlete, a patron of sport and a theoretical writer of sport, from the 1870s made conscious efforts for the spread of new forms of physical activities in Hungary.[1] As the result of his efforts, the Hungarian Athletic Club, with 300 founding members, was formed in April 1875. This club, later a dominant entity in the development of the Hungarian sport system, has increasingly built its structure on the middle class; only a quarter of the founding members were of aristocratic descent.

Even though the aristocracy referred to sport as a means for national education, they considered it as a form of leisure, a free-time activity. In contrast, the bourgeoisie conventionalised sport as a potential for the development of the personality, skills and abilities, and therefore, raised new demands and expectations towards sporting organisations. Some of the members demanding racing competitions of the Neptune Rowing Club (Neptun Evezős Egylet) became independent in 1884 because *social* rowing was not enough of a challenge for them any longer. Organisation of competitions and competition systems had a backlash effect on club life. Besides the more intensive social life and the possibility for heterogeneous social relations a new attraction appeared: club loyalty, the experience of association to and identification with a social unit, a sporting community. This was particularly marked in the case of football, which recreated the map of Hungarian sport life. This new form of communal sports draws new age groups, social segments and settlements; high school students, *petty bourgeoisie* and citizens of rural areas became equally involved with football. Around the increasing number of teams and resolute supporter groups, passive sports fans emerged. Club colours gained increasing importance in the construction of the local masculine identity. Along with the appearance of tens of thousands of supporters, money and also professionalism in sport had appeared. By the 1920s not only sport club foundation *fever* characterised sport, but a sport facility construction wave had also appeared. Both the societal (civil) and the political (governmental) support for the sport increased during this period. The latter is underlined by the fact that the Physical Education Act of 1921 ruled to incorporate the teaching of physical education in schools and sporting practices in factories. Any plant with a number of workers exceeding 1,000 had to provide sporting opportunities for workers. This made sport organisations connected to

[1] In the series of his articles promoting athletics stated: "… *if we had a centre, an organisation, a club we could have a starting point to accelerate athletics*". In Atletikai gyakorlatok [Athletic Exercises]. (text by Count Maximilian Esterhazy (Viador) printed with 143 figures, Budapest, 1879; text by count Maximilian Esterhazy and Lajos Molnár in Vadász és Versenylap [Hunter and Contest-journal], 1874).

factories or other corporations appear more prominent in sports. Besides, workers could join other forms of sport organisations, as trade unions and political parties also established sports clubs (Földes et al. 1989).

In 1930 official state statistical surveys on sport were also published, which draw a rather capital (Budapest)-centred picture of Hungarian competition sport in comparison to the number of inhabitants. The capital outperformed the country region in all measured indexes. In comparison to the 12 % of the total population of the country living in Budapest, 44 % of competitive athletes and 25 % of the sports facilities were located there (Ghimessy 1935; Mike 1938, 1943). Sports attracting the upper and middle layers of society and having high sport facility demand, such as field hockey, skiing, golf and swimming, had formed and operated their sport clubs dominantly here. All large sports clubs that incorporated multiple sports and high memberships were in Budapest. Also, all international sporting events that were staged in Hungary before World War II were located in Budapest. The combination of these advantageous elements also gave the capital a head start in sport professional knowledge and quality in comparison to the rural areas of the country. Despite the weak sports political aspirations, a strong social, economic, sport professional and regional dominance characterised the domestic sporting life, concentrated around the capital.

Looking at the operation of sports clubs of this era, it could be concluded that they could meet more and more demand of civil society. In addition to their basic function—to provide sporting opportunities—their community and identity-forming power became increasingly appreciated. Sport had widened the circle of social contacts; new ranges of opportunities for entertainment and community activities were formed. However, this modernity had redrawn society: a *tribal culture* crept back as sporting clubs were formed based on ethnic, religious and occupational backgrounds. Sport has given the opportunity for people to emphasise the core elements of their own identities. However, before World War II, it was offered to and accessible mainly to men in Hungarian sport.

### *13.2.2 Communist: State-Socialist Era*

The communist transformation after World War II had fundamentally changed the Hungarian political and economic system, and as part of that, it also affected the subsystem of sport. The resolution of the Presidential Council in 1951 stated that the development and centralised management of physical education and sports are state responsibility. For this reason it is a critical issue for the nation; which can be developed through the cooperation of state agencies and civil organisations. Based on the characteristics of the era *state agencies and civil organisations* meant communist, later socialist, party or party-related satellite organisations, such as unions or political youth organisations. Similar to other communist countries, sport in Hungary also became part of the central direction of the party in power. This centralisation was necessary in order to urgently and effectively transform the values and functions that civil sport held. The power of a sport club system in creation of identity and community was a threatening and useless element to the party. This uselessness resulted in different ways of treatment such as merging, termination or restructuralisation of sports clubs that were stereotyped by dangerous bourgeois/civilian traditions. New leadership was appointed where it was necessary to create these organisations to be *trustworthy* for the purposes of the party. At the same time, using the central order, new sporting clubs were established in small countryside settlements, where these organisations had not existed before. All this was necessary because the values carried by civil sport organisation needed a fast and efficient conversion. The party also made people *realise* their need for sport and physical exercise, which also served the goal of artificially structuring and continuously controlling citizens' free time. Sport became an indirect but efficient tool for the suppression of civil initiatives. Based on the Soviet model the sporting gatherings called *spartakiads* or *olimpiads* and other sporting movements were organised by the party. From time to time these events were renamed, and reorganised under *people* or *mass sport* gatherings.

The emerging professionalisation in sport by the 1920s was also discontinued. Sport, which was considered to be a state task of this era, became entirely funded by the state budget. The importance of membership fees and local revenues representing personal commitment became marginal. The ministries, local governments and state-owned enterprises took over the responsibility of the financing of clubs out of their own budget. As time progressed though, the system developed its own inequality; there were no equal chances for clubs to access financial support; elite sport playing a political role gradually pushed mass sport to a weak position. Soft budget constraints, a characteristic of state socialism, and the personal and in most cases informal social capital were in favor for competitive sport.

In this type of sport funding system, mass sport fell into a more disadvantageous position. Its financial resources gradually declined, as the trade unions and also the control of free time had lost its political weight. Both were allocated high priority during the time when the communist regime was established as 90 % of employees were members of labour unions or similar organisations requiring less or no political commitment at that time. However during consolidation after the 1956 revolution, the party changed methodology, well illustrated by the slogan. *Whoever is not against us is with us.*[2] Hungary became the happiest *barrac* of the socialist block by the release of *careful consumption* policy. The party allowed an opportunity for the purchase of some products, services and property by overtime work—at the expense of free time previously blocked from most segments of society. This was a much more reliable and effective tool to control and manage time and privacy of people than spartakiads or the whole sport movement. This is also the reason why the observed leisure wave of the Western world during the 1960s did not reach our

[2]The famous saying was attributed to the first secretariat of the communist party, János Kádár (1912–1989), even though it was a citation by him. The writer Méray Tibor (1924–) living in French emigration wrote these words for the fifth annual celebration of the Hungarian revolution. Kádár started to use Méray's phrase by 1961.

country. The spread of club and recreational sports in Hungary experienced deficits as the investment of free time headed in the direction of the so-called *second economy*.[3] The leaders of the sport policy makers constantly perceived the contradictions of the state-socialist political system in which people and youth were the basic point of reference. In reality, however, these were the dimensions of society where results could not be shown in the continuous struggle between the two World Orders. The policy statements that appeared from time to time during this era urged for a change; however, the notions in words for resolution were never followed by actions in reference to action plans and funding for school and mass (recreational) sport.

The differences had also increased between sports clubs within the competitive sports system. Access to the *soft budget constraints*[4] was not equally approachable to all stakeholders of sport. This access to the additional central funds was based on two basic criteria: political reliability and Olympic success. The intensification of the economic difficulties of socialist economy created an increasingly widening economic gap among the different sports associations and clubs. Consequently, because of the centralised and unprincipled leadership in sports, those who had direct contacts to decision makers became the more advantaged. For example, the *Honvéd* sport club with its base to the army and the Ministry of Defence or *Vasas* SC with its connection to the labour party could provide better financial support and sporting environment to their athletes than, for example, *Ferencváros* with a larger spectator support but fewer party connections.[5] The guild hierarchy among the clubs was stabilised by the reinforcement of the evaluation categories (points) based on the achievements at the Olympic Games and World Championships; these points were converted into financial support levels. Such an evaluation system is still used today.

The industrial background that was appointed behind the different sporting clubs in the beginning served the purpose of the hidden financial support of elite athletes. Besides such so-called *sport-employment* their amateur status was still maintained (Földesiné 1999). Later, the reduction of central funds and intensifying economic difficulties raised the pressure on and the expectation from those state companies and organisations in relation to financial support of clubs. Consequently, in the industrially undeveloped regions the disadvantages of sport clubs were growing.

---

[3] People were given legal permission to engage in a second job in order to gain more discretional income to spend on "authorised" products or properties. The second job option is still a dominant practice in most segments of society (teachers and also blue-collar workers) in order to provide a more comfortable living for families.

[4] Soft budget constraints: A characteristic phenomenon of mixed economies especially apparent in socialist systems described by János Kornai, accumulated when the strict relation of expenditures and earnings relaxed and the difference is paid by an outside institution, usually by the state (Kornai 1986). The meaning in this paper refers to the informal power of sport organisations to get additional funding opportunities based on high political connections, overruling of "five-year plans" and strict budget constraints of the socialist era.

[5] Multiple sport large clubs playing a central role in Hungarian sport: Honvéd SC, Budapest, founded in 1909; Vasas SC Budapest, founded 1911; Ferencváros SC Budapest, founded 1899.

A threefold group breakdown of sports clubs was formulated by the time of the political and economic transition (Barts 1987):

- *Accentuated sports clubs*: 20–25 clubs fell under this category, which had 10–15 sport divisions (szakosztály), and were successful at international competitions. Their supply of equipment and infrastructure was outstanding in comparison to other clubs. Their funding came from different resources. They received significant state and local government support, but could also count on income from the public as they attracted spectators/viewers as well. They employed full-time sports coaches and leaders. The proportion of social workers (volunteers) was insignificant.
- *Mid-size clubs* with nationally accepted performance level: Approximately 120–150 of these clubs functioned in the country at this time, mainly in the countryside, the big cities or municipality centres. They had 5–8 sport divisions each. Their task was talent identification to maintain the *production* of the elite athletic performance of the nation. Talents were mostly transferred to *accentuated* sports clubs of the first group. With few exceptions, part-time work (full employment elsewhere) was employed to serve for managerial and coaching assignments.
- *Small sport clubs*: The majority of the approximately 3,700 small sport organisations designed to serve the local needs. These clubs usually operated one sport division, and this was in most cases football. They typically used social (voluntary) work.

The anomaly of the state-socialist sports system was the latent professionalism. Less attention was paid to the fact that the operation of the illusory amateurism required a large number of professional, full-time sports leaders and coaches. Especially up until the 1970s, a very large apparatus organised the Hungarian sport life, providing employment for both athletes and sport professionals. In the upper levels of the system these jobs were increasingly awarded based on *trust* and political affiliation. Sport professional qualifications were not considered in all cases. For sport leaders the primary requirement was the maintenance of social relations with the related organisations; a strong social and political connection (the so-called *kijárás* in Hungarian) was needed (Kornai 1992). To do this, the aforementioned skills were not necessary. Even though the clubs were operating as employers, like any other work place, they did not reach the management quality of an average enterprise. The presidents of clubs not only outwardly but also inwardly used informal tools and methods in their work. The political resolutions mentioned before identified these managerial errors, such as lavishness (irresponsible spending), despotic management, authoritarianism and inadequate professional skills, favouritism and unfounded decisions. Critical voices, however, did not reach the right decision-making levels; sports leaders' professionalism and management style have not changed fundamentally. This also added to the circumstances that emerged during the period of 1989–1990, when the political and economic transition time and the start of the democratisation process were not entered by sport organisations with ready management scenarios feasible in a market economy.

Overall, before the political transition in 1989–1990, the internal characterisation of sport consisted of three pairs of opposite dimensions: *capital–countryside*; *competitive sport–recreational sport* and *Olympic sportsnon–Olympic sports*. Competition sport was operated on central and state management and funding, and recreation sport on decentral bases, local control and self-financing. The sport clubs of this time had entered the increasingly globalised sporting arena and a new era with a rundown sporting infrastructure, limited professional support related to physiology, sports medicine, psychology and information technology or economy-related management experiences. During this very challenging era the only tool for the survival of sports organisations was to maintain their athletic performance, translated specifically into Olympic success. This led Hungary to perform among the top ten nations at the games among countries with incomparably higher economic strength.

In addition to Olympic success that has been well maintained over the 40 years of state socialism, another positive legacy was the involvement of women. As athletes they caught up with men's sports' success; fencers, swimmers, kayakers and handball players just to name a few brought medals in increasing numbers. As for participation in decision-making entities, however, they were not able to cross the line of the critical mass. Being a female coach still remained a challenge; however, being a former Olympic athlete as an entry requirement and the development of survival strategies made it possible for successful female coaches to maintain their position for a long term in their clubs (Bodnár 2006). These career strategies included the ownership of highest possible coaching qualifications combined with other university degrees mostly in pedagogy or in psychology, which raised them above the average qualification level in their sport. Also, the reduction of feminine behaviour and physical signs and strong separation of work and family were characteristic in their practices.

If not on the drafted extent in political resolutions, diversification of the membership of sports clubs along social, demographic and regional variables started an incline (Table 13.1).

**Table 13.1** Number of sport club and sport club division members between 1955 and 1985 (MTS 1966, p. 1–2; MTS 1986, p. 5–6)

| Year | Sport club | Sport club division | Sport club member[a] | Division member |
|---|---|---|---|---|
| 1955 | 4,391 | 19,105 | 532,707 | 415,390 |
| 1960 | – | – | – | – |
| 1965 | 4,755 | 17,639 | 997,843 | 451,303 |
| 1970 | 4,575 | 14,703 | 1,155,139 | 471,501 |
| 1975 | 4,154 | 11,187 | 1,134,113 | 389,654 |
| 1980 | 3,891 | 10,788 | 1,172,442 | 450,047 |
| 1985 | 3,893 | 9,999 | 1,219,741 | 455,902 |
| 1990 | 2,716 | 5,887 | 477,499[b] | 290,999 |

[a]Mostly sports clubs of workers union, who participated only in sporting events

[b]27 % is female

Based on the yearly report of the State Statistical Agency (Table 13.1) it seems that clubs showed a stable appearance between 1955 and 1975, but the number of sport divisions gradually decreased. Interestingly, the number of sport club members doubled during the same period, which may be due to the state effort to increase mass sport participation primarily through establishing mass sport in state companies. A slight decline in the number of clubs and club sport divisions started as early as the 1980s, which did not reflect in membership. A more drastic decline is noticeable by 1990, as there was a 30 % decline in the number of clubs, and more than 42 % in the number of club sport divisions. This reduction by 1990 had a multiplying effect on the number of members as well. While sport club members (referring to leisure sport) decreased to one-third, the division members (referring to competition sport) had a decline by 37 %. It seems that the destructuralisation affected mass sport the most. Due to the limitation of budgets available to sport, the rationalisation of operation allowed maintenance only to competition and elite sport. That could be a reason for the lower degree of reduction in the members of sport divisions in comparison to club membership as a whole (Table 13.1).

Due to the decentralisation process following the changes, sport became a local, municipality task. However, as the degree to which sport was to be supported on the local level was not regulated centrally, how to allocate funding for the support of sport programmes and sport organisations became the decision of the local city councils. Therefore it became dependent on the financial abilities of local municipalities to support sport. Consequently in more developed regions sport gained a more advantageous position while regions with less economic strength had fewer resources to invest money in the support of sport. Also, the settlement composition of regions and municipalities had an influence as the higher distribution of small settlements created more challenges for sport facility development, and the creation or maintenance of diversity in offering sporting practices for example.

### *13.2.3 The New Democratic Era*

The era following the democratic changes can be further divided into two periods: first the time started by the political and economic changes from 1989–1990 up until 2010, and the one following 2010 up until today. The following sections of this chapter describe these periods together, but using a thematic approach and in parts continue to provide some socio-historic links.

## 13.3 Role of Sport Clubs in Policy and Society

The Hungarian sport sector had arrived at the political and economic changes with no experience in independent democratised operations and practices based on civil initiatives as in general it was state funded and state directed before. Also, high-performance elite sport was a value and priority in sport policy with the role of reinforcing the success and strength of state-socialist world order (Földesi 1996; Dóczi 2012). The motion related to elite athleticism measured in medals at that time is reflected in the focus accumulated in sport strategies also of today (National Sport Strategy 2007). The glory of Hungarian elite performances on the international scene of competition sport is still in central focus. This, however, is not paired with a high degree of involvement in physical activities and sport, as the participation of the general public in sports was reported around 8–18 % during the 1990s (Falussy 2002; Gáldi 2002).

### 13.3.1 National Data on Sport Club Participation

The demolishing effect of the transition period is well demonstrated by the decrease of clubs, club divisions and club members as presented in Table 13.1. Additionally Földesi (1996) also reported substantial reduction in the number of coaches (27 %) and outlined that the rise of unemployment in sport reached a higher level than in other segments. Sport participation has not recovered from this trauma ever since; it is still very low in Hungary in comparison to other EU countries.

The most physically active segment of society is limited to the young generations still studying and not out in the job market. Rates drastically drop by age, and it is starting as early as the age of 15 (Fig. 13.1). There is another drop as people enter the job market or start establishing families. Also, cultural capital plays a very strong role; those with low education are the ones who report the lowest involvement in physically active living. Ethnic groups' involvement is marginal (below 20 %) in all

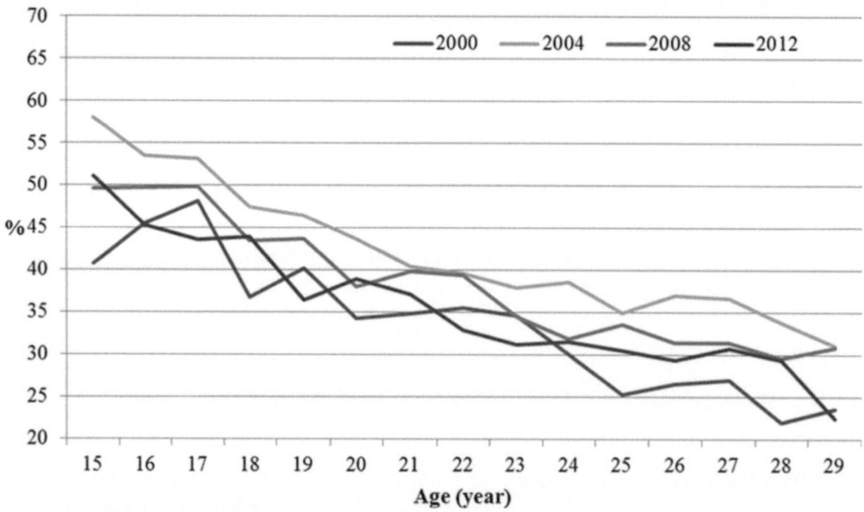


**Fig. 13.1** Sport participation rates (%) of Hungarian youth (age 15–29) between 2000 and 2012 ($N$=8,000). Youth 2000–2012 Survey (Perényi 2013a)

levels of sport and physical activities (Perényi 2011); opportunities are opening mainly in boxing and martial arts (Dóczi 2014). Even though the young generations seem to be the most active their rates are also quite low. The recent results of the Youth 2012 survey reported 35 % participation of the 15–29-year-old youth. It is interesting that these rates did not change since the year of 2000. There was a slight incline by 2004, but numbers dropped back and were pending during the past 12 years. These results are not in harmony with the results gained by the recent Eurobarometer survey of 2014, which shows a 10 % increase in Hungary (the differences may be due to different methodological approaches).

In terms of the popularity of sports, data shows the relevance of football among youth, which is followed by running, cycling and swimming. Football is the most popular among young men as 23 % of those reporting their participation in sport choose football as their primary sporting activity. Young women mainly choose aerobics and other fitness-related activities as their primary activity (Youth 2000, 2004). Team sports other than football show lower popularity among the 15–29-year-olds with 5 % in basketball, 3 % in handball and 1 % in volleyball in the year of 2004. Female proportion in football is marginal, only half a percent of those involved with football as players on the different levels. In handball, however, gender balance is complete; close to half of the registered players are women, while in volleyball more females participate than males (Perényi 2011).

As mentioned before, informal sports such as running, walking, cycling and swimming have become more popular in Hungary today than club-organised sports. Only 2 % of youth reported their membership in sport clubs. Fitness-related activities are also gaining popularity. At present, there are approximately 600–800 fitness clubs that provide services to approximately 300,000 members (Szabó 2012), but the numbers are growing daily. The average frequency in visiting fitness clubs is about two occasions per week and the general entry price is around 30–40 euro per month. This industry is not completely transparent. Very limited information is available on this segment. Based on the mandatory yearly taxation report, one-third of fitness clubs reported operation with financial loss in 2010.

New initiatives of the sport subsystem and an opening to the promotion of sport and movement were represented in the organisation of mass movement gatherings, such as the *Night of movement* that drew 15,000 people to the historic heart of Budapest, Hero Square, in 2014. The initiative represents a wide range of intersectional stakeholder cooperation in sport and state/municipality-NGO-private levels, including the restructured NOC. Even though such events are promoting the relation between movement, exercise and healthy living for citizens of all ages, exposure of or links to sport clubs as the organisational basis of sporting involvement can be hardly identified. The change in the perception of what is accepted as sport or meaningful movement is giving more leverage to activities such as dancing or yoga.[6]

[6]The composition of activities contained popular physical activities such as running, bicycle and fitness activities (Zumba, cardio machines); activities that wanted more proportion such as dancing (salsa), nordic walking, yoga and korfball; but also sports of the Olympic program needing more exposure and promotion such as badminton, table tennis, kajak-canoe and dragonboat.

### 13.3.2 Societal and Political Embedding

Following the political and economic changes, sport organisations were facing fundamental requirements for legal and thus operational transformations. Regulated in the new Civil Law (1991) federations became independent from the state; their funding did not come from direct and automatic resources any longer. The first lawful regulation specific to sport was enacted only in 1996; before that, sport organisations needed to operate with no legal guidance specific to their societal subsystem.

Since the first act on sport (1996) a series of acts ruled lawful changes, such as the Act on Sports in 2000 and in 2004, which all constantly redesigned the structure of sport since the beginning of the 1990s. The National Sport Federation, National Leisure Sport Federation and Paralympic Committee were formed in 2000 and gained special NGO tax status by law. The Hungarian University Sport Federation (MEFS) and the Hungarian Student Sport Federation (MDSZ) operated as independent umbrella organisations of their own area.[7] The funding of sport in this structure was primarily distributed by the respective umbrella organisations; however, it left a range of opportunities for multiplication funding at all levels. As described by Kornai (1992) in relation to the state-socialist era, lobby power or social networks in some cases gave advantages to some federations of different sports. Thus, distinguished clubs, star coaches or athletes could access extra funding for their own activities and operations from different state sources without any systematic distribution logic (Földesi and Gál 2008). These structural modifications did redesign the non-governmental umbrella organisation system of sport, but none of these actions solved and regulated the challenge of funding sports programmes and sport organisations.

Twenty years following the political changes, sport was financially so neglected by central budgets[8] that even the historically and traditionally successful sports started to experience a decline in their performance in delivering medals from continental and world events, and especially the Olympic Games. In Athens and Beijing the Hungarian team fell from the first ten of the unofficial rank of participating nations. A tendency of decline became clear, which alerted the sport subsystem and policymakers. On the other hand, the political and economic climate for reforms in all areas on Hungarian society in the economic crisis period required the introduction of reforms also in the subsystem of sport.

In 2010 sport *became a strategic area in the* political views of the acting government. *New* and substantial changes have been installed into the societal subsystem of sport by the 2011 Amendments of the 2004 Act on sport. This resulted in a com-

[7] Hungarian University Sport Federation (Magyar Egyetemi és Főiskolai Sport Szövetség, MEFS) established in 1906 responsible for organising sport in higher education and the participation on the Universiade; Hungarian Student Sport Federation (Magyar Diáksport Szövetség, MDSZ) established in 1987, responsible for running a national competition sport system, called Student Olympics (diákolimpia) for students in primary and secondary schools.

[8] Share of sport funding of the state budget was below 0.3 %.

plete restructuring in the governance of sports and presented solutions to the funding of sport as well. The effects and challenges of such sudden and fundamental transformations, which Hungarian sport is presently going through, may be quite similar in the extent of the changes in the beginning of the 1990s. It should be emphasised that all these reforms became necessary in the governance of sport; however, it became a top-down procedure and more in-depth civil debate could have added to its development. Changes directly affected the upper segment of larger umbrella organisations and sport federations but indirectly brought serious consequences also to the micro levels, such as sport clubs and other forms of non-profit sport organisations.

The 2011 Amendments of Act on Sport 2004 placed the Hungarian Olympic Committee[9] as the main umbrella organisation and channelled all the other non-governmental umbrella organisations underneath. By this, all previously independent sport umbrella organisations covering different areas of sport became part of the Olympic Committee as one of its branches. In the newly structured HOC there were five new branches created: (1) Olympic sports, (2) non-Olympic sports, (3) disabled sports, (4) leisure sports and (5) student and university sports. These five branches continued to operate their respective areas through their member sport federations and the clubs. Presently 83 NOC-endorsed national sport federations operate in Hungary, 42 in Olympic sports and 41 in non-Olympic sports. The structural changes also granted the responsibility for the Olympic Committee to distribute all state funding to all sport organisations. This task was also paired with controlling functions, which modified the NOC's pure civil organisation function and in reality made it a *quasi-civil* organisation with functions[10] taken over from the state (Perényi 2013b).

A new sport financing approach was implemented in Hungarian sport that opened up new funding channels and presented increased amounts of support. The new funding system contains three different channels. The Hungarian Olympic Committee, through its new structure, distributes funding allocated by the central governmental budget to sport, which is supplemented by a new *program financing* approach, a tax-benefit scheme given to athletes and sport professionals, and the newly developed financial support scheme called *TAO* was implemented.[11] The TAO support was especially important for providing funding solutions for clubs; however, clubs in only five sports were eligible to apply, all of which were team sports only,[12] but not to all team sports. The new process was meant to add new

[9] Hungarian Olympic Committee (HOC)—in Hungarian: Magyar Olimpiai Bizottság (MOB)—established in, 1895 in Budapest.

[10] From a rather small organisation of 15 employees before 2010, with its new functions HOC has grown to be a mid-size organisation with more than 80 full-time employees.

[11] Tax reduction given to companies on their corporate tax upon support given to sport (the process in more detail can be followed in the chapter on Hungary (Perényi 2013b) in the book by Hallmann and Petry: *Comparative Sport Development—System, Participation and Public Policy*).

[12] Five team sports (football, basketball, handball, ice hockey and water polo) defined as spectator-team sports (látvány-csapatsport) by 1996. LXXXI. Act (4.§ 41).

resources from the private sector and to make sport financing more transparent and controllable (Bardóczy 2012).[13] It was also intended to develop these sports on the grass-roots level.

A series of documents and declarations stated the goal of increasing sport participation among citizens (National Sport Strategy 2007; MOB 2012), but the distribution of financial support among the branches of sport has always seemed disproportionate. It was elite sport, specifically Olympic sports of which perceived prestige was granted with high financial support in return. This privilege was maintained over historic times and different political actors and not only the characteristic of the state-socialist era. It must be acknowledged that there were initiatives to move Sport for All funding up the scale, for example in 2000, when for the first time distinguished attention and larger amounts of funding were allocated to Sport for All. This process though did not show a continuum. In 2008 for example 96 % of state sport funds were allocated to the support of elite sport, and the remaining 4 % given to support Sport for All (MOB 2012).

## 13.4 Characteristics of Sport Clubs

### *13.4.1 General Characteristics*

In the Hungarian sport sector civil organisations, non-profit private organisations and profit-oriented enterprises can operate and provide sport services. The 2004 Act on sport defined sports clubs and sport enterprises as the two basic organisational forms in the sport subsystem. Within this framework sport enterprises can choose from several legal forms based on complicated regulation logic. Limited companies and shareholder groups are allowed in competition sports, while in leisure sport independent sole traders and forms of joint companies also permitted besides the classical and traditional form of sport clubs. Sport clubs and sport foundations represent the non-profit sector in sport, but non-profit limited companies can also be found within sport.

However, sports clubs are the traditional and basic units of the Hungarian sport sector. They can be formed as civil initiatives by an association of ten individuals, according to its legal statutes, and must be registered in court (1989. II . Act, 2-3.§;6-7.§). Clubs have their own bank accounts, and are subject to tax payments. Clubs must have their annual general assemble where professional and financial reports of the past and budgets for the following year are being approved; in between these meetings a voluntary board is responsible for daily operation. In general boards are led by a president and board members. In most of the cases clubs attempt to appoint

---

[13] Companies' share in funding sports has increased by 300 % upon the introduction of the tax-benefit scheme.

economically or politically influential individuals to their boards with the hope of additional support for their programmes.

Five different forms of clubs are outlined by Sterbenz and Gulyás (2012) describing clubs in contemporary society of sport. This grouping is partially similar to the one by Barts (1987) described before in this publication. *Accentuated sports clubs, mid-size clubs and small clubs* are attributed the same characteristics; however, two additional groups are identified:

*Leisure sport clubs*: These clubs usually do not participate in the national competition system, offer activities in several sports and organise different activities such as excursions, competitions, events, festivals or gatherings. They focus on local communities, a work environment or asocial group; their numbers are increasing continuously.

*Student sport and university sport clubs*: They are organised by students and their academic institutions in different sports around the country. Their funding is assisted by student fees; they organise competitions and run different activities; their primary target is youth.

Football and football clubs create a separate *island* in Hungarian sport society. The memories of the glorious past dating back to the 1950s induce continuous efforts to rebuild a successful football nation. According to lawful regulations, division I. football clubs must be operated as private companies. Grass-roots football teams, however, continued to be operated by the base clubs of these teams. In most cases the base club is one of the owners of these private companies. For example the football club and the football company in MTK and Honvéd are completely separate, while at Ferencváros (FTC) the club owns the majority of the shares.[14]

The number of non-profit organisations engaged in sport grew between 2003 and 2008 by 12 %. This growth was followed by a slight decrease (Table 13.2).[15] The data also showed a decrease in the number of reported full-time employees over the years. The lowest number reported was in 2010. Following that there is a noticeable increase, which most likely is in accordance with the more beneficial taxing options created for athletes and coaches. Since 2003 the mandatory data submission of non-profit organisations also contains data on the number of volunteers engaged with their operations. Based on these reports, in Hungarian sport organisations an average of 45,000 volunteers were involved during the 10 years between 2003 and 2012 (KSH 2014).

[14] Ferencváros Torna Club (FTC) was founded in 1899. From 2003 it operates as a public limited company (Kft) and is listed on the Budapest Stock Exchange.

[15] Unfortunately, data up until 1990 detailed in Table 13.1 may not be comparable as it may define sport non-profit organisations in a different way.

**Table 13.2** Number of non-profit sport organisations (all legal forms included), their employees and volunteers between 2003 and 2012 (KSH 2014)[16]

| Year | Number of non-profit sport organisations | Number of employees | Number of volunteers |
|---|---|---|---|
| 2003 | 7,008 | 4,172 | 49,825 |
| 2004 | 7,117 | 3,532 | 54,506 |
| 2005 | 7,049 | 3,649 | 38,398 |
| 2006 | 7,190 | 3,316 | 52,623 |
| 2007 | 7,638 | 2,895 | 48,253 |
| 2008 | 7,938 | 3,045 | 40,465 |
| 2009 | 7,860 | 2,974 | 40,446 |
| 2010 | 7,526 | 2,915 | 38,526 |
| 2011 | 7,563 | 3,437 | 43,582 |
| 2012 | 7,649 | 4,778 | 44,254 |

**Table 13.3** Number of registered athletes in the five team (TAO) sports between 2011 and 2014 (NSI 2013; Bardóczy 2014)

| TAO sports | 2011 | 2012 | 2013 | 2014[a] |
|---|---|---|---|---|
| Ice hockey | 2,305 | 2,378 | 2,996 | 3,777 |
| Handball | 24,000 | 25,000 | 29,788 | 31,227 |
| Basketball | 24,642 | 30,957 | 36,618 | 40,551 |
| Football | 179,328 | 205,000 | 228,334 | 250,000 |
| Water polo | 4,223 | 4,754 | 5,223 | 5,400 |
| Total | 234,498 | 268,089 | 302,959 | 330,955 |

[a]Projection

In case of the TAO sports, Table 13.3 shows the dominance of football in comparison to other team sports. It has six times more registered players in comparison to handball and basketball. It is revealing that ice hockey and water polo account for below 6,000 players nationally. Their low representation could be due to their high dependency on special and high maintenance cost facilities. In case of football, both the number of clubs and the number of players are low in comparison to those of other European countries. For example, Denmark counts more than twice as many players in 1,672 clubs than Hungary with 2,778 clubs, even though Hungary has

[16]Data on sport clubs available only from the Central Statistical Agency today (KSH 2014).The National Sport Information System is operated by the NOC, but this system is incomplete and it provides non-consistent data resource. Some sports are very keen on providing accurate, up-to-date information, while some sports do not keep track of their members and do not require them to submit membership information. For this reason, only estimates are available about the number of clubs or the number of registered sport participants. The Hungarian Handball Federation (HHF), established in 1933, is one of the sports federations that records considerable up-to-date information about its member organisations and its members. HHF reported more than 30,000 players in 2,344 teams around the country including the whole spectrum of players from Division I clubs to children's soft-handball teams. The teams are distributed through 460 independent handball clubs and 99 schools, in addition to the 527 handball divisions of multiple sporting clubs (HHF 2014).

double the population of Denmark. There is a noticeable difference in the number of female players as well: over 70,000 in Denmark, and less than 4,000 in Hungary.

It is also worth noting that outside of football the TAO sports are low in popularity among the youth generations (ages of 15–29). Handball is still within the first 15 most popular sports, but water polo and ice hockey are very low on the ranking of the preferred sports; they show participation rates below 1 %. The introduction of TAO reported 30 % growth in the number of youth engaged in the five team sports (Table 13.3). This growth is yet not reflected in national samples as in the 2012 survey a decline was registered (Perényi 2013d).

Student sport organisations operate in most municipalities. All together 424 legally registered, independent Student Sports Clubs and 2,908 Student Sport Club (kör) function within the legal entity of the schools. The umbrella organisation for all these student sport organisations is the Hungarian Student Sport Federation (MDSZ), which operated its national competition system, the so-called *Student Olympics*, in 18 sports during the past 26 years including more than 2,000 schools annually (MDSZ 2014).

### *13.4.2 Experienced Bottlenecks and Challenges by Sport Clubs*

The biggest perceived challenges for clubs are clearly funding and access to facility use. The constantly changing legal environment and tax regulations require civil organisations' flexibility and the ability to frequently and quickly adapt to change. In lots of cases they need to involve legal and accounting experts, which creates additional financial burden. For sports clubs in general, but especially for smaller clubs, it is hard to cover the costs for travelling and lodging for competition events. Since the first years of the political changes these costs gradually became costs that parents paid in full. By introducing the new funding methods, such as TAO, clubs can pay, for example, the cost of competition and travel for youth athletes.

Besides the above-mentioned financial problems of the clubs, their biggest problem is not recognised or given enough attention. An interlocking effect is created around a triangle of (1) low number of members and participants, (2) lack of training services offered to the general public and (3) lack of sport- and non-sport-related activities offered to members. Maintaining the clear competition sport profile, clubs do not serve the expansion of sport participants in the country. A higher level of their both social inclusion and societal integration could foster more opportunities to activate additional volunteer forces and in parallel additional income from club membership fees.

Also, in multiple-sport clubs the individual sport division may gain legal independence and run a sub-account for their budgets. In these cases their incomes from possible supporters and also membership fees are accounted for separately. This, however, puts sports divisions under pressure for gaining quantity in members for raising fee income, but also develops quality for sponsors' exposure and success state/municipality incentives. Most club sponsorship funds and *mecena* contributions come from parents of athletes running their own private businesses.

### 13.4.3 Recreational Sport and Professional Sport in Sport Clubs

Recreation and competition sports have a clear break-off from each other. Most clubs are either competition clubs or recreational clubs. In very few sports do those two functions come together, for example in triathlon or karate. The number of licences issued by sport varies. Some 3,000–5,000 licences were issued in sports such as aerosports. Sport like dancesport, chess, karate, floorball, modelling, kick-boxing and bowling[17] account for 500 to 1,500 licences, while sports like dogsport, darts, diving and auto sport issued below 50. The 24 sports federations in non-Olympic sports all together issued 22,000 competition licences in 2014 (MOB 2012).[18]

Recreational participants of sport in most cases follow the individualisation trend and exercise outside of any organisation or any sporting facility. More and more people like to exercise alone outdoors walking or running, or to stay at home using stationary exercise bicycles or video tapes, but not having any engagement in any club-related sports (Perényi 2011; Gál 2008). However, there is an expansion noticeable in amateur running clubs, with a large proportion of them related to work places (Perényi in press). Also, club membership for mountaineering clubs has increased; they organise walking excursions for their members in nature. Attempts are being made to gather and register all sport for all participants, which purpose is meant to be served by the *sport card* system.

### 13.4.4 Activities for Sport Club Members

The activities for club-based sport are nearly all discretionally organised around providing training opportunities for athletic development, registration and travel for competitions and organising competitions, all with the clear focus on athletic excellence from an early age on. As the largest proportion of central funding is targeted on youth sport from the prospect of talent identification and management, most clubs operate youth divisions to *grow* the next generation of athletes. Club members other than the athletes with competition licence mostly exist in leisure sport or non-Olympic sports but also on a limited level. Therefore, training services for average club members are not in the focus of the majority of the clubs. Also, sporting activities are limited to the sport itself in which each athlete is registered; non-sport-activities in an average club are not characteristic.

Also, physical educators of schools create their student team in their specific sport and conduct training sessions two or three times a week. They pay rent for the sport hall of their school and take monthly fees from participating students. These

[17] Teke: Traditional Hungarian rolling ball game similar to bowling with no holes on the ball. It is widely played in the country side, by people of older age groups.

[18] Source: Incomplete data from the National Sport Information System operated by the NOC.

teams may enter the *student Olympics* organised by the mentioned National Student Sport Federation (MDSZ) or by sport federation programmes, such as the *Bozsik Program* in football.

Club life cooperates with school sports as well. On one hand, clubs rent school sport facilities for their programmes, and they cooperate in the recent daily school PE programme. Students who take part in organised sports of clubs at least three times a week may be exempt from the two additional physical education classes by a certificate issued by sport clubs. Starting in 2012, mandatory daily physical education classes were introduced by law in both primary and secondary schools. This regulation substantially added to the physical activity level of Hungarian children and youth. However, it raised some relevant implementation issues as well. It called attention to the limited number of available qualified PE teachers in schools especially in primary schools, and the lack of available spaces (closed sport halls and open sport courts) for conducting these classes on a daily basis. Presently, additional personnel are being trained and a school sport gymnasium construction programme (similar to the one in 1991) is under development by governmental agencies.

Elite athletes of clubs in different sports with talent prosperity have special connections to schools with an altered educational programming. In the country presently 55 state-funded and an additional 20 not-funded educational institutions, so-called *sportschool*, operate. These sportschools are part of the education structure overseen by the ministry but have special educational programmes for athletes. These schools have very close connections to clubs, making efficient coordination between training and competition schedules with schooling responsibilities. So-called *club-based sportschools* also exist; these units are sports clubs with no academic programmes. Athletes of such clubs are enrolled in neighbouring schools in classes with special programmes allowing young athletes to maintain daily schedules with multiple trainings. The two types of sportschool forms altogether take approximately 20,000 young athletes between the ages of 6 and 20 (Sterbenz and Gulyás 2012). In 1997 sportschools formed their own umbrella organisation, the National Sportschool Federation,[19] with the goal of representation, lobby activities, expansion with new members and organisation of conferences.

### 13.4.5 Professionalisation

The development of the coach occupation in Hungary dates back to the 1930s (Bodnár and Perényi 2012). Their professionalisation was institutionalised by the establishment of the first higher educational institution in 1925, the Hungarian University of Physical Education. Since then it became widely accepted that the education of school physical exercise and sport should be conducted by specially trained sport professionals. This also applies to coaches in sport clubs. Most, if not

[19] In Hungarian: Sportiskolák Országos Szövetsége (SIOSZ).

all, sport federations regulate the ownership of a coaching certificate as a prerequisite to an involvement in sport training processes.

The employment of administrative and managerial staff on a full-time basis can only be seen in multi-discipline sporting clubs. For example, a 12-sports-division club with 1,500 athletes would have fewer than 20 full-time employees. Most clubs, even the big multiple-sport-division clubs, employ coaches on a part-time basis. Most of the coaches are teachers of physical education or perhaps of other subjects, and have their coaching as an afternoon second job.

Volunteer work became more of an option in small clubs with one sport only. In many cases parents of young athletes contribute their time to help the clubs by organising transportation or accommodation for their competitions. Since the Sports Act of 2004 allowed clubs to re-register as non-for-profit companies, the operation of the clubs became more business-like, using managerial methods known in enterprises. This process also brought the practice of paid management staff in the leadership of these *companies* over the volunteer position of presidents of clubs as a civil organisation. Volunteerism in terms of performing professional work such as coaching is not very usual nor is accepted for one not having coaching qualifications. However, low payment or even non-payment of sport-qualified coaches is very frequent, and thus, this could be considered as volunteer work. The classical volunteer involvement more frequently occurs and is actually becoming more and more popular in international and continental or world events in Hungarian cities. In some cases big events such as a European Championship in swimming would have more than twice the number of volunteers registering than these events could actually take. Most of these volunteers are high school or university students. Older age groups and blue-collar workers rarely participate (Perényi 2013c).

### 13.4.6 Finances

The cut-off of state control and automatic state funding in 1989–1990 eliminated federations' ability to channel funds to their member clubs. Also large state companies previously funding sport clubs lost their ability due to the privatisation or, in frequent cases, bankruptcy. Due to this *separation* process and frequent budget cuts combined with the lack of experience and managerial skills, sport organisations found themselves in jeopardy (Bakonyi 2004; Földesi 1996). This process was also strongly influenced by the new tax regulations in 1991. The introduction of income tax and social security created an additional financial burden for clubs on salaries of athletes and coaches. Also VAT was applied to all purchases, which also applied to sports organisations' purchases in buying, for example, equipment, uniforms or transport services. Without the protective hand of the state the emerging discrepancies resulted in the demolishment of the sport structure, membership, organisations/clubs and facilities between 1990 and 2010.

The new sport financing system implemented by 2010, mentioned before, aimed to tackle the overall funding issues of sport. The TAO programme helped sporting clubs in the five team sports to pay salaries of coaches and rent for the use of facilities, send teams for competition, train coaches and other sport professionals and buy equipment and uniforms specifically in their youth programmes. Within the scheme, construction of new and rehabilitation of old sporting facilities were possible by utilising private tax money for funding purposes. The positive discrimination of some sports (the five team sports in this case) may automatically result in negative discrimination on the side of the excluded. On the micro levels this especially formulated conflicts in multiple-sport clubs, where TAO-benefited team sports and other mainly individual sport divisions such as swimming, track and field or fencing work side by side. The differences in financial opportunities in relation to salaries or abilities of purchasing equipment became very clear to all involved such as managers, coaches, even to athletes and parents engaging in different sport divisions.

The selection of team sports and only five team sports within the support scheme (TAO) called attention to the funding issues of the excluded sports. As a solution the government launched a new funding programme for 16 selected successful Olympic Sports on a programme-financing basis. The selection criteria for inclusion in this programme was complex; however, performance in continental, world events and the Olympic Games was critical in the process. The selected sport federations were required to build long-term strategies for the development of their sport. In this way, the signs of poor professionalism in financial and organisational planning of sport organisations that remained from the state-socialism era were intended to be tackled. The requirement, a so-called *sport development plan*, was needed to be developed outlining the foreseen directions by sport federations for the period up until 2020. The completion of these plans was a prerequisite for applying for and receiving funding from the NOC.

The TAO programme also tackled the issue of run-down and insufficient sport facilities. As mentioned, during the privatisation process around the political changes many sports facilities and properties were closed and used for other purposes (e.g. building of shopping malls). One of the last sport facility developments was in 1991 when 650 school sport gymnasiums were built around the country. Since then rehabilitation or new constructions were rarely made. Sports clubs had difficulty in satisfying their facility needs, which resulted in cutting programmes or closing clubs.

Sporting facilities in general are not owned by sport clubs.[20] The ownership of these facilities is attached to municipalities or the state. Their operation is managed by municipality-owned companies or by schools. Accordingly, sports clubs are obliged to pay rent while using school or municipality sports halls or fields. The sport facility problem was assisted by the TAO programme. In the first year of its introduction more than a hundred artificial grass football fields were built, as well as arenas for basketball and handball, and ice rinks for ice hockey; furthermore, swimming

[20] Some exceptions, however, do exist. The Debrecen Fencing Club received the exclusive long-term right of use for a municipality-owned sport hall (previously a school gymnasium) and operates it following its renovation. Today it offers sporting opportunities (services) to a wide range of age groups, abilities and ethnic backgrounds; counts more than 900 membership-paying members and covers its funding needs with no direct state or municipality resources.

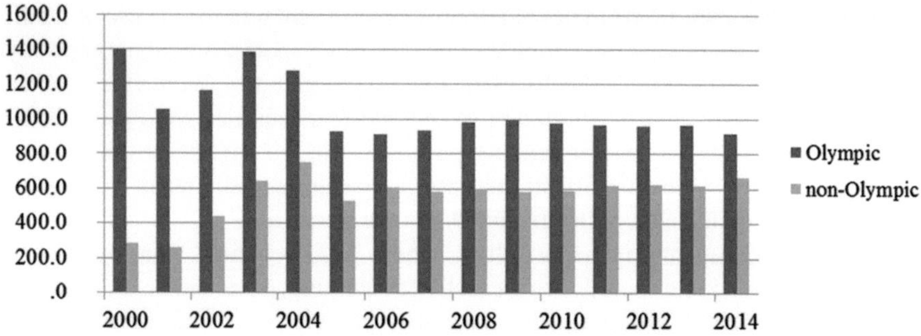


**Fig. 13.2** Distribution of governmental funding by NOC to Olympic and non-Olympic sports between 2000 and 2014 in 1,000 euros (National Sport Information System (NSIS) 2014)

pools for water polo were constructed (Bardóczy 2012, 2014; Géczi et al. 2013). The maintenance of these municipality facilities is assisted by TAO funds, as clubs may apply for support for facility rentals as well. The regulations require all newly built sporting facilities to allocate 20 % of operation capacity to public usage, specifically for sport for all purposes (Act on Sport 2004 modification).

The regulations (Act on Sport 2004) also require municipalities to support sport. Today municipality support to local clubs is realised mostly in the form of free use of city-owned sporting facilities. In this aspect the operation of sport clubs is largely dependent upon the support given by municipalities and local governments. Accordingly, the attitude of municipality leaders towards sport remained a critical factor in the funding and development of sports on the local level even today. In cities where the mayor likes and supports sport, both sport facilities and sports programmes became part of the city strategy and were also used in city marketing; thus their funding was more appropriate than in locations where the leadership of the cities had no such devotion to sport.

Regardless of all sport reforms, however, some of the internal disparity areas identified around the period of the political changes are still present in Hungarian sport. While the *capital–countryside* dimension reflects significant democratisation around the country, the two other areas, *competitive sport–recreational sport* and *Olympic sports–non-Olympic sports*, still show substantial inequality. On one hand, based on the documentation of the Hungarian Olympic Committee (2012), 95 % of the total governmental funding goes to competitive sport both in Olympic and non-Olympic sports. Leisure sports is still waiting for reforms and funding solutions in order to tackle Hungary's tasks with low sport participation. On the other hand, there is a noticeable difference for the favour of Olympic sports over non-Olympic sports (Fig. 13.2). It should be noted that it is more characteristic of clubs in non-Olympic sports to maintain a structure that provides opportunities also for leisure sport or clear amateur sport participation.

The difference in the funding of Olympic and non-Olympic sports was reduced over the years, but only in funds distributed by the NOC. Olympic sports do receive additional funds, for example, through the above-mentioned programme for the 16 selected success sports from which the non-Olympic sports and the leisure sport segment are completely excluded at present. The disparity is more evident if one considers that the large numbers, the crowds, are behind the non-Olympic sport and the sport for all segment; sports club membership of all engaged in sport, as mentioned, is very low (Youth 2004).

In Hungary the debts generated by clubs not only in football but especially due to the reluctance of paying appurtenance (social security, VAT)[21] have been a haunting issue since the changes in 1989–1990.[22] Large traditional sport clubs (mostly having also a football division) have been consolidated by the government several times since that period. Only recently has it been decided that football clubs of Budapest such as Budapest Honvéd, MTK, Újpest, Vasas and BVSC will receive a fund injection and their debts will be taken over by the government. Until 2020, MTK Football club, for example, will receive all together close to three million euros for operation costs and facility development, in addition to the debt consolidation. Some of the countryside clubs also gain facility reconstruction funds (Győr) or constructions of new stadiums such as in Debrecen.[23]

The new financial support scheme introduced in 2010 for the five team sports (Vörös 2011) also reported a participant increase by 30 % since 2011 as the government agency stated (NSI 2013). The increase is explained by the growth in the number of members of existing sports clubs and also by the foundation of new team sport academies predominantly in football and basketball, but also in handball. These academies operate as non-profit private organisations. In some cases they function as umbrella organisations, such as the Debrecen Basketball Academy (Becsky 2014). This academy, for example, through its member clubs offers young players the opportunity for continuous participation throughout the age categories. Parallel, this congregation of clubs raises their chances for TAO fund applications. It must be noted, however, that the permission of EC for the funding solution of TAO shall expire in 2017. This will leave the five team sports and the new sport facilities with a funding and maintenance question. Questions are being raised and survival solutions and methods are being presently developed.

## 13.5 Conclusion

Regardless of the main historical ranges of events in the country, state interventions in civil activities were always present starting as early as the 1920s. This was especially a characteristic in the formulation of civil initiatives in sport, as sport in the later state-socialist countries was a symbol of political existence. The period since

[21] The new Hungarian civil code 2014 requires sport clubs to adhere to stricter documentation procedures.

[22] FTC was even expelled from first division stated in the 2005–2006 season for not meeting the financial requirements of the Hungarian Football Association (MLSZ 2011).

[23] Twenty thousand seating new stadium opened in May 2014 in Debrecen, constructed on municipality property by government funds (tax-payer money) of 5.3 million euros.

the pluralistic changes had a special importance during which civil society attempted to widen its roots in the country, to gain its democracy and autonomy in sport. The fight with the discrepancies that were associated with this process resulted in a weak and neglected sport club system in Hungary (Bakonyi 2004; Földesi 1996; Frenkl 2003; Sárközy 1992). Since the political changes, sport policy development, sport structure and the financing system of sport were reluctant to make efficient connections. In addition sport rather failed than succeeded to integrate as one of the main new players of the developing free-market economy.

The years of 2010–2011 shall be emphasised as a focal point in the development of sport in Hungary as a series of events in political actions were taken for the *rescue* of sport in a form of fundamental legal, structural and funding changes. Sport was declared to be a strategic area of the acting government 2010 (Kele 2012). A new financial support scheme was implemented and approved by the European Commission (2011a; 2011b) to fund five team sports, additional funding channels for 16 sports were opened and the Act on Sports of 2004 was modified. This created a complete re-structuring of the governance of sport in the country and all of this also had an effect on how sports clubs are functioning in the country today.

Such and similar state interventions have been accompanying sport along its developing history throughout dating back to the 1920s. It was, however, most characteristic to the era of state-socialism sport, as at that time elite sport was given prime attention, and even during the hardship of economy resources, it represented the nation as a whole (Földesi 1996; Földesi et al. 2002). As socialisation processes are gaining importance in sport (Bandura 1977; Coakley 1993), today it seems that the habitus for the need of political domination had been passed over to the upcoming generation of leaders in sport, reproducing the era in which they were socialised as athletes and later as coaches, administrators or leaders. Even today the methods and the procedures that govern the subsystem of sport remain along the dimensions of dominance and control regardless of the fact that the actual political power changes almost every 4 election years in the new pluralistic society. It must be stated that the structure of sport without the present strategic governmental intervention and direct fund intervention, if it had not collapsed, would have continued to be demolished.

The organisational culture of the private sector has demonstrated a huge development in Hungary since the political changes, due to their inner initiatives and also the examples given by multinational companies entering the Hungarian market. The management and operation processes of Hungarian sport clubs have been experiencing some struggles in catching up to the conduct of professionalism. However today, formal business-like work procedures are more frequent and project management methods and approaches are also used in sport clubs. Enhanced attention is given to the economic sustainability of club activities. These new processes hope to give a foundation and a chance to sports organisations to start a more independent, efficient and self-sufficient working non-governmental system in sport in the future.

### *13.5.1 Notes*

*Data of this chapter came from* the archives of national sports federations, reports of the state governing bodies, national sports strategy and reports to the sports committee of the Hungarian Parliament. Also, *sport development* reports provided by sports federations to the Hungarian Olympic Committee and the National Sports Institution by the five team sports (football, handball, basketball, ice hockey, water polo) and the 16 sports eligible for extra state funding in 2012 (kayak-canoe, wrestling, judo, ice skating, fencing, gymnastics, modern pentathlon, swimming, track and field, boxing, table tennis, rowing, cycling, tennis, volleyball) were used. Official data sets related to the number of sports clubs from the Central Statistical Office (KSH) were used starting from 1920s. Furthermore, the relevant sport participation data from the Youth 2000/2004/2008/2012 data sets on national youth samples and the analysis of the 2008 survey on national sample were used.

## References


Bakonyi T (2004) Civil álom és politikus állam. Adalékok a civil sportszervezetek státuszának legújabb-kori politikatörténetéhez Magyarországon. Semmelweis University, Faculty of Physical Education and Sport Sciences, Budapest

Bandura A (1977) Self-efficacy: toward a unifying theory of behavioral change. Psychol Rev 84(2):191–215

Bardóczy G (2012) Látványcsapat sportágak finanszírozásának tapasztalatai, a TAO. MSTT konferencia, Budapest

Bardóczy G (2014) A látvány-csapatsport támogatások helyzete, perspektívái. In: Petridis L (ed) A felsőoktatás szerepe a sportban, élsportban és az olimpiai mozgalomban, különös tekintettel a társasági adóból (TAO) támogatott sportágak helyzetére és a támogatások hasznosíthatóságára konferencia kötet. Debreceni Egyetem, Debrecen

Barta O (1987) Sportszervezés. Testnevelési Főiskola, Budapest

Becsky I (2014) A Debreceni Kosárlabda Akadémia vízió és megvalósulás. Presentation on TAO conference. University of Debrecen, Debrecen

Bodnár I (2006) Sikeres edzőnők pályaválasztásának és pályakezdésének elemzése. Kalokagathia 44(1-2):106–116

Bodnár I, Perényi S (2012) A socio-historical approach to the professionalisation of sporting occupations in Hungary during the first decades of the twentieth century: the coach. Int J Hist Sport 29(8):1097–1124

Coakley J (1993) Socialization and sport. In: Singer RN, Murphy M, Tennant LK (eds) Handbook of research on sport psychology. Macmillan, New York, pp 571–586

Dóczi T (2012) Gold fever? Sport and National Identity—The Hungarian case. Int Rev Sociol Sport 47(2):165–182

Dóczi T (2014) Sport and the Social Inclusion of Marginalized Groups: a map of Hungary. EASS Conference, Utrecht

European Commission (2011a) SA.31722—Hungary. Supporting the Hungarian sport sector via tax benefit scheme.http://ec.europa.eu/competition/state_aid/cases/240466/240466_1271180_52_3.pdf. Accessed 23 Feb 2012

European Commission (2011b) State aid: commission clears Hungarian sport support scheme. http://europa.eu/rapid/press-release_IP-11-1322_en.htm. Accessed 23 Feb 2012

Falussy B (2002) Társadalmi-gazdasági trendek a népesség időfelhasználásában. Stat Szle 80(9):847–868

Földes É, Kun L, Kutassi L (1989) A magyar testnevelés és sport története. Magyar Testnevelési Egyetem, Sport, Budapest

Földesi SG (1996) Sport policy in Hungary. In: Johnson A, Stachura L, Chalip L (eds) National Sports Policies. An international handbook. Greenwood Press, London, Westport, CT, pp 187–211

Földesi SG, Egressy J (2005) Post-transformational trends in Hungarian sport (1995-2004). Eur J Sport Soc 2(2):85–96

Földesi SG, Gál A (2008) Válaszút előtt a politika. Magyar Sporttud Szle 2:4–10

Földesi SG, Nagy J, Jakabházy L (2002) Hungary: the development of sport for all in a sporting nation. In: DaCosta L, Miragaya A (eds) Worldwide experiences and trends in sport for all. Meyer and Meyer, Oxford, pp 449–474

Földesiné SG (1999) Félamatőrök, félprofik, Magyar olimpikonok (1980-1996). Magyar Olmpiai Bizottság, Budapest

Frenkl R (2003) Rendszerváltás a magya r sportban. In: Frenkl R (ed) A TF és a magyar sport belülrol. Fair Play Sport, Budapest, pp 53–59

Gál A (2008) A Lakosság egészségtudatossága és szabadidő-sportolási szokásai. In: Földesi SG, Gál A, Dóczi T (eds) Társadalmi riport a sportról. ÖM-MSTT, Budapest, pp 9–39

Gáldi G (2002) Fizikai aktivitás Magyarországon az ezredfordulón. Magyar Sporttud Szle 3–4:16–18

Géczi G, Gergely I, Nagy A, Bardóczy G (2013) Létesítményfejlesztési tendenciák a TAO-s támogatási rendszer tükrében. Semmelweis Egyetem, Budapest

Ghimessy L (1935) A magyar versenyzősportolók statisztikája. Stat Szle 13(2):134–151

Hungarian Handball Federation (2014) Sportágfejlsztési Terv. Magyar Kézilabda Szövetség: Budapset

Hungarian Olympic Committee (2012) A Magyar Olimpiai Bizottság sportfejlesztési irányai és területei 2012

Kele J (2012) Hogyan lesz a sportból "stratégiai ágazat"?—kérdések és válaszok a sportfinanszírozás átalakításáról II. http://www.hatharom.com/2012/01/21/hogyan_lesz_a_sportbol_strategiai_agazat_kerdesek_es_valaszok_a_sportfinanszirozas_atalakitasarol_ii_. Accessed 21 Jan 2012

Kornai J (1986) The soft budget constraint. Kyklos 39:3–30

Kornai J (1992) Socialist economy. Princeton University Press, Princeton

KSH (Central Statistical Agency) (2014) Statistics on non-profit sports organisations. http://statinfo.ksh.hu/Statinfo/haViewer.jsp. Accessed 15 Sep 2014

Mike G (1938) Magyarország sportlétesítményei. Stat Szle 16(4):548–552

Mike G (1943) Magyarország sportegyesületei 1941-ben. Stat Szle 19(4):182–208

MDSZ (2014) Student Olympics (Diákolimpia®) description. Magyar Diáksport Szövetség, Budapest. http://www.mdsz.hu/en/diakolimpia-2/about-us/. Accessed 14 July 2014

MLSZ (2011) A Magyar Labdarúgás Stratégiája. A megújulás évtizede 2011-2020.http://www.sporttamogatas.hu/uploads/file/MLSZ.pdf. Accessed 16 Jan 2012

MOB (2012) A Magyar Olimpiai Bizottság Sportfejlesztési irányai és területei 2012. Magyar Olimpiai Bizottság, Budapest

Monspart S (2012) In: Bartha Cs, Lehmann L (eds) A Magyar Olimpiai Bizottság Sportfejlesztési irányai és területei 2012. Magyar Olimpiai Bizottság, Budapest, pp 36–40

MTS (1966) Összesítő jelentés, 1965, 1-2. Magyar Testnevelési és Sporthivatal, Budapest

MTS (1986) Statisztikai adatok 1985, 5-6. Sportpropaganda, Budapest

National Sport Strategy (NSS) (2007) Sport XXI Nemzeti Sportstratégia. Önkormáyzati és Területfejlesztési Minisztérium Sport Szakállamtitkárság, Budapest

National Sport Information System (2014) Dataset on sportferedetaions. Nemzeti Sportközpontok, Budapest

Perényi S (2011) Sportolási szokások: Sportolási esélyek és változástrendek. In: Bauer B, Szabó A (eds) Arctalan(?) Nemzedék. Belvedere Meridionale Kiadó, Szeged, pp 159–184

Perényi S (2013a) Alacsonyan stagnáló mozgástrend: A fizikai inaktivitás újratermelődése. In: Székely L (ed) Magyar Ifjúság 2012 Tanulmánykötet. Kutatópont, Budapest, pp 229–249
Perényi S (2013b) Hungary. In: Hallmann K, Petry K (eds) Comparative Sport Development—system, participation and public policy. Springer Science+Business Media, New York, pp 87–100
Perényi S (2013c) Egy hazai kontinentális-bajnokság önkéntes programjának menedzsmentje és értékelése. VI. Országos Sporttudományi Kongresszus, Magyar Sporttudományi Társaság, Nyíregyháza. Magyar Sporttudományi Társaság, Budapest
Perényi S (2013d) Ifjúság, sportolási részvétel és a TAO sportágak. A felsőoktatás szerepe a sportban, élsportban és az olimpiai mozgalomban, különös tekintettel a társasági adóból (TAO) támogatott sportágak helyzetére és a támogatások hasznosíthatóságára. University of Debrecen, Debrecen
Perényi S (2015) Hungary. The popularisation and expansion of amateur running culture. In: Scheerder J, Breedveld K, Borgers J (eds) Running across Europe. The rise and size of one of the largest sport markets. Palgrave Macmillan, Basingstoke, pp 63–86
Sárközy T (1992) A privatizáció. In: Gyekiczky A (ed) A váltás rendszere Tanulmányok a kormány politikájáról. Politikai Tanulmányok Intézete Alapítvány, Budapest, pp 47–56
Sterbenz T, Gulyás E (2012) A klubban. In: Sterbenz T, Géczi E (eds) Sportmenedzsment. Semmelweis Egyetem Testnevelési és Sporttudományi Kar, Budapest, pp 147–170
Szabó Á (2012) A magyar szabadidősport működésének vizsgálata. Piacok, értékteremtés, feladatok a szabadidősportban. Doktori Disszertáció, Corvinus University: Budapest
TAO riport (2013) Nemzeti Sport Intézet, Budapest
Youth (2000) Database. (Ifjúság2004 adatbázis). Nemzeti Ifjúságkutató Intézet, Budapest
Youth (2004) Database. (Ifjúság2004 adatbázis). Mobilitás Ifjúságkutatási Iroda, Budapest
Vörös T (2011) A szabadidősport által nyújtott társadalmi haszon—a sportoló lakosság arányát befolyásoló tényezők vizsgálata európai országok vonatkozásában. XXX Országos Tudományos Diákköri Konferencia Testnevelés és Sporttudományi Szekció. OTDK dolgozat. Budapesti Műszaki és Gazdaságtudományi Egyetem, Budapest
Zeidler M (2006) English influences on modern sport in Hungary. 1-2. The Hungarian Quarterly, 47(181)(Spring), 36–54; (182)(Summer), 27–47
Zeidler M (2012) Clair Ignác testgyakorlati iskolája. In: Zeidler M (ed) A labdaháztól a Népstadionig. Sportélet pesten és Budán a 18-20. században. Kalligram, Pozsony, pp 105–130

# Chapter 14
# Sport Clubs in Italy

**Antonio Borgogni, Simone Digennaro, and Davide Sterchele**

## 14.1 Introduction

Italy is a parliamentary republic in southern Europe. It is one of the most populated nations in the European Union—61 million inhabitants—and the fourth largest economy (the ninth in the world). In a similar way to many other European countries, Italy has developed a dynamic and efficient sport system. Especially in top-elite sport it represents one of the most successful nations in terms of Olympic medals and victories in international competitions. Since the establishment of the Italian Republic, after the end of the Second World War and the collapse of the Fascist regime, the Italian sport system has taken on uncommon and specific features. The peculiar role played by the Italian Olympic Committee (Comitato Olimpico Nazionale Italiano, here and henceforth CONI), along with the distinctive features of some of the actors operating in the system—like for instance the Sport Promotion Bodies (Enti di Promozione Sportiva, here and henceforth EPSs) representing some of the most innovative experiences of sport for all organisations in Europe—has defined an almost unique form and an interesting field of investigation.

The paper aims to explain the main features of the Italian sport system and its distinctive characteristics through a detailed analysis of one of its important components: sport clubs. To this aim, after a socio-diachronic analysis of the Italian sport

A. Borgogni (✉) • S. Digennaro
Department of Human Sciences, Society, and Health,
University of Cassino and Southern Lazio, Cassino, Italy
e-mail: a.borgogni@unicas.it; s.digennaro@unicas.it

D. Sterchele
Institute for Sport, Physical Activity and Leisure, Carnegie Faculty,
Leeds Beckett University, Leeds, UK
e-mail: d.sterchele@leedsbeckett.ac.uk



C. Breuer et al. (eds.), *Sport Clubs in Europe*, Sports Economics,
Management and Policy 12, DOI 10.1007/978-3-319-17635-2_14

system, a detailed description of the main features and the role of sport clubs in the Italian society are proposed. Finally, as an important case study, the main results of a 4 year action-research project carried out with the sport club Polisportiva Giovanni Masi are described in detail.

## 14.2 History and Context

Sports clubs play a fundamental role in the current Italian sport system, which is strongly underpinned by these voluntary-based associations. It is estimated that almost all the 12,867,000 Italians who practise regular sport activity (22 % of the population) are members of some sports club (CONI 2012).

Moreover, sports clubs were also pivotal in the historical development of the country's sporting culture. The *massification* and democratisation of sports participation was completed in the second part of the twentieth century, with two-thirds of all sport clubs mapped up to 1996 having been created from the 1970s onward (Baglioni 2010; Nomisma 1999).

Nonetheless, the importance of sports clubs can be traced back to the nineteenth century; 734 of the clubs currently active in Italy are older than 100 years (UNASCI n.a), and their sporting history is intimately intertwined with the everyday history of the cities they belong to (Colsante 2003).

### *14.2.1 From Italian Unification to World War I*

Italy became a nation-state in 1861 and the Kingdom of Piedmont-Sardinia, whose political-administrative structures were gradually extended to the whole country, led the unification process. The first and most prestigious gymnastic and multisport club (Societa' Ginnastica Torino, SGT) had already been operating in Turin since 1844 and became a model for other gymnastic clubs of the newly-unified country (Bonini 2006).

Most gymnastic clubs were set up as private initiatives, usually started by PE teachers who also worked in government schools. Italian law supported the freedom of association and did not regulate the activity of these clubs. In the social and political climate of the newly unified nation-state, physical activity was primarily given a pedagogic and patriotic role besides its recreational and even philanthropic character (Fabrizio 1977; Ferrera 1992). Formative gymnastics, shooting and fencing were therefore the main sports practised in the first clubs. Physical activity in the nineteenth century remained an elitist practice for an increasing but still small number of aristocratic and bourgeois males, despite philanthropic attempts to involve workers, women and youth. Nonetheless, sports clubs contributed to building and reinforcing the social fabric of the fragile newborn nation-state (Verrati 2012).

Mostly developed around the first industrialised cities of north-west Italy (Martin 2011), gymnastic clubs tried to challenge the appeal of English sports or at least control and co-opt them but ended up becoming a vehicle of their diffusion. Many clubs gradually created specific sections for swimming, road racing, wrestling, skating, rowing, equitation and *velocipedestrianism*, as well as football, rugby, lawn tennis and basketball. The football team Pro Vercelli, for instance, which later became seven-times national champion between 1908 and 1922, was born as a football section of the gymnastic club of the same name; 'its players, during the half-time break, used to compete in 60 and 200 m races, and after the match they even engaged in cycling competitions' (Verrati 2012, p. 24).

In 1880, Italy had 26 million inhabitants and 82 gymnastic (multisport) clubs, a higher number per capita than France and the USA, though lower than Germany, Switzerland, Belgium and Austria-Hungary.[1] In 1882, two out of three gymnastic clubs were in the north of the country, whilst less than one third were located in central and a very limited number in southern Italy (Verrati 2012). This geography also reflected the different sociocultural environments, with the new bourgeois sports adopted in the gradually modernising/industrialising north and more aristocratic forms of athletic sociability like riding, hunting and fencing prevailing in the backward south (Verrati 2012). The Gymnastic Federation was the first sports federation to be created in Italy in 1869, followed by the Italian Shooting Union in 1885. Although these initiatives were not run by the State, they were monitored and supported by different Ministries—such as Education, War and Domestic Affairs—in an attempt to reinforce the military-pedagogical role of physical activity, in which shooting clubs also played a significant part. However, this political-ideological project, which also involved the schools, led to only limited results in terms of participation: in 1908 there were 770,000 gymnastic clubs in Germany, 250,000 in France, 50,000 in Switzerland and only 12,000 in Italy (Verrati 2012).[2]

In parallel, other organisations were developing competing concepts of physical activity. From different perspectives, both the Church and, more slowly, the Socialist movements gradually elaborated their own specific sports provision for the popular classes. Notably, the Catholic organisation FASCI had 16 affiliated clubs when it was founded in 1906 and as many as 224 six years later with more than 10,000 members, despite the fact that it was initially ostracised by the monarchist Gymnastic Federation. At the same time, the competitive model of *British* and Olympic sports was rapidly threatening the initial predominance of the Gymnastic Federation through the emergence of several private clubs (associations of citizens) that quickly formed new sports federations. The Italian Cycling Federation was founded in Turin in 1885, and included 95 out of the 170 then existing clubs, and would become the wealthiest federation in the following decades with the number of affiliated clubs increasing to 555 by 1914 (whilst a separate body, the Italian Touring Club, took the

[1] By total number Germany had more than 1,500 clubs, the USA 172, Austria-Hungary 130, France 120, Switzerland 119, Belgium 56 and the Netherlands 45 (Verrati 2012, p. 22).

[2] In 1913 the Italian Gymnastic Federation comprised 130 affiliated clubs, only 40 of which also had a female section.

lead in tourist cycling). The Italian Rowing Federation was born in Turin in 1888 and the Italian Running Union was initiated in Milan in 1897 to later become the Italian Athletics Federation, with 85 affiliated clubs in 1913 (82 % from northern Italy, 18 % from the centre and none from the south) (Verrati 2012). The Italian Football Federation was founded in Turin in 1898 and included clubs such as the Genoa Cricket & Football Club (born in 1893), Juventus (1897) and Milan (1899), and developed a competition system as an alternative to the one organised by the Gymnastic Federation. As noted by Verratti (2012) the cultural clash was also evident in the anglicised names of the new football clubs as opposed to the Latin and classical names of the gymnastic clubs. The Football Federation soon became the dominant body in its field, gradually absorbing the football sections of the gymnastic clubs (Giuntini 2011) and rising from 15 member clubs in 1905 to 262 in 1914. Meanwhile, with the Football Federation focusing on elite competitions, the Free Italian Union of Football was founded in Milan in 1917 to engage youth and working class people. This rapidly expanding organisation held its first national championship in 1920 and comprised 190 affiliated teams by 1922.

With the growing sportisation of the athletic culture and the rising of the Olympic movement, the CONI was founded in 1914 with a distinctiveness that would mark the Italian sport system up to the present day. In fact, besides simply dealing with the preparation and selection of athletes for the Olympics, the CONI was also given the power to control and coordinate the sports federations and thus the development of the whole system (Marani Toro and Marani Toro 1977).

### *14.2.2 Fascism*

This process was suddenly stopped by the outbreak of World War I, whose consequences led to the establishment of the Fascist regime. Aiming to use sport as a tool for both controlling the masses and strengthening its international reputation, the totalitarian government soon took hold of the sport system by taking two main steps. On the one hand, it created specific institutions (the Opera Nazionale Balilla, the Gioventu' Italiana del Littorio and the Opera Nazionale Dopolavoro) to manage the whole provision of pedagogic/recreational physical activity for youth and workers, dissolving all the rival institutions, notably socialist and Catholic sports clubs and centres belonging to worker organisations (Dogliani 2000). On the other hand, it boosted the development of competitive sport by taking full control of the CONI (and thus the sports federations) and in practice making it a governmental body by law.

The impact of Fascism on the Italian sports system was therefore ambivalent. On the one hand, by centralising physical activities and making them almost mandatory, the regime impaired the traditional role of voluntarism and free initiative in the creation and management of sports clubs. On the other hand, by defining and strengthening the institutional structure of the sport system and massively expanding the provision of sport facilities, it strongly accelerated the *massification* of sports participation, involuntarily providing the basis for its subsequent democratisation and the proliferation of sports clubs in the second part of the twentieth century. According to Porro (1996), this was the period of authoritarian modernisation of the Italian sport system in which the governing body of sport was turned into a control apparatus of the regime.

The number of Federations founded supports this theory. In fact, in the period between 1916 and 1942, 16 sports federations were established against 13 during the period 1872–1915 and 14 after the World War II. Moreover, one current sport club out of ten was established prior to 1941.

In 1933 the Italian Federation of Athletics had 1,550 affiliated clubs with 7,500 members, whilst the Italian Federation of Winter Sports had 350 clubs with more than 16,000 members. The Rugby Federation grew from 32 clubs in 1932 to 106 in 1937. On the threshold of World War II, Italy had 11,267 sports clubs within the *fascistised* CONI (with 657,038 athletes, nearly half million of which were hunters) and 520 clubs within the Fascist pedagogical/recreational institutions (with 420,000 athletes, mostly bowlers) (Verrati 2012).

### 14.2.3 After World War II: The Reconstruction

Following the fall of the Fascist regime and the end of World War II, sports clubs were re-democratised (with officials elected by the members rather than imposed from above) and continued their activity within the powerful coordination and ramified structure of the CONI, whose leading role was confirmed by a new law. Municipalities also played an important role at the local level by organising sport events and providing clubs with financial support. In 1946 the CONI was allowed to manage the *Totocalcio*, the state monopoly for gambling on football, which soon became a huge financial resource for the whole sports system. The income from *Totocalcio* allowed the CONI to foster sports development at both elite and grassroots/amateur level, as well as support military sports groups (which were both multisports clubs and military units, specialising in training elite athletes for high performance sports) and the creation of School Sports Groups. A new public body named ENAL was created in 1945 to organise recreational sports for workers and gradually grew to 6,000 clubs[3] with 300,000 members in 1972.

Within the Catholic area, the Italian Sports Centre (CSI) was founded in 1944 to replace the FASCI as a provider of *sport for all*. Despite criticising the monopoly of the CONI on the Italian sport system, CSI acted as a complement to rather than an antagonist of the CONI and the sports federations (for instance by serving them in the organisation of the Youth School Games). CSI rapidly grew to have 1,500 sports clubs in 1951, 2,400 in 1954 and more than 3,000 in 1960. Other important Catholic

[3] These clubs were affiliated to different sport federations, such as: bowling (2,000), billiards (500), chess (300), diving (300), tamburello (240), elastic ball (120), checkers (100), rowing (80) and karate (30) (Verrati 2012).

sports bodies were founded in 1944: the Sporting Union ACLI (by the Catholic workers unions) and the National Centre Libertas (by the Christian Democrat party), the latter already grown to 1,400 multisport clubs in 1956. Within the other main political area, left-wing parties created the Italian Union Popular Sports (UISP) in 1948, which later became the main competitor of the Catholic CSI among the non-federal sports providers (UISP grew from 1,700 clubs in 1953 to 3,900 with 250,000 members in 1973). Another important provider of cultural and sports activities within the left-wing area was ARCI, with 2,000 clubs in 1959 and 3,000 in 1962. The diffusion of these Enti di Promozione Sportiva (EPSs) followed the political geography of the parties they were closely linked to, with CSI more developed in the Lazio Region and UISP strongly rooted in the left wing areas, notably Emilia Romagna and Tuscany. Following the examples of CSI and UISP, in the pluralist political system of post-war Italy, each party created its own EPS, characterised by both outreach ambitions and a socially-oriented concept of physical activity. The EPSs developed a parallel system by setting up their own separate competitions outside those organised by the sports federations within the CONI. Meanwhile, they jointly advocated formal recognition and equal treatment in relation to the high performance system managed by CONI and the sports federations.

The parallel system of EPSs steadily grew throughout the second part of the twentieth century. In 1976 UISP had 8,000 clubs, CSI (jointly with its female section FARI) had 6,500, AICS more than 3,000, Libertas 2,500, CSEN 2,000, ACSI 1,117, UsACLI 1,000, Fiamma 800, ENDAS 374 and CUS (University Sports Clubs) had 33. In the subsequent decades, the overall number of clubs affiliated to the EPSs grew to 45,750 clubs in 1997 and 83,155 in 2005 (Verrati 2012). The end of political *collateralism* in the late twentieth century partially freed EPSs from ideological outreach duties and increased their focus on the sociocultural aspects of sports provision and practice. Nine EPSs obtained a first formal recognition from the CONI in 1974, which enabled them to receive public financial support, although this was much lower than the investment in the Sports Federations. Between 1980 and 1990, several EPSs also obtained specific recognition from individual Ministries for providing social services in particular sectors (such as home affairs, social inclusion, environment, work, and welfare). Despite their high significance though, EPSs are still fighting to democratise the Italian sports system and obtain equal treatment in relation to the sports federations. The latter dominated the *official* statistics of sport in the second part of the twentieth century, growing to 66,501 clubs in 2012, when the CONI included 45 National Sports Federations (FSN) and 19 Associated Sports Disciplines (DSA).[4]

The current articulation of the Italian sports system is thus the result of its origins and history, as it is inappropriately dominated by the CONI (a public institution not juridical belonging to the State but acting as a Ministry of Sport) and based on a crowded landscape of voluntary sports clubs operating throughout the

[4]Among others, DSA include for instance the federations of the following activities: climbing, billiards, ten-pin bowling, bridge, cricket, tamburello, American football, rafting, traditional games and sports, chess and twirling (CONI 2012).

country (Verrati 2012). The majority of these clubs are affiliated either to sports federations (and associated disciplines) within the CONI or EPSs. The latter usually have different characteristics from the former, since many of them are multi-sport clubs and their range of activities tends to be broader (from competitive sports to social, cultural and/or formative programmes, from regular events to intermittent initiatives). Therefore, the data regarding the number of clubs and members are gathered according to more inclusive and extensive criteria than those followed by the CONI to monitor the clubs affiliated to its federations, thus making comparisons more difficult (Verrati 2012). However, the role of EPSs within the Italian sports system can be considered to be as important as that of sports federations in both quantitative and qualitative terms, notably in providing *sport for all* opportunities and making a claim for the social role of sport. Nonetheless, it would be wrong to outline a clear dichotomy considering all clubs affiliated to sports federations as being oriented towards selectivity and performance, as opposed to the clubs of EPSs purely oriented to *social sports*. The reality is more nuanced, with tensions around the concept of competitiveness also permeating the EPSs, as well as significant social and educational efforts carried on by thousands of clubs affiliated to the sports federations. The historical divide between north and south has narrowed in recent years. Although in northern Italy we can still find more sports clubs by total number, the difference is much lower considering the number of clubs pro capita, with some central or even southern provinces ranked higher than many northern ones. Moreover, the rate at which new clubs were founded between 2001 and 2008 was higher in the south than elsewhere in the country (CONI 2001).

For many decades the juridical status of sports clubs remained poorly defined, despite several attempts to improve their regulation. CONI is a public institution but it is constituted of sports federations that from a juridical viewpoint belong to the private sector. Professional clubs, which since 1996 have been for-profit corporations, nonetheless remain part of the same institutional network with sports federations and the Olympic committee. Regardless of their important contribution to the Italian Third Sector, sports clubs were overlooked by the law on no-profit associations in the late 1990s, on the assumption that an allegedly forthcoming law on amateurism, which nonetheless has not yet been enacted, would define their status. Only recently, sports clubs were acknowledged for their social role and granted tax breaks and other small benefits. From the economic point of view, the huge growth of football indirectly benefited all other sport through *Totocalcio*. At the local level, municipalities also provided sports clubs with financial support and notably the provision and maintenance of sports facilities. However, the voluntary commitment of thousands of passionate members was the main asset underpinning the birth and proliferation of Italian sports clubs. This characteristic also enabled most sports clubs to survive the recent dramatic decrease of funding from both the CONI and local authorities, as well as limit the loss of members despite the growing competition from commercial sports providers and the appeal of new unstructured outdoor and lifestyle practices (Fig. 14.1).

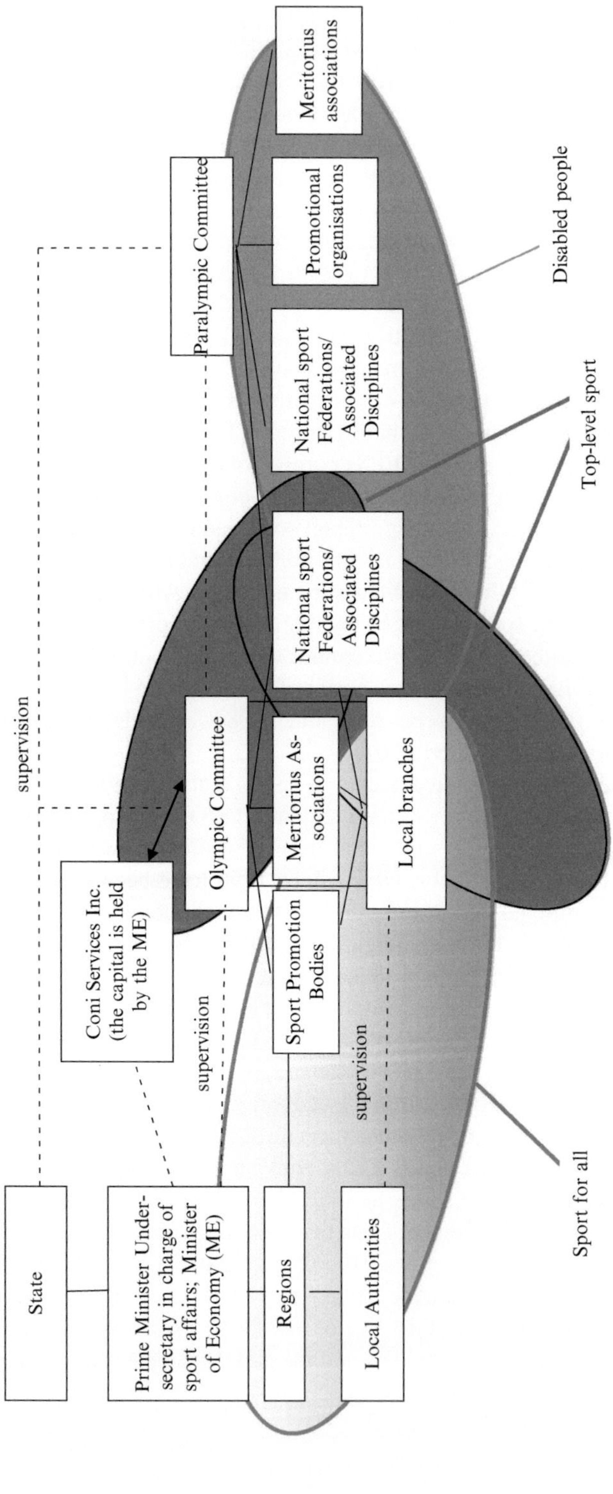


**Fig. 14.1** The Italian Sport System 2014 (Digennaro 2011; modified)

## 14.3 The Role of the Sport Clubs in Policy and Society

In Italy, as in most western industrialised societies, grassroots sport at local and regional levels is organised and delivered by a vast network of local organisations. Nowadays, this network represents the backbone of the sport system numbering approximately 64,000 organisations and a workforce of 850,000 people (CENSIS 2008).

As already argued in the previous paragraph, the Italian sports system is significantly different from those of other European countries because of the dominating role of CONI and the relations of the latter with other players. In this light, from a sociological point of view, the system can be represented as the combination of two different subsystems; one related to the Olympic Sport Movement in which the main actors are the CONI, as a reference point, and Federations that play a crucial role in promoting and supporting, above all, elite and competitive sport; the other one is linked to the realm of the sport for all and inspired by the principles of subsidiarity, adequacy and differentiation. The latter is led by the Regions and EPSs that have a crucial role in making the whole system more dynamic, fostering an often harsh debate between the actors, and between the paradigms of competitive and societal sport. The juxtaposition of these two coalitions witnessed an increase of the level of conflict during the 1990s. The shock provoked by the financial crisis described earlier was further affected by the emergence of the widespread crisis of welfare systems, which were increasingly beleaguered by often-intractable social emergencies. Governments reacted in different and innovative ways, focusing on leaner and more efficient solutions, in the process singling out grassroots sports associations as an area of interest. Over the past 15–20 years we have witnessed what we can call *the season of the sports system as a welfare system* characterised by a strong request—with subsequent allocation of financial resources—of sports-based projects developed within the sphere of social intervention (Digennaro 2013; Madella 2006). These trends have consolidated also because players operating outside the world of sport administration and politics are increasingly seeing sport as having a strong social potential. Also as a result of these *new* social demands, combined with new trends originating during the 1980s, a change in the direction of a growing professionalisation has emerged in Italy. Strategic planning, rational evaluation of the performance and professional systems of governance became part of the approach adopted and commonly mentioned in formal/informal communication. At the same time, a shifting toward a more commercial orientation of the sport activities emerged. The voluntary character of the involvement of many staff members, which for long time had been considered as the key factor for the success of the organisations, was recognised as a possible limitation to the reform of management that was deemed necessary to face the perceived increasing complexity of the environment (Madella and Digennaro 2009). The process of professionalisation was further stimulated by various external and internal events that have taken a central position in the definition of the strategies adopted by sport organisations. Strategic decisions were taken both as a reaction to changes emerging in the system and as a means to try to outline the zone of uncertainty in which many organisations were forced to operate.

The most relevant changes in the external environment included, among others: the effect of European laws and the globalisation of the market; a general, renewed trend toward the use of sport as a means of social intervention utilised to respond to the needs emerging from modern society and to support the action of the welfare state; the reform of the Italian sport system, which established a sort of a dual governance in which the CONI was regarded as assuming a more limited role and expected to operate within the domain of elite sport and the Olympic Movement while regions along with local authorities were required to assume more and more responsibilities in the domain of the sport for all and in the promotion of a large participation among the population; the reduction of the public funds at the disposal for the sport system as effects of the above-mentioned reform; the reduction of the income coming from Totocalcio and the parallel high degree of uncertainty in the access to financial resources.

At the same time, internal factors also produced important effects on sport organisations. It is difficult to draw a complete and detailed picture of such factors because they were contextual and various. The need to put more emphasis on service/product quality in combination with the demand for new forms of governance and the request for new internal structures has produced, as argued by Slack (1997), a general pressure for change. The reaction was not linear, with decisions and strategies that assumed the condition of a schizoid state (Hinings and Greenwood 1988) with modes of functioning and structures adopted that seemed partially contradictory. Only a limited number of organisations were able to define internal programmes of change based on deliberate strategies (Mintzberg 1979) that enabled them to proactively manage the situation. On the contrary, the pressure coming from the external environment forced the majority of organisations to react, in a sort of *struggle to survive* with the adoption of the so-called emergent strategy (Mintzberg 1979) often based on unplanned and unclear actions and decisions.

It is worth noting that, even when there was the adoption of a deliberate strategy grounded in the generic idea of increasing effectiveness, in many cases, the intentions were not realised exactly as intended. Unintended consequences (Gouldner 1954) occurred at micro-level—within the organisation—and at macro-level, as a general effect, in the system. Sport organisations came to be characterised by a mix of cultural and organisational approaches originating forms of cohabitation between divergent strategies and attitudes: profit vs. non-profit, associative vs. managerial logic, participation vs. selection, etc. The process of professionalisation, for instance, has been interpreted as the progressive insertion of expert professionals, without a deliberate strategy affecting internal structures and processes. This generated conflicts between the voluntary human resources—that represent the core of many sport organisations and that have a key role in the decision-making processes—and professional human resources, that try to operate on the strategic planning and the rational evaluation of the outcomes with a clear and decisive impact on the decision-making procedures.

## 14.4 Characteristics of Sport Clubs

The last Census of Industry, Services and Non-profit Sectors (ISTAT[5] 2012) offered a global overview of the status quo and a comparative analysis with the 2001 data. Data about the Non-profit sector, in which the sport sector is included, show the significance of the former in the Italian economic system and its remarkable growth since 2001: 301,191 non-profit organisations (+28 % in comparison with 2001), 4.7 million volunteers (+43 %), 680,000 staff members (+39 %), 270,000 external workers (+169 %) and 5,000 temporary workers (+48 %). Considering only the sector including Culture, Sport and Leisure, the Sport sector accounts for 47 % of the organisations, 37 % of volunteers, and 29 % of staff members with a mean of 14.4 volunteers and 0.2 staff members for each organisation. The Artistic, Cultural and Sport subsector shows that the latter had raised the number of organisations since 2001–2011 (79,024–92,837), and the numbers of volunteers (967,628–1,051,879), reduced the number of staff members (19,164–13,139) witnessing, at the same time, a sharp increase in external workers (17,692–75,475).

Additionally, the latest available statistics on the specific area of sports organisations may offer empirical grounds to further describe the above-reported dynamics. In 2008, CENSIS[6] carried out an investigation with a sample of 11,000 sport clubs with the aim of identifying and describing, from a statistical point of view, some of the most interesting features of the organisations operating in the Italian sport system. Given the significant size of the sample, it can be safely maintained that evidence collected can be generalised with a robust level of confidence and used to draw a general picture of some of the most interesting characteristics of the sport clubs. Broadly, sport clubs in Italy tend to be small, informal organisations with 65 members enrolled on average. They are largely basic associations without legal status (87 %) and with a short-term strategising based on informal governance arrangements and, generally speaking, a low resource allocation. Strategies are, above all, defined *spontaneously* and closely tied to processes of local learning and action on the ground.

The analysis of the distribution of the sport clubs throughout the country can support a more in-depth discussion about the so-called Southern Question, already outlined in the historical description, as a crucial aspect to understand, generally speaking, the North–South gradient in development and quality of services and life, and, more specifically, the irregular development of the Italian sport system and the huge differences in the rates of sport participation and physical inactivity, making any generalised description of the sport system very difficult.

The spread of the sport clubs is, in fact, nationwide but with a higher presence in the north (55 %). In connection with the development of the sport system in Italy, which witnessed a significant increase in terms of participants during the 1970s, a

[5] Istituto Nazionale di Statistica, the Italian National Statistical Institute.

[6] Centro Studi Investimenti Sociali, foundation commissioned by the State with a focus on socio-economic issues.

large proportion of the sport clubs represented in the sample were established between 1976 and 2000 with a remarkable growth in southern and island regions between 2001 and 2008 (38 % vs. 31 % of the national mean). According to CENSIS interpretation, the latter dynamics are probably due to the increased vitality in the southern third sector, which led a filling of the gap that emerged during the previous decades. Nonetheless, Porro (2005) argues that the number of sport clubs established in the South was not completely accompanied by a mobilisation of an adequate number of human resources. Specifically, in the third sector, the South presents 24 % of the human resources (both volunteers and paid staff) and 28 % of the sport organisations. By contrast, the North embraces 51 % of the organisations that involve 56 % of all the human resources involved in the sport sector on a national scale. Moreover, the important rise of sport clubs has not been accompanied with a similar growth in sport participation. During the period 2001–2008, in fact, sport participation did not increase in the South and the islands, showing an unchanged, very low, rate at around 23 %.

In the same period, participation in physical activity in the South shifted by 1.2 % from discontinuous to regular. However, the percentage of inactive people slightly increased in the South (0.6 %) and more significantly in the islands (+5 %) (ISTAT 2013).

According to this data and to Porro's arguments, we can maintain that the southern and insular parts of Italy had witnessed, in that period, a process of fragmentation of the already sports-involved people without, so to speak, any true social and health enhancement.

In common with many European countries, sport clubs tend to establish an alliance with a Sport Federation or an EPS. In this regard, 57 % of the sample reported an affiliation to a National Sport Federation, 23 % to both a National Sport Federation and an EPS and 20 % only to the latter.

In accordance with the law and the Olympic Committee's rules, the internal organisation, ruled by the Articles of Association, includes the Assembly of the members, the Council and the President. A steering committee can also be added, although it is not mandatory. A critical reflection on the management of the sport clubs suggests that the sport system is inclined to comprise formally structured bodies, governed by structured boards, but may also include more informal procedures of governance. Considering the small size that sport clubs tend to have, especially taking into account the economic aspect, it can be inferred that the second, informal structure is the most commonly used.

In fact, it should be highlighted that 60 % of the organisations reported an overall budget of less than €25,000, 15 % between €26,000 and €50,000. Not surprisingly, the majority reported a high degree of uncertainty and difficulty in accessing the financial resources available, both private and public. 57 % did not benefit, in the previous period considered by CENSIS (2008), from any kind of financial support coming from private sponsors; where available, sponsorships tend to be local (56 %). Moreover, 32 % did not receive any public funds and support from the local authorities; such kinds of financial resources derive from the Municipalities (49 %). Only 5 % of the sport clubs own a facility, 46 % use them for free taking care of the maintenance costs, and 38 % pay a rental. The financial aspects (sponsors and public funding) are considered the most binding issues, true bottlenecks challenging the survival of the clubs, followed by the management of the continuous changes in the legislation related to budget accounting and bureaucracy, the recruitment of volunteers, and the availability of facilities (CENSIS 2008). In this regard sport clubs may have particular challenges and constraints that need to be actively considered in the near future by defining and adopting new strategies. Traditional approaches to fundraising, for instance, are unlikely to provide the strategic clarity and level of decisiveness or responsiveness needed to both survive and prosper in the contemporary context.

In the same vein, sport clubs are also required to vary the offer of activities for members in order to match the requests emerging from society. Porro (2005) maintains that individuals tend to prefer the commercial offer because it is considered high-grade and more inclined to fulfil individual needs. This demand creates an *unbalanced* access to the sport sector, which tends to be more commercial, putting significant economic barriers to access for those groups of the population that are not able to afford the costs. Considering the social value of active participation in a sport club both as member and as participant in the sport activities, and the need to enlarge the participation of all the segments of the population, there is the urgency to find new forms of activity, probably with direct action by the State that will support the participation of less privileged individuals with specific financial support.

Focusing more specifically on the human resources, the role of volunteers is still relevant: 85 % of the staff members operate, in fact, as volunteers, representing the main pillar of the whole system. It is important to observe here that the statistics, following Italian law, describe as volunteers also all those sports operators that have an income of €7,500 per year or less. The percentage of volunteers is 94 % among managers, 69 % among instructors and 81 % among administrative staff.

By analysing the subsample of 8,500 organisations affiliated to a National Sport Federation (CENSIS 2008) there were 142,000 staff members with a mean of 16.7 per club, 50 % of them managers, 30 % instructors, 7 % administrative staff and a slightly smaller proportion maintenance staff.

Volunteer human resources have represented for years one of the main features of the Italian sport system that has been strongly linked with the ideology and the rhetoric of the voluntary service. However, as also argued in the report edited by CENSIS, the abundant presence of volunteer human resources and the adoption of non-structured forms of governance have slowed the transition toward a more complex and rational organisational structure that is intended to be more ready to respond to the complexity of today's commercial and competitive landscape. This transition is commonly related, even not exclusively, to the presence of professional human resources, and in this sense, it can be argued that Italian sport clubs, in particular, and the Italian sport system, in general, have witnessed a process of *partial professionalisation* (Madella and Digennaro 2009).

Notably, trained specialists have been employed to perform a range of organisational and, above all, administrative activities. This process has increased the horizontal differentiation within the organisations as a result of task differentiation and functional specialisation (Slack 1997). Usually, the increase in horizontal differentiation is related to a process of vertical differentiation that produces the growth of the numbers of levels in an organisation (Mintzberg 1979; Slack 1997). The vertical differentiation is often assumed to represent the hierarchy of authority (Hall 1982) and it is also a means to solve problems of communication and coordination among the different levels. In this instance, volunteers who traditionally managed sport organisations in Italy have witnessed a reduction of their level of control in favour of professionally trained managers. This has generated a conflicting dual hierarchy that has slowed down the process of professionalisation of many sport organisations. In certain cases, especially in the case of big sport clubs, the management of the conflict has passed through an excessive formalisation and bureaucratisation of the internal procedures.

## 14.5 Participation and Change: The Case of the Polisportiva Giovanni Masi

The fourth part of our chapter concerns the description of a case study: the Masi Sport Club (PGM). The club, located in Casalecchio di Reno—a Municipality of 38,000 inhabitants bordering Bologna—today has about 8,000 members. From a sociological point of view, the case study takes on high importance in the understanding of sports organisations. It is characterised, in fact, by a mix of cultural variables with a strong history of voluntary service and a solid connection with the community. An associative logic based on the ideology of volunteerism, sport for all, participation, informal decision-making, not-for-profit, is today in cohabitation with a managerial logic that pays attention to the idea of profit, effectiveness and efficiency. Then, considering the fact that it was established in 1954, it has witnessed and faced some of the most important changes which have emerged in the Italian sport system during the last decades. Such changes and the impact that they have had on PGM can be detected, analysed and generalised as dynamics that many sports clubs have faced during the last 60 years.

Since 2010, directly funded by PGM, a research group led by the scientific coordinator of this chapter has carried out a longitudinal in-depth research project. This research has focused primarily on the period from September 2010 and the subsequent 4 years until today. As will be discussed later, this time frame has encompassed a period of unprecedented organisation changes in PGM. The study has particularly focused on: (a) the quality of the services provided; (b) the main features of the general structure and organisational processes; (c) dynamics underpinning the interaction between PGM and the main stakeholders (both public and private); (d) members' levels of satisfaction; (e) the effects on the organisation determined by changes occurring within the Italian sport system. Additionally, the work has tried to fill the gap left by the absence of research enabling the description of the influence of a system and its subsystems on organisational structure and performance.

The research framework was ideographic and longitudinal in nature. Based on the case-study approach, it adopted a multidimensional system of data collection and data analysis implemented over a period of 4 years. According to Yin's classification (2009) the research was based on an embedded single-case study design: the main unit of analysis, the PGM, was the focus of the study along with several intermediary units (such as PGM's departments). Different research tools such as questionnaires, in-depth interviews, focus groups, life-histories, documentary analysis and field observations were employed.

Initially, secondary data were collected. Afterward, to investigate the levels of members' satisfaction concerning services and activities provided, the modalities of members' participation as well as new trends in terms of practice, success factors, and organisational critical issues a structured questionnaire ($n=853$. 30 % of the adult members population; LOC=95 %, CI=3.83 %) was submitted to adults' members (>18 years). Additionally, data concerning young members (13–17 years old) were collected via another structured questionnaire ($n=169$. 25 % of the young member population, LO=95 %, CI=6.54 %). Finally, data concerning members under 12 were collected through a guided interview administered to the parents ($n=186$) (Borgogni et al. 2013).

In parallel, the analysis of the organisational dynamics and performances was carried out through focus-groups ($n=9$) involving representatives of members, managers, boards, employees, educators and sector supervisors. This level of analysis was interpolated with a second level based on in-depth interviews ($n=7$) carried out with internal and external key informants. With this interpolation, data collected stemmed from three different points of view: internal (employees, sectors responsible, board members, managers), intermediate (members and educators), and external (e.g., the Major, the Deputy Major and the main competitors). Finally, within a socio-diachronic approach, in-depth interviews ($n=4$) with long-term members were conducted. Focus groups discussions and interviews were recorded and transcribed verbatim, resulting in a substantial pool of qualitative data. Common patterns and themes were identified through a thematic analysis and coding of the transcripts. The diverse levels of analysis and tools allowed researchers to obtain a wide and multidimensional picture of the organisation from a bird's eye perspective to a detailed examination (Fig. 14.2) (Glaser and Strauss 2009).

Findings showed that PGM is recognised as a high quality organization both in terms of services provided and organisational structure/processes. Services provided are perceived as aligned to members' personal expectations; the proportion of adults that reported to be satisfied with services is astonishingly high (97 %) (Fig. 14.3).

Specifically, respondents identified the relationship between members and sports educators/coaches as well as their high level of competence, knowledge, and quality of didactics, as key determinants for PGM's success and quality. PGM provided its main actors with a specific form of training module that tried to embrace and promote PGM's culture within the logic of the lifelong learning approach. This was done mostly through specific training processes that tried to meet the PGM's needs by improving, at the same time, people's skills and changing their attitude. The latter

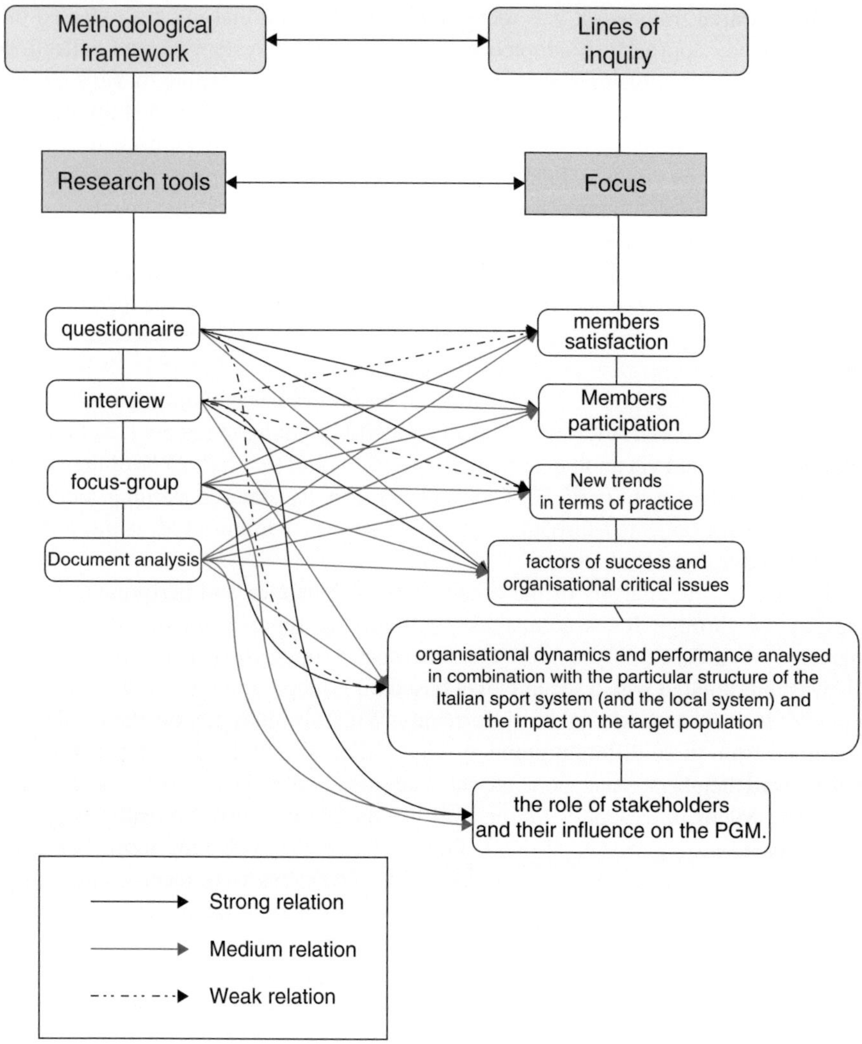


**Fig. 14.2** The methodological framework and the design of the research

point is recognised as a fundamental strategic factor: the adoption of what it is called the *Masi style*—a combination of values, creeds and principles that represents the backbone of the PGM's organisational culture—is considered as a key factor for all the human resources involved in the activities (Fig. 14.4).

From an organisational point of view, PGM is the result of inter-organisational linkages between a large number of units ($n=26$); each unit is expected to develop and promote specific disciplines or ad hoc initiative or specific areas of interest. During the last 10 years, such units have faced a further process of differentiation and separation, above all as result of the process of pluralisation and differentiation

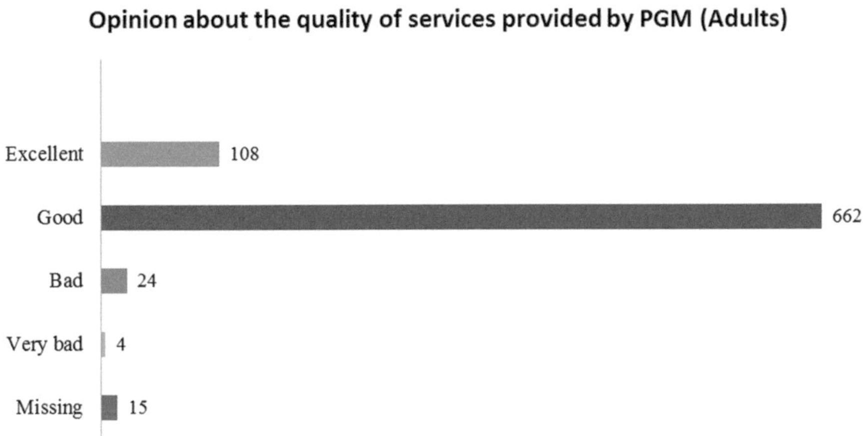


**Fig. 14.3** Opinion about the quality of services provided by PGM (adults)

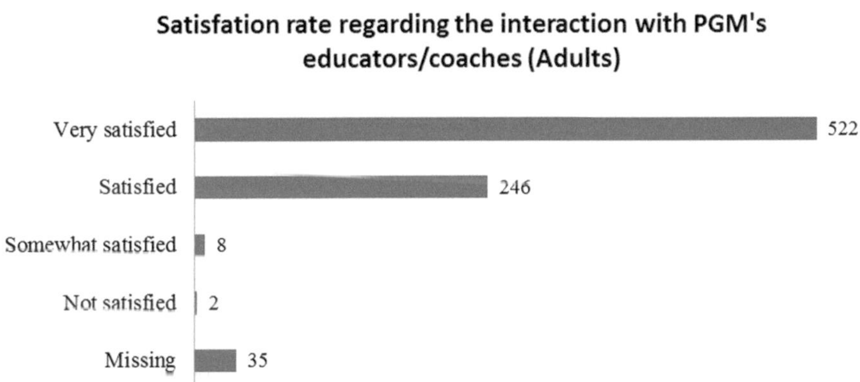


**Fig. 14.4** Satisfaction rate regarding the interaction with PGM's educators/coaches (adults)

of the services and activities. Recreational and sport for all activities were combined with competitive sport activities and not-for-profit projects were placed side by side with pure commercial activities. In parallel, a change in the legitimate forms of capital has emerged (Oakes et al. 1998; O'Brian and Slack 2003). Key actors partially shifted their emphasis on intrinsic forms of cultural and social capital—the tradition of the PGM, the impact on the community, the social value of the activities provided, etc.—to the pursuance of economic capital.

Overall, the vast SWOT analysis carried out by including a legitimate mix of qualitative and quantitative data, highlighted, among many others considerations, that the PGM strengths lay in the territorial ramification, the extent and the diversity of the services, the economic autonomy and the solidarity among units as well as specific aspects concerning the topic of this article like the educator-member relationship and the continuity in the educators' training. The main weaknesses were the facilities' running costs, the lack of turnover and training for managers, and the *mixed* organisational form remaining in between the non-profit and the commercial logic. The process of change undergone during the last 2 years was closely tied with the latter point and conceived to support an enhancement of PGM's performance. In terms of organisational changes, the process of professionalisation was developed as an effective reaction to the growing complexification of the environment that was accompanied also by a more sophisticated demand for new services and activities that both the Municipality of Casalecchio and members addressed to PGM. Such a process of professionalisation was based on deliberative strategies aimed at increasing the standardisation of the roles—also with their parallel enhancement in numbers—formalising the procedures, and reformulating the decision processes in the view to decentralising the decision-making internal knots and increasing their number. The current Council is composed of several new members and the on-going fourth year of the research focuses precisely on the decision making processes. This had not stopped the acceptance of a managerial attitude within such a group of volunteers that was in some ways reinforced by the presence of external professionals involved in the shaping of possible strategies and actions.

This situation determined a strong resistance to change related in particular to two internal coalitions standing for different organisational paradigms. One coalition, based on the ideology of voluntarism, wanted to keep the *pure essence* of PGM with a strong ethos on amateurism, the simplicity of the internal procedures, the informality of decision processes and the internal solidarity between the different units. The other coalition supported, by contrast, a managerial logic focussed on high attention to profit and effectiveness, wishing for a growing presence of professionals. At that point, the organisation entered a period that we can define *competing logic*, which determined the presence of an original form of cohabitation between the two logics that, to some extent, increased the organisational inertia to change. This status soon became apparent when the Executive board, in an attempt to increase predictability and stability in the organisation, decided to postpone the decision concerning some crucial aspects of the future of the organisation. Some interviewees, referring to the strategies adopted by the PGM during the last years, reported the condition of a sort of schizoid state, by describing the decisions adopted as partially contradictory and not linear. The latter is an interesting point that can also be identified and generalised as an important issue in the analysis of the trends concerning a large numbers of Italian sport clubs.

## 14.6 Conclusions

Delayed by the slowness in the country's modernisation, industrialisation and urbanisation, the origin of Italian sport clubs dates back to the very late nineteenth century.

Despite their relatively late origin, Italian sport clubs have played an important social and political role in modern Italy, their development being shaped (and often exploited) by the intervention of powerful institutions such as the Catholic Church, the Socialist movements and notably the Fascist regime. The complex and fragmented history of the country has generated very different economic environments and political cultures at the regional and local level, which also impacts on the development of sport clubs, leading to different organisational and institutional cultures.

The Italian sports system is dominated by the CONI, inappropriately acting as a Ministry of Sport, and is organised in two different subsystems. One is related to the Olympic Sport Movement, with clubs oriented towards elite and competitive sport and affiliated to Sports Federations coordinated by the CONI. The other subsystem, led by the regions and involving the EPSs, is linked to the realm of *sport for all* and inspired by the principles of subsidiarity, adequacy and differentiation. This dichotomy nourishes an often harsh debate between the paradigms of competitive and societal sport, which is nonetheless also fostered by the thousands of clubs that carry on significant social and educational efforts within the sports federations.

Nowadays, sport organisations represent in Italy one of the pillars of the third sector and an interesting object of study for the domains of sociology of organisations and sociology of sport. A mix of cultural and structural variables characterises sports clubs, with a growing evidence of original forms of cohabitation among different organisational logics (associative logic vs. managerial logic, above all). This results in a variety of structures and models of governance with a significant degree of penetration in society.

Drawing some general conclusion from the analysis proposed above and trying to generalise some of the main findings from the case study of Polisportiva Giovanni Masi, it can be argued that within a socio-diachronic perspective the complex process of changes affecting Italian sports clubs in the last decades cannot be interpreted as a linear evolution. This assertion is particularly true for the Italian case in which the lack of a Sport Act means that the changes must be analysed and understood together with the contextual and specific provisions and trends that are closely tied with the peculiar organisational culture of the local authorities and sport clubs. The latter derives from its tradition, history and, above all, from the values and attitudes developed by the dominating coalition(s). Furthermore, the process of leadership selection and the power relationships within the organisation, both influenced by the cultural organisation, are two important factors that shape the adopted strategies and the way decisions are taken. Additionally, the distinctiveness of the Italian context—with its aforementioned not replicated features—and the interaction between internal and external factors, are crucial aspects that must be taken into account to understand the character and direction of the changes undergone by the Italian sport clubs in their recent history. In this regard, there is robust evidence to argue that a significant transformation of the social demands coming from the stakeholders (government, local authorities, individuals, etc.), together with a change in the resources available and the ways to access them, are crucial drivers that have stimulated Italian sport organisations to react appropriately.

During the last 20 years a significant proportion of Italian sports clubs have undergone a process of evolution towards a greater professionalisation, as reaction to the pressure coming from the external environment. Since sport clubs in Italy tend to be small organisations with a limited budget and a small numbers of staff members, this process has determined the collapse of several organisations that were not able to proactively carry out the appropriate organisational changes. In a few cases, however, in those organisations belonging above all to the elite sport subsystem, the tradition of the professional work was further emphasised with a more widespread managerial logic that sought to enhance the degree of specialisation of the professional staff, as well as the standardisation and formalisation of the procedures and the level of hierarchy. These clubs were also successful in developing clear objectives for the supportive plans during the transition process.

However, in most Italian sport clubs, a restricted group of volunteers, often earning small salaries, as has been mentioned, continue to play a vital role in the decision making process, limiting the turnover and the participation of more trained volunteers and professionals and only partially accepting the managerial logic and approach. The mythology of effectiveness and efficiency has become integrated with the traditional set of values underpinned by voluntary commitment; this form of cohabitation represents an interesting discussion topic within the Italian scenario.

## References

Baglioni S (2010) Third sector organizations: the case of sport in Italy. In: Evers A, Zim A (eds) Third sector organizations facing turbulent environments. Nomos, Baden-Baden, pp 73–78

Bonini F (2006) Le istituzioni sportive italiane. Storia e politica. Giappichelli, Torino

Borgogni A, Digennaro S, Vannini E, Manzo S (2013) Partecipazione e Cambiamento. Ricerca quali-quantitativa sul caso studio Polisportiva Giovanni Masi. Educazione Fisica Nella Scuola 239(240):40–49

Censis M (2008) 1 Rapporto Sport e Società. Censis Servizi and CONI, Rome

Colsante G (2003) L'organizzazione dello sport nel mondo e in Italia nella societa moderna. Enciclopedia dello Sport. http://World Warw.treccani.it/enciclopedia/l-organizzazione-dello-sport-nel-mondo-e-in-italia-nella-societa-moderna_%28Enciclopedia-dello-Sport%29/. Retrieved 18 Mar 2014

CONI (2001). Monitoraggio Coni. http://www.coni.it/it/numeri-sport.html. Last Access 19 Mar 2014. Retrieved 19 Mar 2014

CONI (2012) I numeri dello sport 2012. http://www.coni.it/it/numeri-sport.html. Retrieved 19 Mar 2014

Digennaro S (2011) L'intervento sociale attraverso lo sport: aspetti culturali e strategie politiche. Il caso del Centro Sportivo Italiano e dell'Unione Italiana Sport per Tutti. University of Rome Tor Vergata, University of Strasbourg

Digennaro S (2013) Le istituzione sportive tra politiche europee e nuovi diritti di cittadinanza. In: Pioletti AM, Porro N (eds) Lo sport degli europei. FrancoAngeli, Milano, pp 169–198

Dogliani P (2000) Sport and fascism. J Mod Ital Stud 5(3):326–348

Fabrizio F (1977) Storia dello sport in Italia: dalle società ginnastiche all'associazionismo di massa. Guaraldi, Firenze-Rimini

Ferrera P (1992) L'Italia in palestra: storia, documenti e immagini della ginnastica dal 1833 al 1973. La Meridiana, Roma
Giuntini S (2011) I calciatori delle palestre. Football e Società ginnastiche in Italia. Bradipolibri, Turin
Glaser BG, Strauss AL (2009) The discovery of grounded theory: strategies for qualitative research. Transaction Publisher, Piscataway, NJ
Gouldner AW (1954) Patterns of industrial bureaucracy. Collier-Macmillan, Toronto
Hall RH (1982) Organisations: structure and process. Prentice Hall, Englewood Cliffs, NJ
Hinings CR, Greenwood R (1988) The dynamics of organizational change. Basil Blackwell, London
ISTAT (2012) Censimento dell'Industria e dei Servizi. ISTAT, Rome
ISTAT (2013) Aspetti della vita quotidiana. ISTAT, Rome
Madella A (2006) Sport e intervento sociale: miti e fatti. SDS Rivista di Cultura Sportiva 70:7–18
Madella A, Digennaro S (2009) Sociologia dello sport. Analisi del fenomeno e studio delle organizzazioni sportive. SDS Edizioni, Rome
Marani Toro I, Marani Toro A (1977) Gli ordinamenti sportivi. Giuffré, Milan
Martin S (2011) Italian sport and the challenges of its recent historiography. J Sport Hist 38(2):199–209
Mintzberg H (1979) The structuring of organisations: a synthesis of the research. Prentice-Hall, Englewood Cliffs
NOMISMA (1999) Sport ed Economia 1999. Nomisma, Bologna
O'Brian D, Slack T (2003) An analysis of change in an organisational field: the professionalization of English Rugby Union. J Sport Manage 17(4):417–448
Oakes LS, Townley B, Cooper DJ (1998) Business planning as pedagogy: language and control in a changing institutional field. Adm Sci Q 43(2):257–292
Porro N (1996) Sport, political system and sociology in Italy. Int Rev Sociol Sport 27(4):329–340
Porro N (2005) Cittadini in movimento. Meridiana, Molfetta
Slack T (1997) Understanding sport organisation: the application of organisation theory. Human Kinetics, Champaign, IL
UNASCI (n.a.) Censimento delle Società Sportive Centenarie d'Italia. http://www.unasci.com/web/index.php?option=com_unascisocietacen&Itemid=36. Retrieved 18 Mar 2014
Verrati V (2012) Società civile e tessuto sociale in italia. Una storia istituzionale. Bradipolibri, Turin
Yin RY (2009) Case study research: design and methods. Sage, London

# Chapter 15
# Sport Clubs in The Netherlands

**Harold van der Werff, Remco Hoekman, and Janine van Kalmthout**

## 15.1 Introduction

The Netherlands are a prosperous country. Compared to other countries wage differences and social inequality are low, and the standards for education, health, safety and security are high. Furthermore, with approximately 500 inhabitants per square kilometre it is dense populated. The culture of the Dutch is characterised by co-operation and making compromises rather than emphasising differences. With regard to sport these conditions can be considered favourable, as higher income and educational levels are often associated with higher rates of sport participation. Furthermore, the willingness to co-operate and looking for shared interests are essential for the existence of sport clubs with their voluntary staff. Finally, the high population density ensures limited distances to sport facilities and sport clubs.

It therefore should come as no surprise that the Netherlands is also characterised by high sport participation and sport membership rates. The Eurobarometer survey 2009 and 2013 (European Commission 2014) showed that the Netherlands rank at the top with regard to the participation in sport clubs. 27 % of the Dutch population is a member of a sport club, compared to a European average of 12 %. With this, sport clubs are one of or the most important sport providers in the Netherlands

In this chapter we provide some context to the position of sport clubs in the Netherlands. We start off by outlining the history of sport clubs in the Netherlands and their (changing) role in policy and society. Furthermore we provide an overview of the general characteristics of the sport clubs, such as the number of members,

H. van der Werff (✉) • R. Hoekman • J. van Kalmthout
Mulier Institute, Utrecht, The Netherlands
e-mail: h.vanderwerff@mulierinstituut.nl; r.hoekman@mulierinstituut.nl; j.vankalmthout@mulierinstituut.nl



C. Breuer et al. (eds.), *Sport Clubs in Europe*, Sports Economics, Management and Policy 12, DOI 10.1007/978-3-319-17635-2_15

financial situation, experienced bottleneck, provided activities and degree of professionalisation. A specific paragraph is devoted to the role of sport clubs in the national policy programme *To a saver sports environment*, to illustrate the current position of sports clubs in policy and in society. Finally, we give some concluding remarks on the position of sport clubs and shed light on the future development of sport clubs in the Netherlands.

## 15.2 History and Context

### *15.2.1 Origin of Sport Clubs*

Sport as a regulated and competitive form of physical activity emerged in the Netherlands in the second half of the nineteenth century. From England new sport were introduced in the Netherlands, like rugby and badminton. Also already existing recreational activities and public entertainment forms like ice skating, swimming, running and horse riding were transformed into sports. In contrast to England where boarding schools were essential in spreading and developing sports, in the Netherlands sport clubs founded by private initiatives became the main suppliers of sports. However, this did not mean that sport was excluded from the educational system. At the same time that sport clubs emerged gymnastics was introduced in the curriculum, moulded after the German and Scandinavian gymnastic. At present Dutch primary schools are by law required to include physical education in their curriculum and many still refer to the physical educations lessons as *gym*.

It is uncertain when the first sport club was founded in the Netherlands. In the period that sport clubs began to emerge a good administration of sport clubs was lacking. It is known that in 1846 the first rowing club Royal Dutch Yacht Club was founded by Prince Hendrik, brother of King Willem III. After that equestrian sports, fencing, billiards and gymnastic clubs were emerging. The oldest field sport clubs in the Netherlands that still exists is the first cricket club U.D. from Deventer, which dates from 1875. The first soccer club H.F.C. from Haarlem was founded in 1879. Most contemporary sports appear much later (Engels 1960).

Many of the first sport clubs are founded not only to accommodate their members, but to stimulate other goals, like promoting ship building (rowing), to promote self-reliance and personal hygiene (swimming), and to increase the quality of horse breeding (equestrian sports). For sport clubs that were founded at the end of the nineteenth century or later these goals were of no concern. They were focused primarily on the recreation of their own members. Balloting committees made sure that candidate members would fit in the club (Stokvis 2010).

The emergence of clubs in the second half of the nineteenth century is also visible outside the world of sport, such as in the context of labour, charity, culture and science. This increase in clubs coincides with industrialisation and urbanisation, which led to a decrease in the class differences and an increase in social mobility. In the Netherlands the industrial revolution took place in the second half of the nineteenth century, much later than in other countries (De Vries 2003). The new industries were concentrated in the cities and many people left the countryside and moved to the cities. The development of trade, industry and science introduced new professions. In general prosperity rose and people became emancipated. Traditional bonds that provided a cadre for community activities lost a great part of their social meaning. For city dwellers clubs became the new networks in which same minded people connected to achieve mutual goals, like sports participation (Wilterdink 1984). Stokvis (2010) sees club formation as an aspect of the modernisation process.

Sport as a democratic phenomenon in which people from all groups in society participate arose after the 8 h working day was introduced in 1919, though only a small number of sports were involved. Later on, in the 1960s and 1970s, another substantial increase in sport participation occurred (Hoekman and Van der Poel 2009). It is also from this period on that sport clubs are no longer the one and only context of sport participation. As a result of the individualisation and health and fitness orientation, people started to participate in sport outside an official context. Furthermore, the commercialisation led to a wide variety of commercial sport providers that offered all kind of sport activities for the individual. Nowadays, commercial sport providers, especially fitness centres, are an important sport provider (Breedveld 2014). One out of five people in the Netherlands is a member of a fitness centre.

The growth in sport participation in the Netherlands in recent years can mainly be ascribed to the commercial sector and individual sport participation outside the sport club context. Nevertheless, membership rates for sport clubs are quite stable and sport clubs are undeniably one of the main sport providers in the Netherlands (Collard and Hoekman 2013).

### *15.2.2 Position of Sport Clubs within the National Sport Structure*

In this paragraph we describe the place that sport clubs have within the Dutch sport structure. We start at the local level (sport clubs, municipalities), then we describe the regional level and we end with the national level, including the two ministries that are involved with sports, sport federations and the National Olympic Committee*Netherlands Sport Confederation (NOC*NSF), which is the national umbrella organise for sports in the Netherlands. Fig. 15.1 displays an overview of the various organises and the level at which they act.

In 2012, there were 24,727 sport clubs in the Netherlands affiliated to sport federations (Fig. 15.2), which in their turn were affiliated to NOC*NSF. Van Kalmthout and Lucassen (2008) estimated that 90 % of the sport clubs in the Netherlands are member of a sport federation that is affiliated to NOC*NSF. With this, it is estimated that in 2012 there were approximately 27,500 sport clubs in the Netherlands.

In the last decennia, the number of sport clubs in the Netherlands has decreased (Fig. 15.2). However, in the last years, the number of sport clubs remains quite stable. In that same period the number of sport federations affiliated to NOC*NSF rose from 70 in 2002 till 75 in 2012, but these were mainly small federations.

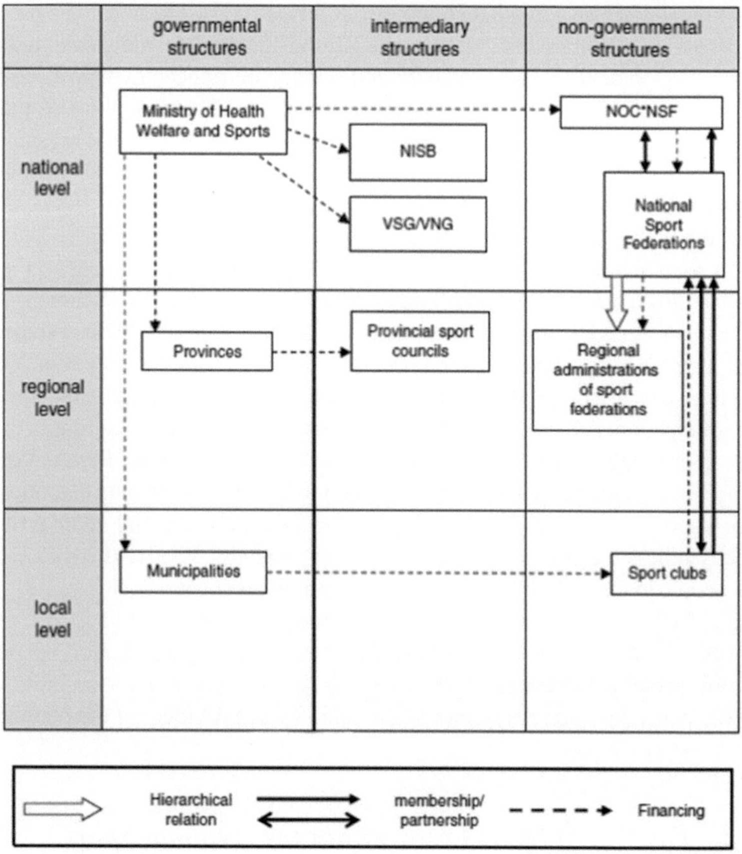


**Fig. 15.1** The organisation of sport in the Netherlands (Hoekman and Breedveld 2013, p. 121). Note: *NISB* National Institute for Sport and Exercise, *VSG* Union of Local Authorities and *VNG* Association of Netherlands Municipalities. For an easier comprehension of the general structure bodies like commercial sport providers and sport for disabled specific elite sport organises were excluded from the figure. Also the ministry of Education, Culture and Science is excluded since it is not involved directly in policies regarding organised sport

Local governments play an important role for local sport. Many have drafted a specific sport policy document in which they lay out their plans for building and maintaining sport facilities and promoting sport participation. Most of the local sport budget is spend on sport facilities, by providing these facilities with reduced fees to sport clubs. Without these reduced fees for sport facilities and additional subsidies of municipalities, sport clubs would have a hard time balancing their budget.

In addition to the local support system for sport clubs, there are also regional organisations that do support sport clubs. The 12 provinces mainly support local development programmes and act as an intermediary between the local and national levels. Furthermore, the provinces finance the provincial sport councils to support

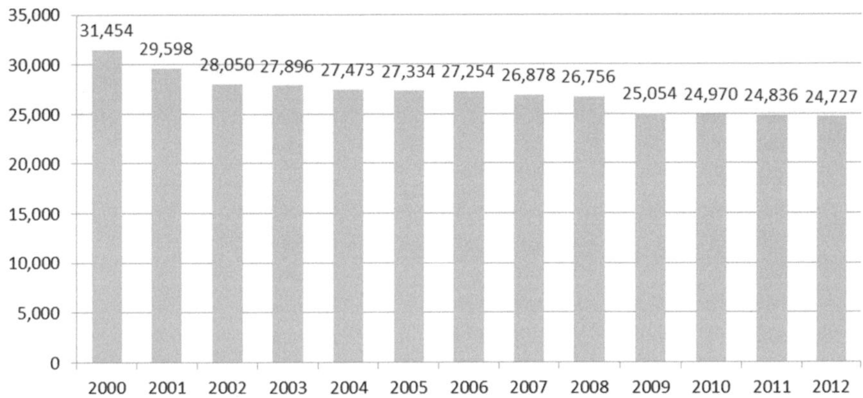


**Fig. 15.2** Number of sport clubs that are member of federations affiliated to NOC*NSF (NOC*NSF, 2000–2012)

sport organisations, such as sport clubs, within the province. The provincial sport council mainly provide information, knowledge and advice to sport clubs.

On the national level, the sport federations, NOC*NSF and the ministry of Health, Welfare and Sports are most important to sport clubs. In the Netherlands the ministry of Health, Welfare and Sports is responsible for the national policies on sports and regularly includes sport clubs in these policies. This ministry focuses on sport and health, sport participation for all and talent development. The ministry of Education, Culture and Science determines the policies with regard to sports at school. Two main issues at this ministry at the moment are the realisation of a third hour of physical education at primary schools and stimulation of the use of professional teachers for the lessons in physical education.

The sport federations look after the interests of all their members and clubs. Sport federations organise competitions on various sport levels, from local competitions to matches on the highest levels, including national championships and international tournaments. Furthermore, the federations provide training courses for technical staff, management and administrative staff and referees. Most of the federations also organise conferences to keep the clubs and their representatives informed on the latest developments in their field.

In 1904, there were 12 sport federations. In 1975 that number has increased to 53 and after that year the number of sports federation continued to grow steadily. In 2012 there were 75 sport federations that are connected to the Dutch Olympic Committee (NOC*NSF).

Looking at the numbers of sport participants the Dutch Soccer Federation is the largest, boosting over 1.2 million members (Table 15.1). The second largest federation is the Dutch Tennis Federation, which has approximately 675,000 members. With only 18 members the Dutch Racquetball Association is the smallest federation. The 12 smallest federations together have fewer members (5,400) than two-thirds of the other federations by themselves. The five biggest federations have more members than all the other 70 together. This shows that the number of sport club members varies enormously between various sports.

**Table 15.1** Sport federation ranked by the number of sport clubs and by their number of members. Top 10 in 2012 (NOC*NSF 2012)

| | Sport | Sport clubs | Sport | Members |
|---|---|---|---|---|
| 1 | Football | 3,325 | Football | 1,209,413 |
| 2 | Tennis | 1,711 | Tennis | 674,696 |
| 3 | Billiards | 1,431 | Golf | 388,043 |
| 4 | Equestrian sports | 1,248 | Gymnastics | 241,500 |
| 5 | Volleyball | 1,119 | Hockey | 232,933 |
| 6 | Bridge | 1,074 | Equestrian sports | 213,009 |
| 7 | Gymnastics | 1,057 | Swimming | 144,613 |
| 8 | Judo | 766 | Athletics | 137,425 |
| 9 | Shooting | 763 | Volleyball | 116,539 |
| 10 | (Ice) skating | 724 | Bridge | 116,169 |

Measured in the number of affiliated sport clubs the largest sport federations are the Dutch Soccer Federation (3,325), Dutch Tennis Federation (1,711) and the Dutch Billiard Federation (1,431). That the latter holds the number 3 position may come as a surprise, but in the Netherlands there are many small billiard clubs, with an average of only 24 members. The Dutch Curling Federation (4), Dutch Bob and Sled Federation (3), Dutch Racquetball Association (2), Dutch Climb and Mountain Sport Association (1) and Dutch Association for Aviation (1) have the smallest number of sport clubs.[1]

NOC*NSF is the national sport umbrella organisation for all federations. However, one should be aware that there are also sport federations that are not affiliated to NOC*NSF where sport clubs can decide to become a member. For example, student swimming clubs with their high mutation in members can choose to join the Dutch Cultural Sport Federation (NCS) which has less strict rules about entering a swimming competition than the Royal Dutch Swimming Federation (KNZB). Some of these federations have a status of extraordinary member of NOC*NSF.

NOC*NSF arose in 1993 when the Dutch Olympic Committee (NOC) and Netherlands Sport Confederation (NSF) merged. In 2012 NOC*NSF celebrated the 100th anniversary of NOC. NOC*NSF represent the interests of its member sport federations, stimulates collaboration between organisations in the world of sports, including schools and business, and coordinates the participation of Dutch top sport participants in the Olympic (Youth) Games and Paralympic (Youth) Games. It strives for an increase in the sport participation in the Netherlands, for more sport club members and for an improvement of the quality of the national and local sport organisations. Another NOC*NSF ambition is to have and keep the Netherlands in the top ten of top sport countries in the world. Furthermore, NOC*NSF represents national sport interests in various national and international partnerships.

In a NOC*NSF additional meeting in June 2014 the members approved of a statutes amendment. The new statutes provide in the possibility for *associates* to

[1] The Dutch Surfing Association has no sport clubs.

join NOC*NSF as a member organisation. Not-for-profit organisations that want to contribute significantly to NOC*NSF and the values for which it stands, can join the umbrella organisation. With this amendment NOC*NSF will develop itself from an interest group for sport federations and their affiliated sport clubs to an organisation that represents the complete sports sector.

## 15.3 Role of Sport Clubs in Policy and Society

In this paragraph we look into national data on sport club participation. We illustrate how sport club participation relates to sport participation patterns in general and provide an overview of which groups mainly participate within the sport club setting. In addition we describe how sport clubs are socially and politically embedded in their environment.

### *15.3.1 National Data on Sport Club Participation*

National sport participation surveys show that 68 % of the Dutch population (6–79 year old) participate in sport at least 12 times per year[2] (Table 15.2). As mentioned earlier NOC*NSF aims to increase this to 75 % in 2016. The most popular sports[3] are aerobics/fitness (22 %), swimming (18 %), hiking (15 %) and running (14 %). About half of the population (56 %) is active in sport on a weekly basis (at least 40 times a year). About 30 % is a sport clubs member. In recent years these numbers are quite stable, despite various local and national initiatives to stimulate sport participation.

Membership of sport clubs differs among certain groups. Within the group of 6–79 years old 34 % of the males and 26 % of the female is a sport club member.

Membership also varies clearly with age. 83 % of the youth group 6–11 years old are a sport club member. Within the group of 12–17 years that is 70 %. Within the older age groups far less people practice their sport within a sport club (Fig. 15.3).

There is a correlation between sport club membership and household income level. 37 % of the people belonging to a household with an above modal income are a sport club member. For the group with a modal income (29 %) and especially a below modal income (20 %) membership is less common.

For comparing membership by educational level we selected people of at least 25 years old. Over the years the percentages per level practically do not vary.

[2] In the Guidelines Sport Research someone is considered being a sport participant if he/she participates in sport activities at least 12 times a year. Some in the field of sports consider this a low threshold. In 'Report Sport 2010' (Tiessen-Raaphorst 2010) a weekly sport participant was defined as someone who participates in sports at least 40 times per year.

[3] Practised at least once during a year.

**Table 15.2** Sport participation and sport club membership, people aged 6 to 79 years old, 2006–2013 (in %, Mulier Institute 2014)

| | 2006 | 2007 | 2008 | 2009 | 2010 | 2011 | 2012 | 2013 |
|---|---|---|---|---|---|---|---|---|
| At least 12× per year | 64 | 66 | 64 | 65 | 65 | 64 | 66 | 68 |
| At least 40× per year (weekly sport participant) | 52 | 53 | 53 | 52 | 53 | 53 | 55 | 56 |
| Sports club membership | 33 | 31 | 31 | 31 | 29 | 29 | 30 | 30 |

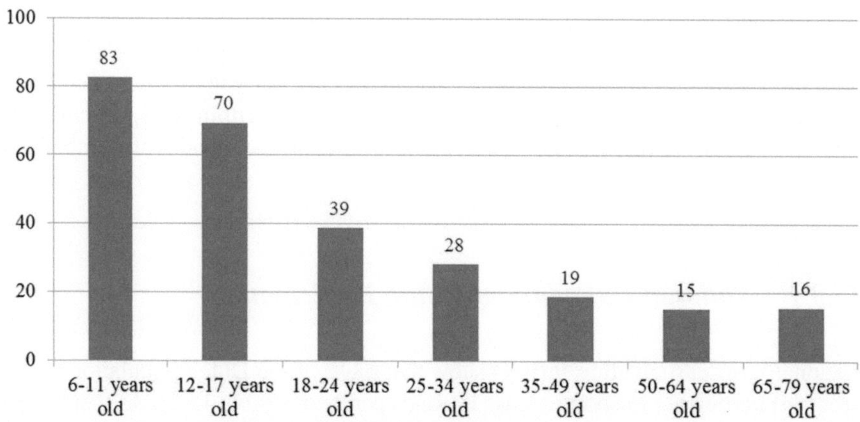


**Fig. 15.3** Membership of sport clubs in the Netherlands by age group, people aged 6 to 79 years old; 2013 (in %, Mulier Institute 2014)

In 2012, 28 % of the people with the highest education level (university for the applied sciences, universities) are a sport club member. Within the middle (18 %) and lower education level (12 %) club membership is less common.

## *15.3.2 Societal and Political Embedding*

National, regional and local government acknowledge that sport clubs attract people from all levels of society and that the societal value of sport clubs goes well beyond that of their own club members. Therefore, the local government provides subsidies to sport clubs, for example by charging low rates for hiring sport facilities. As said earlier, without this support most sport clubs would have a hard time balancing their budget.

However, the governmental support comes with conditions and it seems that these conditions are becoming more demanding. After World War II the local governments demanded that in order to receive a subsidy sport clubs had to abolish the balloting committees, which meant that clubs lost the ability to refuse people

(Stokvis 2010). Everybody who wanted to become a member should have the chance to do so. Since the 1960s the sport clubs were urged to offer more services, for example in playing a role in the integration in society of ethnic minorities, something the staff of the clubs were not prepared for and that put a stress on the clubs and their staff.

In recent years national and local governments have focused on intensifying the involvement of sport clubs within national and local policies, again asking for something in return for subsidies. Several national programmes (e.g. *Sports and physical activity in the neighbourhood*) and local programmes promote local initiatives and co-operations between several local organisations and sectors, like education, health, welfare, civil organisation, neighbourhood organisation, police and entrepreneurs. These programmes rarely focus only on the intrinsic benefits of sports, many times sport is used as a catalyst to stimulate a variety of goals, e.g. social participation, social integration, a healthy lifestyle (e.g. reducing overweight, diabetes and cardiovascular diseases) or a safe neighbourhood. In most cases sport clubs offer low threshold activities like sport activities in the neighbourhood or at school.

Sport clubs are being stimulated to take more social responsibility. However, not all sport clubs are willing and able to provide these additional services and are likely to lose (a part of) their subsidies. The clubs that did participate had to invest time and energy in new activities for people of which the majority would not become a member. Van der Werff et al. (2012) found that sport clubs that participated in these programmes experienced that trainings and clinics for schools do not yield many new youth members, still the clubs continue to organise these activities to contribute to society like the municipalities wanted them to do (enhance the youth health). Other reasons are to get visibility and maybe attract new members in the future.

In order to support the sport clubs to fulfill their societal obligations several parties, including the ministry of Health, Welfare and Sports (VWS) and the ministry of Education, Culture and Science (OCW), umbrella organisations for education and for local municipalities and NOC*NSF, initiated the programme *Impulse community schools, sports and culture*, in which so-called combination officials were tasked to increase the supply of sport activities[4] by stimulating the local co-operation between schools, sport clubs and other social organisation. The aim was to have 2,250 full-time jobs of combination officials in 2012. The first combination officials started in 2008. In 2012 the minister of VWS decided to expand the number of combination officials to 2,900 full-time jobs and to broaden their tasks. As a result in this new programme *Sports and physical activities in the neighbourhood* the name combination official was changed into neighbourhood sport coaches (Von Heijden and Boers 2012).

The concept of so called *open clubs*, recently launched by NOC*NSF, is another initiative that aims to increase the co-operation between sport clubs and other local organisations. These are clubs that not only focus on the needs of their own members, but also of (potential) sport participants and the community at large. Open clubs are

[4] Most combination official were either active in the field of sports or in the field of culture. Some were active in both fields.

able to transcend the interests of their own sport and work together with other sport suppliers and/or other sectors (e.g. health care, community work, education). They participate in all kinds of local activities like organising sport activities at schools and in the National Sport Week, but also participating in local networks. In co-operation with sport federations and local sport organisations NOC*NSF organises local briefings to enthuse sport clubs for the *open club* concept. Daamen et al. (2013) found that 32 % of the sport clubs meet the criteria of an open club. However, they also found that 45 % of the sport clubs in the Netherlands believe that sport clubs only exist to provide for an adequate sport climate for their member and nothing else. Just a quarter of the sport clubs stress that they feel that a sport club should play a larger role within the community and participate in policy programmes. So policy makers should be aware that only a minority of the sport clubs are willing and are able to act as a full partner in local policies.

## 15.4 Characteristics of Sport Clubs

In this fourth paragraph we focus on the characteristics of sport clubs, like size, the way they are organised, bottlenecks and challenges, recreational sport and professional sport, activities for sport club members, professionalisation and finance. Based on data of the Sport Club Monitor (2000–2012; NOC*NSF/Mulier Institute) we present an actual and historic overview. The Sport Club Monitor is a representative panel survey in which yearly over 1,200 sport clubs are interviewed on all kinds of sport related questions, like type of sports, sport facilities, sport activities, members, staff, policies and finances.

### *15.4.1 Basic Characteristics*

In the Netherlands a sport club has on average approximately 300 members,[5] including about 260 active sporting members and 45 non-active members/donors. A quarter of the clubs has 1–100 members (*small*), another quarter 101–250 members (*middle*) and half more than 250 members (*large*). In general larger sport clubs are more associated with outdoor team sports and having their own facilities, whereas smaller clubs tend to offer more often individual indoor sports and most of them do not have facilities of their own (Table 15.3).

In 2012 81 % of the sport clubs are single sport clubs, 14 % offer two types of sports and 5 % is a so called omnisport clubs in which three or more sports can be practised. In 2007 4 % of the clubs are multi- or omnisport clubs. In 2012 57 % of the sport clubs owned a sports facilities and/or a canteen. In 2007 that was 54 %.

[5] The median is 160 members. In the Sport Club Panel (1,200 sport clubs) large(r) clubs are to some extend overrepresented. According to NOC*NSF a sport club has on average 201 members.

**Table 15.3** Type of sport club in the Netherlands by club size, percent by row, 2012 (Sport Club Monitor 2012, NOC*NSF/Mulier Institute)

| | Type of sport | | | Indoor or outdoor | | With own sport facilities | |
|---|---|---|---|---|---|---|---|
| | Team | Semi-individual | Individual | Indoor sports | Outdoor sports | Yes/more or less | No |
| Small (–100 members) | 20 | 29 | 51 | 59 | 41 | 32 | 68 |
| Middle (101–250 members) | 31 | 27 | 42 | 50 | 50 | 43 | 57 |
| Large (251+ members) | 42 | 17 | 41 | 19 | 81 | 76 | 24 |
| Total | 32 | 24 | 45 | 42 | 58 | 51 | 49 |

Teamsport: e.g. soccer (field), basketball, volleyball; semi-individual: e.g. tennis, badminton, judo; individual: e.g. swimming, hiking, equestrian sports
Indoor: e.g. bridge, gymnastics, chess; outdoor: e.g. athletics, cycling, ice skating

### 15.4.2 The Way Sport Clubs Are Organised

Almost all clubs have the legal form of an association of members. Some are a foundation. In some cases a sport club is both an association and a foundation. Whereas the voluntary board is responsible for the daily management, in associations the main decisions are being made by the members themselves. For this an associations has to organise a member meeting at least once a year. In 2012 the clubs reported that on average 27 % of their members attended the annual member meeting.

In most cases the board of a sport club has an odd number of members, so if decisions have to be made there is always a majority, unless someone votes blank. Every board consists of at least three members, a chairman, a treasurer and a secretary. In addition a board can have general board members or any other kinds of members. Almost all board members are volunteers.

In the Netherlands the three main board positions are usually filled by men, ageing 55 years or older. This is especially the case with chairmen, of which 90 % is male and two-thirds is 55 years or older. Half of the board members hold their current position for 11 years or longer. 91 % of the board members did not follow any specific training or education to practice their function. On the other hand it is known that most board members are over qualified for their position within the sport club, like the bank director who is the treasurer of the club. Furthermore, more than half of the board members have finished an education at the highest level (university or university of applied sciences).

### 15.4.3 Bottlenecks and Challenges of Sport Clubs

Though for many years sport clubs form the back bone of the organised sport in the Netherlands they are not without concern. In 2012 87 % of the sport clubs experienced at least one type of bottleneck (Fig. 15.4). Two thirds of all clubs had difficulties with regard to members. The main issues were recruitment of new members,

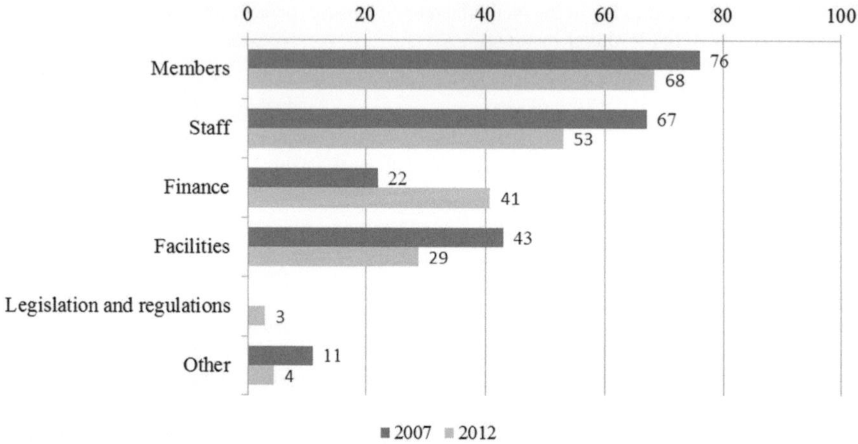


**Fig. 15.4** Bottlenecks and challenges of sport clubs, 2007 and 2012 (in %; Sport Club Monitor, 2007 and 2012; NOC*NSF/Mulier Institute)

decline in the number of members and the fact that on average the total group of members is ageing.

Another bottleneck concerns the staff (shortage, capabilities, retention). About half of the clubs had difficulties with it, especially with finding enough board members and volunteers who are adequate in doing their various tasks. A third bottleneck was finances. 41 % of the sport clubs had problems with this, mainly with increasing costs (hiring sport facilities), retaining old sponsors and finding new ones, and balancing the budget. A fourth important bottleneck concerned the sport facilities. 29 % of the clubs had problems with their facilities. The issue the clubs mentioned the most are quality and maintenance of the facilities. It is important to know that approximately half of the clubs made use of facilities for which the responsibility for management and maintenance lie with the local municipality.

In comparison to 2007 less sport clubs experienced the bottlenecks mentioned above, except for financial bottlenecks. In 5 years the number of clubs that experienced financial bottlenecks have almost doubled. Because of the economic recession sport clubs are faced with a decrease in revenues. For example, it is more difficult to acquire sponsor funds and local governmental subsidies are decreasing. In addition the costs are rising. Though local governments try to spare the sport sector user fees for sport facilities are increasing. Sport clubs are reluctant to increase membership subscriptions, because they want to be a low threshold organisation and are afraid to lose members.

In the Sport Club Monitor 2012 clubs were asked on which policy issues they would focus in the next year (Fig. 15.5). The bottlenecks that were mentioned above are high on the priority lists. 66 % of the sport clubs said that retention and recruiting of members was in their top three of policy issues to which they will pay extra attention in the next year and 37 % of the clubs will give priority to retention and recruiting of volunteers. 22 % will focus on the financial situation.

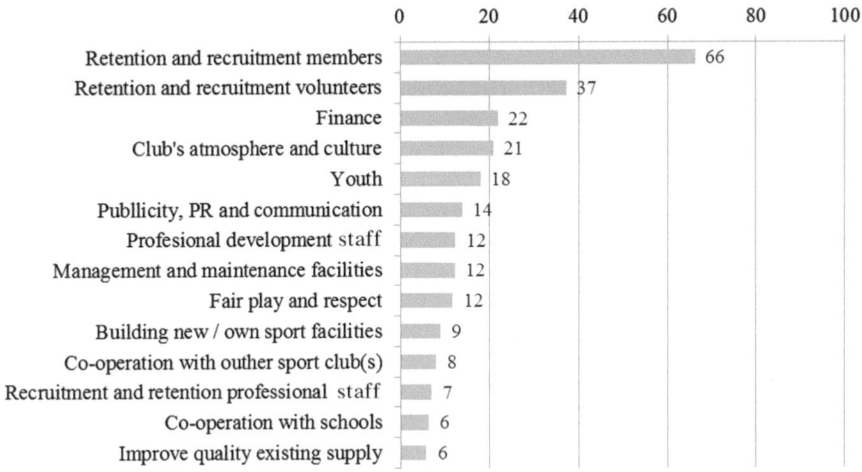


**Fig. 15.5** Main policy issues for the next year (maximum 3; in %; Sport Club Monitor, 2012; NOC*NSF 2012)

## *15.4.4 Activities for Sport Club Members*

The main purpose of sport clubs is to offer sport activities for their members. They provide for adequate sport facilities and training staff and make it possible for members to compete in a competition or other sport events.

87 % of the clubs have members that do compete in an official competition. 53 % of these clubs have at least half of their members participating in an official competition. When looking at team sport clubs (e.g. soccer, hockey) 93 % of them have at least half of their member competing in an official competition. With semi-individual sports (e.g. tennis, badminton) and individual sports (e.g. running, swimming) this is just over 30 %.

In addition to training and competition activities 88 % of the sport clubs offered other activities for their members, mostly social activities like holiday camps, clinics, bingo nights, New Year's activities, special tournaments and other events. In most cases these activities were organised by the clubs themselves, sometimes in collaboration with other clubs, the sport federation or other organisation. Some activities were organised by the municipality and the clubs were asked to participate. Most of the activities organised by sport clubs are for their members only. However, 77 % of the sport clubs have organised activities that were open to non-members.

Also 30 % of the sport club offer activities and facilities that are not (directly) related to the sport they offer. These include physiotherapy (11 %), office facilities (e.g. Internet; 8 %), work, homework and meeting rooms (7 %), and fitness (6 %). It is expected that more sport clubs, especially clubs that have their own sport facilities, will offer such facilities to accommodate their members and by doing so retain them.

**Table 15.4** Number of volunteers and paid staff by club size, 2012 (Sport Club Monitor 2012; NOC*NSF/Mulier Institute)

| | Small (≤100 members) | Middle (101–250 members) | Big (>250 members) | Total |
|---|---|---|---|---|
| Volunteers | 12 | 31 | 89 | 48 |
| Paid staff | 0 | 1 | 5 | 2 |
| Total staff | 13 | 32 | 94 | 51 |

People who receive no pay or less than € 1.500 (expenses, tax free volunteer remuneration) annually for their activities for a club are considered as volunteers

## *15.4.5 Professionalisation*

As sport clubs are voluntary organisations people can join or leave them as they see fit. The existence of the club depends on how many people want to spend time and energy in maintaining all the activities that are needed to manage an organisation. Normally with voluntary organisations there is no paid staff. Sport clubs thrive on volunteers, though many sport clubs now employ paid staff.

In the Netherlands volunteers can receive a tax free compensation for expenses with a maximum of €1,500 per year. Almost half of the Dutch sport clubs have volunteers that benefit from this tax measure. When some receive a fee for which taxes and social contributions have to be paid, they are considered to be paid staff.

It is estimated that approximately one million people are active as a volunteer for sport organisations (Van der Werff and Lucassen 2006). No other sector has more volunteers than sport and on average they spend more than 4 h per week on their voluntary sport activities. In 2012 on average a Dutch sport club has 51 staff members, of which 48 are volunteers and 2 are paid employees (Table 15.4). In total 42 % of the sport clubs have at least one paid employee. This is more the case with clubs with over 250 members (64 %), than with clubs with 101–250 members (37 %) and those with 100 members or less (17 %).

Earlier it was said that finding adequate staff is a mayor bottleneck for clubs and for clubs staff usually means volunteers. In 2012 27 % of the sport clubs said they have enough volunteers and are not looking for new volunteers. 53 % had enough volunteers, but the club was still looking for more and 20 % indicates that they do not have enough volunteers and are in need of more.

The need for volunteers has always been a main issue with sport clubs and somehow they manage to find new volunteers, or reshuffle activities over the available staff. But that is not always the case. For 43 % of the clubs that report staff bottlenecks (67 % of all clubs) these bottlenecks are a (very) serious issue and for 2 % this is a problem that threatens the existence of the sport club.

To some extend the need for volunteers could be decreased if more paid staff would be employed, but that would affect the essence of being a voluntary organisation. And of course, the question is whether there is enough budget for paid staff, as the member's contribution is not adapted to finance many paid staff. In 2012 9 % of the sport clubs thought that the club could benefit if more paid staff were employed and two-thirds disagrees. But only 3 % of the clubs would like to appoint more paid staff in the next year. This is a strong indication that sport clubs still like to be a voluntary organisation.

Within the various staff functions coaches are a very important one, especially with competitive sports. Most sport federations offer coach courses on different levels, from novice to expert on the highest level and many sport clubs volunteers participate in these courses.

In 2012 84 % of the sport clubs have coaches, either volunteers or paid staff. 69 % of the clubs say that they (also) work with coaches that are formally not qualified to act as a coach. The question is whether not formally qualified means not skilled, a question frequently asked, for example when a coach gives a clinic for non-members, like children of a nearby school. The main reasons these unqualified coaches are active in sport clubs are that there are not enough qualified coaches, the unqualified coaches are very experienced, they perform tasks for which it is deemed that no qualification is needed and the unqualified coaches are cheaper than qualified ones. Sometimes sport clubs just have to make do with what coaches are available.

### *15.4.6 Finance*

Sport clubs are non-profit organisations and a positive budget result should benefit the members. For most sport clubs the member's contributions are the main means of income. In addition there are subsidies and revenues from sport activities and events. For sport clubs that have their own canteen catering revenues are also very important. Costs include costs for maintenance of facilities, sport equipment, energy costs, staff, law and regulation (alcohol licence, building taxes).

In 2012 more than one third of the sport clubs had a yearly budget of less than 10,000 euro and 1 out of 5 could spend 100,000 euro per year. 67 % of the sport clubs indicate that their financial situation is (very) healthy, 27 % report a solid situation and 8 % experience a less healthy or even a critical financial situation. In comparison to 2000 and thereafter this has not changed. Though finances were mentioned as one of the main bottlenecks for sport clubs, it seems that most sport clubs can balance their budget.

Looking at the revenues it becomes clear that sport clubs finds themselves in challenging times (Fig. 15.6). Though one-third sees an increase in the member contributions, a quarter have less revenues from these contributions. With catering revenues it is the same. The effects from the economic recession can be seen in the fact that half of the clubs now have (far) less revenues from sponsoring and advertising. Striking is that almost two-third of the sport clubs have to cope with decreasing subsidies from their local municipality. Hoekman and Breedveld (2013) found that 93 % of the Dutch local municipalities have made economic cuts in their sport budget or are planning to do so in the near future. Sport clubs have to face a decrease in the subsidies and higher rates for hiring sport facilities. Still, though these measures

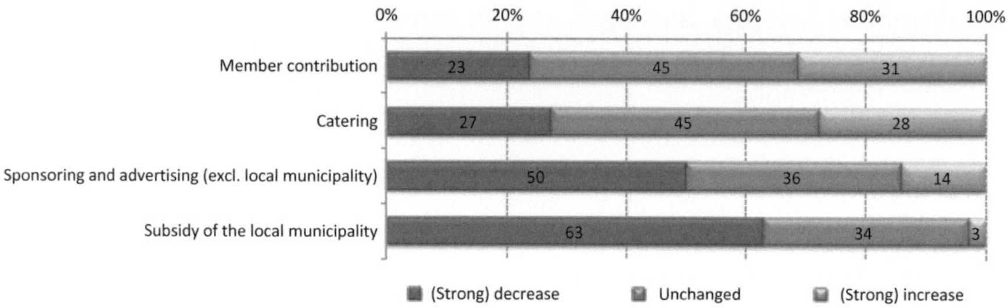


**Fig. 15.6** Development in revenues as compared with the year before, 2012 (in %; Sport Club Monitor 2012; NOC&NSF/Mulier Institute)

have a serious impact it looks like that local municipalities try to spare the sport sector. In other policy areas the economic cuts seems to be more severe.

In the Sport Club Monitor there were some additional questions about the club's financial situation. More than half of the sport clubs experience difficulties in finding new financial resources. Only 8 % say that they are successful in that. Furthermore two-thirds of the clubs find it increasingly difficult to collect the member contributions. Still, over three-quarters manage to balance the club's budget and half of the clubs have some financial room if unexpected costs have to be paid. On the other hand 15 % of the sport clubs have no reserve funds if such costs would suddenly appear.

## 15.5 Safe Sports Environment

In this paragraph we focus on a national policy programme in which sport clubs are heavily involved. With this policy programme *Safe Sports Climate* (VSK) and the role of sport clubs within this policy project, we illustrate the extended social role of sport clubs and their role as policy implementers. The socialisation of sport and the wide media attention of certain abhorrent incidents have turned undesirable behaviour in sport, safe sports environment into a topical and relevant issue in the Netherlands. In the opinion of the Dutch population (73 %) there is coarser and harder aggression in amateur sports in recent years (Van der Werff and Van Kalmthout 2012). They also think that growing aggression in sports is a result of growing aggression in society (72 %).

Since 2005 the Dutch government and sport federations work together in national programmes to stimulate desirable behaviour in sports and to prevent and tackle undesirable behaviour. The recent national programme: *To a safer sports environment* (2012–2016) is performed by NOC*NSF. Numerous sport federations are participating, representing about 18,000 sport clubs (Romijn et al. 2013). The programme focuses on board members of sport clubs, trainers and coaches, referees and sport clubs in dealing with undesirable behaviour, sanctioning and preventing.

**Table 15.5** Perception of undesirable behaviour in sport clubs by type of sport (board members, in %; Romijn et al. 2013)

| | Sport clubs | | | 2013 | | |
|---|---|---|---|---|---|---|
| | 2008 | 2011 | 2013 | Football | Other team sports | Other sports |
| No problem | 43 | 47 | 46 | 10 | 44 | 54 |
| Small problem | 54 | 50 | 51 | 78 | 54 | 45 |
| Major problem | 3 | 3 | 2 | 11 | 3 | 0 |

Sport clubs, actually board members are seen as important in this programme to achieve desirable behaviour in sports.

During the different programmes on preventing undesirable behaviour in sport there were several sports club surveys on the incidence, prevention and sanctioning of undesirable behaviour in sport clubs. The surveys were performed on a representative sports club panel in the Netherlands and consisted generally of the same questions. Undesirable behaviour is a broad concept which encompasses theft, vandalism, threats, physical and verbal aggression, discrimination and nuisance (smoking, alcohol or noise).

In the perception of board members undesirable behaviour didn't pose a major problem in their clubs (Romijn et al. 2013). Nearly half of the board members indicated no problem at all on undesirable behaviour. Half of the board members reported a small problem (Table 15.5.) The perception of undesirable behaviour differs among sports. Board members of football clubs reported more often a (small or major) problem than other sports.

In 2013, half of the board members (49 %) received complaints about or were confronted with undesirable behaviour in their club (Romijn et al. 2013). The clubs were mostly confronted with verbal abuse (29 %), vandalism (24 %), bullying (22 %) and theft (17 %). There were no differences over years. There seemed to be an increase in complaints about nuisance (noise, alcohol, drugs and smoke) since 2011. Clubs were mostly confronted once a year with undesirable behaviour. Verbal abuse of vandalism happened a few times a year within clubs.

One of the focuses of the national programmes on undesirable behaviour is the availability of rules of conduct in sport clubs and paying attention to the rules by club members. Most of the board members believed that it is important to have rules of conduct in sport and to observe them (Table 15.6). The number of sport clubs with any kind of rules of conduct had increased last years (from 74 % in 2008 till 85 % in 2013) (Table 15.2). There were some differences between sports; almost every football club had procedures available. Every sports club brought their rules to attention to their club members in one way or another (make accountable for, new members are noted on).

Other ways in which sport clubs promoted desirable behaviour and prevent undesirable behaviour were: perpetrators are held accountable for their inappropriate behaviour (98 %), presence of an administrator/manager to discuss complaints (76 %), attention devoted to sportsmanship and respect during training (71 %).

**Table 15.6** Available rules with regard to undesirable behaviour by type of sport (sports clubs, %; Romijn et al. 2013)

| | Sport clubs | | | 2013 | | |
|---|---|---|---|---|---|---|
| | 2008 | 2011 | 2013 | Football | Other team sports | Other sports |
| At least one of following procedures available | 74 | 82 | 85 | 95 | 82 | 84 |
| House rules | 52 | 59 | 64 | 83 | 55 | 63 |
| Rules of conduct in statues or domestic regulations | 40 | 42 | 52 | 77 | 42 | 35 |
| Code of conduct/rules of conduct | 26 | 35 | 41 | 23 | 10 | 7 |
| Complaints procedures | 8 | 8 | 18 | 23 | 18 | 18 |
| Disciplinary rules | 6 | 8 | 10 | 58 | 46 | 52 |
| Other agreements with regard to values and standards | 10 | 8 | 10 | 19 | 15 | 7 |

There was a little increase in sport clubs with a trust named contact (for example for discussing sexual harassment) (36 %). There was a decrease of sport clubs paying attention to knowing the game rules or contest rules by their members.

In 2013 more clubs took action in case of complaints about verbal abuse, vandalism, physical violence and sexual harassment than in 2011. One of three board members reported that complaints could always be settled to the satisfaction of the board member concerned; three-fifths reported that this is usually the case. This is an increase compared to 2008.

Sport clubs were familiar with the developed activities and products of the national programme (82 %) but on average, one third of these clubs made use of more activities or products.

The recent national programme *To a safer sports environment* runs until 2016. The number of sport federations and sport clubs participating in the programme will increase the next few years. Also the awareness of working together on desirable behaviour in sports will increase. It takes time to reach everybody involved in sport (athletes, parents, supporters, trainers/coaches, referees etc.) and make them aware of their responsibility on this subject. Last years there has been some progress in realising a safer sports environment. We can speak of an increase of awareness and responsibility among board members of sport clubs to work on desirable behaviour in sport and creating a safer sport environment. But it takes time and endurance to achieve the goals of the national programme and to reach every sports club member.

## 15.6 Conclusion

For over 160 years sport clubs have played an important role in Dutch society, and their role has hardly diminished over these years. Sport clubs are nowadays still an important sport provider and hold a central position in sport policy because of their contribution to the society at large. The Netherlands has an evident sport club culture and ranks on top in European perspective based on the sport club membership rates of the population. Nevertheless, sport clubs still appear to be more appealing to youth, higher educated and higher income groups, than to elderly, lower educated and low income groups. However, these differences in participation between these groups are also visible in the overall sport participation and therefore not typical for sport club membership.

From a policy perspective, we noted that the position of sport clubs has changed considerably. Sport clubs have become policy partners of municipalities and play a central role in national policy programmes, such as *Sports and physical activity in the neighbourhood* and *To a safer sports environment*. With this, the responsibilities and tasks of sport clubs have widened. Sport clubs are encouraged to develop and employ activities that do not only benefit their members, but also the local community. As a result an increasing number of sport clubs work together with their municipality and different other local organisations to contribute to broader societal goals, such as improving health, social integration and safety.

However, this changing position of sport clubs in policy and society does not suit every sport club. Half of the sport clubs stress that their role is primarily to provide activities for their members. This might also be related to the problems that clubs face in finding volunteers for their regular activities, which makes it more difficult to consider providing additional activities in the neighbourhood or at schools. Finding volunteers is still one of the most mentioned bottlenecks for sport clubs, together with retaining old members and finding new members. Nevertheless, a large number of volunteers are active in sport clubs and sport clubs still float on the energy and dedication of these volunteers. The number of paid staff remain very limited within sport clubs. On average one or two people within a sport club is paid. This mainly concerns the trainer or head coach of the first team. This illustrates that the changing role of sport clubs in policy is not coincided with a severe professionalisation of sport clubs to be equipped to the new responsibilities.

Based on current developments it is expected that more sport clubs will be encouraged to widen their perspective to remain eligible for funding. However, not all sport clubs will have the possibilities or the desire to live up to these widened expectations of the municipalities. As a result several sport clubs will most certainly face budget cuts in the years to come, with uncertain consequences. Although the studies related to the current economic recession have indicated that the financial situation of sport clubs is quite stable, sport clubs mention more often financial bottlenecks and have expressed their concerns on the future financial situation of the sport club. It is therefore to be seen how the financial situation of sport clubs will develop in the near future, especially in light of the announced budget cuts of municipalities and the increased responsibilities of sport clubs and their financial implications.

However, the sport clubs in the Netherlands can place themselves lucky to have a diverse support system at their disposal. The NOC*NSF, sport federations, sport councils and municipalities pay due attention to club support in order to strengthen the sport clubs in the Netherlands and to uphold the fine sport infrastructure of the Netherlands. All together the sport clubs are the core of the sport activity in the Netherlands. Sport clubs are still the main sport provider and have enough potential, with their dedicated volunteers, to uphold their position. However, the changing context in which sport clubs are ought to operate brings forward new challenges and new requirements. With the limited professionalization of sport clubs in the Netherlands, it has to be seen whether sport clubs are capable to live up to these expectations.

## References

Breedveld K (2014) Sportparticipatie: uitdagingen voor wetenschap en beleid. Radboud Universiteit Nijmegen, Nijmegen

Collard D, Hoekman R (2013) Sportdeelname in Nederland: 2006–2012. Factsheet. Mulier Instituut, Utrecht

Daamen T, Veerman H, van Kalmthout J, van der Werff H (2013) SportAanbiedersMonitor 2012: facts & figures. NOC*NSF/Mulier Instituut, Arnhem

de Vries BMA (2003) Hoe Jan Salie op stoom kwam: Nederland en de Industriële Revolutie. Stichting Redactie Spiegel Historiael, Amsterdam

Engels A (1960) 100 jaar sport in Nederland, een historische documentatie over de sport en het sportleven gedurende een eeuw. Strengholt, Amsterdam

European Commission (2010) Eurobarometer 72.3. Sport and physical activity. TNS Opinion & Social, Brussels

European Commission (2014) Special Eurobarometer 412. Sport and physical activity. TNS Opinion & Social, Brussels

von Heijden A, Boers E (2012) Impuls lokaal bekeken: verbinders in de tweede tranche. Verdiepingsonderzoek naar effecten én processen van de inzet van combinatiefunctionarissen. Mulier Instituut/Kennispraktijk, Utrecht/Nijmegen

Hoekman R, Breedveld K (2013) The Netherlands. In: Hallmann K, Petry K (eds) Comparative sport development: systems, participation and public policy, vol 8, Sports economic, management and policy. Springer Science+Business Media, New York, pp 119–134

Hoekman R, van der Poel H (2009) Sport: speelbal voor ruimtelijke ontwikkeling. In: Maarse A, Jonkman A (eds) Rooilijn. Faculteit der Maatschappij en Gedragswetenschappen, Amsterdam, pp 458–465, Afdeling Planologie en Internationale Ontwikkelingsstudies. Universiteit van Amsterdam. Jaargang 42, nr.7

Mulier Institute (2014) Injuries and physical activity in the Netherlands (OBiN). http://www.veiligheid.nl/onderzoek/ongevallen-en-bewegen-in-nederland-obin. Retrieved 30 Apr 2014

NOC*NSF (2012) Ledental NOC*NSF over 2012. NOC*NSF, Papendal

Romijn D, van Kalmthout J, Breedveld K, Lucassen J (2013) VSK-monitor 2013: voortgangsrapportage actieplan "naar een veiliger sportklimaat". Mulier Instituut, Utrecht

Stokvis R (2010) De sportwereld: een inleiding. Arko Sports Media, Nieuwegein

Tiessen-Raaphorst A (2010) Sport: een leven lang. Rapportage Sport 2010. Sociaal en Cultureel Planbureau/Mulier Institute, Den Haag/Den Bosch

van der Werff H, van Kalmthout J (2012) Minder klappen, meer applaus?: beeldvorming Nederlands publiek rondom voorkomen onwenselijk gedrag in de sport, 2011. Mulier Instituut, Utrecht

van der Werff H, Wisse E, Stuij M (2012) Sport en onderwijs verbonden. Mulier Instituut, Utrecht

van der Werff H, Lucassen J (2006) Arbeidsmarktmonitor Sport: een meting van sportgerelateerde arbeid in Nederland :nulmeting. IVA Beleidsonderzoek en Advies, Tilburg

van Kalmthout J, Lucassen J (2008) Verenigingsmonitor 2007: de stand van zaken bij sportverenigingen in het perspectief van modernisering. W.J.H. Mulier Instituut, Hertogenbosch

Wilterdink N (1984) Vermogensverhoudingen in Nederland. Ontwikkelingen sinds de negentiende eeuw. De Arbeiderspers, Amsterdam

# Chapter 16
# Sport Clubs in Northern Ireland

**Paul Donnelly, Simon Shibli, and Simon Toole**

## 16.1 Introduction

Northern Ireland is one of the four home nations that constitute the United Kingdom of Great Britain and Northern Ireland. It is the smallest of the home nations both in terms of geography (13,843 $km^2$, 6 %) and population (1.8 m, 2.8 %). The economy of Northern Ireland is heavily dependent on the public sector for employment and it has some of the highest levels of unemployment in the UK. Since the signing of the Good Friday Agreement in 1998, Northern Ireland is emerging from a 30-year conflict known as the troubles into a vibrant service sector lead economy with considerable tourism and inward investment. Sport Northern Ireland (Sport NI) is the leading public body for sport development in the region and enjoys the status of being a National Lottery fund distributor. Since the launch of the National Lottery in 1994, Sport Northern Ireland has benefited from approximately £9.3 m per year for sport. This has been used to develop and enhance Northern Irelands' sporting infrastructure including financial investment in sport clubs. Like the rest of the UK, sport clubs are integral part of community life and provide the majority of opportunities for people to take part in organised sport. Consequently as part of the UK, the historical perspective of sport clubs in Northern Ireland is largely the same as for England as outlined in Chap. 7 by Nichols and Taylor. There are however some issues which are specific to Northern Ireland and these are covered later in this chapter.

P. Donnelly (✉) • S. Toole
Sport Northern Ireland, Belfast, UK
e-mail: pauldonnelly@sportni.net; simontoole@sportni.net

S. Shibli
Sport Industry Research Centre, Sheffield Hallam University, South Yorkshire, UK
e-mail: S.Shibli@shu.ac.uk



C. Breuer et al. (eds.), *Sport Clubs in Europe*, Sports Economics, Management and Policy 12, DOI 10.1007/978-3-319-17635-2_16

### 16.1.1 A Brief Overview of the Position of Sport Clubs Within a National Structure

The structure of sport in the UK is very complex and Fig. 16.1 actually represents something of a simplification as far as Northern Ireland is concerned (Sport Northern Ireland 2012). For example, although Northern Ireland is part of the UK, its athletes have the choice of competing for either the UK or the Republic of Ireland (ROI). Northern Ireland tends to compete in international competition in its own right, in Association Football as well as in the Commonwealth Games, which are held every 4 years. Furthermore, some sports such as rugby union and boxing are organised on an all-Ireland basis in partnership sporting bodies based in the Republic of Ireland. For all four home nations the key point of note about clubs is that their place in the sporting hierarchy is that they are fed into at the bottom via community sport and governed from the top by National Governing of Sport (NGBs). In terms of revenue funding some clubs in Northern Ireland receive income from NGBs which itself is most likely to be sourced from Sport NI.

### 16.1.2 Policy Context

Sport clubs play an important role in government plans to increase sports participation for its associated health benefits and other social benefits—particularly for the young, such as reducing crime, enhancing social cohesion, improving educational attainment and strengthening employment opportunities. The policy importance is recognised in Sport Matters: The Northern Ireland Strategy for the Development of Sport and Physical Recreation in Northern 2009–2019 (hereafter Sport Matters).

Sport Matters presents a strategic framework for the development of sport in Northern Ireland over the 10-year period, 2009–2019 (Department of Culture, Arts and Leisure 2009). It identifies 26 high-level targets that will measure the overall success of the strategy, including PA5 "By 2014 to have increased the number of people in Northern Ireland in membership of at least one sport club" (p. 17).

Sport NI recognises the essential and significant role that sport clubs have to play in the development of sport in Northern Ireland. Sport clubs impact upon sport by providing outlets for people to participate in sport and develop their skills. Sport

**Fig. 16.1** The complex structure of sport in the UK. Abbreviations: *BOA* British Olympic Association, *BPA* British Paralympic Association, *DCMS* Department for Culture Media and Sport, *EIS* English Institute of Sport, *INGBs* Irish National Governing Bodies, *NCSS* National Council for School Sports, *NGOs* Non-Governmental Organisations, *NISF* Northern Ireland Sports Forum, *OCI* Olympic Council of Ireland, *PCI* Paralympic Council of Ireland, *SINI* Sports Institute Northern Ireland, *SIS* Scottish Institute of Sport, *SRA* Sport and Recreation Alliance, *SSA* Scottish Sports Association, *SSS* Scottish Student Sport, *WIS* Welsh Institute of Sport, *WSA* Welsh Sports Association

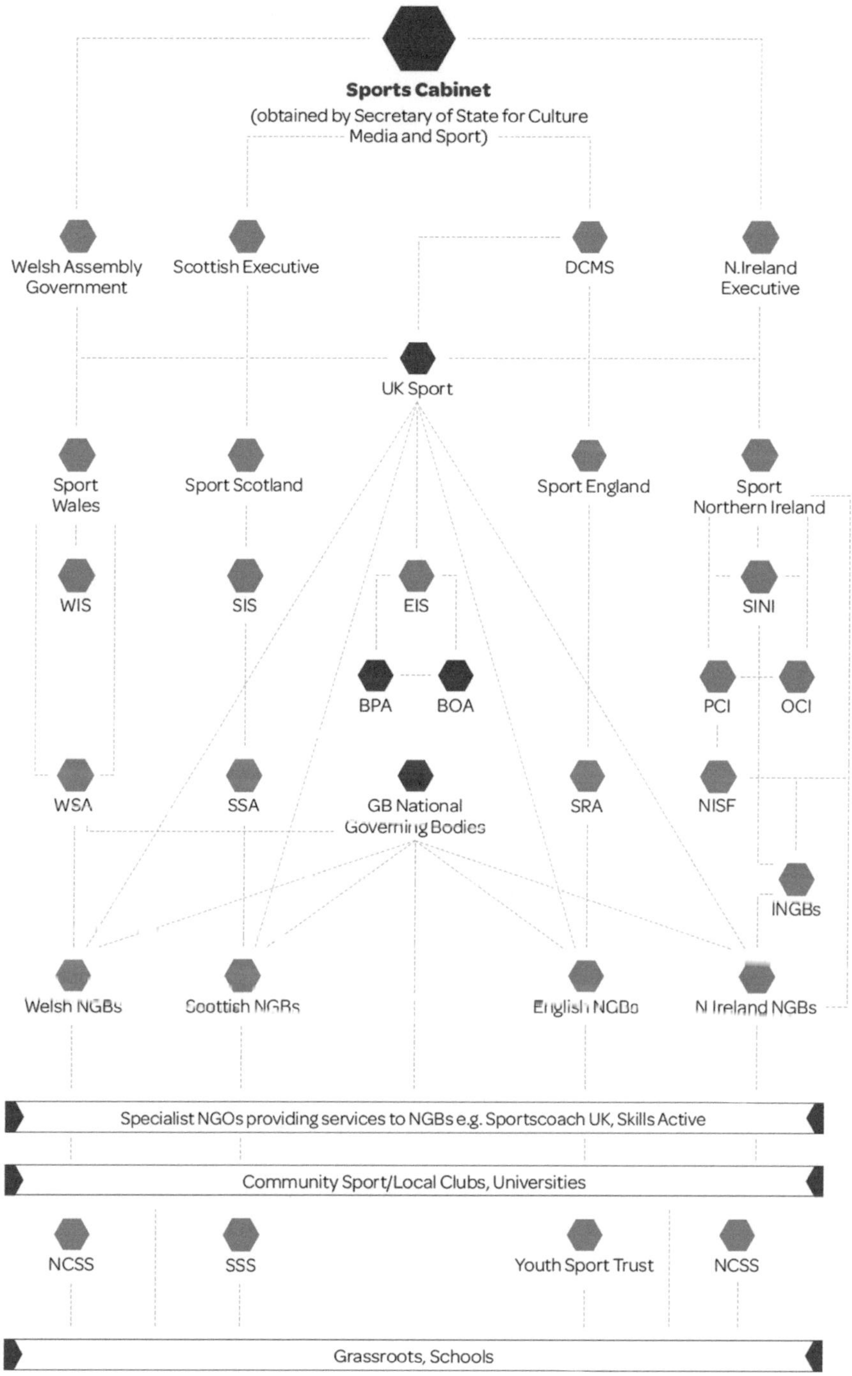
Sports Cabinet
(obtained by Secretary of State for Culture Media and Sport)
Welsh Assembly Government
Scottish Executive
DCMS
N.Ireland Executive
UK Sport
Sport Wales
Sport Scotland
Sport England
Sport Northern Ireland
WIS
SIS
EIS
SINI
BPA
BOA
PCI
OCI
WSA
SSA
GB National Governing Bodies
SRA
NISF
INGBs
Welsh NGBs
Scottish NGBs
English NGBs
N Ireland NGBs
Specialist NGOs providing services to NGBs e.g. Sportscoach UK, Skills Active
Community Sport/Local Clubs, Universities
NCSS
SSS
Youth Sport Trust
NCSS
Grassroots, Schools

Matters further acknowledges the importance of increasing sport club membership, developing school/club links, introducing a new quality accreditation standard and accrediting 1,200 quality clubs.

In Northern Ireland sport clubs have been incorporated into government policy to promote sports participation through local government and governing bodies of sport by developing and agreeing investment plans with Sport NI. Sport NI provides funding for 34 national governing bodies of sport and 11 district councils, in most cases grants in exchange for agreeing to raise participation by specific levels in their sport over a set time period. As is the case in England, sport clubs in Northern Ireland are largely independent self-interest groups and it is only a subset of them who at any point in time will engage in wider government and NGB initiatives related to social policy.

## 16.2 Role of Sport Clubs in Policy and Society

The most contemporary evidence on sports participation for the adult population of Northern Ireland (16 years +) is contained in the Northern Ireland Adult Sport and Physical Activity Survey [also known as SAPAS] (Donnelly 2011). This includes data relating to membership levels in a variety of different types of sport clubs and settings including those in the commercial sector, the public sector and the voluntary sector including traditional NGB-affiliated clubs as well as community-, charitable and church-based clubs.

### *16.2.1 Club Membership in Northern Ireland*

The SAPAS survey revealed that 23 % of adults in Northern Ireland are members of a club in which they can participate in sport or physical activities, as highlighted in Fig. 16.2, and that 73 % of club members participate in moderate or vigorous intensity activities on at least 1 day per week. Furthermore, the proportion of those with club membership increases to 30 % among those who have participated in any sport in the last 12 months and 45 % who participated for at least 30 min with at least moderate intensity in the last 7 days.

Among those who are members of at least one club, 20 % are members of more than one club. Club membership is below average for women, people with disabilities, older people and people in lower social classes. These findings are developed in Sect. 16.2.3 and reinforce the inequalities which are already known about in sports participation generally in the UK (Shibli et al. 1999). Interestingly, there is no significant difference in club membership levels among the two dominant religious groups (Roman Catholics and Protestants) but as will be shown later, the types of club to which they belong are different.

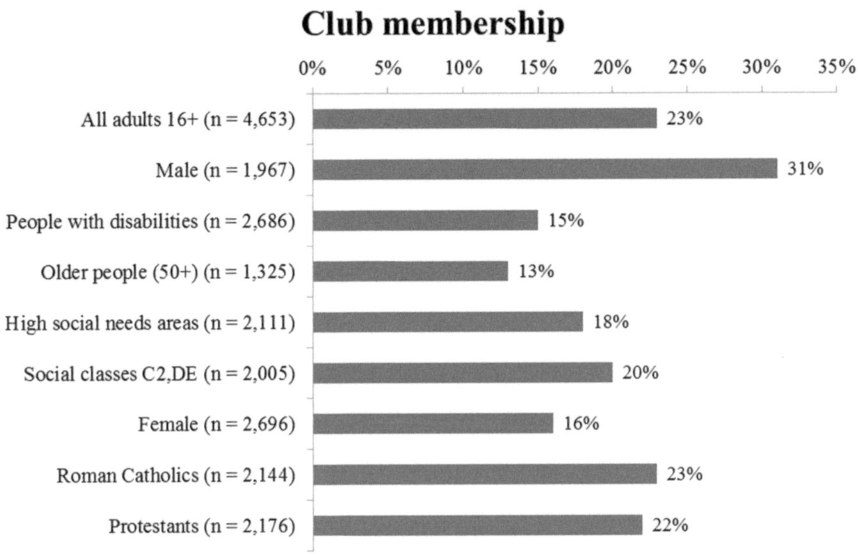


**Fig. 16.2** Club membership levels in Northern Ireland (Donnelly 2011)

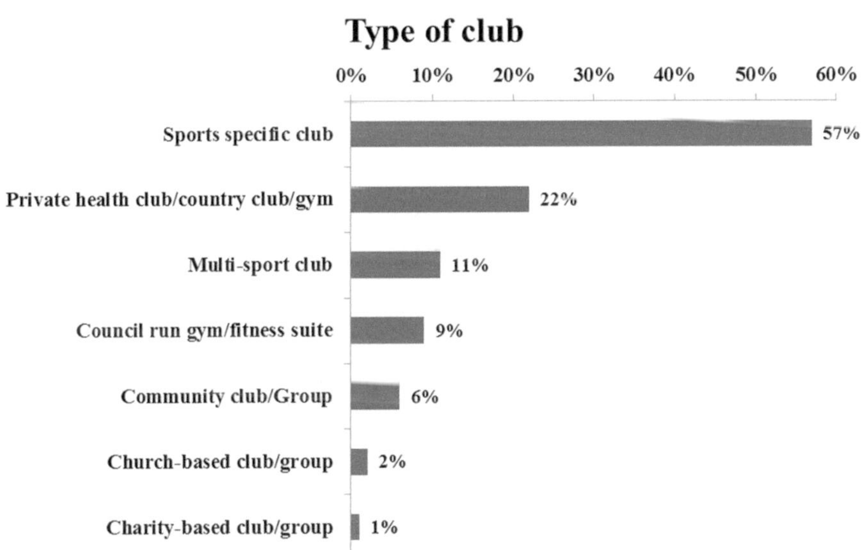


**Fig. 16.3** Types of clubs and activities in Northern Ireland (Donnelly 2011)

### 16.2.2 *Types of Sport Clubs and Activities in Northern Ireland*

Sports-specific clubs are by far the most popular types of clubs (57 %), as demonstrated in Fig. 16.3. This is followed by private health clubs (22 %) and multi-sport clubs (11 %).

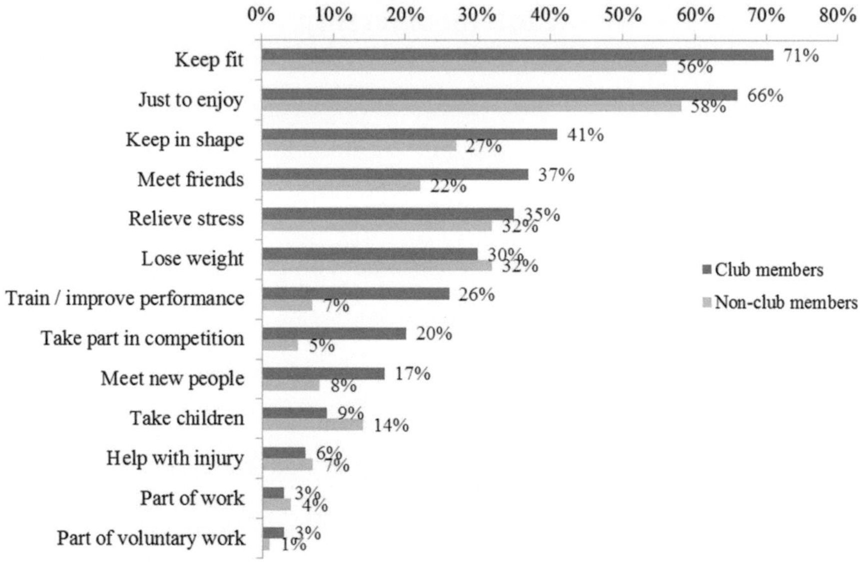


**Fig. 16.4** Motivators for sport participation by club membership (Donnelly 2011)

Unsurprisingly, sport participation among people who are members of clubs is high, with 73 % having participated on at least 1 day in the last week, which compares very favourably with the national average of 37 %. In addition to high level of personal participation in sport, club members are more involved in other aspects of sport as well; for example they are more likely to:

- Participate in competitions (49 % compared to 10 % among non-members)
- Provide coaching to other participants (17 % compared to 3 %)
- Carry out sports' voluntary work (21 % compared to 5 %)
- Watch live sporting events[1] (56 % compared to 32 %)

Although the most important reasons for participating in sports are the same among club members and non-club members—keeping fit and enjoyment—there are some key differences between the two groups, as shown in Fig. 16.4. In particular, social reasons are much more important for club members with 37 % stating that meeting friends is a motivation compared to 22 % among non-members. Furthermore, competition and performance-related factors are more important among this group.

It is worthwhile noting how respondents' reported motivations for participation are intrinsic and not related to concerns with government policy. People do not join clubs with the primary purpose of providing others with a pathway into sport. For some participants, particularly those who also volunteer, there may be degrees of

[1] In Northern Ireland, in the last 12 months.

altruism along the lines of wanting to make a positive difference to society, but for the most part people play sport and join clubs because they want to keep fit and enjoy themselves.

### 16.2.3 Club Membership by Demography, Health and Well-Being

Secondary analysis of the SAPAS data identifies the demographic structure of participation in sport clubs of different types and its relationship with health and well-being. This helps to identify the extent to which clubs cater for different parts of society and their relationship with other health-related factors such as smoking, alcohol consumption and self-reported health and happiness.

### 16.2.4 Gender

There is a significant gap between men and woman with regard to club membership as shown earlier in Fig. 16.2. The proportion of men who are members of clubs in which they can participate in sports or physical activity is more than twice as high as among women (31 % compared to 15 %) and this gap is evident across all age groups. Even when analysing only those who participated in the last week (at least moderate intensity) the difference between men and women with regard to club membership remains substantial (53 % compared to 35 %). This suggests that even women who participate frequently are less likely to join clubs compared with their male counterparts.

One explanation is that many typical club sports, for example, golf, football and Gaelic football (a national sport on the island of Ireland, played predominantly by the Roman Catholic community), are more popular among men than among women. Typical sports that women participate in as members of clubs are fitness-related activities such as using exercise machines (29 %), keep fit/aerobics (23 %) and swimming (14 %).

### 16.2.5 Age

Figure 16.5 highlights that club membership decreases considerably with age. Major decreases occur when people enter the age group of 21–30 years and when people reach the age group of 51–60 years.

However, it is interesting to note that among people who participated in the last 7 days (at least moderate intensity) an opposite trend can be observed, as illustrated in Fig. 16.6. Sport club membership increases beyond the age of 40, having dropped from the age of 20 years.

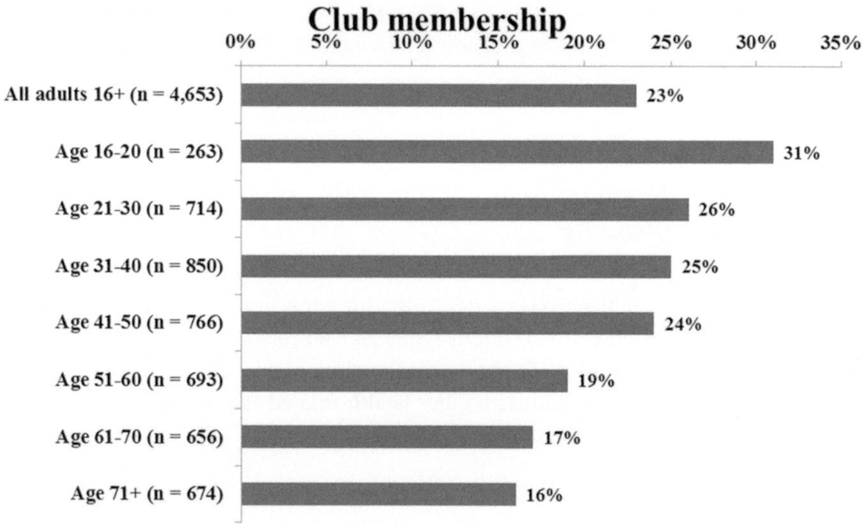


**Fig. 16.5** Club membership and age (Donnelly 2011)

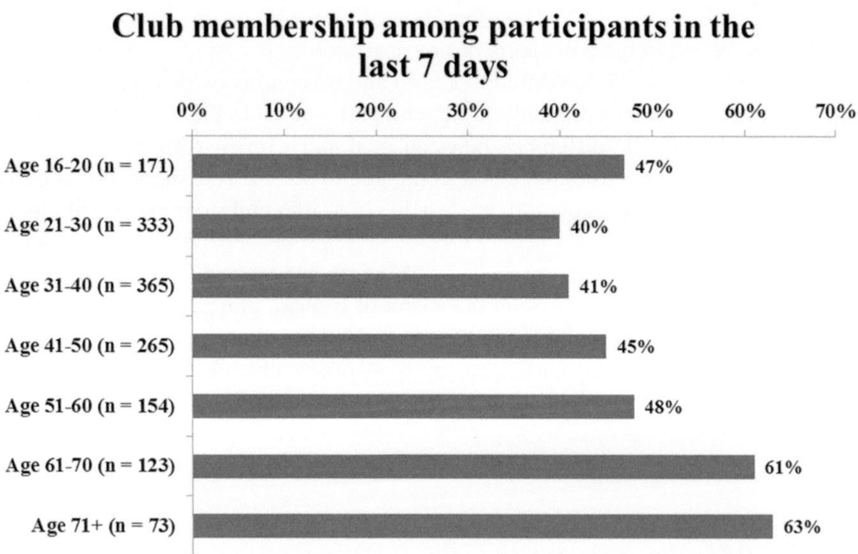


**Fig. 16.6** Club membership and frequency of sport participation (Donnelly 2011)

This finding suggests that sport club membership has a positive effect on people's general sport participation among middle and older age groups. However, the finding that sport club membership increases when participants are older may also reflect the fact that some typical club sports are more popular among older people, for example bowls.

There are also interesting differences by age with regard to the types of clubs of which people are members. Sport-specific clubs are most popular in all age groups but their relevance decreases with age (72 % among club members aged 16–20 compared to 49 % among club members aged 71+). Community clubs become important in the highest age group (71+) with 17 % of all club members having joined a community club/group in which they can participate in sport compared with 5 % among those aged 16–20.

### 16.2.6 Working Status and Educational Attainment

Club membership is highest among students (35 %), followed by working people (27 %). Retired (18 %) and unemployed people (13 %) are less likely to be members of clubs. There is also a strong relationship between educational attainment and club membership. 37 % of those with a university degree are club members compared to 23 % whose highest education is GCSE or equivalent and 12 % of those with no qualifications.

### 16.2.7 Disability

People with disabilities are less likely to be members of sport clubs (13 % compared to 23 % of the total adult population). This is partly due to a higher average age of people with disabilities. In the 30–49 age group the difference between people with disabilities and the total adult population is much smaller although still significant (19 % compared to 24 %). The most popular sports that people with disabilities participate in as members of a club are golf (24 %), and especially among older age groups, swimming (16 %) and indoor bowls (12 %).

### 16.2.8 Areas of Social Need and Social Class

Sports' club membership is slightly lower than average in high social need areas (20 % compared to 23 % overall) and substantially lower among lower social classes (C2DE: 16 %). The gap regarding club membership widens with age and again differences with regard to social class are more significant than differences with regard to deprivation. For young people aged 16–29 club membership varies significantly by socio-economic status with 34 % of those from higher socio-economic groups (ABC1) belonging to a club, whereas for people from lower socio-economic groups (C2DE) the corresponding statistic is 25 %. A similar but more pronounced pattern is found among people aged 30–49 (32 % vs. 15 %) and people aged 50 and over (26 % vs. 12 %). The most popular activities that people in both deprived areas and lower social classes participate in as members of a club are fitness-related activities, golf, football and swimming.

### *16.2.9 Health and Well-Being*

Findings from SAPAS suggest that club membership seems to go *hand in hand* with a healthy lifestyle. The proportion of smokers is lower (21 % among club members compared with 30 % among non-members) as is the proportion of people who eat the recommended amount of fruit and vegetable per day (50 % compared to 43 %). However, the proportion of those who consume more alcohol than recommended is slightly higher among club members (8 % vs. 5 %), even when analysing age groups separately.[2] Club members rate their health considerably better than non-members (82 % good/very good compared with 61 % among non-members), even when analysing age groups separately. Finally, there is also a relationship between club membership and happiness (73 % of club members state that they are very happy compared to 63 % of non-members) and again, this relationship persists across all age groups.[3]

### *16.2.10 Characteristics of Sport Clubs in Northern Ireland*

Table 16.1 outlines the number of clubs currently thought to be operating within each of the 34 sports that have received recurrent public investment in Northern Ireland in the 5 years, 2009–2014. The table reveals a total figure of 3,084 clubs in Northern Ireland, of which the vast majority are affiliated to the relevant governing body of their sport. However, it is important to note that further clubs which are not affiliated to a governing body of sport may exist within these sports. The common casual/recreational or unstructured nature of unaffiliated clubs can make them more difficult to identify than those with an affiliation as they are unlikely to have identified themselves to the body governing the sport in the region. Whilst unaffiliated club sport is known about, its very nature prevents any accurate estimate as to its scale.

There are a further 60 recognised sports within Northern Ireland whose clubs are not represented within Table 16.1. This is because as they have not received funding, the relevant governing bodies have not been required to provide high-level governance data such as censuses of clubs and membership levels. It is estimated that these sports probably account for a further 400–600 clubs, providing an estimated total of approximately 3,600 sport clubs in Northern Ireland.

[2] For example age group 30–49: 10 % above recommended among club members versus 6 % among non-members.

[3] This is partly due to other third variables, for example participation in sport.

**Table 16.1** Clubs in the sports receiving Sport NI funding, 2009–2014 (Sport Northern Ireland 2013)

| Sport | Number of clubs |
|---|---|
| Archery | 47 |
| Association Football | 1,169 |
| Athletics | 71 |
| Badminton | 108 |
| Basketball | 30 |
| Bowling | 82 |
| Boxing | 92 |
| Camogie | 110 |
| Canoeing | 24 |
| Cricket | 61 |
| Cycling | 84 |
| Equestrian | 87 |
| Fencing | 8 |
| Gaelic games | 268 |
| Golf | 95 |
| Gymnastics | 46 |
| Hockey | 80 |
| Judo | 73 |
| Motor sport | 77 |
| Mountaineering | 7 |
| Netball | 37 |
| Orienteering | 4 |
| Rowing | 14 |
| Rugby | 54 |
| Sailing | 46 |
| Shooting | 62 |
| Squash | 21 |
| Swimming | 37 |
| Table tennis | 63 |
| Taekwondo | 54 |
| Tennis | 40 |
| Triathlon | 13 |
| Volleyball | 12 |
| Wrestling | 8 |
| Total | 3,084 |

High-level knowledge about the nature of sport clubs in Northern Ireland is limited as there has been no systematic research conducted on the sector to date. The Sport and Recreation Alliance (SRA) however conducts a biennial survey of sport clubs in the UK and from this it is possible to extract the responses from clubs based in Northern Ireland. In the 2013 survey responses were received from 74 clubs based in Northern Ireland.

Overall 74 clubs from 29 sports responded to the SRA 2013 survey and whilst this cannot be considered to be a representative survey of the sector, it is the best data available at the time of writing and helps to give an insight into the characteristics of clubs in Northern Ireland and the issues they face. For the purposes of this chapter we focus on four key areas: volunteers and staff; finances; responses made by clubs to challenging operating conditions and links with the wider community.

### 16.2.11 Volunteers and Staff

Volunteers are clearly the lifeblood of sport clubs in Northern Ireland with 70/74 clubs (95 %) stating that they had at least one volunteer. The sample is skewed somewhat by larger more formal clubs as can be seen by the difference between the median number of volunteers (5) and the mean (9). By contrast only 17/74 clubs (23 %) reported that they had paid staff and these are combinations of full-time staff such as club managers through to part-time staff such as coaches and those who help with bar and catering activities. Paid staff was invariably found in larger clubs. It was subsequently found that the 17 clubs with staff employed 83 people and of these 41 were employed by just two clubs. The first was a bowls club with over 1,000 members which ran an extensive catering operation; and the other was a gymnastics club with nearly 1,200 junior members which employed an array of part-time coaches. These findings point to sport clubs in Northern Ireland being run predominantly by volunteers and conforming to the mutual aid theory of volunteering.

### 16.2.12 Finances

Almost all of the clubs described themselves as being non-profit organisations that were run by members with a constitution and a committee. For the three clubs that gave different answers they stated that they were other forms of non-profit organisation such as charities or companies limited by guarantee. The non-profit dimension of clubs' operations can be seen by the average income, expenditure and net surplus/deficit statistics shown in Table 16.2.

Of the 74 clubs in the sample 22 made a loss, 21 broke even and 31 made a profit in 2013. Table 16.2 shows considerable disparity between the median and the average scores because of the influence of a minority of large clubs with high levels of

**Table 16.2** Financial performance (Sport and Recreation alliance 2013)

| Measure | Median score | Average score |
|---|---|---|
| Total income | 10,000 | 33,591 |
| Total expenditure | 10,000 | 34,385 |
| Surplus/(deficit) | 0 | −794 |

income. The seven largest clubs had incomes of £100,000 or more and accounted for 59 % of the total income reported by all 74 clubs. The basic point emerging from the data is that the finances of clubs in 2013 reveal something of a *hand-to-mouth* existence whereby income is matched almost exactly by expenditure. Consequently surpluses to reinvest in facilities, equipment and training are few and far between.

### *16.2.13 Responses Made by Clubs to Challenging Operating Conditions*

It follows that if sport clubs overall are breaking even or making small losses as shown in Table 16.2, then trading conditions must be challenging for them. It is therefore interesting to examine the steps that clubs take in order to protect their financial positions and to ensure that they at least operate within the resources available to them. The nature of sport clubs, particularly those with their own infrastructure such as buildings and pitches, is that the majority of costs will be fixed and will not fluctuate significantly with the number of members in the club or the amount of activity which takes place within the club. Under these circumstances, the only logical course of action is measures designed to increase income. The clubs seem to have grasped this point and Table 16.3 shows the number and proportion of clubs that stated that they took specified income-raising measures in the last 12 months.

Nearly half of clubs (49 %) said that they had increased fundraising efforts for the club and almost as many (43 %) reported that membership fees had been increased. These measures indicate at least implicitly that clubs see themselves as the principal source for solving their own financial issues. Although 42 % stated that they had applied for additional funding (an external source) the majority of the answers relate to internal self-help measures including recruiting more members (39 %) and holding more social events (36 %).

By contrast, examples of attempts to save money by reducing expenditure were of a much smaller scale than income generation measures as shown in Table 16.4.

The top three expenditure reducing items all relate to lowering the quality of the sporting experience either by not renewing equipment (20 %) or by carrying out less

**Table 16.3** Income-raising measures (Sport and Recreation Alliance 2013)

| Method | Total | % |
|---|---|---|
| Increasing fundraising efforts for the club | 36 | 49 |
| Increasing membership fees | 32 | 43 |
| Applying for additional funding | 31 | 42 |
| Actively recruiting more members | 29 | 39 |
| Holding more social events | 27 | 36 |
| Developing new ways to make money for the club | 14 | 19 |
| Hiring out the club's facilities | 11 | 15 |

**Table 16.4** Expenditure-reducing measures (Sport and Recreation Alliance 2013)

| Method | Total | % |
|---|---|---|
| Not renewing equipment | 15 | 20 |
| Carrying out less maintenance on our infrastructure facilities | 9 | 12 |
| Carrying out less maintenance on playing or training facilities | 7 | 9 |
| Changing facilities provider | 6 | 8 |
| Sharing services with another club | 5 | 7 |
| Changing utility (e.g. gas, electricity, water) | 4 | 5 |
| Reducing subsidies for member's match/competition fees | 4 | 5 |
| Stopping paying expenses to volunteers | 3 | 4 |
| Making paid staff redundant | 2 | 3 |

maintenance on clubs' facilities and wider infrastructure. Whilst these measures might be storing up problems for future years, they are items over which there is a degree of discretion, as opposed to being fixed costs. Furthermore, the finding that cost cutting is less prevalent than income generation also suggests that clubs are tight-run ships which are already run cost effectively with little scope for further operating efficiencies. Clubs are therefore dependent upon their local communities to provide sufficient demand for their offering and to provide the revenue to at least meet the fixed costs. The relevance of clubs to their communities and the opportunities that can arise by working with schools is outlined in the following section.

### *16.2.14 Links with the Wider Community*

The majority of clubs (49/73, 66 %) describe themselves as being open to both able-bodied and disabled sports participants. There were three clubs in the sample that were exclusively for disabled people and 22 for able-bodied people only. The similar majority of clubs (50/74, 68 %) report having a link with at least one school and in 96 % of cases the links are said to be successful. The major reasons as to why these links are successful are listed in the bullet points below:

- Clubs sharing facilities with the school.
- Clubs sharing equipment with the school.
- Club coaches/officials assisting in PE lessons or school competition.
- Advertising for club is displayed in schools.
- Students from the school join the club.

- It's an opportunity to identify talent.
- It's an opportunity to recruit new volunteers.

Whilst the clubs in the sample are atypical of all sport clubs in Northern Ireland, there is good evidence that in at least a minority of cases there are inclusion initiatives in place for disabled people and school children. Furthermore, working with schools and sharing facilities and equipment provides clubs with a source of financial competitive advantage which can only benefit their long-term sustainability.

## 16.3 Sport and Religion

This section raises some issues about sport and religion in Northern Ireland. It has often been said that Protestants and Roman Catholics in Northern Ireland are divided by many things, including sports that they play (Kremer et al. 1997). Research evidence accumulated over the years would suggest that this claim is only partially true (Sugden and Bairner 1993). The suggestion that Protestants and Roman Catholics play different sports has always been linked to the fact that, in practice if not law, separate school systems operate in Northern Ireland for the two main religious communities. One of first major studies to explore some of the consequences of separate schooling in Northern Ireland and the type of sports that Protestant and Roman Catholic schools offered to their pupils found that the wide variety of sports available in schools fell into three categories (Darby et al. 1977):

1. Gaelic sports, including football, hurling and camogie, were not played on any Protestant schools.
2. Rugby, cricket and hockey were popular in Protestant schools and were markedly less popular in Roman Catholic schools, although all of them except cricket were played to some extent in Roman Catholic schools.
3. A range of sports that were available generally across all the schools (e.g. association football, tennis, netball and basketball).

An additional piece of evidence relating to the theme of sport and religion which deserves acknowledgement is a study carried out by Sugden and Harvie (1995) which examined the role played by sport in community relations in Northern Ireland. These researchers were particularly interested in governing bodies for sports and among their many conclusions was the suggestion that sports' preferences and patterns of participation are governed by cultural traditions and community affiliation, particularly for major team games. They also suggested that differential sports affiliation is embedded in the system of separate Protestant and Roman Catholic schools, because this provides a divided games curriculum. Further weight was given to this claim by their conclusion that sports which were not grounded in the school curriculum appeared to offer greater opportunities for cross-community interaction.

**Table 16.5** Club membership by religious background (Donnelly 2011)

| Sport/activity | Protestant (%) | Roman Catholic (%) | Other (%) | All (%) |
|---|---|---|---|---|
| Keep fit | 44 | 38 | 18 | 100 |
| Jogging | 32 | 62 | 5 | 100 |
| Gaelic football | 0 | 100 | 0 | 100 |
| Football outdoors | 51 | 46 | 3 | 100 |
| Gym | 45 | 41 | 13 | 100 |
| Dance | 69 | 31 | 0 | 100 |
| Rugby | 70 | 15 | 15 | 100 |

From the perspective of sport clubs it has already been shown (Fig. 16.2) that there is no difference in the incidence of sport club membership among Roman Catholics and Protestants in Northern Ireland. However, building on the evidence above that people from different religious backgrounds have different sporting preferences, it is possible to test whether these differences are prevalent in the nature of club membership. The 23 % of the SAPAS survey respondents who were members of a sport club were reanalysed by religion and the most popular sports as shown in Table 16.5.

There are two key findings of note from Table 16.5 that warrant further explanation. First, the starkest finding is that for Gaelic football club membership appears to be 100 % Roman Catholic. In some respects this is not a surprise given that Gaelic football, one of the five sports provided by the Gaelic Athletic Association (GAA), is actively promoted in Roman Catholic primary and post-primary schools as well as the wider Roman Catholic community more generally. Children from Protestant backgrounds would have no or limited exposure to GAA sports. Similarly, in the case of rugby union 70 % of club members are Protestants with the remaining 30 % made up of Roman Catholics (15 %) and other denominations (also 15 %). Rugby union is a popular sport in Protestant schools and Roman Catholic children would be relatively unlikely to experience it. In both cases the tastes and preferences formed in childhood prevail into adulthood and there are some sports which therefore become symbolic of a community divide. Following the Good Friday Agreement of 1998 considerable efforts have been made by both the Irish Rugby Football Union and the GAA to address under-representation by certain communities within their sport. For sports and activities that do not have cultural connotations such as football, keep fit and gym membership the variation in club membership by different religious groups is much less marked.

## 16.4 Conclusions

There is an emerging change in the nature of sport clubs in Northern Ireland. Whilst the majority of clubs are either sports specific or multi-sport clubs, these are not the only club formats in which people consume sport. There is for example considerable evidence of a vibrant private sector providing health and fitness-type activities within a club environment, particularly for those who take part in sport for health reasons and particularly among women. There is some evidence of traditional sport clubs in Northern Ireland responding to these changing patterns of demand by offering wider opportunities such as the use of gym-type equipment to people who are not necessarily playing members of the club's principal sport. For example, St Paul's Gaelic Athletic Club based in Belfast is primarily a GAA sport club offering hurling, camogie, Gaelic football (men and women) and handball. More recently it has developed its facilities to allow its playing and non-playing members to make use of its gym facilities. These are available throughout the day and usage of them is not linked to training for the competitive sports provided by the club. In this respect St Paul's can be said to be a direct rival to private sector provision at a much reduced cost. The increased throughput in the club as well as its wider community relevance help to sustain a healthy social club which via bar sales, catering, hires and fruit machines generates a profit that can be ploughed back into the running of the club.

Sport club membership reflects what people choose to do in their leisure time with their discretionary income. As such clubs are self-help groups in which the primary motivations are to keep fit and enjoyment. This poses an interesting challenge for government and agencies such as Sport NI who have aspirations to use clubs as vehicles for social change linked to funding. Whilst there is a minority of clubs that will sign up for this funding and have the capacity to deliver wider social objectives, this is slightly at odds with the primary motivations as to why people choose to join such sport clubs.

It is perhaps no surprise that sport clubs reflect and in some cases amplify the inequalities that are found in sport generally throughout the UK. Sport club members are for example even more likely to be male, able bodied, relatively young and reasonably affluent compared with the population as a whole. Delivering on social objectives invariably means addressing inequalities experienced by less well-off people and this may well be alien territory and indeed a distraction for the members of traditional sport clubs. There is however some mileage in persuading clubs to embrace wider social objectives as club membership is linked positively with healthier lifestyles such as higher physical activity levels, lower levels of smoking, better healthy eating habits and higher levels of self-reported health and happiness.

Clubs exist in a challenging financial environment in which survival from being able to balance the books each year is a considerable achievement. Typically clubs break even or make a calculated loss. This occurs despite the fact that so much of the production process of providing sporting opportunities and managing a club is done by volunteers with no financial remuneration. The challenging operating environment has forced clubs to be more proactive in their management and most realise that when costs are essentially fixed the only logical strategy is to increase income. Various measures to do this internally (e.g. more social events) and externally (e.g. recruiting new members) are in evidence among sport clubs in Northern Ireland. To a lesser extent there is also evidence of cost-saving measures such as deferring maintenance and the upgrade of equipment, but this tends to have the downside of lowering the quality of the sporting experience and storing up potential problems in the future.

It is also apparent that even at the highest level within Northern Ireland relatively little is known about sport clubs and how they operate. It has proved very difficult to acquire seemingly simple information such as an accurate number of clubs by sport and the size of club membership by sport. If clubs are to be used as potential instruments of social change then much more needs to be known about them, their reach and the extent to which they can be used as instruments of social change. Some major positive features of clubs in Northern Ireland are that they are resilient, innovative and valued by a significant minority (23 %) of the population. From these basic raw ingredients there is hope for their long-term survival and their ability to adapt to the often turbulent world around them.

## References

Darby J, Dunn S, Murray D, Farren S, Batts D, Harris J (1977) Education and community in Northern Ireland: schools apart? Centre for the Study of Conflict, Coleraine

Department of Culture, Arts and Leisure (2009) Sport matters: the Northern Ireland Strategy for Sport and Physical Recreation 2009–2019. DCAL, Belfast

Donnelly P (2011) The Northern Ireland Sport and Physical Activity Survey 2010. Sport Northern Ireland, Belfast

Kremer J, Trew K, Ogle S (1997) Young people's involvement in sport. Routledge, London

Shibli S, Taylor P, Nichols G, Gratton C, Kokolakakis T (1999) The characteristics of volunteers in UK sport clubs. Eur J Sport Manage 6:10–27

Sport and Recreation Alliance (2013) Survey of Sport clubs 2013. Sport and Recreation Alliance, London, http://www.sportandrecreation.org.uk/policy/SSC. Retrieved on 8 Jan 2014

Sport Northern Ireland (2012) Sports policy factors leading to international sporting success: an audit of the Elite Sport Development System in Northern Ireland. Sport Northern Ireland, Belfast

Sport Northern Ireland (2013) Governing body information returns. Sport Northern Ireland, Belfast

Sugden J, Bairner A (1993) Sport, Sectarianism and Society in a Divided Ireland. Leicester University Press, Leicester

Sugden J, Harvie S (1995) Sport and community relations in Northern Ireland. Centre for the Study of Conflict, Coleraine

# Chapter 17
# Sport Clubs in Norway

**Ørnulf Seippel and Eivind Å. Skille**

## 17.1 Introduction

This chapter is about sport clubs in Norway. Norway is a constitutional monarchy with about five million inhabitants. It is part of the Scandinavian tradition of social democratic welfare states which comprises both a strong state and a relatively large civil sector (Esping-Andersen 1990). The largest proportion of the civil sector is voluntary sport organisations (Seippel 2008; Ibsen and Seippel 2010; Sivesind 2012). In this chapter Norwegian sport clubs are first presented as a historical phenomenon and as part of a societal context. Then there are two main sections: on the role of sport clubs in policy and society, and on the characteristics of sport clubs. Next, we discuss a central characteristic of Norwegian sport as the special topic, namely, the close and intricate state–sport relationship and some current trends challenging this relationship. We end the chapter with a conclusion.

## 17.2 History and Context

Sport has a long history in Norway. At least back to the Nordic (Norse) middle-ages—the Viking era—the existence of activities or skills which we today would call sport can be documented. Such skills—sprint oriented as well as endurance

Ø. Seippel (✉)
Department for Culture and Society, Norwegian School of Sport Sciences, Oslo, Norway
e-mail: ornulf.seippel@nih.no

E.Å. Skille
Faculty for public health sciences, Hedmark University College, Elverum, Norway
e-mail: eivind.skille@hihm.no



C. Breuer et al. (eds.), *Sport Clubs in Europe*, Sports Economics, Management and Policy 12, DOI 10.1007/978-3-319-17635-2_17

oriented running, swimming and use of various weapons (sword, axe and javelin)—were all related to what gained status among young men in the Viking community (Goksøyr 2008). In a similar vein, based on desired competences for young men, the first sport clubs were established in order to prepare for military readiness. While shooting skills were always a prioritised element in the first sport clubs, gymnastics and skiing were also important. When the first national umbrella sport organisation was established in 1861, several sport clubs already existed both in the cities and in countryside (*i by og bygd*). For example in Oslo (Christiania), *Christiania weapon exercise club* (Norwegian: *Christiania Vaabenøvelsesforening*) was established in 1959 (Olstad 1987, p. 11), and *Trysil shooting and ski club* (Norwegian: *Trysil Skytte-og Skiløberforening*) was established in 1961 (Goksøyr 2011, p. 12).

The dominance of the military element of sports lasted until the detachment from the union with Sweden in 1905. It should be noted that it was a peaceful process, where the shooting skills of the sport clubs were never needed. From the start in the 1860s the sport organisation has received economic subsidies from public actors (Goksøyr 1992). During the first decades sport was mostly a matter for the Ministry of defence, but there have been multiple interests in and influences upon sport. These changes reflect the shifts in the sport trends, the political foci from the state and from the wider society.

Norwegian sports have been influenced by national traditions as well as international trends. As a start, skiing and gymnastics were often added to shooting in the work of the first sport clubs. Interestingly, skiing and gymnastics represent two different traditions of sport in Norway. First, skiing is the typical Norwegian *idrett*. Second, gymnastics in Norwegian sport clubs is a result of influence from the German *turnen* and the Swedish gymnastics. Both skiing and gymnastics were considered good supplements to shooting in preparing military fitness, as skiing represented endurance and ability to stay out in the winter cold, and gymnastics represented bodily exercise combined with discipline in a group (Olstad 1987; Goksøyr 2011). During the last half of the nineteenth century, shooting, gymnastics and the Norwegian winter sports were all main features of Norwegian sport clubs.

Around the turn of the century (1900 that is) a new influence of international sport trends came over Norway. Unlike the gymnastics, which could fit into the existing sport clubs and sport organisation, the English sport represented another value system and partly challenged the then hegemonic Norwegian *idrett*. Since the Viking literature, the Norwegian or Norse word *idrett* (or *idrott* in Old Norse) has had a special standing. It is the Norwegian word for sport, and today both words as used more or less interchangeably. However, *idrett* refers more to the old and traditional Norwegian sports such as skiing and ice skating, while sport refers more to the English sports such as typically football. The point is that for Norwegians (at least for those with influence in the sport organisations), the new sports were considered a threat to the traditional Norwegian *idrett*. Nevertheless, English sport, especially football (soccer) gained popularity; the Norwegian football association was established in 1902 and has been the largest sport for most of its more than 100 years of existence (Goksøyr and Olstad 2002).

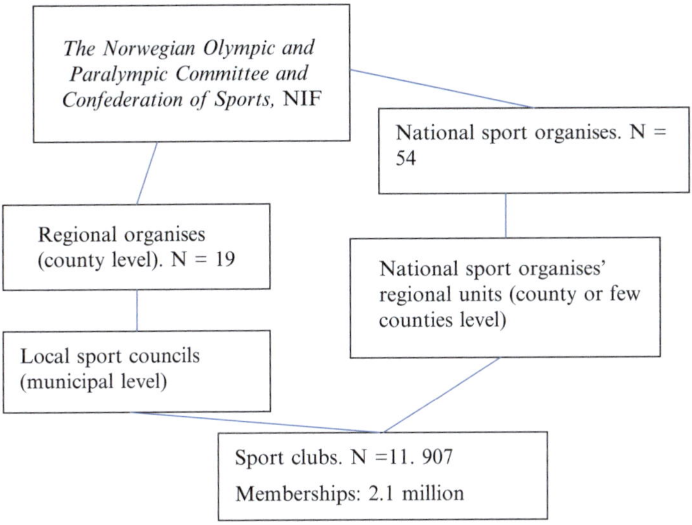


**Fig. 17.1** The NIF system, with the two lines of organisation: the national sport associations and their regional extensions on *right side*; the district sport organises and local sport councils on the *left side*. It shows the umbrella organise NIF on *top*, and the sport clubs at the *bottom*

Historically, a most consequential incidence for the organisational development of Norwegian sport took place in the interwar period with the establishment of a workers' sport federation in 1924. This was a reaction to the bourgeois profile of the existing sports federation (a successor of *Centralforeningen*). For the sport clubs, the everyday sport was split into two systems, often with two sets of competitions (i.e. leagues) for each sport. In 1939 it was agreed, after governmental pressure, to merge the two sport organisations. The formal merger was delayed due to World War II, and was formalised in 1946, in the name of the Norwegian Confederation of Sports (Norwegian: *Norges idrettsforbund*, NIF).[1] However, since both sport organisations were hesitant to change their organisational structure, the outcome was the *double line* organisation seen in Fig. 17.1. NIF's and the district sport organisations' focus on sport for all stem from the mass-oriented worker organisation, while the special national sport federations' focus on competitive sport stems from the bourgeois organisation (Skille and Säfvenbom 2011; Tønnesson 1986).

After World War II sports have developed into important actors for societal development and sport is concerning more and more people. Supplementary activities based on the population's needs and desires were developed and during the 1970s, organised sport appeared as a recreational activity for everybody. From 1965 to 1985 the number of members almost quadrupled, from 430,000 to 1.6 million,

[1] In 1996, NIF merged with The Norwegian Olympic Committee into The Norwegian Olympic Committee and Confederation of Sports. In 2008, The Norwegian Paralympic Committee was also included; the name is now The Norwegian Olympic and Paralympic Committee and Confederation of Sports. It is still abbreviated NIF in Norwegian (Skille and Säfvenbom 2011).

first and foremost by recruiting youth and women. Sport historians have labelled this period *the sport revolution* (Tønnesson 1986), a revolution which was made possible by the construction of new sport facilities and—as indicated above—by opening the sport clubs to new groups of the population: women, children and youth. Since then, NIF has been Norway's largest voluntary organisation, mainly built up by a member base and the vision—shared by public authorities and the voluntary sport organisation—has been *sport for all* (Meld. St. 26 2011–2012; NIF 2011; St. meld. nr. 41 1991–1992; St. meld. nr 14 1999–2000) Moreover, the ideology, understood as the dominant view of how best to organise sport in Norway, has been to join all sport into one organisation.

This unitary organisation then includes mass sport as well as elite sport. There are, nevertheless, challenges to this ideology, from both the inside and the outside of the conventional sport system. Within the sport system, processes of commercialisation and professionalisation challenges the traditional and voluntary culture of Norwegian sport (Enjolras et al. 2011). Moreover, the old tension between mass sport and elite sport has gained new relevance and a new form after the introduction of the concept of elite youth sport; elite youth sport has entered the scene paralleled with the establishment of the Youth Olympic Games (YOG) which is to be hosted in Norway in 2016 (Skille and Houlihan 2014). From the outside of the sport organisation, the most visible development in the field of physical activity, and therefore, a potential challenge for the sport organisation is the establishment and popularity of fitness centres as well as the very fact that the—by far—most popular form of exercising is unorganised/self-organised. (See empirical part below, Figs. 17.6 and 17.7). Let us elaborate a bit on the elite youth sport issue.

The concept of elite youth sport is ambiguous. On the one hand, it can be interpreted as a continuation of a history and process of uniting apparently different interests into one organisation (cf. the two lines model). However, within that one organisation there used to be relatively clear divisions of labour, where one side takes care of elite sport and the other takes care of youth sport. This division of labour is institutionalised through a mutual understanding between the sport organisations (as it is evident in NIF's sport policy document; NIF 2011) and the representatives of society (as in White Papers from the Government to the Parliament; Meld. St. 26 2011–2012). Hence, the very expression of *elite youth sport* contains a contradiction, as the word 'elite' for many Norwegians—laypersons and policymakers alike—does not have a positive connotation when used in association with youth sport (Skille and Houlihan 2014). However, while this distinction is still recognised, it is perhaps less clear than it has been previously. The tensions involved in attempting to maintain the distinction are evident in the most recent report into Norwegian elite sport (NIF 2013b), which treats the relationship between youth sport and elite sport as more closely intertwined and even interdependent.

Moreover, there are—in addition to the elite sport versus mass sport tensions—a number of more general tensions in the NIF system: between large/popular sports and small sports, between rich sports and poor sports (often related to sponsor incomes and media coverage), between the concerns given from the international federations versus national or regional/local concerns, between sport in itself versus sport for societal goods (health, social integration, etc.), focusing on the talents versus protecting drop-outs, between volunteerism and professionalism, and so on. In sum, it could be claimed that the strength of the Norwegian sport model also is its weakness: the aim of uniting all types of sport into one organisation. Leaning on this historical sketch, we move on to present data on the contemporary situation in Norwegian sport, focusing upon Norwegian sport clubs.

Even though we could always wish for more, better and more recent data, we have a relatively rich source of information on Norwegian sport clubs. In the next sections, we address three topics which each illustrates both the situation and the development of Norwegian sport clubs. First, we look at some basic numbers. For clubs we will ask how many and how large. For members we ask how many, which genders and which sports. Second, some of the derivative sides of sports (reflected in the political arguments in favour of sports) are looked into: What are the aims of the clubs? Why are people active in sport? As in many other nations, voluntary work is the foundation for large parts of the sport sector and a third perspective relevant for sport clubs concerns volunteering. In the last section before conclusion, we discuss a central characteristic of the Norwegian sport, namely, the state–sport relationship and current trends challenging these institutional relations.

## 17.3 Role of Sport Clubs in Policy and Society

Regarding the role of sport clubs in the Norwegian society, we highlight two main features: one more internally oriented and one more externally oriented. First, we treat the characteristics of Norwegian sport clubs including issues into members and activity; second, we treat organised sport and its social aspects.

Regarding characteristics of sport clubs, the single most illustrative picture of the development and situation of organised sport in Norway is the number of memberships in Norwegian sport clubs. As we see from Fig. 17.2, there has been an enormous growth during the last 60 years: From—as shown in the history section above—being an organisation primarily for young and adult men, to being an organisation also for women and children and youth. Figure 17.3, on the growth in number of sport clubs, shows reasonably enough, a similar pattern to the figure of memberships. There is, however, one difference between the two: the growth of clubs stops and even reverses in the late 1990s, indicating that there are more large clubs now than previously. Looking into the development of the sizes of sport clubs more specifically, Fig. 17.4 shows how many members there are—on average—per Norwegian sport club during the period from 1954 until 2010.

The growth represented in these figures is basically reflecting the latter part of the modernisation in Norway. It reflects a nation with a tradition for sport and outdoor life which has become a more prosperous nation, but also a nation with a specific policy toward sports and especially the building of sport facilities (Goksøyr

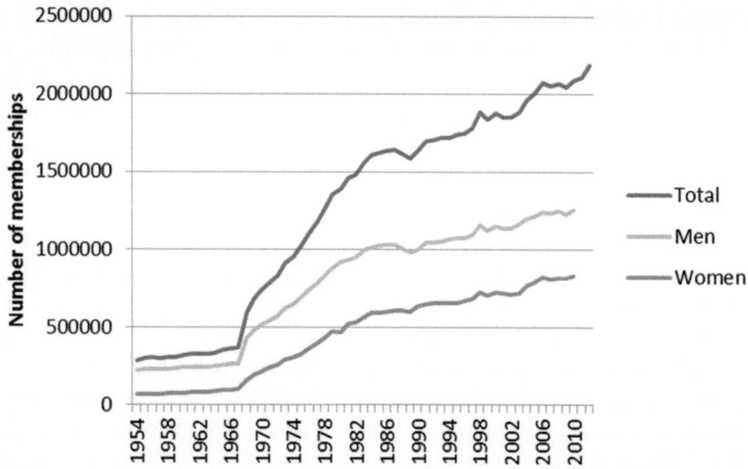


**Fig. 17.2** The development of the number of memberships in Norwegian sport clubs from 1954 until 2012

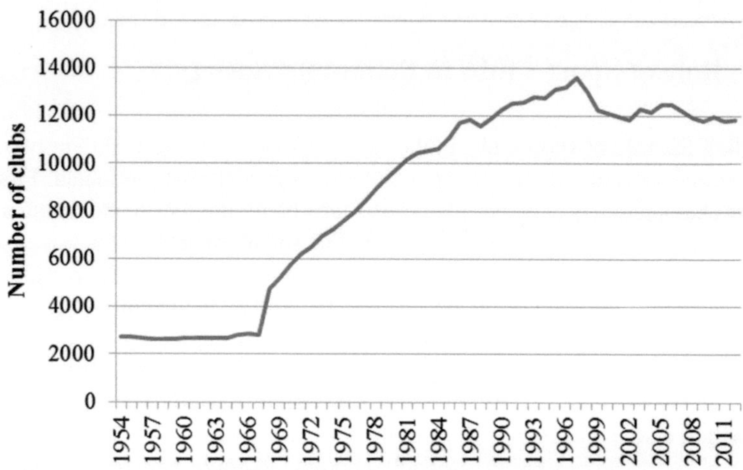


**Fig. 17.3** The development of number of Norwegian sport clubs from 1954 until 2012

et al. 1996), a nation where children have a more central and active place, a more gender equal society, a less elitist society. These characteristics of equality are valid on a general economic and political level of the Norwegian society (Wilkinson and Picket 2010) as well as for sport (Bairner 2010).

Behind the expansive figures we also find a process of differentiation where a third indication of growth within the organised sport system is the number of

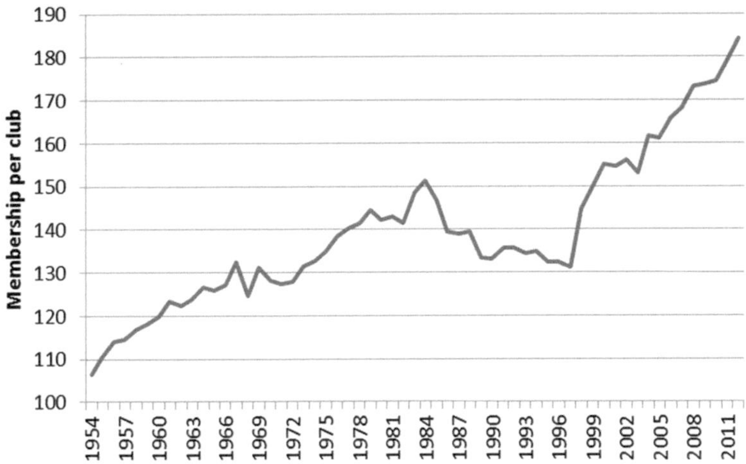


**Fig. 17.4** The development of number of membership per sport club from 1954 until 2012

associations, where each association in principle offers and governs one specific sport.[2] In 1946, there were 24 associations, while in 2014 there are 54 associations.[3] The two most popular sports, counted by memberships in associations, which are based on reports of memberships in sport clubs, are football (369,305 members) and skiing (178,091 members) (NIF 2013a). That indicates that the outcome of the historical tension between English sport and Norwegian/Norse *idrett* is that both survived and live well. This is shown in Fig. 17.5a, while Fig. 17.5b shows next four sports according to size (company sports not included).

The societal development reflected in the growth of sport clubs and members do also reflect shifts within the more general picture of physical activity. We do not have as good data as we could have hoped for this development, but we do have survey results (Norsk Monitor) going back 30 years and which document how the Norwegian adult population exercises. Figure 17.6 shows how the Norwegian population above the age of 15 is physically active in sport clubs, at fitness centres and on their own.

[2] It should be noted that there are huge differences across the associations, both in size (from 337 members in the Sledge, bobsleigh and skeleton association, to 369,305 members in the football association), and regarding structure and sports. Taking two apparently similar sports as examples, the biathlon association governs one sport discipline only (although there is a huge number of competition forms), while the ski association governs six disciplines and have six specific committees (sub-boards with a relative autonomy and responsibility): cross country skiing, ski jumping, Nordic combined, alpine skiing, freestyle skiing and telemark skiing.

[3] There have actually been as many as 56 associations, but some (of the small ones) have merged aiming at more effective administration. For example, tae kwon do, karate, jiu-jitsu used to have separate organisers, and are now federated in the same association (called the martial arts association).

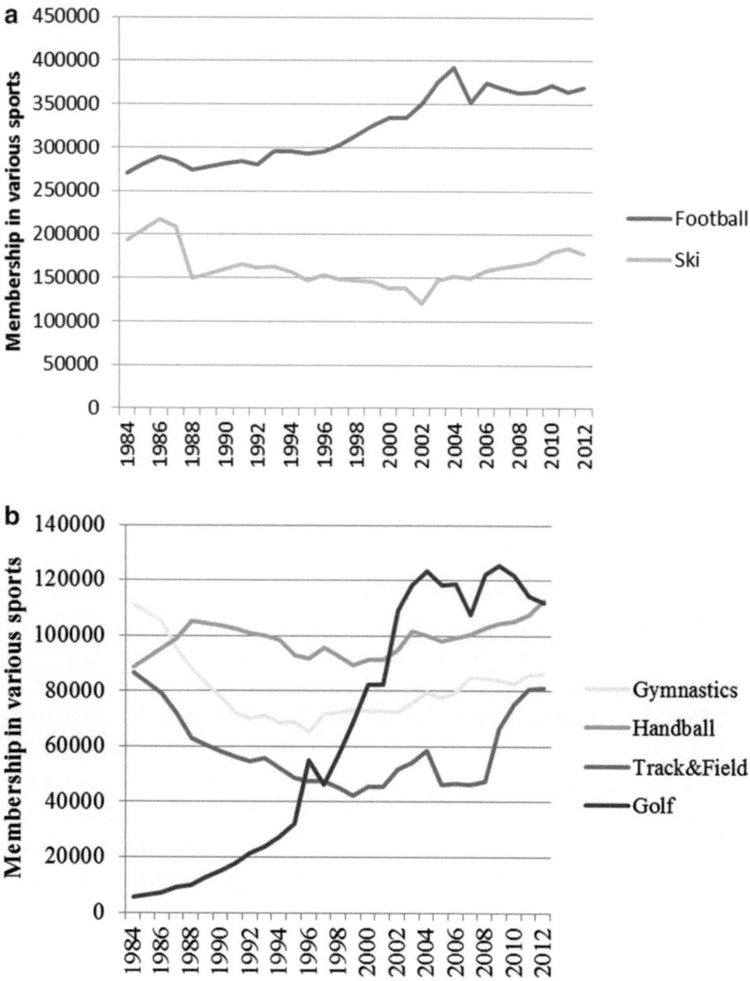


**Fig. 17.5** The development of the five largest sports in 1982 and 2012 (which adds up to six sports (Golf on the rise, Track and field on the wane) largest organised sports from 1982 and until today

The results presented in Fig. 17.6 give important additional information to the above picture about sport clubs. First, we see that exercise in sport clubs among adults have decreased in the same period as the number of memberships in general has increased. This indicates or confirms that the sport clubs have specialised more than previously in being an organisation for children and youth. Second, we see that there has been a strong growth in the proportion of the population saying that they exercise at fitness centres. While the proportion of adults in Norway training in sport clubs have decreased steadily the last two decades, the proportion of adults training at fitness centres have increased steadily; the lines actually mirrors each

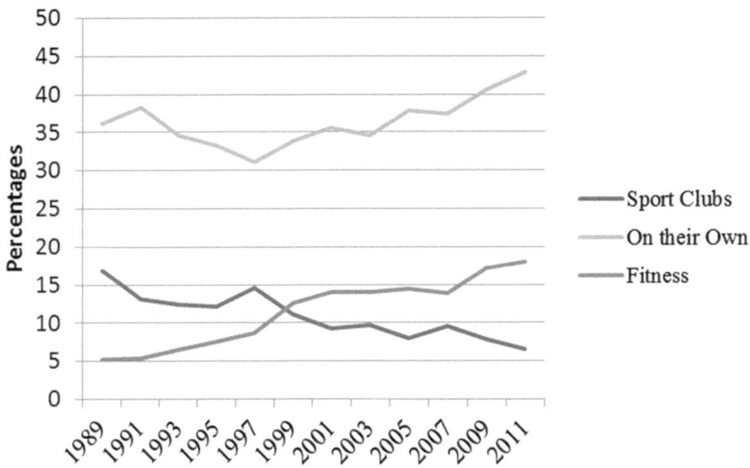


**Fig. 17.6** Percentage of the population over the age of 15 in Norway (2010) being physically active in sport clubs, fitness centres, and on their own, respectively

other, crossing just before the turn of the millennium. Both for sport clubs and fitness centres the data indicate trends which if continued will imply a serious shift in the pattern of physical activity in the Norwegian population and they do also imply challenges for the policies towards these areas. The final finding emanating from Fig. 17.6 is that exercise *on their own* is by far the most used form of physical activity among the adult population in Norway.

Further insights into the question of the role of sport clubs are found in youth research, where studies shows how very large proportions of young people take part in sport clubs, but we also see very clearly how this activity drops and how fitness exercise is strengthening its position. Figure 17.7 shows how the proportion of youth being physically active versus inactive from eighth grade to second year of high school.[4] The figure further shows the proportion of youth being active in the three different organisational forms: sport clubs, fitness centres and on their own.

The overall picture of Fig. 17.7 shows a slight decrease of the physically active proportion of the youth population, from 76 % in eighth grade to 71 % in second year of high school, and an increase of the inactive proportion of the population from 24 to 29 % in the same age span. Regarding organisational form of physical activity, there is a clear decrease of the proportion of youth being active in sport clubs, from 55 to 28 % from eighth grade to second year of high school. The most significant drop in sport club participation is between tenth grade (which is the last year at upper primary school) and the first year of high school. This finding is in line with the idea that all transitions in life challenge patterns and habitual behaviour such as sport participation (Roberts 2006). On the other hand, there is a clear

[4] Eighth grade starts in August the year the youth turn 13 (and lasts until June the year after); second year of high school starts the year the youth turn 17.

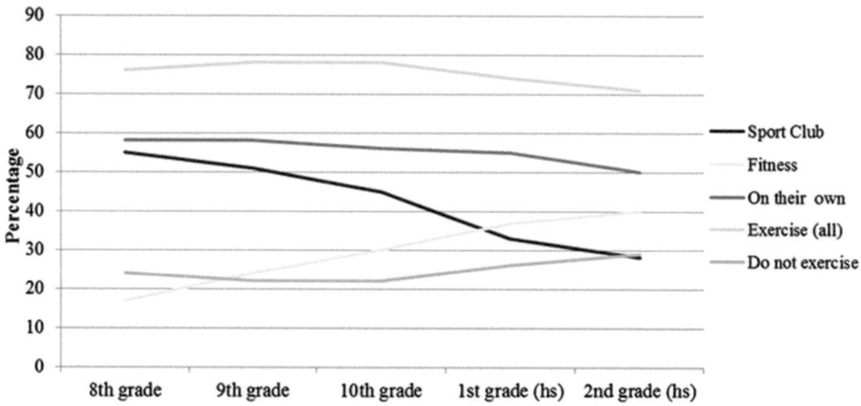


**Fig. 17.7** The proportion (%) of youth (2010) being physically active (in any form; *upper line*), and being inactive (*lower e, line*) from eighth grade until second year in high school; and the proportion of youth being active in sport clubs, fitness centres and on their own (Seippel et al. 2011, p. 64)

increase in the proportion of youth training at fitness centres over the same age span, from 17 to 40 %; there is even similar (contrary to sport clubs figure) leap from tenth grade to first year of high school, from 30 to 37 %. It is, moreover, interesting to see that also for youth, the—by far—most popular organisational form of physical activity is to exercise on their own, which shows a decrease from 58 to 50 % but which is much more stable over the analysed life span than any of the other organisational forms of physical activity among youth.

Regarding organised sport and its social aspects, it was indicated in the historical section that sport is said—both by public policymakers and in the sport organisations (NIF 2011; Meld. St. 26 2011–2012)—to contribute to a broader spectre of goods. Empirically, there are obviously many possible ways to shed light on this question; here we provide three brief answers. First, we take a look at how sport clubs consider their situation. Second, we look at it simply by asking people why they are active in sport, using a 10 year old study of motives for training in sport clubs and motives for training at fitness centres. Third, we refer very briefly to some studies on sport and social capital.

A first approach is to look at what representatives of sport clubs see as the sport clubs' main mission in society. In that respect, we have qualitative data from a case study of sport clubs investigating how sport club leaders (board members) consider the sport club as an institution with a role or a function in society (Skille 2010, 2011). The qualitative empirical evidence can be summed up like this: 'sport club representatives were concerned with sport development and competitiveness, and to varying degrees—or at least with various expressions—were concerned with healthy outcomes of sport'. Sport club representatives are engaged in sport because they see sport participation for their children and their peers as a healthy way of spending leisure time, of growing up, and of personal and social development

**Table 17.1** Motives for exercising in sport clubs and at fitness centres by gender

| | Fitness | | | | Sport Clubs | | | | |
|---|---|---|---|---|---|---|---|---|---|
| Motives | Total | Female | Male | % dif | Total | Female | Male | % dif | % dif |
| To keep fit | 95 (1) | 97 (1) | 90 (1) | 7 | 83 (2) | 90 (1) | 80 (2) | 10 | 12 |
| Mental | 77 (2) | 80 (2) | 69 (2) | 11 | 73 (3) | 80 (3) | 70 (3) | 10 | 4 |
| Joy | 67 (3) | 68 (3) | 65 (3) | 3 | 88 (1) | 89 (2) | 88 (1) | 1 | −21 |
| Appearance | 32 (4) | 36 (4) | 24 (4) | 12 | 9 (7) | 15 (7) | 6 (7) | 9 | 23 |
| Expression | 18 (5) | 20 (5) | 13 (5) | 7 | 37 (5) | 41 (5) | 34 (5) | 7 | −19 |
| Achievement | 5 (6) | 4 (6) | 8 (6) | −4 | 26 (6) | 21 (6) | 29 (6) | −8 | −21 |
| Social | 4 (7) | 3 (7) | 5 (7) | −2 | 46 (4) | 48 (4) | 45 (4) | 3 | −42 |

Percentages reporting that the various motives are important and ranking (in parenthesis; Ulseth 2003, p. 34)

(Skille 2010). Healthy here refers not only to a positive physiological outcome of physical activity, but as much to the social elements related to being part of a group, and a system where rules and fun are integrated in everyday activities. All in all, sport clubs are seen as an arena for social interactions for both youth participants and adult volunteers, which enables development for both parties. In the same qualitative study, it is discussed whether, as long as the competitive sport is the main activity in sport clubs, a consequence of the situation is limited possibilities for the realisation of social goods such as health (Skille 2011). Nevertheless, the main finding is that sport club representatives (the interviewees in the study) consider sport clubs as a total package including a number of ingredients that a healthy upbringing requires. The perhaps most interesting finding from the qualitative sport club study was the taken-for-granted belief in sport as something good, yet the difficulty to express what the goods were. In that respect, the quantitative data below give an important contribution.

A second approach to disclose a picture of what sport club activity implies is simply to ask people why they participate in organised sport and then comparing this to respondents from fitness centres.

The findings shown in Table 17.1 indicate very clearly that doing sport in sport clubs is an activity with unmistakably different qualities from exercise at fitness centres. Starting with the sport clubs, we see that *joy*, followed by a wish to *keep fit* and *mental recreation*, are the most prevalent reasons for being active. The most important comparisons are found in the right-most column showing the differences in prevalence of motives between sport clubs and fitness exercise. Here we see that the largest difference concerns the *social aspects* of exercise, followed by *appearance*, *joy*, *expression* and *achievements*. Overall, the sizes of the differences are remarkable, but also the indication of what we could call existential motives—*joy*, *social* and *achievements*—being so much more important in sport clubs than in fitness are telling. What is clearly more important at fitness centres than in sport clubs is appearance.

A third approach shedding some light on the societal value of sport clubs is studies related to the question of social capital. By time, there are now several approaches to sport which also addresses aspects of social capital related to sport clubs and one of their core characteristics: being organised voluntarily. There is a debate in the international literature on social capital which is concerned with the aspect of social trust and the role civil society actors play in this regard. As a contribution to this debate, a study of members and volunteers of Norwegian sport clubs indicate that—in line with expectations from the literature—being active in a sport club generate more social capital (measured as general trust) than not being active, but less than taking part in more outwardly-directed organisations (Seippel 2006, 2008).

One bottleneck or challenge of the Norwegian sport system is related to the tension between professionalisation and volunteering. Even though there are close bonds between public authorities and the sport clubs, the largest proportion of the clubs' incomes comes from the members: either as member fees or as voluntary work. For a majority of the sport clubs, they are also run without paid staff (Enjolras et al. 2011). This makes the topic of volunteers an important question indeed, and the challenge of how to recruit volunteers is a recurrent theme. So far, the situation seems to be that the level of volunteering is keeping up, at the same time as there are more professionals—both paid and educated—in the clubs (Seippel 2010). This makes the question of how to work with volunteers and what the process of professionalisation implies timely and relevant. The question of volunteering could be approached both from a general (individual) perspective and from the clubs point of view.

From the individual perspective, data from the Norwegian part of the Johns Hopkins Study (Sivesind 2012) show that from 1997 to 2009, sport's proportion of hours volunteered in voluntary organisations has been more or less constant: from 21 to 24 %. For sport, the proportion of volunteers has also been rather stabile: decreasing from 23 to 20 %. Looking at data from Norsk Monitor, we see a similar pattern where about a fourth of the population answers that they have volunteered for a sport association the previous year. Figure 17.8 shows that these numbers have been stable for at least a decade.

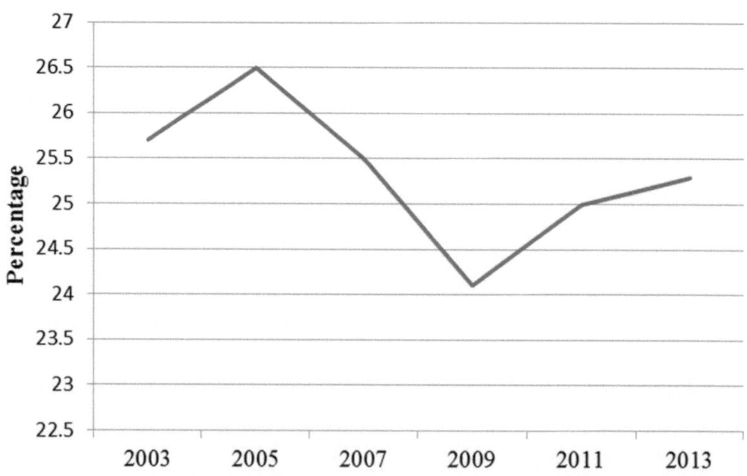


**Fig. 17.8** Percentage of Norwegian population volunteering in sport clubs

From the clubs point of view, the sport clubs study of 2002, shows that in close to 70 % of all sport clubs all work is done by volunteers, whereas more than 90 % of all work is done by volunteers in about 90 % of the clubs (Seippel 2003). Thus, the most striking empirical finding regarding volunteering in sport is that the proposed scenario of a collapse in volunteerism seems exaggerated. We move on to treat other claimed challenges related to sport clubs in the next section.

## 17.4 Special Topic: Sport Policy, Governance and Voluntary Sport Clubs

Above we have focused on Norwegian sport clubs and the voluntary sport system (NIF system). In this section we return to a feature touched upon in the introduction, namely, that, historically, there has been (and is) a strong relationship between the Norwegian authorities and the sport organisation(s). State sport policy and voluntary sport organisations (and thus implementation of the sport policy) have lived in some kind of symbiosis based on a mutual dependency. The traditional division of labour between the public and the voluntary sector is that the government supports the physical and economic infrastructure for sport and the voluntary sport clubs provide activities. As such, there has traditionally been a relatively clear distinction between sport facilities policies on the one hand side, and sport activity policies on the other. The public sector (both state and municipality) has the responsibility for construction of sport facilities, while the sport clubs in the NIF-system have the responsibility to fill these sport facilities with sport activities.

Researchers have discussed whether the state–sport relationship is best conceptualised as corporatism or not (Goksøyr et al. 1996; Mangset and Rommetvedt 2002; Houlihan 1997). Regardless of these discussions, at the national level of sport policy the relationship between the voluntary sport organisation and the public sector is highly institutionalised and has retained its present form since 1946. Recently, three processes of change have been claimed to challenge this institutionalised and corporatist model of sport policy; politisation (Enjolras and Waldahl 2007), governmentalisation (Bergsgard and Rommetvedt 2006) and pluralisation (Bergsgard and Norberg 2010).

Politisation refers to increased lobbying from NIF towards parliament and government. For example, when the formula for distributing the revenues from the state owned gambling agency was changed in favour of sport in 2002, it happened after NIF representatives' extensive parliamentary lobbyism. According to the NIF president, NIF representatives had 100 meetings with politicians in order to persuade them to vote for a raise in the sport share of the revenues (Bergsgard and Rommetvedt 2006).

Governmentalisation is a process reflected in an increased and detailed steering from the state in order to fulfil state policy objectives through the voluntary sport organisations (Bergsgard et al. 2007). In this respect, current sport policy is ambiguous. On the one hand, there are less-targeted subsidies from the state to the NIF compared to earlier periods. On the other hand, the state requires more monitoring on how the subsidies are spent than before (Enjolras 2004, 2005). Nevertheless, the Norwegian sport policy model is, compared to other countries (Bergsgard et al. 2007; Enjolras 2003; Houlihan 1997), relatively stable with regard to the state–sport relationship, the twin organisation of NIF, and the voluntary dependence of sport provision.

While politisation and governmentalisation addresses processes taking place on the national level pluralism refers to developments on the grass roots. Regarding pluralism of sport, it refers first to developments in sport clubs in the NIF system, and it refers to developments outside the NIF system. For example, as we have seen in the empirical part above, there has been a tremendous increase in the number of sports offered by NIF organised sport clubs; at the same time much of the development in the field stems from the increased fitness centre popularity. Another example, although it is rather marginal, is that since 2005 the Sami sport organisation of Norway has received public funding allocated by the gambling revenues (Skille 2012). All these are signs of pluralism in the field of sport/physical activity, inside and outside the NIF system.

Despite some weaker indications of changes, there are few signs of major shifts in the sport policy models in Norway where the lack of interest in sport politics in the parliament is noteworthy, as in the other Scandinavian countries (Bergsgard and Norberg 2010). In sum, the state has limited policy tools to use in order to really control the implication of its sport policies through the voluntary sport clubs. What the state does have is money; two thirds of the state revenues for sport is spent on (building new and recovering established) sport facilities, and about one third is spent on support to NIF and the national sport organisations.[5] Indirectly, these tools support and facilitate sport activity. Nevertheless, some voices speak up for more change and higher degrees of pluralisation in order to reach out to more groups.

Among others, two different points have been presented in order to discuss future development of sport policies, especially for adolescent in the risk-age for dropping out. Skille (2008) argues that there is a need to develop theories which take the sport club as the point of departure for analysis, in order to understand the implementation of sport policy in Norway. The grass-roots implementer has no obligations for the decision-maker in the public policy system, or for the administrators in the central staff of the NIF (Skille 2010, p. 80). Säfvenbom (2010) argues that the point of departure for policy making regarding movement activities and sport among children and youth has to be in contemporary knowledge on how children and adolescents act and develop as modern individuals.

All in all, sport clubs—and all the empirical data presented about sport clubs—must be seen in relation to the special standing sport has in Norway (probably not unique for Norway, though). To understand the sport club participation, the social values of sport, and the volunteerism in sport, it is crucial to have an idea about the NIF relationship, the NIF system, and the relative autonomy of the national sport organisations. Moreover, it is crucial to have an idea about all the expectations

[5] The latter includes 10 % of the state sport budget going directly down to the local sport councils to distribute to activity support for the sport clubs in the council's area.

sport clubs meet, perhaps especially regarding the main target group which is youth and adolescents. It is however, out of the scope of this chapter to go into detailed discussion here.

## 17.5 Conclusion

In this chapter we provide an overview of Norwegian sport clubs; historically but first and foremost with regard to developments in the post war era and regarding the current situation. It is evident that the number of both clubs and members in sport clubs has increased tremendously the last five decades, and that the main membership group contents children and youth. We also show that sport is practised for various reasons, and thus it was what we called existential motives, such as joy, social elements and achievement orientation, which most clearly showed what motives for sport club participation was all about compared to training in fitness centres. And it is evident that volunteerism is crucial for sport clubs in Norway. The patterns painted in the main sections of this chapter seem to be relatively stable, although there are challenging processes of change going on, as discussed in the section above. In that respect, more research should be initiated, in order to find the mechanisms leading to stability in this specific sector of society, when the rest of the social world seems to change rapidly.

## References

Bairner A (2010) What's Scandinavian about Scandinavian sport? Sport Soc 13(4):734–743

Bergsgard NA, Norberg J (2010) Sport policy and politics—the Scandinavian way. Sport Soc 13(4):567–582

Bergsgard NA, Rommetvedt H (2006) Sport and politics: the case of Norway. Int Rev Sociol Sport 41(1):7–29

Bergsgard NA, Houlihan B, Mangset P, Nødland SI (2007) Sport policy—a comparative analysis of stability and change. Butterworth-Heinemann, Oxford

Enjolras B (2003) Statlig idrettspolitikk i Norge og Frankrike [State policy in Norway and France]. Institute for Social Research, Oslo

Enjolras B (2004) Idrett mellom statlig styring og selvbestemmelse [Sport between state steering and autonomy]. Institute for Social Research, Oslo

Enjolras B (2005) Idrettens økonomi og effektivitet [The sport's economy and efficiency]. Institute for Social Research, Oslo

Enjolras B, Waldahl RH (2007) Policy-making in sport. The Norwegian case. Int Rev Sociol Sport 42(2):201–216

Enjolras E, Seippel Ø, Waldahl RH (2011) Norsk idrett [Norwegian sport], 2nd edn. Akilles, Oslo

Esping-Andersen G (1990) The three worlds of welfare capitalism. Cambridge University Press, Cambridge

Goksøyr M (1992) Staten og idretten 1861–1991 [State and sport 1861–1991]. Kulturdepartementet, Oslo

Goksøyr M (2008) Historien om norsk idrett [The history of Norwegian sport]. Abstrakt, Oslo

Goksøyr M (2011) Idrett for alle: Norges idrettsforbund 150 år: 1861–1911. Aschehoug, Oslo

Goksøyr M, Olstad F (2002) Fotball! Norges fotballforbund gjennom 100 år [Football! The Norwegian Football Association through 100 years]. Norges fotballforbund, Oslo
Goksøyr M, Andersen E, Asdal K (1996) Kropp, kultur og tippekamp [Body, culture and TV-football]. Universitetsforlaget, Oslo
Houlihan B (1997) Sport, policy and politics. A comparative analysis. Routledge, London
Ibsen B, Seippel Ø (2010) Voluntary sport in the Nordic countries. Sport Soc 13:593–608
Mangset P, Rommetvedt H (2002) Idrett og politikk [Sport and policy]. Fagbokforlaget, Bergen
Meld. St. 26. (2011) Den norske idrettsmodellen [The Norwegian sports model]. Ministry of Culture, Oslo [White Paper to the Parliament]
NIF (2011) Idrettspolitisk dokument 2011–2015 [The sport policy document 2011–2015]. Norges idrettsforbund og olympiske og paralympiske komite, Oslo
NIF (2013a) Årsrapport 2012 [Annual report 2012]. The Norwegian Olympic Committee and Confederation of Sports, Oslo
NIF (2013b) Den norske toppidrettsmodellen—norsk toppidrett mot 2022 [The Norwegian elite sport model—Norwegian elite sport towards 2022]. The Norwegian Olympic Committee and Confederation of Sports, Oslo
Olstad F (1987) Norsk idretts historie [Norwegian sport history], vol 1. Aschehoug, Oslo
Roberts K (2006) Leisure in contemporary society, 2nd edn. CABI, Oxon
Säfvenbom R (2010) Physical activity and youth. The need for an ecological human development perspective. Norwegian School of Sport Sciences, Oslo, Unpublished paper
Seippel Ø (2003) Norske idrettslag 2002: kunnskap, ledelse og styring. Institutt for samfunnsforskning, Oslo
Seippel Ø (2006) Sport and social capital. Acta Sociol 49:169–185
Seippel Ø (2008) Sport in civil society: network, social capital and influence. Eur Sociol Rev 24:69–80
Seippel Ø (2010) Professionals and volunteers: on the future of a Scandinavian sport model. Sport Soc 13:199–211
Seippel Ø, Strandbu Å, Sletten MA (2011) Ungdom og trening. Endring over tid og sosial skillelinjer. NOVA, Oslo, 3/11
Sivesind KH (2012) Idrettslag og frivillighet i Norge. Notat. Institute for Social Research, Oslo
Skille EÅ (2008) Understanding sport clubs as sport policy implementers. Int Rev Sociol Sport 43(2):181–200
Skille EÅ (2009) State sport policy and the voluntary sport clubs: The case of the Norwegian Sports City Program as social policy. European Sport Management Quarterly 9(1):63.79
Skille EÅ (2010) Competitiveness and health—the work of sport clubs seen from the perspectives of Norwegian sport club representatives. Int Rev Sociol Sport 45(1):73–85
Skille EÅ (2011) The conventions of sport clubs: enabling and constraining the implementation of social goods through sport. Sport Educ Soc 16(2):241–253
Skille EÅ (2012) Ethno-politics and state sport policy—the case of how the Sámi Sport Association–Norway challenged the Norwegian confederation of sport's monopoly for state subsidies to sport. Scand Sport Stud Forum 3:143–165
Skille EÅ, Houlihan B (2014) The contemporary context of elite youth sport. The role of national sport organisations in the UK and Norway. In: Hanstad DV, Parent M, Houlihan B (eds) The youth Olympic games. Routledge, London, pp 34–50
Skille EÅ, Säfvenbom R (2011) Sport policy in Norway. Int J Sport Policy Politics 3(2):283–293
St. meld. nr. 14 (1999–2000) Idrettsliv i endring. [White paper on sport]. Kulturdepartementet, Oslo
St. meld. nr. 41 (1991–1992) Om idretten, folkebevegelse og folkeforlystelse. [White paper on sport]. Kulturdepartementet, Oslo
Tønnesson S (1986) Norsk idretts historie [Norwegian sport history], vol 2. Aschehoug, Oslo
Ulseth A-LB (2003) Treningssentre og idrettslag. Konkurrerende eller supplerende tilbud? [Fitness centres and sport clubs. Competing or complementary offers?]. Institute for Social Research, Oslo
Wilkinson RG, Picket K (2010) The spirit level: why more equal societies almost always do better. Allen Lane, London

# Chapter 18
# Sport Clubs in Poland

**Monika Piątkowska**

## 18.1 Introduction

Poland, officially the Republic of Poland, with a total surface of 312,679 square kilometres is the largest country situated in Central Europe. The 2013 population of Poland is approximately 38.5 million people and has a density of 123,000 inhabitants per square kilometre (GUS 2014, p. 587). Poland became an independent state in 1918, but in World War II was overrun by both Nazi Germany and the Soviet Union. After the war, Poland was transformed into a Soviet satellite. Poland's economy is considered to be one of the healthiest of the post-Communist countries and is one of the fastest growing within the EU (Cienski 2012). Although EU membership and access to EU structural funds have provided a major boost to the economy since 2004, GDP per capita remains significantly below the EU average.

The appearance of the non-profit sector in Poland is not only the result of changes of the turn of 1989–1990. The history of philanthropy has a long tradition in Poland as it is closely linked with the Christian tradition of medieval Europe (Leś 1999). For years, large (over one-third) part of the sector is the non-governmental organisers active in the field of sports, tourism, recreation and hobbies. In 2012 the number of organisations dealing with these issues amounted to 55 %; for 38 % it was the main area of activity (Przewłocka et al. 2013). Therefore, it may seem that sport clubs are one of or the most important sport providers in Poland. On the other hand the Eurobarometer survey 2013 (European Commission 2014) showed that Poland rank at the bottom with regard to the participation in sport clubs. Only 3 % of the Polish population is a member of a sport club, compared to a European average of 12 %.

M. Piątkowska (✉)
Department of Organisation and History of Sport, University of Physical Education in Warsaw, Warsaw, Poland
e-mail: monika.piatkowska@awf.edu.pl



C. Breuer et al. (eds.), *Sport Clubs in Europe*, Sports Economics, Management and Policy 12, DOI 10.1007/978-3-319-17635-2_18

The chapter provides a brief overview of sport clubs in Poland. The first part deals with the origin and the position of sport clubs within the national sport structure. The second paragraph is devoted to the role of sport clubs in the national policy program. The national data on sport club participation are presented. Finally, main characteristics of sport clubs in Poland are provided. This includes basic characteristics such as size and organisational form, challenges and bottlenecks experienced by sport clubs as well as activities and degree of professionalisation of sport club members.

## 18.2 History and Context

### *18.2.1 Origin of Sport Clubs*

Sport movement in Poland has drawn from national traditions and Western, especially English and German, models. The origin of Polish sport dates back to 1867 when students in Lviv established the Polish Gymnastic Society *Sokół*, the first bourgeois–intelligentsia association in the territory of Poland (Chełmecki and Wilk 2013). The main aim of *Sokół* was, of course, to organise gymnastic exercises for its members and later for school students. From the beginning of the 1880s, most *Sokół* branches were similar to contemporary sport clubs in that they opened divisions (called *sections*) for cycling, shooting, fencing, rowing and other disciplines. Apart from sport activity, *Sokół* branches engaged in cultural, educational and social activities with strong patriotic aspects.

Private gymnastics centres that offered sport classes also played an important role in the development of sport in Poland. The turn of the nineteenth century was a period of peak development for sport associations and organisations.

Polish sport clubs originated in the beginning of the twentieth century (Chełmecki and Wilk 2013). The first clubs were established in Galicia, in particular, in Lviv and Kraków. Initially, the clubs comprised of only a football section. Later, the track and field, tennis and other sections were added. The origins of Polish sport clubs are strictly connected with the school environment. The first sport club *Lechia Lwów* was established in 1903 by the students of Gymnasium No. 3 and the members of the Football Division at the Lviv *Sokół* Society (Chełmecki and Wilk 2013), followed by the *Sława* club (renamed later *Czarni Lwów*), also in 1903, and by the *Pogoń* club in 1904 (renamed later to *Pogoń Lwów*). Still before World War I, *Pogoń* and *Czarni Lwów* became major, multi-section clubs, and Lviv became the largest centre of Polish sport within the partitioned territories. The oldest clubs in Kraków, *Cracovia* and *Wisła* were established in 1906 by university and gymnasium students. Constituent meetings were held in the Jordan Park.

In the same period, attempts were also made to organise a football association in Galicia (Chełmecki and Wilk 2013). Between 1910 and 1911, *Cracovia*, *Pogoń* and *Wisła* belonged to the Austrian Football Association. In 1911, the Polish Football Association in Galicia was created, belonging to the Austrian Football Association, and thus to FIFA.

## 18.2.2 Sport Clubs within the National Sport Structure

Polish sport is managed by governmental and non-governmental structures (Fig. 18.1).

The central organ within the governmental structure is the Ministry of Sport and Tourism, the main task of which is to develop competitive and recreational sport and to supervise all sport federations in Poland (Żyśko 2013).

Divisions in voivodeship offices operate on a regional level. Their main aim is to carry out tasks related to physical culture, often connected with other aspects of social life, such as tourism, education or health. Furthermore, Sport Boards operate on a local level under units of local (county and municipal) self-governments. Their aim is to create development strategies, sport-based programs, sport and recreational event plans, Acts and county and municipality budget projects in respect to tasks related to sport.

As far as non-governmental organisations are concerned, the primary national, central-level organisation is the Polish Olympic Committee (POC). POC carries out aims and tasks of the Olympic Movement as well as activities related to the development of Polish sport, i.e. developing qualified sport, promoting sport for everyone, supervising the participation of the Polish National Representation in the Olympic Games, combating doping, conducting education and promoting fair play. The Polish Paralympic Committee performs the same function for persons with disabilities.

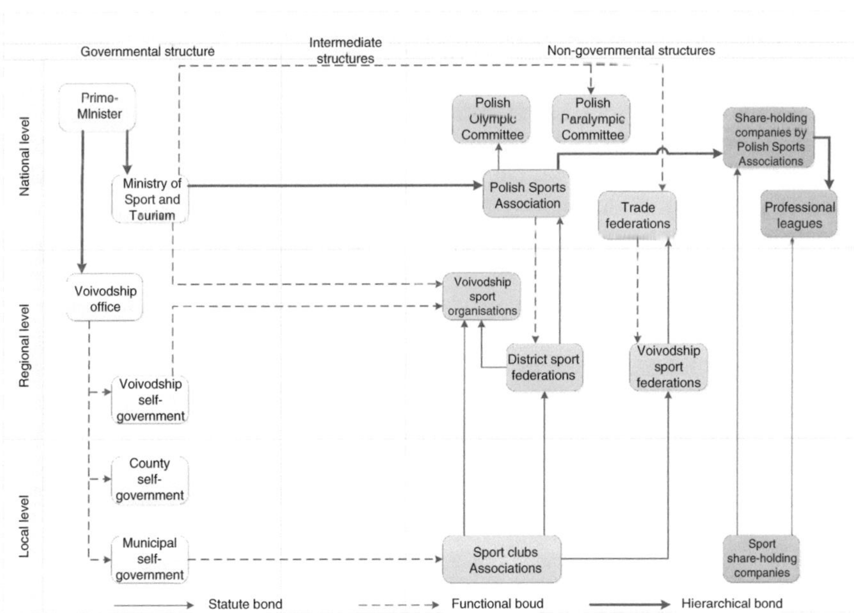


**Fig. 18.1** Structure of sport in Poland (Żyśko 2008, p. 123)

The central level also involves sport associations and Polish sport associations. Sport associations constitute of at least three sport clubs. They are interdisciplinary. Their primary aims are conducting activities related to sport and physical recreation, organising sport and recreational competitions and events, conducting educational and popularising activities related to physical culture and professional training of coaches and instructors. Sport associations include the following:

- The University Sports Association, a student-led, nationwide organisation for academic sport in Poland that aims to popularise and develop physical culture in the academic environment. Nowadays the University Sports Association Poland has over 40,000 members and over 250 university clubs.
- The *Rural Sports Clubs* Association is the Polish national sport organisation which is active primarily in rural areas and small towns. It aims to popularise and develop sport, recreation, physical education and tourism. Within the scope of professional sport, its activity is generally based on Rural Sports Clubs, and within the scope of physical recreation it is based on Rural Sports Clubs, Rural Tourist Clubs, Rural Tourist Teams and also, since 1994, Student Sports Clubs.
- The School Sports Association is an organisation which is active among children and students at primary, lower secondary, upper post-primary and upper secondary schools. Within the scope of professional sport, its activity is based on competitive inter-school sports clubs. Recreational activities are provided by school sports associations and, since 1994, by Student Sports Clubs.

Polish sport associations are a special form of a nationwide sport association that operate within one sport discipline and require permission from the Minister of Sport and Tourism to be established. There are currently 70 active Polish sport associations. However, the number has changed over the years.

Many sport associations within the structure of non-governmental organisations have their own intermediary structures on a regional level. Polish sport associations as well as multi-discipline associations have their own structures on a voivodeship level. The aim of these structures is to secure conditions for the development of non-school sport of children and youth.

On a local level, the basic organisational unit that carries out aims and tasks related to sport is a sport club. In legal terms, most clubs operate as associations, which means that they belong to the non-profit sector.

Professional leagues also operate on a national level. These leagues can be created by a Polish sport association for a discipline in which competition involves league championships and for which over half of the sport clubs participating in the championships are joint-stock companies. Four professional leagues are currently active in Poland: Ekstraklasa S.A. for football, Profesjonalna Liga Piłki Siatkowej S.A. for volleyball, Ekstraliga Żużlowa sp. z o.o. for motorcycle speedway and Polska Liga Koszykówki and Polska Liga Koszykówki Kobiet for basketball.

## 18.3 Role of Sport Clubs in the Policy and the Society

### *18.3.1 National Data on Sport Club Participation*

The presented data are derived from the KFT-1 report developed by the Central Statistical Office (Główny Urząd Statystyczny, GUS). The report constitutes a source of data on sport clubs, students' sport clubs and religious sport clubs. Since 2004, the report has been developed as a cyclic assessment, conducted every 2 years. The assessment includes sport clubs operating primarily within competitive sports as well as students' sport clubs and religious sport clubs where the main activity is physical recreation.

Analysis of the participation of Poles in activities conducted at sport clubs shows that there were 567.4 thousand registered members in 2012 (GUS 2013). The number has more than doubled over 50 years (Fig. 18.2). Men constituted a great majority of the practising persons (83.5 %). Over 60 % of practising persons were aged 18 or below. The share of boys among the practising youth was similar to the share of men among the total practising population and amounted to 80.8 %.

Another source of data on the participation of Poles in the activities organised by sports clubs is the Special Eurobarometer 412 Sport and Physical Activity (2014) report. The data presented in the report differ slightly from those provided by national statistics. According to the Eurobarometer, 3 % of Poles above 15 years of age declare their membership in a sports club, which taking into account the number of Polish citizens constitutes approx. 945.4 thousand (Fig. 18.3). The report also shows a 1 % decrease compared to 2009 while the national statistics reveal constant increase since the 1990s (Fig. 18.2). Eurobarometer also included other places

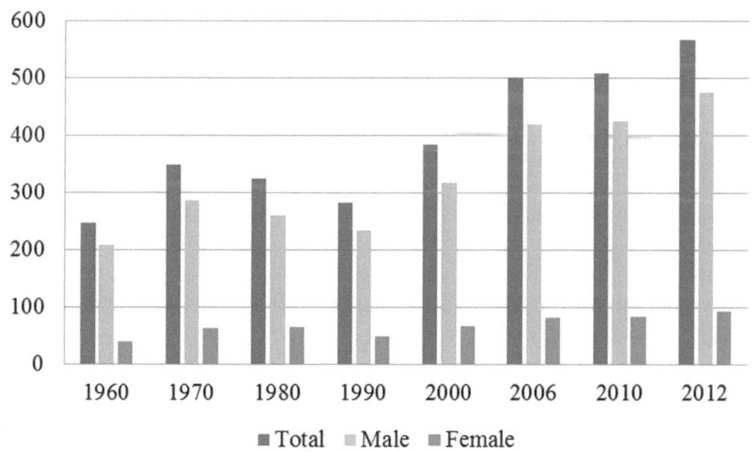


**Fig. 18.2** Number of persons practising at sport clubs between 1960 and 2012 (GUS 2013, p. 57)

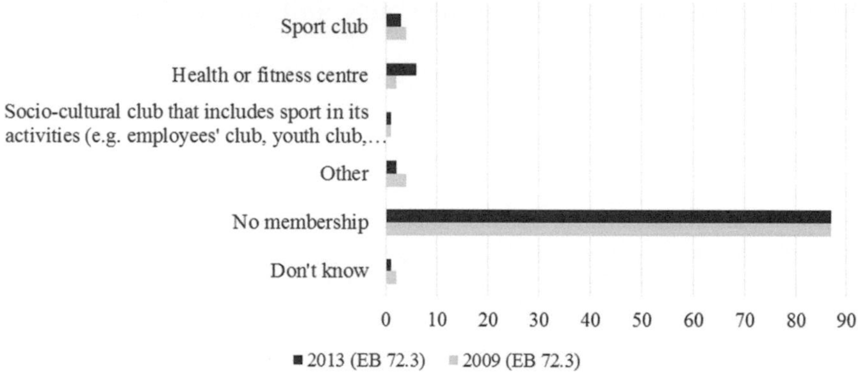


**Fig. 18.3** Participation of Poles in sport or recreational physical activity clubs (European Commission 2014)

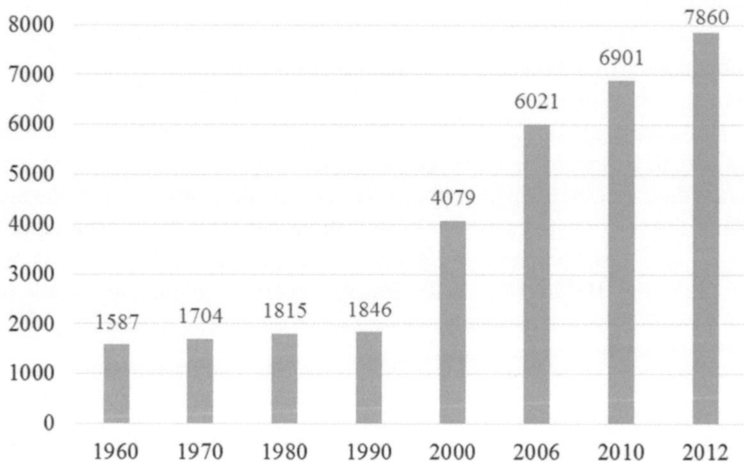


**Fig. 18.4** The number of sport clubs in Poland between 1960 and 2012 (GUS 2013, p. 57)

where one can practise organised forms of physical activity (Fig. 18.4). In 2013 only 6 % of Poles belonged to a health or fitness center and 1 % were members of sociocultural clubs that include sport in its activities, such as an employees' club, a youth club or a club related to school or university. It should be noted, however, that the national statistics are filled in by employees of sports clubs, while the Eurobarometer deals with declarations of Poles. Such discrepancies may also result from differences in definitions and in the way question and answer categories were formulated.

As for sport disciplines in 2012 and before, football was the most popular sport in Poland, taken up by about 48 % of persons practising at sport clubs (Table 18.1).

**Table 18.1** Percentage of persons practising sports in sport sections in 2012 (GUS 2013, pp. 70–75)

| Sport | Persons practising sports in sport sections in 2012 (%) |
|---|---|
| Football | 48.4 |
| Combat sports | 7.7 |
| Volleyball | 4.6 |
| Karate | 3.8 |
| Sport shooting | 2.8 |
| Basketball | 2.8 |
| Athletics | 2.6 |
| Swimming | 2.3 |
| Handball | 1.9 |
| Table tennis | 1.9 |
| Others | 21.2 |

The number of persons engaged in this discipline ($n=279,702$) was over ten times greater than the number of persons engaged in the second most popular sport, i.e. volleyball ($n=26,212$). In 2012, karate occupied third place, followed by basketball and shooting. Track and field sports and swimming were also popular among practising persons. As much as 7.7 % of persons practising at clubs chose martial arts, such as judo, jujutsu, kendo, kickboxing, sumo, taekwondo or wrestling (not taking karate into account) (GUS 2013).

## 18.3.2 *Societal and Political Embedding*

Polish sport policy is described in a governmental document called Strategy of Sport Development in Poland up to 2015 (Strategia rozwoju sportu w Polsce do roku 2015). The document specifies the direction of activities and how aims and tasks related to physical culture and sport should be carried out by adjusting them to high European standards (taking into account Polish traditions, conditions, needs and capabilities). The strategy unambiguously determines a vision whereby sport will occupy an increasingly stronger position in the broadly defined system of individual and social values and benefit a comprehensive development of human beings (including maintaining health and fitness and spending one's leisure time in a worthwhile manner). An active and fit society is the main strategic aim. Carrying this out will help:

- Improve the constitution and physical fitness among children and youth
- Limit the tendency of a sedentary lifestyle
- Reduce the number of persons who are overweight and obese

- Reduce the risk of diseases of affluence
- Improve societal health indicators
- Reduce the number of pathological phenomena and aggression (especially among youth)
- Develop awareness among society of the value of active leisure and positive habits of spending one's leisure time
- Increase citizen participation in physical recreation
- Increase the capability for sport and physical recreation among persons with disabilities

The document defines three priorities: popularising sport for everyone, improving sport results and developing sport and recreation infrastructure.

Currently, the ministry is working on a new strategy for the development of sport, which is to set goals and priorities for the coming years. State policy will be more focused on areas related to sport for all, especially for children and youth. The ministry set new programs: *Little Master*, *Multi Sport*, *Classy PE*, *Animator's Academy* and *I can swim*. Their primary purpose is to enrich the offer, increase the attractiveness of recreation and sports activities and improve the competences of persons engaged in such activities.

The main idea of the *Little Master* project is to encourage students in grades I–III of primary schools to acquire new motor skills and improve physical fitness. The project is also designed to help early childhood education teachers in gaining new knowledge and skills necessary to conduct interesting activities that encourage young Poles to take up new activities, as well as enhance the attractiveness of physical education classes.

The *I can swim* project is addressed to students of classes III primary schools throughout the country. It assumes a systematic and universal children's participation in extracurricular and after-school sports activities in the field of *learning to swim*.

The *Multisport* program is aimed at students in grades IV–VI schools. The main objective of the program is to promote physical activity through participation in regular and free sports activities. It is also important to identify sports talents and to ensure the effective transition from school to sports clubs and the participation in sport competition.

The programs also carry the potential for changes in the functioning of the sports environment, because their implementation requires new management mechanisms, close co-operation of sports organisations, local governments and schools.

Programmes are accompanied by actions *Classy PE* and *No sick leave because of PE*. The first one supports teachers in developing innovative programs of sports activities. The second one encourages parents to send their children to physical education classes. These programs are set in order to combat the health problems of Polish children, such as Europe's fastest weight gain, incorrect posture and steadily declining levels of physical fitness, resulting from a sedentary lifestyle. The programs also support PE teachers to raise professional qualifications.

## 18.4 Characteristics of Sport Clubs

### 18.4.1 Recreational Sport and Professional Sport

According to Article 3 of the Act on Sport of June 25, 2010, sport activity is conducted by sport clubs that have a legal personality (Journal of Laws 2010. No. 127, Item 857). The act does not specify what legal personality a sport club should have; it only indicates that it needs to have one (which means that the club cannot operate as, e.g., an economic activity of an individual). The establishers of a sport club may decide on its legal form themselves according to their needs and capabilities. Thus, sport clubs may operate as:

- Associations or foundations registered in the National Court Register.
- Students' sport clubs.
- Associations registered under the head of county administration appropriate to the club's location; such entities cannot conduct economic activity.
- Limited companies, i.e. joint-stock companies and limited-liability companies, registered in the National Court Register; these entities are entrepreneurs who conduct economic activity. Clubs participating in sport competition as part of a professional league operate under this legal form.

Since 1960, the number of sport clubs in Poland has been growing systematically. In 2012, there were 7,860 active sport clubs in Poland, which is almost five times more than over 50 years ago (Fig. 18.4). This number does not include the 6,370 students' sport clubs that operate in schools or under sport and recreation centres and 77 religious sport clubs.

Among all sport clubs, as much as 31.9 % were clubs that belonged to Rural Sports Clubs Association ($n$=2,508). School Sports Association included 1.0 % of clubs ($n$=108), as did University Sports Associations ($n$=82).

Discussing recreational and competitive activity of Polish sport clubs is difficult, as data on the subject are lacking. However, results are available on the number of persons and clubs participating in national sport competitions.

Among all persons practising at sport clubs, almost two-thirds (65.1 %) were registered in national or district sport associations (GUS 2013). As far as youth and senior national level sports competition is concerned, 4,140 sport clubs (52.7 %) declared participation (Table 18.2).

### 18.4.2 Challenges and Bottlenecks Experienced by Sport Clubs

Polish sport and sport clubs are in a systematically worsening situation due to numerous financial, organisational and training problems.

Poland occupies one of the last positions in Europe in terms of the amount of public spending on sport per citizen (about €25, compared to about €200 in the

**Table 18.2** National level sports competition in 2010 and 2012 (*n*/%) (GUS 2013, p. 59)

| | 2010 | 2012 |
|---|---|---|
| Clubs | 3,742 | 4,140 |
| Sections | 6,203 | 6,883 |
| Club members | 336,096 | 355,127 |
| Persons practising sports (total) | 316,974 | 344,739 |
| Males | 254,463/80.3 | 275,127/79.8 |
| Females | 62,511/19.7 | 69,612/20.2 |
| Up to the age of 18 | 199,335/62.9 | 199,335/57.8 |
| 18 and over the age of 18 | 117,639/37.1 | 145,404/42.2 |

leading countries) (OSPS 2014). According to the model of financing, which has been in force for many years, the main source of finances for sport is the public sector (*The sport…* 2007). The structure of public spending indicates a significant share of self-governmental units in the financing of sport. Only about one-third of total spending comes from the national budget and surcharges to stakes in games of chance, which constitute a state monopoly. For Poland to achieve European standards of popularity and accessibility of sports and maintain a high position in sport competition, an appropriate increase in spending on sport needs to take place. Rules for financing youth and competitive sport should be changed. Tasks should be divided among self-governments, the central budget and private entities (sponsors). Public spending and the need to relate public spending with sport results are frequently considered as being crucially important in ensuring the effectiveness of the system of financing. However, it should be noted that in Poland, promoting and financing on the part of central and self-governmental budgets have for a long time focused on team sports, especially football. Other sports disciplines are expected to be self-financing.

The next problem is related to sport infrastructure. Even though over 3,200 sport facilities have been opened since 1995, qualified sports and recreational infrastructure do not meet European standards in terms of both quantity and quality. A vast majority of sport facilities are dilapidated, often require comprehensive repair work and are usually difficult to access by persons with disabilities. Local sport clubs face extreme locale problems. On the one hand, sport halls are expensive to rent, and on the other, the possibilities to rent facilities for 5 or 6 h on 5 days every week are limited. This also entails problems with storing sports equipment for clubs that have it. Modern training involves professional equipment that requires considerable financial input. Many clubs experience a progressive decapitalisation of sport facilities and equipment. Equipment and auxiliary tools, used successfully in the preceding years, have in many cases been excluded from the training process.

Insufficient funds are another obstacle for employing coaches and instructors. Usually, coaches and instructors work part time and are paid poorly.

The unsatisfactory professional qualifications of persons engaged in sport make developing this area of life significantly more difficult. Compared to other countries in this respect, Poland shows a significant backlog that manifests itself on most pitches and in sport halls and sport fields. These facilities are dilapidated, underfunded and either empty or not used to their full potential. One of the reasons for this state of affairs is the lack of well-trained managerial staff (Zdebel 2007). It is emphasised that marketing activities conducted by sport clubs have great potential. In organisations with a small number of employees, marketing is either the board's or no one's responsibility. In large clubs, marketing is supervised by an appropriate person or branch. Nonetheless, in Poland, most persons responsible for marketing in sport clubs are still unprepared for the task; that is, they have not completed any training or university courses on the subject.

One of the aims of sport clubs is to participate in sport competition, and one of the aims of athlete training is to enable them to take part in the competition. In small clubs, a problem already arises on the stage of constructing a training pyramid (Zdebel 2007). To pave the road for top-level sport competition, a particular number of groups need to be created that would allow the creation of such a pyramid and athletes need to be given access to modern training and tools that allow modern training. Therefore, clubs should have a maximal number of children groups, a smaller number of junior groups and a relatively small number of athlete groups. In these circumstances, maintaining recreational groups would be pointless. However, several conditions must be met in order to construct such a model, i.e. a large number of training groups, solid equipment and staff resources, access to sport halls, access to training for all interested persons and a strong emphasis on children training. These conditions entail considerable expenditures to cope with which clubs introduce membership fees or training fees. This makes it necessary to maintain numerous recreational groups or to allow many persons who practise sports recreationally to train in competitive groups. Thus, club activity shifts its focus from a strictly competitive range to recreational functions. Another problem concerns children groups, which, from the viewpoint of sports theory, should be the most numerous ones. However, combining the self-financing of clubs with a wide accessibility to training proves difficult. Unfortunately, experience shows that selection criteria are most often based not on physical fitness, motivation or ambition of future athletes, but on their parents' financial resources. Thus, an enormous number of potentially good athletes never signs up for training.

Sport clubs are also accused of a lack of perspective thinking and strategic management. The truth is that the boards of many small sport clubs focus on finding funds for current activity. They simply have no time left to develop long-term plans.

Sport clubs also face social problems. They carry out actions aimed at combating pathological phenomena in sports, especially doping, hooliganism, xenophobia and symptoms of intolerance.

### 18.4.3 Professionalisation

Organised classes in a sport club participating in competition organised by a Polish sport association can only be conducted by a coach or a sport instructor (Article 41 of the Act on Sport). The tasks of a coach or a sport instructor include conducting

**Table 18.3** Coaching and administrative staff in sport clubs according to selected sport sections in 2012 (GUS 2013, p. 99)

| Sport sections | Coaches | | | | Instructors | Other persons conducting sport classes | Medical and wellness staff | Administrative staff |
|---|---|---|---|---|---|---|---|---|
| | Total | Master class | I class | II class | | | | |
| Total | 9,313 | 779 | 1,777 | 6,757 | 14,398 | 5,666 | 1,794 | 7,693 |
| Including | | | | | | | | |
| USA | 646 | 59 | 148 | 439 | 381 | 112 | 61 | 171 |
| RSCA | 1,792 | 192 | 298 | 1,302 | 3,027 | 1,899 | 434 | 2,071 |
| SSA | 247 | 9 | 27 | 211 | 301 | 62 | 13 | 56 |

*USA* University Sports Association, *RSCA* Rural Sports Clubs Association, *SSA* School Sports Association

classes and sharing current theoretical and practical knowledge on sport training and sport competition in a given discipline. A coach or a sport instructor in a discipline handled by Polish sport associations must be a person who

- Is 18 or older
- Has at least middle education
- Has knowledge, experience and skills required to perform the tasks of a coach or a sport instructor

In 2012, coaching staff comprised of 29.4 thousand persons (including community service workers) (GUS 2013). Over 31 % of the staff were coaches (master, I, and II class[1]), 49 % were instructors[2] and about 20 % were other persons conducting sports classes (Table 18.3). Compared to 2010, coaching staff increased by 11.4 %, the number of coaches and instructors by 14.1 % and the number of other persons conducting sports classes by 1.6 %.

Volunteers also play a major role in sport club activity. While voluntary work in Poland is dynamically developing and an increasing number of Polish organisations, associations and clubs seek volunteers who can support their activities and development, it still functions on a much smaller scale than in other European countries. It should be emphasised that full-fledged voluntary work has existed in Poland only since 1990. According to the Act of Law of April 24, 2003, on Public Benefit and Volunteer Work, a volunteer is a person who willingly and without remuneration performs services for a volunteer organisation (Journal of Laws of

[1] A coach conducts sport training for athletes qualified in a given sports discipline who take part in the national competition system (first level) and the international competition system (second level).

[2] An instructor is a specialist who conducts basic training for children, youth and adults. The basic tasks of an instructor are developing physical fitness, teaching technical and tactical skills necessary to take part in sports competition and supervising the participants of sports competition.

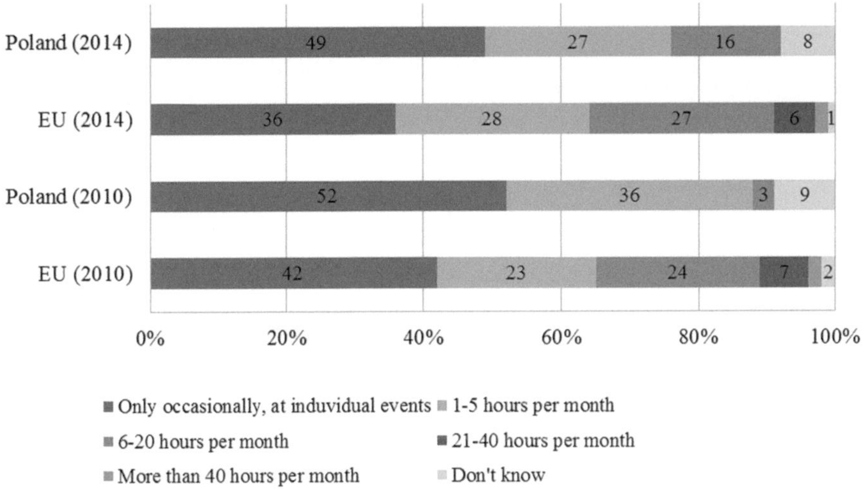


**Fig. 18.5** Time spent on voluntary work in sport in Poland and other EU countries (European Commission 2010, 2014, p. 72)

2010, No. 234, Item 1536, as amended). Two basic forms of voluntary work exist in sports:

– Action (short-term) volunteering: Volunteers are hired to assist at a one-time or cyclic event that takes place once every 6 or 3 months; this type of voluntary work is characteristic for such events as marathons or half marathons, i.e. local and national sports events.
– Permanent (indefinite) volunteering: Volunteers are close tied with an organisation and perform specific work for it. Under permanent volunteering, volunteers constantly cooperate with a given organisation or institution and perform work regularly, e.g. two or three times per week, at a specific time. Permanent volunteers work, for instance, in academic, students' and professional league sport clubs, associations and foundations related to sports. Permanent volunteers also work with persons with disabilities and individuals.

According to a Eurobarometer study (European Commission 2010, Wave 72.3), volunteer participation in organising and conducting sports classes in Poland was the lowest in Europe, amounting to only 2 %, with a mean European participation of 7 %. The newest Eurobarometer report (European Commission 2014, Wave 412) indicates an increase in the share of voluntary workers by 1 %, with the same European mean.

Analysis of data on time spent on activity confirms again that Poles are uninterested in community work in this area. In 2010, half the Poles (52 %) who spent their time on sports projects (2 %) declared that they did so only sporadically. Over one-fourth of volunteers (27 %) worked up to 5 h per month. In 2014, the percentage increased to 36 %. Unfortunately, however, no one declared participation in voluntary work for more than 20 h per month. Figure 18.5 shows detailed data on the subject.

**Table 18.4** Types of activities undertaken in sport organisations (Eurobarometer 2014, p. 75)

| Type of activity | Poland (%) | EU (%) |
|---|---|---|
| Being a member of a board or a committee | 11 | 22 |
| Administrative tasks | 8 | 16 |
| Being a coach or a trainer | 12 | 29 |
| Being a referee or other official | 19 | 9 |
| Organising or helping to conduct a sport event | 10 | 35 |
| Supporting day-to-day club activities (bar, food or merchandising) | 15 | 20 |
| Providing transport | 11 | 15 |
| Maintaining sport facilities | 16 | 10 |
| Maintaining sport equipment | 4 | 8 |
| Other | 13 | 10 |
| Respondent does not know | 9 | 1 |

A Eurobarometer study published in 2014 also analysed activities undertaken by voluntary workers in sport organisations. Table 18.4 shows a comparison between the results from the Polish and the English sample.

What is the reason for such a low interest among Poles in sport volunteering? The results of a qualitative study conducted under the Social Project 2012 on a sample of 24 sport organisations show numerous barriers to the development of sport voluntary work in Poland (*Wolontariat w sporcie…* 2010). These barriers include the following:

- A lack of an in-depth diagnosis of the sport volunteering in Poland, which hampers conducting a social policy adjusted to real needs in the area of this non-governmental sector: In particular, the lack of data concerns the number of sport volunteers, their types of engagement, their motivation and needs, the potential and needs of organisations in terms of hiring volunteers, methods of communication, resources available to sport organisations and conditions that must be met for organisations to use these resources.
- Insufficient knowledge about voluntary work among the representatives of sport organisations, which prevents voluntary work from being recognised as a resource that allows sport organisations to develop: The lack of knowledge concerns benefits for an organisation that stem from engaging volunteers, competences of organisation representatives in coordinating volunteer work (including constructing different offers, effective recruitment, training, motivating and taking advantage of volunteer competences, especially in relation to permanent volunteers), legal knowledge on voluntary work and knowledge and skills related to various sources of funding for engaging volunteers.
- Limited co-operation between sectors and branches aimed at creating conditions for the development of sport voluntary work, which reduces the quality of voluntary work and prevents effective sharing of resources and knowledge on voluntary work and undertaking coordinated activities in the area.

- A low awareness about sport voluntary work among Poles, which results in one of the lowest number of volunteers in Europe (in sport and in total) and a low recognition of the value of voluntary work.

As far as staff training is concerned, up to 2013, a permission to work as a coach or sport instructor could be obtained through education, in particular through:

1. Sport instructor and coach courses in a given sports discipline that realise a curriculum with a required number of hours (instructor: a minimum of 150 h of specialist classes and 70 h of theoretical foundations; trainer: a minimum of 300 h, including 60 % spent on specialist classes) and are organised by universities, teacher training centres and facilities that obtained permission from the Minister of Sport and Tourism.
2. Courses at universities of physical education (full-time and part-time programmes) based on curricula with a different number of hours, approved by the authorities of each university (Kielak 2008).

Professional training took place through:

1. First and master class coach courses (40-h and 60-h curricula, respectively), organised by the Central Sport Centre and universities of physical education.
2. Professional training courses organised by Polish sport associations; the curricula (in terms of subjects covered and the number hours) were determined by the appropriate organs of these associations.

In 2013, the Act on the Deregulation of Professions in Poland of June 13, 2013, was issued, which improved the accessibility of the coach and sport instructor professions. The administrative load has been decreased by eliminating the procedure of obtaining permission for conducting specialist coach and sport instructor courses from the appropriate minister for matters concerning physical culture. It is the employment market that now decides which specialists to hire. To prevent a lack of professionalism among staff working with children and youth, the Ministry of Sport and Tourism plans to introduce a unified qualification system for these two professions.

## 18.5 Conclusions

One of the goals of social policy in EU countries is to improve the awareness of educational and sport organisations about the need for co-operation aimed at developing education through sport, applying the values brought by sport to broaden knowledge and qualifications and promoting the benefits of youth exchange by organising sport and cultural events as part of school, youth organisation and sport club activity.

The number of sport clubs and persons practising at them in Poland is constantly rising. Unfortunately, the rise does not entail a modernisation of the sport financing system, which would allow club funds to increase. Now that sport clubs have operated for many years, they need to be thoroughly analysed and assessed for effectiveness in terms of participating in national and, more importantly, international competitions, i.e. the UEFA European Championship, the World Cup and the Olympic Games. The role of sport clubs in popularising sport for everyone and promoting physical activity should not be underestimated.

The situation of Polish clubs stems from the fact that since the political transformation, Polish sport has visibly halted in development. Sport clubs were managed by persons unadjusted to operating in a market economy. In Western Europe, sport underwent commercialisation, while in Poland, sport clubs did not see the need for marketing professionals.

The key to success in sport financing is educating sport organisations and sharing knowledge with them about how to obtain, manage and maintain sponsors. Guaranteed central funding for sport, instead of forcing sport organisations to acquire funds on their own, makes them slothful when it comes to self-financing. Sport clubs in Poland should assume a more business-oriented approach, as money earned through one's own efforts is spent more reasonably and more efficiently.

Better financial resources will greatly improve the situation in many clubs, especially those that operate locally. This in turn will not only allow a greater number of qualified coaching and medical staff to be hired (both of which are lacking in many environments), but will also help modernise equipment and facilities.

One should not forget about the key role that science and sport medicine play. Without material support for research, the level of studies that enrich training methodology will not improve. Systematically updated coaching knowledge on the part of persons supervising modern training is also indispensable. Countries that occupy top positions in sport rankings put a considerable emphasis on scientific recruitment into sport, which allows them to save funds and direct talented youth into qualified sport.

When creating training standards for sport specialists, a country should assume that sport staff need to be prepared not only for coaching, but also for managing sport organisations. Consequently, the specialists will create employment for other specialists, thus motivating societal development and increasing the significance of sport within the national economy.

Monitoring and controlling processes that tie sport with the economy require creating a concept for a system of sport information that would combine databases on sport results, facilities, sport clubs and coaching staff maintained by different institutions. Currently, such institutions gather and analyse data on sport on different levels, often creating redundancy. The proposed solution will allow for a rational management of assessment programmes and qualification results within the existing systems of coaching and competition.

## References

Chełmecki J, Wilk S (2013) Zarys historii sportu/An outline of the history of sport/. Wydawnictwo WSEWS, Warszawa

Cienski J (2012) Poland's growth defies eurozone crisis. Financial Times, 1 July 2012. http://www.ft.com. Retrieved 8 Jan 2014

European Commission (2010) Special Eurobarometer 334—Wave 72.3. Sport and physical activity. TNS Opinion & Social, Brussels
European Commission (2014) Special Eurobarometer 214. Sport and physical activity. TNS Opinion & Social, Brussels
GUS (2013) Physical education in Poland in 2011 and 2012. http://www.stat.gov.pl. Retrieved 15 Jun 2014
GUS (2014) Demographic yearbook of Poland. Warsaw. http://stat.gov.pl. Retrieved 8 Jan 2014
Kielak D (2008) How to improve training of coaches and instructors in Poland? Sport Wyczynowy 4–6:520–522
Leś E (1999) Działalność dobroczynna w Europie i Ameryce. Tradycje i współczesność. Częśc III (Charity in Europe and America. Traditions and modernity. Part III). Cooperation Fund, Warszawa
OSPS (2014) Spotkanie Zespołu ds. Finansowania Sportu (Meeting devoted to financing sport). http://www.olimpijski.pl. Retrieved 15 Jun 2014
Przewłocka J, Adamiak P, Herbst J (2013) Podstawowe fakty o organizacjach pozarządowych—raport z badania 2012 (Basic facts about non-governmental organizations—the audit report 2012). Stowarzyszenie Klon/Jawor, Warszawa
The Ministry of sport (2007) The sport development strategy in Poland for 2015. http://www.msport.gov.pl/fs/paragraph_download/download_file/433/815Finalna_strategia–_12_01.doc_2.pdf. Retrieved 15 Jun 2014
Ustawa o działalności pożytku publicznego i o wolontariacie z dn. 24.04.2003 r. / Act on Public Benefit and Volunteer Work/ (Dz.U. z 2010 r., Nr 234, poz. 1536 z późn. zm.). http://isap.sejm.gov.pl/. Accessed 15 Jun 2014
Ustawa o sporcie z dn. 25.06.2010 r. /Act on sport/ (Dz.U. 2010 nr 127 poz. 857). http://isap.sejm.gov.pl/. Accessed 15 Jun 2014
Wolontariat Sportowy 2012+ (2010) Wolontariat w sporcie. Sport dla wolontariatu/Volunteering in sport. Sport for volunteering. http://www.azs.pl/fck/files/newsy_10/wolontariat_w_sporcie-rekomendacje.pdf. Retrieved 15 Jun 2014
Zdebel D (2007) Finanse i ich wpływ na rozwój klubu (Finance and its impact on sport club's development). Sztuki Walki 2:24–25
Żyśko J (2008) Zmiany we współczesnych systemach zarządzania sportem wyczynowym w wybranych krajach europejskich/Changes in contemporary sport management systems in professional sport in selected European countries/. Wydawnictwo AWF Warszawa, Warszawa
Żyśko J (2013) Poland. In: Hallman K, Petry K (eds) Comparative sport development. Systems, participation and public policy. Springer, New York, pp 135–148

# Chapter 19
# Sport Clubs in Sweden

**Josef Fahlén**

## 19.1 Introduction

Sweden is home to Upsala Simsällskap, founded in 1796, often mentioned as the oldest sport club in the world still competing in regular contests. Since then, Swedish voluntary and membership-based club sport has grown exponentially and come to embrace nearly a third of the Swedish population. This phenomenon is often credited in international comparisons of physical activity and civic engagement but also often claimed as an explanation for the success of Zlatan Ibrahimovic, Annika Sörenstam, Björn Borg and Sarah Sjöström. For many Swedes, sport is an integral part of everyday life as pastime, entertainment, physical exercise, competition or volunteer work. In this chapter, the background to and specifics of these features are outlined together with an analysis of current tensions in the landscape of Swedish club sport.

## 19.2 History and Context

Sweden, with its 9.6 million inhabitants, has become known for its social engineering leading up to what has been termed the Nordic social welfare system or the Scandinavian welfare policy model. It has during most parts of the twentieth century been governed by the Social Democratic party, which has promoted heavy taxing in order to finance far-reaching welfare measures to level out social and economic differences in the population. Today, Sweden has become a multicultural nation due to significant immigration. Some 15 % of the population is foreign born

J. Fahlén (✉)
Department of Education, Umeå University, Umeå, Sweden
e-mail: Josef.fahlen@umu.se



C. Breuer et al. (eds.), *Sport Clubs in Europe*, Sports Economics, Management and Policy 12, DOI 10.1007/978-3-319-17635-2_19

and an additional 5 % is born to immigrant parents. It is, since 2006, governed by a centre-right alliance and is rated as the seventh-richest country in the world with a gross domestic product per capita of €42,000.

The official starting point for voluntary and membership-based club sport in Sweden, in its present form and organisation, was in 1903 when the Swedish Sports Confederation (SSC) was established. With the growing associationism, voluntarism and nationalism typical for its time, competitive sports imported from England got foothold in the Swedish society. Aided by strong connections to the government, royal house, military officials and representatives from the business and industrial spheres, the sport's movement could grow in strength and numbers. Armed with the success of the 1912 Stockholm Olympics, as well as with arguments that sport was beneficial for health, physical and moral character, sobriety, national defence capabilities and national unity (Norberg 2004), supporters of sport managed to push through a parliamentary decision on an annual government grant to sport in 1913. With that decision, a long-standing relationship characterised by an intimate and corporative partnership between the state and voluntary and membership-based club sport was established.

This relationship, which has been described as a mutual dependency governed by a so-called implicit contract (Norberg 2002), has since its inception been paramount to the growth of voluntary and membership-based club sport in Sweden (Bergsgard and Norberg 2010). Included in what was later developed into the Scandinavian welfare policy model, voluntary and membership-based club sport gained access to public funds. Welfare, in this Scandinavian take, was not limited to health care and schools but also included citizens' access to recreation and leisure activities in which voluntary and membership-based club sport was given a leading role. However, the government chose to support sport in its voluntary organisational form, and not to nationalise it under suitable department. The support was help to self-help, to safeguard autonomy and to protect against commercial forces, and it was granted to membership-based sport organisations, to stimulate civic engagement and democratic associationism. With these features came a dependence on government funds which resulted in recipient responsiveness—an implicit contract regulating the right to state support under responsibility to contribute to societal benefits and restrain excesses (Norberg 2004). But it also allowed sports with less public attraction to develop and contribute to an increased plurality in Swedish sport.

Due to geographical and social propagation, voluntary and membership-based club sport grew exponentially during the subsequent decades. Its expansion was further propelled by the extension of sport facilities as part of public relief work, the establishment of a state-controlled gambling institution and the decision to allocate the revenues to sport, which multiplied the government support many times over (Norberg 2004). The affiliation to the SSC went from 25 sport federations (NSF), 730 sport clubs and 93,000 members in 1920 to 45 NSFs, 9,500 sport clubs and 790,000 members in 1950 (Norberg 2002). Simultaneously, the competitive element in voluntary and membership-based club sport was accentuated by the detachment of exercise, keep-fit and outdoor activities to organisations not affiliated to the SSC such as the Swedish Federation for Company Sports and the Swedish Outdoor Association.

During the post-World War II rehabilitation, the *Swedish model* in politics was formed where increased cooperation between state and third-sector organisations became important for the continuing growth of voluntary and membership-based club sport. Fuelled by arguments such as sport's ability to decrease health care costs, rural emigration, youth delinquency and drinking and to stimulate productivity, the government grant was 18-fold between 1945 and 1970 (in practice it was 50-fold, counting other grants benefitting sport such as an extensive support to youth organisations) which made it possible to professionalise leaders. The affiliation to the SSC grew further to 53 NSFs, 13,467 sport clubs and 2,200,000 members in 1970 (Lindroth 2011). Key to the extensive increase in government funding was two government commissions of inquiry (SOU 1922, 1957). Both ascertained that sport had developed into a real popular movement and a means for public health and upbringing and recommended a substantial increase of the grant, resources for training of leaders and an extension of sport facilities. But with the third government commission of inquiry (SOU 1969), the sport's movement not only was granted yet another increased financial grant but more importantly was formally granted the right to exercise government agency authority (Österlind and Wright 2014). This decision, often referred to as a formative moment in Swedish sport politics, marked the end of a drawn-out process deciding whether to rely on a corporative arrangement between state and sport or to install a government agency relieving the SSC of its informal yet effective mandate. It also made it formally possible for the confederation to exercise mandate and financial influence over a policy area which had more than one organisation aspiring to represent the sport, exercise, keep-fit and outdoor interests of individuals (Norberg 2004). By granting the SSC this mandate, the government gave prerogative to competitive sport at the expense of outdoor and exercise activities, which in its extension further strengthened sport clubs' position in the Swedish society and their focus on competitive activities as opposed to exercise, keep-fit and outdoor activities.

From 1970 and onwards, voluntary and membership-based club sport continued its expansion and integration with surrounding society. While the government's initial and enduring trust in voluntary organisations to administer and develop sport had effectively restrained the development of sport in the commercial sector, the SSC abandoned its long-standing amateur rules in 1967 which had prohibited professional athletes since 1904. The decision gave further momentum to the bourgeoning professionalisation and opened up for academic training of professional coaches and managers in 1973, training of future professional athletes at upper secondary elite sport schools in 1979, limited sport companies in 1999 and foreign investors in 2000 (Fahlén 2007). The affiliation to the SSC increased to 70 NSFs, 20,164 sport clubs and 3,147,000 members in 2010 (Centrum för idrottsforskning 2013).

The defining character of and main organising principle for contemporary voluntary and membership-based club sport is that of individuals forming and/or taking part as members in voluntary and membership-based sport clubs which are affiliated to some 1,000 district sport federations (DSF, with regional authority over one specific sport), to one of the 21 regional sports federations (RSF, with regional authority over all sports) and to one or several of the 70 NSF (with national authority over one specific sport). This organisational design, based on horizontal (by sport) and vertical (by geography) specialisation, has availed for local, regional, national and international competition between individuals and teams in competitions, cups, leagues and tournaments in which sporting merits have formed the basis for representation, promotion and demotion in contrast to professional leagues and circuits where profitability and competitive balance is used to decide opponents.

The individual sport club member can, by the club's annual meeting, be elected to represent the club at the annual meeting of the DSF. If elected to the board of the DSF, the individual can in turn be elected representative in the RSF in question, and in the NSF for the given sport. If elected to one of these two boards, the individual can, in extension, be elected to the board of the SSC and to represent the sport in question in international federations and the Olympic movement. This representative democracy is often referred to as one cornerstone of Swedish voluntary and membership-based club sport, and also as one main contribution to the civic education of Swedish citizens. The biannual national meeting for the elected representatives constitutes the parliament, and the board of the SSC constitutes the government. The meeting has the mandate to appoint the board, auditors, the doping commission, the doping authority, the arbitral commission and the caucus, and to admit new sports into the confederation. It also accepts or rejects motions and make decisions on the confederation's direction for the following 2 years.

The confederation's principal tasks are to represent voluntary and membership-based club sport in communication with authorities, officials and the surrounding society, to support and service affiliated organisations, to administer and distribute the government funds to affiliated organisations, to stimulate sport development and research, to coordinate social and ethical issues, to lead and coordinate the anti-doping work, to coordinate international cooperation, to protect sport's historical legacy and to act as government authority for the 51 upper secondary elite sport schools with some 1,200 students in 30 sports.

## 19.3 Role of Sport Clubs in Policy and Society

Voluntary and membership-based club sport is nowadays an integral part of the Swedish society. As the tables in the following will show, most Swedes have a connection to voluntary and membership-based club sport as participants or leaders. As described in the historical account it is also closely intertwined with the state in terms of extensive public funding and as means for realising social policy. For the latter, voluntary and membership-based club sport enjoys an annual government grant of €210 million (Centrum för idrottsforskning 2013). The grant has more than tripled since the end of the 1990s (€61 million in 1998, SOU 2008). To that amount comes municipal support of €490 million (€360 million to facilities and €130 million to activities and leaders, Bergsgard and Norberg 2010). The value of volunteer work, calculated by multiplying the 176 million hours put in by some 600,000 leaders and the mean wage in the private sector (Olsson 2007), amounts to some €3,400 million.

In addition, members contribute some €420 million in fees (Riksidrottsförbundet 2005b), and spectators contribute some €360 million in entrance (SOU 2008). On top of the government grant, mostly financed by gambling revenues, sport also benefits from its own lotteries to the estimated value of some €45 million (SOU 2008). Resources from the commercial sector are roughly estimated to some €280 million (SOU 2008).

These resources go out to and are used by sport club members in the 20,164 sport clubs in Sweden. In Table 19.1 (Riksidrottsförbundet 2011), the distribution of members by sex and age group is described. It shows that almost half of the population between the ages of 7 and 70 are members of a sport club. It shows how the proportion of men is higher than the proportion of women, and that membership rates are highest in younger ages. The biggest dropout occurs between the age groups 7–14 and 15–19, which coincides with an increased focus on competition noted by the Swedish research community (Sjöblom and Fahlén 2012).

When dividing the memberships by sport, in Table 19.2 (Centrum för idrottsforskning 2013), it is evident that football holds a special position, being by far the most popular sport. Table 19.2 shows that despite the Nordic climate, winter sports such as ice hockey, skiing, bandy and bobsleigh and luge are gathering far less members. Worth noticing is the high membership numbers in athletics, golf and gymnastics despite their character as individual sports. Popular sports internationally such as basketball, table tennis and badminton are relatively small in Sweden, while a few sports with less attraction internationally has gained strong footholds such as floorball, equestrian and sailing. The popularity of football has been consistent for almost a century, doubling its membership base from 1970 to 2013, while skiing has taken a severe decrease in members from 309,000 in 1970 to 91,000 in 2013, falling from third place to 11th. In contrast, golf has evolved in the other direction to a third place in 2013 (Lindroth 1988; Norberg 2002).

While Tables 19.1 and 19.2 provide valuable information on memberships, which can be taken as a token of the societal embedding of club sport and its force of attraction with the Swedish population, they tell less about how active in sport

**Table 19.1** Sport club members by sex and age group (age 7–70, $n = 7,558,000$)

| | | Active members | % | Supporting members | % | Total | % |
|---|---|---|---|---|---|---|---|
| Total | | 2,274,000 | 30 | 873,000 | 12 | 3,147,000 | 42 |
| Sex | Women | 1,056,000 | 28 | 341,000 | 9 | 1,397,000 | 38 |
| | Men | 1,217,000 | 32 | 532,000 | 14 | 1,749,000 | 46 |
| Age group | 7–14 | 577,000 | 72 | 43,000 | 5 | 620,000 | 77 |
| | 15–19 | 249,000 | 44 | 42,000 | 8 | 291,000 | 51 |
| | 20–29 | 280,000 | 23 | 99,000 | 8 | 379,000 | 31 |
| | 30–39 | 305,000 | 25 | 143,000 | 12 | 448,000 | 37 |
| | 40–49 | 410,000 | 31 | 207,000 | 16 | 617,000 | 47 |
| | 50–59 | 232,000 | 20 | 154,000 | 13 | 386,000 | 33 |
| | 60–70 | 222,000 | 18 | 185,000 | 15 | 407,000 | 32 |

**Table 19.2** Sport club members by sport

| National sport federation | Members | National sport federation | Members |
|---|---|---|---|
| Football | 1,050,000 | Karate | 16,132 |
| Athletics | 503,000 | Boule | 13,563 |
| Golf | 491,401 | Boxing | 13,500 |
| Gymnastics | 209,733 | Taekwondo | 11,733 |
| Company sports | 208,261 | Wrestling | 10,516 |
| Floorball | 185,500 | Diving | 10,377 |
| Equestrian | 151,006 | Ice sailing | 10,000 |
| School sports | 133,302 | American football | 9,450 |
| Sailing | 120,167 | Biathlon | 9,125 |
| Swimming | 118,750 | Triathlon | 9,000 |
| Ice hockey | 108,925 | Volleyball | 8,339 |
| Tennis | 105,766 | Rowing | 7,242 |
| Motor sports | 101,393 | Climbing | 6,727 |
| Handball | 100,000 | Casting | 6,506 |
| Skiing | 91,032 | Bandy | 6,375 |
| Shooting | 86,835 | Archery | 6,375 |
| Orienteering | 85,795 | [Mångkamp][a] | 6,000 |
| Basketball | 80,000 | Squash | 5,977 |
| Academic sports | 70,329 | Mini golf | 5,835 |
| Motorcycle | 54,827 | Frisbee | 5,800 |
| Cycling | 40,000 | Rugby | 5,281 |
| Dance sports | 38,641 | Deaf sports | 4,967 |
| Table tennis | 37,513 | Curling | 4,621 |
| Budo and martial arts | 36,885 | Hockey | 4,461 |
| Power lifting | 35,000 | Fencing | 4,324 |
| Paralympic sports | 33,000 | Water skiing | 4,012 |
| Walking | 31,000 | Sled dog racing | 3,700 |
| Bowling | 30,582 | Boat racing | 2,879 |
| Canoeing | 28,800 | Darts | 2,491 |
| Badminton | 27,433 | Varpa | 2,100 |
| Judo | 23,999 | Baseball and softball | 2,000 |
| Air sport | 21,359 | Tug of war | 832 |
| Figure skating | 19,000 | Billiards | 767 |
| Skating | 19,000 | Bobsleigh and luge | 725 |
| Weightlifting | 17,588 | | |

[a]Modern Pentathlon, Military Pentathlon, Military Biathlon Orienteering

activities the members are. Therefore, information on the proportion of the population, ages 7–70, actively training and competing is provided in Table 19.3 (Riksidrottsförbundet 2011). These data are similar to those on memberships in Table 19.1 but also show that the membership itself is no guarantee for being active in training and competition. This is especially true for the older age groups.

**Table 19.3** Training and competition in sport clubs, proportionate to the total population in each age group (%)

| Age group | Women | Men | Total |
|---|---|---|---|
| 7–14 | 64.1 | 73.6 | 69.0 |
| 15–19 | 31.8 | 44.9 | 38.6 |
| 20–29 | 15.9 | 26.1 | 21.1 |
| 30–39 | 5.6 | 24.9 | 15.4 |
| 40–49 | 6.6 | 20.0 | 13.4 |
| 50–59 | 3.7 | 13.6 | 8.7 |
| 60–70 | 5.6 | 13.3 | 9.4 |

**Table 19.4** Exercise activities, proportionate to the total population in each age group (%)

| Age group | Women | Men | Total |
|---|---|---|---|
| 7–14 | 95 | 93 | 94 |
| 15–19 | 85 | 70 | 77 |
| 20–29 | 82 | 73 | 77 |
| 30–39 | 70 | 64 | 67 |
| 40–49 | 77 | 67 | 72 |
| 50–59 | 79 | 59 | 69 |
| 60–70 | 84 | 68 | 76 |

In comparison it is evident that membership rates for age groups 7–14, 15–19 and 20–29 are on average some 10 percentage points higher than those for training and competition in sport clubs. For the older age groups the difference is on average some 25 percentage points.

These proportions can be compared to the overall levels of physical activity in the population. Table 19.4 (Riksidrottsförbundet 2011) shows the proportion of the population ages 7–70, exercising at least once a week for 20 min. When comparing the rates for training and competition in sport clubs in Table 19.3 and those for exercise activities in Table 19.4 it is evident that while club sport activities are popular with the younger age groups, large proportions of the population in each age group are active outside voluntary and membership-based club sport, assumedly in self-organised forms and/or at private gyms and fitness clubs. These proportions grow with increasing age. The turning point seems to occur between the age groups 15–19 and 20–29, which coincides with the shift from junior to adult participation in most sports.

An indicator on how training and competition is distributed by sport is provided by looking into the number of activities sport clubs receive public funding for. But since funding is granted only to children and youth 7–20 years old, Table 19.5 shows the ten sports with the most activities for participants 7–20. Table 19.5 (Centrum för idrottsforskning 2013) shows that football gathers the most participants and also arranges the most activities. But despite its sixth position in the number of memberships in Table 19.2, floorball is number two when it comes to number of participants 7–20 years old, thus placing itself as the second biggest sport for children and youth in Sweden. Continuing the comparison with Table 19.2 it becomes clear how football, despite its large numbers of participants and activities,

**Table 19.5** Sport club activities by sport

| Sport | Number of participants | Sport | Number of activities |
|---|---|---|---|
| Football | 18,344,900 | Football | 1,675,160 |
| Floorball | 5,129,520 | Equestrian | 438,337 |
| Ice hockey | 4,194,882 | Floorball | 424,888 |
| Handball | 2,970,865 | Tennis | 340,230 |
| Equestrian | 2,711,726 | Ice hockey | 316,645 |
| Basketball | 2,557,718 | Swimming | 298,374 |
| Gymnastics | 2,134,892 | Basketball | 270,654 |
| Swimming | 1,989,275 | Handball | 269,084 |
| Tennis | 1,609,469 | Gymnastics | 225,729 |
| Athletics | 1,439,162 | Athletics | 194,399 |

**Table 19.6** Participation in sport club activities by sex, age group, family situation, ethnicity and socioeconomic background, proportionate to the total population in each age group (%)

| | Team sports | | Other sports | |
|---|---|---|---|---|
| | Girls | Boys | Girls | Boys |
| All children, ages 7–15 | 36 | 52 | 38 | 32 |
| Ages 7–9 | 35 | 54 | 40 | 32 |
| Ages 10–12 | 40 | 55 | 37 | 37 |
| Ages 13–15 | 32 | 48 | 36 | 27 |
| Children in single-parent households | 23 | 46 | 33 | 27 |
| Children in two-parent households | 38 | 54 | 38 | 33 |
| Children to parents born abroad | 16 | 38 | 12 | 15 |
| Children to parents born in Sweden | 38 | 54 | 40 | 34 |
| Children to parents with blue-collar occupations | 31 | 50 | 28 | 26 |
| Children to parents with white-collar occupations | 40 | 55 | 43 | 36 |

gathers less participants than floorball, ice hockey and handball relative to their number of members. One possible explanation could be the shorter season for football, practised mainly outdoors, compared to the relatively longer seasons for floorball, ice hockey and handball, practised almost exclusively indoors. Worth noticing is that half of the sports on the *Top-ten list* is individual sports.

Sport club participation is also socially stratified, especially for children and youth. By looking into parameters such as whether a child is brought up by one or two parents in the household, if the parents are born in another country, the parents' line of work and the household's financial situation, it is evident that sport club activities are not equally accessible to all social groups. Table 19.6 (Centrum för idrottsforskning 2013) shows how participation in voluntary and membership-based club sport is distributed along these parameters. It also shows the distribution by type of sport. Data show that club sport activities are less accessible for girls in general, for children in single-parent households than for children in two-parent households, for children to parents born abroad than for children to parents born in

**Table 19.7** Sport leaders

| | | Women | | Men | | | |
|---|---|---|---|---|---|---|---|
| | | Numbers | % | Numbers | % | Total | % |
| Total | | 227,000 | 6.1 | 430,000 | 11.2 | 657,000 | 8.6 |
| Age group | 7–14 | 18,000 | 4.7 | 9,000 | 2.1 | 27,000 | 3.4 |
| | 15–19 | 43,000 | 15.2 | 22,000 | 7.7 | 65,000 | 11.4 |
| | 20–29 | 26,000 | 4.2 | 48,000 | 7.5 | 73,000 | 5.9 |
| | 30–39 | 43,000 | 7.3 | 76,000 | 12.2 | 119,000 | 9.9 |
| | 40–49 | 66,000 | 10.2 | 154,000 | 23.3 | 220,000 | 16.9 |
| | 50–59 | 23,000 | 3.9 | 69,000 | 11.8 | 92,000 | 7.9 |
| | 60–70 | 10,000 | 1.6 | 50,000 | 8.1 | 61,000 | 4.8 |

Sweden and for children to parents with blue-collar occupations compared to children to parents with white-collar occupations. Combining these parameters, club sport activities become least accessible for girls with parents born abroad, living in single-parent households, with parents holding blue-collar occupations. Team sports are in general more accessible than individual sports, with regard to social stratification, even if this particular pattern is less conclusive.

However, being part of a sport club is not just about training and competing. Table 19.7 (Riksidrottsförbundet 2011) shows the numbers and proportion of the population taking on leadership positions in sport divided by sex and age group. A leadership position is defined as formal duties as trainers, coaches, board members and similar assignments. The data show that 657,000 individuals are engaged as leaders in voluntary and membership-based club sport, nearly 10 % of the population aged 7–70. They also show that men are more likely to be sport leaders than women and that the typical sport leader is a man in his 40s.

The distribution of leader positions in sport is similar to the social stratification of participation in sport club activities in terms of socioeconomic background. Table 19.8 (Centrum för idrottsforskning 2013) shows the numbers and proportions of the population taking on leadership positions in sport divided by educational level. The data shows that the proportion with leadership positions increases with educational level, suggesting that volunteer engagement is connected to educational background. Another explanation is connected to professionalisation, suggesting that university and college programmes for coaches, administrators and managers contribute to the high proportion of sport leaders with post-upper secondary school education to some extent.

The aforementioned numbers point to the importance of sport clubs to the Swedish society. It is by far the most popular organised leisure time activity for Swedish citizens and especially for children and youth (Hvenmark 2008). It is also the civic engagement gathering the largest group by far. One-fifth of all volunteer work in Sweden is carried out within sport (the second largest group—10 %—is volunteering for tenant unions, Olsson et al. 2005). If these leaders would dedicate 5 h per week, 36 weeks per year, to their engagement, it would be equivalent to some 70,000 jobs (Riksidrottsförbundet 2010).

**Table 19.8** Leadership positions by educational background

| Education | Numbers | % | Population |
|---|---|---|---|
| Pre-upper secondary school level | 168,000 | 7 | 2,501,000 |
| Upper secondary school level | 266,000 | 9 | 2,909,000 |
| Post-upper secondary school level | 224,000 | 10 | 2,148,000 |

## 19.4 Characteristics of Sport Clubs

As conveyed under previous headings, Swedish sport clubs are forced to be organised in the voluntary, non-profit and membership-based form in order to be eligible for membership in a NSF and the SSC, which in turn is a condition for receiving government support. It is also a condition for participating in competitive sport since each NSF has monopoly on authorising competitions, tournaments, cups and leagues in the sport in question. The monopoly has no legal jurisdiction but is upheld by the national sport federations' exclusive right to appoint national teams and international representation by their affiliation to an international sport federation (Lindholm 2013). These conditions taken together work in practice in excluding commercial actors, at least in the more traditional sports. Certainly, some traditionally commercialised sports such as harness racing or traditionally professionalised sports such as professional boxing are examples on sports not affiliated to the SSC. But such examples are still few, even if newer sports such as mixed martial arts and roller derby are challenging the traditional competition system arranged by NSFs affiliated to the SSC with competition systems franchised by international actors and based on commercial principles. Given these circumstances, most leisure-time sport activities are arranged in voluntary and membership-based sport clubs, regardless of form, intensity and purpose of the activities. Hence, recreational and professional, children's and adult, sport-for-all and elite, keep-fit and competitive sport activities coexist within the same organisational form. This is often referred to as another cornerstone of Swedish voluntary and membership-based club sport. Certainly there are physical and competitive activities arranged by training centres, fitness clubs, fun runs and similar, but such activities are not considered to be part of Swedish club sport.

The characteristics of Swedish sport clubs can be portrayed in many ways (Riksidrottsförbundet 2005b). In terms of size, 38 % are to be considered as small sport clubs (<50 members), 36 % as medium-sized clubs (50–199 members) and 26 % as big clubs (200< members). In terms of age, 36 % are established before 1960, and 17 % are established after 1995. In terms of gender, 41 % are to be considered as male sport clubs (>70 % male members) and 12 % as female sport clubs (>70 % female members). Gender is also visible with regard to type of sport. Table 19.9 (Centrum för idrottsforskning 2014) shows the distribution in terms of gender. Ice hockey and shooting are less surprisingly typical male domains while equestrian and figure skating are the traditional female domains.

**Table 19.9** Distribution of members in terms of gender and sport (%)

| Sports with low proportions of female members | % | Sports with equal distribution of members | % | Sports with high proportions of female members | % |
|---|---|---|---|---|---|
| Ice hockey | 6 | Handball | 50 | Equestrian | 90 |
| Shooting | 17 | Basketball | 49 | Figure skating | 84 |
| Table tennis | 20 | Deaf sports | 49 | Gymnastics | 77 |
| Floorball | 21 | Rowing | 49 | Judo | 71 |
| Cycling | 22 | Walking | 47 | Athletics | 63 |
| Motor cycling | 23 | Swimming | 53 | Volleyball | 62 |
| Bowling | 25 | School sports | 46 | Dance sports | 60 |

One way of looking at activities arranged by sport clubs is by dividing them by target group and primary purpose. Table 19.10 (Riksidrottsförbundet 2005b) shows a relatively proportionate distribution of activities with competitive sport activities for adults and sport activities for children together constituting the main part of a sport club's repertoire. Sport activities for children under 12 are not divided by purpose since the policy programme guiding all sport club's activities stipulates that children's sport should not be competitive in its primary nature but focus on fun, play and games (Riksidrottsförbundet 2005a).

Another way of looking at sport club activities is by categorising them as single- or multiple-sport clubs. The absolute majority of Swedish sport clubs are single-sport clubs (85 %). Less than 3 % carry more than three sports on their repertoire (Riksidrottsförbundet 2005b). Sport club activities can also be categorised as being performed in teams or individually. Almost half (48 %) of the Swedish sport clubs carry so-called individual sports on their repertoire, while a third (29 %) offer team sports. A mere 4 % of the clubs have both individual and team sports represented (18 % carry sports that are classified as neither individual nor team sports such as gymnastics, bobsleigh and luge, deaf sports, Paralympic sports and school sports). Clubs with team sports exclusively on their repertoire are in general larger clubs, both in terms of number of members and in turnover (Centrum för idrottsforskning 2014).

Apart from sport activities, 16 % of the Swedish sport clubs run extracurricular activities such as youth recreation centres and similar, 43 % run and/or own sport facilities and 34 % cooperate with schools at field days, in physical education classes or as part of the training in upper secondary elite sport schools (Riksidrottsförbundet 2005b), showing how Swedish sport clubs are acting as more than just organisers of sport activities but are an integral part of both the public and the private sector, engaged in several different industrial branches such as social work, real estate and education.

As previously mentioned, sport activities are led and managed by some 657,000 leaders. But 27 % of the Swedish sport clubs also have employed staff, 7 % have one or more female full-time employees and 15 % have one or more male full-time employees, 10 % have one or more female part-time employees and 12 % have one or more male part-time employees (Riksidrottsförbundet 2005b). These proportions

**Table 19.10** Sport club activities by target group and purpose (%)

| Activities | % |
|---|---|
| Competitive sport activities for adults (21<) | 24 |
| Sport activities for children (<12) | 23 |
| Recreational sport activities for adults (21<) | 20 |
| Recreational sport activities for youth (13–20) | 19 |
| Competitive sport activities for youth (13–20) | 14 |

**Table 19.11** Proportions of sport clubs with paid staff by sport (%)

| Sport | % |
|---|---|
| Golf | 68 |
| Ice hockey | 65 |
| Tennis | 63 |
| Football | 55 |
| Handball | 51 |
| Swimming | 48 |
| Basketball | 42 |
| Floorball | 42 |
| Equestrian | 41 |
| Table tennis | 40 |
| Gymnastics | 37 |
| Athletics | 35 |
| Volleyball | 32 |
| Badminton | 32 |
| Boule | 31 |
| Skiing | 29 |
| Dance sports | 28 |
| Sailing | 26 |
| Orienteering | 22 |
| Cycling | 17 |
| School sports | 15 |
| Bowling | 11 |
| Motor cycling | 11 |
| Budo and martial arts | 8 |
| Shooting | 4 |

indicate that some 5,500, at the very least, are employed by Swedish sport clubs. The actual number is probably higher given the nature of the question *one employee or more*. In clubs participating in the higher divisions for larger team sports, the number is probably much higher since most players in such teams are listed as employees. A football or an ice hockey club playing in one of the two highest divisions, for instance, would have up to 30 employees counting players only. In addition, such clubs would most probably have also administrative staff employed adding to that number. Table 19.11 (Centrum för idrottsforskning 2014) shows the proportion of clubs employing paid staff, divided by sport. It shows how paid staff

**Table 19.12** Proportions of clubs with paid staff by type of duties (the ten sports where paid staff is most common, %)

| Sport | One employee or more | Administration | Performance |
|---|---|---|---|
| Golf | 68 | 63 | 44 |
| Ice hockey | 65 | 59 | 37 |
| Tennis | 63 | 43 | 55 |
| Football | 55 | 44 | 33 |
| Handball | 51 | 46 | 28 |
| Swimming | 48 | 37 | 37 |
| Floorball | 42 | 35 | 22 |
| Basketball | 42 | 34 | 33 |
| Equestrian | 41 | 22 | 40 |
| Table tennis | 40 | 32 | 24 |
| Mean for all sports | 31 | 22 | 22 |

are more common in clubs offering team sports and in clubs with facilities in need of caretaking and administration.

Being employed, however, involves different duties in different sports. By separating duties connected to the performance of sport such as those performed by athletes and leaders/coaches, and the administration of sport such as those performed by clerks and managers, Table 19.12 (Centrum för idrottsforskning 2014) shows that employments for duties connected to the administration of sport and employments for duties connected to the performance of sport are equally common on an average. In tennis and equestrian, however, employments for duties connected to the performance of sport are more common. For team sports in general it is more common to have staff performing administrative duties while for individual sports in general it is more common to have staff performing duties connected to the performance of sport.

The professionalisation of voluntary and membership-based club sport in Sweden is also shown in the constitution of boards of sport clubs. During the last few decades it has become more and more common to engage professionals from the business sphere for the club's strategic operations. There are, however, differences between clubs with large and small financial turnovers (Centrum för idrottsforskning 2014). Among clubs with large financial turnovers 64 % have at least one business executive on the board. Corresponding proportion among clubs with small financial turnovers is 24 %. Business executives are more common in clubs offering team sports than in clubs offering individual sports, a fact that might be connected to their proportionately larger size and financial turnover. Golf, however, is the deviant case where 72 % of the clubs have at least one business executive on the board. In addition, 43 % of them also have a professional marketer on the board. Table 19.13 (Centrum för idrottsforskning 2014) shows the proportions of clubs with business professionals on their boards. Equally common is to have at least one business executive on the board as having no business professionals at all on the board.

**Table 19.13** Proportions of clubs with business professionals on their boards (%, possible to mark more than one alternative)

| Professional competence | % |
|---|---|
| Business executive | 38 |
| Salesperson | 25 |
| Business administrator | 20 |
| Accountant | 19 |
| Marketer | 14 |
| Communicator | 10 |
| Lawyer | 5 |
| None of the above | 38 |

**Table 19.14** Sport clubs' expenses (%)

| Cost | % |
|---|---|
| Training and competition | 26.5 |
| Rent for facilities | 15.8 |
| Equipment | 14.4 |
| Miscellaneous | 13.2 |
| Facilities (running costs, interest, depreciation) | 12.1 |
| Salaries | 7.1 |
| Administration (postage, phone, etc.) | 5.8 |
| Remuneration to athletes and leaders | 5.0 |

**Table 19.15** Proportions of sport clubs remunerating members with official duties (%, possible to mark more than one alternative)

| Official duty | % |
|---|---|
| Leaders/coaches | 38 |
| Others | 14 |
| Athletes | 7 |
| Board members | 7 |
| Officials | 5 |
| No remuneration | 55 |

The cost of having employees constitutes some 7 % of sport clubs' expenses. Table 19.14 (Riksidrottsförbundet 2005b) shows the total distribution of expenses. The proportions show that while salaries might be a large expenditure and a problem for clubs participating in elite sport they constitute only 7.1 % of the average sport club's expenditure. Even if this proportion is added to the costs for remuneration to athletes and leaders, which is essentially the same type of cost, the total proportion is still lower than those for miscellaneous, equipment, facilities, travels, training and competition (travels, accommodation and entry fees). The costs associated with training and competition constitute the largest cost for the average Swedish sport club.

Concerning remuneration to athletes and leaders specifically, Table 19.15 (Centrum för idrottsforskning 2014) shows how remuneration is distributed among athletes, leaders/coaches, board members, officials and others. It shows that most clubs are not remunerating their members with official duties in any way at all. In addition, as indicated in Table 19.14, even if 45 % of Swedish sport clubs report

**Table 19.16** Distribution of type of remuneration (%, possible to mark more than one alternative)

| Type of remuneration | % |
|---|---|
| Money | 90 |
| Products | 13 |
| Other | 8 |
| Services | 4 |
| Don't know | 1 |

**Table 19.17** Sport clubs' revenues (%)

| Revenues | % |
|---|---|
| Membership fees | 22.8 |
| Lotteries | 17.5 |
| Miscellaneous | 10.3 |
| Municipal grants (to activities) | 8.8 |
| Events (entry fees, tickets) | 8.0 |
| Corporate sponsoring and advertisements | 6.8 |
| Government grants | 6.7 |
| Training fees | 6.5 |
| Municipal grants (to facilities) | 4.6 |
| Sales | 4.1 |
| Miscellaneous grants and donations | 3.8 |

remuneration to leaders/coaches and athletes, the size of the remuneration is probably small since it constitutes a mere 5 % of the average sport club's expenditure. Remuneration to leaders/coaches is most common in sport clubs offering gymnastics, football, ice hockey, tennis and swimming. Remuneration to others is most common in sport clubs offering ice hockey and golf, probably due to the nature of the administrative operations surrounding the facilities for such sports. Remuneration to athletes is most common in sport clubs offering ice hockey, handball and athletics. No remuneration is most common in clubs offering shooting, bowling, orienteering, cycling, budo and martial arts and motor sports.

Remuneration is however a broad concept. It spans from proper salaries to more informal gifts and barter transactions. Table 19.16 (Centrum för idrottsforskning 2014) shows that money is by far the most common form of compensation. In the category *Other*, examples provided are gift cards, reduced membership fees, free admissions to the club's Christmas party and mileage. Again worth noticing is that while money is the most common type of remuneration, it is probably small amounts given the small proportion of the average club's total expenditure as displayed in Table 19.14.

Sport club's costs are covered by membership and training fees to large parts, amounting to some 30 % of the sport clubs' revenues. Table 19.17 (Riksidrottsförbundet 2005b) shows the total distribution of revenues. It shows that Swedish sport clubs are self-funded to large extent since membership fees, lottery sales, entry fees and tickets, training fees and sales together combine into almost 60 % of the revenues of a Swedish sport club. So even if Swedish sport often is portrayed as being heavily dependent on public subsidies, they only constitute some 24 % of the total revenues.

**Table 19.18** Sport clubs' financial turnover (%)

| Financial turnover | % |
|---|---|
| € –2,000 | 10 |
| €2,001–5,000 | 11 |
| €5,001–10,000 | 12 |
| €10,001–25,000 | 16 |
| €25,001–50,000 | 16 |
| €50,001–100,000 | 11 |
| €100,001–250,000 | 11 |
| €250,001–500,000 | 5 |
| €500,001– | 3 |

Some differences between sports can however be noted. For clubs offering golf, sailing, cycling and motor sports, public subsidies seem to be of less importance, while corporate sponsoring seems to be more important for clubs offering golf, ice hockey and football. In general, corporate sponsoring is a more important revenue source for clubs offering team sports than for clubs offering individual sports. The same relationship exists between clubs located in rural areas compared to clubs located in cities (Centrum för idrottsforskning 2014). Possible explanations could be related to the higher costs associated with certain sports and the higher competition over corporate sponsors in urban areas.

In terms of financial turnover, many clubs are to be considered as small clubs. Table 19.18 (Centrum för idrottsforskning 2014) shows the distribution of sport clubs in relation to financial turnover. Almost half of the Swedish sport clubs' turnover is less than €25,000. Only a very small proportion of the clubs has a financial turnover above €500,000. Golf affiliates the most clubs with a turnover above €100,000 (68 %). Other sports affiliating clubs with large turnovers are ice hockey, tennis, handball and football. Budo and martial arts, shooting, badminton and boule are found at the other end of the spectrum.

As evident in Table 19.18, resources are scarce for most sport clubs and making ends meet is reported by many club treasurers as a significant challenge for the club. Table 19.19 shows treasurers' assessments of sport clubs' financial situation. It shows how treasurers' perceptions about sport clubs' financial situation in general are rather pessimistic. Nearly 40 % of them estimate the financial situation for sport clubs in general as poor. Paradoxically enough, they report fairly good or very good finances for the club they represent themselves. On the one hand this phenomenon could be a result of the rather pessimistic image of sport clubs' economy portrayed in the media, leading to pessimistic estimates of other sport clubs' economy. On the other hand, it could be a result of an attempt to idealise the responding treasurer's own effort, leading to optimistic estimates of the treasurer's own club.

Clubs offering team sports report to a larger extent poor financial situations than do clubs offering individual sports. So do smaller clubs compared to larger, and clubs with employed staff compared to clubs without employed staff. Clubs offering athletics, skiing, orienteering, boule and cycling have in general brighter financial

**Table 19.19** The financial situation of sport clubs (%)

| | My club | Other clubs in the same sport | Sport clubs in general |
|---|---|---|---|
| Very good | 12 | 0 | 0 |
| Fairly good | 39 | 9 | 6 |
| Neither good nor bad | 29 | 28 | 29 |
| Fairly poor | 15 | 27 | 36 |
| Very poor | 4 | 4 | 3 |
| Don't know | 0 | 31 | 26 |

**Table 19.20** Experienced threats against club development (%, possible to mark more than one alternative)

| Threats | % |
|---|---|
| Recruiting leaders/coaches/officials | 71 |
| Retaining youth | 58 |
| Recruiting and retaining corporate sponsors | 55 |
| Recruiting members | 47 |
| Applying for subsidies and grants | 45 |
| Reaching sporting goals and ambitions | 29 |
| Competition from private sector alternatives | 18 |

outlooks, while clubs offering ice hockey and equestrian experience the opposite (Centrum för idrottsforskning 2014).

Financial turnover, costs and revenues are not the primary concerns for Swedish sport clubs though. Experienced bottlenecks and challenges are instead decreasing volunteer efforts. Table 19.20 (Centrum för idrottsforskning 2014) shows how sport clubs experience the biggest threats against the development of the club. In practice, three of the four most experienced threats are essentially the same—a lack of members needed for running the operations of the club.

Concerning experienced difficulties in recruiting leaders/coaches/officials specifically, the experiences differ slightly between clubs in different sports. In Table 19.21 (Centrum för idrottsforskning 2014), these differences, yet small, are displayed. More sport clubs offering team sports experience difficulties in recruiting leaders/coaches/officials than clubs offering individual sports do, which could depend on their relatively bigger need for many volunteers due to the relatively larger size of operations.

Regarding experienced difficulties in retaining youth specifically, the experiences again differ slightly between clubs in different sports. In Table 19.22 (Centrum för idrottsforskning 2014), these differences are displayed. Again, more sport clubs offering team sports experience difficulties in retaining youth than clubs offering individual sports do.

In relation to the experienced difficulties in recruiting and retaining corporate sponsors specifically, the experiences again differ slightly between clubs. However, given the nature of the question, results are not only divided by type of sport but also by scope, local demography and financial turnover. Table 19.23 (Centrum för idrottsforskning 2014) shows that more clubs with elite ambitions experience

**Table 19.21** Experienced difficulties in recruiting leaders/coaches/officials by sport (response alternatives very challenging and challenging, %)

| Sport | % |
|---|---|
| Gymnastics | 80 |
| Football | 78 |
| Swimming | 77 |
| Ice hockey | 75 |
| Athletics | 75 |
| Average for team sports clubs | 74 |
| Average for all sport clubs | 70 |
| Average for individual sports clubs | 68 |
| Golf | 60 |

**Table 19.22** Experienced difficulties in retaining youth by sport (response alternatives very challenging and challenging, %)

| Sport | % |
|---|---|
| Orienteering | 73 |
| Golf | 69 |
| Ice hockey | 68 |
| Average for all clubs | 58 |
| Basketball | 46 |
| Swimming | 44 |
| Volleyball | 41 |

**Table 19.23** Experienced difficulties in recruiting and retaining corporate sponsors by scope, type of sport, local demography and financial turnover (response alternatives very challenging and challenging, %)

| Scope | % |
|---|---|
| Elite focus | 68 |
| No elite focus | 49 |
| **Type of sport** | |
| Team sports clubs | 65 |
| Individual sports clubs | 54 |
| **Local demography** | |
| Large city | 59 |
| City | 54 |
| Rural area | 52 |
| **Financial turnover** | |
| High | 73 |
| Medium | 57 |
| Low | 42 |
| Average for all sport clubs | 55 |

difficulties than clubs with no such ambitions do, which could depend on the fact that these clubs are in greater need of such resources. It also shows how more clubs offering team sports and more clubs located in the larger cities experience difficulties than their counterparts offering individual sports and being located in smaller cities or in rural areas do. One explanation to this phenomenon could be these clubs' greater need of resources and tougher competition over corporate sponsors in the more densely populated areas.

**Table 19.24** Experienced difficulties in recruiting members by sport (response alternatives very challenging and challenging, %)

| Sport | % |
|---|---|
| Golf | 72 |
| Shooting | 55 |
| Ice hockey | 54 |
| Average for all sport clubs | 47 |
| Equestrian | 45 |
| Athletics | 38 |
| Tennis | 36 |
| Swimming | 28 |

With regard to experienced difficulties in recruiting members specifically, the experiences again differ slightly between clubs in terms of the sport they offer, the size of the club and the size of the financial turnover. More of the smaller clubs and of the clubs with low financial turnovers find recruiting members difficult than their large counterparts and those with high financial turnovers do. In Table 19.24 (Centrum för idrottsforskning 2014), some of these differences are displayed. For most sports in Table 19.24, the difficulties could have their background in the clubs' greater need for many members in order to cover the costs for their often expensive facilities.

## 19.5 The Political Programming and Governance of Sport Clubs Through Policy Programmes

As shown in Table 19.20, decreasing membership base is one of the main concerns for Swedish sport clubs. This has also been a concern for the government when providing funds for activating the Swedish population—physically and civically. Since much of the legitimacy of supporting voluntary and membership-based club sport with taxpayers' money rests on organised sport's ability to engage large parts of the population, it has become vital for organised sport and the government alike to account for high membership numbers. Aiming at high numbers and an equal distribution of government funds to different social groups, the government has on a number of occasions launched special programmes targeting more or less specific groups and/or aims. From the end of the 1990s, four large programmes of this kind have been initiated (SOU 2008): *Project Local Sport Development*, 1998–2002 (€7 million), *The large children's and youth venture*, 2001–2004 (€13.5 million), *The Handshake*, 2002–2006 (€100 million) and *The lift for Sport*, 2007–2011 (€200 million).

In these examples, it becomes evident though that the supplementary support to sport is more than just about extra funding. It is also about political programming of sport. In a large-scale evaluation of the latest programme, The Lift for Sport, data show how sport clubs specifically are made responsible for meeting explicit and societal, non-sport goals (Karp et al. 2012). In the programme, the government commissioned the SSC to develop activities for more children and youth and develop activities, so they choose to be active in sport longer. The basic idea of the programme was to stimulate development work in NSFs and to let sport clubs apply for funding for projects aimed at working towards the ambitions in the programme manifesto corresponding to the guidelines in the regular sport policy programme (Riksidrottsförbundet 2005a).

By analysing policy documents, interviews with 27 key personnel in distributing the programme funds in five NSFs, 2,563 project applications to these federations made by sport clubs for programme funding and 486 questionnaires filled out by representatives of the sport clubs applying for funding, results show how the increase of political programming of club sport has taken form. They show that the government ambition is to govern sport in a specific direction, both in terms of content (widened recruitment) and in terms of governing per se (NSFs are provided with resources to develop themselves). In addition, the government formulated key performance indicators which show that accountability is key to the process and that evidence, in terms of numbers, is the way of keeping scores.

This responsibilisation of the recipient, evident in the relationship between the government and sport, is clearly expressed also in the relationship between the SSC and the NSFs. The NSFs were expected to provide data to an overall programme evaluation and to account for how they plan to follow up on their development plan. They were also responsible for the appropriate use of allotted resources and for monitoring club activities by establishing contracts with clubs receiving project funds. The contracts should regulate project conformity with programme aims and accounts from receiving clubs. The analyses of the NSFs' development plans show that the NSFs have taken up the governing principles in the above-mentioned relationships—pushing the responsibility for development further down the chain of command. However, they have not regulated themselves as desired by the government and the SSC, i.e. identifying their own specific needs and developing their own specific strategies to address those needs. Instead, aims are mirror images of the general ambitions formulated by the government and the SSC (expansion, i.e. more leaders, facilities and clubs, which, in turn, are expected to result in more participants that will participate longer), even if the issue of facilities for example is not a problem for the NSF in question. The development plans show how the NSFs reproduce the model used by the government in its governing of the SSC and, in turn, by the confederation in its governing of the NSFs, implying that the governing body relinquishes the responsibility for the design of the programme to the governed one. In the development plans it is noticeable how the processes of autonomisation and responsibilisation continue with the NSFs as senders and the sport clubs as recipients. These new modes of governing work in passing the responsibility for reaching programme goals to the next organisation in line.

Signs of these processes are also visible in the analyses of the interviews. In these analyses, it appears that the programme is a much welcomed initiative and that the representatives are receptive to the demands, direction and follow-ups inherent in the programme. Governing in terms of checks and balances is perceived as a natural part of the development and something that must be expected as part of these types of directed grants. Their own explanation of that is the experienced concordance between programme aims and the NSFs' aims for regular activities. It is evident that programme aims are merged with the NSFs' aims for regular activities, thereby making it possible for them to tone down expectations and relieve themselves of some of the responsibility laid upon them for reaching key performance indicators.

However, in the analyses of project applications for programme funds, a slightly different picture emerges. Certainly, the projects that clubs seek funds for are in the broad outlines aligned with overall government aims, guidelines from the SSC and NSFs' development plans. However, many of the guidelines in the regular policy programme, which applications should adhere to, are conspicuous by their absence in the analysed project applications. The analysis of the contents of the project applications in relation to the regular policy programme guidelines shows very few applications explicitly expressing ambitions relating to promoting respect for others (0.15 %), considering participants' views (0.15 %) and promoting fair play (0.35 %). These proportions can be compared to those of developing leaders (22.40 %), developing facilities (12.00 %) and developing rules and policies (22.45 %).

The processes of self-regulation and responsibilisation observed between the government and the SSC and between the confederation and the NSFs are also in play between the NSFs and the sport clubs. However, the processes have not resulted in the self-regulation and accepted responsibility aimed for, at least not by judging from the content in the applications for programme funds. When left free to formulate project ideas, sport clubs conform to the main ideas of the programme rather than tailoring projects to their specific needs. As a result, some aspects of development agreed on in the regular policy programme are unattended. Another example of that is visible in the analysis of the focus in the applications in relation to the overall aim of increasing gender and class equality. Very few applications explicitly express ambitions to increase gender equality (2.25 %), increase class equality (2.80 %) or increase gender and class equality (4.35 %).

The analyses of the questionnaires also show how the alignment with overall government aims, SSC guidelines and NSFs' development plans is high, at least in broad outlines. But only half of the respondents actually know about the content of the NSF development plan (53 % fairly poor knowledge/very poor knowledge/no knowledge). This result suggests that half of the programme activities arranged are designed without regard to the programme aims even if many activities show concordance per se. The result also lends further support to the previous analysis, suggesting that the self-regulation and responsibility handed down from the NSFs are not acted upon by the sport clubs.

This impression is strengthened by the analysis of target groups for project activities. Children and youth in general represent the main target group for 68 % of the studied projects while children with immigrant backgrounds (19 %), children with disabilities (19 %) and children from low-income households (13 %) are targeted less. This result shows that the overarching aim of the programme, that *all work should consider gender and class equality*, is not a high priority for the sport clubs.

The sport clubs' priorities are also visible in the analysis of their experiences regarding the programme as a means for club development, which was another overarching aim of the programme. This analysis shows that the programme has, to the least extent, contributed to increased class equality and increased gender equality. A similar impression is gained from the analysis of perceived results of project activities. This analysis shows that sport club representatives perceive recruitment of children from low-income households and recruitment of leaders from low-income households to be the least visible results of arranged programme activities. These analyses show how sport clubs prioritise and how they have not accepted responsibility for some of the specific features in the programme ambitions, handed down from the government via the SSC and the NSFs.

While The Lift for Sport as the latest and largest government intervention in sport has brought with it more specific and more instrumental goals for sport to attain through new governing instruments leaning on responsibilisation and demands on accountability, it has not been able to stimulate the self-regulation aimed for. Instead, each organisation in the chain of command has forwarded the responsibility for development, accountability for results and demands on self-regulation to the next organisation in line, leaving sport clubs with the lion's share of the responsibility for the development of voluntary and membership-based club sport in Sweden. However, this responsibility has been disregarded to large parts also at club level. Although applications adhere to some of the main ideas of the programme, many of them are left unattended. Ironically enough, many of the guidelines left unattended are the ones considered most important by the Swedish research community (SOU 2008), government (Regeringen 2011) and SSC (Riksidrottsförbundet 2005b) in addressing many of the problems Swedish sport is facing, such as unhealthy pressure from coaches, peers and parents; dropout in early years and poor recruitment from underrepresented groups. It is evident that neither government missives, programme guidelines and development plans nor additional and earmarked resources have been able to stimulate development through self-regulation and, in the end, to secure envisioned effects. On the contrary, it seems the power and informal authority to govern the grass-roots activities in sport remain in the hands of the implementers: the sport clubs.

In understanding these phenomena, Fahlén et al. (2014) propose moving beneath surface explanations, such as "policy implementation in the end comes down to the people who actually implement it" (Lipsky 1980, p. 8) and "sport policy [is] a 'weak' policy area" (Grix 2010, p. 169). They suggest instead that the SSC and the NSFs, on one hand, are, in their capacity as representative organs, more concerned with acting in accordance with official politics and dependent on the legitimacy connected with that compliance. The sport clubs, on the other hand, are, in their capacity as membership-based organisers, more concerned with the needs and wishes of their existing members (and dependent on their resources), rather than with answering to political expectations regarding recruitment of new participants and equality (Stenling 2013). Fahlén et al. (2014) argue that it is easier to align oneself with organisations higher up in the hierarchy when the costs for alignments are low (i.e. the SSC and the NSFs can align their operations by simply rephrasing policy documents and guidelines) compared to when they are high (i.e. sport clubs actually have to change the basic idea of their activities from we-for-us to us-for-them). Similar to the findings reported by Keat and Sam (2013), they claim that if costs appear too high, the risk of sports clubs opting out increases.

In sum, while political programming of sport clubs increases, their influence over core activities seems unaffected. This result is the opposite of what has been reported on in research on sport in, for example, the UK (Goodwin and Grix 2011), and Fahlén et al. (2014) suggest that this deviation is associated with the Scandinavian and Swedish pattern of institutional arrangements, organisational and cultural, hallmarked by large national voluntary sports organisations with almost a monopoly on competitive sports as described earlier. In contrast to Norberg's (2011) suggestion that the implicit contract is on its way to being renegotiated to the benefit of more government control, they argue that the component of voluntariness inherent in SSC's part of the contract trumps the government's stake in providing resources. As long as the government depends on voluntary efforts for reaching more instrumental goals, power will remain with sport. This argument also resonates with the findings reported in the studies of the Danish (The Sport Policy Idea Programme) and Norwegian (The Sports City Programme) counterparts to The Lift for Sport, showing that the voluntary-based institutional arrangement in the Scandinavian countries still provides a stronghold against top-down initiatives with external goals differing too much from sports clubs' core activities (Ibsen 2002; Skille 2008).

## 19.6 Summary and Concluding Remarks

In summary it can be concluded that voluntary and membership-based club sport is an integral part of the Swedish society and acts as a trusted partner in the Swedish welfare system, for which it enjoys extensive financial support. Most Swedes are or have been involved in a sport club in one capacity or the other, which often places Sweden on top in international comparisons of sport participation. Its voluntary and non-profit organisational form has availed for high participation rates in most social groups. In parallel, however, sport has begun experiencing challenges in recruiting volunteers, counteracting social stratification in participation patterns, decreasing dropouts, competing with private sector alternatives and raising necessary funds. In addition, societal expectations on sport's delivery of social goods in general has increased, placing many sport clubs in an area of tensions between their members' needs and wishes and the conditions that increasingly follow with the financial support from the public. The latter is particularly evident in the more recent political programming of sport which has become increasingly common through various sport policy programmes aiming at increased participation and the attainment of non-sport goals. That notwithstanding, the autonomy of voluntary and membership-based sport clubs seems intact, still providing an outlet for the self-determination needed for civic engagement.

## References

Bergsgard NA, Norberg J (2010) Sports policy and politics—the Scandinavian way. Sport Soc Cult Commerce Media Politics 13:567–582

Centrum för idrottsforskning (2013) Statens stöd till idrotten—uppföljning 2012 [Government support to sport—follow up 2012]. Centrum för idrottsforskning, Stockholm

Centrum för idrottsforskning (2014) Etik och ekonomi i idrottsföreningar [Ethics and economy in sport clubs]. Centrum för idrottsforskning, Stockholm

Fahlén J (2007) Från Ulf Sterner till Harry Harkimo—En analys av transformeringen av svensk ishockey 1967–2000 [From Ulf Sterner to Harry Harkimo—an analysis of the transformation of Swedish ice hockey 1967–2000]. Idrott, Historia och Samhälle 2007:100–120

Fahlén J, Wickman K, Eliasson I (2014) Resisting self-regulation: an analysis of sport policy programme making and implementation in Sweden. Int J Sport Policy Politics. doi:10.1080/19406940.2014.925954

Goodwin M, Grix J (2011) Bringing structures back in: The 'governance narrative', the 'decentred approach' and 'asymmetrical network governance' in the education and sport policy communities. Public Adm 89(2):537–556

Grix J (2010) The 'governance debate' and the study of sport policy. Int J Sport Policy Politics 2(2):159–171

Hvenmark J (2008) Reconsidering membership: a study of individual members' formal affiliation with democratically governed federations. Handelshögskolan, Stockholm

Ibsen B (2002) Evaluering af Det Idrætspolitiske Idéprogram [Evaluation of the sport policy idea programme]. Københavns Universitet and Institut for forskning i Idræt og Folkelig Oplysning, København

Karp S, Eliasson I, Fahlén J, Löfgren K, Wickman K (2012) Specialidrottsförbunden och Idrottslyftet - Extern utvärdering av Budo & Kampsortförbundet, Gymnastikförbundet, Handikappidrottsförbundet, Innebandyförbundet och Skidförbundet [The National Sport Federations and The Lift for Sport – The external evaluation of the Swedish Budo & Martial Arts Federation, the Swedish Floorball Federation, the Swedish Gymnastics Federation, the Swedish Ski Association, and the Swedish Sports Organisation for the Disabled and the Swedish Paralympic Committee. Riksidrottsförbundet, Stockholm

Keat RA, Sam MP (2013) Regional implementation of New Zealand sport policy: new instrument, new challenges. Int J Sport Policy Politics 5(1):39–54

Lindholm J (2013) The impact of SBF v KKV on sport: Swedish fender-bender or European pileup? Eur Competition Law Rev 34(7):367–372

Lindroth J (1988) Från "sportfåneri" till massidrott. Den svenska idrottsrörelsens utveckling 1869–1939 [From "sport-heads" to mass-sport. The development of the Swedish sport's movement 1869–1939]. Stockholms universitet, Stockholm

Lindroth J (2011) Idrott under 5000 år [Sport during 5000 years]. SISU idrottsböcker, Stockholm

Lipsky M (1980) Street-level bureaucracy: dilemmas of the individual in public services. Russell Sage, New York

Norberg J (2002) Idrottsrörelsen och staten. In: Lindroth J, Norberg JR (eds) Riksidrottsförbundet 1903–2003 [The Swedish Sports Confederation 1903–2003]. Informationsförlaget, Stockholm, pp 181–231

Norberg J (2004) Idrottens väg till folkhemmet. Studier i statlig idrottspolitik 1913–1970 [Sport's road to the welfare state. Studies in Swedish government sport policy, 1913–1970]. SISU Idrottsböcker, Stockholm

Norberg J (2011) A contract reconsidered? Changes in the Swedish state's relation to the sports movement. Int J Sport Policy Politics 3(3):311–325

Olsson L-E (2007) Frivilligt arbete inom idrotten [Volunteer work in sport]. Riksidrottsförbundet, Stockholm

Olsson L-E, Svedberg L, Jeppsson Grassman E (2005) Medborgarnas insatser och engagemang i civilsamhället—några grundläggande uppgifter från en ny befolkningsstudie [Citizens' efforts and engagement in the civil society—basic facts from a new population study]. Justitiedepartementet, Stockholm

Österlind M, Wright J (2014) If sport's the solutions then what's the problem? The social significance of sport in the moral governing of 'good' and 'healthy' citizens in Sweden 1922–1998. Sport Educ Soc 19(8):973–990

Regeringen (2011) Regeringsbeslut 15 [Government decision 15]. Kulturdepartementet, Stockholm

Riksidrottsförbundet (2005a) Idrotten vill [What sports wants]. Riksidrottsförbundet, Stockholm

Riksidrottsförbundet (2005b) Idrottens föreningar—En studie om idrottsföreningarnas situation [Sport clubs—a study of sport clubs' situation]. Riksidrottsförbundet, Stockholm

Riksidrottsförbundet (2010) Sport in Sweden. A presentation of the Swedish Sports Confederation. Riksidrottsförbundet, Stockholm

Riksidrottsförbundet (2011) Idrotten i siffror [Sport in numbers]. Riksidrottsförbundet, Stockholm

Sjöblom P, Fahlén J (2012) Good sport environments: a study of collective fundamental values and their importance for activity principles in Swedish club sport. Swed J Sport Res 1:1–28

Skille EÅ (2008) State sport policy and voluntary sport clubs: the case of the Norwegian sports city program as social policy. Eur Sport Manag Q 9(1):63–79

SOU (1922) Statsunderstöd för idrottens främjande, avgiven av tillkallade sakkunniga [State support for the promotion of sport, given by summoned advisers]. Ecklesastikdepartementet, Stockholm

SOU (1957) Idrotten och samhället. Betänkande om statens stöd till idrott och friluftsliv [Sport and society. Commission report on the government support to sport and outdoor activities]. Handelsdepartmentet, Stockholm

SOU (1969) Idrott åt alla. Betänkande avgivet av Idrottsutredningen [Sport for all. Commission report given by the sports commission]. Handelsdepartmentet, Stockholm

SOU (2008) Föreningsfostran och tävlingsfostran En utvärdering av statens stöd till idrotten [Democratic fostering and competition fostering. An evaluation of the government support to sport]. Fritzes, Stockholm

Stenling C (2013) Sport programme implementation as translation and organizational identity construction: the implementation of Drive-in sport in Swedish sports as an illustration. Int J Sport Policy Politics 6(1):55–69

# Chapter 20
# Sport Clubs in Slovenia

**Simona Kustec Lipicer and Mojca Doupona Topič**

## 20.1 Introduction

Slovenia has a population of two million. With the changes of political system (1991), significant changes in commercialisation and the partnership between state and private capital occurred also in the area of financing of sport. Today, sports organisations at all levels are financed from public and private funds.

Sport represents one of the important symbolic features of national identity in Slovenia. Besides culture sport has always been regarded to be one of the central positive and bright cornerstones of the states' national and international image. A lot of public and media attention has been already from the Yugoslav times devoted to sport activities, so far predominantly to the international elite sport competitions and national system of sport education.

## 20.2 History and Context

The aim of this contribution is to give a descriptive overview of the existing evolution of sport in Slovenia from the perspective of the historical, organisational, financial and public attitudes and perceptions of the position of sport clubs in the sport system of the state. Based on the fact that the whole idea of sport system has been

S.K. Lipicer (✉)
Faculty of Social Sciences, University of Ljubljana, Ljubljana, Slovenia
e-mail: Simona.Kustec-Lipicer@fdv.uni-lj.si

M.D. Topič
Faculty of Sport, University of Ljubljana, Ljubljana, Slovenia
e-mail: mojca.doupona@fsp.uni-lj.si



C. Breuer et al. (eds.), *Sport Clubs in Europe*, Sports Economics, Management and Policy 12, DOI 10.1007/978-3-319-17635-2_20

until so far founded on the sport clubs' structural arrangements, our expectation is that this contribution will point to the evolving importance and growth of the role and position of sport clubs in the national sport system architecture.

Development of sport in Slovenia has always been importantly based on the association culture. Up until current times all the important sport activities—be it at the grass-roots or elite level—have had their foundations in sport associational structures and policies.

The first sport clubs in the country were formed more than 150 years ago, in times when current Slovenian territory belonged to the Austro-Hungarian Empire. In that period gym became one of the components of the *school system* legally prescribed by a special act first in 1869[1] and then expanded in 1869 and 1871 when the government introduced the gym as a compulsory subject in all levels of education (Šugman 1999). Later on, mainly with the emergence of parliamentarianism in the middle of the nineteenth century and in the frameworks of the already established sport association practices the formation of the first *political parties* in Slovenian territory had importantly influenced the forthcoming work of sport associations of that times. Different sports associations occurred under the political parties' umbrella and the two most important ones, called Hawk (*Sokol*) and Eagle (*Orel*), were directly related to the two most powerful political parties. Sport retained its pre-war importance in civil as well as political life after the end of the World War II, too. Later on Federal Assembly on physical culture was formed at the governmental side in 1968, introducing the first elements of decentralisation and de-etatisation of sport, resulting in a shift of all activities from the federal to the national level which was a very distinct political act in the times of a high centralisation of the Yugoslav state.

In the late 1980s when political processes connected with Slovenian independence became very straightforward, the legal and institutional changes of the whole system affected the field of sport as well. In the late 1980s Slovenian communist governmental authorities as well as democratic opposition supported the democratic processes in the society, while they accepted the changes of Slovenian federal constitution, introducing the prevalence of Slovenian constitution under the federal Yugoslavian, the right of national self-determination, independence and free elections (Socialist Republic of Slovenia 1989). According to the plebiscite results from December 23rd in 1990 Slovenia declared its independence on 25th June 1991 and afterwards introduced democratic institutional and regulation changes. Even though the key democratic institutions and responsibilities were defined in 1991, the sports field suffered from a lack of contextual changes to the old socialist legislation before 1998 when the Sports Act finally came into force. Pursuant to Articles 1–3 of the Sports Act (1992) sport encompasses the broader aspects of human life and foresees the involvement of both state and civil society players, who should work together cooperatively. The most important legislation supplementing the Sports Act is the National Programme of Sport in Slovenia introduced in 2000, according to which

[1] In that period gym was only an optional subject at school.

the state co-creates the conditions for the development of sport at the national and local level, and through international and bilateral cooperations (NPS 2000), as stated:

> The state of Slovenia will promote the development of sport with financial and expert support, especially in fields which importantly influence the development of sport, such as education, training of experts, sport infrastructure, expert and research activities. Local communities mainly co-finance the programmes for children and youth, sport recreation and sport infrastructure. (p. 1)

According to the Sport Act (1998) sport organisations are the holders (e.g. also the implementers of governmental sport policy) of sport activities at the national and local state levels.[2] After the independence on the regulation of sport organisations has been based on the Societies Act (2006, 2011) and is being understood as free association for recreational or professional sport activities. Sport associations' organisational structures are typically pyramid based. On the peak of the national sport organisation system is the Olympic Committee of Slovenia—the Association of Sport Federations (OCS-ASF), followed by national sports federations, other sports associations and associations at the local level.

Slovenian citizens are known of giving a remarkably high value to the top athletes' results on the world sport stages, and being themselves at the same time highly active in the recreational part of sport activity in comparison with other European citizens, and regardless of various socio-demographic determinants (ISSP 2009).

## 20.3 Role of Sports Clubs in Politics and Society

The role of the government in the field of sport has always been very supportive, even stimulating in the beginning years. On the basis of the stated the organisation of sport in the country can be classified as regulatory (Chaker 1999, 2004), meaning that sport is regulated by the state's and local communities' regulatory frameworks on one side while still remaining its own sport self-regulation that is founded on the organisational self-autonomy principles.

Organisation of Slovenian sport has always been in accordance with a traditional European pyramid model of sport (EC 2007) according to which the major part of sport organisations is being represented in the frameworks of the grass-roots sport clubs at the local level of municipalities, followed by the regional and national sport associations and the National Olympic Committee—Association of Sport Federations on the top of the pyramid. Sport in general is supposed to be governed by the principles of high self-autonomy and cooperation between individual sport organisational levels.

[2] A special legal status was given to the expert workers in sport (Articles 26–33) and private work in sport (Articles 34–45).

From the evolution perspective sport in Slovenia can be marked as a relatively stable and not much changing filed of social activity in which the role of government and also politics have always been recognised.

When it comes to organisational sport activities Slovenian men are above average active in sport organisations (clubs and associations), while this is not the case for Slovenian women who in 77 % reported that they have not participated in organised sport activities in the last year, which is more than one percentage point less than European average. Below average organised sport activity is also evidenced in relation to age, education and assessment of own health conditions (EC 2007).

The studies in Slovenia (Doupona Topič 2010) show that the frequency of a person's engagement in a sport activity still reflects their social status and the social stratification patterns which are characteristic of the Slovenian society. These social differences could be summarised as follows:

- The number of men engaging in sport is higher than that of women.
- Sport activity is proportional to the age (the higher the age, the lower the sport activity).
- People with a higher socio-economic status are more sport active.
- People who live in urban areas are more sport active than those from rural areas.

Nevertheless, sports without any doubts enjoy a very high level of reputation in societal system in general publics, showing that respondents are among various achievements in their societal, political and economic system far more proud of sport successes.

On the other side also Slovenian elite athletes report about a high value and are proud of sport achievements of Slovenian nation (Doupona Topič et al. 2012; Toš 2014). Namely, Slovenian athletes are prouder of the sports achievements of their nation than their American counterparts, and the organisation of sports events means much more to them than for the US athletes. In contrast to Slovenian natural beauties and tourism the athletes also report no feelings of pride in the Slovenian economy or in Slovenian politics (Doupona Topič et al. 2012).

## 20.4 Characteristics of Sport Clubs

In Slovenia, associations are interest organisations. Their members share a common interest which is not political but most often involves associating based on sport and other interests. Associations can be artistic, scientific or sports associations. When we use the term *club*, we have in mind associations that deal with competitive sport.

The official register of all associations registered at the Ministry of the Interior in Slovenia at the end of 2003 showed that out of 18,577 associations officially registered in Slovenia, 5,518 of them with some 350,000 members were from the sports field (Statistical Office of the Republic of Slovenia 2004). In 2009 there were 21,503 associations registered in Slovenia, most of which were sport clubs (7,699), of which 189 basketball clubs (Central Register of Associations 2009). These data

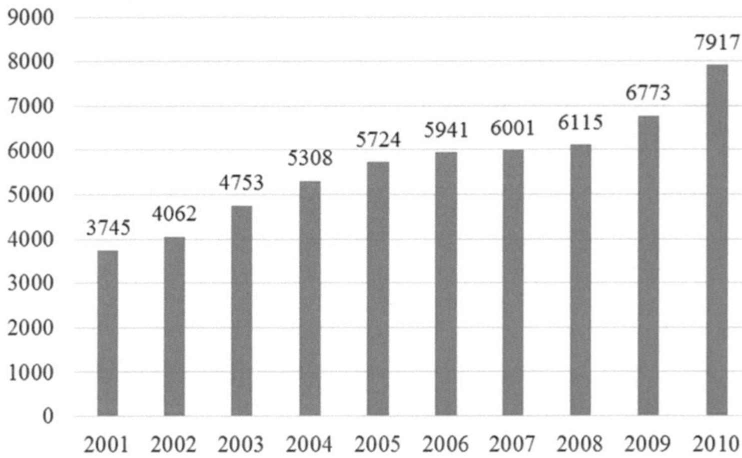


**Fig. 20.1** Growth in a number of sport associations, 2001–2010

show that almost 30 % of all registered associations in Slovenia come from sports, followed by the cultural field with 14 % and fire brigade associations with 8 %, where the majority of the associations work on the local levels. Associations or clubs are structured differently. Some operate only within one sport, while others cover several sports. However, there are different types of sports associations with various patterns of structural design.

Very similar figures are revealed if we analyse the establishment of new associations in the last years, for the highest number of new associations again comes from the sports field (28 %). It is also worth mentioning that the statistics on defunct and deleted associations show that most associations that cease activity are again coming from the field of sport, although the percentage is somewhat higher than expected and represents 33 % in the last year (Central Register of Associations 2011) (Fig. 20.1).

From the perspective of geographical distribution majority of the sport associations are based in central Slovenian region in the capital city of Ljubljana and its surroundings, followed by Podravska region where the second biggest city of Maribor is based, and then Gorenjska and Savinjska region, both known to be sport-oriented regions of winter sports (Gorenjska) and team sports and martial arts (Savinjska) (Fig. 20.2).

In 2011 we evidenced around 7,500 sport associations (NOC-ASF 2013), among which associations for sport recreation and then football clubs and skiing dominate. Around two-thirds of all sport clubs are individual and the rest team sport or mental sport games run (Zavod za šport Planica 2012).

Three thousand three hundred and fifty-five sport associations or something less than half of all sport associations were members of national sport federations (Zavod za šport Planica 2012). We can assume that the members of the sports federations are those sport associations (clubs) that deal with competitive sport (Table 20.1).

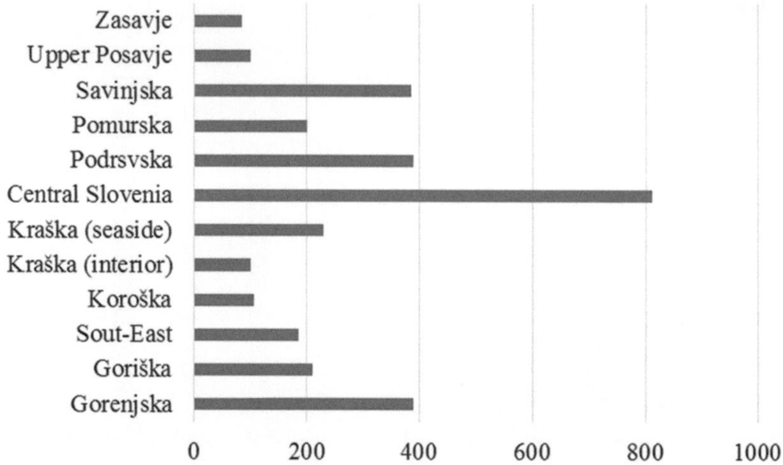


**Fig. 20.2** Sport associations by region (Zavod za šport Planica 2012)

According to the lately conducted web survey data on sport participation of Slovenian citizens (Kustec Lipicer et al. 2012)[3] around 25 % of respondents claim to be members of some sort of sport associations. Around 15 % claim to be members of sport associations, while similar percentage reports to be a member of sport association in the past. Respondents report that their average week sport activity is related to walking and gym and stretching at home and that their direct connection with sport association is rare, except if they are elite athletes.

From the EU perspective Slovenian data related to sport association participation seem to be close to EU average, but at the same time still quite far away from the best practices in the Netherlands (27 %), Denmark (25 %) and Germany (24 %) (EC 2014).

Although sport associations are a central and most widespread organisational holder of sport activities in Slovenia, they have so far not been really much researched so far.

Data on detailed characteristics of sport association would rarely exist and are besides the official data about the number of registered clubs and associations mostly not publically available, also due to the fact that in various recent attempts both at the governmental and sport organisational level (e.g. OCS-ASF) monitoring system has still been establishing (Zavod za sport Planica 2012, 2013).

[3]Web survey of everyday and physical activities, based on a non-random sample of 1,467 respondents (ibid).

**Table 20.1** Sport associations by sport federations in 2011 (selected, out of 3,357 in total) (Zavod za šport Planica 2012)

| Federation | |
|---|---|
| Athletics | 65 |
| Auto-motor | 79 |
| Badminton | 28 |
| Billiard | 12 |
| Bob | 2 |
| Bowing | 32 |
| Bowling | 143 |
| Bridge | 9 |
| Curling | 6 |
| Fishing | 72 |
| Floorball | 16 |
| Golf | 47 |
| Gymnastics | 40 |
| Hockey | 19 |
| Ju-jitsu | 21 |
| Judo | 63 |
| Sailing | 79 |
| Skiing | 225 |
| Kayak | 25 |
| Karate | 66 |
| Cycling | 89 |
| Aviation | 109 |
| Football | 415 |
| Volleyball | 77 |
| Handball | 94 |
| Hiking | 266 |
| Swimming | 36 |
| Equestrian | 39 |
| Dancing | 75 |
| Shooting | 112 |
| Handball | 94 |
| Chess | 99 |
| Triathlon | 20 |
| Water polo | 10 |
| Tennis | 67 |
| Disabled | 129 |

According to various types of sport associations sport system in the country distinguishes between the following types, while they can be either profit or non-profit oriented for active or passive users of sport services (Bednarik et al. 2002):

- According to the founder criteria: private, public and mixed types of associations.
- According to the users: associations that deliver sport services for passive or active participants.

- According to the content of the working filed: recreational sport clubs, open sport associations, mixed types of sport associations, sport associations of a specific sport discipline and sport associations that work in the forms of managerial entrepreneurships.
- According to the profile of the workers in sport: amateurs, volunteers or paid professionals.

Sport clubs are without doubts the elementary holders of sport activities, where at the grass-roots and recreational level this function is implemented by sport associations (*društva*), while at the elite level the key holders are national sport federations.

Over the time the number of sport associations has been increasing, but it is Professor Šugman who warns that sport associations have been changing importantly in their organisational and also contextual character (Šugman 1999). According to his assessment this fact leads to the decrease in the elementary importance and power of sport associations to be a key holder of sport activities in a country (Sugman: 7).

Similar assessment was traced also through the semi-structured interviews that were conducted with the representatives of various types of sport associations, where the problems of various kinds of inequalities between associations at various levels and of various forms were disclosed (Kustec Lipicer et al. 2012). It turned out that sport associations and in this relation also sport clubs distinguish between themselves according to the type of sport activities (also disciplines) that they cover and access to the decision-making bodies. As a consequence usually less popular sport activities, as well as those that relate to the specific social minorities groups, are frequently put on the edge of decision-making and further implementation processes.

"Disabled people are splendid, but in our system it means that you work with them on the basis of charity, from a kind of a mercy. This is absurd for me. They need to be given the same conditions as to other sport organisations because nowadays disabled sport is losing its own rights. Current logic goes in a direction: oh, they have been given something, so now you can shut up. But it should not be like this, they need to have the same" (interview with the representative of sport club that is not close to decision-making bodies) (Kustec Lipicer et al. 2012, p. 80).

"Many of us work voluntarily, but this means that we don't have any initiations, no rewards in the whole process. … In our system voluntary work has no value and you need to establish a kind of entrepreneurship if you want to work in sport. Faculty of sports produces many new cadres which is on the work market and they are those who at the end do this kind of voluntary work in the stated circumstances" (interview with the representative of sport club that is not close to decision-making bodies) (Kustec et al. 2012, p. 58).

## 20.5 Basketball Clubs in Slovenia

The organisation of basketball in Slovenia is based on more than 190 clubs or associations which differ substantially in terms of size, organisation, financial standing and competitive performance. The purpose of this part is to shed light on some organisational-administrative and financial characteristics of the selected basketball clubs and establish whether the clubs, which participate at different competitive levels with their top (senior-men) teams, differ in terms of the above-mentioned characteristics.

The study encompassed all basketball associations (clubs) which in the 2011/2012 season competed with their first (senior-men) teams at one of the three highest competitive levels in Slovenia, 1.A Slovenian basketball league (hereinafter: 1.A SKL), 1.B Slovenian basketball league (hereinafter: 1.B SKL) and the 2nd Slovenian basketball league (hereinafter: 2. SKL). The data were acquired through a survey questionnaire sent by regular mail and e-mail to 45 basketball clubs. The questionnaire consisted of 63 questions divided into four sets: the first set of variables covered personnel management in associations, the second covered their financial operations, the third covered their organisational characteristics and the fourth inquired about association (club) identity.

The results show that basketball associations in Slovenia are quite similar in terms of organisational structure, regardless of their competitive quality. On average, the associations have 150 members, which means that, in the continuation, we will deal with fairly small basketball associations and clubs which, nonetheless, have the same characteristics as larger ones.

On average, the associations are run by slightly more than seven professional staff not on the payroll or administrative and organisational staff covering various fields of activity. On average, a 1.A SKL club employs slightly more than two professional staff, while the clubs ranking lower employ fewer people. The clubs' managing boards consist of slightly less than nine members on average; they meet almost ten times a year on average and an interesting observation is that the least active in this respect are the managing boards of the 1.A SKL clubs.

Basketball clubs in Slovenia are financed in a variety of ways. A considerable item of revenue is that of sponsorship funds as well as public, state and donation funds, while revenues from admission tickets and TV coverage rights are relatively low in most of the clubs for the already mentioned reason. Parts of funds are obtained from participation of some members, membership fees or playing fees. All clubs of the 1.A National League earn their finances through sales of admission tickets. In the 1.B league such clubs account for only slightly more than one-half, whereas in 2. SKL none of the clubs earns revenues from admission tickets. By and large, basketball clubs own no real property or only rarely own those office premises in which they are based. Almost 90 % of the clubs have lease contracts for the use of training and competition facilities and there are practically no differences between them in this respect. Such contracts are usually limited to a period of 1 year.

Fifty-eight percent of clubs use a meeting room and generally have a PC with access to the Internet and their own website. The clubs also provide training for their coaches in the form of coaching education courses. The clubs whose first team plays in the 1.A SKL provide training courses to their coaches more frequently than other clubs competing at lower levels. Nevertheless, it could be said that the clubs do not provide sufficient training courses to their coaches, as on average only one coach in a year attends a basketball coaching course.

Regardless of their quality and competitive performance, even the best Slovenian basketball clubs and teams do not yet stand on an equal footing when compared to the best European, let alone US clubs and teams. What is meant here is the organisational and financial aspects of the sport. The reason lies primarily in the previously mentioned small population and the economic (under)development and companies' (un)willingness to finance, or respectively to sponsor basketball clubs. Another reason is also the gradual withdrawal of the state from the financing of the elite sport and the amendments to the tax policy at the expense of clubs and athletes. All of the above and also the poor financial sources from TV coverage and entrance tickets are reflected in the fact that clubs suffer from scarce finances.

## 20.6 Conclusion

In Slovenia sport is perceived as an important element of national identity when it comes to top sport achievements on one side and educational and health promoter when it comes to recreational or sport for all perception on the other side. Sport associations and in this regard sport clubs have been given a central role of being an organisational holder of the sport-related activities from the same beginnings on.

Sport associations and in this regard clubs have been undertaken a long and rich history. In the times of former Yugoslavia and first decades of independence they had been gaining in importance and growth as key and fundamental holders of sport activities in the country. Their organisational and functional capacities have, despite their self-autonomy, always been quite tightly related to the governmental regulations and financial distribution that besides the evidenced problems with non-transparent and unequal positions play a role in weakening roles of sport associations and clubs nowadays.

Since the early nineteenth century on, and even in socialist times when the private initiatives were suppressed due to political ideology, we can speak about lively sport associational activities. Sport association culture has remained at a high level of self-organisation and independence and still evidences one of the highest ranks of associational life in the country. The state's regulation has always played an important role in the development of sport, be it as a promoter or as a regulator of sport in general and the work of sport associations and clubs. As it can be revealed out of the stated historical overview sport clubs' evolution praxis in the state has always been very tightly interrelated with the current political interests and priorities, where the latter were more related to the educational motives in the beginning periods, but have quite soon been transferring into the tool for founding and maintaining national identity characters. In the stated circumstances sport clubs have been quite early regarded as the central holder of sport activities for recreational as well as increasingly elite sport policy goals not only of the sport clubs themselves, but also of state, national and local politics.

Many environmental as well as internal sports association factors have challenged their work and positions in the last periods. Mainly survival motives due to the state policy regulations, bounded transparency and often clientelistic and corrupt relations among the stakeholders on the top positions of sport subsystem are frequently traced in this regard. Sport organisations as the central holders of the policy have experienced problems of favourising selected top-level sports, as well as tight and close connections and interdependency of the selected organisations with governmental policies and even individual political parties and politicians in the everyday practices.

## References


Bednarik J, Kolarič B, Doupona Topič M, Rauter M, Tušak M (2002) Športni menedžment (Sport management). Fakulteta za šport, Ljubljana

Central Register of Associations (2009, 2011) http://mrrsp.gov.si/rdruobjave/dr/index.faces. Accessed 3 Jan 2012

Chaker A-N (1999) Study of national sports legislation in Europe. Council of Europe Publishing, Strasbourg

Chaker A-N (2004) Good governance in sport. A European survey. Council of Europe Publishing, Strasbourg

European Commission (2007) The white paper on sport, 2007/0391. COM, Brussels

Doupona Topič M (2010) Vpliv socialne stratifikacije na značilnosti športno rekreativne dejavnosti v Sloveniji (The impact of social stratification on the characteristics of sport-recreational activity in Slovenia). Šport 58(1/2):100–104

Doupona Topič M, Rauter S, Žvan M, Coakley J (2012) Nacionalni identitet vrhunskih sportaša. (National identity of athletes). Sport Mont 34,35,36./X:372–377

European Commission (2014) Eurobarometer on sport and physical activity. Special Eurobarometer 412/Wave EB80.2. http://ec.europa.eu/public_opinion/archives/ebs/ebs_412_en.pdf. Accessed 20 Apr 2014

ISSP Research Group, International Social Survey Programme (ISSP) (2009) Leisure time and sports, 2007. GESIS, Cologne

Kustec Lipicer S, Slabe Erker R, Bartolj T (2012) Javnopolitični ukrepi in modeli športne politike v Sloveniji (Public policy actions and models of sports policy in Slovenia). Fakulteta za družbene vede, Ljubljana

National Programme of sport in the Republic of Slovenia (2000) Official Gazette of the Republic of Slovenia. http://www.pisrs.si/Pis web/pregledPredpisa?id=NACP24. Accessed 6 May 2014

NOC- ASF (2013) Caleidoscope. http://www.olympic.si/o-oks/osnovni-podatki. Accessed 22 Mai 2014

Socialist Republic of Slovenia (1989) The constitutional amendments to the constitution of the Socialist Republic of Slovenia, 1989, adopted on 27th September 1989. Available in the Official Gazette of the Socialist Republic of Slovenia 32.http://unpan1.un.org/intradoc/groups/public/documents/UNTC/UNPAN014895.pdf. Accessed 1 Dec 2015

Sports Act (1998) Official Gazette of the Republic of Slovenia, no. 22/98, 97/01 – ZSDP and 15/03 – ZOPA.http://www.uradni-list.si/1/objava.jsp?urlid=199822&stevilka=929. Accessed 5 Apr 2014

Statistical Office of the Republic of Slovenia (2004) Culture and sport. http://www.stat.si/letopis/index_vsebina.asp?poglavje=8&leto=2003&jezik=en. Accessed 17 Nov 2004

Šugman R (1999) Prelomno obdobje slovenskega športa 1988-1994 [A Landmark Period of Slovene Sports, 1988-1994]. Fakulteta za šport, Ljubljana

The Societies Act (2011) Official Gazette of the Republic of Slovenia, no. 91/2008 Odl.US: U-I-380/06-11, 95/2008 Skl.US: U-I-380/06-15, 102/2008 Odl.US: U-I-57/07-7, 58/2009, 39/2011, 64/2011-UPB2

Toš N (Ed) (2014) Slovensko javno mnenje 2013/1: National Identity III, ISSP 2013, Citizenship II, ISSP 2014, Public opinion mirror. Overview and comparisions [data set]. Fakulteta za družbene vede, Center za raziskovanje javnega mnenja in množičnih komunikacij, Ljubljana

Zavod za šport Republike Slovenije Planica (2012) Pregled vrhunskega in kakovostnega športa. http://www.zsrs-planica.si/wp-content/uploads/2011/11/%C5%A0port-v-%C5%A1tevilkah_021.pdf. Accessed 3 Jan 2014

Zavod za šport Republike Slovenije Planica (2013) Sport in numbers. http://www.zsrs-planica.si/informatika-v-sportu/sport-v-stevilkah. Accessed 3 Jan 2014

# Chapter 21
# Sport Clubs in Spain

**Ramon Llopis-Goig and Anna Vilanova**

## 21.1 Introduction

Spain is a decentralised state with an approximate population of 47.1 million. It is a European Union member state since 1986 and the 13th largest economy in the world. According to the latest survey of sporting habits conducted in Spain (2010), 19 % of people over the age of 15 engage in some kind of sport or physical activity through a sports club or association. The corresponding figures in previous surveys were 24 % in 2005 and 25 % in 2000. Although the number of sports clubs in Spain has increased over the last 10 years, there has been an even greater rise in the number of people taking up recreational sport or physical activity without being formally linked to any sports federation or organisation. This chapter presents an analysis of sports clubs in Spain, doing so on the basis of information gathered from secondary sources, previous research, and studies conducted by the authors of this chapter.

The chapter begins by analysing the historical development of sports clubs in Spain, from their creation during the last quarter of the nineteenth century through to the present day. This first section offers an interpretation of the defining characteristics of sports clubs in Spain and their relatively late emergence, and discusses the principal milestones in their social and organisational development. The analysis here focuses specifically on the place of sports clubs within the wider national system of sport, and examines how the relationships between sports clubs and the state has

R. Llopis-Goig (✉)
Department of Sociology and Social Anthropology, Faculty of Social Sciences, Universitat de València, Valencia, Spain
e-mail: ramon.llopis@uv.es

A. Vilanova
Institut Nacional d'Educació Física de Catalunya, Universitat de Barcelona, Barcelona, Spain
e-mail: anna.vilanova@gencat.cat



C. Breuer et al. (eds.), *Sport Clubs in Europe*, Sports Economics, Management and Policy 12, DOI 10.1007/978-3-319-17635-2_21

evolved into what can be described as a highly interventionist model. The next section provides a quantitative overview concerning the number of sports clubs and their membership within Spanish society. This section is organised into two parts. The first examines the main statistics available on the number of federated sports clubs in Spain, while the second analyses the role of sports clubs with respect to the practice of sport by the Spanish population, and examines how this relationship has evolved over the last 30 years. In addition, a broad socio-demographic description of the membership of sports clubs and associations is presented. The data source for this part of the chapter is the 5-yearly surveys of sporting habits that have been conducted in Spain over the last 30 years, with the socio-demographic analysis being based on the most recent survey.

Following this broad analysis the third section of the chapter focuses on the characteristics of sports clubs. Given the absence of research for the Spanish population as a whole, the analysis in this section is based on studies that have been carried out in two of Spain's autonomous regions (Catalonia and Galicia). The aspects addressed includes the organisational features of clubs, such as their size, age and number of sections, the number and profile of members, the executive and management bodies, voluntary work, financial resources, range of sporting activities on offer, equipment and facilities, and relationships with the local area and other institutions. The chapter concludes with a discussion of the results, integrating the various data, drawing key conclusions from the analysis and proposing suggestions for future research.

The initial expansion of sport in Western Europe was tightly bound up with the English model of sports clubs. In Spain, modern sporting practices began to develop in the second half of the nineteenth century in urban, dockland and industrial areas as well as areas characterised by the development of energy resources by professionals who were European in origin. The first sports clubs were set up later than in other European countries, specifically in the last quarter of the nineteenth century (García 1986). The creation of clubs in Spain was closely associated with foreign professionals and specialists who came to the country to work in the industries then being set up. One of the best-known examples is FC Barcelona, founded by Hans Gamper, a Swiss engineer. To a large extent, the creation of clubs was also connected to young people who went to other European countries for their studies or to learn languages and later came back with new habits, including sport. Together, these factors brought English sport into Spanish society and introduced the idea of a democratically run, volunteer-based sports club (Heinemann 1999). Initially, the process took place in the more highly industrialised areas of the country, namely, Catalonia, the Basque Country and Madrid, but also in mining areas and in small centres of industrial activity in other regions of Spain (Puig et al. 1999a, b).

The historians Xavier Pujadas and Carles Santacana have identified the features characteristic of the majority of sports clubs emerging in Spain in the late nineteenth and early twentieth centuries (Pujadas and Santacana 2003). The first of these features is the adoption of a number of prescripts followed by early British clubs: equality among their sportspeople, the social standing of their directors, and their members' competitive ethos. The second feature is related to the fact that, although they acted as platforms for sociability and they had a collective function, they were private bodies. Thirdly, the earliest Spanish sports clubs fostered amateurism as a core value, such that the sportspeople themselves were the managers and organisers of the club. This feature entailed a strong commitment to the club and it worked as a membership selection mechanism that precluded the participation of individuals whose social class was more modest. A fourth feature of the early clubs was an internal structure built on strict regimentation that enjoyed a certain degree of democratisation over time and gradually drew a distinction between practising sportspeople and club directors.

When the Franco regime (1939–1975) took power at the end of the Spanish Civil War (1936–1939), radical change came to the structure of sport. This change occurred in the very conception of sport, which ceased being part of civil society and was assimilated into the structure of the state. The political authorities appropriated sport and the new Francoist state transferred its control to the single party Falange in line with a theory that predicated absolute one-party control over society. The new Francoist state understood that sports clubs and associations were not merely social groups devoid of ideological content (Llopis-Goig 2006). It had a clear notion of the cultural, social and political significance of the various traditions fostered by sports associations throughout the first third of the twentieth century (Pujadas and Santacana 2003). Indeed, until 1964, the sports clubs were almost the sole associations permitted beyond the network of bodies controlled by the Minister Secretary-General of the Movement, through which the Falange Española y de las JONS was to play a monolithic role during the first half of the dictatorship. As a result, sports clubs became the only place with a certain margin for freedom of association and, until the passage of the Law of Associations in 1964; they remained, to some extent, the last redoubt of opposition against the regime (Rodríguez 2008). Even so, the clubs' latitude of freedom was extremely limited. Sports organisations were forced under the control of a state body set up in 1938, the National Sports Council (later renamed the National Sports Delegation), which was overseen by the Falange Española y de las JONS. In this way, sports clubs and federations lost their private character, their autonomy and their democratic ethos. How they operated was turned completely on its head. The National Sports Delegation took over the appointment of key executive figures in the national federations and these figures, in turn, named regional delegates, who would later become the ones to endorse or block the appointment of club directors (Santacana 2011).

With the subordination of sports clubs to the state apparatus, their organisational autonomy and their management structures were dismantled. This had a decisive effect on their internal functioning and led to the demise of the original liberal democratic approach that had conceived of the clubs as peer-based associations. Members lost the power to select their clubs' top officials, because club officials were appointed by bodies ultimately responsible to the state. Although this panorama saw modest changes in the nineteen-fifties (for example, with the introduction of elections by delegates), the selections of the members' general assembly still had to be ratified by the pertinent sports federation, which reserved the right to appoint club officials directly if the initial slate proposed by members was rejected twice (Pujadas and Santacana 2003). As a result of restructuring, the clubs were no longer run on the basis of democratic participation, but this was not the only change. The framework by which they had worked with the sports federations was also replaced. The federations, which had provided a space where clubs could reach agreement as free and equal agents, turned into bodies reporting to the National Sports Delegation and charged with overseeing clubs' activities. In their statutes, clubs had to acknowledge their subordination to the provisions and authority of the National Sports Delegation. If they failed to do so, they were refused legal recognition and denied authorization to take part in sporting competitions.

Club structures continued to adapt to the requirements of the regime during its nearly four decades of rule. With the advent of democracy, however, the clubs embarked on a process of modernisation that enabled them to regain their former status, although their organisational culture and operating procedures were still permeated with the regime's authoritarianism. The end of the Franco regime also witnessed broad-based growth in the number of sports clubs, which had to find their own space in a context in which, on one hand, sport was run mainly by the state and, on the other hand, a strong market dynamic began to take hold (Heinemann 1999).

During the transition to democracy, sport began to undergo democratisation. Sport was introduced into the Spanish constitution (adopted in 1978) and the General Law of Physical Culture and Sport was enacted in 1980. These years were crucial to the process of modernisation. They made it possible to include sport in the legal framework of the state. The first half of the nineteen-eighties saw a strong push in the construction of sports infrastructure, one of the most nagging shortcomings of the Spanish sports system at the time. Municipal governments woke up to the need to promote *sport for all* and this led to a booming sports movement in Spanish society that some have dubbed the *municipalisation of Spanish* sport.

In the nineties, Spanish sport experienced significant events that contributed to its development and legal regulation. Democracy found a firm footing; the country became a member of the European Union (in 1986) and the Spanish economy embarked a cycle of economic growth that would last over 10 years. At the beginning of the decade, in 1990, the enactment of a new Sports Law (Law 10/1990 of 15 October) once again regulated the responsibilities and functions of the state on the subject of sport, drawing a line between professional sport, top-class sport and sport for everyone. Associative bodies in sport were defined as private associations formed by natural or legal persons, whose purpose is to promote one or more sports, encourage members to engage in one or more sports and foster their participation in sporting activities and competitions. As the Sports Law stipulated, the associative bodies were classified as elementary clubs, basic clubs, professional sports clubs and limited companies operating in the field of sport. Thus, a new legal framework was created by which professional sports (the first and second divisions of Spanish football and the top-flight Liga ACB in basketball) were separated from non-professional sports. Professional clubs were turned into Sociedades Anónimas Deportivas (SADs), or sports-based public limited companies. This was a new legal form that brought with it a number of prerequisites and required the application of a series of controls by various state bodies (Llopis-Goig 2013). It was a matter of no small significance for Spanish sport that Barcelona hosted the Olympic Games of

1992. Indeed, the organisation and running of the event provided a major impetus to push Spanish sport out of its marginal position and finally make it a significant factor in the social and cultural life of the country. Since that time, sports clubs and associations have grown in importance and gained autonomy within the Spanish sports system, despite the unquestionable dominance that the state continues to exert as a supplier and financial supporter of numerous sporting activities.

The eighties had also witnessed the first steps toward the decentralisation of competencies in the area of sport. A number of autonomous communities were allowed to enact their own sports laws. Thus, while the body of legislation governing sports associations had been limited and weak in the Franco period, the new democracy saw a veritable barrage of sports legislation at the level of the autonomous communities. By the nineties, all seventeen of Spain's autonomous communities had adopted their own sports laws, with specific provisions on sports associations spelled out in decrees, ordinances, plans and programmes (Rodríguez 2008). Over time, these different legislative developments, as well as the historical and cultural differences among the various autonomous communities, have given rise to an essential feature of the Spanish sports system, namely, its territorial heterogeneity.

In addition to decentralisation, a second feature of the Spanish sports model relates to the position of the sports clubs. As the Spanish sports model is based on the state's collaboration with sports clubs, the state provides resources to the clubs in exchange for the clubs' promotion of the practice of sport by the public. Moreover, the state is not merely an ancillary promoter of the clubs' activities, but also involves itself in the provision of a wide range of opportunities for the practice of sport. Thus, the model can be viewed as interventionist, because their collaboration with the state makes the clubs reliant on the state's financial help (Burriel and Puig 1999; Rodríguez 2008). A stark consequence of this is that sports clubs in some regions play a weak role in the provision of sport, which is left very much in the hands of municipalities and other bodies to which the promotion and development of sporting activities is delegated.

Heinemann has put forward an interesting interpretation of the relationship between the state and organised sport in Spain. His idea is that the chief weakness of the Franco dictatorship was not that the state exercised a wide ranging influence on sport, but rather that this influence was not articulated with sufficient efficiency (Heinemann 1999). Thus, with the advent of democracy, the challenge facing Spanish sport did not centre on the state's withdrawal from sport. Instead, it was a question of achieving a more effective realisation of its influence. This was because a widely held belief in Spanish society viewed the practice of sport to be not only an individual right, but also a service that the state is required to provide to its citizens. Obviously, state interventionism has historical roots and rests on a cultural ethos that took hold in Spanish society in the seventeenth, eighteenth and nineteenth centuries thanks to an enormous confidence in the capacity of the state to satisfy the needs of the population. Nor was the aristocracy's and the Catholic Church's stranglehold on civil society unrelated to this belief. Both institutions enjoyed a clear-cut hegemony in the society and they strongly resisted any change or proposal for modernisation that might undermine their position of power. The bourgeoisie only emerged in a few regions and it did not have the strength or influence that it attained in other areas of Europe (Giner 2000). Consequently, there was a certain distrust of volunteer-based private organisations. They were suspected of being answerable largely to the Catholic Church and, therefore, of standing in the way of progress. In the same vein, the belief spread that any substantial change would have to be carried out by the state. Taken together, these factors elicited in the society a rather aloof view of private associations and clubs.

## 21.2 An Empirical Approach to the Study of Sports Clubs

This section offers an empirical approach to the study of sports clubs in Spanish society. As noted in the introduction, the section is broken into two parts. The first part examines the key statistical data available on the number of sports clubs in Spain, while the second part looks at the clubs' role in the practice of sport by Spaniards and takes a nuanced view of the characteristics of club members.

The data examined in the first part come from Spain's National Institute of Statistics (INE 2014) and the annual reports on sports statistics issued by the National Sports Council (CSD 2013, 2014). The data on sports clubs appearing in the CSD reports are compiled from figures submitted annually by each Spanish sports federation to the National Sports Council in order to facilitate its role of oversight and coordination as assigned under the Sports Law, Law 10/1990 of 15 October. While the CSD reports are an up-to-date and highly credible source of statistical information, they do not cover all of the sports clubs in Spain because not all clubs are members of a sports federation. As there is no national register of sports clubs, one possible solution would be to aggregate the information from the general association registers for each autonomous community. This alternative, however, seems unsuitable, given that the autonomous communities use different ways of classifying associations. We must also bear in mind that this type of register does not make use of an updating procedure and associations that cease to exist do not always delete their listing from the register. In future, it will be necessary to carry out empirical research to establish an in-depth sociological analysis of sports clubs across the whole of Spanish society.

The data examined in the first half of the section come specifically from the 5-yearly surveys on sporting habits conducted by the National Sports Council. Most of the information used in the analysis has been taken directly from the main publications in which the data have been explored (García-Ferrando 2006; García-Ferrando and Llopis-Goig 2011a, b).

### *21.2.1 Federated Sports Clubs*

Figure 21.1 shows changes in the number of federated sports clubs over the past 14 years. Over the first decade of the twenty-first century, the number rose, reaching its highest point in 2010, when 94,511 sports clubs were registered in Spain. From this

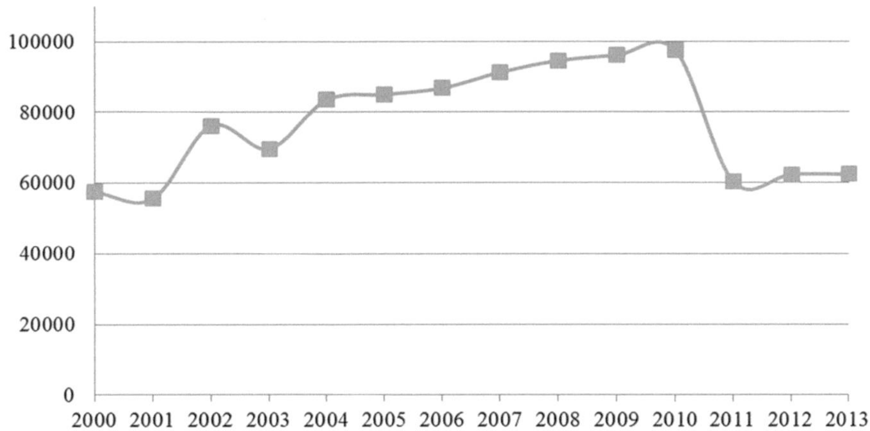


**Fig. 21.1** Changes in the number of federated clubs in Spain since 2000 (INE 2014)

point, the trend-line shows a sharp fall in 2011, reflecting a loss of more than a third of the clubs. The economic crisis affecting Spanish society since 2008 and the cutbacks in the social expenditure that the Government began to implement in 2010 might be related to this sharp fall. In the subsequent 2 years, there was a weak recovery and the number of federated sports clubs registered in Spain in 2013 stood at 62,363.

Of the total number of federated sports clubs registered in 2013, over a third (34.6 %) were football clubs. There are 21,584 federated football clubs in Spain, making this one of the most typical features of the Spanish sports system (see Table 21.1). The football figure is far above the figure for the second-ranking sport in terms of club numbers—hunting (5,398)—and it is seven times higher than sports such as basketball and cycling, which have 3,968 and 3,177 clubs, respectively. Other sports with over a thousand federated clubs are climbing and mountaineering, karate, fishing, tennis, athletics and pigeon sports. Next comes a group of seven sports with overall figures slightly below a thousand: judo, underwater activities, skating, *petanca*, motorcycle sports, chess and triathlon. Lastly, there are six sports that have between 600 and 900 clubs: handball, *padel* tennis, equestrian sports, swimming, Olympic shooting and taekwondo. A further 45 sports account collectively for 14.1 % of all federated clubs registered in Spain, but their individual figures fall below 1 % of total clubs.

It is also useful to examine the breakdown of federated sports clubs among the various autonomous communities into which the country is divided administratively. As Table 21.2 shows, Andalusia and Catalonia have the greatest number of sports clubs, together accounting for 30 % of all sports clubs in Spain. Behind them are Aragón and Valencia with slightly over 5,000 clubs each. Then come three autonomous communities in the vicinity of 4,000 clubs each: Castile and León, Galicia and Castile-La Mancha. Ranked seventh is the Community of Madrid, with 3,941 clubs, followed by a group of seven whose club numbers range from 1,000 to

**Table 21.1** Federated sports clubs in 2013, by sport (INE 2014, p. 97)

| | Federated sports clubs | | Average number of registered members per club |
|---|---|---|---|
| | Total | % | |
| Football | 21,584 | 34.6 | 39.7 |
| Hunting | 5,398 | 8.7 | 65.0 |
| Basketball | 3,968 | 6.4 | 100.8 |
| Cycling | 3,177 | 5.1 | 20.6 |
| Climbing and mountaineering | 2,083 | 3.3 | 81.2 |
| Karate | 1,376 | 2.2 | 44.6 |
| Fishing and casting | 1,354 | 2.2 | 42.0 |
| Tennis | 1,252 | 2.0 | 71.7 |
| Athletics | 1,203 | 1.9 | 51.8 |
| Pigeon sports | 1,033 | 1.7 | 22.2 |
| Judo | 996 | 1.6 | 106.9 |
| Underwater activities | 991 | 1.6 | 32.0 |
| Skating | 966 | 1.5 | 46.8 |
| *Petanca* | 950 | 1.5 | 24.4 |
| Motorcycle sports | 946 | 1.5 | 18.8 |
| Chess | 911 | 1.5 | 24.3 |
| Triathlon | 904 | 1.4 | 26.8 |
| Handball | 848 | 1.4 | 108.3 |
| *Padel* tennis | 788 | 1.3 | 55.0 |
| Equestrian sports | 766 | 1.2 | 62.4 |
| Swimming | 723 | 1.2 | 84.7 |
| Olympic shooting | 712 | 1.1 | 78.1 |
| Taekwondo | 627 | 1.0 | 54.7 |
| Other sports | 8,807 | 14.1 | 74.1 |
| Total | 62,363 | 100 | 54.4 |

3,000. The remainder have fewer than a thousand clubs each and they include Cantabria, La Rioja and the autonomous cities of Ceuta and Melilla. Clearly, in the case of federated sports clubs, there are deep-seated differences by region. This is underscored by the fact that the eight highest-ranking communities account for 74.7 % of the total.

Table 21.2 also provides information on the number of clubs for every 10,000 residents in each community. The inclusion of population numbers demonstrates that the regions with the highest per-capita number of clubs are Aragón, La Rioja, Extremadura, Castile-La Mancha and the autonomous city of Ceuta. Conversely, the regions with the lowest percentage of clubs for each 10,000 residents are the Basque Country, the Balearic Islands, Valencia, the Canary Islands, Catalonia and Madrid. In the absence of empirical research addressing this issue and bearing in mind the higher level of economic development and the greater population of these last autonomous communities, we might venture that this is related to the existence of alternative sports associations and other ways to engage in sport.

**Table 21.2** Federated sports clubs in 2013, by autonomous community (INE 2014, p. 98)

| Autonomous communities | Federated sports clubs | | Population in 2013 | Clubs per 10,000 residents |
|---|---|---|---|---|
| | Total | % | | |
| Andalusia | 11,023 | 17.7 | 8,393,159 | 13.1 |
| Catalonia | 7,666 | 12.3 | 7,480,921 | 10.2 |
| Aragón | 5,271 | 8.5 | 1,338,308 | 39.4 |
| Valencia | 5,220 | 8.4 | 4,987,017 | 10.5 |
| Castile and León | 4,807 | 7.7 | 2,518,528 | 19.1 |
| Galicia | 4,409 | 7.1 | 2,761,970 | 16.0 |
| Castile-La Mancha | 4,230 | 6.8 | 2,094,391 | 20.2 |
| Madrid | 3,941 | 6.3 | 6,414,709 | 6.1 |
| Basque Country | 2,673 | 4.3 | 2,177,006 | 12.3 |
| Murcia | 2,595 | 4.2 | 1,461,987 | 17.7 |
| Extremadura | 2,402 | 3.9 | 1,100,968 | 21.8 |
| Canary Islands | 2,166 | 3.5 | 2,105,232 | 10.3 |
| Asturias | 1,443 | 2.3 | 1,067,802 | 13.5 |
| Balearic Islands | 1,358 | 2.2 | 1,110,115 | 12.2 |
| Navarre | 1,133 | 1.8 | 638,949 | 17.7 |
| Cantabria | 958 | 1.5 | 590,037 | 16.2 |
| La Rioja | 699 | 1.1 | 318,639 | 21.9 |
| Ceuta | 259 | 0.4 | 84,534 | 30.6 |
| Melilla | 110 | 0.2 | 83,619 | 13.2 |
| Total | 62,363 | 100 | 46,727,890 | 13.3 |

### *21.2.2 Participation in Sports and Sports Clubs*

From the data gathered through the surveys on sporting habits conducted in the past decade, it is apparent that the rise in sport and physical activity has occurred outside the associations with which they have been integrally connected in earlier periods. This trend is logical if we bear in mind that the gradual spread of sport and physical activity among the Spanish population is increasingly oriented to recreation, health and keeping in shape. This is why sports clubs—despite, as seen earlier, their continued growth over the past decade—have been losing their previous supremacy. Against this, studies conducted in recent years (García-Ferrando 2006; García-Ferrando and Llopis-Goig 2011a, b) have shown a gradual move toward more individualised and non-competitive forms of sport and physical activity. For example, 75 % of the people who engaged in some type of sport or physical activity in 2010 (García-Ferrando and Llopis-Goig 2011a) stated that they did so on their own, a rise of seven percentage points since 2005, nine percentage points since 2000 and twelve since 1990. In other words, the percentage of people doing sport on their own has climbed in the past two decades from 63 to 75 %. Consistent with this rise, there have also been fewer people doing sport as an activity organised by a sports club, association or organisation. At present, the figure stands at 19 %, a drop of five percentage points since 2005.

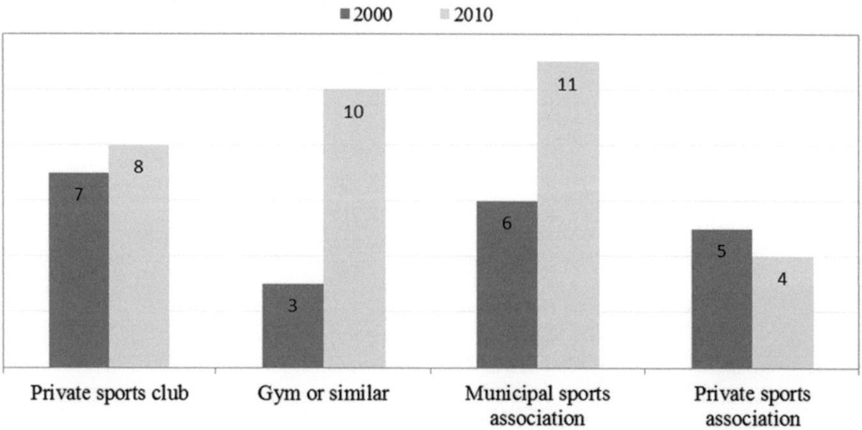


**Fig. 21.2** Membership in sports clubs and other sports bodies (García-Ferrando and Llopis-Goig 2011a, b)

However, the growth of sport and physical activity outside the clubs is not incompatible with the growth of membership in clubs and other types of sports bodies or associations. After all, the proportion of Spaniards engaged in some kind of sport or physical activity has risen from 37 % in 2000 to 43 % in 2010 (García-Ferrando and Llopis-Goig 2011a). In other words, the number of people who are members of a sports club or association has grown, although they have lost relative weight within the sports systems as a whole, because of the increase in activities pursued outside the club structure. This explains why, as Fig. 21.2 shows, there could nonetheless be an increase between 2000 and 2010 in the proportion of Spaniards who were members of a private sports club, a gym or similar, a private sports association or a municipal sports association.[1]

The largest growth has occurred among members of gyms or similar: from 3 % in 2000 to 10 % in 2010. This is followed by increased membership in municipal sports associations, which has risen from 6 to 11 %. Private club membership has grown only minimally, climbing one percentage point from 7 to 8 %. Lastly, membership in private sports associations has declined by a percentage point, falling from 5 % in 2000 to 4 % in 2010. Aggregating the various percentages, we can see that the overall membership in some kind of sports body has gone up from 21 % in 2000 to 33 % in 2010. An additional piece of data to consider in relation to the information in Fig. 21.2 is that 18.4 % of the Spanish population belongs to some kind of sports body, 4.8 % belong to two and 1.4 % belongs to three or more.

Table 21.3 examines the relationship between membership in some kind of sports body and gender, age, education level, social class and size of place of residence.

[1]These are the categories adopted by the survey on sport participation in 2010 and before to measure the membership of Spaniards in sports bodies. A private sports club refers to a sport club in the strict sense of the term while a gym or similar corresponds to sports centres of a commercial nature. On the other hand, a sports association is any private association created to promote sports while a municipal sports association refers to those associations restricted to a municipal sphere.

**Table 21.3** Characteristics of the population who are members of sports bodies (García-Ferrando and Llopis-Goig 2011a, p. 77)

| Socio-demographic characteristics | Private sports club | Gym or similar | Municipal association | Private association |
|---|---|---|---|---|
| Sex | | | | |
| Men | 11 | 11 | 12 | 6 |
| Women | 5 | 9 | 10 | 2 |
| Age | | | | |
| 15–17 Years | 11 | 10 | 19 | 10 |
| 18–34 Years | 10 | 18 | 14 | 6 |
| 35–64 Years | 7 | 8 | 11 | 4 |
| 65 Years and over | 4 | 2 | 8 | 1 |
| Education level | | | | |
| No studies | – | 1 | 3 | – |
| Primary | 5 | 6 | 9 | 3 |
| Secondary | 11 | 12 | 12 | 5 |
| Vocational training | 8 | 14 | 16 | 6 |
| University | 13 | 18 | 16 | 6 |
| Advanced | 16 | 19 | 14 | 9 |
| Social class | | | | |
| Upper/upper-middle class alta/media-alta | 15 | 17 | 16 | 8 |
| New middle classes | 9 | 14 | 11 | 5 |
| Old middle classes | 5 | 7 | 10 | 3 |
| Skilled workers | 6 | 7 | 10 | 3 |
| Unskilled workers | 3 | 4 | 8 | 2 |
| Size of place of residence | | | | |
| Less than 10,000 | 5 | 6 | 11 | 3 |
| 10,001–50,000 | 6 | 8 | 12 | 3 |
| 50,001–100,000 | 7 | 11 | 11 | 4 |
| 100,001–400,000 | 9 | 12 | 10 | 5 |
| 400,001 and higher | 11 | 13 | 11 | 5 |
| Total | 8 | 10 | 11 | 4 |

Private clubs and sports associations have a higher percentage of male members than female members: 11 % of men and 5 % of women belong to private clubs, while 6 and 2 %, respectively, belong to private associations. However, there is a much more balanced distribution by gender in gyms and municipal sports associations: 11 % of men and 9 % of women in gyms and 12 and 10 %, respectively, in municipal associations.

Sports bodies are visited more frequently by young people than by older people, and by people with university educations than by people with primary and secondary studies. The highest percentages of membership correspond to the population between 15 and 34 years of age, while the lowest percentages relate to people of 65 years and over. In the case of education level, private clubs and associations present the most differentiated profiles. Socioeconomic status is the most distinguishing feature among the members of private clubs (15 % of the upper/upper-middle class and 8 % of the new middle classes compared to 6 % of skilled workers and 2 % of unskilled workers). This is also the case with private associations (8 % of the upper/upper-middle class compared to 2 % of unskilled workers) and especially with gyms (17 % of the upper/upper-middle class and 14 % of the middle class compared to 7 % of skilled workers and 4 % of unskilled workers). Conversely, municipal sports associations offer the most inclusive profile (16 % of the upper/upper-middle class compared to 8 % of unskilled workers).

In cities with more than 100,000 inhabitants, the percentage of people belonging to some sports body is significantly greater than in smaller cities and, especially, than in smaller municipalities. The dividing line in the case of gyms is 50,000 inhabitants, with gym membership being much higher in cities above this size. Conversely, municipal sports associations show hardly any differences by population size. The various figures are only a point above or below the total average value. This appears to be the clearest and most rigorous demonstration of the fact that municipal sports services are evenly distributed among most of the towns and cities of Spain. As for private sports associations, their distribution does not present any notable differences, with percentages varying between 3 and 5 %.

In short, private clubs and associations coincide in more often having men, aged 15–34, with university studies, from the upper/upper-middle class and new middle classes, and living in cities with more than 50,000 inhabitants. Gyms and municipal associations have a greater balance between men and women, with gyms having a younger membership (15–34 years old) and municipal associations having a membership spread across all ages. Gyms are more classist and municipal associations are more inclusive. And gyms correspond to cities of more than 50,000 inhabitants, while municipal associations correspond to towns and cities of all sizes.

## 21.3 Characteristics of Sport Clubs

This section seeks to show the basic characteristics of sports clubs in Spain. Unfortunately, there is no comprehensive study on the situation of sports clubs for the country as a whole. As a result, we focus fundamentally on two recent studies carried out in Catalonia and Galicia. The Catalan study was done by the Catalan Sports Observatory for the Secretaria General de l'Esport in 2012, while the Galician study was prepared by Vicente Gambau in 2002. The two studies, which are based on the study carried out by Heinemann and Schubert in 1994, are the most thorough ones currently available in Spain (Heinemann and Schubert 1994). The aspects addressed will include the organisational features of clubs, such as year founded, size, range of sporting activities on offer, equipment and facilities, voluntary versus paid staff, financial resources and relationships with the local area and other institutions.

### 21.3.1 General Characteristics of Sports Clubs

Looking at the date of their founding, we do find older clubs, but as noted in the previous sections, a large proportion of sports clubs have been created since the end of the Franco regime. In Catalonia, 68 % of clubs have been set up since the advent of democracy (Catalan Sports Observatory 2010). In Galicia, 76.6 % of clubs have been set up since the year 1976 (Gambau 2002). Of the clubs with more than a thousand members, 28 % were founded before 1920. This percentage falls to 2.8 % for the smallest clubs. The oldest on record is the Cercle Sabadellès in Sabadell, founded in 1856 (Puig et al. 1999a, b). The first sports club in Spain is the R. C. Mediterranean nautical club, founded in Málaga in 1873 (García 1986).

In Spain, small sports clubs of less than 300 members predominate. In Catalonia, for example, the greater part of the network of associations is made up of small clubs, with 84.1 % of clubs having between 3 and 300 members. Medium-sized clubs, which have between 301 and 1,000 members, account for 10.6 % of the total, while the largest clubs, with over 1,000 members, account for only 5.3 % of the total (Catalan Sports Observatory 2010). The findings from the study of Galicia conducted by Gambau (2002) are similar. More specifically, 64.5 % of clubs have fewer than 300 members and only 3.1 % of clubs have over a thousand members. Although the number of large clubs is very small, they are of major importance, because they include a fourth of all members, have the most professional structures and can more readily attract public attention (Fig. 21.3).

Another factor that reveals the selective nature of clubs is the activities on offer. Most clubs focus on traditional competitive sports, such as football, basketball, indoor football, cycling and athletics (Catalan Sports Observatory 2010; Gambau 2002). In Catalonia, 88 % of all sports clubs entered in the register of sports clubs and associations overseen by the Secretaria General de l'Esport signed up as federated sports clubs, while the remaining 12 % did so as leisure clubs. If we analyse the range of sporting activities on offer, we find that a majority of clubs—77.3 % in

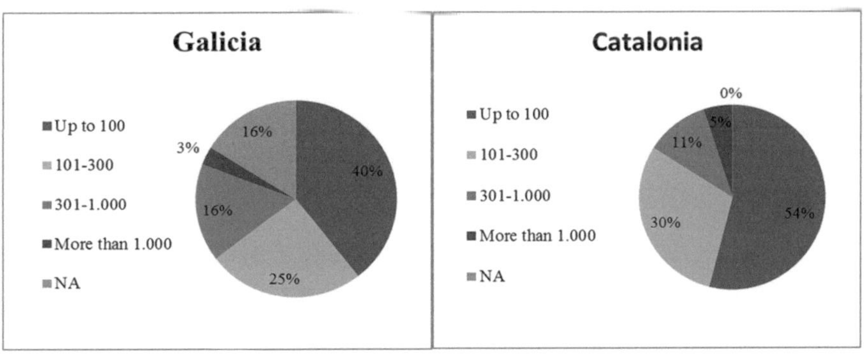


**Fig. 21.3** Distribution of sport clubs in Catalonia and Galicia by size (Catalan Sports Observatory 2010; Gambau 2002, p. 21)

**Table 21.4** Number of teams, by level of competition (%) (Catalan Sports Observatory 2010; Gambau 2002)

| Level | Catalonia (2012) | Galicia (2002) |
|---|---|---|
| Local or district | 48 | 32 |
| Regional | [a] | 23 |
| Autonomous community | 42 | 28 |
| Spain | 8 | 3 |
| International | 2 | 2 |

[a]Not collected

Catalonia and 67 % in Galicia—have only one section. The clubs with a greater number of sections are the large ones. Notably, this figure is lower than the number of clubs belonging to a single federation, which is 85.4 % in the case of Catalonia. This suggests, therefore, that not all of the sports sections of the clubs have competition as their purpose. If we look at competitive sport, we find that the predominant level of competition is local or district, which accounts for 48 % of the teams in Catalonia and 32 % of the teams in Galicia. As Table 21.4 shows, the number of sports teams decreases at higher levels of competition.

The largest clubs are also represented by the most sports people on the national teams. Over half of the large clubs with over 1,000 members have sportspeople on the Spanish and Catalan national squads. By contrast, the small clubs have only 19 % of the sportspeople on the Catalan squads and 8.7 % of those on the Spanish squads.

In addition, some sports clubs initially founded to engage in competitive sport have expanded their provision to include recreational sport. The data show that, aside from sections for competitive sport, 71 % of Catalan sports clubs have an additional offering that is made up of non-sporting activities in 72 % of cases. These include outings, dinners, parties and one-off sporting activities (tournaments, hikes, courses, ski trips, etc.). In 55.2 % of cases, they offer ongoing sporting activities such as, notably, sports campuses, recreational sports leagues and supervised activities. In addition, 20.8 % offer activities for specific groups (children, disabled people, people with difficulties reintegrating into society) (Catalan Sports Observatory 2010).

Ongoing sporting activities are the ones that provide regular income for clubs beyond membership fees. The provision of activities outside the sections for competitive sport enables clubs to reach a broader segment of the population who may potentially be interested in membership. Also, the entire family can engage in physical activity in the same sports organisation or facilities, because while children are engaged in a sporting activity, parents can pursue another activity within the club.

In the Galician study (Gambau 2002), 66 % of clubs offered a single sport, although 63 % also had additional sociocultural offerings. The additional offering is not as pronounced as in Catalonia, but we need to see what has happened in the intervening 12 years in order to better determine any trends in the provision of sporting activities.

Another fact that shows the range of non-competitive activities aimed at recreation and health is the prevalence of subscription members. People with day passes are entitled to use a club's services, but they do not have the same rights as members. For example, they cannot vote. In this respect, more than 25 % of sports clubs in Catalonia have subscription members (Catalan Sports Observatory 2010) and these are the clubs that have facilities such as sports halls, swimming pools and racquet courts that the clubs own or lease.

A clear relationship can be observed between the public administration and voluntary organisations in the use made by the clubs of sports facilities. Of the clubs, 74.3 % in Catalonia and 55.4 % in Galicia use publicly owned facilities, while only 18.7 % of Catalan clubs and roughly 19 % of Galician clubs have their own facilities (Catalan Sports Observatory 2010; Gambau 2002). The public administration clearly plays a vital role in leasing facilities to clubs so that they can carry out their activities.

According to data provided by the Catalan Sports Observatory, the most utilised facilities in Catalonia are indoor sports halls (41.1 %), where participants can engage in sports such as basketball, indoor football, handball, hockey, figure skating, etc. This group of facilities is immediately followed by outdoors sports facilities (29.1 %). Football pitches are used by 25 % of clubs. In addition, 25 % of clubs use the natural environment.

### 21.3.2 Professionalisation and Other Socioeconomic Factors

Sports clubs have two profiles of people working at them: volunteers (39.2 %) and paid staff (60.8 %), in the case of Catalonia. Volunteers perform a service within the club, but do not receive any kind of financial compensation for their contribution, while paid individuals do. The data show that, irrespective of whether the work is voluntary or paid, the people working in Catalan clubs are largely men (75.4 %).

Firstly, we find board members that are made up mostly of men whose contribution is entirely voluntary. Both in Catalonia and in Galicia, the typical profile of all board members (president, vice-president, secretary, treasurer) is male, devoting less than 10 h a week to the post, aged between 36 and 65, and of the upper or upper-middle class. No clear tendency is observed in terms of board members' education level, which can range from primary studies to higher education.

We can also see a vertical segregation by gender. The greater the power of a post, the fewer women there are in possession.

Table 21.5 shows a breakdown of paid and voluntary staff by club size. It includes paid management posts, specialist positions and operational jobs and shows that increasing club size is tied to a higher level of professionalisation.

Professionalisation is also evident in the types of posts, with 70 % of clubs with over 1,000 members have general managers and 61 % have technical directors. By contrast, only 5 % of clubs with fewer than 300 members have general managers and 35 % have technical directors. In Catalonia, with the exception of the post of team delegate, most posts reflect a predominance of paid staff over voluntary staff.

Table 21.5 Breakdown of staff by job profile and club size (%) (Catalan Sports Observatory 2010)

| Size | Paid staff[a] | Voluntary staff |
|---|---|---|
| 100 Members or less | 51.4 | 48.6 |
| 101–300 Members | 57.7 | 42.3 |
| 301–1,000 Members | 59.8 | 40.2 |
| More than 1,000 members | 89.8 | 10.2 |
| Total | 60.8 | 39.2 |

[a]Paid staff may carry out some voluntary work, but most of their work is remunerated

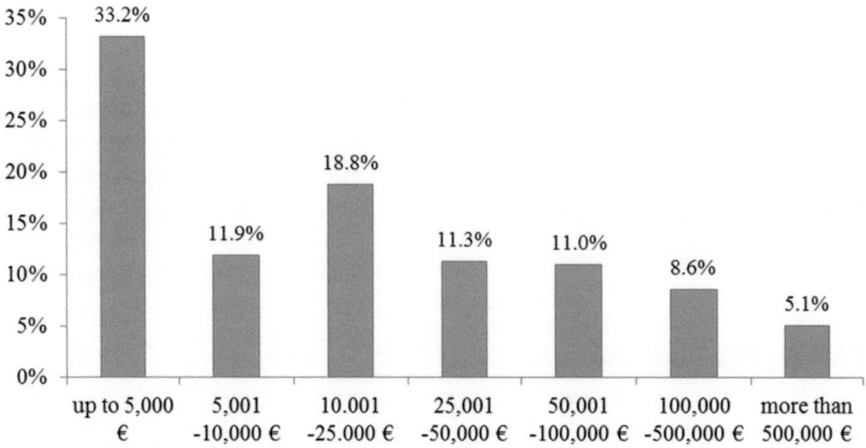


**Fig. 21.4** Size of club budgets (Catalan Sports Observatory 2010, p. 34)

If we analyse club budgets, we can see significant differences among them. The amounts vary from less than 5,000 euros (33 % for Catalonia and 35 % for Galicia) to over 500,000 euros (5.1 % for Catalonia). Figure 21.4 shows the homogeneous distribution of clubs across the different budget sizes.

As Table 21.6 below shows, membership fees are the primary income source for clubs. As a result, the number of members and the size of fees are two significant factors. Unsurprisingly, the largest clubs boast the largest budgets.

However, 26.8 % of clubs with more than a thousand members have a budget lower than 5,000 euros. This is because some of the clubs have very low membership fees, reflecting low levels of activity and, in some cases, a focus on sports that do not necessarily require a licence, such as hiking. Additionally, 10 % of clubs with fewer than 100 people have budgets above 50,000 euros. This can be explained by the fact that, in these cases, the main revenues come from sponsors and not membership fees, such as clubs involved in motorsport. If we look at budgets as a function of membership size, we see that 40 % of clubs have annual budgets below 100 euros per member. At the other extreme, 26 % have budgets above 500 euros per member.

**Table 21.6** Breakdown of income (%) (Catalan Sports Observatory 2010; Gambau 2002)

| | Catalonia | Galicia |
|---|---|---|
| Membership fees | 48.8 | 26.7 |
| Entrance fees | 1.9 | [a] |
| Donations | 1.8 | [a] |
| Sports services | 12.6 | 3.4 |
| Subsidies | 5.3 | 37.5 |
| Rentals | 2.5 | [a] |
| Tickets to events | 1.6 | [a] |
| Advertising and sponsors | 9.2 | 13 |
| Management of assets | [a] | 2.9 |
| Self-funding | [a] | 12.7 |
| Other income | 16.3 | 3.4 |

[a]Not collected

Heinemann and Horch (1991) suggested that one of the main characteristics of sports clubs is their independence from third parties. A club can take decisions and manage its future autonomously if there is no influence from third parties. In this respect, if we analyse the breakdown of club revenues, we see that in Catalonia the main source is membership fees (48.8 %), while in Galicia grants and subsidies (37.5 %) are the main source. This reflects a major difference between the two regions. In the case of Galicia, we observe substantial public administration intervention in the network of associations as a result of the hegemonic social representation of the state described in the first section.

If we look at income by club size, we find in Catalonia that an important source of revenues for large clubs is sports services (12.4 %), while the smallest clubs rely not only on sports services as a key source of revenue, but also on subsidies.

The highest expenditure in Catalonia relates to staff costs (44.4 %). We can also see that clubs with more members have a lower proportion of expenditure that is directly related to the practice of sport. In the case of Galicia, the highest expenditure relates to material resources needed for the practice of sport (40.2 %). This may stem from the fact that sports clubs in Galicia are less professionalised than Catalan sports clubs and also from the fact that the data from the Galician survey date back to 2002. It would be necessary see whether a process of professionalisation can be observed in Galicia's clubs during the intervening 10 years (Table 21.7).

#### 21.3.2.1 Bottlenecks and Challenges Facing Sports Clubs

In the view of board members running Catalan and Galician sports clubs, the biggest problem confronting sports clubs is the economic situation (e.g. covering budget shortfalls and achieving more secure revenues). Their second problem concerns club membership. There is a need in their view to reduce the fluctuations in membership numbers and even out the participation of men and women. The third

**Table 21.7** Breakdown of club expenditure (%) (Catalan Sports Observatory 2010; Gambau 2002)

| | Catalonia | Galicia |
|---|---|---|
| Staff | 44.4 | 19.2 |
| Sports-related expenditure | 23.5 | 40.2 |
| Taxes and fees | 6.0 | 11.7 |
| General expenditure | 18.2 | 23.2 |
| Capital expenditure | 8.0 | 6.5 |

issue is a question of the offering, which they believe needs to be made more appealing and expanded with new activities and services. Lastly, they are concerned about voluntarism; it is becoming increasingly difficult to find people who will give their time and get involved in club-related tasks. In some cases, board members believe that when they leave the club it will collapse, because it is unlikely that anyone will take their place and carry on.

When board members consider their club's success, the first thing they mention is that it is a product of the financial support received from institutions—a belief that reflects "the syndrome of dependence on subsidies" (Gambau 2004, p. 78) and the major dependence of clubs on third parties. The second most important success factor is the active participation of members. Third in Catalonia is the initiative shown by the board members, while the third ranked item in Galicia is viewed as the financial support provided by the federations.

In this respect, Gambau (2004, p. 78) suggests that there is a "discrepancy between the beliefs of current sports managers and the theoretical notions of sports management, suggesting the value of investing more resources in training sports managers and in changing their mind-set."

## 21.4 Conclusions

In the first section of this chapter, we look at the emergence of sports clubs in Spain, a development closely linked to the English model and the arrival of European professionals and workers, and we examine the main features of the earliest clubs, which appeared in civil society as platforms for sociability and were private in nature and operated in an increasingly democratic manner. When the Franco regime took power, however, a radical change came to the structure of sport, making sport subordinate to the state apparatus and stripping clubs of their organisational autonomy and management system. With the restoration of democracy, clubs regained their previous status. However, their organisational culture and operating precepts were still permeated with the authoritarianism of the Franco regime. During the eighties and nineties, Spanish sport underwent modernisation, a process heavily indebted to legal reforms that were conducive to decentralised competencies in the area of sport and a municipalisation of the public provision of sports services.

At this point, an interventionist model took shape, based on state collaboration with clubs. This was a model rooted in the confidence that Spanish society has historically placed in the state's ability to solve problems and meet the needs of the population, going as far back as the seventeenth, eighteenth and nineteenth centuries.

The second section sets out an overview of sports clubs in Spanish society, drawing on quantitative data. A first level of analysis looked at federated sports clubs, which rose in number in the first decade of the twenty-first century from roughly 60,000 to over 94,000. However, since 2011, their numbers have fallen back to their levels at the beginning of the century, obviously as a consequence of the enormous impact of the economic crisis that has affected the country for some years. The analysis of census data for federated sports clubs in Spain has also shown that more than a third (34.6 %) are football clubs. Together with football, eight other sports (basketball, cycling, hunting, climbing, karate, fishing, tennis and athletics) account for 66.4 % of all federated clubs in Spain.

According to data provided through Spain's survey on sporting habits, the last decade has witnessed only a slight growth in the proportion of people belonging to a sports club (from 7 % in 2000 to 8 % in 2010). Greater growth has been seen in gyms or similar (from 3 to 10 % over the same period) and in sports associations (from 6 to 11 %). However, a much steeper rise has occurred in the proportion of people engaging in sport on their own, increasing from 63 % in 2000 to 75 % in 2010. These trends are compatible if we bear in mind that the period involved has also seen a significant growth in sports participation in Spain, rising from 37 % in 2000 to 43 % in 2010. According to the survey, the profile of members of sports clubs and associations is comprised of men, aged 15–34, with university studies, in the upper/upper-middle class, living in cities of more than 50,000 inhabitants.

The third section examines the general characteristics of clubs in greater detail, specifically turning to the autonomous communities of Catalonia and Galicia. The data clearly show that a large number of clubs have been created since the end of the Franco regime. There is a predominance of small clubs with between 3 and 300 members. Also, clubs are not merely competitive in nature, but have expanded their provision to include recreational sport. In addition, the data show the clubs' dependence on the public sector economically and in terms of sports facilities. This reflects the interventionist model described in the first section. However, it must be noted that differences exist between Catalonia and Galicia, particularly in relation to the financial dependence of Galician clubs on the public sector and on their lower level of professionalisation in comparison to Catalan clubs, attesting to the historical and cultural differences that exist among the various autonomous communities. Future research will be needed to address the characteristics of sports clubs across the whole of Spain.

**Acknowledgments** The English translation of this chapter was supported by the Institut Nacional d'Educació Física de Catalunya (INEFC).

## References

Burriel JC, Puig N (1999) Responsabilidades y relaciones entre el sector público y el privado en el sistema deportivo. In: Subirats J (ed) Existe sociedad civil en España? Responsabilidades colectivas y valores públicos. Fundación Encuentro, Madrid, pp 178–200

Catalan Sports Observatory (2010) Els clubs esportius a Catalunya. Secretaria General de l'Esport, Esplugues de Llobregat. http://www.observatoridelesport.cat/uploads/pdf/clubs2010.pdf. Accessed 30 June 2014

CSD (2013) Anuario de Estadísticas Deportivas. Consejo Superior de Deportes, Madrid

CSD (2014) Anuario de Estadísticas Deportivas. Consejo Superior de Deportes, Madrid

Gambau V (2002) Estudio de la organización de los clubes deportivos en Galicia: un análisis empírico. A Coruña: Universidade da Coruña [Doctoral dissertation]

Gambau V (2004) Estudio sobre la gestión de los Clubes Deportivos en Galicia. Investigación y Marketing 83:71–78

García M (1986) Notas para una historia del deporte en España. Revista de Occidente 62–63, 35–49

García-Ferrando M (2006) Postmodernidad y Deporte. Entre la individualización y la masificación. Encuesta sobre hábitos deportivos de los españoles 2005. Consejo Superior de Deportes/Centro de Investigaciones Sociológicas, Madrid

García-Ferrando M, Llopis-Goig R (2011a) Ideal democrático y bienestar personal. La encuesta de hábitos deportivos en España 2010. Centro de Investigaciones Sociológicas, Madrid

García-Ferrando M, Llopis-Goig R (2011b) El deporte en España. Un enfoque sociológico. In: Informe España 2011 (ed) Una interpretación de su realidad social. Fundación Encuentro, Madrid, pp 3–57

Giner S (2000) Los españoles. Plaza y Janés Editores, Barcelona

Heinemann K, Horch HD (1991) Elemente einer Finanzsoziologie freiwilliger Vereinigungen. Verlag Siebek-Mohr, Stuttgart

Heinemann K, Puig N, López C, Moreno A (1997) Clubs esportius a Espanya i Alemanya: una comparació teòrica i empírica. Apunts Educació Física i Esports 49:40–62

Heinemann K, Schubert M (1994) DerSportverein: Ergebnisse einer repräsentativen Untersuchung. Karl Hofmann, Schorndorf

Heinemann K (1999) Sociología de las organizaciones voluntarias. El ejemplo del club deportivo. Editorial Tirant lo Blanch, Valencia

INE (2014) Clubes deportivos federados en España. Datos del Consejo Superior de Deportes. Instituto Nacional de Estadística/Ministerio de Educación, Cultura y Deporte, Madrid

Llopis-Goig R (2006) Clubes y selecciones nacionales de fútbol: la dimensión etnoterritorial del fútbol español. Revista Internacional de Sociología LXIV(45):37–66

Llopis-Goig R (2013) Los clubes de fútbol como organizaciones. Un análisis sociológico referido al origen, evolución y configuración estructural de los principales clubes de fútbol españoles. In: Fabra A, Giménez A (eds) El cambiante mundo de las organizaciones. Teoría, metododología e investigación. Publicaciones de la Universiad Jaume I, Castellón de la Plana, pp 595–614

Puig N, García O, López C (1999a) Clubes deportivos en España. Investigación en Ciencias del Deporte 24:69–77

Puig N, García O, López C (1999b) Sport clubs in Spain. In: Heinemann K (ed) Sport clubs in various European countries. Karl Hofmann, Schorndorf, pp 71–100

Pujadas X, Santacana C (2003) El club deportivo como marco de sociabilidad en España. Una visión histórica (1850-1975). LXIII, Hispania

Rodríguez A (2008) El deporte en la construcción del espacio social. Centro de Investigaciones Sociológicas, Madrid

Santacana C (2011) Espejo de un régimen. Transformación de las estructuras deportivas y su uso político y propagandístico, 1936-1961. In: Pujadas X (ed) Atletas y ciudadanos. Historia Social del Deporte en España 1870-2010. Alianza Editorial, Madrid, pp 205–232

# Chapter 22
# Sport Clubs in Switzerland

**Hanspeter Stamm, Adrian Fischer, Siegfried Nagel, and Markus Lamprecht**

## 22.1 Introduction

This chapter examines the development and characteristics of sport clubs in Switzerland. Starting from a historical overview and some remarks on sport clubs' relevance for Swiss sport and society (Sect. 22.2), we look at some general features of the club system (Sect. 22.3) as well as a number of specific characteristics of the clubs such as their size, finances and the importance of voluntary and paid work (Sect. 22.4). Section 22.5 then examines differences in the structure of sport clubs between the three major Swiss language regions.

There are several data sources on sport clubs in Switzerland on which the chapter has drawn. A number of reviews and studies on (sport) clubs as well as data from the following recent surveys have been used:

(a) In the framework of the *Sport Switzerland 2014* survey, a representative sample of the Swiss population aged between 15 and 74 ($n=10{,}652$) was interviewed regarding their sport participation and sport club membership in mid-2013 (Lamprecht et al. 2014).[1] In some instances, results from the two preceding Sport Switzerland studies of 1999 (Lamprecht and Stamm 2000) and 2007 (Lamprecht et al. 2008) were used to analyse changes over time.

[1]The survey was carried out by the Swiss Observatory for Sport and Physical Activity in close co-operation with the following partners: Swiss Federal Office for Sport (BASPO), Swiss Federal Statistical Office (BFS), Swiss Olympic, Swiss Accident Insurance Fund, Swiss Council for Accident Prevention (bfu) as well as several cantons and towns.

H. Stamm (✉) • A. Fischer • M. Lamprecht
Swiss Observatory for Sport and Physical Activity, Zurich, Switzerland
e-mail: info@sportobs.ch

S. Nagel
Institute of Sport Science, University of Berne, Bern, Switzerland
e-mail: siegfried.nagel@ispw.unibe.ch



C. Breuer et al. (eds.), *Sport Clubs in Europe*, Sports Economics, Management and Policy 12, DOI 10.1007/978-3-319-17635-2_22

(b) More detailed information on the structure and problems of sport clubs comes from two surveys carried out in 1996 (Stamm and Lamprecht 1998) and 2010 (Lamprecht et al. 2011, 2012) with representatives of sport clubs. The more recent study was undertaken in close co-operation with Swiss Olympic (SO), the umbrella organisation of Swiss sport associations and clubs, the Federal Office for Sport and a German project on sport clubs (Breuer 2011). The survey included questions on membership structure, organisational features, offers, goals and finances as well as an assessment of various problems that the clubs face. The most recent study covered about a third of all Swiss sport clubs ($n=6,221$) and is highly representative. In addition, this study also included interviews with representatives from all associations affiliated with SO.

(c) Finally, some results from a recent survey on voluntary work in sport clubs (Schlesinger et al. 2014) were used. The survey was based on case studies of 63 sport clubs and interviews of 1,717 members on their volunteering, motivation, expectations and other factors influencing one's participation and engagement in clubs.

Unless otherwise stated, the results in the following sections are from these three sources.

## 22.2 Historical Background and Context

Sport clubs have been an important feature of Swiss sport for quite a long time. In fact, taking a broad perspective, one could even claim that the establishment of sport clubs preceded the introduction of modern sport in Switzerland. The earliest cross-bow and shooting associations were founded as early as the late medieval times (e.g. in the mid-fourteenth century in the town of Lucerne). However, military defence rather than sport was the primary objective of these early shooting clubs that did not see themselves a sports clubs until well into the twentieth century.

Somewhat the same applies to a second type of early sport clubs. German gymnastics (*Turnen*) were introduced into Switzerland in the early eighteenth century, and from 1819 onwards the first gymnastic clubs started to emerge. Rather than offering competitive sport activities, gymnastic clubs had primarily social and political goals and saw themselves as a setting to build and improve members' bodies, health and characters. Consequently, and similar to shooting, throughout the nineteenth century there was a strong linkage of gymnastics with military defence considerations. Some more decades had to pass before modern sports in the true sense made their way into Switzerland in the wake of industrialists and students who had gotten to know sports in England. The first cycling club was established in Geneva in 1860, followed by the Swiss Alpine Club (1863), St. Gall football club (1879) and the rowing (1986) and tennis associations (1896) to name but a few important dates.

At the beginning of the twentieth century Switzerland thus had three distinctive traditions of sport clubs. Whereas shooting and gymnastics were predominant with a total number of about 1,500 clubs, modern sports clubs were still quite marginal and only started to take off seriously in the twentieth century. However, all three types of clubs had at least two common features that still exist: First, clubs are voluntary organisations with democratic structures that exist because members share a common goal, namely, practising sport (e.g. Nagel 2008). Second, and to the extent that the number of clubs was growing, coordinating mechanisms integrating clubs of the same sport, so-called sport associations, were established.

As the number of clubs and associations increased during the first decades of the twentieth century, a further need for coordination beyond single sports was felt, and in 1922 the first umbrella organisation of Swiss sport associations was founded by nine associations including gymnastics but not shooting.[2] The remainder of the twentieth century saw a more or less steady rise in the number of sport clubs and an increasing differentiation into different sports. Currently, SO has 84 member associations representing roughly 20,000 clubs which means that there are more than 2.5 clubs per 1,000 inhabitants. All important Olympic sports federations are members of SO. The only sport of some importance in Switzerland currently not being a member of SO is *Schwingen*, a traditional form of wrestling. At the same time, however, SO also integrates a number of associations and clubs only loosely associated with sport in the strict sense as, for example, (boy) scouts or an association aimed at improving school sports. Apart from the scout movement (602 clubs in 2009), these associations do not play a major role in SO and in the system of sport clubs, however.

As can be seen from Table 22.1, in 2009, shooting and gymnastics were still the most important club sports in terms of the number of clubs. Yet, other sports such as football, tennis, skiing, volleyball, cycling, athletics, riding and floorball have gained ground over the past 100 years. In terms of active members, gymnastics, football, *academic sports*, tennis, shooting and the Swiss Alpine Club are most important with over 100,000 members each. In total, there are currently about 2.7 million persons in Switzerland belonging to one or more sport clubs, 2.2 million of which are classified as *active members*. Correcting for persons that are members in more than one club, the total number of club members is estimated at 1.6 million or about 20 % of the Swiss population (see also Fig. 22.1).

Despite these impressive numbers, sport clubs are currently not the only and not even the most important setting for practising sport in Switzerland. There are no figures regarding general sports participation during the nineteenth and the first half of the twentieth century but it is safe to say that until the 1960s, most sports took place in the framework of clubs. Since then, the sport system has expanded and integrated ever more persons in an increasing number of sports and settings (Lamprecht and Stamm 2002).

[2] Shooting joined the sports movement only in 1941. It is also important to note that the Swiss Olympic Committee had already been founded in 1912 but only joined forces with the general umbrella organisation of Swiss sport clubs and associations in 1987.

**Table 22.1** Most important club sports and their associations in Switzerland (2009)[a]

| Sport | Number of active members | Number of clubs |
|---|---|---|
| Gymnastics | 297,000 | 3,288 |
| Football | 272,000 | 1,450 |
| Tennis | 189,000 | 839 |
| Academic Sports Association[b] | 133,000 | 16 |
| Shooting | 131,000 | 3,125 |
| Swiss Alpine Club | 125,000 | 122 |
| Skiing | 91,000 | 810 |
| Golf | 69,000 | 94 |
| Riding | 62,000 | 475 |
| Judo and Ju-Jitsu | 49,000 | 303 |
| Swimming | 47,000 | 200 |
| Athletics | 45,000 | 479 |
| Swissfit[c] | 42,000 | 488 |
| Company Sports Association[d] | 36,000 | 421 |
| Volleyball | 34,000 | 611 |
| Floorball | 29,000 | 446 |
| Cycling | 16,000 | 517 |
| Basketball | 15,000 | 205 |

[a]Associations with more than 15,000 members; excluding non-sports organisations
[b]The Academic Sports Association integrates universities' sport clubs (one per university)
[c]Association made up of the former *Workers' Sport Association* and the Catholic *Women's Gymnastic Association*

[d]Sport clubs existing in the framework of enterprises

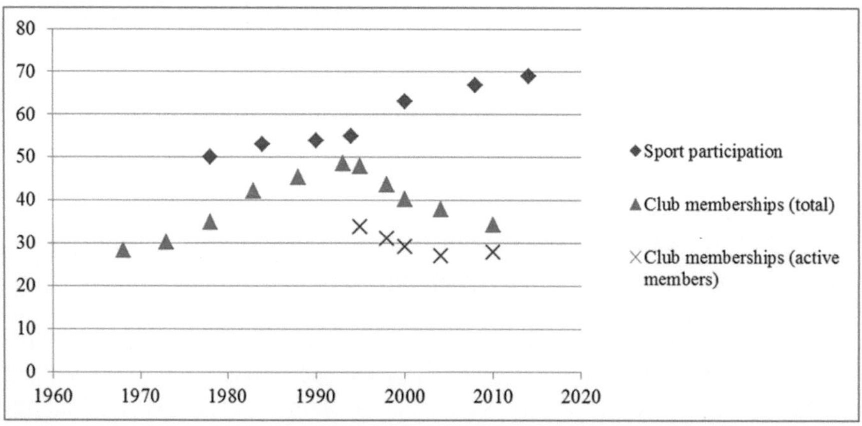


**Fig. 22.1** Sport participation and sport club memberships (per cent of the population), late 1960s to early 2010s (Lamprecht et al. 2012, 2014). Note: Sport participation: percentage of persons claiming to participate at least once per week in sport; Club memberships: total club memberships (including passive members and double counts) and active members (including double counts) as a percentage of total population

The data in Fig. 22.1 suggest, that club sports have initially profited from this development but that sport outside of clubs has grown even more strongly over the past few decades. The decline of total sport club memberships in Fig. 22.1 is somewhat misleading, however, for two reasons: On the one hand, membership rosters have been improved since the 1990s leading to a decrease in double counts and nominal member figures. On the other hand, compulsory membership of conscripts in shooting clubs was abandoned in 1997 leading to a sharp drop in membership figures of about 350,000 members in the following years. In addition, the number of active club members appears to have increased slightly over the past few years. In fact, if we exclude shooting clubs from the calculation, we find a net gain in active memberships of 10 % for the period of 1995–2009.

Still, the total number of clubs has dropped from an all-time high of 27,090 in 1995 to 20,728 in 2010 (see also Sect. 22.3) due to a number of factors: mergers of (small) clubs, the disappearance of small clubs (shooting clubs in particular) and improved accounting procedures in the sense that up to the 1990s clubs were often counted more than once when they were members of more than one association (e.g. gymnastic clubs that also have volleyball and handball teams, see also Sect. 22.3).

## 22.3 Role of Sport Clubs in Policy and Society

Even though sport clubs no longer appear to be the dominant framework for practising sport they still hold an important position in the Swiss sport system: According to the recent *Sport Switzerland 2014* survey, about three quarters of the Swiss population aged between 15 and 74 years (74 %) participate in sports, and about a third of these persons (25 %) also hold a club membership (see Fig. 22.1 and Table 22.2 below). Sport clubs are particularly important when it comes to regular and competitive activities: 84 % of all club members and 76 % of all *independent* sport participants claim to be active for at least 2 h per week, and 50 % of all club members but only 10 % of the other respondents are involved in competitions that are usually organised and coordinated by sport associations. In this connection, it also needs to be mentioned that team sports are hardly ever played outside of clubs.

The Sport Switzerland survey also contains data on the general relevance and structure of club sports in Switzerland. Whereas Fig. 22.1 above shows the overall participation in sport and sport clubs, selected characteristics of sport club members and other sport participants are being compared in Table 22.2. As can be seen from the table, men are predominant in sport clubs—in fact, only 42 % of all club members are women—whereas general sport participation does not vary greatly between men and women. In addition, there are also differences with respect to citizenship in the sense that migrants are underrepresented in Swiss sport clubs.

There is also a distinctive age structure in the sense that sport clubs have a considerably higher share of young athletes than the general population. A further analysis on the basis of the 2010 sport clubs survey shows this in more detail

**Table 22.2** Characteristics of active sport club members and other sport participants, 2013 (per cent of total population aged 15–74 years) (Federal Statistical Office for Population Data 2014, Sport Switzerland 2014 for sport and club participants)

| | | Total population (distribution %) | All sport participants[a] (% of total population) | Active sport club members (% of total population) |
|---|---|---|---|---|
| Overall | | | 73.7 | 25.2 |
| Gender | Female | 50.7 | 74.1 | 19.9 |
| | Male | 49.3 | 73.3 | 31.0 |
| Age | 15–29 Years | 24.1 | 79.8 | 34.7 |
| | 30–44 Years | 28.6 | 75.4 | 24.6 |
| | 45–59 Years | 28.1 | 72.4 | 22.0 |
| | 60–74 Years | 19.2 | 68.2 | 21.3 |
| Citizenship | Swiss | 77.6 | 76.0 | 27.2 |
| | Foreign | 22.4 | 61.1 | 13.7 |

[a]All persons claiming to participate in sport at least occasionally

**Table 22.3** Age and gender of active club members, 2010 (Lamprecht et al. 2012)

| | Population share[a] | Share of all active members | Share of women in age group |
|---|---|---|---|
| 10 Years and less | 11 | 9 | 49 |
| 11–20 Years | 11 | 26 | 37 |
| 21–40 Years | 27 | 34 | 35 |
| 41–60 Years | 29 | 23 | 36 |
| Over 60 years | 22 | 9 | 31 |

[a]Share of age group in the total Swiss population of 2010

(see Table 22.3): The share of persons 20 years old or younger in all sport clubs amounts to 35 %, even though the share of this group in the population is only 22 %. On the other hand, elderly persons are underrepresented in sport clubs: only 9 % of all club members are older than 60 years, even though this group also accounts for 22 % of the total population. As is shown by Table 22.3, there is also a relationship between age and gender in the sense that in the youngest group there are about equal shares of boys and girls. During adolescence, the number of women drops sharply, however.

Of course, the social composition of a club depends to a large extent on the sport(s) it offers. The club survey of 2010 suggests, for example, that volleyball, ice skating and gymnastics have elevated shares of women whereas there are, not surprisingly, hardly any women in ice hockey, wrestling and weight lifting. Children and adolescents are particularly often found in ice skating, swimming, taekwondo and karate, and almost absent in bowling, boules or pétanque clubs. Finally, the share of foreign nationals is above average in football, basketball and karate. Conversely, winter sports such as skiing and curling as well as crossbow and rifle shooting have a low proportion of migrants thus reflecting differing cultural preferences for selected sports in the Swiss and migrant population.

Before analysing the structure of sport clubs in somewhat more detail, a few further remarks on the significance of sport clubs in the Swiss sport system are suitable. There are two important reasons why sport clubs have played a decisive role in the development of sport in Switzerland and keep on being a major force in Swiss sport.

1. *Club friendly environment*: The establishment and operation of clubs has always been simple in Switzerland and was seldom opposed by the authorities as was, for example, the case in Germany, where gymnastics were banned on political grounds from 1820 to 1842. Currently, Swiss law only has two prerequisites for establishing a club: First, clubs are voluntary organisations of members sharing a common goal and must not be oriented towards making an economic profit, and, second, they need to have written statutes stating their aims and organisational characteristics.

   In this connection it should be noted, that most sport clubs have a secular background. Even though there was a number of explicitly catholic clubs during the twentieth century they have all but vanished. In a similar fashion, *class-based* sport clubs are no longer of major importance. Interestingly, the *Swiss Association of female Catholic gymnasts* has merged with the *Swiss Workers' Gymnastic Union* to form a new organisation called *swissfit* in 2003 (see also Table 22.1). To be sure, there are still social differences between clubs, but these usually do no longer proceed along conventional social class or occupational lines (academic clubs, -workers' clubs etc.) but rather correspond to economic wealth (via membership fees), one's citizenship (clubs of migrants, e.g. *FC Portugal*, *Stella Italia*) and differing preferences for certain sports in different milieus.
2. *Clubs as a partial substitute for public initiatives*: When sport and the first sport clubs emerged, there was not yet a central government that could play a role in shaping sports. In fact, in the absence of strong public authorities, early clubs—not only in sports but also in areas such as science, education and politics—have often assumed official functions. Even after the foundation of the Swiss Confederation in 1848 the central government remained weak, and somewhat the same applies to regional and municipal authorities that keep on relying to a considerable extent on contributions by clubs and other non state actors. Thus, sport and other clubs are to some extent a private and officially encouraged alternative to public interventions and have become an important feature of Swiss civil society.[3] Sports clubs and associations are the main promoters of leisure sport and top level sports in Switzerland whereas public authorities are responsible for sport and physical activities at school.

However, it would be wrong to assume that there is no political support for sport in Switzerland. The key word in this connection is *subsidiarity*, i.e. a system in which the initiative is left to individuals and private organisations such as sport

[3] For 2007, Helmig, Gmür, Bärlocher & Bächtold (2010) have estimated the total number of clubs in Switzerland to be about 76,500. This translates into about ten clubs per 1,000 inhabitants. More than a quarter of all clubs in Switzerland are sport clubs.

clubs whose activities are supported by the authorities if they are perceived as contributing to the common good (for details concerning Switzerland's public sport policy see Chappelet 2010). An important kind of support already mentioned above entails providing a favourable legal framework that facilitates the establishment and operation of sport clubs. In addition, sport clubs are supported either indirectly or directly by public authorities on the national, regional or municipal level. An example of direct support is the national *Youth and Sport* programme in whose framework over 50 million Swiss Francs per year are distributed by the Federal Office of Sport to clubs and schools engaged in the promotion of youth sports. In addition, about ten million francs of public funds per year are channelled into organised sport via SO. Sport facilities are an important type of indirect support as they are usually built, maintained and operated by local authorities but made available to sport clubs and individuals at concessional rates (Balthasar et al. 2013). According to the sport club survey of 2010, about three quarters of all sport clubs (73 %) rely exclusively or partially on public sport facilities.[4]

Thus, despite a lack of far-reaching direct interventions, sport clubs are effectively being supported by public authorities and are acknowledged as an important pillar of the Swiss sport system. In general, they are supposed to fulfil several welfare functions in the context of health promotion, the socialisation of children and adolescents and the social integration. Sport clubs, in turn, are aware of the role they play in sport and society. In the 2010 survey, large proportions of all interviewed officials claimed that their clubs *offer cheap sport opportunities* (83 %), *are interested in leisure and popular sport* (80 %), integrate young (68 %) as well as elderly people (68 %), *low income* groups (66 %) and migrants (66 %) and *play an important role in community life* (53 %) as well as in *health sports* (43 %) to name but a few of the positive functions that clubs associate with their activities.

## 22.4 Characteristics of Sport Clubs

As stated above, there are over 20,000 sport clubs in Switzerland. As Table 22.4 illustrates, these clubs are on average rather small: Somewhat less than two thirds of all clubs have 100 or less active members. Large clubs with more than 500 active members are quite rare (2.7 %).

Since the late 1990s, these figures have not changed fundamentally, but there is a slight trend towards bigger clubs: The share of large clubs with more than 500 members has doubled, the share of mid-sized clubs has also increased, and average membership figures per club have increased by 19 %. At the same time, and as noted in Sect. 22.2, the overall number of clubs has dropped by 23 %, but the number of active members increased by 10 % if one does not take into account the

[4]Thirty-two percent of all clubs also use facilities belonging to the club and 19 % use privately owned facilities. The sum of these numbers is more than 100 % because some clubs use different types of facilities.

**Table 22.4** Size of sport clubs, 1996 and 2010 (percentage of clubs in different size categories)

| | 1996 | 2010 |
|---|---|---|
| 1–50 Active members | 40.7 | 40.9 |
| 51–100 Active members | 26.4 | 23.5 |
| 101–200 Active members | 21.1 | 19.5 |
| 201–500 Active members | 10.7 | 13.4 |
| More than 500 active members | 1.3 | 2.7 |
| Average number of active members per club[a] | 89 | 106 |

[a]Figures calculated from overall membership and club figures for 1995 (2.4 million active members in 27,090 clubs) and 2007 (2.2 million active members in 20,728 clubs)

shrinking rifle clubs. These conflicting figures suggest that many clubs have vanished or merged into bigger units while other clubs appear to have thrived.[5]

More than two thirds of all sport clubs restrict their activities to one sport (68 %), with the remainder having a more varied offer. For example, many gymnastic clubs also have team sports and special fitness trainings in their programme. Taking these multiple offers into account, we find that traditional gymnastics (*Turnen*) are most widespread in the Swiss club system with 16 % of all clubs offering this sport. Further important sports are shooting (13 % of all clubs), football (13 %), fitness training (12 %), general gymnastics (11 %), athletics (10 %), volleyball (10 %), floorball (9 %), aerobics training (8 %), tennis (7 %) and skiing (5 %). Overall, the clubs in the 2010 survey offer 150 different sports, many of which (as for example synchronised swimming, modern pentathlon or American football) are only practised in a handful of clubs.

An important feature of Swiss sport clubs is their interest in competitive sports: 85.5 % of all clubs participate in competitions at the regional (33 %), national (34 %) or even international level (19 %), and 61 % claim to be proud of their success in competitive sport. However, participation in competitions is not a prerequisite for membership in most clubs. In fact, the 2010 survey shows, that less than half of all active members (42 %) engage in competitive sports. As a consequence, most clubs (80 %) subscribe to the view that they are primarily aimed at leisure and popular sports (which may or may not be competitive). In addition, clubs often have different departments for recreational and competitive sports. A further differentiation is usually found with respect to the age of participants: Depending on the size of the club and the sport being played, one may find one or more branches for kids and adolescents as well as different recreational and competitive teams for adults. In addition, most clubs are not only interested in sport but organise further activities such as parties (88 % of all clubs) and claim to be engaged in the prevention of tobacco, alcohol and drug abuse (69 %).

[5]Of the 84 member associations of SO, 44 have increased their membership figures between 1995 and 2009, and 30 have lost members during the same period. There are no data for the remaining 8 associations. The biggest winners for this period were football, golf and riding, the biggest losers were shooting, company sports and tennis.

**Table 22.5** Earnings and expenses of sport clubs by size, 2010 (rounded median mean values in €)

| | Earnings (€) | | Expenses (€) | |
|---|---|---|---|---|
| | Total | Per active member | Total | Per active member |
| Small clubs (up to 100 members) | 6,400 | 166 | 6,000 | 160 |
| Mid-sized clubs (101–300 members) | 33,800 | 203 | 31,100 | 191 |
| Large clubs (more than 300 members) | 94,700 | 204 | 94,700 | 208 |
| Average (median) | 10,800 | 177 | 10,200 | 169 |

Note: The use of median average values may explain the surprising finding that earnings and expenses appear to be balanced in large clubs

Club size appears to play an important role with respect to a number of further features of the clubs. Table 22.5 shows a summary of earnings and expenses of clubs according to their size. Not surprisingly, small clubs have considerably lower total earnings and expenses than bigger clubs. In addition, they also appear to generate and spend less money per member. Overall, the finances of clubs appear to be in order as earnings usually exceed expenses slightly. In fact, only 28 % of all clubs in the 2010 survey report a financial deficit which is rather small in most cases: In only a fifth (22 %) of these clubs the deficit amounts to more than 100 Swiss Francs (about €68) per active member. At the same time, over half of all clubs (54 %) report a profit. Again, only one fifth of these clubs have a substantial gain of more than 100 Swiss Francs per active member.

Figure 22.2 shows, that membership fees and public grants account for about half of a club's budget. Advertising and sponsoring also plays a role, and a further important source of income are events organised by the clubs. If we have stated earlier that most clubs organise events and competitions we now find that these activities have often an important economic rationale. In addition, the importance of different income sources varies according to club size: Large clubs rely more heavily on membership fees (51 % of all earnings) than small clubs (31 %) which, in turn, generate a larger proportion of earnings with advertising and sponsoring (18 % vs. 12 %) and events (16 % vs. 8 %). In addition, the share of different income sources varies according to the sport that is practised in a club: Golf (71 %) and tennis clubs (64 %) are much more dependent upon membership fees than handball (19 %), rifle shooting (18 %) and cycling clubs (13 %). Golf and tennis clubs also have comparatively high membership fees (golf: median value of CHF 2000, tennis: CHF 400). Average values for all clubs are considerably lower ranging from CHF 50 per year for kids to about CHF 150 per year for licensed athletes. Conversely, advertising and sponsoring appear to play a comparatively large role in team sports such as handball (52 %), football (32 %) and ice hockey (29 %) as well as in cycling (32 %).

With respect to expenses, staff and operative costs are most important (see Fig. 22.2), but, once again, there are substantial variations with respect to club size and sport. Small clubs have a lower share of staff costs (21 %) than big clubs (42 %), whose operation costs are comparatively lower (36 % vs. 52 %). The share of staff

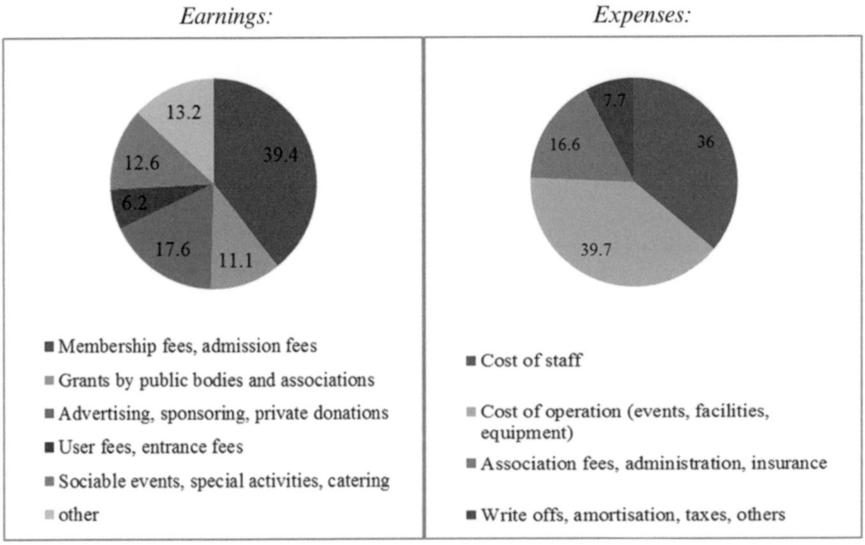


**Fig. 22.2** Share of different categories of earnings and expenses in an average sports club, 2010 (percentages) (Lamprecht et al. 2012)

costs is highest in swimming (55 %), football (54 %) and handball (51 %) and lowest in shooting (8 %), yachting (10 %) and cycling (12 %). In cycling clubs, operation costs (67 %) are much higher than in the above mentioned team sports (about 30 %).

The high share of staff costs in an average club would at first glance suggest that Swiss sport clubs are highly professionalised. This is not the case, however, as is shown in Table 22.6. Keeping in mind that most clubs only have small earnings and expenses, staff cost usually refers to comparatively small compensations and allowances for travel cost, equipment etc. In fact, most work in clubs is done by volunteers that earn less than CHF 2000 per year (about €1,350). An average club has 14 volunteers[6] but less than one person earning more than CHF 2000 per year. In sum, Swiss sport clubs rely on about 285,000 volunteers and 17,500 paid persons, only 3,500 of which have a paid workload of 50 % or more. In other words, paid work is still comparatively unimportant and amounts only to about 20 % of all the work done in the framework of Swiss sport clubs.

Yet, it is important to note that paid work has become more important since 1996 when it only accounted for about 10 % of the whole work effort in the Swiss sport clubs. Since then, the number of paid workers has almost doubled while the number of volunteers (minus 19 %) as well as the total work done by them (minus 13 %) has decreased substantially. However, this trend towards a higher share of paid work

[6] Of these 14 persons, six hold a position in the club's board (president, CFO, secretary etc.), a further seven are directly involved in sports as coaches, managers or referees and one person has other tasks such as caring for the equipment.

**Table 22.6** Voluntary and paid work in Swiss sport clubs, 1996 and 2010

| | 1996 | 2010 |
|---|---|---|
| Voluntary work[a] | | |
| Number of volunteers per club | 13 | 14 |
| Number of volunteers per 100 active members | 13 | 13 |
| Average work load per month | 11 h | 12 h |
| Total number of volunteers | 350,000 | 285,000 |
| Number of full-time equivalents | 24,000 | 21,000 |
| Economic value | 1.0–1.3 billion € | 1.0–1.3billion € |
| Paid work[b] | | |
| Number of paid workers per club | <1 | <1 |
| Share of clubs with paid workers | 15 % | 14 % |
| Share of workload of paid workers of total club work | 10 % | 20 % |
| Average work load per month | 45 h | 48 h |
| Total number of paid workers | 10,000 | 17,500 |
| Number of full-time equivalents | 2,800 | 5,300 |
| Economic value | 120–160 million € | 250–330 million € |

[a]Unpaid personnel and personnel receiving less than 1,350 € per year. The number of volunteers excludes persons doing informal auxiliary services (see text)

[b]Persons getting paid more than 1,350 € per year

appears to be confined to bigger clubs and has not yet spread to the club system as a whole: As in the 1990s, only about one in seven clubs has currently paid workers at all.

Voluntary work keeps on being a decisive resource of club sports. In fact, 92 % of all clubs in the 2010 survey subscribe to the view that their club lives primarily on voluntary work. In addition, professional work does not appear to be a viable alternative to voluntary work on a large scale. Our estimates regarding the economic value of voluntary and paid work done in the clubs in Table 22.6 suggest that membership fees and other earnings would have to increase beyond most members' willingness to pay if voluntary work were to be substituted by professional work. The more so, because the numbers in Table 22.6 only refer to formal volunteers (board members, coaches, referees etc.) and not to all persons who occasionally help in the club, e.g. when organising a sociable event or when kids need driving to facilities. A further estimate suggests that there are an additional 450,000 persons doing such auxiliary services amounting to about 6 h per person and month in the clubs.

Furthermore, the current study of Schlesinger et al. (2014) shows that there is only a marginal correlation between club size and the relative number of volunteers. However, there are more volunteers in rural regions compared to sport clubs in an urban environment, and in traditional sport clubs supporting competitive sports volunteering is more important than in clubs with growth-oriented goals (Schlesinger and Nagel 2013). Multilevel analyses indicate that besides these structural characteristics also individual determinants play a role with regard to the engagement of club members as volunteers. Whereas the percentage of women in volunteer

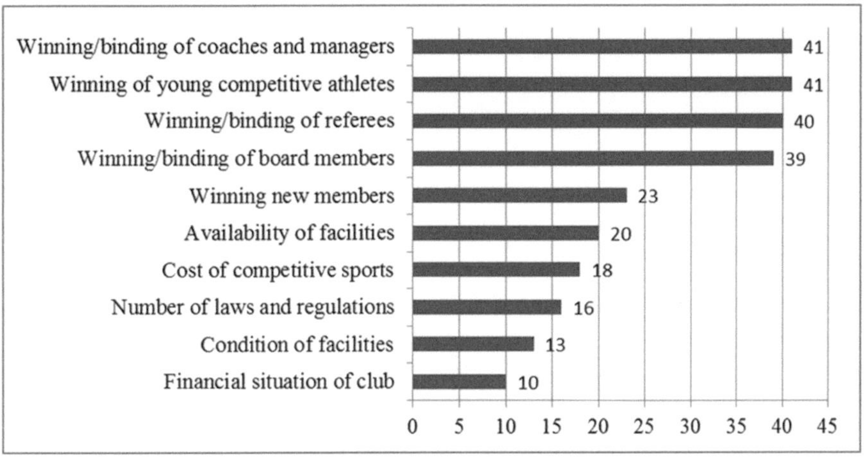


**Fig. 22.3** Ranking of selected problems faced by Swiss sport clubs, 2010 (per cent share of clubs which regard the problems as major). Note: Of a total of 22 problems assessments were asked; the figure only includes a number of problems that were particularly often claimed to be major

positions is nearly equal to their membership rates, higher income and education, children belonging to the same club, long-term club membership and especially a strong identification with the club have a positive effect on the willingness to volunteer. In addition, the satisfaction with the job as volunteer correlates positively with the willingness of long-term volunteering. The following factors are relevant for the volunteer job satisfaction (see Schlesinger et al. 2013): task design, leadership, support, recognition, material incentives. Finally, it has to be pointed out that about half of the volunteers could be characterised as stable whereas the other half occasionally or often think about terminating their volunteering.

Against this background it is hardly surprising that finding volunteers and helpers is one of the most serious problems faced by many clubs. As Fig. 22.3 shows, about 40 % of all clubs claim that winning and binding coaches, referees and board members are major problems. A similar share of clubs also mention recruitment problems with respect to young athletes whereas general membership problems appear to affect less than a quarter of the clubs. Facilities, cost and financial issues as well as legal ramifications also appear to be an important challenge for between 10 and 20 % of all clubs.

Looking at the results in Fig. 22.3 one could also conclude that only a minority of all clubs mention the quoted major problems and that it is anyway not entirely clear what a major problem implies. Against this background, the 2010 club survey included an additional question asking which of the problems clubs saw as *life-threatening*. More than two thirds of all clubs (68 %) do not mention any life-threatening problems despite occasionally identifying some problems as major. However, a rough fifth of all clubs (18 %) report one life-threatening problem and a further 14 % two or more such problems. As suggested by Fig. 22.3, *life-threatening* problems most often refer to voluntary work and the winning and binding of members. Small clubs (37 %) appear to be affected by life-threatening problems more often than large clubs (22 %) which suggests that some of these clubs may vanish or merge in the future thus confirming the trend towards a smaller number of, on average, larger clubs mentioned above.

## 22.5 Differences Between the Swiss Language Regions

According to the discussion in Sects. 22.3 and 22.4 the system of sport clubs in Switzerland is highly differentiated, and there is variation with respect to club size and the sport that is done in the framework of the club. Further differences with respect to community size as well as gender and age structure are discussed in the full study (Lamprecht et al. 2012) that also includes analyses of a special feature of the Swiss sport system that are discussed briefly in this section: differences with respect to language region.

In the context of a book on sport clubs in Europe the three major language regions of Switzerland—German (72 % of the population), French (24 %) and Italian (5 %)—are of interest for two reasons: First, there is the question whether there are differences between the three culturally different regions, and second, whether these differences are in any way related to general (cultural) characteristics of the neighbouring countries, i.e. whether clubs from the German speaking part of Switzerland are more similar to German and Austrian clubs than to clubs from the French speaking part of Switzerland which might, in turn, be more similar to French clubs.

As other analyses have shown (Lamprecht et al. 2008, 2014; Stamm and Lamprecht 2011; Studer et al. 2011), sports participation in general differs substantially between the three regions: 71 % of the German speaking population claims to participate in sport at least once per week whereas these shares are considerably lower in the French (63 %) and Italian (56 %) speaking parts of Switzerland. According to the latest Eurobarometer study (European Commission 2014), these differences correspond to differences in the neighbouring countries of Switzerland: Germany (48 %) has the highest participation rate of persons doing sport at least once a week, followed by Austria (45 %), France (43 %) and Italy (30 %).

Against this general background it is not surprising that the German speaking part of Switzerland has more sport clubs per 1,000 inhabitants than the other language regions (see Table 22.7). As Table 22.7 shows, there is also a number of further differences: Clubs tend to be bigger but have less voluntary workers in the French speaking part of the country which might explain the higher share of staff cost in total expenses. In the Italian speaking region, the share of young members and the number and workload of volunteers is bigger than in the other two areas. These two findings may well be connected as a large number of children may lead to a greater demand for youth coaches. In view of the fact that children's membership fees usually are a lot lower than adults' fees, it is also striking that membership fees appear to be more important in the Italian speaking part of Switzerland than in the other regions.

**Table 22.7** Selected characteristics of Swiss sport clubs by language region, 2010 (Lamprecht et al. 2014)

| | German | French | Italian | Switzerland |
|---|---|---|---|---|
| Active club members as a percentage of population[a] | 26 | 25 | 14 | 25 |
| Club memberships as a percentage of population[a] | 30 | 30 | 18 | 29 |
| No. of clubs per 1000 inhabitants | 2.8 | 2.2 | 2.2 | 2.5 |
| Average size of clubs (members) | 123 | 153 | 129 | 110 |
| 5 Sports most often practised in clubs | Gymnastics<br>Fitness training<br>Rifle shooting<br>Football<br>Athletics | Football<br>Rifle shooting<br>Gymnastics<br>Volleyball<br>Skiing | Football<br>Gymnastics<br>Athletics<br>Floorball<br>Basketball | Gymnastics<br>Rifle shooting<br>Football<br>Fitness training<br>Athletics |
| Share of children and adolescents[b] | 37 | 32 | 43 | 35 |
| No. of volunteers per 100 active members | 14 | 11 | 17 | 14 |
| Average workload of volunteers per month | 11 | 11 | 15 | 12 |
| Membership fees as a percentage of earnings | 40 | 35 | 52 | 39 |
| Cost of staff as a percentage of expenses | 31 | 50 | 32 | 36 |
| Percentage of clubs with one or more life-threatening problems | 31 | 36 | 34 | 32 |

[a]All data were taken from Lamprecht et al. (2012) except active and general club memberships
[b]Persons aged 20 years and younger

In sum, there appears to be a marked difference between the reliance on voluntary work and the share of young members between the Italian and French speaking parts of Switzerland with the German speaking part taking the middle ground between these two poles. It is difficult to relate these finding to general cultural preferences in the three language regions in Switzerland or to the characteristics of clubs in the neighbouring countries Austria, France, Germany and Italy. Overall, the French and Italian regions appear to react somewhat differently to the generally lower interest in sport and sport clubs: In the Italian speaking part of Switzerland, clubs are particularly popular with children but do not appear to be too attractive for adults. This conforms to data from the Sport Switzerland 2008 study that shows similar sport participation rates for kids and adolescents in all three language regions but a particularly steep drop in sports participation for adults in the Italian part of Switzerland. In the French speaking part of Switzerland, on the other hand, the interest in voluntary work appears to be smaller than in the German speaking part which also appears to be the case in the corresponding neighbouring countries.

This finding corresponds with the results of current studies on volunteering in Switzerland (e.g. Stadelmann-Steffen et al. 2010) that show generally higher rates of volunteering in the German speaking part for different fields of the club system. Thus, the sports clubs in the French speaking part need some compensation with paid work that is—as shown before—more prevalent in larger clubs that may be able to afford it.

Interestingly, however, the larger average size of clubs in the French speaking part of Switzerland contradicts the findings from the neighbouring countries because the average size of clubs appears to be bigger in Germany and Austria than in France. Overall, however, clubs in Switzerland tend to be smaller than in the neighbouring countries. Together with the fact that (club) sport appears to be particularly popular in Switzerland, this explains the higher density of clubs in Switzerland. Apart from these findings, there are no clear correspondences between the Swiss language regions and the neighbouring countries, however.

## 22.6 Summary and Concluding Remarks

We can conclude that there is a differentiated and important system of sport clubs in Switzerland that has a long tradition and nowadays includes over 20,000 clubs and about 20 % of the country's population. Public authorities in Switzerland usually do not initiate—apart from sport at school—their own sport programmes. However they support private initiatives, especially sport clubs which are still the most important organisational *player* in the private sport sector. Even though they are no longer the most important setting for sports participation—independent sports are even more popular—clubs still play a crucial role in the sport system, particularly with respect to regular, competitive, youth and team sports. As participation in competitions is usually no prerequisite to become an active member, clubs often need to maintain differentiated internal structures for recreational as well as competitive members and for different age groups with specific needs. Particularly for children and adolescents they offer a broad range of different sports and about half of the population aged between 10 and 19 years is currently member of a sport club.

Voluntary work is the most important resource of sport clubs but also constitutes their biggest challenge: If clubs report *major* or *life-threatening* problems these very often relate to voluntary work. Yet, it is also important to note that there is no way around voluntary work despite it becoming an increasingly scarce resource. Although the majority of the sport clubs in Switzerland has less than 200 members, some strain appears to have been taken from clubs in the past few years by merging or growing into bigger and more work-effective units without becoming overly professionalised. Against this background, the claim that sport clubs are doing much for the common good has quite a lot going for it: Sport clubs integrate large groups of people and promote their health, are operating at a comparably low cost and appear to offer something that is in demand by around a fifth of the population. And most likely they will achieve these various welfare functions also in the future.

## References


Balthasar A, Bieri O, Laubereau B, Arnold T, Rütter H, Höchli C, Rieser A, Stettler J, Wehrli R. Sportanlagenstatistik Schweiz 2012. Statistische Grundlagen mit betriebs- und energiewirtschaftlichen Vertiefungen. Lucerne and Rüschlikon: Interface/Rütter and Partner/ITW Luzern; 2013.

Breuer C. Sportentwicklungsbericht 2009/10. Analyse zur Situation der Sportvereine in Deutschland. Köln: Strauss; 2011.

Chappelet J-L. Switzerland. Int J Sport Pol. 2010;2:99–110.

European Commission. Special Eurobarometer 412. Sport and physical activity. Brussels: European Commission; 2014.

Federal Statistical Office (2014) Population data tables on website. http://www.bfs.admin.ch/bfs/portal/de/index/themen/01/02/blank/key/bevoelkerungsstand/02.html. Accessed 2 June 2014

Helmig B, Gmür M, Bärlocher C, Bächtold C. Statistik des Dritten Sektors in der Schweiz. In: Helmig B, Lichtsteiner H, Gmür M, editors. Der Dritte Sektor der Schweiz Länderstudie zum Johns Hopkins Comparative Nonprofit Sector Project. Bern: Haupt; 2010. p. 173–205.

Lamprecht M, Stamm H. Sport Schweiz 2000. Sportaktivität und Sportkonsum der Schweizer Bevölkerung. Basel, Bern, Zürich: SOV, STG, LSSFB; 2000.

Lamprecht M, Stamm H. Sport zwischen Kultur, Kult und Kommerz. Zürich: Seismo; 2002.

Lamprecht M, Fischer A, Stamm H. Sport Schweiz 2008. Das Sportverhalten der Schweizer Bevölkerung. Magglingen: Bundesamt für Sport; 2008.

Lamprecht M, Fischer A, Stamm H. Sportvereine in der Schweiz. Zahlen, Fakten und Analysen zum organisierten Sport. Magglingen: Bundesamt für Sport; 2011.

Lamprecht M, Fischer A, Stamm H. Die Schweizer Sportvereine. Strukturen, Leistungen, Herausforderungen. Zürich: Seismo; 2012.

Lamprecht M, Fischer A, Stamm H. Sport Schweiz 2014. Sportaktivität und Sportinteresse der Schweizer Bevölkerung. Zürich: Seismo; 2014.

Nagel S. Goals of sports clubs. Eur J Sport Soc. 2008;5:121–41.

Schlesinger T, Klenk C, Nagel S. Freiwillige Mitarbeit im Sportverein analyse individueller Faktoren und organisationaler Entscheidungen. Zürich: Seismo; 2014.

Schlesinger T, Nagel S. Who will volunteer? Analysing individual and structural factors of volunteering in Swiss sports clubs. Eur J Sport Sci. 2013;13:707–15.

Schlesinger T, Egli B, Nagel S. Continue or terminate? Determinants of long term volunteering in sports clubs. Eur Sport Manag Q. 2013;13:32–53.

Stadelmann-Steffen I, Traunmüller R, Gundelach B, Freitag M. Freiwilligen-Monitor Schweiz 2010. Zürich: Seismo; 2010.

Stamm H, Lamprecht M. Sportvereine in der Schweiz. Probleme – Fakten – Perspektiven. Chur. Zürich: Rüegger; 1998.

Stamm H, Lamprecht M. Swiss sports participation in an international perspective. Eur J Sport Soc. 2011;8(1):15–29.

Studer F, Schlesinger T, Engel C. Socio-economic and cultural determinants of sports participation in Switzerland from 2000 to 2008. Eur J Sport Soc. 2011;8:147–66.

# Chapter 23
# A Cross-National Comparative Perspective on Sport Clubs in Europe

**Remco Hoekman, Harold van der Werff, Siegfried Nagel, and Christoph Breuer**

## 23.1 Introduction

The preceding 20 chapters have presented national perspectives on sport clubs based on quantitative and descriptive information on the origin of sport clubs, the position of sport clubs within policy and society, and characteristics of sport clubs. In this chapter we offer a cross-national comparison focusing on more general findings. To optimise the comparative approach we developed a framework for international comparison that served as a guideline for the authors for their country chapters (see Chap. 1). This, however, does not mean that we can directly compare the quantitative data that is provided in the country chapters, as the availability of data differs between the countries and there is by no means a comparable data set between the countries. The framework for comparison does enable us to focus on differences between groups, and on patterns and trends that can be observed throughout Europe or in specific regions or countries. In this chapter we focus on these similarities and differences in patterns and trends between countries.

In the following we offer a systematic and comprehensive analysis of the characteristics of sport clubs and their embedding in society and in national sport systems in various European countries. For this analysis we use the multilevel model that

R. Hoekman (✉) • H. van der Werff
Mulier Institute, Utrecht, Netherlands
e-mail: r.hoekman@mulierinstituut.nl; h.vanderwerff@mulierinstituut.nl

S. Nagel
Institute of Sport Science, University of Bern, Bern, Switzerland
e-mail: siegfried.nagel@ispw.unibe.ch

C. Breuer
Department of Sport Economics and Sport Management, German Sport University Cologne, Cologne, Germany
e-mail: breuer@dshs-koeln.de



C. Breuer et al. (eds.), *Sport Clubs in Europe*, Sports Economics, Management and Policy 12, DOI 10.1007/978-3-319-17635-2_23

was outlined in the theoretical chapter (Chap. 2), including a macro perspective and a meso perspective. From a macro perspective we pay attention to the origin and development of sport clubs and the way sport clubs are embedded in the national sport system. Furthermore, we focus on the position of sport clubs within society and within policy, including the position of sport clubs within sport policy and within the more general social welfare policies. From a meso perspective we illustrate differences and similarities in the characteristics of sport clubs and identify the main bottlenecks and challenges of sport clubs in the context of the current developments in modern sports and society.

The central question of this chapter can be formulated as follows:

*What are the similarities and differences in the 20 contributions with regard to the development of sport clubs within the national sport structure, their role in policy and society and their characteristics and bottlenecks and challenges?*

Before we address this question we provide a general overview of sport club participation in the countries in this book based on Eurobarometer data and national data of Switzerland and Norway, as these countries are not part of the European Union. This provides a further context to the interpretation of the differences that are found between the countries and adds to the comparative perspective that forms the core of this chapter.

## 23.2 Comparative Data from Eurobarometer

The Eurobarometer provides information on sport club participation in all EU-member states. Data from Switzerland and Norway are available from national studies. Figure 23.1 shows that the Netherlands have the highest sport club membership, followed by Switzerland and the Western and Northern European countries; Denmark, Germany, Sweden and Belgium. In comparison to other Northern European countries the sport clubs participation in Norway is quite low.[1] Three of the participating Eastern European countries have about the same participation as the EU mean. Hungary and Poland deviate from that picture. Looking at the Mediterranean countries it is noticeable that in France the participation is somewhat above the EU average, while Spain, Italy and Greece are at the bottom of the list.

In the Eurobarometer people were asked whether local sport clubs and other local providers offer many opportunities to be physically active (statement). Again Western and Northern European countries form the top of the ranking. Citizens from these countries are the most satisfied with the opportunities that sport clubs and other local providers offer, especially in Denmark and the Netherlands. And again Eastern European countries do not deviate from the average of the EU

[1] In some cases results from the Eurobarometer study differ from national studies that are presented in the country chapters. These differences are caused by differences in definitions, sampling and research methods. In general the Eurobarometer results reflect the general tendencies that were observed in the respective countries.

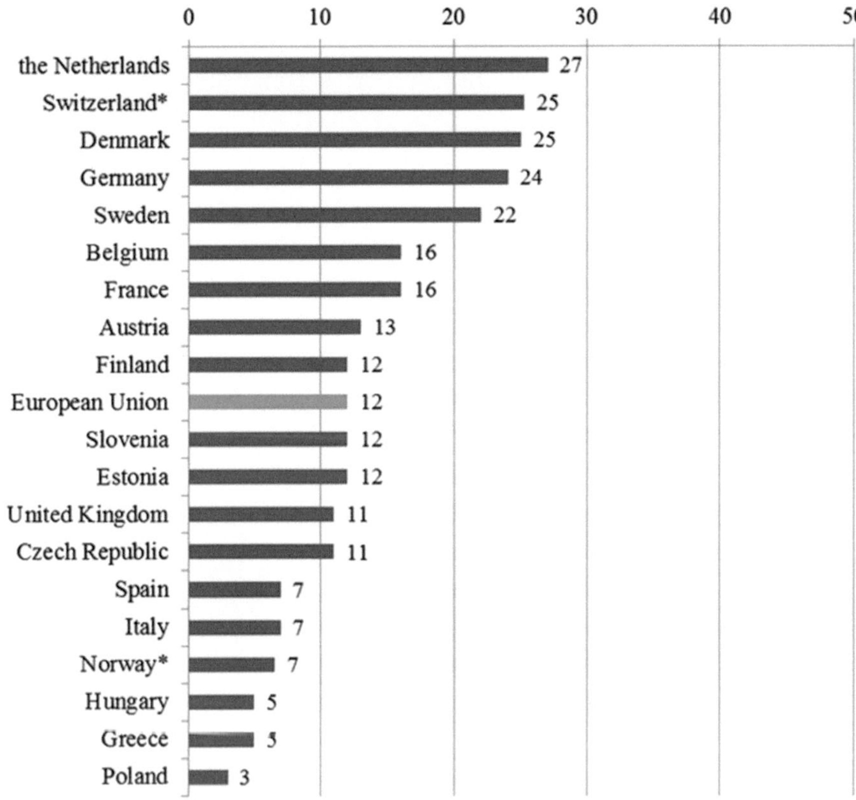


**Fig. 23.1** Sport club participation (people 15 years and older). Special Eurobarometer 412 "Sport and physical activity" (European Commission 2014); Norway (see Chap. 17) and Switzerland, people 15–74 years old (Lamprecht et al. 2014)

member states, with the exception of Poland and Hungary. When comparing the Mediterranean countries the opportunities are quite different. France is in the top of the ranking, Spain is somewhere in the middle and Italy and Greece are at the bottom (Fig. 23.2).

In the Eurobarometer citizens were asked if they were engaged in voluntary work that supports sporting events. Figure 23.3 clearly shows that volunteering in sport is high in the Northern European countries, especially in Norway and Sweden, and in Switzerland. Also in the Netherlands there are relatively many volunteers. The Eastern European countries Estonia, Slovenia and Czech Republic are a bit above the EU average and Hungary is about average. It is remarkable that in the four Mediterranean countries participating in this book volunteerism in sport is the lowest.

The Eurobarometer provides great insights in sport involvement in general and more specific in the participation in sport and the report reveals many differences between member states. There are clear differences between the countries with

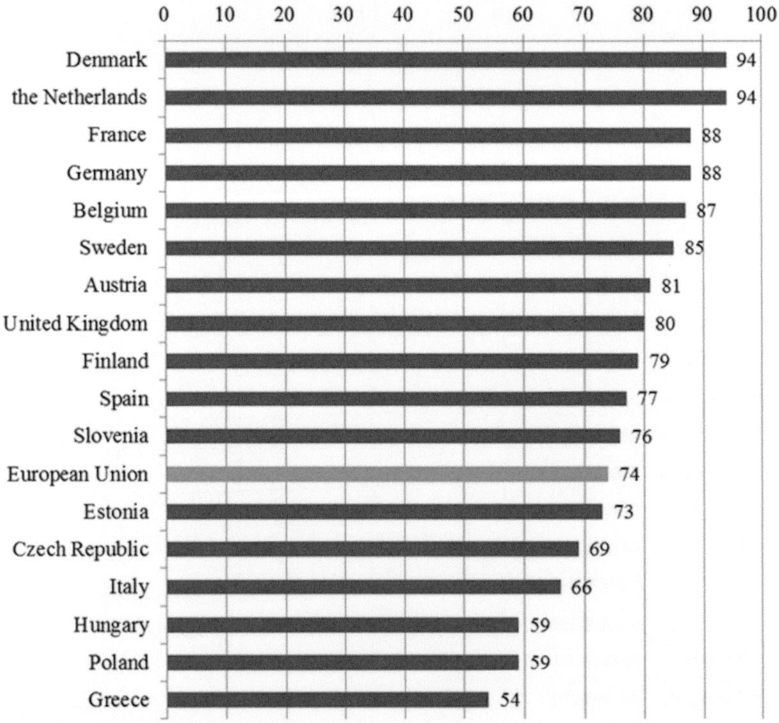


**Fig. 23.2** The extent to which citizens (people 15 years and older) agreed that local sport clubs and other local providers offer many opportunities to be physically active. Special Eurobarometer 412 "Sport and physical activity" (European Commission 2014)

regard to membership and volunteering in sport clubs as well as the relevance of sport clubs as local sport providers. In general, the Northern European countries rank on top. The countries in Western and Central Europe are a little behind, whereas the relevance of sport clubs in South and Eastern Europe is considerably lower.

## 23.3 Historical Origin of Sport and Their Current Position in National Sport Structures

Though the countries have different social, cultural and political backgrounds, they share to a great extent the same roots with regard to sport and sport clubs. In the presented countries the first sport clubs offered sports that had a link with the military, like fencing, shooting, equestrian sports, swimming, running and sailing. Furthermore the gymnastic movement from Sweden or the German *Turnen*

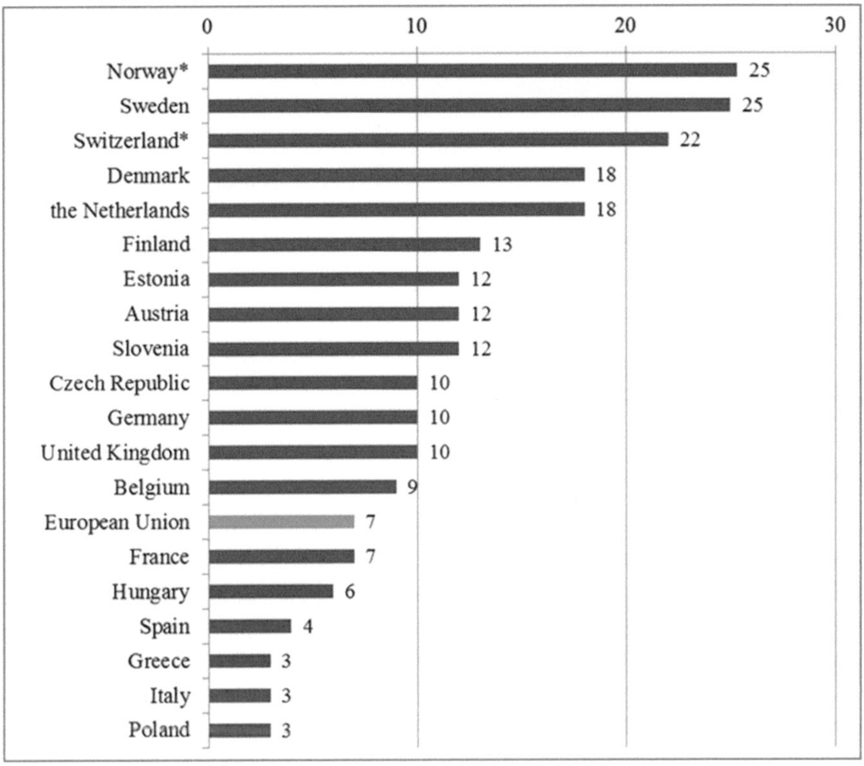


**Fig. 23.3** Participating in voluntary work that support sporting activities (people 15 years and older). Special Eurobarometer 412 "Sport and physical activity" (European Commission 2014); Norway (see Chap. 17) and Switzerland, people 15–74 years old (Lamprecht et al. 2014)

influenced the development of sport clubs within the countries. In the Northern and Western European countries it mainly concerned voluntary sport clubs, while in parts of Eastern Europe and Southern Europe private clubs also played an important role (see for instance the chapters of Italy, Hungary and Poland). The emphasis of the gymnastic movement, that was present throughout Europe, was mainly on health, strengthening the body and building character.

Another wave of sports emerged in England. There the industrial revolution lead to urbanisation and emancipation, but it was the reduction of the working hours in the second half of the nineteenth century that made it possible for the mass to participate in sport or be a spectator. Also common rules in sports were established, which made it possible to compete between schools, universities and so on. People who visited England, e.g. foreign students, became acquainted with typical Anglo-Saxon sports like football, rugby and tennis with its focus on performance and competition and they introduced these sports in their home countries. Starting in the UK modern sports spread out throughout Europe, showing up first in countries with a closer relation to UK and later in the Eastern European countries. These sports were becoming for instance immense popular in countries like France, Italy, the Netherlands, Spain and the Czech Republic.

The modern sport with its competition element and elite sports found its way to other countries in a different manner. In the Eastern European countries there is a noticeable higher involvement of the government and allegedly a stronger focus on performance and elite sports given the *sport schools* that are organised by the state and a less presence of the mostly grassroots sport oriented democratic sport clubs in the beginning stages of the development of sport clubs. Furthermore, in Hungary and Poland sport was also connected with the school system, as was partly the case in the UK. This positions Hungary and Poland as school sporting countries, more than as sport club countries (see also Van Tuyckom 2011). Other European countries incorporated gymnastic in the school system and sport clubs were the main venue for the modern sports.

Sport clubs really started to develop in the beginning of the twentieth century in all parts of Europe. Countries with a full political support for the development of the voluntary sector of sport and a vivid civil society grew more rapidly (e.g. Sweden, Finland, the Netherlands, Austria, Denmark). The increase in the popularity of sport and the expansion of sport clubs made it necessary to organise sport in a more formal way. In most countries sport federations are responsible for organising local, regional and national competitions, the training of talents and the representation of their sport in other national forums. In addition every country has a national Olympic committee in which the interests of all sports are represented. The configuration of sport federation differs between the European countries as a result of differences in ideological, political and religious background. In Spain the Franco dictatorship has had its influence on the development of sport clubs and the limited willingness to participate in volunteer-based organisations. Furthermore, in Belgium there are two sport federations per sport, reflecting the national political situation, with a Flemish and a Walloon part. On the other hand, the national Olympic committee is not divided along those lines and it holds a strong position in Belgium. Austria even has three umbrella sport organisation of which two have a specific political alignment (SPORTUNION and ASKÖ) and the third (ASVÖ) is independent and unifies the sport clubs that do not feel associated with the other two umbrella organisations. Also in Denmark there are three national umbrella organisations active, namely, DIF and DGI, supplemented by the more specialised DFIF. This division is in Denmark not political but ideological. DIF represents modern sports with competitions and national championships. DGI represents the sports and exercise movement, while DFIF mainly focuses on company sports. In Italy two subsystems exist in juxtaposition, on the one hand CONI and sport federations and on the other hand the regions and sport promotion bodies.

Furthermore, the chapters illustrate to some extent that the world war period affected the development of sport clubs and their position within policy. This is for instance noticeable in Italy with regard to the collapse of the Fascist Regime. In Eastern Europe sport clubs experienced a central controlled state after World War II.

In the communist era daily life, including sports, was controlled by the central government. Sport became entirely funded by the state. Though financial thresholds for sport participation were non-existent, mass sport found itself in a weak position because the state favoured elite sport, because the latter could be used to strengthen the state's international reputation. After the fall of the iron curtain the Eastern European countries changed for the better and a democratic organisation of sport is developing.

The different historical roots of sport within the countries and the political anchor points in these countries in the last century result in different configurations of the current sport system. Camy et al. (2004) refer to four basic configurations of sport systems in Europe: (1) bureaucratic configuration, (2) missionary configuration, (3) entrepreneurial configuration, and (4) social configuration. Table 23.1 presents the basic characteristics of these systems.

Camy et al. (2004) described for 16 out of the 25 EU member states the configuration of sport systems as bureaucratic and six as missionary. In the UK and Ireland an entrepreneurial system was in place and only in the Netherlands the system was seen as social. Camy et al. emphasise that the typology is a tool in comparing different sport systems and that we should not lose sight of the dynamics that can be seen in the field of sports. The observed developments are not univocal, although Camy et al. perceive a general strengthening of 'entrepreneurial' and 'social' positions in many countries.

On the basis of the country chapters it is hard to make clear statements whether this grouping is still valid, because not all grouping criteria that Camy et al. have used were included in the analyses of the country chapters. Still, general tendencies can be found.

In the classification by Camy et al. the bureaucratic system is dominant. Today in many countries the state still plays a key role in sports, but it is not as dominant as it used to be. For instance, in countries like the Czech Republic and Estonia, a decentralisation can be seen as the state delegates its roles in the domain of sport to local authorities.

To a certain extent a shift is observed from bureaucratic and missionary towards a entrepreneurial and a social system. In Austria, Denmark, Germany, Italy and Sweden the sport clubs still hold a very strong position. CONI in Italy is an example of how sport can be independent from state interference. However, in the last decades mainly due to the emergence of commercial sport providers, sport clubs lost their hegemony, though in most cases sport clubs still have a leading role in the sport landscape.

In 2004 the UK was positioned as the only country with an entrepreneurial system. Even now England and Northern Ireland are a bit different from the other participating countries in the way the sport system is organised. The same holds true for the Netherlands that was positioned as having a social sport system. Sport clubs in the Netherlands are still very autonomous. Furthermore, central and local governments try to reach their sport for all policy more and more through sport clubs, using subsidies as a tool to involve sport clubs in reaching people that are underrepresented in the clubs. In addition commercial sport providers have a significant

**Table 23.1** Configuration of sport systems according to Camy et al. (2004)

| | Bureaucratic | Missionary | Entrepreneurial | Social |
|---|---|---|---|---|
| Characteristics | • State plays a dominant role<br>• Legislative framework to field of sport<br>• Voluntary sports movement acts by 'delegation'<br>• Almost no social partners<br>• Users/consumers and private entrepreneurs yield low impact | • Dominant and autonomous voluntary sports movement<br>• State/regional government delegate much responsibility for orienting the sport policy<br>• Little presence of social partners<br>• Legitimacy more with voluntary managers than with employees<br>• Users rarely have the chance to adopt the position of consumer; private entrepreneurs act on the fringes of the dominant system (with a variable role) | • Regulation of the system arises from the social or economic "demand" for sport. There is little to prevent the supply/demand relationship being directly regulated by the market<br>• The public authorities' role consists essentially in setting a framework to enable this market logic to express itself<br>• The voluntary sports movement must adapt to its requirements which correspond to the tendencies of private entrepreneurs and to attempt to maintain its positions, in this context | • Presence of the social partners within a multifaceted system<br>• Cohabitation/collaboration between public, voluntary and commercial players<br>• The employee and employer representatives called upon to provide "governance" are mostly concerned with the "common good" that sport brings |

portion of the market. Still, as with almost all policy issues in the Netherlands all parties involved are open for collaboration. As a result of the economic recession the system is even more 'social' than before, though not all clubs are ready to embrace the new challenges and as a result frictions between clubs and local government may arise. The rise of the commercial sport providers and public sport providers, and decentralisation can also be seen in other European countries. Gradually they show more and more characteristics of a 'social' sport system as mentioned before.

In general, we can conclude that the current position of sport clubs in the sport system in the different countries is to a large extent the result of historical milestones in these countries, such as the World War and political shifts. All in all sport clubs are increasingly positioned within a sport market and are more and more intertwined with local sport policy. During the years the position of sport clubs within the sport system has evolved and in most cases was strengthened. Sport clubs are with no doubt the core of the sport system in Europe. In the following paragraph we illustrate the importance of sport clubs within the sport system by focusing on the role of sport clubs in policy and society.

## 23.4 Role of Sport Clubs in Policy and Society

The social and political significance of sport has grown considerably over the past decades. This is amongst others illustrated by the acceptance of the European Sport for All Charter (Council of Europe 1975) and by the White Paper on Sport (European Commission 2007), in which the European Commission addressed for the first time sport-related issues in a comprehensive manner. The White Paper on Sport addressed three core fields of sport: (1) the societal role of sport, (2) the economic aspect of sports, and (3) the organisation of sport. Especially the social role of sport and the organisation of sport is relevant with regard to the position of sport clubs in policy and society. Active sport participation, among which participation within a sport club context, is considered beneficial from a social and health perspective. It is for these social, health, educational and cultural functions of sport that central and local government invest in sport, and more particularly support sport clubs.

In all European countries the sport clubs can count on support of the government. This support is mainly related to the facilitating role of the local government. Municipalities build and maintain sport facilities for grassroots sport and offer them free of charge, or with reduced fees to sport clubs. This holds true for all countries presented in this book and is in line with the Sport for All Charter which stresses the task of the government to facilitate sport activities. It is the ideology of sport for all that is used to position sport clubs within policy and to issue programmes to stimulate sport club participation. In the countries where sport clubs are more present and a higher share of the population participates in sport clubs, it seems that sport clubs also hold a stronger position within policy. In countries such as Austria, Denmark, the Netherlands, Switzerland, Germany, France, Northern Ireland, England, Sweden and Belgium there is a broad agreement on the social significance of sport clubs and their ability to contribute to policy objectives with regard to for instance social inclusion, health and safety. Sport clubs are positioned as the cornerstones of the sports movement and very important at a local level. It is especially in these countries that the citizens are satisfied with the opportunities to be physical active provided by the local sport clubs and other local providers (see Fig. 23.2). The large representation of sport clubs in these countries, and their local significance, offers policy makers the opportunity to position sport clubs more centrally in their policy. An example is the *Sport Matters* programme in Northern Ireland that recognises the important role of sport clubs in achieving governmental objectives for sport participation and its associated health benefits and other social benefits. While in countries such as Hungary, Poland, Czech Republic and Greece, the focus has been or still is mostly on elite sport and less on the social benefits of sport for all and the societal values of sport clubs. Most likely related to this a lower representation of sport clubs and lower sport club participation and lower sport participation in general are noticed in these countries. Nevertheless, an increase in the importance of sport for all and sport clubs is also visible in these countries. In a way Slovenia is ahead of these countries and combines elite sport, as an important element for national identity, with the educational value and health benefits of sport for all, and consequently puts sport clubs central in policy.

## 23.5 Characteristics of Sport Clubs

The 20 country chapters provide an overview of the nationally available information on sport clubs in the respective countries. A first look at these chapters learns that there is a clear difference in the availability of data on characteristics of sport clubs. The Eastern European countries in general lack information on most of the characteristics of sport clubs, while Western European and the Northern European countries have in most cases national monitoring systems for sport clubs providing ample information on the characteristics of sport clubs. This coincides with the policy attention for sport clubs in these countries, and with this most likely a higher interest in information on the development of sport clubs and their strengths, weaknesses, challenges and opportunities.

In the following sections we give a comparative overview on important structural characteristics of sport clubs that were part of the multilevel framework (Chap. 2).

### *23.5.1 Size*

According to the concept of club goods, size is a relevant factor for understanding sport clubs. The average size of sport clubs differs between the countries. In general it holds true that larger clubs tend to organise both competitive and recreational sport, whereas smaller clubs usually focus on the latter. The majority of the clubs are organised as single sport clubs. This is especially the case in Belgium (85 %), Sweden (85 %) the Netherlands (81 %) and Spain (70 %). In Finland, Germany and Austria, a more substantial group are multiple sport clubs with different sports. On average multisport clubs have more members than single sport clubs.

### *23.5.2 Members' Age and Gender*

In regard to sport club members and demographic factors, there are differences between age groups and gender. Sport clubs appeal more to youth—especially in the preliminary school age groups—than to elderly though there are differences between sports and disparities are diminishing. Furthermore, sport club membership is more common for male than female and again there are differences between sports. Some are dominated by males (martial arts, football) and others by females (equestrian sports). Surveys also show that the educational level has an influence on sport club participation. This pattern of overrepresentation of higher educated holds true for all of the countries where data was presented of.

### *23.5.3 Sport Activities*

According to the changing role of sport clubs in policy, especially in the Western European and Northern European countries, sport clubs have been expanding their activities. Traditionally sport clubs organise training sessions and opportunities to participate in competitions and tournaments. This is still mainly the case in some countries such as Poland, Greece and Hungary. In most other countries the majority of the clubs also organise—in the context of the sport for all agenda—non-competitive sport activities as well as non-sport activities to enhance social cohesion among their members or to raise funds. Such activities include youth camps, celebrations, thematic dinners, bingo nights, carnival parties and New Year's receptions. Furthermore, sport clubs participate in local events with a focus other than sport. In most cases the activities are for members only, but there are also various activities that are also open to non-members (family-tournaments) or in some cases are especially targeted at them (introduction days, activities for the elderly or disabled people, clinics at schools). In addition, gatherings in the sport canteen after trainings and matches—the Austrians call it *Anschlussgeselligkeit*—are very popular, illustrating the social value of sport clubs.

### *23.5.4 Volunteering and Paid Staff*

To organise the sport activities and other activities, sport clubs mainly call upon their volunteers. Volunteering of the members is a basic characteristic of sport clubs all over Europe. However, in the context of professionalisation of modern sports an increase of paid staff is visible in certain countries (e.g. Switzerland, Sweden, Norway, Italy, Finland). In Finland there was a successful experiment in which the government supported clubs for hiring paid staff. In Poland a contradictory development of increasing voluntary work is visible, and can be explained by the currently low threshold of voluntary work, compared to the other countries. The paid staff appeared to be mainly appointed as coach or instructor.

In the countries included in this book most sport clubs thrive almost exclusively on volunteers for positions as board member, coach, referee/jury member or committee member, volunteer at sport events, or for canteen or maintenance duties. Roughly nine out of ten staff members are volunteers. The number of volunteers per club member varies between different kinds of sports. Team sports need relatively more volunteers, whereas recreational sport activities have a lower demand. In Hungary and Poland it is more common to have paid staff, due to limited voluntary work and part-time contracts for coaches.

In some countries volunteers qualify for remuneration, sometimes with a legal maximum (the Netherlands €1,500 per year). In Italy someone who earns up to €7,500 annually is still considered a volunteer.

There is a big variety between countries as well as between clubs in the attitude of sport clubs with regard to facilitating training and education for volunteers. For some clubs investment in volunteers is standard practice whereas others do not invest in this. Though most clubs have enough volunteers, recruiting and retaining volunteers is one of the main challenges they face (see *bottlenecks of sport clubs* below).

### *23.5.5 Finances*

Since sport clubs are traditionally non-profit organisations in which likeminded people organise activities for their own and common benefit, the revenues and costs at least have to be balanced. For most clubs the membership fees are the most important revenue. In addition, there are subsidies from local governments, club activities for fund raising and sponsoring/advertising, which provide revenues for sport clubs. In some countries lottery money (Sweden, Austria) and paid services can also be substantial.

Other revenues are responsible for only a small part of the total income. Sport clubs that have their own facility usually also have a canteen and this is a great advantage in comparison to clubs that do not have such a facility available, not only for generating important revenues, but also as a place to host club activities.

In most countries the central or local governments provide the sport facilities. Sport clubs have to pay a limited rent for the use of the facilities. However, for sport clubs these facility-related costs are still substantial. Other important costs are the fees that have to be paid to the governing sport federation, the salaries and remunerations, water and energy, taxes, insurances and costs for sport materials.

In most cases the greater part of the costs for sport clubs are fixed. This makes it hard to keep the budget in balance in times of financial hardship. Due to the economic recession sport clubs find it harder to find sponsors. However, almost all clubs are able to balance their revenues and costs and when asked (Belgium, the Netherlands) the greater part of the clubs regard their financial situation as (very) healthy or at least as stable. Only a small part of the sport clubs stress that they have a poor financial situation, though in Sweden (fairly/very poor 19 %) this share of sport clubs is substantial. Nonetheless, many sport clubs do mention their financial situation as one of the bottlenecks they face.

## 23.6 Bottlenecks of Sport Clubs

Though in most European countries sport clubs are traditionally the main suppliers for organised sport, in the last decades commercial suppliers have successfully penetrated the sport market. Especially those that focus on body and health, like fitness centres, and less to competition appeal to a greater extend to women. This makes recruiting and retaining members somewhat harder than before, especially for smaller clubs (Sweden, Switzerland). Another reason is that individualism in society is also recognisable in sports. People are less motivated to commit themselves for a long period to a sport club (training and competition on fixed times), making recruiting and retaining of members harder. A third reason why recruiting is getting harder is related to the enrolment of young athletes. As a result of a drop in birth rate in several European countries (e.g. Austria, Czech Republic, the Netherlands) there are simply less children to recruit.

Individualism also has a noticeable effect on recruiting and retaining volunteers (board members, coaches, officials), especially for team sport clubs, since they need more staff for training and matches than individual sport clubs. Many sport clubs find it hard to find staff that is willing to commit themselves to the club for the long-term.

Besides quantity also the quality of staff is an issue a club has to consider. In many cases the volunteers are overqualified, for example a local bank director as the treasurer, but when there are not that many volunteers, e.g. in small clubs, the quality might decrease. In other countries (Hungary, Poland) for some staff functions, like coaches, professionals are hired but the wages are low and in many cases a second occupation is needed, which does not make sport an appealing sector to work in.

Furthermore, in return for subsidies governments require sport clubs to help solving societal problems for which most clubs are not equipped. These tasks demand other qualities than what is needed for managing a club or providing sport activities.

In addition, sport clubs are faced with more administrative tasks and legal procedures, which ask for specific knowledge. This all requires more professionalism in sport clubs. This conflicts with the idea in most countries that a sport club in itself is an independent organisation that exists for and by its members.

Another bottleneck concerns funding, the worldwide economic recession also has consequences for sports. In general governments have less money to spend and have to make choices. This has an impact on the building and maintenance of sport facilities. Also on the national level choices have to be made, for example which sports to favour. As mentioned, on the local level sport clubs find it harder to find sponsors. Furthermore, clubs are reluctant to increase membership fees because it goes against the principle of sport for all.

In some countries there were also other major problems in funding sports. In the Czech Republic the lottery company SAZKA, a main source for funding amateur's sport, went bankrupt, resulting in far lower municipal budgets for sports. On the opposite, in Austria funding from the Lotto-Toto lottery for sport increased substantially.

In some countries there is a huge demand for sport activities, but there are not enough facilities available. In Austria many football clubs do not have their own pitch and it is hard to afford the rent for these basic facilities. In Poland the sport infrastructure does not meet normal standards of quantity and quality for sport accommodations. Many are dilapidated and need comprehensive repair works.

## 23.7 Future of Sport Clubs in Europe

### *23.7.1 Fundamentals of Sport Clubs*

The contributions have made it clear that sport clubs are well rooted in the European society. Even though there are unmistakably differences between countries, one could say that sport clubs are the core of the grassroots sport in Europe. Furthermore, it is noticeable that sport clubs are seen as valuable contributors to society. Sport in itself is considered beneficial for one's health, social wellbeing and many other aspects of life and sport club participation is deemed to be even more beneficial due to its social structure, shared norms and values and attention for fair play and respect. As a result sport clubs are also well mentioned in sport policies and are put to use for exactly these purposes.

In Western and Northern European countries this process has started longer ago than in Eastern and to a less extent Southern European countries. Nevertheless, the Eastern part of Europe is slowly catching up, and paying specific attention to the position of sport clubs within the broader society. In times where sport policy is more oriented towards cooperation with other policy fields and contributing to their goals, sport clubs and sport governing bodies are important partners to achieve the common objectives.

### *23.7.2 Environmental Influence*

For the near future sport clubs will experience several exogenous developments in Europe, which may affect their daily activities. For starters the ageing of society is a negative development for most of the sport clubs. The contributions illustrated the attractiveness of sport clubs for the younger population and a strong decline in membership rates by increasing age. With this the ageing of society is not beneficial for sport clubs in Europe, unless sport clubs find ways to increase the enrolment of older age groups within sport clubs.

Another development that can be noticed is that of consumerism and a growing sport market. Sport clubs are experiencing more competition by other sport providers than a few decades ago. Furthermore, on the one hand the expected quality of sport services increases, while on the other hand there is a decreasing interest to volunteer and a higher focus on consuming instead of contributing to services of sport clubs. This is among others reflected in the bottlenecks that were expressed by sport clubs in several countries. Recruiting volunteers and the quality of the volunteers to fulfil the higher demands of society is a problem that many sport clubs face, irrespectively of which country they are in.

The problem of volunteers also relates to the increasing workload of sport clubs with the decentralisation of tasks and responsibilities from local government to sport clubs, as well as due to the expansion of the role of sport clubs within policy. This development is mainly observed in the Western European countries and some Northern European countries. One example of the decentralisation is the maintenance of sport facilities, that is for instance in the Netherlands not seldom in the hands of sport clubs. So far this development is not reflected in an increasing number of paid employees in sport clubs. Even though sport clubs do have to a small extent paid staff, most of the work is done by volunteers. Furthermore, the training and development of volunteers seem to have little attention at the sport clubs. It remains to be seen if this will change with the higher demands of society and increasing responsibilities for sport clubs. It seems evident that this will require a higher degree of professionalisation of sport clubs.

A positive change is the development of transnational economies including Eastern European socialist countries. Sport clubs are profiting from this in especially the Eastern European countries. Negative though is the current financial crisis that has an influence on the European economy as well as on the financial situation within countries. Although most sport clubs report a healthy financial situation, they are also experiencing the negative effects of this with decreasing sponsorship budgets and less financial support of local governments. It is to be expected that the impact of the financial recession is not over yet. Also in the years to come the sport clubs will face financial challenges that relate to the drawbacks of the financial recession.

## 23.8 Research Programme: Research Agenda on Sport Clubs

This book has provided an overview of the current state of knowledge on sport clubs in Europe and with this a general understanding of the playing field. Throughout the book a general multilevel framework is used to get this overview of sport clubs in Europe. Using this general guideline also made it clear that the presence of data on sport clubs was quite different from one country to another. We signal in general a lack of data in the Eastern European countries, as well as in some Southern European countries, such as Greece. It is in the best interest for these sport clubs and for their contribution to society, that more data will be collected on sport clubs in these countries, to be able to optimise the utilisation of sport clubs and provide ample support attuned to the problems of sport clubs.

In this context, it is furthermore useful to have data that can compare the situation in different European countries more exactly by using the same method and questionnaires.

Within joint research projects, it would be possible to exchange knowledge on sport clubs and their role in sport policy in order to discuss best practice models which are collected in the participating countries (e.g. with regard to volunteering, recruiting new members or societal tasks). This could be the basis for a better sport club management in the context of current challenges, e.g. personal resources, finances, social inclusion.

In order to carry out comparable joint research, a collective theoretical framework is also necessary. Therefore, the theoretical concepts and particularly the multi level model presented in Chap. 2 could be helpful as an analytic framework. However, depending on the specific research question appropriate theoretical concepts have to be selected.

Given the developments of sport clubs in the last decades in Europe and the prospects for the future, it would be important to enhance the knowledge on sport clubs in Europe. Special attention should be paid to the following topics and questions (see also the current research topics in Chap. 2):

- The increasing attention for social values of sport and role for sport clubs within policy to reach objectives or contribute to them;
- The role of sport clubs in the context of the changing landscape of sport providers—e.g. private, municipal, commercial, school.—and the growing competition on the sports market
- The financial situation and financial responsibilities of sport clubs;
- The professionalisation and volunteering in sport clubs;
- The recruitment and retaining of members in the context of developments in society (e.g. demographic transitions)

This book has offered interesting perspectives on sport clubs in different European countries and highlighted some interesting challenges for the future. In general it can be concluded that sport clubs have evolved over time and hold a strong position within the national sport systems and are valuable to sport for all and increasing the societal benefits of sport. Nevertheless there are clear differences between European countries that need further attention. Foremost, the potential of sport clubs justifies a stronger focus on sport clubs in research and monitoring on a European level as well as on a national level, especially in the Eastern European and some Southern European countries.

## References

Camy J, Clijsen L, Madella A, Pilkington A (2004) Improving employment in the field of sport in Europe through vocational training. VOCASPORT project. DG Education and Culture, Brussels

Council of Europe (1975) European sport for all charter. Retrieved 2 Feb 2015 from http://www.coe.int/t/dg4/sport/resources/texts/spchart2_en.asp

European Commission (2007) White paper on sport. European Commission, Brussels

Lamprecht M, Fischer A, Stamm H (2014) Sport Schweiz, 2014. Sportaktivität und Sportinteresse der Schweizer Bevölkerung. Seismo, Zürich

European Commission (2014) Special Eurobarometer 412 "Sport and physical activity". European Commission 2014, Brussels

van Tuyckom C (2011) Sport for all: fact or fiction?: individual and cross-national differences in sport participation from a European perspective. Charlotte Van Tuyckom, Ghent

MIX
Papier aus verantwortungsvollen Quellen
Paper from responsible sources
FSC® C105338

If you have any concerns about our products, you can contact us on
**ProductSafety@springernature.com**

In case Publisher is established outside the EU, the EU authorized representative is:
**Springer Nature Customer Service Center GmbH**
**Europaplatz 3, 69115 Heidelberg, Germany**

Printed by Libri Plureos GmbH
in Hamburg, Germany